The
Oxford Book
of English Verse
of the
Romantic Period
1798–1837

Oxford University Press, Ely House, London W. 1

GLASGOW   NEW YORK   TORONTO   MELBOURNE   WELLINGTON
CAPE TOWN   SALISBURY   IBADAN   NAIROBI   DAR ES SALAAM   LUSAKA   ADDIS ABABA
BOMBAY   CALCUTTA   MADRAS   KARACHI   LAHORE   DACCA
KUALA LUMPUR   SINGAPORE   HONG KONG   TOKYO

The
Oxford Book
of English Verse
of the Romantic Period

1798–1837

Chosen by

H. S. Milford

Oxford

At the Clarendon Press

One name only appears on the title-page
and at the end of the preface: but the
selection is at least equally the work of
the editor's two friends and collaborators,
Mr. Frederick Page and Mr. Charles
Williams; it owes much also to the advice,
censure, and encouragement of Professor
David Nichol Smith.

First published 1928
as *Oxford Book of Regency Verse*
Reissued 1935
as *Oxford Book of Romantic Verse*

REPRINTED LITHOGRAPHICALLY IN GREAT BRITAIN
AT THE UNIVERSITY PRESS, OXFORD
1946, 1951, 1957, 1963, 1967, 1971

PREFACE

THIS book is intended to bridge the gap between the *Oxford Book of Eighteenth Century
Verse* and the *Oxford Book of Victorian Verse*:
between the *Lyrical Ballads* of Wordsworth and
Coleridge, and the earlier volumes of Tennyson
and Browning; between 1798 and 1837. This
period of forty years thus begins with two very
great poets, and ends with two not unworthy of
them; in its course it comprises also the whole
poetical career of Scott, Byron, Shelley, and Keats,
most of Landor's and Hood's, and much of
Crabbe's, Clare's, and Blake's. The mere recital
of these names calls attention to one of the two
main difficulties which have faced the selectors—
the amount of first-rate poetry which was written
in these forty years. This difficulty was of course
obvious at the outset; some half of the book must,
whoever its selector, have been occupied by
poems which all readers will know, and many will
know by heart. There can be no apology for this,
because there can be no need for apology.

The other difficulty, however, only disclosed
itself clearly when the lesser poets were read in
their enormous and depressing bulk. Not only
are ' the majors so very major ', but the minors
' are so very minor '; and yet a book of this
kind, besides giving the greatest things of the
majors, must also represent the minors—it must
be historical, must show what was, in effect,

happening, what was being written and read. It must omit a lesser glory of Keats to make room for Mrs. Hemans and John Wilson, for Praed and Luttrell. It is hoped that the flats are not too long or too flat, and that the reader's descent from the heights of the *Prelude* or *Adonais* may be beguiled by the humour of *Anster Fair* or *Peter Bell* 'the First'.

Nor is that pleasure to be underrated which is found in the recognition of 'the real thing' when it exists. Leyden's line ' The ancient snakes, the favourites of the sun ' is received with sudden satisfaction; and, good though Clare usually is, it is with joy that the reader finds even in him such perfect verses as

> And little footpaths sweet to see
> Go seeking sweeter places still.

Towards the end of the period the contrast between majors and minors becomes less apparent. There are at least two names which have hardly yet received their proper honour as poets—those of Hood and Darley. The chronological limit ruled out Hood's most famous poems—the *Song of the Shirt*, the *Bridge of Sighs*; but it left in a great deal of remarkably fine work. There is in him the suggestion of a great poet; the suggestion may be false, but it appears as it does not appear in the work, for example, of Macaulay. Keats's *Ode to Autumn* is, without doubt, greater than

Hood's. But it is conceivable that Keats himself might have had momentary doubts.

Hood has been misjudged—his puns have been remembered and his poems forgotten. But Darley, though lyrics of his have appeared in anthologies—' Wherefore, unlaurelled Boy ', with its admirable opening; ' The Serenade of a Loyal Martyr ', which anticipated by so many years the movement of *Love in a Valley*; the seventeenth-century ' It is not Beauty I demand ' —has not been judged at all. He was neglected in his lifetime; he has been neglected since. ' It is time something was done about it ', and a small beginning is here made.

The principles of selection are closer to those of the *Oxford Book of Eighteenth Century Verse* than to the *Oxford Book of Victorian Verse*, which confines itself almost entirely to lyrics. Extracts from long poems have been freely admitted; and it is no extreme claim that the greatness of Byron, for instance, is far more clearly displayed than if he had been represented only by *The Isles of Greece* and *There be none of Beauty's Daughters* for the hundredth time. Scott, too, in his introductory verses to *Marmion* and to the other narrative poems, appears an almost unexpectedly outstanding figure as a poet.

Passages from plays have been excluded, although songs from them have been admitted.

There is, it is true, a passage from *Prometheus Unbound*, but no one would call that a play. Translations also have been generally omitted.

The authors are arranged in order of birth; their work, under each, in order of publication. The date of first publication is given at the end of each poem, but the text (as in the *Oxford Book of Eighteenth Century Verse*) sometimes follows a later version. Nowhere, however, has a text later than 1837 been used, and the result of this is most noticeable in the poems chosen from Tennyson. The early versions of *Œnone* and *The Lady of Shalott*, for instance, explain, if they do not justify, the virulence of the *Quarterly* and Bulwer Lytton.

The editor's thanks are due to Mr. Edmund Blunden and Mr. Cobden-Sanderson for permission to print poems by John Clare; to Messrs. Longmans for the poem by Jane Carlyle; and to Miss Phyllis Jones for her ungrudging secretarial labours.

H. S. M.

WILLIAM COMBE

1741–1823

I

In search of the picturesque

(i)

THE Sun, as hot as he was bright,
   Had got to his meridian height;
'Twas sultry noon—for not a breath
Of cooling zephyr fann'd the heath—
When Syntax cried—' 'Tis all in vain
' To find my way across the plain;
' So here my fortune I will try,
' And wait till some one passes by:
' Upon that bank awhile I'll sit,
' And let poor Grizzle graze a bit;
' But as my time shall not be lost,
' I'll make a drawing of the post;
' And, tho' your flimsy tastes may flout it,
' There 's something *picturesque* about it:
' 'Tis rude and rough, without a gloss,
' And is well cover'd o'er with moss;
' And I've a right—(who dares deny it?)
' To place yon group of asses by it.
' Aye! this will do: and now I'm thinking,
' That self-same pond where Grizzle 's drinking,
' If hither brought 'twould better seem,
' And faith I'll turn it to a stream;
' I'll make this flat a shaggy ridge,
' And o'er the water throw a bridge;

' I'll do as other sketchers do—
' Put any thing into the view;
' And any object recollect,
' To add a grace, and give effect.
' Thus, tho' from truth I haply err,
' *The scene preserves its character.*
' What man of taste my right will doubt,
' To put things in, or leave them out?
' 'Tis more than right, it is a duty,
' If we consider landscape beauty:—
' He ne'er will as an artist shine,
' Who copies nature line by line:
' Whoe'er from nature takes a view,
' Must copy and improve it too:
' To heighten ev'ry work of art,
' Fancy should take an active part:
' Thus I (which few, I think, can boast)
' *Have made a Landscape of a Post.*'

(*ii*)

' THE first, the middle, and the last,
' In *picturesque* is *bold contrast*;
' And painting has no nobler use
' Than this grand object to produce.
' Such is my thought, and I'll pursue it;
' There 's an example—you shall view it:
' Look at that tree—then take a glance
' At its fine, bold protuberance;
' Behold those branches—how their shade
' Is by the mass of light display'd;
' Look at that light, and see how fine
' The backward shadows make it shine:

2

IN SEARCH OF THE PICTURESQUE

‘ The sombre clouds that spot the sky
‘ Make the blue vaulting twice as high;
‘ And where the sunbeams warmly glow,
‘ They make the hollow twice as low.
‘ The Flemish painters all surpass
‘ In making pictures smooth as glass:
‘ In Cuyp’s best works there ’s pretty painting :
‘ But the bold *picturesque* is wanting.
   ‘ Thus, tho’ I leave the birds to sing,
‘ Or cleave the air with rapid wing—
‘ Thus, tho’ I leave the fish to play
‘ Till the net drags them into day—
‘ Kind Nature, ever-bounteous mother !
‘ Contrives it in some way or other,
‘ Our proper wishes to supply
‘ In infinite variety.
‘ The world of quadrupeds displays
‘ The painter’s art in various ways;
‘ But, ’tis some shaggy, ragged brute
‘ That will my busy purpose suit;
‘ Or such as, from their shape and make,
‘ No fine-wrought high-bred semblance take.
‘ A well-fed horse, with shining skin,
‘ Form’d for the course, and plates to win,
‘ May have his beauties, but not those
‘ That will my graphic art disclose :
‘ My raw-bon’d mare is worth a score
‘ Of these fine pamper’d beasts, and more,
‘ To give effect to bold design,
‘ And decorate such views as mine.
‘ To the fine steed you sportsmen bow,
‘ But *picturesque* prefers a cow;

' On her high hips and horned head
' How true the light and shade are shed.
' Indeed I should prefer by half,
' To a fine colt, a common calf:
' The unshorn sheep, the shaggy goat,
' The ass with rugged ragged coat,
' Would, to a taste-inspir'd mind,
' Leave the far-fam'd *Eclipse* behind:
' In a grand stable he might please,
' But ne'er should graze beneath my trees.'

(*iii*)

' HAIL, favour'd casement!—where the sight
' Is courted to enjoy delight!
' T'ascend the hill, and trace the plain,
' Where lavish Nature 's proud to reign;
' Unlike those pictures that impart
' The windows of Palladian art,
' From whence no other object 's seen
' But gravel-walk, or shaven green;
' Plann'd by the artist on his desk;—
' Pictures that are not *picturesque*.
' But I should not perform my duty
' Did I relinquish all this beauty;
' Nor snatch, from this expansive view,
' Some pretty little scene or two.
  ' The cot that 's all bewhiten'd o'er,
' With children playing at the door;
' A peasant hanging o'er the hatch,
' And the vine mantling on the thatch,

4

IN SEARCH OF THE PICTURESQUE

' While the thick coppice, down the hill,
' Throws its green umbrage o'er the rill,
' Whose stream drives on the busy mill;
' In pleasing group their forms combine,
' And suit a pencil such as mine.
' Nor shall I miss the branchy screen
' Of those fine elms, that hide the green,
' O'er which the tap'ring spire is seen.
' I'll add no more—for, to my mind,
' The scene 's complete—and well design'd.
' There are, indeed, who would insert
' Those pigs, which wallow in the dirt;
' And, tho' I hold a pig is good
' Upon a dish, prepar'd for food,
' I do not fear to say the brute
' Does not my taste in painting suit;
' For I most solemnly aver,
' That he from genuine taste must err,
' Who flouts at grace or character;
' And there 's as much in my old wig
' As can be found about a pig;
' For, to say truth, I don't inherit
' This self-same *picturesquish* spirit,
' That looks to nought but what is rough,
' And ne'er thinks Nature coarse enough.
' Their system does my genius shock,
' Who see such graces in a dock.
' Whose eye the *picturesque* admires
' In straggling brambles, and in briers;
' Nay, can a real beauty see
' In a decay'd and rotten tree.
' I hate with them the trim of Art;

5

WILLIAM COMBE

' But from this rule I'll ne'er depart.—
' In grandame Nature's vast collection,
' To make a fair and fit selection,
' Which, when in happy contrast join'd,
' Delights th'inform'd, well-judging mind.'

The Tour of Dr. Syntax, 1812

ANNA LÆTITIA BARBAULD

1743–1825

2

Life

Animula, vagula, blandula

LIFE! I know not what thou art,
   But know that thou and I must part;
And when, or how, or where we met,
I own to me 's a secret yet.
But this I know, when thou art fled,
Where'er they lay these limbs, this head,
No clod so valueless shall be,
As all that then remains of me.
O whither, whither dost thou fly,
Where bend unseen thy trackless course,
   And in this strange divorce,
Ah tell where I must seek this compound I?

To the vast ocean of empyreal flame,
   From whence thy essence came,
   Dost thou thy flight pursue, when freed
From matter's base encumbering weed?
      Or dost thou, hid from sight,
      Wait, like some spell-bound knight,
Through blank oblivious years the' appointed hour,
To break thy trance and reassume thy power?

6

ANNA LÆTITIA BARBAULD

Yet canst thou without thought or feeling be?
O say what art thou, when no more thou'rt thee?

Life! we've been long together,
Through pleasant and through cloudy weather;
'Tis hard to part when friends are dear;
Perhaps 't will cost a sigh, a tear;
Then steal away, give little warning,
        Choose thine own time;
Say not Good night, but in some brighter clime
        Bid me Good morning.

Collected Works, 1825

GEORGE CRABBE

1754–1832

3   *From ' Reflections '*

WE'VE trod the maze of error round,
    Long wand'ring in the winding glade;
And now the torch of truth is found,
    It only shows us where we stray'd:
Light for ourselves, what is it worth,
    When we no more our way can choose?
For others, when we hold it forth,
    They, in their pride, the boon refuse.

By long experience taught, we now
    Can rightly judge of friends and foes,
Can all the worth of these allow,
    And all their faults discern in those;
Relentless hatred, erring love,
    We can for sacred truth forgo;
We can the warmest friend reprove,
    And bear to praise the fiercest foe:

To what effect? Our friends are gone,
   Beyond reproof, regard, or care;
And of our foes remains there one,
   The mild relenting thoughts to share?

Now 'tis our boast that we can quell
   The wildest passions in their rage;
Can their destructive force repel,
   And their impetuous wrath assuage:
Ah! Virtue, dost thou arm, when now
   This bold rebellious race are fled;
When all these tyrants rest, and thou
   Art warring with the mighty dead?

Poems, 1807

4   *From ' The Parish Register '*

(i)

BEHOLD the Cot! where thrives th' industrious swain,
  Source of his pride, his pleasure, and his gain;
Screen'd from the winter's wind, the sun's last ray
Smiles on the window and prolongs the day;
Projecting thatch the woodbine's branches stop,
And turn their blossoms to the casement's top:
All need requires is in that cot contain'd,
And much that taste untaught and unrestrain'd
Surveys delighted; there she loves to trace,
In one gay picture, all the royal race;
Around the walls are heroes, lovers, kings;
The print that shows them and the verse that sings.
  Here the last Lewis on his throne is seen,
And there he stands imprison'd, and his Queen;

8

THE PARISH REGISTER

To these the mother takes her child, and shows
What grateful duty to his God he owes;
Who gives to him a happy home, where he
Lives and enjoys his freedom with the free;
When kings and queens, dethroned, insulted, tried,
Are all these blessings of the poor denied.

There is King Charles, and all his Golden Rules,
Who proved Misfortune's was the best of schools:
And there his Son, who, tried by years of pain,
Proved that misfortunes may be sent in vain.

The Magic-mill that grinds the gran'nams young,
Close at the side of kind Godiva hung;
She, of her favourite place the pride and joy,
Of charms at once most lavish and most coy,
By wanton act the purest fame could raise,
And give the boldest deed the chastest praise.

There stands the stoutest Ox in England fed;
There fights the boldest Jew, Whitechapel bred;
And here Saint Monday's worthy votaries live,
In all the joys that ale and skittles give.

Now lo! in Egypt's coast that hostile fleet,
By nations dreaded and by NELSON beat;
And here shall soon another triumph come,
A deed of glory in a day of gloom;
Distressing glory! grievous boon of fate!
The proudest conquest, at the dearest rate.

On shelf of deal beside the cuckoo-clock,
Of cottage-reading rests the chosen stock;
Learning we lack, not books, but have a kind
For all our wants, a meat for every mind:
The tale for wonder and the joke for whim,
The half-sung sermon and the half-groan'd hymn.

No need of classing; each within its place,
The feeling finger in the dark can trace;
' First from the corner, farthest from the wall,'
Such all the rules, and they suffice for all.

There pious works for Sunday's use are found;
Companions for that Bible newly bound;
That Bible, bought by sixpence weekly saved,
Has choicest prints by famous hands engraved;
Has choicest notes by many a famous head,
Such as to doubt have rustic readers led;
Have made them stop to reason *why?* and *how?*
And, where they once agreed, to cavil now.
Oh! rather give me commentators plain,
Who with no deep researches vex the brain;
Who from the dark and doubtful love to run,
And hold their glimmering tapers to the sun;
Who simple truth with nine-fold reason back,
And guard the point no enemies attack.

Bunyan's famed Pilgrim rests that shelf upon;
A genius rare but rude was honest John:
Not one who, early by the Muse beguiled,
Drank from her well the waters undefiled;
Not one who slowly gain'd the hill sublime,
Then often sipp'd and little at a time;
But one who dabbled in the sacred springs,
And drank them muddy, mix'd with baser things.

Here to interpret dreams we read the rules,
Science our own! and never taught in schools;
In moles and specks we Fortune's gifts discern,
And Fate's fix'd will from Nature's wanderings learn.

Of Hermit Quarll we read, in island rare,
Far from mankind and seeming far from care;

Safe from all want, and sound in every limb;
Yes! there was he, and there was care with him.

    Unbound and heap'd, these valued tomes beside,
Lay humbler works, the pedlar's pack supplied;
Yet these, long since, have all acquired a name;
The Wandering Jew has found his way to fame;
And fame, denied to many a labour'd song,
Crowns Thumb the Great, and Hickathrift the strong.

    There too is he, by wizard-power upheld,
Jack, by whose arm the giant-brood were quell'd:
His shoes of swiftness on his feet he placed;
His coat of darkness on his loins he braced;
His sword of sharpness in his hand he took,
And off the heads of doughty giants stroke:
Their glaring eyes beheld no mortal near;
No sound of feet alarm'd the drowsy ear;
No English blood their pagan sense could smell,
But heads dropt headlong, wondering why they fell.

    These are the Peasant's joy, when, placed at ease,
Half his delighted offspring mount his knees.

Part I (Introduction)

(ii)

NEXT at our altar stood a luckless pair,
    Brought by strong passions and a warrant there;
By long rent cloak, hung loosely, strove the bride,
From ev'ry eye, what all perceived, to hide.
While the boy-bridegroom, shuffling in his pace,
Now hid awhile and then exposed his face;
As shame alternately with anger strove,
The brain confused with muddy ale to move:

In haste and stammering he perform'd his part,
And look'd the rage that rankled in his heart;
(So will each lover inly curse his fate,
Too soon made happy and made wise too late:)
I saw his features take a savage gloom,
And deeply threaten for the days to come.
Low spake the lass, and lisp'd and minced the while,
Look'd on the lad, and faintly tried to smile;
With soften'd speech and humbled tone she strove
To stir the embers of departed love:
While he, a tyrant, frowning walk'd before,
Felt the poor purse, and sought the public door,
She sadly following in submission went,
And saw the final shilling foully spent;
Then to her father's hut the pair withdrew,
And bade to love and comfort long adieu!
Ah! fly temptation, youth, refrain! refrain!
I preach for ever; but I preach in vain!

Part II (Marriage)

(iii)

MY Record ends:—But hark! e'en now I hear
The bell of death, and know not whose to fear:
Our farmers all, and all our hinds were well;
In no man's cottage danger seem'd to dwell;—
Yet death of man proclaim these heavy chimes,
For thrice they sound, with pausing space, three times.
' Go; of my sexton seek, Whose days are sped?—
What! he, himself!—and is old *Dibble* dead?'
His eightieth year he reach'd, still undecay'd,
And rectors five to one close vault convey'd:—

But he is gone; his care and skill I lose,
And gain a mournful subject for my Muse:
His masters lost, he'd oft in turn deplore,
And kindly add,—' Heaven grant, I lose no more!'
Yet, while he spake, a sly and pleasant glance
Appear'd at variance with his complaisance:
For, as he told their fate and varying worth,
He archly look'd,—' I yet may bear thee forth.'
' When first '—(he so began)—' my trade I plied,
Good master *Addle* was the parish-guide;
His clerk and sexton, I beheld with fear
His stride majestic, and his frown severe;
A noble pillar of the church he stood,
Adorn'd with college-gown and parish-hood:
Then as he paced the hallow'd aisles about,
He fill'd the sevenfold surplice fairly out!
But in his pulpit, wearied down with prayer,
He sat and seem'd as in his study's chair;
For while the anthem swell'd, and when it ceased,
Th' expecting people view'd their slumbering priest:
Who, dozing, died.—Our Parson *Peele* was next;
" I will not spare you," was his favourite text;
Nor did he spare, but raised them many a pound;
Ev'n me he mulct for my poor rood of ground;
Yet cared he nought, but with a gibing speech,
" What should I do," quoth he, " but what I preach?"
His piercing jokes (and he'd a plenteous store)
Were daily offer'd both to rich and poor;
His scorn, his love, in playful words he spoke;
His pity, praise, and promise, were a joke:
But though so young and bless'd with spirits high,
He died as grave as any judge could die:

13

The strong attack subdued his lively powers,—
His was the grave, and Doctor *Grandspear* ours.
   ' Then were there golden times the village round;
In his abundance all appear'd t' abound;
Liberal and rich, a plenteous board he spread,
E'en cool Dissenters at his table fed;
Who wish'd, and hoped,—and thought a man so kind
A way to Heaven, though not their own, might find;
To them, to all, he was polite and free,
Kind to the poor, and, ah! most kind to me:
" Ralph," would he say, " *Ralph Dibble,* thou art old;
" That doublet fit, 'twill keep thee from the cold:
How does my Sexton?—What! the times are hard;
Drive that stout pig, and pen him in thy yard."
But most, his rev'rence loved a mirthful jest:—
" Thy coat is thin; why, man, thou'rt *barely* dress'd;
It 's worn to th' thread: but I have nappy beer;
Clap that within, and see how they will wear! "
   ' Gay days were these; but they were quickly past:
When first he came, we found he cou'dn't last:
A whoreson cough (and at the fall of leaf)
Upset him quite:—but what 's the gain of grief?
   ' Then came the *Author-Rector*: his delight
Was all in books; to read them, or to write:
Women and men he strove alike to shun,
And hurried homeward when his tasks were done:
Courteous enough, but careless what he said,
For points of learning he reserved his head;
And when addressing either poor or rich,
He knew no better than his cassock which:
He, like an osier, was of pliant kind,
Erect by nature, but to bend inclined;

14

Not like a creeper falling to the ground,
Or meanly catching on the neighbours round:—
Careless was he of surplice, hood, and band,—
And kindly took them as they came to hand :
Nor, like the doctor, wore a world of hat,
As if he sought for dignity in that:
He talk'd, he gave, but not with cautious rules:—
Nor turn'd from gipsies, vagabonds, or fools;
It was his nature, but they thought it whim,
And so our beaux and beauties turn'd from him :
Of questions, much he wrote, profound and dark,—
How spake the serpent, and where stopp'd the ark;
From what far land the Queen of Sheba came;
Who Salem's Priest, and what his father's name;
He made the Song of Songs its mysteries yield,
And Revelations, to the world, reveal'd.
He sleeps i' the aisle,—but not a stone records
His name or fame, his actions or his words:
And truth, your reverence, when I look around,
And mark the tombs in our sepulchral ground,
(Though dare I not of one man's hope to doubt),
I'd join the party who repose without.
 ' Next came a Youth from Cambridge, and, in truth,
He was a sober and a comely youth;
He blush'd in meekness as a modest man,
And gain'd attention ere his task began;
When preaching, seldom ventured on reproof,
But touch'd his neighbours tenderly enough.
Him, in his youth, a clamorous sect assail'd,
Advised and censured, flatter'd,—and prevail'd.—
Then did he much his sober hearers vex,
Confound the simple, and the sad perplex;

To a new style his reverence rashly took;
Loud grew his voice, to threat'ning swell'd his look;
Above, below, on either side, he gazed,
Amazing all, and most himself amazed:
No more he read his preachments pure and plain,
But launch'd outright, and rose and sank again:
At times he smiled in scorn, at times he wept,
And such sad coil with words of vengeance kept,
That our best sleepers started as they slept.
" Conviction comes like lightning," he would cry;
" In vain you seek it, and in vain you fly;
'Tis like the rushing of the mighty wind,
Unseen its progress, but its power you find;
It strikes the child ere yet its reason wakes;
His reason fled, the ancient sire it shakes;
The proud, learn'd man, and him who loves to know
How and from whence these gusts of grace will blow,
It shuns,—but sinners in their way impedes,
And sots and harlots visits in their deeds:
Of faith and penance it supplies the place;
Assures the vilest that they live by grace,
And, without running, makes them win the race."
    ' Such was the doctrine our young prophet taught;
And here conviction, there confusion wrought;
When his thin cheek assumed a deadly hue,
And all the rose to one small spot withdrew:
They call'd it hectic; 'twas a fiery flush,
More fix'd and deeper than the maiden blush;
His paler lips the pearly teeth disclosed,
And lab'ring lungs the length'ning speech opposed.
No more his span-girth shanks and quiv'ring thighs
Upheld a body of the smaller size;
16

But down he sank upon his dying bed,
And gloomy crotchets fill'd his wandering head.—
  ' " Spite of my faith, all-saving faith," he cried,
" I fear of worldly works the wicked pride;
Poor as I am, degraded, abject, blind,
The good I've wrought still rankles in my mind;
My alms-deeds all, and every deed I've done,
My moral-rags defile me every one;
It should not be:—what say'st thou? tell me, Ralph."
Quoth I, " Your reverence, I believe, you're safe;
Your faith's your prop, nor have you pass'd such time
In life's good-works as swell them to a crime.
If I of pardon for my sins were sure,
About my goodness I would rest secure."
  ' Such was his end; and mine approaches fast;
I've seen my best of preachers,—and my last.'—
  He bow'd, and archly smiled at what he said,
Civil but sly:—' And is old Dibble dead?'

Part III (Burials)
The Parish Register, &c., 1807

5   *From ' The Borough '*

(*i*)

CAN scenes like these withdraw thee from thy wood,
  Thy upland forest or thy valley's flood?
Seek then thy garden's shrubby bound, and look,
As it steals by, upon the bordering brook; ·
That winding streamlet, limpid, lingering, slow,
Where the reeds whisper when the zephyrs blow;
Where in the midst, upon her throne of green,
Sits the large Lily as the water's queen;

And makes the current, forced awhile to stay,
Murmur and bubble as it shoots away;
Draw then the strongest contrast to that stream,
And our broad river will before thee seem.

   With ceaseless motion comes and goes the tide,
Flowing, it fills the channel vast and wide;
Then back to sea, with strong majestic sweep
It rolls, in ebb yet terrible and deep;
Here samphire-banks and salt-wort bound the flood,
There stakes and sea-weeds withering on the mud;
And higher up, a ridge of all things base,
Which some strong tide has roll'd upon the place.

                     Letter I (General Description)

(ii)

NOW is it pleasant in the summer-eve,
   When a broad shore retiring waters leave,
Awhile to wait upon the firm fair sand,
When all is calm at sea, all still at land;
And there the ocean's produce to explore,
As floating by, or rolling on the shore;
Those living jellies which the flesh inflame,
Fierce as a nettle, and from that its name;
Some in huge masses, some that you may bring
In the small compass of a lady's ring;
Figured by hand divine—there 's not a gem
Wrought by man's art to be compared to them;
Soft, brilliant, tender, through the wave they glow,
And make the moonbeam brighter where they flow.
Involved in sea-wrack, here you find a race,
Which science doubting, knows not where to place;

THE BOROUGH

On shell or stone is dropp'd the embryo-seed,
And quickly vegetates a vital breed.

    While thus with pleasing wonder you inspect
Treasures the vulgar in their scorn reject,
See as they float along th' entangled weeds
Slowly approach, upborne on bladdery beads;
Wait till they land, and you shall then behold
The fiery sparks those tangled fronds infold,
Myriads of living points; th' unaided eye
Can but the fire and not the form descry.
And now your view upon the ocean turn,
And there the splendour of the waves discern;
Cast but a stone, or strike them with an oar,
And you shall flames within the deep explore;
Or scoop the stream phosphoric as you stand,
And the cold flames shall flash along your hand;
When, lost in wonder, you shall walk and gaze
On weeds that sparkle, and on waves that blaze.

    The ocean too has winter-views serene,
When all you see through densest fog is seen;
When you can hear the fishers near at hand
Distinctly speak, yet see not where they stand;
Or sometimes them and not their boat discern,
Or half-conceal'd some figure at the stern;
The view 's all bounded, and from side to side
Your utmost prospect but a few ells wide;
Boys who, on shore, to sea the pebble cast,
Will hear it strike against the viewless mast;
While the stern boatman growls his fierce disdain,
At whom he knows not, whom he threats in vain.

    'Tis pleasant then to view the nets float past,
Net after net till you have seen the last;

And as you wait till all beyond you slip,
A boat comes gliding from an anchor'd ship,
Breaking the silence with the dipping oar,
And their own tones, as labouring for the shore;
Those measured tones which with the scene agree,
And give a sadness to serenity.

Letter IX (Amusements)

(iii)

ALAS! for Peter not a helping hand,
   So was he hated, could he now command;
Alone he row'd his boat, alone he cast
His nets beside, or made his anchor fast;
To hold a rope or hear a curse was none,—
He toil'd and rail'd; he groan'd and swore alone.

   Thus by himself compell'd to live each day,
To wait for certain hours the tide's delay;
At the same times the same dull views to see,
The bounding marsh-bank and the blighted tree;
The water only, when the tides were high
When low, the mud half-cover'd and half-dry;
The sun-burnt tar that blisters on the planks,
And bank-side stakes in their uneven ranks;
Heaps of entangled weeds that slowly float,
As the tide rolls by the impeded boat.

   When tides were neap, and, in the sultry day,
Through the tall bounding mud-banks made their way,
Which on each side rose swelling, and below
The dark warm flood ran silently and slow;
There anchoring, Peter chose from man to hide,
There hang his head, and view the lazy tide
In its hot slimy channel slowly glide;

20

Where the small eels that left the deeper way
For the warm shore, within the shallows play;
Where gaping muscles, left upon the mud,
Slope their slow passage to the fallen flood;—
Here dull and hopeless he'd lie down and trace
How sidelong crabs had scrawl'd their crooked race;
Or sadly listen to the tuneless cry
Of fishing gull or clanging golden-eye;
What time the sea-birds to the marsh would come,
And the loud bittern, from the bull-rush home,
Gave from the salt-ditch side the bellowing boom:
He nursed the feelings these dull scenes produce,
And loved to stop beside the opening sluice;
Where the small stream, confined in narrow bound,
Ran with a dull, unvaried, sadd'ning sound;
Where all, presented to the eye or ear,
Oppress'd the soul with misery, grief, and fear.

Letter XXII (Peter Grimes)
The Borough, 1810

6   *From ' The Frank Courtship '*

GRAVE *Jonas Kindred*, Sybil Kindred's sire,
Was six feet high, and look'd six inches higher;
Erect, morose, determined, solemn, slow,
Who knew the man, could never cease to know;
His faithful spouse, when Jonas was not by,
Had a firm presence and a steady eye;
But with her husband dropp'd her look and tone,
And Jonas ruled unquestion'd and alone.

He read, and oft would quote the sacred words,
How pious husbands of their wives were lords;

Sarah called Abraham Lord! and who could be,
So Jonas thought, a greater man than he?
Himself he view'd with undisguised respect,
And never pardon'd freedom or neglect.

They had one daughter, and this favourite child
Had oft the father of his spleen beguiled;
Soothed by attention from her early years,
She gain'd all wishes by her smiles or tears:
But *Sybil* then was in that playful time,
When contradiction is not held a crime;
When parents yield their children idle praise
For faults corrected in their after days.

Peace in the sober house of Jonas dwelt,
Where each his duty and his station felt:
Yet not that peace some favour'd mortals find,
In equal views and harmony of mind;
Not the soft peace that blesses those who love,
Where all with one consent in union move;
But it was that which one superior will
Commands, by making all inferiors still;
Who bids all murmurs, all objections cease,
And with imperious voice announces—Peace!

They were, to wit, a remnant of that crew,
Who, as their foes maintain, their Sovereign slew;
An independent race, precise, correct,
Who ever married in the kindred sect:
No son or daughter of their order wed
A friend to England's king who lost his head;
Cromwell was still their Saint, and when they met,
They mourn'd that Saints were not our rulers yet.

Fix'd were their habits; they arose betimes,
Then pray'd their hour, and sang their party-rhymes:

Their meals were plenteous, regular, and plain;
The trade of Jonas brought him constant gain;
Vender of hops and malt, of coals and corn—
And, like his father, he was merchant born:
Neat was their house; each table, chair, and stool,
Stood in its place, or moving moved by rule;
No lively print or picture graced the room;
A plain brown paper lent its decent gloom;
But here the eye, in glancing round, survey'd
A small recess that seem'd for china made;
Such pleasing pictures seem'd this pencill'd ware,
That few would search for nobler objects there—
Yet, turn'd by chosen friends, and there appear'd
His stern, strong features, whom they all revered;
For there in lofty air was seen to stand
The bold Protector of the conquer'd land;
Drawn in that look with which he wept and swore,
Turn'd out the Members, and made fast the door,
Ridding the House of every knave and drone,
Forced, though it grieved his soul, to rule alone.
The stern still smile each friend approving gave,
Then turn'd the view, and all again were grave.

There stood a clock, though small the owner's need,
For habit told when all things should proceed;
Few their amusements, but when friends appear'd,
They with the world's distress their spirits cheer'd;
The nation's guilt, that would not long endure
The reign of men so modest and so pure:
Their town was large, and seldom pass'd a day
But some had fail'd, and others gone astray;
Clerks had absconded, wives eloped, girls flown
To Gretna-Green, or sons rebellious grown;

Quarrels and fires arose;—and it was plain
The times were bad; the Saints had ceased to reign!
A few yet lived, to languish and to mourn
For good old manners never to return.

Tales, 1812

7   *Young Paris*

YOUNG Paris was the shepherd's pride,
    As well the fair Ænone knew;
They sat the mountain stream beside,
    And o'er the bank a poplar grew.

Upon its bark this verse he traced,—
    Bear witness to the vow I make;
Thou, Xanthus, to thy source shalt haste,
    E'er I my matchless maid forsake.

No prince or peasant lad am I,
    Nor crown nor crook to me belong,
But I will love thee till I die,
    And die before I do thee wrong.

Back to thy source now, Xanthus, run,
    Paris is now a prince of Troy;
He leaves the Fair his flattery won,
    Himself and country to destroy.

He seizes on a sovereign's wife,
    The pride of Greece, and with her flies;
He causes thus a ten years' strife,
    And with his dying parent dies.

24

YOUNG PARIS

Oh! think me not this Shepherd's Boy,
   Who from the Maid he loves would run:
Oh! think me not a Prince of Troy,
   By whom such treacherous deeds are done.

(Tale XIX)
Posthumous Tales, 1834

8
His Wife's Wedding Ring

THE ring so worn, as you behold,
   So thin, so pale, is yet of gold:
The passion such it was to prove;
Worn with life's cares, love yet was love.

Written *c.* 1813–14;
Poetical Works, vol. i, 1834 (in the ' Life ' by his son)

WILLIAM BLAKE

1757–1827

9
From ' Milton '

(*i*)

AND did those feet in ancient time
   Walk upon England's mountains green?
And was the holy Lamb of God
   On England's pleasant pastures seen?

And did the Countenance Divine
   Shine forth upon our clouded hills?
And was Jerusalem builded here
   Among these dark Satanic Mills?

Bring me my bow of burning gold!
   Bring me my arrows of desire!
Bring me my spear! O clouds, unfold!
   Bring me my chariot of fire!

WILLIAM BLAKE

I will not cease from mental fight,
  Nor shall my sword sleep in my hand,
Till we have built Jerusalem
  In England's green and pleasant land.

Preface

(*ii*)

LOS is by mortals nam'd Time; Enitharmon is nam'd Space;
  But they depict him bald and agèd who is in eternal
  youth,
All powerful, and his locks flourish like the brows of morning:
He is the Spirit of Prophecy, the ever apparent Elias.
Time is the mercy of Eternity; without Time's swiftness,
Which is the swiftest of all things, all were eternal torment.
All the Gods of the Kingdoms of Earth labour in Los's
  Halls:
Everyone is a fallen Son of the Spirit of Prophecy.
He is the Fourth Zoa, that stood around the Throne Divine.

    .   .   .   .   .   .

This Wine-press is call'd War on Earth: it is the Printing-
  Press
Of Los; and here he lays his words in order above the mortal
  brain,
As cogs are form'd in a wheel to turn the cogs of the adverse
  wheel.

Timbrels and violins sport round the Wine-presses; the little
  Seed,
The sportive Root, the Earth-worm, the Gold-beetle, the wise
  Emmet
Dance round the Wine-presses of Luvah; the Centipede is
  there,

26

The Ground-spider with many eyes, the Mole clothèd in
        velvet,
The ambitious Spider in his sullen web, the lucky Golden-
        spinner,
The Earwig arm'd, the tender Maggot, emblem of immor-
        tality,
The Flea, Louse, Bug, the Tape-worm; all the Armies of
        Disease,
Visible or invisible to the slothful, Vegetating Man;
The slow Slug, the Grasshopper, that sings and laughs and
        drinks—
Winter comes: he folds his slender bones without a murmur.

The cruel Scorpion is there, the Gnat, Wasp, Hornet, and
        the Honey-bee,
The Toad and venomous Newt, the Serpent cloth'd in gems
        and gold:
They throw off their gorgeous raiment: they rejoice with loud
        jubilee,
Around the Wine-presses of Luvah, naked and drunk with
        wine.

There is the Nettle that stings with soft down, and there
The indignant Thistle, whose bitterness is bred in his milk,
Who feeds on contempt of his neighbour; there all the idle
        Weeds,
That creep around the obscure places, show their various
        limbs
Naked in all their beauty, dancing round the Wine-presses.

                                        Book I

(iii)

THOU hearest the Nightingale begin the Song of Spring:
　The Lark, sitting upon his earthy bed, just as the morn
Appears, listens silent; then, springing from the waving corn-
　　field, loud
He leads the Choir of Day—trill! trill! trill! trill!
Mounting upon the wings of light into the great Expanse,
Re-echoing against the lovely blue and shining heavenly Shell;
His little throat labours with inspiration; every feather
On throat and breast and wings vibrates with the effluence
　　Divine.
All Nature listens silent to him, and the awful Sun
Stands still upon the mountain looking on this little Bird
With eyes of soft humility and wonder, love and awe.
Then loud from their green covert all the Birds begin their
　　song:
The Thrush, the Linnet and the Goldfinch, Robin and the
　　Wren
Awake the Sun from his sweet revery upon the mountain:
The Nightingale again assays his song, and thro' the day
And thro' the night warbles luxuriant; every Bird of song
Attending his loud harmony with admiration and love.
This is a Vision of the lamentation of Beulah over Ololon.

Thou perceivest the Flowers put forth their precious Odours;
And none can tell how from so small a centre comes such
　　sweet,
Forgetting that within that centre Eternity expands
Its ever-during doors, that Og and Anak fiercely guard.
First, ere the morning breaks, joy opens in the flowery
　　bosoms,
28

Joy even to tears, which the Sun rising dries: first the Wild
    Thyme
And Meadow-sweet, downy and soft, waving among the
    reeds,
Light springing on the air, lead the sweet dance; they wake
The Honeysuckle sleeping on the oak; the flaunting beauty
Revels along upon the wind; the White-thorn, lovely May,
Opens her many lovely eyes; listening the Rose still sleeps—
None dare to wake her; soon she bursts her crimson-curtain'd
    bed
And comes forth in the majesty of beauty. Every Flower,
The Pink, the Jessamine, the Wallflower, the Carnation,
The Jonquil, the mild Lily opes her heavens; every Tree
And Flower and Herb soon fill the air with an innumerable
    dance,
Yet all in order sweet and lovely. Men are sick with love!

Book II, 1804

10   *From 'Jerusalem'*

(i)

WHAT are those Golden Builders doing? Where was
    the burying-place
Of soft Ethinthus? near Tyburn's fatal Tree? Is that
Mild Zion's hill's most ancient promontory, near mournful
Ever-weeping Paddington? Is that Calvary and Golgotha
Becoming a building of Pity and and Compassion? Lo!
The stones are Pity, and the bricks well-wrought Affections
Enamell'd with Love and Kindness; and the tiles engraven
    gold,
Labour of merciful hands; the beams and rafters are For-
    giveness,

29

The mortar and cement of the work tears of Honesty, the nails
And the screws and iron braces are well-wrought Blandish-
    ments
And well-contrivèd words, firm fixing, never forgotten,
Always comforting the remembrance; the floors Humility,
The ceilings Devotion, the hearths Thanksgiving.
Prepare the furniture, O Lambeth, in thy pitying looms!
The curtains, woven tears and sighs, wrought into lovely forms
For Comfort; there the secret furniture of Jerusalem's
    chamber
Is wrought. Lambeth! the Bride, the Lamb's Wife loveth
    thee;
Thou art one with her, and knowest not of Self in thy supreme
    joy.
Go on, Builders, in hope! tho' Jerusalem wanders far away
Without the Gate of Los, among the dark Satanic wheels.

Chapter I

(ii)

THE fields from Islington to Marybone,
    To Primrose Hill and Saint John's Wood,
Were builded over with pillars of gold;
    And there Jerusalem's pillars stood.

Her Little Ones ran on the fields,
    The Lamb of God among them seen,
And fair Jerusalem, His Bride,
    Among the little meadows green.

Pancras and Kentish Town repose
    Among her golden pillars high,
Among her golden arches which
    Shine upon the starry sky.

JERUSALEM

The Jew's-harp House and the Green Man,
　　The Ponds where boys to bathe delight,
The fields of cows by Willan's farm,
　　Shine in Jerusalem's pleasant sight.

She walks upon our meadows green;
　　The Lamb of God walks by her side;
And every English child is seen,
　　Children of Jesus and His Bride;

Forgiving trespasses and sins,
　　Lest Babylon, with cruel Og,
With Moral and Self-righteous Law,
　　Should crucify in Satan's Synagogue.

What are those Golden Builders doing
　　Near mournful ever-weeping Paddington,
Standing above that mighty ruin,
　　Where Satan the first victory won;

Where Albion slept beneath the fatal Tree,
　　And the Druid's golden knife
Rioted in human gore,
　　In offerings of Human Life?

They groan'd aloud on London Stone,
　　They groan'd aloud on Tyburn's Brook:
Albion gave his deadly groan,
　　And all the Atlantic mountains shook.

Albion's Spectre, from his loins,
　　Tore forth in all the pomp of War;
Satan his name; in flames of fire
　　He stretch'd his Druid pillars far.

WILLIAM BLAKE

Jerusalem fell from Lambeth's vale,
  Down thro' Poplar and Old Bow,
Thro' Malden, and across the sea,
  In war and howling, death and woe.

The Rhine was red with human blood;
  The Danube roll'd a purple tide;
On the Euphrates Satan stood,
  And over Asia stretch'd his pride.

He wither'd up sweet Zion's hill
  From every nation of the Earth;
He wither'd up Jerusalem's Gates,
  And in a dark land gave her birth.

He wither'd up the Human Form
  By laws of sacrifice for Sin,
Till it became a Mortal Worm,
  But O! translucent all within.

The Divine Vision still was seen,
  Still was the Human Form Divine;
Weeping, in weak and mortal clay,
  O Jesus! still the Form was Thine!

And Thine the Human Face, and Thine
  The Human Hands, and Feet, and Breath,
Entering thro' the Gates of Birth,
  And passing thro' the Gates of Death.

And O Thou Lamb of God! whom I
  Slew in my dark self-righteous pride,
Art Thou return'd to Albion's land,
  And is Jerusalem Thy Bride?

JERUSALEM

Come to my arms, and nevermore
    Depart; but dwell for ever here;
Create my spirit to Thy love;
    Subdue my Spectre to Thy fear.

Spectre of Albion! warlike Fiend!
    In clouds of blood and ruin roll'd,
I here reclaim thee as my own,
    My Selfhood—Satan arm'd in gold!

Is this thy soft Family-love,
    Thy cruel patriarchal pride;
Planting thy Family alone,
    Destroying all the World beside?

A man's worst Enemies are those
    Of his own House and Family;
And he who makes his Law a curse,
    By his own Law shall surely die!

In my Exchanges every land
    Shall walk; and mine in every land,
Mutual shall build Jerusalem,
    Both heart in heart and hand in hand.

To the Jews

(iii)

AH! weak and wide astray! Ah! shut in narrow doleful
    form,
Creeping in reptile flesh upon the bosom of the ground!
The Eye of Man, a little narrow orb clos'd up and dark,
Scarcely beholding the Great Light, conversing with the
    ground;

The Ear, a little shell, in small volutions shutting out
True Harmonies, and comprehending great as very small;
The Nostrils, bent down to the earth, and clos'd with sense-
    less flesh,
That odours cannot them expand nor joy on them exult;
The Tongue, a little moisture fills, a little food it cloys,
A little sound it utters, and its cries are faintly heard.

Chapter II

(iv).

I SAW a Monk of Charlemaine
  Arise before my sight:
I talk'd with the Grey Monk as we stood
In beams of infernal light.

Gibbon arose with a lash of steel,
And Voltaire with a racking wheel;
The Schools, in clouds of learning roll'd,
Arose with War in iron and gold.

' Thou lazy Monk!' they sound afar,
' In vain condemning glorious War;
And in your cell you shall ever dwell:
Rise, War, and bind him in his cell!'

The blood red ran from the Grey Monk's side,
His hands and feet were wounded wide,
His body bent, his arms and knees
Like to the roots of ancient trees.

When Satan first the black bow bent
And the Moral Law from the Gospel rent,
He forg'd the Law into a sword,
And spill'd the blood of Mercy's Lord.

34

JERUSALEM

Titus! Constantine! Charlemaine!
O Voltaire! Rousseau! Gibbon! Vain
Your Grecian mocks and Roman sword
Against this image of his Lord;

For a Tear is an Intellectual thing;
And a Sigh is the sword of an angel king;
And the bitter groan of a Martyr's woe
Is an arrow from the Almighty's bow.

To the Deists

(v)

I GIVE you the end of a golden string;
  Only wind it into a ball,
It will lead you in at Heaven's gate,
  Built in Jerusalem's wall.

To the Christians

(vi)

ENGLAND! awake! awake! awake!
  Jerusalem thy sister calls!
Why wilt thou sleep the sleep of death,
  And close her from thy ancient walls?

Thy hills and valleys felt her feet
  Gently upon their bosoms move:
Thy gates beheld sweet Zion's ways;
  Then was a time of joy and love.

And now the time returns again:
  Our souls exult, and London's towers
Receive the Lamb of God to dwell
  In England's green and pleasant bowers.

To the Christians
Jerusalem, 1804?–20

11 *From ' The Everlasting Gospel '*

(i)

THE Vision of Christ that thou dost see
  Is my vision's greatest enemy.
Thine has a great hook nose like thine;
Mine has a snub nose like to mine.
Thine is the Friend of all Mankind;
Mine speaks in parables to the blind.
Thine loves the same world that mine hates;
Thy heaven doors are my hell gates.
Socrates taught what Meletus
Loath'd as a nation's bitterest curse,
And Caiaphas was in his own mind
A benefactor to mankind.
Both read the Bible day and night,
But thou read'st black where I read white.

(ii)

WAS Jesus chaste? or did He
  Give any lessons of chastity?
The Morning blushèd fiery red:
Mary was found in adulterous bed;
Earth groan'd beneath, and Heaven above
Trembled at discovery of Love.
Jesus was sitting in Moses' chair.
They brought the trembling woman there.
Moses commands she be ston'd to death.
What was the sound of Jesus' breath?
He laid His hand on Moses' law;
The ancient Heavens, in silent awe,

THE EVERLASTING GOSPEL

Writ with curses from pole to pole,
All away began to roll.
The Earth trembling and naked lay
In secret bed of mortal clay;
On Sinai felt the Hand Divine
Pulling back the bloody shrine;
And she heard the breath of God,
As she heard by Eden's flood:
' Good and Evil are no more!
Sinai's trumpets cease to roar!
Cease, finger of God, to write!
The Heavens are not clean in Thy sight
Thou art good, and Thou alone;
Nor may the sinner cast one stone.
To be good only, is to be
A God or else a Pharisee.
Thou Angel of the Presence Divine,
That didst create this Body of Mine,
Wherefore hast thou writ these laws
And created Hell's dark jaws?
My Presence I will take from thee:
A cold leper thou shalt be.
Tho' thou wast so pure and bright
That Heaven was impure in thy sight,
Tho' thy oath turn'd Heaven pale,
Tho' thy covenant built Hell's jail,
Tho' thou didst all to chaos roll
With the Serpent for its soul,
Still the breath Divine does move,
And the breath Divine is Love.
Mary, fear not! Let me see
The seven devils that torment thee.

Hide not from My sight thy sin,
That forgiveness thou may'st win.
Has no man condemnèd thee?'
'No man, Lord.' 'Then what is he
Who shall accuse thee? Come ye forth,
Fallen fiends of heavenly birth,
That have forgot your ancient love,
And driven away my trembling Dove.
You shall bow before her feet;
You shall lick the dust for meat;
And tho' you cannot love, but hate,
Shall be beggars at Love's gate.
What was thy love? Let Me see it;
Was it love or dark deceit?'
'Love too long from me has fled;
'Twas dark deceit, to earn my bread;
'Twas covet, or 'twas custom, or
Some trifle not worth caring for;
That they may call a shame and sin
Love's temple that God dwelleth in,
And hide in secret hidden shrine
The naked Human Form Divine,
And render that a lawless thing
On which the Soul expands its wing.
But this, O Lord, this was my sin,
When first I let these devils in,
In dark pretence to chastity
Blaspheming Love, blaspheming Thee,
Thence rose secret adulteries,
And thence did covet also rise.
My sin Thou hast forgiven me;
Canst Thou forgive my blasphemy?

Canst Thou return to this dark hell,
And in my burning bosom dwell?
And canst Thou die that I may live?
And canst Thou pity and forgive?'
Then roll'd the shadowy Man away
From the limbs of Jesus, to make them His prey,
An ever devouring appetite,
Glittering with festering venoms bright;
Crying ' Crucify this cause of distress,
Who don't keep the secrets of holiness!
The mental powers by diseases we bind;
But He heals the deaf, the dumb, and the blind.
Whom God has afflicted for secret ends,
He comforts and heals and calls them friends.'
But, when Jesus was crucified,
Then was perfected His galling pride.
In three nights He devour'd His prey,
And still He devours the body of clay;
For dust and clay is the Serpent's meat,
Which never was made for Man to eat.

Gilchrist's Life, 1863 (part)

[Epilogue]

I AM sure this Jesus will not do,
Either for Englishman or Jew.

Written c. 1810
Aldine edition, 1874

12   *Auguries of Innocence*

TO see a World in a grain of sand,
And a Heaven in a wild flower,
Hold Infinity in the palm of your hand,
And Eternity in an hour.

WILLIAM BLAKE

A robin redbreast in a cage
Puts all Heaven in a rage.
A dove-house fill'd with doves and pigeons
Shudders Hell thro' all its regions.
A dog starv'd at his master's gate
Predicts the ruin of the State.
A horse misus'd upon the road
Calls to Heaven for human blood.
Each outcry of the hunted hare
A fibre from the brain does tear.
A skylark wounded in the wing,
A cherubim does cease to'sing.
The game-cock clipt and arm'd for fight
Does the rising sun affright.
Every wolf's and lion's howl
Raises from Hell a Human soul.
The wild deer, wandering here and there,
Keeps the Human soul from care.
The lamb misus'd breeds public strife,
And yet forgives the butcher's knife.
He who shall hurt the little wren
Shall never be belov'd by men.
He who the ox to wrath has mov'd
Shall never be by woman lov'd.
The wanton boy that kills the fly
Shall feel the spider's enmity.
He who torments the chafer's sprite
Weaves a bower in endless night.
The caterpillar on the leaf
Repeats to thee thy mother's grief.
Kill not the moth nor butterfly,
For the Last Judgement draweth nigh.

AUGURIES OF INNOCENCE

He who shall train the horse to war
Shall never pass the polar bar.
The beggar's dog and widow's cat,
Feed them, and thou wilt grow fat.
The bat that flits at close of eve
Has left the brain that won't believe.
The owl that calls upon the night
Speaks the unbeliever's fright.
The gnat that sings his summer's song
Poison gets from Slander's tongue.
The poison of the snake and newt
Is the sweat of Envy's foot.
The poison of the honey-bee
Is the artist's jealousy.
A truth that 's told with bad intent
Beats all the lies you can invent.

Joy and woe are woven fine,
A clothing for the soul divine;
Under every grief and pine
Runs a joy with silken twine.
It is right it should be so;
Man was made for joy and woe;
And when this we rightly know,
Thro' the world we safely go.

The babe is more than swaddling-bands;
Throughout all these human lands
Tools were made, and born were hands,
Every farmer understands.
Every tear from every eye
Becomes a babe in Eternity;

This is caught by Females bright,
And return'd to its own delight.
The bleat, the bark, bellow, and roar
Are waves that beat on Heaven's shore.
The babe that weeps the rod beneath
Writes revenge in realms of death.
He who mocks the infant's faith
Shall be mock'd in Age and Death.
He who shall teach the child to doubt
The rotting grave shall ne'er get out.
He who respects the infant's faith
Triumphs over Hell and Death.

The child's toys and the old man's reasons
Are the fruits of the two seasons.
The questioner, who sits so sly,
Shall never know how to reply.
He who replies to words of Doubt
Doth put the light of knowledge out.
A riddle, or the cricket's cry,
Is to Doubt a fit reply.
The emmet's inch and eagle's mile
Make lame Philosophy to smile.
He who doubts from what he sees
Will ne'er believe, do what you please.
If the sun and moon should doubt,
They'd immediately go out.

The prince's robes and beggar's rags
Are toadstools on the miser's bags.
The beggar's rags, fluttering in air,
Does to rags the heavens tear.

AUGURIES OF INNOCENCE

The poor man's farthing is worth more
Than all the gold on Afric's shore.
One mite wrung from the labourer's hands
Shall buy and sell the miser's lands;
Or, if protected from on high,
Does that whole nation sell and buy.
The soldier, arm'd with sword and gun,
Palsied strikes the summer's sun.
The strongest poison ever known
Came from Caesar's laurel crown.
Nought can deform the human race
Like to the armour's iron brace.
When gold and gems adorn the plough
To peaceful arts shall Envy bow.
To be in a passion you good may do,
But no good if a passion is in you.
The whore and gambler, by the state
Licensed, build that nation's fate.
The harlot's cry from street to street
Shall weave Old England's winding-sheet.
The winner's shout, the loser's curse,
Dance before dead England's hearse.

Every night and every morn
Some to misery are born.
Every morn and every night
Some are born to sweet delight.
Some are born to sweet delight,
Some are born to endless night.
We are led to believe a lie
When we see not thro' the eye,
Which was born in a night, to perish in a night,

When the Soul slept in beams of light.
God appears, and God is Light,
To those poor souls who dwell in Night;
But does a Human Form display
To those who dwell in realms of Day.

> Written *c.* 1801–3
> Gilchrist's *Life*, 1863;
> arranged by Mr. John Sampson, 1905

13   ## *Gnomic Verses*

THE Angel that presided o'er my birth
  Said ' Little creature, form'd of joy and mirth,
Go, love without the help of anything on earth.'

> Written *c.* 1806–10
> Gilchrist's *Life*, 1863

14   ## *The Smile*

THERE is a smile of love,
  And there is a smile of deceit,
And there is a smile of smiles
In which these two smiles meet.

And there is a frown of hate,
And there is a frown of disdain,
And there is a frown of frowns
Which you strive to forget in vain,

For it sticks in the heart's deep core
And sticks in the deep backbone—
And no smile that ever was smil'd,
But only one smile alone,

THE SMILE

That betwixt the cradle and grave
It only once smil'd can be;
And, when it once is smil'd,
There 's an end to all misery.

Written *c.* 1801–3
Gilchrist's *Life*, 1863

15   *The Land of Dreams*

AWAKE, awake, my little boy!
Thou wast thy mother's only joy;
Why dost thou weep in thy gentle sleep?
Awake! thy father does thee keep.

' O, what land is the Land of Dreams?
What are its mountains, and what are its streams?
O father! I saw my mother there,
Among the lilies by waters fair.

' Among the lambs, clothèd in white,
She walk'd with her Thomas in sweet delight.
I wept for joy, like a dove I mourn;
O! when shall I again return? '

Dear child, I also by pleasant streams
Have wander'd all night in the Land of Dreams;
But tho' calm and warm the waters wide,
I could not get to the other side.

' Father, O father! what do we here
In this land of unbelief and fear?
The Land of Dreams is better far,
Above the light of the morning star.'

Written *c.* 1801–3
Gilchrist's *Life*, 1863

16 *The Crystal Cabinet*

THE Maiden caught me in the wild,
    Where I was dancing merrily;
She put me into her Cabinet,
And lock'd me up with a golden key.

This Cabinet is form'd of gold
And pearl and crystal shining bright,
And within it opens into a world
And a little lovely moony night.

Another England there I saw,
Another London with its Tower,
Another Thames and other hills,
And another pleasant Surrey bower,

Another Maiden like herself,
Translucent, lovely, shining clear,
Threefold each in the other clos'd—
O, what a pleasant trembling fear!

O, what a smile! a threefold smile
Fill'd me, that like a flame I burn'd;
I bent to kiss the lovely Maid,
And found a threefold kiss return'd.

I strove to seize the inmost form
With ardour fierce and hands of flame,
But burst the Crystal Cabinet,
And like a weeping Babe became—

A weeping Babe upon the wild,
And weeping Woman pale reclin'd,
And in the outward air again
I fill'd with woes the passing wind.

Written *c.* 1801–3
Gilchrist's *Life*, 1863

17 ' *Mock on, mock on, Voltaire, Rousseau* '

MOCK on, mock on, Voltaire, Rousseau;
Mock on, mock on; 'tis all in vain!
You throw the sand against the wind,
And the wind blows it back again.

And every sand becomes a gem
Reflected in the beams divine;
Blown back they blind the mocking eye
But still in Israel's paths they shine.

The Atoms of Democritus
And Newton's Particles of Light
Are sands upon the Red Sea shore,
Where Israel's tents do shine so bright.

Written *c.* 1800–10
Gilchrist's *Life*, 1863

18   *Morning*

TO find the Western path,
Right thro' the Gates of Wrath
I urge my way;
Sweet Mercy leads me on
With soft repentant moan:
I see the break of day.

47

The war of swords and spears,
Melted by dewy tears,
Exhales on high;
The Sun is freed from fears,
And with soft grateful tears
Ascends the sky.

Written *c.* 1800–10
Gilchrist's *Life,* 1863

19 *The Birds*

He. WHERE thou dwellest, in what grove,
Tell me Fair One, tell me Love;
Where thou thy charming nest dost build,
O thou pride of every field!

She. Yonder stands a lonely tree,
There I live and mourn for thee;
Morning drinks my silent tear,
And evening winds my sorrow bear.

He. O thou summer's harmony,
I have liv'd and mourn'd for thee;
Each day I mourn along the wood,
And night hath heard my sorrows loud.

She. Dost thou truly long for me?
And am I thus sweet to thee?
Sorrow now is at an end,
O my Lover and my Friend!

48

THE BIRDS

He.   Come, on wings of joy we'll fly
       To where my bower hangs on high;
       Come, and make thy calm retreat
       Among green leaves and blossoms sweet.

Written *c.* 1800–10
Gilchrist's *Life*, 1863

20   *To Mrs. Ann Flaxman*

A LITTLE Flower grew in a lonely Vale;
   Its form was lovely but its colours pale.
One standing in the Porches of the Sun,
When his Meridian Glories were begun,
Leap'd from the steps of fire and on the grass
Alighted where this little flower was.
With hands divine he moved the gentle Sod,
And took the Flower up in its native Clod;
Then planting it upon a Mountain's brow,
' 'Tis your own fault if you don't flourish now.'

Written *c.* 1800;
Designs for Gray's Poems, 1922

JOANNA BAILLIE

1769–1851

21   *Song*

THOUGH richer swains thy love pursue,
   In Sunday gear, and bonnets new;
And ev'ry fair before thee lay
Their silken gifts with colours gay;
They love thee not, alas! so well
As one who sighs and dares not tell;
Who haunts thy dwelling, night and noon,
In tatter'd hose and clouted shoon.

I grieve not for my wayward lot,
My empty folds, my roofless cot;
Nor hateful pity proudly shown,
Nor alter'd looks, nor friendship flown;
Nor yet my dog with lanken sides
Who by his master still abides;
But how will Nan prefer my boon,
In tatter'd hose and clouted shoon!

The Country Inn, 1804

22   *Song of the Outlaws*

THE chough and crow to roost are gone,
    The owl sits on the tree,
The hush'd wind wails with feeble moan,
    Like infant charity.
The wild-fire dances on the fen,
    The red star sheds its ray,
Uprouse ye, then, my merry men!
    It is our op'ning day.

Both child and nurse are fast asleep,
    And clos'd is every flower,
And winking tapers faintly peep
    High from my lady's bower;
Bewilder'd hinds with shorten'd ken
    Shrink on their murky way,
Uprouse ye, then, my merry men!
    It is our op'ning day.

Nor board nor garner own we now,
    Nor roof nor latched door,
Nor kind mate, bound by holy vow
    To bless a good man's store;

SONG OF THE OUTLAWS

Noon lulls us in a gloomy den,
    And night is grown our day,
Uprouse ye, then, my merry men!
    And use it as ye may.

Orra, 1812

SAMUEL ROGERS

1763–1855

23   *Fond Youth*

WHO spurs his horse against the mountain-side;
    Then, plunging, slakes his fury in the tide?
Draws, and cries ho; and, where the sun-beams fall,
At his own shadow thrusts along the wall?
Who dances without music; and anon
Sings like the lark—then sighs as woe-begone,
And folds his arms, and, where the willows wave,
Glides in the moon-shine by a maiden's grave?
Come hither, boy, and clear thy open brow.
Yon summer-clouds, now like the Alps, and now
A ship, a whale, change not so fast as thou.

He hears me not—Those sighs were from the heart.
Too, too well taught, he plays the lover's part.
He who at masques, nor feigning nor sincere,
With sweet discourse would win a lady's ear,
Lie at her feet and on her slipper swear
That none were half so faultless, half so fair,
Now through the forest hies, a stricken deer,
A banished man, flying when none are near;
And writes on every tree, and lingers long
Where most the nightingale repeats her song;

Where most the nymph, that haunts the silent grove,
Delights to syllable the names we love.

At length he goes—a Pilgrim to the Shrine,
And for a relic would a world resign!
A glove, a shoe-tye, or a flower let fall—
What though the least, Love consecrates them all!
And now he breathes in many a plaintive verse;
Now wins the dull ear of the wily nurse
At early matins ('twas at matin-time
That first he saw and sickened in his prime)
And soon the Sibyl, in her thirst for gold,
Plays with young hearts that will not be controlled.

' Absence from Thee—as self from self it seems! '
Scaled is the garden-wall; and lo, her beams
Silvering the east, the moon comes up, revealing
His well-known form along the terrace stealing.
—Oh, ere in sight he came, 'twas his to thrill
A heart that loved him though in secret still.
' Am I awake? or is it . . . can it be
' An idle dream? Nightly it visits me!
'—That strain,' she cries, ' as from the water rose.
' Now near and nearer through the shade it flows!—
' Now sinks departing—sweetest in its close! '
No casement gleams; no Juliet, like the day,
Comes forth and speaks and bids her lover stay.
Still, like aërial music heard from far,
Nightly it rises with the evening-star.

—' She loves another! Love was in that sigh! '
On the cold ground he throws himself to die.
Fond Youth, beware. Thy heart is most deceiving.
Who wish are fearful; who suspect, believing.

—And soon her looks the rapturous truth avow.
Lovely before, oh say how lovely now!
She flies not, frowns not, though he pleads his cause;
Nor yet—nor yet her hand from his withdraws;
But by some secret Power surprised, subdued,
(Ah how resist? Nor would she if she could.)
Falls on his neck as half unconscious where,
Glad to conceal her tears, her blushes there.

Human Life, 1819

24 *Bologna, and Byron*

'TWAS night; the noise and bustle of the day
Were o'er. The mountebank no longer wrought
Miraculous cures—he and his stage were gone;
And he who, when the crisis of his tale
Came, and all stood breathless with hope and fear,
Sent round his cap; and he who thrummed his wire
And sang, with pleading look and plaintive strain
Melting the passenger. Thy thousand Cries,
So well pourtrayed, and by a son of thine,
Whose voice had swelled the hubbub in his youth,
Were hushed, Bologna, silence in the streets,
The squares, when hark, the clattering of fleet hoofs;
And soon a Courier, posting as from far,
Housing and holster, boot and belted coat
And doublet, stained with many a various soil,
Stopt and alighted. 'Twas where hangs aloft
That ancient sign, The Pilgrim, welcoming
All who arrive there, all perhaps save those
Clad like himself, with staff and scallop-shell,
Those on a pilgrimage. And now approached

53

Wheels, through the lofty porticoes resounding,
Arch beyond arch, a shelter or a shade
As the sky changes. To the gate they came;
And, ere the man had half his story done,
Mine host received the Master—one long used
To sojourn among strangers, every where
(Go where he would, along the wildest track)
Flinging a charm that shall not soon be lost,
And leaving footsteps to be traced by those
Who love the haunts of Genius; one who saw,
Observed, nor shunned the busy scenes of life,
But mingled not, and mid the din, the stir,
Lived as a separate Spirit.

      Much had passed
Since last we parted; and those five short years—
Much had they told! His clustering locks were turned
Grey; nor did aught recall the youth that swam
From Sestos to Abydos. Yet his voice,
Still it was sweet; still from his eye the thought
Flashed lightning-like, nor lingered on the way,
Waiting for words. Far, far into the night
We sat, conversing—no unwelcome hour,
The hour we met; and, when Aurora rose,
Rising, we climbed the rugged Apennine.

Well I remember how the golden sun
Filled with its beams the unfathomable gulfs,
As on we travelled, and along the ridge,
Mid groves of cork and cistus and wild-fig,
His motley household came—Not last nor least,
Battista, who, upon the moonlight-sea
Of Venice, had so ably, zealously,
Served, and, at parting, thrown his oar away

BOLOGNA, AND BYRON

To follow through the world; who without stain
Had worn so long that honourable badge,
The gondolier's, in a Patrician House
Arguing unlimited trust.—Not last nor least,
Thou, tho' declining in thy beauty and strength,
Faithful Moretto, to the latest hour
Guarding his chamber-door, and now along
The silent, sullen strand of Missolonghi
Howling in grief.—He had just left that Place
Of old renown, once in the Adrian sea,
Ravenna! where, from Dante's sacred tomb
He had so oft, as many a verse declares,
Drawn inspiration; where, at twilight-time,
Thro' the pine-forest wandering with loose rein,
Wandering and lost, he had so oft beheld
(What is not visible to a Poet's eye?)
The spectre-knight, the hell-hounds and their prey,
The chase, the slaughter, and the festal mirth
Suddenly blasted. 'Twas a theme he loved,
But others claimed their turn; and many a tower,
Shattered, uprooted from its native rock,
Its strength the pride of some heroic age,
Appeared and vanished (many a sturdy steer
Yoked and unyoked) while as in happier days
He poured his spirit forth. The past forgot,
All was enjoyment. Not a cloud obscured
Present or future.

Italy, 1822

MARY ANN LAMB

1764–1847

25 *Helen*

HIGH-BORN Helen, round your dwelling
   These twenty years I've paced in vain:
Haughty beauty, thy lover's duty
   Hath been to glory in his pain.

High-born Helen, proudly telling
   Stories of thy cold disdain;
I starve, I die, now you comply,
   And I no longer can complain.

These twenty years I've lived on tears,
   Dwelling for ever on a frown;
On sighs I've fed, your scorn my bread;
   I perish now you kind are grown.

Can I, who loved my beloved
   But for the scorn ' was in her eye',
Can I be moved for my beloved,
   When she ' returns me sigh for sigh '?

In stately pride, by my bed-side,
   High-born Helen's portrait 's hung;
Deaf to my praise, my mournful lays
   Are nightly to the portrait sung.

To that I weep, nor ever sleep,
   Complaining all night long to her—
Helen, grown old, no longer cold,
   Said, ' you to all men I prefer.'

         John Woodvil: a Tragedy, &c.
           By C. Lamb, 1802

I SAW a boy with eager eye
Open a book upon a stall,
And read as he'd devour it all:
Which when the stall-man did espy,
Soon to the boy I heard him call,
' You, Sir, you never buy a book,
Therefore in one you shall not look.'
The boy passed slowly on, and with a sigh
He wish'd he never had been taught to read,
Then of the old churl's books he should have had no need.

Of sufferings the poor have many,
Which never can the rich annoy.
I soon perceiv'd another boy
Who look'd as if he'd not had any
Food for that day at least, enjoy
The sight of cold meat in a tavern larder.
This boy's case, thought I, is surely harder,
Thus hungry longing, thus without a penny,
Beholding choice of dainty dressed meat:
No wonder if he wish he ne'er had learn'd to eat.

Poetry for Children, 1809

JAMES GRAHAME

1765–1811

27   *Sunday morning*

HOW still the morning of the hallowed day!
Mute is the voice of rural labour, hushed
The ploughboy's whistle and the milkmaid's song.
The scythe lies glittering in the dewy wreath

Of tedded grass, mingled with fading flowers,
That yester-morn bloomed waving in the breeze.
Sounds the most faint attract the ear—the hum
Of early bee, the trickling of the dew,
The distant bleating midway up the hill.
Calmness seems throned on yon unmoving cloud.
To him who wanders o'er the upland leas,
The blackbird's note comes mellower from the dale;
And sweeter from the sky the gladsome lark
Warbles his heaven-tuned song; the lulling brook
Murmurs more gently down the deep-sunk glen;
While from yon lowly roof, whose curling smoke
O'ermounts the mist, is heard at intervals
The voice of psalms, the simple song of praise.

With dove-like wings Peace o'er yon village broods:
The dizzying mill-wheel rests; the anvil's din
Hath ceased; all, all around is quietness.
Less fearful on this day, the limping hare
Stops, and looks back, and stops, and looks on man,
Her deadliest foe. The toil-worn horse, set free,
Unheedful of the pasture, roams at large;
And, as his stiff unwieldy bulk he rolls,
His iron-armed hoofs gleam in the morning ray.

The Sabbath, 1804

HENRY LUTTRELL

1765?–1851

From 'Advice to Julia'

(i)

Dress

B UT how shall I, unblamed, express
The awful mysteries of DRESS?
How, all unpractised, dare to tell
The art sublime, ineffable,
Of making *middling* men look well;
Men who had been such heavy sailers
But for their shoe-makers and tailors?
So, by the cutler's sharpening skill,
The bluntest weapons wound and kill:
So, when 'tis scarcely fit to eat,
Good cooks, by *dressing*, flavour meat.
And as, by steam impressed with motion
'Gainst wind and tide, across the ocean,
The merest *tub* will far outstrip
The progress of the lightest ship
That ever on the waters glided,
If with an engine unprovided;—
Thus Beaus, in person and in mind
Excelled by those they leave behind,
On, through the world, undaunted, press,
Backed by the mighty power of Dress;
While folks less confident than they
Stare, in mute wonder,—and give way.

(ii)

The Peace

TOO warm, my friend, your anger waxes;
   Consider, pray, the war and taxes.
First 'twas Napoleon and the French.
Now 'tis The Peace.—We *must* retrench.
War was a bitter scourge and curse;
Yet peace is, somehow, ten times worse.
Peace, or (as more than one division
Has gravely voted it) *Transition*,
As Commerce droops and times grow harder,
Shuts here a cellar, there a larder;
By slow, yet sure degrees, disables
Parks, gardens, eating-rooms, and stables;
Nor yet in her career relents,
But mows down whole establishments.
The poor, the middling, shoot a pitch
More and more humble;—ev'n the rich
From whose fat acres milk and honey
Keep flowing in the shape of money,
For lean economy produce
If not a reason, an excuse.
Their rates are high, their rents decrease,
Their corn 's a drug;—'tis all the Peace!
This jade-like Peace! Say, who will father her,
Unless she 's sworn to the tax-gatherer?

ADVICE TO JULIA

(iii)

The Honeymoon

HENCE, flames and darts! ye amorous sighs, hence!
Breathe not without—a *Special licence*!
For what are favors, bride-cakes, honey-
Moons, without equipage and money?
Cupids in vain around them hover,
Unless (the conjuration over
Which makes a husband of a lover)
Four conscious horses, strong and supple,
Whisk from the door the happy couple,
And lodge them in that deep retreat
Impregnable—a country-seat;
There, haply in the sultry season,
Condemned, without one earthly reason,
To struggle through a week's warm weather
In hopeless solitude together.

Strange work of Fate, with Custom leaguing,
To make ev'n happiness fatiguing!
Think how this caging must perplex
Two persons, though of different sex;
Unless kind fortune sends a *third*
To put in, now and then, a word!
For lovers may, when raptures fail,
When tender *tête-à-têtes* grow stale,
And Time creeps on with pinions leaded,
Wax very weary—*though they're wedded.*

Thus many a pair, so lately free,
Take their *first* lesson in Ennui;

And justly may be dunces reckoned,
If not quite perfect in a *second*.
Surely 'twere kinder not to banish
These turtles,—not to bid them vanish
At once into some rustic den,
Far from the cheerful haunts of men,
Till they are reconciled, and broke
A little to the nuptial yoke.
Launched in a life so strange and new,
Society should help them through,
As training makes young colts less wild,
Or as a go-cart props a child,
Until, by practice steady grown,
Its infant limbs can move alone.

Say, why should grots and shrubberies hide
A lawful bridegroom and a bride?
Why must they, lost in shady groves,
Fit shelter for unlicensed loves,
Steal from the' approving world, and seek
A long probationary week
Of close retirement, as profound
As if they both were under ground?
Twelve hours of every four-and-twenty
Left to themselves, methinks, were plenty.
Then why to villas hurry down,
When these, fond pair, are yours in town?

Be counselled.—Stir not, near or far,
But stay, I charge you, where you are.
The dream of passion soon or late
Is broken—don't anticipate.

ADVICE TO JULIA

Haste not to lose your hopes in fears,
Stark mad for moments, dull for years;
Devour not, for your comfort's sake,
At once, like children, *all* your cake;
Truth (on your memory well engrave it)
Whispers, you cannot eat and have it.
Gold is too precious,—lay it not
So thickly on a single spot;
But beat the bullion—husbands, wives—
And spread it over all your lives.

(*iv*)

Lovers and Friends

JULIA, my dear, how long, I wonder,
Must Charles and I be kept asunder,
Lest a friend's precept and example
Should teach him on his chains to trample?
Lest, questioned close and tutored well,
Your weary subject should rebel?
Lest your poor servant, one fine morning,
Should rise, and give his mistress warning?

I war not thus, (dismiss your fears)
For Man's resolves 'gainst Woman's tears.
Whether you quarrel or agree,
Mine is an armed neutrality.
Charles has my full consent to yield,
And leave you mistress of the field;
Or, if despair has made him stout,
With his fair foe to fight it out.

But wherefore thus provoke hostilities?
Think, Julia, think how rash and silly 'tis!
My counsel ends as it began.
Patch up a treaty, while you *can*.
Abate your power,—'tis overgrown.
Unsafe is a despotic throne.
Give up departments you can spare,
And yield a province here and there—
Warned by *his* fate whose stubborn pride
Clung to an empire stretched too wide;
Who, in *one* stake, to end the game,
Heaped power, and liberty, and fame;
Among the royal punters tost it,
Cried ' *Seven 's the main*,' threw crabs, and lost it!

Be not Napoleon's madness thine.
Accept the boundary of the Rhine;
Make promises and resolutions,
And *talk* at least of constitutions;
Or soon the angry Fates will frown
On Beauty in an *iron crown*,
And Fortune tarnish every gem
That glitters in your diadem.

Advice to Julia, 1820

ROBERT BLOOMFIELD

1766–1823

29   *From ' The Farmer's Boy '*

(*i*)

LIVE, trifling incidents, and grace my song,
    That to the humblest menial belong;
To him whose drudgery unheeded goes,
His joys unreckon'd as his cares or woes:

THE FARMER'S BOY

Though joys and cares in every path are sown,
And youthful minds have feelings of their own;
Quick springing sorrows, transient as the dew;
Delights from trifles, trifles ever new.
'Twas thus with GILES: meek, fatherless, and poor;
Labour his portion, but he felt no more;
No stripes, no tyranny his steps pursu'd;
His life was constant, cheerful, servitude:
Strange to the world, he wore a bashful look,
The Fields his study, Nature was his book;
And, as revolving SEASONS chang'd the scene
From heat to cold, tempestuous to serene,
Though every change still varied his employ,
Yet each new duty brought its share of joy.

(ii)

AGAIN, the year's *decline*, midst storms and floods,
The thund'ring chase, the yellow fading woods,
Invite my song; that fain would boldly tell
Of upland coverts, and the echoing dell,
By turns resounding loud, at eve and morn
The swineherd's halloo, or the huntsman's horn.

No more the fields with scatter'd grain supply
The restless wand'ring tenants of the STY;
From oak to oak they run with eager haste,
And wrangling share the first delicious taste
Of fallen ACORNS; yet but thinly found
Till the strong gale have shook them to the ground.
It comes; and roaring woods obedient wave:
Their home well pleas'd the joint adventurers leave:

ROBERT BLOOMFIELD

The trudging sow leads forth her numerous young,
Playful, and white, and clean, the briars among,
Till briars and thorns increasing, fence them round,
Where last year's mould'ring leaves bestrew the ground,
And o'er their heads, loud lash'd by furious squalls,
Bright from their cups the rattling treasure falls;
Hot thirsty food; whence doubly sweet and cool
The welcome margin of some rush-grown pool,
The wild duck's lonely haunt, whose jealous eye
Guards every point; who sits prepar'd to fly,
On the calm bosom of her little lake,
Too closely screen'd for ruffian winds to shake;
And as the bold intruders press around,
At once she starts, and rises with a bound:
With bristles rais'd the sudden noise they hear,
And ludicrously wild, and wing'd with fear,
The herd decamp with more than swinish speed,
And snorting dash through sedge, and rush, and reed:
Through tangling thickets headlong on they go,
Then stop and listen for their fancied foe;
The hindmost still the growing panic spreads,
Repeated fright the first alarm succeeds,
Till Folly's wages, wounds and thorns, they reap:
Yet glorying in their fortunate escape,
Their groundless terrors by degrees soon cease,
And Night's dark reign restores their wonted peace.
For now the gale subsides, and from each bough
The roosting pheasant's short but frequent crow
Invites to rest; and huddling side by side,
The herd in closest ambush seek to hide;
Seek some warm slope with shagged moss o'erspread,
Dry'd leaves their copious covering and their bed.

In vain may *Giles*, through gath'ring glooms that fall,
And solemn silence, urge his piercing call:
Whole days and nights they tarry midst their store,
Nor quit the woods till oaks can yield no more.

The Farmer's Boy, 1800

CAROLINA, LADY NAIRNE

1766–1845

30   *The Laird o' Cockpen*

THE laird o' Cockpen, he 's proud an' he 's great,
His mind is ta'en up wi' things o' the State;
He wanted a wife his braw house to keep,
But favour wi' wooin' was fashious to seek.

Down by the dyke-side a lady did dwell,
At his table head he thought she'd look well,
McClish 's ae daughter o' Clavers-ha Lee,
A penniless lass wi' a lang pedigree.

His wig was well pouther'd and as gude as new,
His waistcoat was white, his coat it was blue;
He put on a ring, a sword, and cock'd hat,
And wha could refuse the laird wi' a' that?

He took the grey mare, and rade cannily,
An' rapp'd at the yett o' Clavers-ha Lee;
' Gae tell Mistress Jean to come speedily ben,—
She 's wanted to speak to the Laird o' Cockpen.'

Mistress Jean was makin' the elder-flower wine;
' An' what brings the laird at sic a like time? '
She pat aff her aprin, and on her silk gown,
Her mutch wi' red ribbons, and gaed awa' down.

fashious] fastidious.   yett] door.   mutch] cap.

An' when she cam' ben he boued fu' low,
An' what was his errand he soon let her know;
Amazed was the laird when the lady said ' Na,'
And wi' a laigh curtsie she turned awa'

Dumfounder'd was he, nae sigh did he gie,
He mounted his mare—he rade cannily;
An' aften he thought, as he gaed through the glen,
' She 's daft to refuse the laird o' Cockpen.'

The Scottish Minstrel, vol. iii, *c.* 1822

31   *Caller Herrin'*

WHA'LL buy caller herrin'?
    They're bonnie fish and halesome farin';
Wha'll buy caller herrin',
New drawn frae the Forth?

When ye were sleepin' on your pillows,
Dream'd ye aught o' our puir fellows,
Darkling as they faced the billows,
A' to fill the woven willows? . . .

Wha'll buy my caller herrin'?
Oh, ye may ca' them vulgar farin',
Wives and mithers, maist despairing,
Ga' them lives o' men. . . .

When the creel o' herrin' passes,
Ladies, clad in silks and laces,
Gather in their braw pelisses,
Cast their heads and screw their faces,
   Wha'll buy caller herrin'? etc.

caller] fresh.

CALLER HERRIN'

Caller herrin's no to lightlie,
Ye can trip the spring fu' tightlie,
Spite o' tauntin', flauntin', flingin',
Gow has set you a' a-singing,
    Wha'll buy caller herrin'? etc.

Neibour wives, now tent my tellin':
When the bonny fish ye're sellin'
At a word aye be your dealin',
Truth will stand when a' thing's failin'.

Wha'll buy caller herrin'?
They're bonny fish and halesome farin';
Wha'll buy caller herrin',
New drawn frae the Forth?

The Scottish Minstrel, vol. v, *c.* 1823

JOHN HOOKHAM FRERE

1769–1846

32   *Bees and Monks*

AS Bees, that when the skies are calm and fair,
    In June, or the beginning of July,
Launch forth colonial settlers in the air,
    Round, round, and round-about, they whiz, they fly,
With eager worry whirling here and there,
    They know not whence nor whither, where, nor why,
In utter hurry-scurry, going, coming,
Maddening the summer air with ceaseless humming;

Till the strong Frying-pan's energic jangle
    With thrilling thrum their feeble hum doth drown;
Then passive and appeas'd, they droop and dangle,
    Clinging together close, and clust'ring down,

trip . . . tightlie] dance lightly.   Gow] Nathaniel Gow
(1766–1831), composer.   tent] attend to.

JOHN HOOKHAM FRERE

Link'd in a multitudinous living tangle
  Like an old Tassel of a dingy brown;
The joyful Farmer sees, and spreads his hay,
And reckons on a settled sultry day.

E'en so the Monks, as wild as sparks of fire,
  (Or swarms unpacified by pan or kettle)
Ran restless round the Cloisters and the Quire,
  Till those huge masses of sonorous metal
Attracted them toward the Tower and Spire;
  There you might see them cluster, crowd, and settle,
Throng'd in the hollow tintinnabular Hive;
The Belfry swarm'd with Monks; it seem'd alive.

King Arthur and His Round Table,
Canto III, 1818

JAMES HOGG
1770–1835

33   *Kilmeny*

BONNY Kilmeny gaed up the glen;
  But it wasna to meet Duneira's men,
Nor the rosy monk of the isle to see,
For Kilmeny was pure as pure could be.
It was only to hear the yorlin sing,
And pu' the cress-flower round the spring;
The scarlet hypp and the hindberrye,
And the nut that hang frae the hazel tree;
For Kilmeny was pure as pure could be.
But lang may her minny look o'er the wa',
And lang may she seek i' the green-wood shaw;

yorlin] yellow hammer.   hindberrye] raspberry.   minny]
mother.

70

KILMENY

Lang the laird o' Duneira blame,
And lang, lang greet or Kilmeny come hame!

When many a day had come and fled,
When grief was calm and hope was dead,
When mess for Kilmeny's soul had been sung,
When the bedes-man had prayed, and the dead-bell rung,
Late, late in a gloamin', when all was still,
When the fringe was red on the westlin hill,
The wood was sere, the moon i' the wane,
The reek o' the cot hung over the plain,
Like a little wee cloud in the world its lane;
When the ingle lowed with an eiry leme,
Late, late in the gloaming Kilmeny came hame!

' Kilmeny, Kilmeny, where have you been?
Lang hae we sought baith holt and den;
By linn, by ford, and green-wood tree,
Yet you are halesome and fair to see.
Where gat you that joup o' the lily scheen?
The bonny snood of the birk sae green?
And these roses, the fairest that ever were seen?
Kilmeny, Kilmeny, where have you been? '—

Kilmeny looked up with a lovely grace,
But nae smile was seen on Kilmeny's face;
As still was her look, and as still was her e'e,
As the stillness that lay on the emerant lea,
Or the mist that sleeps on a waveless sea.
For Kilmeny had been she knew not where,
And Kilmeny had seen what she could not declare;

greet] weep.   lowed] blazed, glowed.   leme] light, flame.
linn] torrent, cascade.   joup] petticoat.

Kilmeny had been where the cock never crew,
Where the rain never fell, and the wind never blew.

But it seemed as the harp of the sky had rung,
And the airs of heaven played round her tongue,
When she spake of the lovely forms she had seen,
And a land where sin had never been;
A land of love and a land of light,
Withouten sun, or moon, or night;
Where the river swa'd a living stream,
And the light a pure celestial beam;
The land of vision, it would seem,
A still, an everlasting dream.

In yon green-wood there is a waik,
And in that waik there is a wene,
And in that wene there is a maike,
That neither has flesh, blood, nor bane;
And down in yon green-wood he walks his lane.

In that green wene Kilmeny lay,
Her bosom happ'd wi' flowerets gay;
But the air was soft and the silence deep,
And bonny Kilmeny fell sound asleep.
She kenn'd nae mair, nor open'd her e'e,
Till waked by the hymns of a far countrye.

She 'waken'd on couch of the silk sae slim,
All striped wi' the bars of the rainbow's rim;
And lovely beings round were rife,
Who erst had travell'd mortal life;

swa'd] swelled.   waik] grassy path, glade.   wene] dwelling.
maike] mate.   his lane] alone, by himself.   happ'd]
covered.

KILMENY

And aye they smiled and 'gan to speer,
' What spirit has brought this mortal here? '—

' Lang have I journey'd the world wide,'
A meek and reverend fere replied;
' Baith night and day I have watch'd the fair,
Eident a thousand years and mair.
Yes, I have watch'd o'er ilk degree,
Wherever blooms femenitye;
But sinless virgin, free of stain
In mind and body, fand I nane.
Never, since the banquet of time,
Found I virgin in her prime,
Till late this bonny maiden I saw
As spotless as the morning snaw:
Full twenty years she has lived as free
As the spirits that sojourn in this countrye.
I have brought her away frae the snares of men,
That sin or death she never may ken.'—

They clasp'd her waist and her hands sae fair,
They kiss'd her cheek and they kemed her hair,
And round came many a blooming fere,
Saying, ' Bonny Kilmeny, ye're welcome here!
Women are freed of the littand scorn:
O blest be the day Kilmeny was born!
Now shall the land of the spirits see,
Now shall it ken what a woman may be!
Many a lang year in sorrow and pain,
Many a lang year through the world we've gane,

speer] inquire.   fere] fellow.   Eident] unintermittently.
kemed] combed.   littand] staining.

Commission'd to watch fair womankind,
For it's they who nurice th' immortal mind.
We have watch'd their steps as the dawning shone,
And deep in the green-wood walks alone;
By lily bower and silken bed,
The viewless tears have o'er them shed;
Have soothed their ardent minds to sleep,
Or left the couch of love to weep.
We have seen! we have seen! but the time must come,
And the angels will weep at the day of doom!

' O would the fairest of mortal kind
Aye keep the holy truths in mind,
That kindred spirits their motions see,
Who watch their ways with anxious e'e,
And grieve for the guilt of humanitye!
O, sweet to heaven the maiden's prayer,
And the sigh that heaves a bosom sae fair!
And dear to heaven the words of truth,
And the praise of virtue frae beauty's mouth!
And dear to the viewless forms of air,
The minds that kyth as the body fair!
O bonny Kilmeny! free frae stain,
If ever you seek the world again,
That world of sin, of sorrow and fear,
O tell of the joys that are waiting here!
And tell of the signs you shall shortly see;
Of the times that are now, and the times that shall be.'—

They lifted Kilmeny, they led her away,
And she walk'd in the light of a sunless day;

kyth] show, appear.

74

KILMENY

The sky was a dome of crystal bright,
The fountain of vision, and fountain of light:
The emerald fields were of dazzling glow,
And the flowers of everlasting blow.
Then deep in the stream her body they laid,
That her youth and beauty never might fade;
And they smiled on heaven, when they saw her lie
In the stream of life that wander'd bye.
And she heard a song, she heard it sung,
She kend not where; but sae sweetly it rung,
It fell on her ear like a dream of the morn:
' O, blest be the day Kilmeny was born!
Now shall the land of the spirits see,
Now shall it ken what a woman may be!
The sun that shines on the world sae bright,
A borrow'd gleid frae the fountain of light;
And the moon that sleeks the sky sae dun,
Like a gouden bow, or a beamless sun,
Shall wear away, and be seen nae mair,
And the angels shall miss them travelling the air.
But lang, lang after baith night and day,
When the sun and the world have elyed away;
When the sinner has gane to his waesome doom,
Kilmeny shall smile in eternal bloom! '—

They bore her away she wist not how,
For she felt not arm nor rest below;
But so swift they wain'd her through the light,
'Twas like the motion of sound or sight;
They seem'd to split the gales of air,
And yet nor gale nor breeze was there.

gleid] spark, glow.   elyed] vanished.   wain'd] carried.

75

Unnumber'd groves below them grew,
They came, they pass'd, and backward flew,
Like floods of blossoms gliding on,
In moment seen, in moment gone.
O, never vales to mortal view
Appear'd like those o'er which they flew!
That land to human spirits given,
The lowermost vales of the storied heaven;
From thence they can view the world below,
And heaven's blue gates with sapphires glow,
More glory yet unmeet to know.

They bore her far to a mountain green,
To see what mortal never had seen;
And they seated her high on a purple sward,
And bade her heed what she saw and heard,
And note the changes the spirits wrought,
For now she lived in the land of thought.
She look'd, and she saw nor sun nor skies,
But a crystal dome of a thousand dyes.
She look'd, and she saw nae land aright,
But an endless whirl of glory and light.
And radiant beings went and came,
Far swifter than wind, or the linked flame.
She hid her e'en frae the dazzling view;
She look'd again, and the scene was new.

She saw a sun on a summer sky,
And clouds of amber sailing bye;
A lovely land beneath her lay,
And that land had glens and mountains gray;
And that land had valleys and hoary piles,
And marled seas, and a thousand isles.

KILMENY

Its fields were speckled, its forests green,
And its lakes were all of the dazzling sheen,
Like magic mirrors, where slumbering lay
The sun and the sky and the cloudlet gray;
Which heaved and trembled, and gently swung,
On every shore they seem'd to be hung;
For there they were seen on their downward plain
A thousand times and a thousand again;
In winding lake and placid firth,
Little peaceful heavens in the bosom of earth.

Kilmeny sigh'd and seem'd to grieve,
For she found her heart to that land did cleave;
She saw the corn wave on the vale,
She saw the deer run down the dale;
She saw the plaid and the broad claymore,
And the brows that the badge of freedom bore;
And she thought she had seen the land before.

She saw a lady sit on a throne,
The fairest that ever the sun shone on!
A lion lick'd her hand of milk,
And she held him in a leish of silk;
And a leifu' maiden stood at her knee,
With a silver wand and melting e'e;
Her sovereign shield till love stole in,
And poison'd all the fount within.

Then a gruff untoward bedesman came,
And hundit the lion on his dame;
And the guardian maid wi' the dauntless e'e,
She dropp'd a tear, and left her knee;

leifu'] wistful.

And she saw till the queen frae the lion fled,
Till the bonniest flower of the world lay dead;
A coffin was set on a distant plain,
And she saw the red blood fall like rain;
Then bonny Kilmeny's heart grew sair,
And she turn'd away, and could look nae mair.

Then the gruff grim carle girn'd amain,
And they trampled him down, but he rose again;
And he baited the lion to deeds of weir,
Till he lapp'd the blood to the kingdom dear;
And weening his head was danger-preef,
When crown'd with the rose and clover leaf,
He gowl'd at the carle, and chased him away,
To feed wi' the deer on the mountain gray.
He gowl'd at the carle, and geck'd at Heaven,
But his mark was set, and his arles given.
Kilmeny a while her e'en withdrew;
She look'd again, and the scene was new.

She saw below her fair unturl'd
One half of all the glowing world,
Where oceans roll'd, and rivers ran,
To bound the aims of sinful man.
She saw a people, fierce and fell,
Burst frae their bounds like fiends of hell;
Their lilies grew, and the eagle flew,
And she herked on her ravening crew,
Till the cities and towers were wrapp'd in a blaze,
And the thunder it roar'd o'er the lands and the seas.

girn'd] snarled.   weir] war.   gowl'd] howled.   geck'd]
mocked.   arles] money paid on striking a bargain.   herked]
urged.

KILMENY

The widows they wail'd, and the red blood ran,
And she threaten'd an end to the race of man;
She never lened, nor stood in awe,
Till caught by the lion's deadly paw.
O, then the eagle swink'd for life,
And brainyell'd up a mortal strife;
But flew she north, or flew she south,
She met wi' the gowl of the lion's mouth.

With a mooted wing and waefu' maen,
The eagle sought her eiry again;
But lang may she cower in her bloody nest,
And lang, lang sleek her wounded breast,
Before she sey another flight,
To play wi' the norland lion's might.

But to sing the sights Kilmeny saw,
So far surpassing nature's law,
The singer's voice wad sink away,
And the string of his harp wad cease to play.
But she saw till the sorrows of man were bye,
And all was love and harmony;
Till the stars of heaven fell calmly away,
Like flakes of snaw on a winter day.

Then Kilmeny begg'd again to see
The friends she had left in her own country;
To tell of the place where she had been,
And the glories that lay in the land unseen;
To warn the living maidens fair,
The loved of Heaven, the spirits' care,

lened] crouched.   swink'd] struggled.   brainyell'd]
stirred, beat.   mooted] moulted.   sey] essay.

That all whose minds unmeled remain
Shall bloom in beauty when time is gane.

With distant music, soft and deep,
They lull'd Kilmeny sound asleep;
And when she awaken'd, she lay her lane,
All happ'd with flowers, in the green-wood wene.
When seven lang years had come and fled,
When grief was calm, and hope was dead;
When scarce was remember'd Kilmeny's name,
Late, late in a gloamin' Kilmeny came hame!

And O, her beauty was fair to see,
But still and steadfast was her e'e!
Such beauty bard may never declare,
For there was no pride nor passion there;
And the soft desire of maiden's e'en
In that mild face could never be seen.
Her seymar was the lily flower,
And her cheek the moss-rose in the shower;
And her voice like the distant melodye,
That floats along the twilight sea.
But she loved to raike the lanely glen,
And keepèd afar frae the haunts of men;
Her holy hymns unheard to sing,
To suck the flowers, and drink the spring.
But wherever her peaceful form appear'd,
The wild beasts of the hill were cheer'd;
The wolf play'd blythly round the field,
The lordly byson low'd and kneel'd;

unmeled] unblemished.   seymar] = cymar, a slight
covering.   raike] range, wander.

KILMENY

The dun deer woo'd with manner bland,
And cower'd aneath her lily hand.
And when at even the woodlands rung,
When hymns of other worlds she sung
In ecstasy of sweet devotion,
O, then the glen was all in motion!
The wild beasts of the forest came,
Broke from their bughts and faulds the tame,
And goved around, charm'd and amazed;
Even the dull cattle croon'd and gazed,
And murmur'd and look'd with anxious pain
For something the mystery to explain.
The buzzard came with the throstle-cock;
The corby left her houf in the rock;
The blackbird alang wi' the eagle flew;
The hind came tripping o'er the dew;
The wolf and the kid their raike began,
And the tod, and the lamb, and the leveret ran;
The hawk and the hern attour them hung,
And the merle and the mavis forhooy'd their young;
And all in a peaceful ring were hurl'd;
It was like an eve in a sinless world!

When a month and a day had come and gane,
Kilmeny sought the greenwood wene;
There laid her down on the leaves sae green,
And Kilmeny on earth was never mair seen.
But O, the words that fell from her mouth,
Were words of wonder, and words of truth!

bughts] milking-pens.   goved] stared, gazed.   corby]
raven.   houf] haunt.   tod] fox.   attour] above.
merle] blackbird.   forhooy'd] forsook.

JAMES HOGG

But all the land were in fear and dread,
For they kendna whether she was living or dead.
It wasna her hame, and she couldna remain;
She left this world of sorrow and pain,
And return'd to the land of thought again.

The Queen's Wake, 1813

WILLIAM WORDSWORTH

1770–1850

34 *Lines*

*Composed a few miles above Tintern Abbey, on revisiting the
banks of the Wye during a tour. July 13, 1798*

FIVE years have past; five summers, with the length
Of five long winters! and again I hear
These waters, rolling from their mountain-springs
With a sweet inland murmur.—Once again
Do I behold these steep and lofty cliffs,
That on a wild secluded scene impress
Thoughts of more deep seclusion; and connect
The landscape with the quiet of the sky.
The day is come when I again repose
Here, under this dark sycamore, and view
These plots of cottage-ground, these orchard-tufts,
Which at this season, with their unripe fruits,
Are clad in one green hue, and lose themselves
Among the woods and copses, nor disturb
The wild green landscape. Once again I see
These hedge-rows, hardly hedge-rows, little lines
Of sportive wood run wild: these pastoral farms,
Green to the very door; and wreaths of smoke

Sent up, in silence, from among the trees!
With some uncertain notice, as might seem
Of vagrant dwellers in the houseless woods,
Or of some Hermit's cave, where by his fire
The Hermit sits alone.

                These beauteous forms,
Through a long absence, have not been to me
As is a landscape to a blind man's eye:
But oft, in lonely rooms, and 'mid the din
Of towns and cities, I have owed to them,
In hours of weariness, sensations sweet,
Felt in the blood, and felt along the heart;
And passing even into my purer mind,
With tranquil restoration:—feelings too
Of unremembered pleasure: such, perhaps,
As have no slight or trivial influence
On that best portion of a good man's life,
His little, nameless, unremembered acts
Of kindness and of love. Nor less, I trust,
To them I may have owed another gift,
Of aspect more sublime; that blessed mood,
In which the burthen of the mystery,
In which the heavy and the weary weight
Of all this unintelligible world,
Is lightened:—that serene and blessed mood,
In which the affections gently lead us on,—
Until, the breath of this corporeal frame
And even the motion of our human blood
Almost suspended, we are laid asleep
In body, and become a living soul:
While with an eye made quiet by the power

Of harmony, and the deep power of joy,
We see into the life of things.
                              If this
Be but a vain belief, yet, oh! how oft—
In darkness and amid the many shapes
Of joyless daylight; when the fretful stir
Unprofitable, and the fever of the world,
Have hung upon the beatings of my heart—
How oft, in spirit, have I turned to thee,
O sylvan Wye! Thou wanderer thro' the woods,
How often has my spirit turned to thee!

    And now, with gleams of half-extinguished thought,
With many recognitions dim and faint,
And somewhat of a sad perplexity,
The picture of the mind revives again:
While here I stand, not only with the sense
Of present pleasure, but with pleasing thoughts
That in this moment there is life and food
For future years. And so I dare to hope,
Though changed, no doubt, from what I was when first
I came among these hills; when like a roe
I bounded o'er the mountains, by the sides
Of the deep rivers, and the lonely streams,
Wherever nature led: more like a man
Flying from something that he dreads, than one
Who sought the thing he loved. For nature then
(The coarser pleasures of my boyish days,
And their glad animal movements all gone by)
To me was all in all.—I cannot paint
What then I was. The sounding cataract
Haunted me like a passion: the tall rock,

TINTERN ABBEY

The mountain, and the deep and gloomy wood,
Their colours and their forms, were then to me
An appetite; a feeling and a love,
That had no need of a remoter charm,
By thought supplied, nor any interest
Unborrowed from the eye.—That time is past,
And all its aching joys are now no more,
And all its dizzy raptures. Not for this
Faint I, nor mourn nor murmur; other gifts
Have followed; for such loss, I would believe,
Abundant recompence. For I have learned
To look on nature, not as in the hour
Of thoughtless youth; but hearing oftentimes
The still, sad music of humanity,
Nor harsh nor grating, though of ample power
To chasten and subdue. And I have felt
A presence that disturbs me with the joy
Of elevated thoughts; a sense sublime
Of something far more deeply interfused,
Whose dwelling is the light of setting suns,
And the round ocean and the living air,
And the blue sky, and in the mind of man:
A motion and a spirit, that impels
All thinking things, all objects of all thought,
And rolls through all things. Therefore am I still
A lover of the meadows and the woods,
And mountains; and of all that we behold
From this green earth; of all the mighty world
Of eye, and ear,—both what they half create,
And what perceive; well pleased to recognise
In nature and the language of the sense,
The anchor of my purest thoughts, the nurse,

The guide, the guardian of my heart, and soul
Of all my moral being.
                    Nor perchance,
If I were not thus taught, should I the more
Suffer my genial spirits to decay:
For thou art with me here upon the banks
Of this fair river; thou my dearest Friend,
My dear, dear Friend; and in thy voice I catch
The language of my former heart, and read
My former pleasures in the shooting lights
Of thy wild eyes. Oh! yet a little while
May I behold in thee what I was once,
My dear, dear Sister! and this prayer I make,
Knowing that Nature never did betray
The heart that loved her; 'tis her privilege,
Through all the years of this our life, to lead
From joy to joy: for she can so inform
The mind that is within us, so impress
With quietness and beauty, and so feed
With lofty thoughts, that neither evil tongues,
Rash judgments, nor the sneers of selfish men,
Nor greetings where no kindness is, nor all
The dreary intercourse of daily life,
Shall e'er prevail against us, or disturb
Our cheerful faith, that all which we behold
Is full of blessings. Therefore let the moon
Shine on thee in thy solitary walk;
And let the misty mountain-winds be free
To blow against thee: and, in after years,
When these wild ecstasies shall be matured
Into a sober pleasure; when thy mind
Shall be a mansion for all lovely forms,

Thy memory be as a dwelling-place
For all sweet sounds and harmonies; oh! then,
If solitude, or fear, or pain, or grief,
Should be thy portion, with what healing thoughts
Of tender joy wilt thou remember me,
And these my exhortations! Nor, perchance—
If I should be where I no more can hear
Thy voice, nor catch from thy wild eyes these gleams
Of past existence—wilt thou then forget
That on the banks of this delightful stream
We stood together; and that I, so long
A worshipper of Nature, hither came
Unwearied in that service: rather say
With warmer love—oh! with far deeper zeal
Of holier love. Nor wilt thou then forget,
That after many wanderings, many years
Of absence, these steep woods and lofty cliffs,
And this green pastoral landscape, were to me
More dear, both for themselves and for thy sake!

Lyrical Ballads, 1798

35　　　　*Expostulation and Reply*

' WHY, William, on that old grey stone,
　　Thus for the length of half a day,
Why, William, sit you thus alone,
And dream your time away?

Where are your books?—that light bequeathed
To Beings else forlorn and blind!
Up! up! and drink the spirit breathed
From dead men to their kind.

WILLIAM WORDSWORTH

You look round on your mother Earth,
As if she for no purpose bore you;
As if you were her first-born birth,
And none had lived before you!'

One morning thus, by Esthwaite lake,
When life was sweet, I knew not why,
To me my good friend Matthew spake,
And thus I made reply:

' The eye—it cannot choose but see;
We cannot bid the ear be still;
Our bodies feel, where'er they be,
Against, or with our will.

Nor less I deem that there are Powers
Which of themselves our minds impress;
That we can feed this mind of ours
In a wise passiveness.

Think you, 'mid all this mighty sum
Of things for ever speaking,
That nothing of itself will come,
But we must still be seeking?

—Then ask not wherefore, here, alone,
Conversing as I may,
I sit upon this old grey stone,
And dream my time away.'

Lyrical Ballads, 1798

The Tables Turned

An evening scene on the same subject.

UP! up! my Friend, and quit your books;
  Or surely you'll grow double:
Up! up! my Friend, and clear your looks;
Why all this toil and trouble?

The sun, above the mountain's head,
A freshening lustre mellow
Through all the long green fields has spread,
His first sweet evening yellow.

Books! 'tis a dull and endless strife:
Come, hear the woodland linnet,
How sweet his music! on my life,
There 's more of wisdom in it.

And hark! how blithe the throstle sings!
He, too, is no mean preacher:
Come forth into the light of things,
Let Nature be your teacher.

She has a world of ready wealth,
Our minds and hearts to bless—
Spontaneous wisdom breathed by health,
Truth breathed by cheerfulness.

One impulse from a vernal wood
May teach you more of man,
Of moral evil and of good,
Than all the sages can.

3353   D   89

Sweet is the lore which Nature brings;
Our meddling intellect
Mis-shapes the beauteous forms of things:—
We murder to dissect.

Enough of Science and of Art;
Close up those barren leaves;
Come forth, and bring with you a heart
That watches and receives.

Lyrical Ballads, 1798

37   *Lines Written in Early Spring*

I HEARD a thousand blended notes,
  While in a grove I sate reclined,
In that sweet mood when pleasant thoughts
Bring sad thoughts to the mind.

To her fair works did Nature link
The human soul that through me ran;
And much it grieved my heart to think
What man has made of man.

Through primrose tufts, in that green bower,
The periwinkle trailed its wreaths;
And 'tis my faith that every flower
Enjoys the air it breathes.

The birds around me hopped and played;
Their thoughts I cannot measure:—
But the least motion which they made,
It seemed a thrill of pleasure.

The budding twigs spread out their fan,
To catch the breezy air;
And I must think, do all I can,
That there was pleasure there.

If this belief from heaven be sent,
If such be Nature's holy plan,
Have I not reason to lament
What man has made of man?

Lyrical Ballads, 1798

38 *To My Sister*

*Written at a small distance from my house, and sent by
my little boy*

IT is the first mild day of March:
Each minute sweeter than before,
The redbreast sings from the tall larch
That stands beside our door.

There is a blessing in the air,
Which seems a sense of joy to yield
To the bare trees, and mountains bare,
And grass in the green field.

My Sister! ('tis a wish of mine)
Now that our morning meal is done,
Make haste, your morning task resign;
Come forth and feel the sun.

Edward will come with you;—and, pray,
Put on with speed your woodland dress;
And bring no book: for this one day
We'll give to idleness.

WILLIAM WORDSWORTH

No joyless forms shall regulate
Our living calendar:
We from to-day, my Friend, will date
The opening of the year.

Love, now a universal birth,
From heart to heart is stealing,
From earth to man, from man to earth:
—It is the hour of feeling.

One moment now may give us more
Than years of toiling reason:
Our minds shall drink at every pore
The spirit of the season.

Some silent laws our hearts will make,
Which they shall long obey:
We for the year to come may take
Our temper from to-day.

And from the blessed power that rolls
About, below, above,
We'll frame the measure of our souls:
They shall be tuned to love.

Then come, my Sister! come, I pray,
With speed put on your woodland dress;—
And bring no book: for this one day
We'll give to idleness.

Lyrical Ballads, 1798

STRANGE fits of passion have I known:
And I will dare to tell,
But in the Lover's ear alone,
What once to me befel.

When she I loved looked every day
Fresh as a rose in June,
I to her cottage bent my way,
Beneath an evening-moon.

Upon the moon I fixed my eye,
All over the wide lea;
With quickening pace my horse drew nigh
Those paths so dear to me.

And now we reached the orchard-plot;
And, as we climbed the hill,
The sinking moon to Lucy's cot
Came near, and nearer still.

In one of those sweet dreams I slept,
Kind Nature's gentlest boon!
And all the while my eyes I kept
On the descending moon.

My horse moved on; hoof after hoof
He raised, and never stopped:
When down behind the cottage roof,
At once, the bright moon dropped.

What fond and wayward thoughts will slide
Into a Lover's head!
' O mercy! ' to myself I cried,
' If Lucy should be dead! '

Lyrical Ballads, &c., 1800

40 *'She dwelt among the untrodden ways'*

SHE dwelt among the untrodden ways
 Beside the springs of Dove,
A Maid whom there were none to praise
 And very few to love:

A violet by a mossy stone
 Half hidden from the eye!
—Fair as a star, when only one
 Is shining in the sky.

She lived unknown, and few could know
 When Lucy ceased to be;
But she is in her grave, and, oh,
 The difference to me!

Lyrical Ballads, &c. 1800

41 *' Three years she grew '*

THREE years she grew in sun and shower,
 Then Nature said, ' A lovelier flower
On earth was never sown;
This Child I to myself will take;
She shall be mine, and I will make
A Lady of my own.

Myself will to my darling be
Both law and impulse: and with me
The Girl, in rock and plain,
In earth and heaven, in glade and bower,
Shall feel an overseeing power
To kindle or restrain.

THREE YEARS SHE GREW

She shall be sportive as the fawn
That wild with glee across the lawn
Or up the mountain springs;
And her's shall be the breathing balm,
And her's the silence and the calm
Of mute insensate things.

The floating clouds their state shall lend
To her; for her the willow bend;
Nor shall she fail to see
Even in the motions of the Storm
Grace that shall mould the Maiden's form
By silent sympathy.

The stars of midnight shall be dear
To her; and she shall lean her ear
In many a secret place
Where rivulets dance their wayward round,
And beauty born of murmuring sound
Shall pass into her face.

And vital feelings of delight
Shall rear her form to stately height,
Her virgin bosom swell;
Such thoughts to Lucy I will give
While she and I together live
Here in this happy dell.'

Thus Nature spake—The work was done—
How soon my Lucy's race was run!
She died, and left to me
This heath, this calm and quiet scene;
The memory of what has been,
And never more will be.

Lyrical Ballads, &c., 1800

42   ' *A slumber did my spirit seal* '

A SLUMBER did my spirit seal;
    I had no human fears:
She seemed a thing that could not feel
    The touch of earthly years.

No motion has she now, no force;
    She neither hears nor sees;
Rolled round in earth's diurnal course,
    With rocks, and stones, and trees.

Lyrical Ballads, &c., 1800

43   ' *There was a Boy* '

THERE was a Boy; ye knew him well, ye cliffs
    And islands of Winander!—many a time,
At evening, when the earliest stars began
To move along the edges of the hills,
Rising or setting, would he stand alone,
Beneath the trees, or by the glimmering lake;
And there, with fingers interwoven, both hands
Pressed closely palm to palm and to his mouth
Uplifted, he, as through an instrument,
Blew mimic hootings to the silent owls,
That they might answer him.—And they would shout
Across the watery vale, and shout again,
Responsive to his call,—with quivering peals,
And long halloos, and screams, and echoes loud
Redoubled and redoubled; concourse wild
Of jocund din! And, when there came a pause
Of silence such as baffled his best skill:
Then, sometimes, in that silence, while he hung

Listening, a gentle shock of mild surprise
Has carried far into his heart the voice
Of mountain-torrents; or the visible scene
Would enter unawares into his mind
With all its solemn imagery, its rocks,
Its woods, and that uncertain heaven received
Into the bosom of the steady lake.

This Boy was taken from his mates, and died
In childhood, ere he was full twelve years old.
Fair are the woods, and beauteous is the spot,
The vale where he was born: the churchyard hangs
Upon a slope above the village-school;
And, through that church-yard when my way has led
On summer-evenings, I believe, that there
A long half-hour together I have stood
Mute—looking at the grave in which he lies!

Lyrical Ballads, &c., 1800

44 *A Poet's Epitaph*

ART thou a Statist in the van
Of public conflicts trained and bred?
—First learn to love one living man;
Then may'st thou think upon the dead.

A Lawyer art thou?—draw not nigh!
Go, carry to some fitter place
The keenness of that practised eye,
The hardness of that sallow face.

Art thou a Man of purple cheer?
A rosy Man, right plump to see?
Approach; yet, Doctor, not too near,
This grave no cushion is for thee.

Or art thou one of gallant pride,
A Soldier, and no man of chaff?
Welcome!—but lay thy sword aside,
And lean upon a peasant's staff.

Physician art thou? one, all eyes,
Philosopher! a fingering slave,
One that would peep and botanize
Upon his mother's grave?

Wrapt closely in thy sensual fleece,
O turn aside,—and take, I pray,
That he below may rest in peace,
Thy ever-dwindling soul, away!

A Moralist perchance appears;
Led, Heaven knows how! to this poor sod:
And he has neither eyes nor ears;
Himself his world, and his own God;

One to whose smooth-rubbed soul can cling
Nor form, nor feeling, great or small;
A reasoning, self-sufficing thing,
An intellectual All-in-all!

Shut close the door; press down the latch;
Sleep in thy intellectual crust;
Nor lose ten tickings of thy watch
Near this unprofitable dust.

But who is He, with modest looks,
And clad in homely russet brown?
He murmurs near the running brooks
A music sweeter than their own.

A POET'S EPITAPH

He is retired as noontide dew,
Or fountain in a noon-day grove;
And you must love him, ere to you
He will seem worthy of your love.

The outward shows of sky and earth,
Of hill and valley, he has viewed;
And impulses of deeper birth
Have come to him in solitude.

In common things that round us lie
Some random truths he can impart,—
The harvest of a quiet eye
That broods and sleeps on his own heart.

But he is weak; both Man and Boy,
Hath been an idler in the land;
Contented if he might enjoy
The things which others understand.

—Come hither in thy hour of strength;
Come, weak as is a breaking wave!
Here stretch thy body at full length;
Or build thy house upon this grave.

Lyrical Ballads, &c., 1800

45   *The Fountain*

A CONVERSATION

WE talked with open heart, and tongue
Affectionate and true,
A pair of friends, though I was young,
And Matthew seventy-two.

We lay beneath a spreading oak,
Beside a mossy seat;
And from the turf a fountain broke,
And gurgled at our feet.

' Now, Matthew!' said I, ' let us match
This water's pleasant tune
With some old border-song, or catch,
That suits a summer's noon;

Or of the church-clock and the chimes
Sing here beneath the shade,
That half-mad thing of witty rhymes
Which you last April made!'

In silence Matthew lay, and eyed
The spring beneath the tree;
And thus the dear old Man replied,
The grey-haired man of glee:

' No check, no stay, this Streamlet fears;
How merrily it goes!
'Twill murmur on a thousand years,
And flow as now it flows.

And here, on this delightful day,
I cannot choose but think
How oft, a vigorous man, I lay
Beside this fountain's brink.

My eyes are dim with childish tears,
My heart is idly stirred,
For the same sound is in my ears
Which in those days I heard.

THE FOUNTAIN

Thus fares it still in our decay:
And yet the wiser mind
Mourns less for what age takes away
Than what it leaves behind.

The blackbird amid leafy trees,
The lark above the hill,
Let loose their carols when they please,
Are quiet when they will.

With Nature never do *they* wage
A foolish strife; they see
A happy youth, and their old age
Is beautiful and free:

But we are pressed by heavy laws;
And often, glad no more,
We wear a face of joy, because
We have been glad of yore.

If there be one who need bemoan
His kindred laid in earth,
The household hearts that were his own;
It is the man of mirth.

My days, my Friend, are almost gone,
My life has been approved,
And many love me; but by none
Am I enough beloved.'

' Now both himself and me he wrongs,
The man who thus complains!
I live and sing my idle songs
Upon these happy plains,

And, Matthew, for thy children dead
I'll be a son to thee!'
At this he grasped my hand, and said,
' Alas! that cannot be.'

We rose up from the fountain-side;
And down the smooth descent
Of the green sheep-track did we glide
And through the wood we went;

And, ere we came to Leonard's rock,
He sang those witty rhymes
About the crazy old church-clock,
And the bewildered chimes.

Lyrical Ballads, &c., 1800

46   *Lucy Gray*

OR, SOLITUDE

OFT I had heard of Lucy Gray:
And, when I crossed the wild,
I chanced to see at break of day
The solitary child.

No mate, no comrade Lucy knew;
She dwelt on a wide moor,
—The sweetest thing that ever grew
Beside a human door!

You yet may spy the fawn at play,
The hare upon the green;
But the sweet face of Lucy Gray
Will never more be seen.

LUCY GRAY

' To-night will be a stormy night—
You to the town must go;
And take a lantern, Child, to light
Your mother through the snow.'

' That, Father! will I gladly do:
'Tis scarcely afternoon—
The minster-clock has just struck two,
And yonder is the moon!'

At this the Father raised his hook,
And snapped a faggot-band;
He plied his work;—and Lucy took
The lantern in her hand.

Not blither is the mountain roe;
With many a wanton stroke
Her feet disperse the powdery snow,
That rises up like smoke.

The storm came on before its time :
She wandered up and down;
And many a hill did Lucy climb:
But never reached the town.

The wretched parents all that night
Went shouting far and wide;
But there was neither sound nor sight
To serve them for a guide.

At day-break on a hill they stood
That overlooked the moor;
And thence they saw the bridge of wood,
A furlong from their door.

They wept—and, turning homeward, cried,
' In heaven we all shall meet; '
—When in the snow the mother spied
The print of Lucy's feet.

Half breathless from the steep hill's edge
They tracked the footmarks small;
And through the broken hawthorn-hedge,
And by the long stone-wall;

And then an open field they crossed:
The marks were still the same;
They tracked them on, nor ever lost;
And to the bridge they came.

They followed from the snowy bank
Those footmarks, one by one,
Into the middle of the plank;
And further there were none!

—Yet some maintain that to this day
She is a living child;
That you may see sweet Lucy Gray
Upon the lonesome wild.

O'er rough and smooth she trips along,
And never looks behind;
And sings a solitary song
That whistles in the wind.

Lyrical Ballads, &c., 1800

47 *Prefatory Sonnet*

NUNS fret not at their convent's narrow room;
 And hermits are contented with their cells;
And students with their pensive citadels:
Maids at the wheel, the weaver at his loom,
Sit blithe and happy; bees that soar for bloom,
High as the highest Peak of Furness-fells,
Will murmur by the hour in foxglove bells:
In truth, the prison, unto which we doom
Ourselves, no prison is: and hence to me,
In sundry moods, 'twas pastime to be bound
Within the Sonnet's scanty plot of ground:
Pleased if some Souls (for such there needs must be)
Who have felt the weight of too much liberty,
Should find brief solace there, as I have found.

Poems in Two Volumes, 1807

48 *To Toussaint l'Ouverture*

TOUSSAINT, the most unhappy man of men!
 Whether the whistling Rustic tend his plough
Within thy hearing, or thy head be now
Pillowed in some deep dungeon's earless den;—
O miserable Chieftain! where and when
Wilt thou find patience? Yet die not; do thou
Wear rather in thy bonds a cheerful brow:
Though fallen thyself, never to rise again,
Live, and take comfort. Thou hast left behind
Powers that will work for thee; air, earth, and skies;

There 's not a breathing of the common wind
That will forget thee; thou hast great allies;
Thy friends are exultations, agonies,
And love, and man's unconquerable mind.

Poems in Two Volumes, 1807

49   ' *It is not to be thought of* '

IT is not to be thought of that the Flood
Of British freedom, which, to the open sea
Of the world's praise, from dark antiquity
Hath flowed, ' with pomp of waters, unwithstood,'
Roused though it be full often to a mood
Which spurns the check of salutary bands,
That this most famous Stream in bogs and sands
Should perish; and to evil and to good
Be lost for ever. In our halls is hung
Armoury of the invincible Knights of old:
We must be free or die, who speak the tongue
That Shakespeare spake; the faith and morals hold
Which Milton held.—In every thing we are sprung
Of Earth's first blood, have titles manifold.

Poems in Two Volumes, 1807

50   ' *When I have borne in memory* '

WHEN I have borne in memory what has tamed
Great Nations, how ennobling thoughts depart
When men change swords for ledgers, and desert
The student's bower for gold, some fears unnamed
I had, my Country!—am I to be blamed?

But, when I think of thee, and what thou art,
Verily, in the bottom of my heart,
Of those unfilial fears I am ashamed.
But dearly must we prize thee; we who find
In thee a bulwark for the cause of men;
And I by my affection was beguiled:
What wonder if a Poet now and then,
Among the many movements of his mind,
Felt for thee as a lover or a child!

Poems in Two Volumes, 1807

51 ' *The world is too much with us* '

THE world is too much with us; late and soon,
 Getting and spending, we lay waste our powers
Little we see in Nature that is ours;
We have given our hearts away, a sordid boon!
This Sea that bares her bosom to the moon;
The winds that will be howling at all hours,
And are up-gathered now like sleeping flowers;
For this, for every thing, we are out of tune;
It moves us not.—Great God! I'd rather be
A Pagan suckled in a creed outworn;
So might I, standing on this pleasant lea,
Have glimpses that would make me less forlorn;
Have sight of Proteus rising from the sea;
Or hear old Triton blow his wreathèd horn.

Poems in Two Volumes, 1807

52 *Thoughts of a Briton on the Subjugation of Switzerland*

TWO Voices are there; one is of the sea,
 One of the mountains; each a mighty Voice:
In both from age to age thou didst rejoice,
They were thy chosen music, Liberty!
There came a Tyrant, and with holy glee
Thou fought'st against him; but hast vainly striven:
Thou from thy Alpine holds at length art driven,
Where not a torrent murmurs heard by thee.
Of one deep bliss thine ear hath been bereft:
Then cleave, O cleave to that which still is left;
For, high-souled Maid, what sorrow would it be
That mountain Floods should thunder as before,
And Ocean bellow from his rocky shore,
And neither awful Voice be heard by thee!

       Poems in Two Volumes, 1807

53 *London, 1802*

MILTON! thou should'st be living at this hour:
 England hath need of thee: she is a fen
Of stagnant waters: altar, sword, and pen,
Fireside, the heroic wealth of hall and bower,
Have forfeited their ancient English dower
Of inward happiness. We are selfish men;
Oh! raise us up, return to us again;
And give us manners, virtue, freedom, power.
Thy soul was like a Star, and dwelt apart:
Thou hadst a voice whose sound was like the sea:

Pure as the naked heavens, majestic, free,
So didst thou travel on life's common way,
In cheerful godliness; and yet thy heart
The lowliest duties on herself did lay.

Poems in Two Volumes, 1807

54 *Composed upon Westminster Bridge, September 3, 1802*

EARTH has not any thing to show more fair:
Dull would he be of soul who could pass by
A sight so touching in its majesty:
This City now doth, like a garment, wear
The beauty of the morning; silent, bare,
Ships, towers, domes, theatres, and temples lie
Open unto the fields, and to the sky;
All bright and glittering in the smokeless air.
Never did sun more beautifully steep
In his first splendour, valley, rock, or hill;
Ne'er saw I, never felt, a calm so deep!
The river glideth at his own sweet will:
Dear God! the very houses seem asleep;
And all that mighty heart is lying still!

Poems in Two Volumes, 1807

55 *On the Extinction of the Venetian Republic*

ONCE did She hold the gorgeous east in fee;
And was the safeguard of the west: the worth
Of Venice did not fall below her birth,
Venice, the eldest Child of Liberty.
She was a maiden City, bright and free;

No guile seduced, no force could violate;
And, when she took unto herself a Mate,
She must espouse the everlasting Sea.
And what if she had seen those glories fade,
Those titles vanish, and that strength decay;
Yet shall some tribute of regret be paid
When her long life hath reached its final day:
Men are we, and must grieve when even the Shade
Of that which once was great, is passed away.

Poems in Two Volumes, 1807

56   *November, 1806*

ANOTHER year!—another deadly blow!
    Another mighty Empire overthrown!
And We are left, or shall be left, alone;
The last that dare to struggle with the Foe.
'Tis well! from this day forward we shall know
That in ourselves our safety must be sought;
That by our own right hands it must be wrought;
That we must stand unpropped, or be laid low.
O dastard whom such foretaste doth not cheer!
We shall exult, if they who rule the land
Be men who hold its many blessings dear,
Wise, upright, valiant; not a servile band,
Who are to judge of danger which they fear,
And honour which they do not understand.

Poems in Two Volumes, 1807

To Sleep

57

A FLOCK of sheep that leisurely pass by,
   One after one; the sound of rain, and bees
Murmuring; the fall of rivers, winds and seas,
Smooth fields, white sheets of water, and pure sky;
I have thought of all by turns, and yet I lie
Sleepless! and soon the small birds' melodies
Must hear, first uttered from my orchard trees;
And the first cuckoo's melancholy cry.
Even thus last night, and two nights more, I lay
And could not win thee, Sleep! by any stealth:
So do not let me wear to-night away :
Without Thee what is all the morning's wealth?
Come, blessèd barrier between day and day,
Dear mother of fresh thoughts and joyous health!

Poems in Two Volumes, 1807

' *Where lies the Land* '

58

WHERE lies the Land to which yon Ship must go?
   Fresh as a lark mounting at break of day,
Festively she puts forth in trim array;
Is she for tropic suns, or polar snow?
What boots the enquiry?—Neither friend nor foe
She cares for; let her travel where she may,
She finds familiar names, a beaten way
Ever before her, and a wind to blow.
Yet still I ask, what haven is her mark?

And, almost as it was when ships were rare,
(From time to time, like Pilgrims, here and there
Crossing the waters) doubt, and something dark,
Of the old Sea some reverential fear,
Is with me at thy farewell, joyous Bark!

Poems in Two Volumes, 1807

59   ' *Scorn not the Sonnet* '

SCORN not the Sonnet; Critic, you have frowned,
   Mindless of its just honours; with this key
Shakespeare unlocked his heart; the melody
Of this small lute gave ease to Petrarch's wound;
A thousand times this pipe did Tasso sound;
With it Camöens soothed an exile's grief;
The Sonnet glittered a gay myrtle leaf
Amid the cypress with which Dante crowned
His visionary brow: a glow-worm lamp,
It cheered mild Spenser, called from Faery-land
To struggle through dark ways; and, when a damp
Fell round the path of Milton, in his hand
The Thing became a trumpet; whence he blew
Soul-animating strains—alas, too few!

Poetical Works, 1827

60   ' *She was a Phantom of delight* '

SHE was a Phantom of delight
   When first she gleamed upon my sight;
A lovely Apparition, sent
   To be a moment's ornament;

SHE WAS A PHANTOM OF DELIGHT

Her eyes as stars of Twilight fair;
Like Twilight's, too, her dusky hair;
But all things else about her drawn
From May-time and the cheerful Dawn;
A dancing Shape, an Image gay,
To haunt, to startle, and way-lay.

I saw her upon nearer view,
A Spirit, yet a Woman too!
Her household motions light and free,
And steps of virgin-liberty;
A countenance in which did meet
Sweet records, promises as sweet;
A Creature not too bright or good
For human nature's daily food;
For transient sorrows, simple wiles,
Praise, blame, love, kisses, tears, and smiles.

And now I see with eye serene
The very pulse of the machine;
A Being breathing thoughtful breath,
A Traveller between life and death;
The reason firm, the temperate will,
Endurance, foresight, strength, and skill;
A perfect Woman, nobly planned,
To warn, to comfort, and command;
And yet a Spirit still, and bright
With something of an angel-light.

Poems in Two Volumes, 1807

61   *' I wandered lonely as a cloud '*

I WANDERED lonely as a cloud
   That floats on high o'er vales and hills,
When all at once I saw a crowd,
A host of golden daffodils;
Beside the lake, beneath the trees,
Fluttering and dancing in the breeze.

Continuous as the stars that shine
And twinkle on the milky way,
They stretched in never-ending line
Along the margin of a bay:
Ten thousand saw I at a glance,
Tossing their heads in sprightly dance.

The waves beside them danced; but they
Out-did the sparkling waves in glee:
A poet could not but be gay
In such a jocund company:
I gazed—and gazed—but little thought
What wealth the show to me had brought:

For oft, when on my couch I lie
In vacant or in pensive mood,
They flash upon that inward eye
Which is the bliss of solitude;
And then my heart with pleasure fills,
And dances with the daffodils.

Poems in Two Volumes, 1807

'My heart leaps up'

MY heart leaps up when I behold
   A rainbow in the sky:
So was it when my life began;
So is it now I am a man;
So be it when I shall grow old,
      Or let me die!
The Child is father of the Man;
And I could wish my days to be
Bound each to each by natural piety.

Poems in Two Volumes, 1807

63 *Lines*

Composed at Grasmere, during a walk one Evening, after a
stormy day, the Author having just read in a Newspaper that the
dissolution of Mr. Fox was hourly expected.

LOUD is the Vale! the Voice is up
   With which she speaks when storms are gone,
A mighty unison of streams!
Of all her Voices, One!

Loud is the Vale;—this inland Depth
In peace is roaring like the Sea;
Yon star upon the mountain-top
Is listening quietly.

Sad was I, even to pain deprest,
Importunate and heavy load!
The Comforter hath found me here,
Upon this lonely road;

And many thousands now are sad—
Wait the fulfilment of their fear;
For he must die who is their stay,
Their glory disappear.

A Power is passing from the earth
To breathless Nature's dark abyss;
But when the great and good depart
What is it more than this—

That Man, who is from God sent forth,
Doth yet again to God return?—
Such ebb and flow must ever be,
Then wherefore should we mourn?

Poems in Two Volumes, 1807

64   ' *I travelled among unknown men* '

I TRAVELLED among unknown men,
   In lands beyond the sea;
Nor, England! did I know till then
   What love I bore to thee.

'Tis past, that melancholy dream!
   Nor will I quit thy shore
A second time; for still I seem
   To love thee more and more.

Among thy mountains did I feel
   The joy of my desire;
And she I cherished turned her wheel
   Beside an English fire.

Thy mornings showed, thy nights concealed,
  The bowers where Lucy played;
And thine too is the last green field
  That Lucy's eyes surveyed.

Poems in Two Volumes, 1807

To H. C.

Six Years Old

65

O THOU! whose fancies from afar are brought;
  Who of thy words dost make a mock apparel,
And fittest to unutterable thought
The breeze-like motion and the self-born carol;
Thou faery voyager! that dost float
In such clear water, that thy boat
May rather seem
To brood on air than on an earthly stream;
Suspended in a stream as clear as sky,
Where earth and heaven do make one imagery;
O blessèd vision! happy child!
That art so exquisitely wild,
I think of thee with many fears
For what may be thy lot in future years.

   I thought of times when Pain might be thy guest,
Lord of thy house and hospitality;
And Grief, uneasy lover! never rest
But when she sate within the touch of thee.
O too industrious folly!
O vain and causeless melancholy!

Nature will either end thee quite;
Or, lengthening out thy season of delight,
Preserve for thee, by individual right,
A young lamb's heart among the full-grown flocks.
What hast thou to do with sorrow,
Or the injuries of to-morrow?
Thou art a dew-drop, which the morn brings forth,
Ill fitted to sustain unkindly shocks,
Or to be trailed along the soiling earth;
A gem that glitters while it lives,
And no forewarning gives;
But, at the touch of wrong, without a strife
Slips in a moment out of life.

Poems in Two Volumes, 1807

66 *A Complaint*

THERE is a change—and I am poor;
   Your love hath been, nor long ago,
A fountain at my fond heart's door,
Whose only business was to flow;
And flow it did; not taking heed
Of its own bounty, or my need.

What happy moments did I count!
Blest was I then all bliss above!
Now, for that consecrated fount
Of murmuring, sparkling, living love,
What have I? shall I dare to tell?
A comfortless and hidden well.

A well of love—it may be deep—
I trust it is,—and never dry:
What matter? if the waters sleep
In silence and obscurity.
—Such change, and at the very door
Of my fond heart, hath made me poor.

Poems in Two Volumes, 1807

67   *The Affliction of Margaret*

I

WHERE art thou, my beloved Son,
      Where art thou, worse to me than dead?
Oh find me, prosperous or undone!
Or, if the grave be now thy bed,
Why am I ignorant of the same
That I may rest; and neither blame
Nor sorrow may attend thy name?

II

Seven years, alas! to have received
No tidings of an only child;
To have despaired, have hoped, believed,
And been for evermore beguiled;
Sometimes with thoughts of very bliss!
I catch at them, and then I miss;
Was ever darkness like to this?

III

He was among the prime in worth,
An object beauteous to behold;
Well born, well bred; I sent him forth
Ingenuous, innocent, and bold:

If things ensued that wanted grace,
As hath been said, they were not base;
And never blush was on my face.

IV

Ah! little doth the young-one dream,
When full of play and childish cares,
What power is in his wildest scream,
Heard by his mother unawares!
He knows it not, he cannot guess:
Years to a mother bring distress;
But do not make her love the less.

V

Neglect me! no, I suffered long
From that ill thought; and, being blind,
Said, ' Pride shall help me in my wrong:
Kind mother have I been, as kind
As ever breathed: ' and that is true;
I've wet my path with tears like dew,
Weeping for him when no one knew.

VI

My Son, if thou be humbled, poor,
Hopeless of honour and of gain,
Oh! do not dread thy mother's door;
Think not of me with grief and pain:
I now can see with better eyes;
And worldly grandeur I despise,
And fortune with her gifts and lies.

THE AFFLICTION OF MARGARET

Alas! the fowls of heaven have wings,
And blasts of heaven will aid their flight;
They mount—how short a voyage brings
The wanderers back to their delight!
Chains tie us down by land and sea;
And wishes, vain as mine, may be
All that is left to comfort thee.

Perhaps some dungeon hears thee groan,
Maimed, mangled by inhuman men;
Or thou upon a desert thrown
Inheritest the lion's den;
Or hast been summoned to the deep,
Thou, thou and all thy mates, to keep
An incommunicable sleep.

I look for ghosts; but none will force
Their way to me:—'tis falsely said
That there was ever intercourse
Between the living and the dead;
For, surely, then I should have sight
Of him I wait for day and night,
With love and longings infinite.

My apprehensions come in crowds;
I dread the rustling of the grass;
The very shadows of the clouds
Have power to shake me as they pass:

I question things, and do not find
One that will answer to my mind;
And all the world appears unkind.

XI

Beyond participation lie
My troubles, and beyond relief:
If any chance to heave a sigh,
They pity me, and not my grief.
Then come to me, my Son, or send
Some tidings that my woes may end;
I have no other earthly friend!

Poems in Two Volumes, 1807

68   *To the small Celandine*

PANSIES, lilies, kingcups, daisies,
    Let them live upon their praises;
Long as there 's a sun that sets,
Primroses will have their glory;
Long as there are violets,
They will have a place in story:
There 's a flower that shall be mine,
'Tis the little Celandine.

Eyes of some men travel far
For the finding of a star;
Up and down the heavens they go,
Men that keep a mighty rout!
I'm as great as they, I trow,
Since the day I found thee out,
Little flower!—I'll make a stir,
Like a sage astronomer.

TO THE SMALL CELANDINE

Modest, yet withal an Elf
Bold, and lavish of thyself;
Since we needs must first have met
I have seen thee, high and low,
Thirty years or more, and yet
'Twas a face I did not know;
Thou hast now, go where I may,
Fifty greetings in a day.

Ere a leaf is on a bush,
In the time before the thrush
Has a thought about her nest,
Thou wilt come with half a call,
Spreading out thy glossy breast
Like a careless Prodigal;
Telling tales about the sun,
When we've little warmth, or none.

Poets, vain men in their mood!
Travel with the multitude:
Never heed them; I aver
That they all are wanton wooers;
But the thrifty cottager,
Who stirs little out of doors,
Joys to spy thee near her home;
Spring is coming, Thou art come!

Drawn by what peculiar spell,
By what charm for sight or smell,
Do those wingèd dim-eyed creatures,
Labourers sent from waxen cells,

Settle on thy brilliant features,
In neglect of buds and bells
Opening daily at thy side,
By the season multiplied?

Comfort have thou of thy merit,
Kindly, unassuming Spirit!
Careless of thy neighbourhood,
Thou dost show thy pleasant face
On the moor, and in the wood,
In the lane;—there 's not a place,
Howsoever mean it be,
But 'tis good enough for thee.

Ill befall the yellow flowers,
Children of the flaring hours!
Buttercups, that will be seen,
Whether we will see or no;
Others, too, of lofty mien;
They have done as worldlings do,
Taken praise that should be thine,
Little, humble Celandine!

Prophet of delight and mirth,
Ill-requited upon earth;
Herald of a mighty band,
Of a joyous train ensuing,
Serving at my heart's command,
Tasks that are no tasks renewing,
I will sing, as doth behove,
Hymns in praise of what I love!

Poems in Two Volumes, 1807

I

THERE was a roaring in the wind all night,
    The rain came heavily and fell in floods;
But now the sun is rising calm and bright;
The birds are singing in the distant woods;
Over his own sweet voice the Stock-dove broods;
The Jay makes answer as the Magpie chatters;
And all the air is filled with pleasant noise of waters.

II

All things that love the sun are out of doors;
The sky rejoices in the morning's birth;
The grass is bright with rain-drops;—on the moors
The hare is running races in her mirth;
And with her feet she from the plashy earth
Raises a mist; that, glittering in the sun,
Runs with her all the way, wherever she doth run.

III

I was a Traveller then upon the moor;
I saw the hare that raced about with joy;
I heard the woods and distant waters roar;
Or heard them not, as happy as a boy:
The pleasant season did my heart employ:
My old remembrances went from me wholly;
And all the ways of men, so vain and melancholy.

IV

But, as it sometimes chanceth, from the might
Of joy in minds that can no further go,
As high as we have mounted in delight
In our dejection do we sink as low,

To me that morning did it happen so;
And fears and fancies thick upon me came;
Dim sadness—and blind thoughts, I knew not, nor could
  name.

v

I heard the sky-lark warbling in the sky;
And I bethought me of the playful hare:
Even such a happy Child of earth am I;
Even as these blissful creatures do I fare;
Far from the world I walk, and from all care;
But there may come another day to me—
Solitude, pain of heart, distress, and poverty.

VI

My whole life I have lived in pleasant thought,
As if life's business were a summer mood;
As if all needful things would come unsought
To genial faith, still rich in genial good;
But how can He expect that others should
Build for him, sow for him, and at his call
Love him, who for himself will take no heed at all?

VII

I thought of Chatterton, the marvellous Boy,
The sleepless Soul that perished in his pride;
Of Him who walked in glory and in joy
Following his plough, along the mountain-side:
By our own spirits are we deified:
We Poets in our youth begin in gladness;
But thereof come in the end despondency and madness.

126

RESOLUTION AND INDEPENDENCE

Now, whether it were by peculiar grace,
A leading from above, a something given,
Yet it befell that, in this lonely place,
When I with these untoward thoughts had striven,
Beside a pool bare to the eye of heaven
I saw a Man before me unawares:
The oldest man he seemed that ever wore grey hairs.

IX

As a huge stone is sometimes seen to lie
Couched on the bald top of an eminence;
Wonder to all who do the same espy,
By what means it could thither come, and whence;
So that it seems a thing endued with sense:
Like a sea-beast crawled forth, that on a shelf
Of rock or sand reposeth, there to sun itself;

X

Such seemed this Man, not all alive nor dead,
Nor all asleep—in his extreme old age:
His body was bent double, feet and head
Coming together in life's pilgrimage;
As if some dire constraint of pain, or rage
Of sickness felt by him in times long past,
A more than human weight upon his frame had cast.

XI

Himself he propped, limbs, body, and pale face,
Upon a long grey staff of shaven wood:
And, still as I drew near with gentle pace,
Upon the margin of that moorish flood

Motionless as a cloud the old Man stood,
That heareth not the loud winds when they call;
And moveth all together, if it move at all.

XII

At length, himself unsettling, he the pond
Stirred with his staff, and fixedly did look
Upon the muddy water, which he conned,
As if he had been reading in a book:
And now a stranger's privilege I took;
And, drawing to his side, to him did say,
' This morning gives us promise of a glorious day.'

XIII

A gentle answer did the old Man make,
In courteous speech which forth he slowly drew:
And him with further words I thus bespake,
' What occupation do you there pursue?
This is a lonesome place for one like you.'
Ere he replied, a flash of mild surprise
Broke from the sable orbs of his yet-vivid eyes.

XIV

His words came feebly, from a feeble chest,
But each in solemn order followed each,
With something of a lofty utterance drest—
Choice word and measured phrase, above the reach
Of ordinary men; a stately speech;
Such as grave Livers do in Scotland use,
Religious men, who give to God and man their dues.

RESOLUTION AND INDEPENDENCE

XV

He told, that to these waters he had come
To gather leeches, being old and poor:
Employment hazardous and wearisome!
And he had many hardships to endure:
From pond to pond he roamed, from moor to moor;
Housing, with God's good help, by choice or chance;
And in this way he gained an honest maintenance.

XVI

The old Man still stood talking by my side;
But now his voice to me was like a stream
Scarce heard; nor word from word could I divide;
And the whole body of the Man did seem
Like one whom I had met with in a dream;
Or like a man from some far region sent,
To give me human strength, by apt admonishment.

XVII

My former thoughts returned: the fear that kills;
And hope that is unwilling to be fed;
Cold, pain, and labour, and all fleshly ills;
And mighty Poets in their misery dead.
—Perplexed, and longing to be comforted,
My question eagerly did I renew,
' How is it that you live, and what is it you do?'

XVIII

He with a smile did then his words repeat;
And said that, gathering leeches, far and wide
He travelled; stirring thus about his feet
The waters of the pools where they abide.

' Once I could meet with them on every side;
But they have dwindled long by slow decay;
Yet still I persevere, and find them where I may.'

XIX

While he was talking thus, the lonely place,
The old Man's shape, and speech—all troubled me:
In my mind's eye I seemed to see him pace
About the weary moors continually,
Wandering about alone and silently.
While I these thoughts within myself pursued,
He, having made a pause, the same discourse renewed.

XX

And soon with this he other matter blended,
Cheerfully uttered, with demeanour kind,
But stately in the main; and when he ended,
I could have laughed myself to scorn to find
In that decrepit Man so firm a mind.
' God,' said I, ' be my help and stay secure;
I'll think of the Leech-gatherer on the lonely moor!'

Poems in Two Volumes, 1807

While my Fellow-traveller and I were walking by the side of Loch Ketterine, one fine evening after sunset, in our road to a Hut where, in the course of our Tour, we had been hospitably entertained some weeks before, we met, in one of the loneliest parts of that solitary region, two well-dressed Women, one of whom said to us, by way of greeting, ' What, you are stepping westward? '

' *WHAT, you are stepping westward?* '—' *Yea.*'
——'Twould be a *wildish* destiny,
If we, who thus together roam
In a strange Land, and far from home,
Were in this place the guests of Chance:
Yet who would stop, or fear to advance,
Though home or shelter he had none,
With such a Sky to lead him on?

The dewy ground was dark and cold;
Behind, all gloomy to behold;
And stepping westward seemed to be
A kind of *heavenly* destiny:
I liked the greeting; 'twas a sound
Of something without place or bound;
And seemed to give me spiritual right
To travel through that region bright.

The voice was soft, and she who spake
Was walking by her native lake:
The salutation had to me
The very sound of courtesy:
Its power was felt; and while my eye
Was fixed upon the glowing Sky,

The echo of the voice enwrought
A human sweetness with the thought
Of travelling through the world that lay
Before me in my endless way.

Poems in Two Volumes, 1807

71   *The Solitary Reaper*

BEHOLD her, single in the field,
    Yon solitary Highland Lass!
Reaping and singing by herself;
Stop here, or gently pass!
Alone she cuts, and binds the grain,
And sings a melancholy strain;
O listen! for the Vale profound
Is overflowing with the sound.

No Nightingale did ever chant
More welcome notes to weary bands
Of travellers in some shady haunt,
Among Arabian sands:
A voice so thrilling ne'er was heard
In spring-time from the Cuckoo-bird,
Breaking the silence of the seas
Among the farthest Hebrides.

Will no one tell me what she sings?—
Perhaps the plaintive numbers flow
For old, unhappy, far-off things,
And battles long ago:
Or is it some more humble lay,
Familiar matter of to-day?
Some natural sorrow, loss, or pain,
That has been, and may be again?

Whate'er the theme, the Maiden sang
As if her song could have no ending;
I saw her singing at her work,
And o'er the sickle bending;—
I listened, motionless and still;
And, as I mounted up the hill,
The music in my heart I bore,
Long after it was heard no more.

Poems in Two Volumes, 1807

72 *Ode to Duty*

' Jam non consilio bonus, sed more eò perductus, ut non tantum
rectè facere possim, sed nisi rectè facere non possim.'

STERN Daughter of the Voice of God!
O Duty! if that name thou love
Who art a light to guide, a rod
To check the erring, and reprove;
Thou, who art victory and law
When empty terrors overawe;
From vain temptations dost set free;
And calm'st the weary strife of frail humanity!

There are who ask not if thine eye
Be on them; who, in love and truth,
Where no misgiving is, rely
Upon the genial sense of youth:
Glad Hearts! without reproach or blot;
Who do thy work, and know it not:
Oh! if through confidence misplaced
They fail, thy saving arms, dread Power! around them cast.

Serene will be our days and bright,
And happy will our nature be,
When love is an unerring light,
And joy its own security.
And they a blissful course may hold
Even now, who, not unwisely bold,
Live in the spirit of this creed;
Yet seek thy firm support, according to their need.

I, loving freedom, and untried;
No sport of every random gust,
Yet being to myself a guide,
Too blindly have reposed my trust:
And oft, when in my heart was heard
Thy timely mandate, I deferred
The task, in smoother walks to stray;
But thee I now would serve more strictly, if I may.

Through no disturbance of my soul,
Or strong compunction in me wrought,
I supplicate for thy control;
But in the quietness of thought:
Me this unchartered freedom tires;
I feel the weight of chance-desires:
My hopes no more must change their name,
I long for a repose that ever is the same.

Stern Lawgiver! yet thou dost wear
The Godhead's most benignant grace;
Nor know we anything so fair
As is the smile upon thy face:
Flowers laugh before thee on their beds;
And fragrance in thy footing treads;

Thou dost preserve the stars from wrong;
And the most ancient heavens, through Thee, are fresh
and strong.

To humbler functions, awful Power!
I call thee: I myself commend
Unto thy guidance from this hour;
Oh, let my weakness have an end!
Give unto me, made lowly wise,
The spirit of self-sacrifice;
The confidence of reason give;
And in the light of truth thy Bondman let me live!

Poems in Two Volumes, 1807

73　　*Character of the Happy Warrior*

WHO is the happy Warrior? Who is he
　　That every Man in arms should wish to be?
—It is the generous Spirit, who, when brought
Among the tasks of real life, hath wrought
Upon the plan that pleased his childish thought:
Whose high endeavours are an inward light
That makes the path before him always bright:
Who, with a natural instinct to discern
What knowledge can perform, is diligent to learn;
Abides by this resolve, and stops not there,
But makes his moral being his prime care;
Who, doomed to go in company with Pain,
And Fear, and Bloodshed, miserable train!
Turns his necessity to glorious gain;
In face of these doth exercise a power
Which is our human nature's highest dower;

Controls them and subdues, transmutes, bereaves
Of their bad influence, and their good receives;
By objects, which might force the soul to abate
Her feeling, rendered more compassionate;
Is placable—because occasions rise
So often that demand such sacrifice;
More skilful in self-knowledge, even more pure,
As tempted more; more able to endure,
As more exposed to suffering and distress;
Thence, also, more alive to tenderness.
—'Tis he whose law is reason; who depends
Upon that law as on the best of friends;
Whence, in a state where men are tempted still
To evil for a guard against worse ill,
And what in quality or act is best
Doth seldom on a right foundation rest,
He labours good on good to fix, and owes
To virtue every triumph that he knows:
—Who, if he rise to station of command,
Rises by open means; and there will stand
On honourable terms, or else retire,
And in himself possess his own desire;
Who comprehends his trust, and to the same
Keeps faithful with a singleness of aim;
And therefore does not stoop, nor lie in wait
For wealth, or honours, or for worldly state;
Whom they must follow; on whose head must fall,
Like showers of manna, if they come at all:
Whose powers shed round him in the common strife,
Or mild concerns of ordinary life,
A constant influence, a peculiar grace;
But who, if he be called upon to face

CHARACTER OF THE HAPPY WARRIOR

Some awful moment to which Heaven has joined
Great issues, good or bad for human kind,
Is happy as a Lover; and attired
With sudden brightness, like a Man inspired;
And, through the heat of conflict, keeps the law
In calmness made, and sees what he foresaw;
Or if an unexpected call succeed,
Come when it will, is equal to the need:
—He who, though thus endued as with a sense
And faculty for storm and turbulence,
Is yet a Soul whose master-bias leans
To homefelt pleasures and to gentle scenes;
Sweet images! which, wheresoe'er he be,
Are at his heart; and such fidelity
It is his darling passion to approve;
More brave for this, that he hath much to love:
'Tis, finally, the Man, who, lifted high,
Conspicuous object in a Nation's eye,
Or left unthought-of in obscurity,—
Who, with a toward or untoward lot,
Prosperous or adverse, to his wish or not—
Plays, in the many games of life, that one
Where what he most doth value must be won:
Whom neither shape of danger can dismay,
Nor thought of tender happiness betray;
Who, not content that former worth stand fast,
Looks forward, persevering to the last,
From well to better, daily self-surpast:
Who, whether praise of him must walk the earth
For ever, and to noble deeds give birth,
Or he must fall and sleep without his fame,
And leave a dead unprofitable name—

Finds comfort in himself and in his cause;
And, while the mortal mist is gathering, draws
His breath in confidence of Heaven's applause:
This is the happy Warrior; this is He
That every Man in arms should wish to be.

Poems in Two Volumes, 1807

74   *The Small Celandine*

THERE is a Flower, the lesser Celandine,
   That shrinks, like many more, from cold and rain;
And, the first moment that the sun may shine,
Bright as the sun himself, 'tis out again!

When hailstones have been falling, swarm on swarm,
Or blasts the green field and the trees distrest,
Oft have I seen it muffled up from harm,
In close self-shelter, like a Thing at rest.

But lately, one rough day, this Flower I passed
And recognised it, though an altered form,
Now standing forth an offering to the blast,
And buffeted at will by rain and storm.

I stopped, and said with inly-muttered voice,
' It doth not love the shower, nor seek the cold:
This neither is its courage nor its choice,
But its necessity in being old.

The sunshine may not cheer it, nor the dew;
It cannot help itself in its decay;
Stiff in its members, withered, changed of hue.'
And, in my spleen, I smiled that it was grey.

To be a Prodigal's Favourite—then, worse truth,
A Miser's Pensioner—behold our lot!
O Man, that from thy fair and shining youth
Age might but take the things Youth needed not!

Poems in Two Volumes, 1807

75   *Elegiac Stanzas*

*Suggested by a picture of Peele Castle, in a storm,
painted by Sir George Beaumont*

I WAS thy Neighbour once, thou rugged Pile!
Four summer weeks I dwelt in sight of thee:
I saw thee every day; and all the while
Thy Form was sleeping on a glassy sea.

So pure the sky, so quiet was the air!
So like, so very like, was day to day!
Whene'er I looked, thy Image still was there;
It trembled, but it never passed away.

How perfect was the calm! it seemed no sleep;
No mood, which season takes away, or brings:
I could have fancied that the mighty Deep
Was even the gentlest of all gentle Things.

Ah! THEN, if mine had been the Painter's hand,
To express what then I saw; and add the gleam,
The light that never was, on sea or land,
The consecration, and the Poet's dream;

I would have planted thee, thou hoary Pile!
Amid a world how different from this!
Beside a sea that could not cease to smile;
On tranquil land, beneath a sky of bliss.

A Picture had it been of lasting ease,
Elysian quiet, without toil or strife;
No motion but the moving tide, a breeze,
Or merely silent Nature's breathing life.

Such, in the fond illusion of my heart,
Such Picture would I at that time have made:
And seen the soul of truth in every part,
A stedfast peace that might not be betrayed.

So once it would have been,—'tis so no more;
I have submitted to a new control:
A power is gone, which nothing can restore;
A deep distress hath humanised my Soul.

Not for a moment could I now behold
A smiling sea, and be what I have been:
The feeling of my loss will ne'er be old;
This, which I know, I speak with mind serene.

Then, Beaumont, Friend! who would have been the Friend,
If he had lived, of Him whom I deplore,
This work of thine I blame not, but commend;
This sea in anger, and that dismal shore.

O 'tis a passionate Work!—yet wise and well;
Well chosen is the spirit that is here;
That Hulk which labours in the deadly swell,
This rueful sky, this pageantry of fear!

And this huge Castle, standing here sublime,
I love to see the look with which it braves,
Cased in the unfeeling armour of old time,
The lightning, the fierce wind, and trampling waves.

ELEGIAC STANZAS

Farewell, farewell the heart that lives alone,
Housed in a dream, at distance from the Kind!
Such happiness, wherever it be known,
Is to be pitied; for 'tis surely blind.

But welcome fortitude, and patient cheer,
And frequent sights of what is to be borne!
Such sights, or worse, as are before me here.—
Not without hope we suffer and we mourn.

Poems in Two Volumes, 1807

76 *To the Cuckoo*

O BLITHE New-comer! I have heard,
    I hear thee and rejoice.
O Cuckoo! shall I call thee Bird,
    Or but a wandering Voice?

While I am lying on the grass
    Thy twofold shout I hear,
That seems to fill the whole air's space
    As loud far off as near.

Though babbling only to the Vale,
    Of sunshine and of flowers,
Thou bringest unto me a tale
    Of visionary hours.

Thrice welcome, darling of the Spring!
    Even yet thou art to me
No bird, but an invisible thing,
    A voice, a mystery;

The same whom in my schoolboy days
　　I listened to; that Cry
Which made me look a thousand ways
　　In bush, and tree, and sky.

To seek thee did I often rove
　　Through woods and on the green;
And thou wert still a hope, a love;
　　Still longed for, never seen.

And I can listen to thee yet;
　　Can lie upon the plain
And listen, till I do beget
　　That golden time again.

O blessèd Bird! the earth we pace
　　Again appears to be
An unsubstantial, faery place,
　　That is fit home for Thee!

Poems in Two Volumes, 1807

77　　Ode

Paulo majora canamus

Intimations of Immortality from Recollections of Early Childhood

The Child is Father of the Man;
And I could wish my days to be
Bound each to each by natural piety.

I

THERE was a time when meadow, grove, and stream,
　　The earth, and every common sight,
　　　　To me did seem
　　　　Apparelled in celestial light,

INTIMATIONS OF IMMORTALITY

The glory and the freshness of a dream.
It is not now as it hath been of yore;—
  Turn wheresoe'er I may,
   By night or day,
The things which I have seen I now can see no more.

II

  The Rainbow comes and goes,
  And lovely is the Rose,
  The Moon doth with delight
Look round her when the heavens are bare;
  Waters on a starry night
  Are beautiful and fair;
 The sunshine is a glorious birth;
 But yet I know, where'er I go,
That there hath past away a glory from the earth.

III

Now, while the birds thus sing a joyous song,
 And while the young lambs bound
  As to the tabor's sound,
To me alone there came a thought of grief:
A timely utterance gave that thought relief,
  And I again am strong:
The cataracts blow their trumpets from the steep;
No more shall grief of mine the season wrong;
I hear the Echoes through the mountains throng,
The Winds come to me from the fields of sleep,
  And all the earth is gay;
   Land and sea

Give themselves up to jollity,
    And with the heart of May
Doth every Beast keep holiday;—
    Thou Child of Joy,
Shout round me, let me hear thy shouts, thou happy Shep-
    herd-boy!

IV

Ye blessed Creatures, I have heard the call
    Ye to each other make; I see
The heavens laugh with you in your jubilee;
    My heart is at your festival,
      My head hath its coronal,
The fulness of your bliss, I feel—I feel it all.
        Oh evil day! if I were sullen
        While Earth herself is adorning,
          This sweet May-morning,
        And the Children are culling
          On every side,
        In a thousand valleys far and wide,
        Fresh flowers; while the sun shines warm,
And the Babe leaps up on his Mother's arm:—
        I hear, I hear, with joy I hear!
        —But there 's a Tree, of many one,
A single Field which I have looked upon,
Both of them speak of something that is gone:
        The Pansy at my feet
        Doth the same tale repeat:
Whither is fled the visionary gleam?
Where is it now, the glory and the dream?

INTIMATIONS OF IMMORTALITY

V

Our birth is but a sleep and a forgetting:
The Soul that rises with us, our life's Star,
  Hath had elsewhere its setting,
   And cometh from afar:
  Not in entire forgetfulness,
  And not in utter nakedness,
But trailing clouds of glory do we come
  From God, who is our home:
Heaven lies about us in our infancy!
Shades of the prison-house begin to close
  Upon the growing Boy,
But He beholds the light, and whence it flows,
  He sees it in his joy;
The Youth, who daily farther from the east
   Must travel, still is Nature's Priest,
   And by the vision splendid
   Is on his way attended;
At length the Man perceives it die away,
And fade into the light of common day.

VI

Earth fills her lap with pleasures of her own;
Yearnings she hath in her own natural kind,
And, even with something of a Mother's mind,
   And no unworthy aim,
  The homely Nurse doth all she can
To make her Foster-child, her Inmate Man,
  Forget the glories he hath known,
And that imperial palace whence he came.

VII

Behold the Child among his new-born blisses,
A six years' Darling of a pigmy size!
See, where 'mid work of his own hand he lies,
Fretted by sallies of his mother's kisses,
With light upon him from his father's eyes!
See, at his feet, some little plan or chart,
Some fragment from his dream of human life,
Shaped by himself with newly-learned art;
  A wedding or a festival,
  A mourning or a funeral;
   And this hath now his heart,
   And unto this he frames his song:
   Then will he fit his tongue
To dialogues of business, love, or strife;
   But it will not be long
   Ere this be thrown aside,
   And with new joy and pride
The little Actor cons another part;
Filling from time to time his ' humorous stage '
With all the Persons, down to palsied Age,
That Life brings with her in her equipage;
   As if his whole vocation
   Were endless imitation.

VIII

Thou, whose exterior semblance doth belie
  Thy Soul's immensity;
Thou best Philosopher, who yet dost keep
Thy heritage, thou Eye among the blind,
That, deaf and silent, read'st the eternal deep,

Haunted for ever by the eternal mind,—
      Mighty Prophet! Seer blest!
      On whom those truths do rest,
Which we are toiling all our lives to find,
In darkness lost, the darkness of the grave;
Thou, over whom thy Immortality
Broods like the Day, a Master o'er a Slave,
A Presence which is not to be put by;
Thou little Child, yet glorious in the might
Of heaven-born freedom on thy being's height,
Why with such earnest pains dost thou provoke
The years to bring the inevitable yoke,
Thus blindly with thy blessedness at strife?
Full soon thy Soul shall have her earthly freight,
And custom lie upon thee with a weight,
Heavy as frost, and deep almost as life!

IX

      O joy! that in our embers
      Is something that doth live,
      That nature yet remembers
      What was so fugitive!
The thought of our past years in me doth breed
Perpetual benediction: not indeed
For that which is most worthy to be blest;
Delight and liberty, the simple creed
Of Childhood, whether busy or at rest,
With new-fledged hope still fluttering in his breast:—
      Not for these I raise
      The song of thanks and praise;
      But for those obstinate questionings
      Of sense and outward things,

Fallings from us, vanishings;
   Blank misgivings of a Creature
Moving about in worlds not realised,
High instincts before which our mortal Nature
Did tremble like a guilty Thing surprised:
     But for those first affections,
     Those shadowy recollections,
   Which, be they what they may,
Are yet the fountain light of all our day,
Are yet a master light of all our seeing;
   Uphold us, cherish, and have power to make
Our noisy years seem moments in the being
Of the eternal Silence: truths that wake,
     To perish never;
Which neither listlessness, nor mad endeavour,
     Nor Man nor Boy,
Nor all that is at enmity with joy,
Can utterly abolish or destroy!
    Hence in a season of calm weather
    Though inland far we be,
Our Souls have sight of that immortal sea
    Which brought us hither,
    Can in a moment travel thither,
And see the Children sport upon the shore,
And hear the mighty waters rolling evermore.

x

Then sing, ye Birds, sing, sing a joyous song!
    And let the young Lambs bound
    As to the tabor's sound!
We in thought will join your throng,
    Ye that pipe and ye that play,

INTIMATIONS OF IMMORTALITY

Ye that through your hearts to-day
Feel the gladness of the May!
What though the radiance which was once so bright
Be now for ever taken from my sight,
Though nothing can bring back the hour
Of splendour in the grass, of glory in the flower;
We will grieve not, rather find
Strength in what remains behind;
In the primal sympathy
Which having been must ever be;
In the soothing thoughts that spring
Out of human suffering;
In the faith that looks through death,
In years that bring the philosophic mind.

XI

And O, ye Fountains, Meadows, Hills, and Groves,
Forebode not any severing of our loves!
Yet in my heart of hearts I feel your might;
I only have relinquished one delight
To live beneath your more habitual sway.
I love the Brooks which down their channels fret,
Even more than when I tripped lightly as they;
The innocent brightness of a new-born Day
Is lovely yet;
The Clouds that gather round the setting sun
Do take a sober colouring from an eye
That hath kept watch o'er man's mortality;
Another race hath been, and other palms are won.
Thanks to the human heart by which we live,
Thanks to its tenderness, its joys, and fears,

To me the meanest flower that blows can give
Thoughts that do often lie too deep for tears.

Poems in Two Volumes, 1807

78   *Influence of Natural Objects*

*In calling forth and strengthening the imagination in
boyhood and early youth*

WISDOM and Spirit of the universe!
    Thou Soul, that art the eternity of thought!
And giv'st to forms and images a breath
And everlasting motion! not in vain,
By day or star-light, thus from my first dawn
Of childhood didst thou intertwine for me
The passions that build up our human soul;
Not with the mean and vulgar works of Man;
But with high objects, with enduring things,
With life and nature; purifying thus
The elements of feeling and of thought,
And sanctifying by such discipline
Both pain and fear,—until we recognise
A grandeur in the beatings of the heart.

Nor was this fellowship vouchsafed to me
With stinted kindness. In November days,
When vapours rolling down the valleys made
A lonely scene more lonesome; among woods
At noon; and 'mid the calm of summer nights,
When, by the margin of the trembling lake,
Beneath the gloomy hills, homeward I went
In solitude, such intercourse was mine:
Mine was it in the fields both day and night,

INFLUENCE OF NATURAL OBJECTS

And by the waters, all the summer long.
And in the frosty season, when the sun
Was set, and, visible for many a mile,
The cottage-windows through the twilight blazed,
I heeded not the summons: happy time
It was indeed for all of us; for me
It was a time of rapture! Clear and loud
The village-clock tolled six—I wheeled about,
Proud and exulting like an untired horse
That cares not for his home.—All shod with steel
We hissed along the polished ice, in games
Confederate, imitative of the chase
And woodland pleasures,—the resounding horn,
The pack loud-bellowing, and the hunted hare.
So through the darkness and the cold we flew,
And not a voice was idle: with the din
Smitten, the precipices rang aloud;
The leafless trees and every icy crag
Tinkled like iron; while the distant hills
Into the tumult sent an alien sound
Of melancholy, not unnoticed while the stars,
Eastward, were sparkling clear, and in the west
The orange sky of evening died away.

Not seldom from the uproar I retired
Into a silent bay, or sportively
Glanced sideway, leaving the tumultuous throng,
To cut across the reflex of a star;
Image, that, flying still before me, gleamed
Upon the glassy plain: and oftentimes,
When we had given our bodies to the wind,
And all the shadowy banks on either side

Came sweeping through the darkness, spinning still
The rapid line of motion, then at once
Have I, reclining back upon my heels,
Stopped short; yet still the solitary cliffs
Wheeled by me—even as if the earth had rolled
With visible motion her diurnal round!
Behind me did they stretch in solemn train,
Feebler and feebler, and I stood and watched
Till all was tranquil as a summer sea.

Poems, 1815

79   *From ' The Excursion '*

(i)

SUCH was the Boy—but for the growing Youth
     What soul was his, when, from the naked top
Of some bold headland, he beheld the sun
Rise up, and bathe the world in light! He looked—
Ocean and earth, the solid frame of earth
And ocean's liquid mass, beneath him lay
In gladness and deep joy. The clouds were touched,
And in their silent faces could he read
Unutterable love. Sound needed none,
Nor any voice of joy; his spirit drank
The spectacle: sensation, soul, and form
All melted into him; they swallowed up
His animal being; in them did he live,
And by them did he live; they were his life.
In such access of mind, in such high hour
Of visitation from the living God,
Thought was not; in enjoyment it expired.

152

No thanks he breathed, he proffered no request;
Rapt into still communion that transcends
The imperfect offices of prayer and praise,
His mind was a thanksgiving to the power
That made him; it was blessedness and love!

Book I, ll. 197–218

(ii)

         ' I SEE around me here
Things which you cannot see: we die, my Friend,
Nor we alone, but that which each man loved
And prized in his peculiar nook of earth
Dies with him, or is changed; and very soon
Even of the good is no memorial left.
—The Poets, in their elegies and songs
Lamenting the departed, call the groves,
They call upon the hills and streams to mourn,
And senseless rocks; nor idly; for they speak,
In these their invocations, with a voice
Obedient to the strong creative power
Of human passion. Sympathies there are
More tranquil, yet perhaps of kindred birth,
That steal upon the meditative mind,
And grow with thought. Beside yon spring I stood,
And eyed its waters till we seemed to feel
One sadness, they and I. For them a bond
Of brotherhood is broken: time has been
When, every day, the touch of human hand
Dislodged the natural sleep that binds them up
In mortal stillness; and they ministered
To human comfort. Stooping down to drink,

Upon the slimy foot-stone I espied
The useless fragment of a wooden bowl,
Green with the moss of years, and subject only
To the soft handling of the elements:
There let it lie—how foolish are such thoughts!
Forgive them;—never—never did my steps
Approach this door but she who dwelt within
A daughter's welcome gave me, and I loved her
As my own child. Oh, Sir! the good die first,
And they whose hearts are dry as summer dust
Burn to the socket. Many a passenger
Hath blessed poor Margaret for her gentle looks,
When she upheld the cool refreshment drawn
From that forsaken spring; and no one came
But he was welcome; no one went away
But that it seemed she loved him. She is dead,
The light extinguished of her lonely hut,
The hut itself abandoned to decay,
And she forgotten in the quiet grave.'

Book I, ll. 469–510

(*iii*)

DIVERGING now (as if his quest had been
Some secret of the mountains, cavern, fall
Of water, or some boastful eminence,
Renowned for splendid prospect far and wide)
We scaled, without a track to ease our steps,
A steep ascent; and reached a dreary plain,
With a tumultuous waste of huge hill tops
Before us; savage region! which I paced
Dispirited: when, all at once, behold!
Beneath our feet, a little lowly vale,

THE EXCURSION

A lowly vale, and yet uplifted high
Among the mountains; even as if the spot
Had been, from eldest time by wish of theirs
So placed, to be shut out from all the world!
Urn-like it was in shape, deep as an urn;
With rocks encompassed, save that to the south
Was one small opening, where a heath-clad ridge
Supplied a boundary less abrupt and close;
A quiet treeless nook, with two green fields,
A liquid pool that glittered in the sun,
And one bare dwelling; one abode, no more!
It seemed the home of poverty and toil,
Though not of want: the little fields, made green
By husbandry of many thrifty years,
Paid cheerful tribute to the moorland house.
—There crows the cock, single in his domain:
The small birds find in spring no thicket there
To shroud them; only from the neighbouring vales
The cuckoo, straggling up to the hill tops,
Shouteth faint tidings of some gladder place.

Book II, ll. 319–48

(iv)

'THE tenour
Which my life holds, he readily may conceive
Whoe'er hath stood to watch a mountain brook
In some still passage of its course, and seen,
Within the depths of its capacious breast,
Inverted trees, rocks, clouds, and azure sky;
And, on its glassy surface, specks of foam,
And conglobated bubbles undissolved,

155

Numerous as stars; that, by their onward lapse,
Betray to sight the motion of the stream,
Else imperceptible. Meanwhile, is heard
A softened roar, or murmur; and the sound
Though soothing, and the little floating isles
Though beautiful, are both by Nature charged
With the same pensive office; and make known
Through what perplexing labyrinths, abrupt
Precipitations, and untoward straits,
The earth-born wanderer hath passed; and quickly,
That respite o'er, like traverses and toils
Must be again encountered.—Such a stream
Is human Life; and so the Spirit fares
In the best quiet to her course allowed;
And such is mine,—save only for a hope
That my particular current soon will reach
The unfathomable gulf, where all is still!'

Book III, ll. 967–91

(v)

WITHIN the soul a faculty abides,
That with interpositions, which would hide
And darken, so can deal that they become
Contingencies of pomp; and serve to exalt
Her native brightness. As the ample moon,
In the deep stillness of a summer even
Rising behind a thick and lofty grove,
Burns, like an unconsuming fire of light,
In the green trees; and, kindling on all sides
Their leafy umbrage, turns the dusky veil
Into a substance glorious as her own,

Yea, with her own incorporated, by power
Capacious and serene; like power abides
In man's celestial spirit; virtue thus
Sets forth and magnifies herself; thus feeds
A calm, a beautiful, and silent fire,
From the encumbrances of mortal life,
From error, disappointment—nay, from guilt;
And sometimes, so relenting justice wills,
From palpable oppressions of despair.

Book IV, ll. 1058–77

(*vi*)

I HAVE seen
A curious child, who dwelt upon a tract
Of inland ground, applying to his ear
The convolutions of a smooth-lipped shell;
To which, in silence hushed, his very soul
Listened intensely; and his countenance soon
Brightened with joy; for murmurings from within
Were heard, sonorous cadences! whereby,
To his belief, the monitor expressed
Mysterious union with its native sea.
Even such a shell the universe itself
Is to the ear of Faith; and there are times,
I doubt not, when to you it doth impart
Authentic tidings of invisible things;
Of ebb and flow, and ever-during power;
And central peace, subsisting at the heart
Of endless agitation. Here you stand,
Adore, and worship, when you know it not;
Pious beyond the intention of your thought;

Devout above the meaning of your will.
—Yes, you have felt, and may not cease to feel.
The estate of man would be indeed forlorn
If false conclusions of the reasoning power
Made the eye blind, and closed the passages
Through which the ear converses with the heart.
Has not the soul, the being of your life,
Received a shock of awful consciousness,
In some calm season, when these lofty rocks
At night's approach bring down the unclouded sky,
To rest upon their circumambient walls;
A temple framing of dimensions vast,
And yet not too enormous for the sound
Of human anthems,—choral song, or burst
Sublime of instrumental harmony,
To glorify the Eternal! What if these
Did never break the stillness that prevails
Here,—if the solemn nightingale be mute,
And the soft woodlark here did never chant
Her vespers,—Nature fails not to provide
Impulse and utterance. The whispering air
Sends inspiration from the shadowy heights,
And blind recesses of the caverned rocks;
The little rills, and waters numberless,
Inaudible by daylight, blend their notes
With the loud streams: and often, at the hour
When issue forth the first pale stars, is heard,
Within the circuit of this fabric huge,
One voice—the solitary raven, flying
Athwart the concave of the dark blue dome,
Unseen, perchance above all power of sight—
An iron knell! with echoes from afar

Faint—and still fainter—as the cry, with which
The wanderer accompanies her flight
Through the calm region, fades upon the ear,
Diminishing by distance till it seemed
To expire; yet from the abyss is caught again,
And yet again recovered!

Book IV, ll. 1132–87;
The Excursion, 1814

80 ' *Surprised by joy* '

SURPRISED by joy—impatient as the Wind
I turned to share the transport—Oh! with whom
But Thee, deep buried in the silent tomb,
That spot which no vicissitude can find?
Love, faithful love, recalled thee to my mind—
But how could I forget thee? Through what power,
Even for the least division of an hour,
Have I been so beguiled as to be blind
To my most grievous loss?—That thought's return
Was the worst pang that sorrow ever bore,
Save one, one only, when I stood forlorn,
Knowing my heart's best treasure was no more;
That neither present time, nor years unborn
Could to my sight that heavenly face restore.

Poems, 1815

81 *Characteristics of a Child Three Years Old*

LOVING she is, and tractable, though wild;
And Innocence hath privilege in her
To dignify arch looks and laughing eyes;
And feats of cunning; and the pretty round

Of trespasses, affected to provoke
Mock-chastisement and partnership in play.
And, as a faggot sparkles on the hearth,
Not less if unattended and alone
Than when both young and old sit gathered round
And take delight in its activity;
Even so this happy Creature of herself
Is all-sufficient; solitude to her
Is blithe society, who fills the air
With gladness and involuntary songs.
Light are her sallies as the tripping fawn's
Forth-startled from the fern where she lay couched;
Unthought-of, unexpected, as the stir
Of the soft breeze ruffling the meadow-flowers;
Or from before it chasing wantonly
The many-coloured images imprest
Upon the bosom of a placid lake.

Poems, 1815

82   *After-thought*

I THOUGHT of Thee, my partner and my guide,
   As being past away.—Vain sympathies!
For, backward, Duddon! as I cast my eyes,
I see what was, and is, and will abide;
Still glides the Stream, and shall not cease to glide;
The Form remains, the Function never dies;
While we, the brave, the mighty, and the wise,
We Men, who in our morn of youth defied
The elements, must vanish;—be it so!
Enough, if something from our hands have power
To live, and act, and serve the future hour;

And if, as toward the silent tomb we go,
Through love, through hope, and faith's transcendent
dower,
We feel that we are greater than we know.

The River Duddon, &c., 1820

83   *Song for the Spinning Wheel*

*Founded upon a belief prevalent among the pastoral vales
of Westmoreland*

SWIFTLY turn the murmuring wheel!
Night has brought the welcome hour,
When the weary fingers feel
Help, as if from faery power;
Dewy night o'ershades the ground;
Turn the swift wheel round and round!

Now, beneath the starry sky,
Couch the widely-scattered sheep;—
Ply the pleasant labour, ply!
For the spindle, while they sleep,
Runs with speed more smooth and fine,
Gathering up a trustier line.

Short-lived likings may be bred
By a glance from fickle eyes;
But true love is like the thread
Which the kindly wool supplies,
When the flocks are all at rest,
Sleeping on the mountain's breast.

The River Duddon, &c., 1820

84 *Mutability*

FROM low to high doth dissolution climb,
 And sinks from high to low, along a scale
Of awful notes, whose concord shall not fail;
A musical but melancholy chime,
Which they can hear who meddle not with crime,
Nor avarice, nor over-anxious care.
Truth fails not; but her outward forms that bear
The longest date do melt like frosty rime,
That in the morning whitened hill and plain
And is no more; drop like the tower sublime
Of yesterday, which royally did wear
His crown of weeds, but could not even sustain
Some casual shout that broke the silent air,
Or the unimaginable touch of Time.

Ecclesiastical Sketches, 1822

85 *Inside of King's College Chapel, Cambridge*

TAX not the royal Saint with vain expense,
 With ill-matched aims the Architect who planned—
Albeit labouring for a scanty band
Of white-robed Scholars only—this immense
And glorious Work of fine intelligence!
Give all thou canst; high Heaven rejects the lore
Of nicely-calculated less or more;
So deemed the man who fashioned for the sense
These lofty pillars, spread that branching roof
Self-poised, and scooped into ten thousand cells,

Where light and shade repose, where music dwells
Lingering—and wandering on as loth to die;
Like thoughts whose very sweetness yieldeth proof
That they were born for immortality.

Ecclesiastical Sketches, 1822

86   ' *If thou indeed derive* '

IF thou indeed derive thy light from Heaven,
  Then, to the measure of that heaven-born light,
Shine, Poet! in thy place, and be content:—
The stars pre-eminent in magnitude,
And they that from the zenith dart their beams,
(Visible though they be to half the earth,
Though half a sphere be conscious of their brightness)
Are yet of no diviner origin,
No purer essence, than the one that burns,
Like an untended watchfire, on the ridge
Of some dark mountain; or than those which seem
Humbly to hang, like twinkling winter lamps,
Among the branches of the leafless trees;
All are the undying offspring of one Sire:
Then, to the measure of the light vouchsafed,
Shine, Poet! in thy place, and be content.

Poetical Works, 1827

87   ' *Why art thou silent* '

WHY art thou silent! Is thy love a plant
  Of such weak fibre that the treacherous air
Of absence withers what was once so fair?
Is there no debt to pay, no boon to grant?

163

Yet have my thoughts for thee been vigilant
(As would my deeds have been) with hourly care,
The mind's least generous wish a mendicant
For nought but what thy happiness could spare.
Speak—though this soft warm heart, once free to hold
A thousand tender pleasures, thine and mine,
Be left more desolate, more dreary cold
Than a forsaken bird's-nest filled with snow
'Mid its own bush of leafless eglantine—
Speak, that my torturing doubts their end may know!

Yarrow Revisited, &c., 1835

88   *The Trosachs*

THERE 's not a nook within this solemn Pass,
   But were an apt confessional for One
Taught by his summer spent, his autumn gone,
That Life is but a tale of morning grass
Withered at eve. From scenes of art which chase
That thought away, turn, and with watchful eyes
Feed it 'mid Nature's old felicities,
Rocks, rivers, and smooth lakes more clear than glass
Untouched, unbreathed upon. Thrice happy quest,
If from a golden perch of aspen spray
(October's workmanship to rival May)
The pensive warbler of the ruddy breast
That moral sweeten by a heaven-taught lay,
Lulling the year, with all its cares, to rest!

Yarrow Revisited, &c., 1835

SMALL service is true service while it lasts;
Of Friends, however humble, scorn not one:
The Daisy, by the shadow that it casts,
Protects the lingering dew-drop from the Sun.

Yarrow Revisited, &c., 1835

WHEN first, descending from the moorlands,
I saw the Stream of Yarrow glide
Along a bare and open valley,
The Ettrick Shepherd was my guide.

When last along its banks I wandered,
Through groves that had begun to shed
Their golden leaves upon the pathways,
My steps the Border-minstrel led.

The mighty Minstrel breathes no longer,
'Mid mouldering ruins low he lies;
And death upon the braes of Yarrow,
Has closed the Shepherd-poet's eyes:

Nor has the rolling year twice measured,
From sign to sign, its steadfast course,
Since every mortal power of Coleridge
Was frozen at its marvellous source;

WILLIAM WORDSWORTH

The rapt One, of the godlike forehead,
The heaven-eyed creature sleeps in earth:
And Lamb, the frolic and the gentle,
Has vanished from his lonely hearth.

Like clouds that rake the mountain-summits,
Or waves that own no curbing hand,
How fast has brother followed brother,
From sunshine to the sunless land!

Yet I, whose lids from infant slumber
Were earlier raised, remain to hear
A timid voice, that asks in whispers,
' Who next will drop and disappear? '

Our haughty life is crowned with darkness,
Like London with its own black wreath,
On which with thee, O Crabbe! forthlooking,
I gazed from Hampstead's breezy heath.

As if but yesterday departed,
Thou too art gone before; but why,
O'er ripe fruit, seasonably gathered,
Should frail survivors heave a sigh?

Mourn rather for that holy Spirit,
Sweet as the spring, as ocean deep;
For Her who, ere her summer faded,
Has sunk into a breathless sleep.

No more of old romantic sorrows,
For slaughtered Youth or love-lorn Maid!
With sharper grief is Yarrow smitten,
And Ettrick mourns with her their Poet dead.

Poems, 1837

(i)

FAIR seed-time had my soul, and I grew up
Foster'd alike by beauty and by fear;
Much favour'd in my birthplace, and no less
In that beloved Vale to which, ere long
I was transplanted. Well I call to mind
('Twas at an early age, ere I had seen
Nine summers) when upon the mountain slope
The frost and breath of frosty wind had snapp'd
The last autumnal crocus, 'twas my joy
To wander, half the night, among the Cliffs
And the smooth Hollows, where the woodcocks ran
Along the open turf. In thought and wish
That time, my shoulder all with springes hung,
I was a fell destroyer. On the heights
Scudding away from snare to snare, I plied
My anxious visitation; hurrying on,
Still hurrying, hurrying onward; moon and stars
Were shining o'er my head; I was alone
And seem'd to be a trouble to the peace
That was among them. Sometimes it befel
In these night-wanderings, that a strong desire
O'erpower'd my better reason, and the bird
Which was the captive of another's toils
Became my prey; and when the deed was done
I heard among the solitary hills
Low breathings coming after me, and sounds

[1] The text of these extracts is that of the 1805–6 MS., first published in 1926.

Of undistinguishable motion, steps
Almost as silent as the turf they trod.
Nor less in springtime, when on southern banks
The shining sun had from his knot of leaves
Decoy'd the primrose flower, and when the Vales
And woods were warm, was I a plunderer then
In the high places, on the lonesome peaks
Where'er, among the mountains and the winds,
The Mother Bird had built her lodge. Though mean
My object and inglorious, yet the end
Was not ignoble. Oh! when I have hung
Above the raven's nest, by knots of grass
And half-inch fissures in the slippery rock
But ill sustain'd, and almost, as it seem'd,
Suspended by the blast which blew amain,
Shouldering the naked crag; Oh! at that time,
While on the perilous ridge I hung alone,
With what strange utterance did the loud dry wind
Blow through my ears! the sky seem'd not a sky
Of earth, and with what motion mov'd the clouds!

Book I, ll. 305–50

(ii)

ONE evening (surely I was led by her[1])
I went alone into a Shepherd's Boat,
A Skiff that to a Willow tree was tied
Within a rocky Cave, its usual home.
'Twas by the shores of Patterdale, a Vale
Wherein I was a Stranger, thither come
A School-boy Traveller, at the Holidays.
Forth rambled from the Village Inn alone,

[1] her = Nature.

No sooner had I sight of this small Skiff
Discover'd thus by unexpected chance,
Than I unloos'd her tether and embark'd.
The moon was up, the Lake was shining clear
Among the hoary mountains; from the Shore
I push'd, and struck the oars and struck again
In cadence, and my little Boat mov'd on
Even like a Man who walks with stately step
Though bent on speed. It was an act of stealth
And troubled pleasure, not without the voice
Of mountain-echoes did my Boat move on,
Leaving behind her still on either side
Small circles glittering idly in the moon,
Until they melted all into one track
Of sparkling light. A rocky Steep uprose
Above the Cavern of the Willow tree
And now, as suited one who proudly row'd
With his best skill, I fix'd a steady view
Upon the top of that same craggy ridge,
The bound of the horizon; for behind
Was nothing but the stars and the grey sky.
She was an elfin Pinnace; lustily
I dipp'd my oars into the silent Lake,
And, as I rose upon the stroke, my Boat
Went heaving through the water, like a Swan;
When from behind that craggy Steep, till then
The bound of the horizon, a huge Cliff,
As if with voluntary power instinct,
Uprear'd its head. I struck, and struck again,
And, growing still in stature, the huge Cliff
Rose up between me and the stars, and still,
With measur'd motion, like a living thing,

Strode after me. With trembling hands I turn'd
And through the silent water stole my way
Back to the Cavern of the Willow tree.
There in her mooring-place, I left my Bark,
And, through the meadows homeward went, with grave
And serious thoughts; and after I had seen
That spectacle, for many days, my brain
Work'd with a dim and undetermin'd sense
Of unknown modes of being; in my thoughts
There was a darkness, call it solitude,
Or blank desertion, no familiar shapes
Of hourly objects, images of trees;
Of sea or sky, no colours of green fields;
But huge and mighty Forms, that do not live
Like living men, mov'd slowly through the mind
By day, and were the trouble of my dreams.

Book I, ll. 372–427

(iii)

FOR I would walk alone,
In storm and tempest, or in starlight nights
Beneath the quiet Heavens; and, at that time,
Have felt whate'er there is of power in sound
To breathe an elevated mood, by form
Or image unprofaned; and I would stand,
Beneath some rock, listening to sounds that are
The ghostly language of the ancient earth,
Or make their dim abode in distant winds.
Thence did I drink the visionary power.
I deem not profitless these fleeting moods
Of shadowy exultation: not for this,

170

That they are kindred to our purer mind
And intellectual life; but that the soul,
Remembering how she felt, but what she felt
Remembering not, retains an obscure sense
Of possible sublimity, to which,
With growing faculties she doth aspire,
With faculties still growing, feeling still
That whatsoever point they gain, they still
Have something to pursue.

Book II, ll. 321–41

(iv)

BESIDE the pleasant Mills of Trompington
I laugh'd with Chaucer; in the hawthorn shade
Heard him (while birds were warbling) tell his tales
Of amorous passion. And that gentle Bard,
Chosen by the Muses for their Page of State,
Sweet Spenser, moving through his clouded heaven
With the moon's beauty and the moon's soft pace,
I call'd him Brother, Englishman, and Friend.
Yea, our blind Poet, who, in his later day,
Stood almost single, uttering odious truth,
Darkness before, and danger's voice behind;
Soul awful!—if the earth has ever lodg'd
An awful Soul, I seem'd to see him here
Familiarly, and in his Scholar's dress
Bounding before me, yet a stripling Youth,
A Boy, no better, with his rosy cheeks
Angelical, keen eye, courageous look,
And conscious step of purity and pride.

Book III, ll. 276–93

WILLIAM WORDSWORTH

(v)

WHEN first I made
Once more the circuit of our little Lake
If ever happiness hath lodg'd with man,
That day consummate happiness was mine,
Wide-spreading, steady, calm, contemplative.
The sun was set, or setting, when I left
Our cottage door, and evening soon brought on
A sober hour, not winning or serene,
For cold and raw the air was, and untun'd;
But, as a face we love is sweetest then
When sorrow damps it, or, whatever look
It chance to wear is sweetest if the heart
Have fulness in itself, even so with me
It fared that evening. Gently did my soul
Put off her veil, and, self-transmuted, stood
Naked as in the presence of her God.
As on I walked, a comfort seem'd to touch
A heart that had not been disconsolate,
Strength came where weakness was not known to be,
At least not felt; and restoration came,
Like an intruder, knocking at the door
Of unacknowledg'd weariness.

Book IV, ll. 127-48

(vi)

IN a throng,
A festal company of Maids and Youths,
Old Men, and Matrons staid, promiscuous rout,
A medley of all tempers, I had pass'd
The night in dancing, gaiety and mirth;

With din of instruments, and shuffling feet,
And glancing forms, and tapers glittering,
And unaim'd prattle flying up and down,
Spirits upon the stretch, and here and there
Slight shocks of young love-liking interspers'd,
That mounted up like joy into the head,
And tingled through the veins. Ere we retired,
The cock had crow'd, the sky was bright with day.
Two miles I had to walk along the fields
Before I reached my home. Magnificent
The morning was, in memorable pomp,
More glorious than I ever had beheld.
The Sea was laughing at a distance; all
The solid Mountains were as bright as clouds,
Grain-tinctured, drench'd in empyrean light;
And, in the meadows and the lower grounds,
Was all the sweetness of a common dawn,
Dews, vapours, and the melody of birds,
And Labourers going forth into the fields,
—Ah! need I say, dear Friend, that to the brim
My heart was full; I made no vows, but vows
Were then made for me; bond unknown to me
Was given, that I should be, else sinning greatly,
A dedicated Spirit. On I walk'd
In blessedness, which even yet remains.

Book IV, ll. 316–45

(vii)

A FAVOURITE pleasure hath it been with me
From time of earliest youth, to walk alone
Along the public Way, when, for the night

Deserted, in its silence it assumes
A character of deeper quietness
Than pathless solitudes. At such an hour
Once, ere these summer months were pass'd away,
I slowly mounted up a steep ascent
Where the road's watery surface, to the ridge
Of that sharp rising, glitter'd in the moon,
And seem'd before my eyes another stream
Creeping with silent lapse to join the brook
That murmur'd in the valley. On I went
Tranquil, receiving in my own despite
Amusement, as I slowly pass'd along,
From such near objects as from time to time,
Perforce intruded on the listless sense
Quiescent, and dispos'd to sympathy,
With an exhausted mind, worn out by toil,
And all unworthy of the deeper joy
Which waits on distant prospects, cliff, or sea,
The dark blue vault, and universe of stars.
Thus did I steal along that silent road,
My body from the stillness drinking in
A restoration like the calm of sleep,
But sweeter far. Above, before, behind,
Around me, all was peace and solitude,
I look'd not round, nor did the solitude
Speak to my eye; but it was heard and felt.
Oh happy state! what beauteous pictures now
Rose in harmonious imagery—they rose
As from some distant region of my soul
And came along like dreams; yet such as left
Obscurely mingled with their passing forms
A consciousness of animal delight,

A self-possession, felt in every pause
At every gentle movement of my frame.

Book IV, ll. 363–99

(*viii*)

A GRACIOUS Spirit o'er this earth presides,
And o'er the heart of man: invisibly
It comes, directing those to works of love,
Who care not, know not, think not what they do:
The Tales that charm away the wakeful night
In Araby, Romances, Legends penn'd
For solace, by the light of monkish Lamps;
Fictions for Ladies, of their Love, devis'd
By youthful Squires; adventures endless, spun
By the dismantled Warrior in old age,
Out of the bowels of those very thoughts
In which his youth did first extravagate,
These spread like day, and something in the shape
Of these, will live till man shall be no more.
Dumb yearnings, hidden appetites are ours,
And they must have their food: our childhood sits,
Our simple childhood sits upon a throne
That hath more power than all the elements.
I guess not what this tells of Being past,
Nor what it augurs of the life to come;
But so it is; and in that dubious hour,
That twilight when we first begin to see
This dawning earth, to recognise, expect;
And in the long probation that ensues,
The time of trial, ere we learn to live
In reconcilement with our stinted powers,
To endure this state of meagre vassalage,

175

Unwilling to forego, confess, submit,
Uneasy and unsettled, yoke-fellows
To custom, mettlesome, and not yet tam'd
And humbled down, oh! then we feel, we feel,
We know when we have Friends. Ye dreamers, then,
Forgers of lawless tales! we bless you then,
Impostors, drivellers, dotards, as the ape
Philosophy will call you: then we feel
With what, and how great might ye are in league,
Who make our wish our power, our thought a deed,
An empire, a possession; Ye whom Time
And Seasons serve; all Faculties; to whom
Earth crouches, the elements are potter's clay,
Space like a Heaven fill'd up with Northern lights;
Here, nowhere, there, and everywhere at once.

Book V, ll. 516–57

(ix)

A SINGLE Tree

There was, no doubt yet standing there, an Ash,
With sinuous trunk, boughs exquisitely wreath'd;
Up from the ground and almost to the top
The trunk and master branches everywhere
Were green with ivy; and the lightsome twigs
And outer spray profusely tipp'd with seeds
That hung in yellow tassels and festoons,
Moving or still, a Favourite trimm'd out
By Winter for himself, as if in pride,
And with outlandish grace. Oft have I stood
Foot-bound, uplooking at this lovely Tree
Beneath a frosty moon. The hemisphere

Of magic fiction, verse of mine perhaps
May never tread; but scarcely Spenser's self
Could have more tranquil visions in his youth,
More bright appearances could scarcely see
Of human Forms with superhuman Powers,
Than I beheld, standing on winter nights
Alone, beneath this fairy work of earth.

Book VI, ll. 90–109

(x)

      THE brook and road
Were fellow-travellers in this gloomy Pass,
And with them did we journey several hours
At a slow step. The immeasurable height
Of woods decaying, never to be decay'd,
The stationary blasts of water-falls,
And every where along the hollow rent
Winds thwarting winds, bewilder'd and forlorn,
The torrents shooting from the clear blue sky,
The rocks that mutter'd close upon our ears;
Black drizzling crags that spake by the way-side
As if a voice were in them, the sick sight
And giddy prospect of the raving stream,
The unfetter'd clouds and region of the Heavens,
Tumult and peace, the darkness and the light
Were all like workings of one mind, the features
Of the same face, blossoms upon one tree,
Characters of the great Apocalypse,
The types and symbols of Eternity,
Of first and last, and midst, and without end.

Book VI, ll. 553–72

(xi)

IN France, the Men who for their desperate ends
 Had pluck'd up mercy by the roots were glad
Of this new enemy[1]. Tyrants, strong before
In devilish pleas, were ten times stronger now,
And thus beset with Foes on every side
The goaded Land waxed mad; the crimes of few
Spread into madness of the many, blasts
From hell came sanctified like airs from heaven;
The sternness of the Just, the faith of those
Who doubted not that Providence had times
Of anger and of vengeance,—theirs who throned
The human Understanding paramount
And made of that their God, the hopes of those
Who were content to barter short-lived pangs
For a paradise of ages, the blind rage
Of insolent tempers, the light vanity
Of intermeddlers, steady purposes
Of the suspicious, slips of the indiscreet,
And all the accidents of life were press'd
Into one service, busy with one work;
The Senate was heart-stricken, not a voice
Uplifted, none to oppose or mitigate;
Domestic carnage now filled all the year
With Feast-days; the old Man from the chimney-nook,
The Maiden from the bosom of her Love,
The Mother from the Cradle of her babe,
The Warrior from the Field, all perish'd, all,
Friends, enemies, of all parties, ages, ranks,
Head after head, and never heads enough

[1] this new enemy = England.

For those that bade them fall: they found their joy,
They made it, ever thirsty as a Child,
If light desires of innocent little Ones
May with such heinous appetites be match'd,
Having a toy, a wind-mill, though the air
Do of itself blow fresh, and make the vane
Spin in his eyesight, he is not content
But with the plaything at arm's length he sets
His front against the blast, and runs amain,
To make it whirl the faster.

Book X, ll. 308–46

(xii)

O PLEASANT exercise of hope and joy!
For great were the auxiliars which then stood
Upon our side, we who were strong in love;
Bliss was it in that dawn to be alive,
But to be young was very heaven; O times,
In which the meagre, stale, forbidding ways
Of custom, law, and statute took at once
The attraction of a Country in Romance;
When Reason seem'd the most to assert her rights
When most intent on making of herself
A prime Enchanter to assist the work,
Which then was going forwards in her name.
Not favour'd spots alone, but the whole earth
The beauty wore of promise, that which sets,
To take an image which was felt, no doubt,
Among the bowers of Paradise itself,
The budding rose above the rose full blown.
What temper at the prospect did not wake
To happiness unthought of? The inert

Were rouz'd, and lively natures rapt away:
They who had fed their childhood upon dreams,
The Play-fellows of Fancy, who had made
All powers of swiftness, subtlety, and strength
Their ministers, used to stir in lordly wise
Among the grandest objects of the sense,
And deal with whatsoever they found there
As if they had within some lurking right
To wield it; they, too, who, of gentle mood,
Had watch'd all gentle motions, and to these
Had fitted their own thoughts, schemers more mild,
And in the region of their peaceful selves,
Did now find helpers to their hearts' desire,
And stuff at hand, plastic as they could wish,
Were call'd upon to exercise their skill,
Not in Utopia, subterraneous Fields,
Or some secreted Island, Heaven knows where,
But in the very world which is the world
Of all of us, the place in which, in the end,
We find our happiness, or not at all!

Book X, ll. 690–728

(xiii)

OH! yet a few short years of useful life,
     And all will be complete, thy [1] race be run,
Thy monument of glory will be raised.
Then, though, too weak to tread the ways of truth,
This Age fall back to old idolatry,
Though men return to servitude as fast
As the tide ebbs, to ignominy and shame
By Nations sink together, we shall still

[1] thy = Coleridge's.

Find solace in the knowledge which we have,
Bless'd with true happiness if we may be
United helpers forward of a day
Of firmer trust, joint labourers in a work
(Should Providence such grace to us vouchsafe)
Of their redemption, surely yet to come.
Prophets of Nature, we to them will speak
A lasting inspiration, sanctified
By reason and by truth: what we have loved,
Others will love, and we may teach them how;
Instruct them how the mind of man becomes
A thousand times more beautiful than the earth
On which he dwells, above this Frame of things
(Which, 'mid all revolution in the hopes
And fears of men, doth still remain unchanged)
In beauty exalted, as it is itself
Of substance and of fabric more divine.

> Book XIII, ll. 428–52
> *The Prelude*: written 1805–6

92   *From ' The Recluse '*

ON Man, on Nature, and on Human Life,
　　Musing in solitude, I oft perceive
Fair trains of imagery before me rise,
Accompanied by feelings of delight
Pure, or with no unpleasing sadness mixed;
And I am conscious of affecting thoughts
And dear remembrances, whose presence soothes
Or elevates the Mind, intent to weigh
The good and evil of our mortal state.

—To these emotions, whencesoe'er they come,
Whether from breath of outward circumstance,
Or from the Soul—an impulse to herself—
I would give utterance in numerous verse.
Of Truth, of Grandeur, Beauty, Love, and Hope,
And melancholy Fear subdued by Faith;
Of blessed consolations in distress;
Of moral strength, and intellectual Power;
Of joy in widest commonalty spread;
Of the individual Mind that keeps her own
Inviolate retirement, subject there
To Conscience only, and the law supreme
Of that Intelligence which governs all—
I sing:—' fit audience let me find though few!'

So prayed, more gaining than he asked, the Bard,
Holiest of Men.—Urania, I shall need
Thy guidance, or a greater Muse, if such
Descend to earth or dwell in highest heaven!
For I must tread on shadowy ground, must sink
Deep—and, aloft ascending, breathe in worlds
To which the heaven of heavens is but a veil.
All strength—all terror, single or in bands,
That ever was put forth in personal form—
Jehovah—with his thunder, and the choir
Of shouting Angels, and the empyreal thrones—
I pass them unalarmed. Not Chaos, not
The darkest pit of lowest Erebus,
Nor aught of blinder vacancy, scooped out
By help of dreams—can breed such fear and awe
As fall upon us often when we look
Into our Minds, into the Mind of Man—

My haunt, and the main region of my song.
—Beauty—a living Presence of the earth,
Surpassing the most fair ideal Forms
Which craft of delicate Spirits hath composed
From earth's materials—waits upon my steps;
Pitches her tents before me as I move,
An hourly neighbour. Paradise, and groves
Elysian, Fortunate Fields—like those of old
Sought in the Atlantic Main—why should they be
A history only of departed things,
Or a mere fiction of what never was?
For the discerning intellect of Man,
When wedded to this goodly universe
In love and holy passion, shall find these
A simple produce of the common day.
—I, long before the blissful hour arrives,
Would chant, in lonely peace, the spousal verse
Of this great consummation:—and, by words
Which speak of nothing more than what we are,
Would I arouse the sensual from their sleep
Of Death, and win the vacant and the vain
To noble raptures; while my voice proclaims
How exquisitely the individual Mind
(And the progressive powers perhaps no less
Of the whole species) to the external World
Is fitted:—and how exquisitely, too—
Theme this but little heard of among men—
The external World is fitted to the Mind;
And the creation (by no lower name
Can it be called) which they with blended might
Accomplish:—this is our high argument.
—Such grateful haunts foregoing, if I oft

Must turn elsewhere—to travel near the tribes
And fellowships of men, and see ill sights
Of madding passions mutually inflamed;
Must hear Humanity in fields and groves
Pipe solitary anguish; or must hang
Brooding above the fierce confederate storm
Of sorrow, barricadoed evermore
Within the walls of cities—may these sounds
Have their authentic comment; that even these
Hearing, I be not downcast or forlorn!
Descend, prophetic Spirit! that inspir'st
The human Soul of universal earth,
Dreaming on things to come; and dost possess
A metropolitan temple in the hearts
Of mighty Poets: upon me bestow
A gift of genuine insight; that my Song
With star-like virtue in its place may shine,
Shedding benignant influence, and secure,
Itself, from all malevolent effect
Of those mutations that extend their sway
Throughout the nether sphere!—And if with this
I mix more lowly matter; with the thing
Contemplated, describe the Mind and Man
Contemplating; and who, and what he was—
The transitory Being that beheld
This Vision; when and where, and how he lived;—
Be not this labour useless. If such theme
May sort with highest objects, then—dread Power!
Whose gracious favour is the primal source
Of all illumination—may my Life
Express the image of a better time,
More wise desires, and simpler manners;—nurse

THE RECLUSE

My Heart in genuine freedom:—all pure thoughts
Be with me;—so shall thy unfailing love
Guide, and support, and cheer me to the end!

Preface to *The Excursion*, 1814;
The Recluse, 1888

SIR WALTER SCOTT

1771–1832

93 *From ' The Lay of the Last Minstrel '*

(i)

THE humble boon was soon obtain'd;
The aged Minstrel audience gain'd.
But, when he reach'd the room of state,
Where she with all her ladies sate,
Perchance he wish'd his boon denied:
For, when to tune his harp he tried,
His trembling hand had lost the ease,
Which marks security to please;
And scenes long past, of joy and pain,
Came wildering o'er his aged brain—
He tried to tune his harp in vain!
The pitying Duchess prais'd its chime,
And gave him heart, and gave him time,
Till every string's according glee
Was blended into harmony.
And then, he said, he would full fain
He could recall an ancient strain
He never thought to sing again.

It was not framed for village churls,
But for high dames and mighty earls;
He had play'd it to King Charles the Good,
When he kept court in Holyrood;
And much he wish'd, yet fear'd, to try
The long-forgotten melody.
Amid the strings his fingers stray'd,
And an uncertain warbling made,
And oft he shook his hoary head.
But when he caught the measure wild,
The old man rais'd his face, and smil'd;
And lighten'd up his faded eye
With all a poet's ecstasy.
In varying cadence, soft or strong,
He swept the sounding chords along:
The present scene, the future lot,
His toils, his wants, were all forgot;
Cold diffidence, and age's frost,
In the full tide of song were lost;
Each blank, in faithless memory void,
The poet's glowing thought supplied;
And, while his harp responsive rung,
'Twas thus the LATEST MINSTREL sung.

I

THE feast was over in Branksome tower,
And the Ladye had gone to her secret bower;
Her bower that was guarded by word and by spell,
Deadly to hear, and deadly to tell—
Jesu Maria, shield us well!
No living wight, save the Ladye alone,
Had dared to cross the threshold stone.

THE LAY OF THE LAST MINSTREL

II

The tables were drawn, it was idlesse all;
   Knight, and page, and household squire,
Loiter'd through the lofty hall,
   Or crowded round the ample fire:
The stag-hounds, weary with the chase,
   Lay stretch'd upon the rushy floor,
And urg'd, in dreams, the forest race
   From Teviot-stone to Eskdale-moor.

III

Nine-and-twenty knights of fame
   Hung their shields in Branksome hall;
Nine-and-twenty squires of name
   Brought them their steeds to bower from stall;
      Nine-and-twenty yeomen tall
      Waited, duteous, on them all:
      They were all knights of mettle true,
      Kinsmen to the bold Buccleuch.

IV

Ten of them were sheath'd in steel,
With belted sword, and spur on heel:
They quitted not their harness bright,
Neither by day, nor yet by night:
      They lay down to rest,
      With corslet laced,
Pillow'd on buckler cold and hard;
      They carv'd at the meal
      With gloves of steel,
And they drank the red wine through the helmet barr'd.

SIR WALTER SCOTT

V

Ten squires, ten yeomen, mail-clad men,
Waited the beck of the warders ten:
Thirty steeds, both fleet and wight,
Stood saddled in stable day and night,
Barb'd with frontlet of steel, I trow,
And with Jedwood-axe at saddlebow;
A hundred more fed free in stall:
Such was the custom of Branksome Hall.

VI

Why do these steeds stand ready dight?
Why watch these warriors, arm'd, by night?
They watch to hear the blood-hound baying:
They watch to hear the war-horn braying;
To see St. George's red cross streaming,
To see the midnight beacon gleaming:
They watch against Southern force and guile,
    Lest Scroop, or Howard, or Percy's powers,
    Threaten Branksome's lordly towers,
From Warkworth, or Naworth, or merry Carlisle.

Introduction, ll. 60–100
Canto I, ll. 1–51

(ii)

IF thou would'st view fair Melrose aright,
  Go visit it by the pale moonlight;
For the gay beams of lightsome day
Gild, but to flout, the ruins grey.

      wight] strong.

When the broken arches are black in night,
And each shafted oriel glimmers white;
When the cold light's uncertain shower
Streams on the ruin'd central tower;
When buttress and buttress, alternately,
Seem fram'd of ebon and ivory;
When silver edges the imagery,
And the scrolls that teach thee to live and die;
When distant Tweed is heard to rave,
And the owlet to hoot o'er the dead man's grave,
Then go—but go alone the while—
Then view St. David's ruin'd pile;
And, home returning, soothly swear,
Was never scene so sad and fair!

Canto II, ll. 1–18

(*iii*)

SWEET Teviot! on thy silver tide
The glaring bale-fires blaze no more;
No longer steel-clad warriors ride
　　Along thy wild and willow'd shore;
Where'er thou wind'st, by dale or hill,
All, all is peaceful, all is still,
　　As if thy waves, since Time was born,
Since first they roll'd upon the Tweed,
Had only heard the shepherd's reed,
　　Nor started at the bugle-horn.

Unlike the tide of human time,—
　　Which, though it change in ceaseless flow,
Retains each grief, retains each crime
　　Its earliest course was doom'd to know;

SIR WALTER SCOTT

And, darker as it downward bears,
Is stain'd with past and present tears.
    Low as that tide has ebb'd with me,
It still reflects to Memory's eye
The hour my brave, my only boy
    Fell by the side of great Dundee.
Why, when the volleying musket play'd
Against the bloody Highland blade,
Why was not I beside him laid!
Enough, he died the death of fame;
Enough, he died with conquering Græme.

Canto IV, ll. 1–25

(iv)

HE paused: the listening dames again
   Applaud the hoary Minstrel's strain.
With many a word of kindly cheer,
In pity half, and half sincere,
Marvell'd the Duchess how so well
His legendary song could tell
Of ancient deeds, so long forgot;
Of feuds, whose memory was not:
Of forests, now laid waste and bare;
Of towers, which harbour now the hare;
Of manners, long since chang'd and gone;
Of chiefs, who under their grey stone
So long had slept, that fickle Fame
Had blotted from her rolls their name,
And twin'd round some new minion's head
The fading wreath for which they bled;

In sooth, 'twas strange, this old man's verse
Could call them from their marble hearse.

    The Harper smil'd, well-pleas'd; for ne'er
Was flattery lost on poet's ear:
A simple race! they waste their toil
For the vain tribute of a smile;
E'en when in age their flame expires,
Her dulcet breath can fan its fires:
Their drooping fancy wakes at praise,
And strives to trim the short-liv'd blaze.

Canto IV, ll. 600–25

(v)

CALL it not vain; they do not err,
  Who say, that when the Poet dies,
Mute Nature mourns her worshipper,
    And celebrates his obsequies:
Who say, tall cliff and cavern lone
For the departed Bard make moan;
That mountains weep in crystal rill;
That flowers in tears of balm distil;
Through his lov'd groves that breezes sigh,
And oaks, in deeper groan, reply;
And rivers teach their rushing wave
To murmur dirges round his grave.

Not that, in sooth, o'er mortal urn
Those things inanimate can mourn;
But that the stream, the wood, the gale,
Is vocal with the plaintive wail

Of those, who, else forgotten long,
Liv'd in the poet's faithful song,
And, with the poet's parting breath,
Whose memory feels a second death.
The Maid's pale shade, who wails her lot,
That love, true love, should be forgot,
From rose and hawthorn shakes the tear
Upon the gentle Minstrel's bier:
The phantom Knight, his glory fled,
Mourns o'er the field he heap'd with dead;
Mounts the wild blast that sweeps amain,
And shrieks along the battle-plain.
The Chief, whose antique crownlet long
Still sparkled in the feudal song,
Now, from the mountain's misty throne,
Sees, in the thanedom once his own,
His ashes undistinguish'd lie,
His place, his power, his memory die:
His groans the lonely caverns fill,
His tears of rage impel the rill:
All mourn the Minstrel's harp unstrung,
Their name unknown, their praise unsung.

Canto V, ll. 1–38

(vi)

TRUE love 's the gift which God has given
    To man alone beneath the heaven:
It is not fantasy's hot fire,
    Whose wishes, soon as granted, fly;
It liveth not in fierce desire,
    With dead desire it doth not die;

THE LAY OF THE LAST MINSTREL

It is the secret sympathy,
The silver link, the silken tie,
Which heart to heart, and mind to mind,
In body and in soul can bind.

Canto V, ll. 217–26

(vii)

BREATHES there the man, with soul so dead,
Who never to himself hath said,
 This is my own, my native land!
Whose heart hath ne'er within him burn'd,
As home his footsteps he hath turn'd,
 From wandering on a foreign strand!
If such there breathe, go, mark him well;
For him no Minstrel raptures swell;
High though his titles, proud his name,
Boundless his wealth as wish can claim;
Despite those titles, power, and pelf,
The wretch, concentred all in self,
Living, shall forfeit fair renown,
And, doubly dying, shall go down
To the vile dust, from whence he sprung,
Unwept, unhonour'd, and unsung.

O Caledonia! stern and wild,
Meet nurse for a poetic child!
Land of brown heath and shaggy wood,
Land of the mountain and the flood,
Land of my sires! what mortal hand
Can e'er untie the filial band,
That knits me to thy rugged strand!

Still as I view each well-known scene,
Think what is now, and what hath been,
Seems as, to me, of all bereft,
Sole friends thy woods and streams were left;
And thus I love them better still,
Even in extremity of ill.
By Yarrow's stream still let me stray,
Though none should guide my feeble way;
Still feel the breeze down Ettrick break,
Although it chill my wither'd cheek;
Still lay my head by Teviot Stone,
Though there, forgotten and alone,
The Bard may draw his parting groan.

Canto VI, ll. 1–36

(viii)

IT was an English ladye bright,
  (The sun shines fair on Carlisle wall,)
And she would marry a Scottish knight,
    For Love will still be lord of all.

Blithely they saw the rising sun,
    When he shone fair on Carlisle wall;
But they were sad ere day was done,
    Though Love was still the lord of all.

Her sire gave brooch and jewel fine,
    Where the sun shines fair on Carlisle wall;
Her brother gave but a flask of wine,
    For ire that Love was lord of all.

For she had lands, both meadow and lea,
   Where the sun shines fair on Carlisle wall;
And he swore her death ere he would see
   A Scottish knight the lord of all!

That wine she had not tasted well,
   (The sun shines fair on Carlisle wall,)
When dead in her true love's arms she fell,
   For Love was still the lord of all!

He pierc'd her brother to the heart,
   Where the sun shines fair on Carlisle wall:
So perish all would true love part,
   That Love may still be lord of all!

And then he took the cross divine,
   (Where the sun shines fair on Carlisle wall,)
And died for her sake in Palestine;
   So Love was still the lord of all.

Now all ye lovers that faithful prove,
   (The sun shines fair on Carlisle wall,)
Pray for their souls who died for love,
   For Love shall still be lord of all!

Canto VI, ll. 191–222

(ix)

NOUGHT of the bridal will I tell,
   Which after in short space befell;
Nor how brave sons and daughters fair
Bless'd Teviot's Flower, and Cranstoun's heir:
After such dreadful scene, 'twere vain
To wake the note of mirth again.

More meet it were to mark the day
   Of penitence, and prayer divine,
When pilgrim-chiefs, in sad array,
   Sought Melrose' holy shrine.

With naked foot, and sackcloth vest,
And arms enfolded on his breast,
   Did every pilgrim go;
The standers-by might hear uneath,
Footstep, or voice, or high-drawn breath,
   Through all the lengthen'd row:
No lordly look, nor martial stride;
Gone was their glory, sunk their pride,
   Forgotten their renown;
Silent and slow, like ghosts they glide
To the high altar's hallow'd side,
   And there they knelt them down;
Above the suppliant chieftains wave
The banners of departed brave;
Beneath the letter'd stones were laid
The ashes of their fathers dead;
From many a garnish'd niche around,
Stern saints and tortur'd martyrs frown'd.

And slow up the dim aisle afar,
With sable cowl and scapular,
And snow-white stoles, in order due,
The holy Fathers, two and two,
   In long procession came;
Taper and host, and book they bare,
And holy banner, flourish'd fair
   With the Redeemer's name.

            uneath] with difficulty.

Above the prostrate pilgrim band
The mitred Abbot stretch'd his hand,
   And bless'd them as they kneel'd;
With holy cross he sign'd them all,
And pray'd they might be sage in hall,
   And fortunate in field.
Then mass was sung, and prayers were said,
And solemn requiem for the dead;
And bells toll'd out their mighty peal,
For the departed spirit's weal;
And ever in the office close
The hymn of intercession rose;
And far the echoing aisles prolong
The awful burthen of the song,—
   DIES IRÆ, DIES ILLA,
   SOLVET SÆCLUM IN FAVILLA,—
While the pealing organ rung.
   Were it meet with sacred strain
   To close my lay, so light and vain,
Thus the holy Fathers sung:

HYMN FOR THE DEAD

That day of wrath, that dreadful day,
When heaven and earth shall pass away,
What power shall be the sinner's stay?
How shall he meet that dreadful day?

When, shriveling like a parched scroll,
The flaming heavens together roll;
When louder yet, and yet more dread,
Swells the high trump that wakes the dead;

Oh! on that day, that wrathful day,
When man to judgment wakes from clay,
Be Thou the trembling sinner's stay,
Though heaven and earth shall pass away!

Canto VI, ll. 486–553
Lay of the Last Minstrel, 1805

94　　　　　　　*From ' Marmion '*

(i)

NOVEMBER'S sky is chill and drear,
November's leaf is red and sear;
Late, gazing down the steepy linn,
That hems our little garden in,
Low in its dark and narrow glen
You scarce the rivulet might ken,
So thick the tangled greenwood grew,
So feeble trill'd the streamlet through:
Now, murmuring hoarse, and frequent seen
Through bush and brier, no longer green,
An angry brook, it sweeps the glade,
Brawls over rock and wild cascade,
And, foaming brown with doubled speed,
Hurries its waters to the Tweed.

No longer Autumn's glowing red
Upon our Forest hills is shed;
No more beneath the evening beam
Fair Tweed reflects their purple gleam;
Away hath pass'd the heather-bell
That bloom'd so rich on Needpath-fell;
Sallow his brow; and russet bare
Are now the sister-heights of Yair.

MARMION

The sheep, before the pinching heaven,
To shelter'd dale and down are driven,
Where yet some faded herbage pines,
And yet a watery sunbeam shines:
In meek despondency they eye
The wither'd sward and wintry sky,
And far beneath their summer hill,
Stray sadly by Glenkinnon's rill:
The shepherd shifts his mantle's fold,
And wraps him closer from the cold;
His dogs no merry circles wheel,
But shivering follow at his heel;
A cowering glance they often cast,
As deeper moans the gathering blast.

   .   .   .   .   .   .

To mute and to material things
New life revolving summer brings;
The genial call dead Nature hears,
And in her glory reappears.
But oh! my country's wintry state
What second spring shall renovate?
What powerful call shall bid arise
The buried warlike and the wise;
The mind that thought for Britain's weal,
The hand that grasp'd the victor steel?
The vernal sun new life bestows
Even on the meanest flower that blows;
But vainly, vainly may he shine
Where glory weeps o'er NELSON's shrine;
And vainly pierce the solemn gloom,
That shrouds, O PITT, thy hallowed tomb!

SIR WALTER SCOTT

Deep grav'd in every British heart,
O never let those names depart!
Say to your sons,—Lo, here his grave,
Who victor died on Gadite wave.
To him, as to the burning levin,
Short, bright, resistless course was given.
Where'er his country's foes were found,
Was heard the fated thunder's sound,
Till burst the bolt on yonder shore,
Roll'd, blaz'd, destroy'd,—and was no more.

Nor mourn ye less his perish'd worth
Who bade the conqueror go forth,
And launch'd that thunderbolt of war
On Egypt, Hafnia, Trafalgar;
Who, born to guide such high emprize,
For Britain's weal was early wise;
Alas! to whom the Almighty gave,
For Britain's sins, an early grave!
His worth who, in his mightiest hour,
A bauble held the pride of power,
Spurn'd at the sordid lust of pelf,
And serv'd his Albion for herself;
Who, when the frantic crowd amain
Strain'd at subjection's bursting rein,
O'er their wild mood full conquest gain'd,
The pride, he would not crush, restrain'd,
Show'd their fierce zeal a worthier cause,
And brought the freeman's arm to aid the freeman's laws.

Had'st thou but liv'd, though stripp'd of power,
A watchman on the lonely tower,

Thy thrilling trump had rous'd the land,
When fraud or danger were at hand;
By thee, as by the beacon-light,
Our pilots had kept course aright;
As some proud column, though alone,
Thy strength had propp'd the tottering throne:
Now is the stately column broke,
The beacon-light is quench'd in smoke,
The trumpet's silver sound is still,
The warder silent on the hill!

Oh think, how to his latest day,
When Death, just hovering, claim'd his prey,
With Palinure's unalter'd mood,
Firm at his dangerous post he stood;
Each call for needful rest repell'd,
With dying hand the rudder held,
Till, in his fall, with fateful sway,
The steerage of the realm gave way!
Then, while on Britain's thousand plains,
One unpolluted church remains,
Whose peaceful bells ne'er sent around
The bloody tocsin's maddening sound,
But still, upon the hallow'd day,
Convoke the swains to praise and pray;
While faith and civil peace are dear,
Grace this cold marble with a tear,—
He, who preserved them, PITT, lies here!

Nor yet suppress the generous sigh,
Because his rival slumbers nigh;
Nor be thy *requiescat* dumb,
Lest it be said o'er Fox's tomb.

For talents mourn, untimely lost,
When best employ'd, and wanted most;
Mourn genius high, and lore profound,
And wit that lov'd to play, not wound;
And all the reasoning powers divine,
To penetrate, resolve, combine;
And feelings keen, and fancy's glow,—
They sleep with him who sleeps below:
And, if thou mourn'st they could not save
From error him who owns this grave,
Be every harsher thought suppress'd,
And sacred be the last long rest.
Here, where the end of earthly things
Lays heroes, patriots, bards, and kings;
Where stiff the hand, and still the tongue,
Of those who fought, and spoke, and sung;
Here, where the fretted aisles prolong
The distant notes of holy song,
As if some angel spoke agen,
' All peace on earth, good-will to men ';
If ever from an English heart,
O, *here* let prejudice depart,
And, partial feeling cast aside,
Record, that Fox a Briton died!
When Europe crouch'd to France's yoke,
And Austria bent, and Prussia broke,
And the firm Russian's purpose brave
Was barter'd by a timorous slave,
Even then dishonour's peace he spurn'd,
The sullied olive-branch return'd,
Stood for his country's glory fast,
And nail'd her colours to the mast!

MARMION

Heaven, to reward his firmness, gave
A portion in this honour'd grave,
And ne'er held marble in its trust
Of two such wondrous men the dust.

Canto I, Introduction, ll. 1–165

(ii)

LIKE April morning clouds, that pass,
　With varying shadow, o'er the grass,
And imitate, on field and furrow,
Life's chequer'd scene of joy and sorrow;
Like streamlet of the mountain north,
Now in a torrent racing forth,
Now winding slow its silver train,
And almost slumbering on the plain;
Like breezes of the autumn day,
Whose voice inconstant dies away,
And ever swells again as fast,
When the ear deems its murmur past;
Thus various, my romantic theme
Flits, winds, or sinks, a morning dream.
Yet pleas'd, our eye pursues the trace
Of Light and Shade's inconstant race;
Pleas'd, views the rivulet afar,
Weaving its maze irregular;
And pleas'd, we listen as the breeze
Heaves its wild sigh through autumn trees:
Then, wild as cloud, or stream, or gale,
Flow on, flow unconfin'd, my Tale!

Canto III, Introduction, ll. 1–22

(*iii*)

THUS while I ape the measure wild
 Of tales that charm'd me yet a child,
Rude though they be, still with the chime
Return the thoughts of early time;
And feelings, rous'd in life's first day,
Glow in the line, and prompt the lay.
Then rise those crags, that mountain tower
Which charm'd my fancy's wakening hour.
Though no broad river swept along,
To claim, perchance, heroic song;
Though sigh'd no groves in summer gale,
To prompt of love a softer tale;
Though scarce a puny streamlet's speed
Claim'd homage from a shepherd's reed;
Yet was poetic impulse given,
By the green hill and clear blue heaven.
It was a barren scene, and wild,
Where naked cliffs were rudely pil'd;
But ever and anon between
Lay velvet tufts of loveliest green;
And well the lonely infant knew
Recesses where the wall-flower grew,
And honey-suckle lov'd to crawl
Up the low crag and ruin'd wall.
I deem'd such nooks the sweetest shade
The sun in all its round survey'd;
And still I thought that shatter'd tower
The mightiest work of human power;
And marvell'd as the aged hind
With some strange tale bewitch'd my mind,

MARMION

Of forayers, who, with headlong force,
Down from that strength had spurr'd their horse,
Their southern rapine to renew,
Far in the distant Cheviots blue,
And, home returning, fill'd the hall
With revel, wassel-rout, and brawl.
Methought that still with trump and clang
The gateway's broken arches rang;
Methought grim features, seam'd with scars,
Glar'd through the window's rusty bars,
And ever, by the winter hearth,
Old tales I heard of woe or mirth,
Of lovers' slights, of ladies' charms,
Of witches' spells, of warriors' arms;
Of patriot battles, won of old
By Wallace wight and Bruce the bold;
Of later fields of feud and fight,
When, pouring from their Highland height,
The Scottish clans, in headlong sway,
Had swept the scarlet ranks away.
While stretch'd at length upon the floor,
Again I fought each combat o'er,
Pebbles and shells, in order laid,
The mimic ranks of war display'd;
And onward still the Scottish Lion bore,
And still the scatter'd Southron fled before.

Canto III, Introduction, ll. 152–207

(*iv*)

Song

WHERE shall the lover rest,
Whom the fates sever
From his true maiden's breast,
Parted for ever?
Where, through groves deep and high,
Sounds the far billow,
Where early violets die,
Under the willow.

Chorus

Eleu loro, &c.   Soft shall be his pillow.

There, through the summer day,
Cool streams are laving;
There, while the tempests sway,
Scarce are boughs waving;
There, thy rest shalt thou take,
Parted for ever,
Never again to wake,
Never, O never!

Chorus

Eleu loro, &c. Never, O never!

Where shall the traitor rest,
He, the deceiver,
Who could win maiden's breast,
Ruin, and leave her?

In the lost battle,
  Borne down by the flying,
Where mingles war's rattle
  With groans of the dying.

Chorus

Eleu loro, &c. There shall he be lying.

Her wing shall the eagle flap
  O'er the false-hearted;
His warm blood the wolf shall lap,
  Ere life be parted.
Shame and dishonour sit
  By his grave ever;
Blessing shall hallow it,
  Never, O never!

Chorus

Eleu loro, &c. Never, O never!

Canto III, ll. 148–183

(v)

WHEN dark December glooms the day,
  And takes our autumn joys away;
When short and scant the sunbeam throws,
Upon the weary waste of snows,
A cold and profitless regard,
Like patron on a needy bard;
When silvan occupation 's done,
And o'er the chimney rests the gun,
And hang, in idle trophy, near,
The game-pouch, fishing-rod, and spear;

When wiry terrier, rough and grim,
And greyhound, with his length of limb,
And pointer, now employ'd no more,
Cumber our parlour's narrow floor;
When in his stall the impatient steed
Is long condemn'd to rest and feed;
When from our snow-encircled home
Scarce cares the hardiest step to roam,
Since path is none, save that to bring
The needful water from the spring;
When wrinkled news-page, thrice conn'd o'er,
Beguiles the dreary hour no more,
And darkling politician, cross'd,
Inveighs against the lingering post,
And answering housewife sore complains
Of carriers' snow-impeded wains;
When such the country cheer, I come,
Well pleas'd, to seek our city home;
For converse, and for books, to change
The Forest's melancholy range,
And welcome, with renew'd delight,
The busy day and social night.

Canto V, Introduction, ll. 1–32

(vi)

Lochinvar

O, YOUNG Lochinvar is come out of the west,
  Through all the wide Border his steed was the best;
And save his good broadsword he weapons had none,
He rode all unarm'd, and he rode all alone.

MARMION

So faithful in love, and so dauntless in war,
There never was knight like the young Lochinvar.

He staid not for brake, and he stopp'd not for stone,
He swam the Eske river where ford there was none;
But ere he alighted at Netherby gate,
The bride had consented, the gallant came late:
For a laggard in love, and a dastard in war,
Was to wed the fair Ellen of brave Lochinvar.

So boldly he enter'd the Netherby Hall,
Among bride's-men, and kinsmen, and brothers, and all:
Then spoke the bride's father, his hand on his sword,
(For the poor craven bridegroom said never a word,)
' O come ye in peace here, or come ye in war,
Or to dance at our bridal, young Lord Lochinvar?'

' I long woo'd your daughter, my suit you denied;—
Love swells like the Solway, but ebbs like its tide—
And now am I come, with this lost love of mine,
To lead but one measure, drink one cup of wine.
There are maidens in Scotland more lovely by far,
That would gladly be bride to the young Lochinvar.'

The bride kiss'd the goblet: the knight took it up,
He quaff'd off the wine, and he threw down the cup.
She look'd down to blush, and she look'd up to sigh,
With a smile on her lips, and a tear in her eye.
He took her soft hand, ere her mother could bar,—
' Now tread we a measure!' said young Lochinvar.

So stately his form, and so lovely her face,
That never a hall such a galliard did grace;
While her mother did fret, and her father did fume,
And the bridegroom stood dangling his bonnet and plume;

And the bride-maidens whisper'd, ' 'Twere better by far,
To have match'd our fair cousin with young Lochinvar.'

One touch to her hand, and one word in her ear,
When they reach'd the hall-door, and the charger stood near;
So light to the croupe the fair lady he swung,
So light to the saddle before her he sprung!
' She is won! we are gone, over bank, bush, and scaur;
They'll have fleet steeds that follow,' quoth young Lochinvar.

There was mounting 'mong Græmes of the Netherby clan;
Forsters, Fenwicks, and Musgraves, they rode and they ran:
There was racing and chasing on Cannobie Lee,
But the lost bride of Netherby ne'er did they see.
So daring in love, and so dauntless in war,
Have ye e'er heard of gallant like young Lochinvar?

Canto V, ll. 313–60;
Marmion, 1808

95 *From ' The Lady of the Lake '*

(*i*)

Song

SOLDIER, rest! thy warfare o'er,
 Sleep the sleep that knows not breaking;
Dream of battled fields no more,
  Days of danger, nights of waking.
In our isle's enchanted hall,
  Hands unseen thy couch are strewing,
Fairy strains of music fall,
  Every sense in slumber dewing.

THE LADY OF THE LAKE

Soldier, rest! thy warfare o'er,
Dream of fighting fields no more:
Sleep the sleep that knows not breaking,
Morn of toil, nor night of waking.

No rude sound shall reach thine ear,
   Armour's clang, or war-steed champing,
Trump nor pibroch summon here
   Mustering clan, or squadron tramping.
Yet the lark's shrill fife may come
   At the day-break from the fallow,
And the bittern sound his drum,
   Booming from the sedgy shallow.
Ruder sounds shall none be near,
Guards nor warders challenge here,
Here 's no war-steed's neigh and champing,
Shouting clans, or squadrons stamping.

   .   .   .   .   .

Huntsman, rest! thy chase is done;
   While our slumbrous spells assail ye,
Dream not, with the rising sun,
   Bugles here shall sound reveillé.
Sleep! the deer is in his den;
   Sleep! thy hounds are by thee lying;
Sleep! nor dream in yonder glen,
   How thy gallant steed lay dying.
Huntsman, rest! thy chase is done,
Think not of the rising sun,
For at dawning to assail ye,
Here no bugles sound reveillé.

Canto I, ll. 624–47, 654–65

SIR WALTER SCOTT

(ii)

Coronach

HE is gone on the mountain,
  He is lost to the forest,
Like a summer-dried fountain,
  When our need was the sorest.
The font, reappearing,
  From the rain-drops shall borrow,
But to us comes no cheering,
  To Duncan no morrow!

The hand of the reaper
  Takes the ears that are hoary,
But the voice of the weeper
  Wails manhood in glory.
The autumn winds rushing
  Waft the leaves that are searest,
But our flower was in flushing,
  When blighting was nearest.

Fleet foot on the correi,
  Sage counsel in cumber,
Red hand in the foray,
  How sound is thy slumber!
Like the dew on the mountain,
  Like the foam on the river,
Like the bubble on the fountain,
  Thou art gone, and for ever!

Canto III, ll. 370–99

correi] hollow side of the hill, where the game lies.
cumber] trouble, perplexity.

(iii)

Roderick Dhu

' TWICE have I sought Clan-Alpine's glen
    In peace; but when I come agen,
I come with banner, brand, and bow,
As leader seeks his mortal foe.
For love-lorn swain, in lady's bower,
Ne'er panted for the appointed hour,
As I, until before me stand
This rebel Chieftain and his band!'
' Have, then, thy wish!' He whistled shrill,
And he was answer'd from the hill;
Wild as the scream of the curlew,
From crag to crag the signal flew.
Instant, through copse and heath, arose
Bonnets and spears and bended bows;
On right, on left, above, below,
Sprung up at once the lurking foe;
From shingles grey their lances start,
The bracken bush sends forth the dart,
The rushes and the willow-wand
Are bristling into axe and brand,
And every tuft of broom gives life
To plaided warrior arm'd for strife.
That whistle garrison'd the glen
At once with full five hundred men,
As if the yawning hill to heaven
A subterranean host had given.
Watching their leader's beck and will,
All silent there they stood, and still.

Like the loose crags, whose threatening mass
Lay tottering o'er the hollow pass,
As if an infant's touch could urge
Their headlong passage down the verge,
With step and weapon forward flung,
Upon the mountain-side they hung.
The Mountaineer cast glance of pride
Along Benledi's living side,
Then fix'd his eye and sable brow
Full on Fitz-James—' How say'st thou now?
These are Clan-Alpine's warriors true;
And, Saxon,—I am Roderick Dhu!'
Fitz-James was brave. Though to his heart
The life-blood thrill'd with sudden start,
He mann'd himself with dauntless air,
Return'd the Chief his haughty stare,
His back against a rock he bore,
And firmly placed his foot before:
' Come one, come all! this rock shall fly
From its firm base as soon as I.'
Sir Roderick mark'd, and in his eyes
Respect was mingled with surprise,
And the stern joy which warriors feel
In foemen worthy of their steel.
Short space he stood, then waved his hand:
Down sunk the disappearing band;
Each warrior vanish'd where he stood,
In broom or bracken, heath or wood;
Sunk brand and spear and bended bow,
In osiers pale and copses low;
It seem'd as if their mother Earth
Had swallow'd up her warlike birth.

THE LADY OF THE LAKE

The wind's last breath had toss'd in air
Pennon, and plaid, and plumage fair;
The next but swept a lone hill-side,
Where heath and fern were waving wide:
The sun's last glance was glinted back,
From spear and glaive, from targe and jack;
The next, all unreflected, shone
On bracken green and cold grey stone.

Fitz-James look'd round, yet scarce believed
The witness that his sight received;
Such apparition well might seem
Delusion of a dreadful dream.
Sir Roderick in suspense he eyed,
And to his look the Chief replied,
' Fear nought—nay, that I need not say—
But doubt not aught from mine array.
Thou art my guest; I pledged my word
As far as Coilantogle ford:
Nor would I call a clansman's brand
For aid against one valiant hand,
Though on our strife lay every vale
Rent by the Saxon from the Gael.
So move we on; I only meant
To show the reed on which you leant,
Deeming this path you might pursue
Without a pass from Roderick Dhu.'
They moved. I said Fitz-James was brave
As ever knight that belted glaive,
Yet dare not say that now his blood
Kept on its wont and temper'd flood,

As, following Roderick's stride, he drew
That seeming lonesome pathway through,
Which yet, by fearful proof, was rife
With lances, that, to take his life,
Waited but signal from a guide,
So late dishonour'd and defied.
Ever, by stealth, his eye sought round
The vanish'd guardians of the ground,
And still, from copse and heather deep,
Fancy saw spear and broadsword peep,
And in the plover's shrilly strain,
The signal-whistle heard again.
Nor breathed he free till far behind
The pass was left; for then they wind
Along a wide and level green,
Where neither tree nor tuft was seen,
Nor rush nor bush of broom was near,
To hide a bonnet or a spear.

Canto V;
The Lady of the Lake, 1810

96 *Two Songs from ' Rokeby '*
(i)

O BRIGNAL banks are wild and fair,
    And Greta woods are green,
And you may gather garlands there
    Would grace a summer queen.
And as I rode by Dalton-hall,
    Beneath the turrets high,
A maiden on the castle wall
    Was singing merrily,—

TWO SONGS FROM 'ROKEBY'

Chorus

' O Brignal banks are fresh and fair,
 And Greta woods are green;
I'd rather rove with Edmund there,
 Than reign our English queen.'

' If, maiden, thou wouldst wend with me,
 To leave both tower and town,
Thou first must guess what life lead we,
 That dwell by dale and down.
And if thou canst that riddle read,
 As read full well you may,
Then to the greenwood shalt thou speed,
 As blithe as Queen of May.'

Chorus

Yet sung she, ' Brignal banks are fair,
 And Greta woods are green;
I'd rather rove with Edmund there,
 Than reign our English queen.

I read you, by your bugle-horn,
 And by your palfrey good,
I read you for a ranger sworn,
 To keep the king's greenwood.'
' A ranger, lady, winds his horn,
 And 'tis at peep of light;
His blast is heard at merry morn,
 And mine at dead of night.'

Chorus

Yet sung she, ' Brignal banks are fair,
  And Greta woods are gay;
I would I were with Edmund there,
  To reign his Queen of May!

With burnish'd brand and musketoon,
  So gallantly you come,
I read you for a bold dragoon,
  That lists the tuck of drum.'
' I list no more the tuck of drum,
  No more the trumpet hear;
But when the beetle sounds his hum,
  My comrades take the spear.

Chorus

And O! though Brignal banks be fair,
  And Greta woods be gay,
Yet mickle must the maiden dare,
  Would reign my Queen of May!

Maiden! a nameless life I lead,
  A nameless death I'll die;
The fiend, whose lantern lights the mead,
  Were better mate than I!
And when I'm with my comrades met
  Beneath the greenwood bough,
What once we were we all forget,
  Nor think what we are now.

TWO SONGS FROM 'ROKEBY'

Chorus

Yet Brignal banks are fresh and fair,
 And Greta woods are green,
And you may gather garlands there
 Would grace a summer queen.'

(ii)

' A WEARY lot is thine, fair maid,
  A weary lot is thine!
To pull the thorn thy brow to braid,
 And press the rue for wine!
A lightsome eye, a soldier's mien,
 A feather of the blue,
A doublet of the Lincoln green,—
 No more of me you knew,

     My love!

 No more of me you knew.

This morn is merry June, I trow,
 The rose is budding fain;
But she shall bloom in winter snow,
 Ere we two meet again.'
He turn'd his charger as he spake,
 Upon the river shore,
He gave his bridle-reins a shake,
 Said, ' Adieu for evermore,

     My love!

 And adieu for evermore.'

      Rokeby, 1812

97 *Gellatley's Song to the Deerhounds*

HIE away, hie away,
    Over bank and over brae,
Where the copsewood is the greenest,
Where the fountains glisten sheenest,
Where the lady-fern grows strongest,
Where the morning dew lies longest,
Where the black-cock sweetest sips it,
Where the fairy latest trips it:
Hie to haunts right seldom seen,
Lovely, lonesome, cool, and green,
Over bank and over brae,
Hie away, hie away.

Waverley, 1814

98 ——— *Jock of Hazeldean*

'WHY weep ye by the tide, ladie?
    Why weep ye by the tide?
I'll wed ye to my youngest son,
    And ye sall be his bride:
And ye sall be his bride, ladie,
    Sae comely to be seen '—
But aye she loot the tears down fa'
    For Jock of Hazeldean.

' Now let this wilfu' grief be done,
    And dry that cheek so pale;
Young Frank is chief of Errington,
    And lord of Langley-dale;

His step is first in peaceful ha',
  His sword in battle keen '—
But aye she loot the tears down fa'
  For Jock of Hazeldean.

' A chain of gold ye sall not lack,
  Nor braid to bind your hair;
Nor mettled hound, nor managed hawk,
  Nor palfrey fresh and fair;
And you, the foremost o' them a',
  Shall ride our forest queen '—
But aye she loot the tears down fa'
  For Jock of Hazeldean.

The kirk was deck'd at morning-tide,
  The tapers glimmer'd fair;
The priest and bridegroom wait the bride,
  And dame and knight are there.
They sought her baith by bower and ha';
  The ladie was not seen!
She 's o'er the Border, and awa'
  Wi' Jock of Hazeldean.

Campbell Albyn's Anthology, 1816

Proud Maisie

99

PROUD Maisie is in the wood,
  Walking so early;
Sweet Robin sits on the bush,
  Singing so rarely.

' Tell me, thou bonny bird,
  When shall I marry me? '

' When six braw gentlemen
 Kirkward shall carry ye.'

' Who makes the bridal bed,
 Birdie, say truly ? '
' The grey-headed sexton
 That delves the grave duly.

' The glow-worm o'er grave and stone
 Shall light thee steady.
The owl from the steeple sing,
 " Welcome, proud lady." '

Heart of Midlothian, 1818

100   ' *Look not thou* '

LOOK not thou on beauty's charming,
 Sit thou still when kings are arming,
Taste not when the wine-cup glistens,
Speak not when the people listens,
Stop thine ear against the singer,
From the red gold keep thy finger;
Vacant heart and hand and eye,
Easy live and quiet die.

Bride of Lammermoor, 1819

101   *County Guy*

AH! County Guy, the hour is nigh,
 The sun has left the lea,
The orange flower perfumes the bower,
 The breeze is on the sea.
The lark, his lay who thrill'd all day,
 Sits hush'd his partner nigh;

Breeze, bird, and flower, confess the hour,
   But where is County Guy?

The village maid steals through the shade,
   Her shepherd's suit to hear;
To beauty shy, by lattice high,
   Sings high-born Cavalier.
The star of Love, all stars above,
   Now reigns o'er earth and sky;
And high and low the influence know—
   But where is County Guy?

Quentin Durward, 1823

102 *Bonny Dundee*

TO the Lords of Convention 'twas Claver'se who spoke,
   ' Ere the King's crown shall fall there are crowns to be
broke;
So let each Cavalier who loves honour and me,
Come follow the bonnet of Bonny Dundee.

   ' Come fill up my cup, come fill up my can,
   Come saddle your horses, and call up your men;
   Come open the West Port, and let me gang free,
   And it 's room for the bonnets of Bonny Dundee! '

Dundee he is mounted, he rides up the street,
The bells are rung backward, the drums they are beat;
But the Provost, douce man, said, ' Just e'en let him be,
The Gude Town is weel quit of that Deil of Dundee.'

   Come fill up my cup, &c.

As he rode down the sanctified bends of the Bow,
Ilk carline was flyting and shaking her pow;

But the young plants of grace they look'd couthie and slee,
Thinking, ' Luck to thy bonnet, thou Bonny Dundee! '
    Come fill up my cup, &c.

With sour-featured Whigs the Grass-market was cramm'd
As if half the West had set tryst to be hang'd;
There was spite in each look, there was fear in each e'e,
As they watch'd for the bonnets of Bonny Dundee.
    Come fill up my cup, &c.

These cowls of Kilmarnock had spits and had spears,
And lang-hafted gullies to kill Cavaliers;
But they shrunk to close-heads, and the causeway was free,
At the toss of the bonnet of Bonny Dundee.
    Come fill up my cup, &c.

He spurr'd to the foot of the proud Castle rock,
And with the gay Gordon he gallantly spoke;
' Let Mons Meg and her marrows speak twa words or three,
For the love of the bonnet of Bonny Dundee.'
    Come fill up my cup, &c.

The Gordon demands of him which way he goes—
' Where'er shall direct me the shade of Montrose!
Your Grace in short space shall hear tidings of me,
Or that low lies the bonnet of Bonny Dundee.
    Come fill up my cup, &c.

' There are hills beyond Pentland, and lands beyond Forth,
If there 's lords in the Lowlands, there 's chiefs in the North;

carline] old woman.   flyting] scolding.   pow] head.
couthie] kindly.   slee] sly.   gullies] large knives.
marrows] companions.

There are wild Duniewassals, three thousand times three,
Will cry *hoigh!* for the bonnet of Bonny Dundee.

Come fill up my cup, &c.

' There 's brass on the target of barken'd bull-hide;
There 's steel in the scabbard that dangles beside;
The brass shall be burnish'd, the steel shall flash free,
At a toss of the bonnet of Bonny Dundee.

Come fill up my cup, &c.

' Away to the hills, to the caves, to the rocks—
Ere I own an usurper, I'll couch with the fox;
And tremble, false Whigs, in the midst of your glee,
You have not seen the last of my bonnet and me! '

Come fill up my cup, &c.

He waved his proud hand, and the trumpets were blown,
The kettle-drums clash'd, and the horsemen rode on,
Till on Ravelston's cliffs and on Clermiston's lee,
Died away the wild war-notes of Bonny Dundee.

Come fill up my cup, come fill up my can,
Come saddle the horses and call up the men,
Come open your gates, and let me gae free,
For it 's up with the bonnets of Bonny Dundee!

Doom of Devorgoil, 1830

JAMES MONTGOMERY

1771–1854

103   *Nativity*

ANGELS, from the realms of glory,
Wing your flight o'er all the earth,
Ye who sang creation's story,

barken'd] tanned.

225

Now proclaim Messiah's birth;
 Come and worship,
Worship Christ the new-born King.

Shepherds, in the field abiding,
 Watching o'er your flocks by night,
God with man is now residing,
 Yonder shines the infant-light;
  Come and worship,
Worship Christ the new-born King.

Sages, leave your contemplations,
 Brighter visions beam afar;
Seek the great Desire of nations;
 Ye have seen His natal star;
  Come and worship,
Worship Christ the new-born King.

Saints before the altar bending,
 Watching long in hope and fear,
Suddenly the Lord, descending,
 In His temple shall appear;
  Come and worship,
Worship Christ the new-born King.

Sinners, wrung with true repentance,
 Doom'd for guilt to endless pains,
Justice now revokes the sentence,
 Mercy calls you,—break your chains;
  Come and worship,
Worship Christ the new-born King.

The Sheffield Trio, Dec. 24, 1816;
Cotterill's Selections, 1819

SAMUEL TAYLOR COLERIDGE

1772–1834

104   *The Rime of the Ancient Mariner*

IN SEVEN PARTS

ARGUMENT

How a Ship having passed the Line was driven by storms to the
cold Country towards the South Pole; and how from thence she
made her course to the tropical Latitude of the Great Pacific
Ocean; and of the strange things that befell; and in what manner
the Ancyent Marinere came back to his own Country.

PART I

IT is an ancient Mariner,
And he stoppeth one of three.
' By thy long grey beard and glittering eye,
Now wherefore stopp'st thou me?

The Bridegroom's doors are opened wide,
And I am next of kin;
The guests are met, the feast is set:
May'st hear the merry din.'

He holds him with his skinny hand,
' There was a ship,' quoth he.
' Hold off! unhand me, grey-beard loon!'
Eftsoons his hand dropt he.

He holds him with his glittering eye—
The Wedding-Guest stood still,
And listens like a three years' child:
The Mariner hath his will.

*An ancient
Mariner meeteth
three Gallants
bidden to a wed-
ding-feast, and
detaineth one.*

*The Wedding-
Guest is spell-
bound by the
eye of the old
seafaring man,
and constrained
to hear his tale.*

227

SAMUEL TAYLOR COLERIDGE

The Wedding-Guest sat on a stone:
He cannot choose but hear;
And thus spake on that ancient man,
The bright-eyed Mariner.

' The ship was cheered, the harbour cleared,
Merrily did we drop
Below the kirk, below the hill,
Below the lighthouse top.

The Mariner tells how the ship sailed southward with a good wind and fair weather, till it reached the line.

The Sun came up upon the left,
Out of the sea came he!
And he shone bright, and on the right
Went down into the sea.

Higher and higher every day,
Till over the mast at noon—'
The Wedding-Guest here beat his breast,
For he heard the loud bassoon.

The Wedding-Guest heareth the bridal music; but the Mariner continueth his tale.

The bride hath paced into the hall,
Red as a rose is she;
Nodding their heads before her goes
The merry minstrelsy.

The Wedding-Guest he beat his breast,
Yet he cannot choose but hear;
And thus spake on that ancient man,
The bright-eyed Mariner.

The ship driven by a storm toward the south pole.

' And now the Storm-blast came, and he
Was tyrannous and strong:
He struck with his o'ertaking wings,
And chased us south along.

THE RIME OF THE ANCIENT MARINER

With sloping masts and dipping prow,
As who pursued with yell and blow
Still treads the shadow of his foe,
And forward bends his head,
The ship drove fast, loud roared the blast,
And southward aye we fled.

And now there came both mist and snow,
And it grew wondrous cold:
And ice, mast-high, came floating by,
As green as emerald.

And through the drifts the snowy clifts
Did send a dismal sheen:
Nor shapes of men nor beasts we ken—
The ice was all between.

The land of ice, and of fearful sounds where no living thing was to be seen.

The ice was here, the ice was there,
The ice was all around:
It cracked and growled, and roared and
   howled,
Like noises in a swound!

At length did cross an Albatross,
Thorough the fog it came;
As if it had been a Christian soul,
We hailed it in God's name.

Till a great sea-bird, called the Albatross, came through the snow-fog, and was received with great joy and hospitality.

It ate the food it ne'er had eat,
And round and round it flew.
The ice did split with a thunder-fit;
The helmsman steered us through!

And lo! the
Albatross
proveth a bird
of good omen,
and followeth
the ship as it
returned north-
ward through
fog and floating
ice.

And a good south wind sprung up behind
The Albatross did follow,
And every day, for food or play,
Came to the mariner's hollo!

In mist or cloud, on mast or shroud,
It perched for vespers nine;
Whiles all the night, through fog-smoke white,
Glimmered the white Moon-shine.'

The ancient
Mariner
inhospitably
killeth the
pious bird of
good omen.

' God save thee, ancient Mariner!
From the fiends, that plague thee thus!—
Why look'st thou so?'—'With my cross-bow
I shot the ALBATROSS.

PART II

The Sun now rose upon the right:
Out of the sea came he,
Still hid in mist, and on the left
Went down into the sea.

And the good south wind still blew behind,
But no sweet bird did follow,
Nor any day for food or play
Came to the mariners' hollo!

His shipmates
cry out against
the ancient
Mariner, for
killing the
bird of good
luck.

And I had done a hellish thing,
And it would work 'em woe:
For all averred, I had killed the bird
That made the breeze to blow.
Ah wretch! said they, the bird to slay,
That made the breeze to blow!

THE RIME OF THE ANCIENT MARINER

Nor dim nor red, like God's own head,
The glorious Sun uprist:
Then all averred, I had killed the bird
That brought the fog and mist.
'Twas right, said they, such birds to slay,
That bring the fog and mist.

But when the fog cleared off, they justify the same, and thus make themselves accomplices in the crime.

The fair breeze blew, the white foam flew,
The furrow followed free;
We were the first that ever burst
Into that silent sea.

The fair breeze continues; the ship enters the Pacific Ocean, and sails northward, even till it reaches the Line.

Down dropt the breeze, the sails dropt down,
'Twas sad as sad could be;
And we did speak only to break
The silence of the sea!

The ship hath been suddenly becalmed.

All in a hot and copper sky,
The bloody Sun, at noon,
Right up above the mast did stand,
No bigger than the Moon.

Day after day, day after day,
We stuck, nor breath nor motion;
As idle as a painted ship
Upon a painted ocean.

Water, water, every where,
And all the boards did shrink;
Water, water, every where,
Nor any drop to drink.

And the Albatross begins to be avenged.

The very deep did rot: O Christ!
That ever this should be!
Yea, slimy things did crawl with legs
Upon the slimy sea.

About, about, in reel and rout
The death-fires danced at night;
The water, like a witch's oils,
Burnt green, and blue and white.

A Spirit had
followed them;
one of the in-
visible inhabi-
tants of this
planet, neither
departed souls
nor angels; con-

And some in dreams assuréd were
Of the Spirit that plagued us so;
Nine fathom deep he had followed us
From the land of mist and snow.

cerning whom the learned Jew, Josephus, and the Platonic Constantinopolitan,
Michael Psellus, may be consulted. They are very numerous, and there is no
climate or element without one or more.

And every tongue, through utter drought,
Was withered at the root;
We could not speak, no more than if
We had been choked with soot.

The shipmates,
in their sore
distress, would
fain throw the
whole guilt on
the ancient
Mariner: in sign
whereof they

Ah! well a-day! what evil looks
Had I from old and young!
Instead of the cross, the Albatross
About my neck was hung.

hang the dead sea-bird round his neck.

Part III

There passed a weary time. Each throat
Was parched, and glazed each eye.
A weary time! a weary time!
How glazed each weary eye,

THE RIME OF THE ANCIENT MARINER

When looking westward, I beheld
A something in the sky.

The ancient Mariner beholdeth a sign in the element far off.

At first it seemed a little speck,
And then it seemed a mist;
It moved and moved, and took at last
A certain shape, I wist.

A speck, a mist, a shape, I wist!
And still it neared and neared:
As if it dodged a water-sprite,
It plunged and tacked and veered.

With throats unslaked, with black lips baked,
We could nor laugh nor wail;
Through utter drought all dumb we stood!
I bit my arm, I sucked the blood,
And cried, A sail! a sail!

At its nearer approach, it seemeth him to be a ship; and at a dear ransom he freeth his speech from the bonds of thirst.

With throats unslaked, with black lips baked,
Agape they heard me call:
Gramercy! they for joy did grin,
And all at once their breath drew in,
As they were drinking all.

A flash of joy;

See! see! (I cried) she tacks no more!
Hither to work us weal;
Without a breeze, without a tide,
She steadies with upright keel!

And horror follows. For can it be a ship that comes onward without wind or tide?

The western wave was all a-flame.
The day was well nigh done!
Almost upon the western wave

233

Rested the broad bright Sun;
When that strange shape drove suddenly
Betwixt us and the Sun.

It seemeth him but the skeleton of a ship.

And straight the Sun was flecked with bars,
(Heaven's Mother send us grace!)
As if through a dungeon-grate he peered
With broad and burning face.

Alas! (thought I, and my heart beat loud)
How fast she nears and nears!
Are those *her* sails that glance in the Sun,
Like restless gossameres?

And its ribs are seen as bars on the face of the setting Sun. The Spectre-Woman and her Death-mate, and no other on board the skeleton ship.

Like vessel, like crew!

Are those *her* ribs through which the Sun
Did peer, as through a grate?
And is that Woman all her crew?
Is that a DEATH? and are there two?
Is DEATH that woman's mate?

Her lips were red, *her* looks were free,
Her locks were yellow as gold:
Her skin was as white as leprosy,
The Night-mare LIFE-IN-DEATH was she,
Who thicks man's blood with cold.

Death and Life-in-Death have diced for the ship's crew, and she (the latter) winneth the ancient Mariner.

No twilight within the courts of the Sun.

The naked hulk alongside came,
And the twain were casting dice;
" The game is done! I've won! I've won! "
Quoth she, and whistles thrice.

The Sun's rim dips; the stars rush out:
At one stride comes the dark;
With far-heard whisper, o'er the sea,
Off shot the spectre-bark.

THE RIME OF THE ANCIENT MARINER

We listened and looked sideways up!
Fear at my heart, as at a cup,
My life-blood seemed to sip!
The stars were dim, and thick the night,
The steersman's face by his lamp gleamed
    white;
From the sails the dew did drip—
Till clomb above the eastern bar
The hornéd Moon, with one bright star
Within the nether tip.

One after one, by the star-dogged Moon,
Too quick for groan or sigh,
Each turned his face with a ghastly pang,
And cursed me with his eye.

Four times fifty living men,
(And I heard nor sigh nor groan)
With heavy thump, a lifeless lump,
They dropped down one by one.

The souls did from their bodies fly,—
They fled to bliss or woe!
And every soul, it passed me by,
Like the whizz of my cross-bow!'

Part IV

' I fear thee, ancient Mariner!
I fear thy skinny hand!
And thou art long, and lank, and brown,
As is the ribbed sea-sand.

At the rising of the Moon,

One after another,

His shipmates drop down dead.

But Life-in-Death begins her work on the ancient Mariner.

The Wedding-Guest feareth that a Spirit is talking to him;

235

I fear thee and thy glittering eye,
And thy skinny hand, so brown.'—

But the ancient
Mariner assureth
him of his bodily
life, and proceed-
eth to relate his
horrible penance.

' Fear not, fear not, thou Wedding-Guest!
This body dropt not down.

Alone, alone, all, all alone,
Alone on a wide wide sea!
And never a saint took pity on
My soul in agony.

He despiseth
the creatures
of the calm,

The many men, so beautiful!
And they all dead did lie:
And a thousand thousand slimy things
Lived on; and so did I.

I looked upon the rotting sea,
And drew my eyes away;
I looked upon the rotting deck,
And there the dead men lay.

And envieth
that *they* should
live, and so
many lie dead.

I looked to heaven, and tried to pray;
But or ever a prayer had gusht,
A wicked whisper came, and made
My heart as dry as dust.

I closed my lids, and kept them close,
And the balls like pulses beat;
For the sky and the sea, and the sea and the sky
Lay like a load on my weary eye,
And the dead were at my feet.

But the curse
liveth for him
in the eye of
the dead men.

The cold sweat melted from their limbs,
Nor rot nor reek did they:
The look with which they looked on me
Had never passed away.

THE RIME OF THE ANCIENT MARINER

An orphan's curse would drag to hell
A spirit from on high;
But oh! more horrible than that
Is the curse in a dead man's eye!
Seven days, seven nights, I saw that curse,
And yet I could not die.

The moving Moon went up the sky,
And no where did abide:
Softly she was going up,
And a star or two beside—

Her beams bemocked the sultry main,
Like April hoar-frost spread;
But where the ship's huge shadow lay,
The charméd water burnt alway
A still and awful red.

In his loneliness and fixedness he yearneth towards the journeying Moon, and the stars that still sojourn, yet still move onward; and every where the blue sky belongs to them, and is their appointed rest, and their native country and their own natural homes, which they enter unannounced, as lords that are certainly expected and yet there is a silent joy at their arrival.

Beyond the shadow of the ship,
I watched the water-snakes:
They moved in tracks of shining white,
And when they reared, the elfish light
Fell off in hoary flakes.

By the light of the Moon he beholdeth God's creatures of the great calm.

Within the shadow of the ship
I watched their rich attire:
Blue, glossy green, and velvet black,
They coiled and swam; and every track
Was a flash of golden fire.

O happy living things! no tongue
Their beauty might declare:
A spring of love gushed from my heart,

Their beauty and their happiness.

He blesseth
them in his
heart.

And I blessed them unaware:
Sure my kind saint took pity on me,
And I blessed them unaware.

The spell begins
to break.

The self-same moment I could pray;
And from my neck so free
The Albatross fell off, and sank
Like lead into the sea.

Part V

Oh sleep! it is a gentle thing,
Beloved from pole to pole!
To Mary Queen the praise be given!
She sent the gentle sleep from Heaven,
That slid into my soul.

By grace of the
holy Mother,
the ancient
Mariner is re-
freshed with rain.

The silly buckets on the deck,
That had so long remained,
I dreamt that they were filled with dew;
And when I awoke, it rained.

My lips were wet, my throat was cold,
My garments all were dank;
Sure I had drunken in my dreams,
And still my body drank.

I moved, and could not feel my limbs:
I was so light—almost
I thought that I had died in sleep,
And was a blesséd ghost.

He heareth
sounds and
seeth strange
sights and com-
motions in the
sky and the
element.

And soon I heard a roaring wind:
It did not come anear;
But with its sound it shook the sails,
That were so thin and sere.

THE RIME OF THE ANCIENT MARINER

The upper air burst into life!
And a hundred fire-flags sheen,
To and fro they were hurried about!
And to and fro, and in and out,
The wan stars danced between.

And the coming wind did roar more loud,
And the sails did sigh like sedge;
And the rain poured down from one black
    cloud;
The Moon was at its edge.

The thick black cloud was cleft, and still
The Moon was at its side:
Like waters shot from some high crag,
The lightning fell with never a jag,
A river steep and wide.

The loud wind never reached the ship,
Yet now the ship moved on!
Beneath the lightning and the Moon
The dead men gave a groan.

The bodies of
the ship's crew
are inspired
and the ship
moves on;

They groaned, they stirred, they all uprose,
Nor spake, nor moved their eyes;
It had been strange, even in a dream,
To have seen those dead men rise.

The helmsman steered, the ship moved on;
Yet never a breeze up-blew;
The mariners all 'gan work the ropes,
Where they were wont to do;
They raised their limbs like lifeless tools—
We were a ghastly crew.

The body of my brother's son
Stood by me, knee to knee:
The body and I pulled at one rope,
But he said nought to me.'

' I fear thee, ancient Mariner!'
' Be calm, thou Wedding-Guest!
'Twas not those souls that fled in pain,
Which to their corses came again,
But a troop of spirits blest:

But not by the souls of the men, nor by dæmons of earth or middle air, but by a blessed troop of angelic spirits, sent down by the invocation of the guardian saint.

For when it dawned—they dropped their arms,
And clustered round the mast;
Sweet sounds rose slowly through their mouths,
And from their bodies passed.

Around, around, flew each sweet sound,
Then darted to the Sun;
Slowly the sounds came back again,
Now mixed, now one by one.

Sometimes a-dropping from the sky
I heard the sky-lark sing;
Sometimes all little birds that are,
How they seemed to fill the sea and air
With their sweet jargoning!

And now 'twas like all instruments,
Now like a lonely flute;
And now it is an angel's song,
That makes the heavens be mute.

It ceased; yet still the sails made on
A pleasant noise till noon,
A noise like of a hidden brook
In the leafy month of June,
That to the sleeping woods all night
Singeth a quiet tune.

Till noon we quietly sailed on,
Yet never a breeze did breathe:
Slowly and smoothly went the ship,
Moved onward from beneath.

Under the keel nine fathom deep,
From the land of mist and snow,
The spirit slid: and it was he
That made the ship to go.
The sails at noon left off their tune,
And the ship stood still also.

The lonesome Spirit from the south-pole carries on the ship as far as the Line, in obedience to the angelic troop, but still requireth vengeance.

The Sun, right up above the mast,
Had fixed her to the ocean:
But in a minute she 'gan stir,
With a short uneasy motion—
Backwards and forwards half her length
With a short uneasy motion.

Then like a pawing horse let go,
She made a sudden bound:
It flung the blood into my head,
And I fell down in a swound.

How long in that same fit I lay,
I have not to declare;
But ere my living life returned,
I heard and in my soul discerned
Two voices in the air.

" Is it he? " quoth one, " Is this the man?
By him who died on cross,
With his cruel bow he laid full low
The harmless Albatross.

The spirit who bideth by himself
In the land of mist and snow,
He loved the bird that loved the man
Who shot him with his bow."

The other was a softer voice,
As soft as honey-dew:
Quoth he, " The man hath penance done,
And penance more will do."

Part VI

FIRST VOICE

" But tell me, tell me! speak again,
Thy soft response renewing—
What makes that ship drive on so fast?
What is the ocean doing? "

SECOND VOICE

" Still as a slave before his lord,
The ocean hath no blast;
His great bright eye most silently
Up to the Moon is cast—

242

THE RIME OF THE ANCIENT MARINER

If he may know which way to go;
For she guides him smooth or grim.
See, brother, see! how graciously
She looketh down on him."

FIRST VOICE

" But why drives on that ship so fast,
Without or wave or wind?"

SECOND VOICE

" The air is cut away before,
And closes from behind.

Fly, brother, fly! more high, more high!
Or we shall be belated:
For slow and slow that ship will go,
When the Mariner's trance is abated."

I woke, and we were sailing on
As in a gentle weather:
'Twas night, calm night, the moon was high;
The dead men stood together.

All stood together on the deck,
For a charnel-dungeon fitter:
All fixed on me their stony eyes,
That in the Moon did glitter.

The pang, the curse, with which they died,
Had never passed away:
I could not draw my eyes from theirs,
Nor turn them up to pray.

The Mariner hath been cast into a trance; for the angelic power causeth the vessel to drive northward faster than human life could endure.

The supernatural motion is retarded; the Mariner awakes, and his penance begins anew.

The curse is finally expiated.

And now this spell was snapt: once more
I viewed the ocean green,
And looked far forth, yet little saw
Of what had else been seen—

Like one, that on a lonesome road
Doth walk in fear and dread,
And having once turned round walks on,
And turns no more his head;
Because he knows, a frightful fiend
Doth close behind him tread.

But soon there breathed a wind on me,
Nor sound nor motion made:
Its path was not upon the sea,
In ripple or in shade.

It raised my hair, it fanned my cheek
Like a meadow-gale of spring—
It mingled strangely with my fears,
Yet it felt like a welcoming.

Swiftly, swiftly flew the ship,
Yet she sailed softly too:
Sweetly, sweetly blew the breeze—
On me alone it blew.

And the ancient Mariner beholdeth his native country.

Oh! dream of joy! is this indeed
The light-house top I see?
Is this the hill? is this the kirk?
Is this mine own countree?

We drifted o'er the harbour-bar,
And I with sobs did pray—
O let me be awake, my God!
Or let me sleep alway.

THE RIME OF THE ANCIENT MARINER

The harbour-bay was clear as glass,
So smoothly it was strewn!
And on the bay the moonlight lay,
And the shadow of the Moon.

The rock shone bright, the kirk no less,
That stands above the rock:
The moonlight steeped in silentness
The steady weathercock.

And the bay was white with silent light,
Till rising from the same,
Full many shapes, that shadows were,
In crimson colours came.

The angelic spirits leave the dead bodies,

A little distance from the prow
Those crimson shadows were:
I turned my eyes upon the deck—
Oh, Christ! what saw I there!

And appear in their own forms of light.

Each corse lay flat, lifeless and flat,
And, by the holy rood!
A man all light, a seraph-man,
On every corse there stood.

This seraph-band, each waved his hand:
It was a heavenly sight!
They stood as signals to the land,
Each one a lovely light;

This seraph-band, each waved his hand,
No voice did they impart—
No voice; but oh! the silence sank
Like music on my heart.

But soon I heard the dash of oars,
I heard the Pilot's cheer;
My head was turned perforce away
And I saw a boat appear.

The Pilot and the Pilot's boy,
I heard them coming fast:
Dear Lord in Heaven! it was a joy
The dead men could not blast.

I saw a third—I heard his voice:
It is the Hermit good!
He singeth loud his godly hymns
That he makes in the wood.
He'll shrieve my soul, he'll wash away
The Albatross's blood.

Part VII

The Hermit of
the Wood,

This Hermit good lives in that wood
Which slopes down to the sea.
How loudly his sweet voice he rears!
He loves to talk with marineres
That come from a far countree.

He kneels at morn, and noon, and eve—
He hath a cushion plump:
It is the moss that wholly hides
The rotted old oak-stump.

The skiff-boat neared: I heard them talk,
" Why, this is strange, I trow!
Where are those lights so many and fair,
That signal made but now? "

THE RIME OF THE ANCIENT MARINER

"Strange, by my faith!" the Hermit said—
"And they answered not our cheer!
The planks looked warped! and see those sails,
How thin they are and sere!
I never saw aught like to them,
Unless perchance it were

Approacheth
the ship with
wonder.

Brown skeletons of leaves that lag
My forest-brook along;
When the ivy-tod is heavy with snow,
And the owlet whoops to the wolf below,
That eats the she-wolf's young."

"Dear Lord! it hath a fiendish look—
(The Pilot made reply)
I am a-feared "—"Push on, push on!"
Said the Hermit cheerily.

The boat came closer to the ship,
But I nor spake nor stirred;
The boat came close beneath the ship,
And straight a sound was heard.

Under the water it rumbled on,
Still louder and more dread:
It reached the ship, it split the bay;
The ship went down like lead.

The ship sud-
denly sinketh.

Stunned by that loud and dreadful sound,
Which sky and ocean smote,
Like one that hath been seven days drowned
My body lay afloat;
But swift as dreams, myself I found
Within the Pilot's boat.

The ancient
Mariner is saved
in the Pilot's
boat.

Upon the whirl, where sank the ship,
The boat spun round and round;
And all was still, save that the hill
Was telling of the sound.

I moved my lips—the Pilot shrieked
And fell down in a fit;
The holy Hermit raised his eyes,
And prayed where he did sit.

I took the oars: the Pilot's boy,
Who now doth crazy go,
Laughed loud and long, and all the while
His eyes went to and fro.
" Ha! ha! " quoth he, " full plain I see,
The Devil knows how to row."

And now, all in my own countree,
I stood on the firm land!
The Hermit stepped forth from the boat,
And scarcely he could stand.

The ancient Mariner earnestly entreateth the Hermit to shrieve him; and the penance of life falls on him.

" O shrieve me, shrieve me, holy man! "
The Hermit crossed his brow.
" Say quick," quoth he, " I bid thee say—
What manner of man art thou? "

Forthwith this frame of mine was wrenched
With a woful agony,
Which forced me to begin my tale;
And then it left me free.

And ever and anon throughout his future life an agony constraineth him to travel from land to land;

Since then, at an uncertain hour,
That agony returns:
And till my ghastly tale is told,
This heart within me burns.

248

THE RIME OF THE ANCIENT MARINER

I pass, like night, from land to land;
I have strange power of speech;
That moment that his face I see,
I know the man that must hear me:
To him my tale I teach.

What loud uproar bursts from that door!
The wedding-guests are there:
But in the garden-bower the bride
And bride-maids singing are:
And hark the little vesper bell,
Which biddeth me to prayer!

O Wedding-Guest! this soul hath been
Alone on a wide wide sea:
So lonely 'twas, that God himself
Scarce seeméd there to be.

O sweeter than the marriage-feast,
'Tis sweeter far to me,
To walk together to the kirk
With a goodly company!—

To walk together to the kirk,
And all together pray,
While each to his great Father bends,
Old men, and babes, and loving friends
And youths and maidens gay!

Farewell, farewell! but this I tell
To thee, thou Wedding-Guest!
He prayeth well, who loveth well
Both man and bird and beast.

And to teach,
by his own
example, love
and reverence
to all things
that God made
and loveth.

He prayeth best, who loveth best
All things both great and small;
For the dear God who loveth us,
He made and loveth all.'

The Mariner, whose eye is bright,
Whose beard with age is hoar,
Is gone: and now the Wedding-Guest
Turned from the bridegroom's door.

He went like one that hath been stunned,
And is of sense forlorn:
A sadder and a wiser man.
He rose the morrow morn.

Lyrical Ballads, &c., 1798
Marginalia added 1815–16

105   *From ' The Nightingale '*

'TIS the merry Nightingale
That crowds, and hurries, and precipitates
With fast thick warble his delicious notes,
As he were fearful that an April night
Would be too short for him to utter forth
His love-chant, and disburthen his full soul
Of all its music!
                        And I know a grove
Of large extent, hard by a castle huge,
Which the great lord inhabits not; and so
This grove is wild with tangling underwood,
And the trim walks are broken up, and grass,
Thin grass and king-cups grow within the paths.

But never elsewhere in one place I knew
So many nightingales; and far and near,
In wood and thicket, over the wide grove,
They answer and provoke each other's songs,
With skirmish and capricious passagings,
And murmurs musical and swift jug jug,
And one low piping sound more sweet than all—
Stirring the air with such an harmony,
That should you close your eyes, you might almost
Forget it was not day! On moonlight bushes,
Whose dewy leaflets are but half-disclosed,
You may perchance behold them on the twigs,
Their bright, bright eyes, their eyes both bright and full,
Glistening, while many a glow-worm in the shade
Lights up her love-torch.

Lyrical Ballads, &c., 1798

106   *Frost at Midnight*

THE Frost performs its secret ministry,
  Unhelped by any wind. The owlet's cry
Came loud—and hark, again! loud as before.
The inmates of my cottage, all at rest,
Have left me to that solitude, which suits
Abstruser musings: save that at my side
My cradled infant slumbers peacefully.
'Tis calm indeed! so calm, that it disturbs
And vexes meditation with its strange
And extreme silentness. Sea, hill, and wood,
This populous village! Sea, and hill, and wood,
With all the numberless goings-on of life,
Inaudible as dreams! the thin blue flame

Lies on my low-burnt fire, and quivers not;
Only that film, which fluttered on the grate,
Still flutters there, the sole unquiet thing.
Methinks, its motion in this hush of nature
Gives it dim sympathies with me who live,
Making it a companionable form,
Whose puny flaps and freaks the idling Spirit
By its own moods interprets, every where
Echo or mirror seeking of itself,
And makes a toy of Thought.

                                But O! how oft,
How oft, at school, with most believing mind,
Presageful, have I gazed upon the bars,
To watch that fluttering *stranger*! and as oft
With unclosed lids, already had I dreamt
Of my sweet birth-place, and the old church-tower,
Whose bells, the poor man's only music, rang
From morn to evening, all the hot Fair-day,
So sweetly, that they stirred and haunted me
With a wild pleasure, falling on mine ear
Most like articulate sounds of things to come!
So gazed I, till the soothing things, I dreamt,
Lulled me to sleep, and sleep prolonged my dreams!
And so I brooded all the following morn,
Awed by the stern preceptor's face, mine eye
Fixed with mock study on my swimming book:
Save if the door half opened, and I snatched
A hasty glance, and still my heart leaped up,
For still I hoped to see the *stranger's* face,
Townsman, or aunt, or sister more beloved,
My play-mate when we both were clothed alike!

FROST AT MIDNIGHT

Dear Babe, that sleepest cradled by my side,
Whose gentle breathings, heard in this deep calm,
Fill up the intersperséd vacancies
And momentary pauses of the thought!
My babe so beautiful! it thrills my heart
With tender gladness, thus to look at thee,
And think that thou shalt learn far other lore,
And in far other scenes! For I was reared
In the great city, pent 'mid cloisters dim,
And saw nought lovely but the sky and stars.
But *thou*, my babe! shalt wander like a breeze
By lakes and sandy shores, beneath the crags
Of ancient mountain, and beneath the clouds,
Which image in their bulk both lakes and shores
And mountain crags: so shalt thou see and hear
The lovely shapes and sounds intelligible
Of that eternal language, which thy God
Utters, who from eternity doth teach
Himself in all, and all things in himself.
Great universal Teacher! he shall mould
Thy spirit, and by giving make it ask.

Therefore all seasons shall be sweet to thee,
Whether the summer clothe the general earth
With greenness, or the redbreast sit and sing
Betwixt the tufts of snow on the bare branch
Of mossy apple-tree, while the nigh thatch
Smokes in the sun-thaw; whether the eave-drops fall
Heard only in the trances of the blast,
Or if the secret ministry of frost
Shall hang them up in silent icicles,
Quietly shining to the quiet Moon.

Frost at Midnight, 1798

107   *Something Childish, but very Natural*

IF I had but two little wings
   And were a little feathery bird,
      To you I'd fly, my dear!
But thoughts like these are idle things,
      And I stay here.

But in my sleep to you I fly:
   I'm always with you in my sleep!
      The world is all one's own.
But then one wakes, and where am I?
      All, all alone.

Sleep stays not, though a monarch bids:
   So I love to wake ere break of day:
      For though my sleep be gone,
Yet while 'tis dark, one shuts one's lids,
      And still dreams on.

Annual Anthology, 1800;
Sibylline Leaves, 1817

108   *Dejection: an Ode*

I

WELL! If the Bard was weather-wise, who made
   The grand old ballad of Sir Patrick Spence,
This night, so tranquil now, will not go hence
Unroused by winds, that ply a busier trade
Than those which mould yon cloud in lazy flakes,
Or the dull sobbing draft, that moans and rakes
Upon the strings of this Æolian lute,
   Which better far were mute.

254

DEJECTION : AN ODE

For lo! the New-moon winter-bright!
    And overspread with phantom light,
   (With swimming phantom light o'erspread
   But rimmed and circled by a silver thread)
I see the old Moon in her lap, foretelling
    The coming-on of rain and squally blast.
And oh! that even now the gust were swelling,
    And the slant night-shower driving loud and fast!
Those sounds which oft have raised me, whilst they awed,
      And sent my soul abroad,
Might now perhaps their wonted impulse give,
Might startle this dull pain, and make it move and live!

II

A grief without a pang, void, dark, and drear,
   A stifled, drowsy, unimpassioned grief,
   Which finds no natural outlet, no relief,
      In word, or sigh, or tear—
O Lady! in this wan and heartless mood,
To other thoughts by yonder throstle woo'd,
   All this long eve, so balmy and serene,
Have I been gazing on the western sky,
   And its peculiar tint of yellow green:
And still I gaze—and with how blank an eye!
And those thin clouds above, in flakes and bars,
That give away their motion to the stars;
Those stars, that glide behind them or between,
Now sparkling, now bedimmed, but always seen:
Yon crescent Moon, as fixed as if it grew
In its own cloudless, starless lake of blue;
I see them all so excellently fair,
I see, not feel, how beautiful they are!

III

My genial spirits fail;
    And what can these avail
To lift the smothering weight from off my breast?
    It were a vain endeavour,
    Though I should gaze for ever
On that green light that lingers in the west:
I may not hope from outward forms to win
The passion and the life, whose fountains are within.

IV

O Lady! we receive but what we give,
And in our life alone does Nature live:
Ours is her wedding garment, ours her shroud!
    And would we aught behold, of higher worth,
Than that inanimate cold world allowed
To the poor loveless ever-anxious crowd,
    Ah! from the soul itself must issue forth
A light, a glory, a fair luminous cloud
    Enveloping the Earth—
And from the soul itself must there be sent
    A sweet and potent voice, of its own birth,
Of all sweet sounds the life and element!

V

O pure of heart! thou need'st not ask of me
What this strong music in the soul may be!
What, and wherein it doth exist,
This light, this glory, this fair luminous mist,
This beautiful and beauty-making power.
  Joy, virtuous Lady! Joy that ne'er was given,

Save to the pure, and in their purest hour,
Life, and Life's effluence, cloud at once and shower,
Joy, Lady! is the spirit and the power,
Which wedding Nature to us gives in dower
   A new Earth and new Heaven,
Undreamt of by the sensual and the proud—
Joy is the sweet voice, Joy the luminous cloud—
     We in ourselves rejoice!
And thence flows all that charms or ear or sight,
   All melodies the echoes of that voice,
All colours a suffusion from that light.

VI

There was a time when, though my path was rough,
   This joy within me dallied with distress,
And all misfortunes were but as the stuff
   Whence Fancy made me dreams of happiness:
For hope grew round me, like the twining vine,
And fruits, and foliage, not my own, seemed mine.
But now afflictions bow me down to earth:
Nor care I that they rob me of my mirth;
     But oh! each visitation
Suspends what nature gave me at my birth,
    My shaping spirit of Imagination.
For not to think of what I needs must feel,
   But to be still and patient, all I can;
And haply by abstruse research to steal
   From my own nature all the natural man—
   This was my sole resource, my only plan:
Till that which suits a part infects the whole,
And now is almost grown the habit of my soul.

VII

Hence, viper thoughts, that coil around my mind,
    Reality's dark dream!
I turn from you, and listen to the wind,
   Which long has raved unnoticed. What a scream
Of agony by torture lengthened out
That lute sent forth! Thou Wind, that rav'st without,
   Bare crag, or mountain-tairn, or blasted tree,
Or pine-grove whither woodman never clomb,
Or lonely house, long held the witches' home,
   Methinks were fitter instruments for thee,
Mad Lutanist! who in this month of showers,
Of dark-brown gardens, and of peeping flowers,
Mak'st Devils' yule, with worse than wintry song,
The blossoms, buds, and timorous leaves among.
   Thou Actor, perfect in all tragic sounds!
Thou mighty Poet, e'en to frenzy bold!
     What tell'st thou now about?
     'Tis of the rushing of an host in rout,
  With groans, of trampled men, with smarting wounds—
At once they groan with pain, and shudder with the cold!
But hush! there is a pause of deepest silence!
   And all that noise, as of a rushing crowd,
With groans, and tremulous shudderings—all is over—
   It tells another tale, with sounds less deep and loud!
     A tale of less affright
     And tempered with delight,
As Otway's self had framed the tender lay,—
     'Tis of a little child
     Upon a lonesome wild,
Not far from home, but she hath lost her way:

And now moans low in bitter grief and fear,
And now screams loud, and hopes to make her mother hear.

VIII

'Tis midnight, but small thoughts have I of sleep:
Full seldom may my friend such vigils keep!
Visit her, gentle Sleep! with wings of healing,
    And may this storm be but a mountain-birth,
May all the stars hang bright above her dwelling,
    Silent as though they watched the sleeping Earth!
        With light heart may she rise,
        Gay fancy, cheerful eyes,
    Joy lift her spirit, joy attune her voice;
To her may all things live, from pole to pole,
Their life the eddying of her living soul!
    O simple spirit, guided from above,
Dear Lady! friend devoutest of my choice,
Thus mayest thou ever, evermore rejoice.

Morning Post, Oct. 4, 1802;
Sibylline Leaves, 1817

109   *From 'A Tombless Epitaph'*

SICKNESS, 'tis true,
Whole years of weary days, besieged him close,
Even to the gates and inlets of his life!
But it is true, no less, that strenuous, firm,
And with a natural gladness, he maintained
The citadel unconquered, and in joy
Was strong to follow the delightful Muse.
For not a hidden path, that to the shades
Of the beloved Parnassian forest leads,

Lurked undiscovered by him; not a rill
There issues from the fount of Hippocrene,
But he had traced it upward to its source,
Through open glade, dark glen, and secret dell,
Knew the gay wild flowers on its banks, and culled
Its med'cinable herbs. Yea, oft alone,
Piercing the long-neglected holy cave,
The haunt obscure of old Philosophy,
He bade with lifted torch its starry walls
Sparkle, as erst they sparkled to the flame
Of odorous lamps tended by Saint and Sage.
O framed for calmer times and nobler hearts!
O studious Poet, eloquent for truth!
Philosopher! contemning wealth and death,
Yet docile, childlike, full of Life and Love!

The Friend, Nov. 23, 1809;
Sibylline Leaves, 1817

110 *Christabel: Part I*

'TIS the middle of night by the castle clock,
　And the owls have awakened the crowing cock;
Tu—whit!——Tu—whoo!
And hark, again! the crowing cock,
How drowsily it crew.
Sir Leoline, the Baron rich,
Hath a toothless mastiff bitch;
From her kennel beneath the rock
She maketh answer to the clock,
Four for the quarters, and twelve for the hour;
Ever and aye, by shine and shower,

CHRISTABEL

Sixteen short howls, not over loud;
Some say, she sees my lady's shroud.

Is the night chilly and dark?
The night is chilly, but not dark.
The thin gray cloud is spread on high,
It covers but not hides the sky.
The moon is behind, and at the full;
And yet she looks both small and dull.
The night is chill, the cloud is gray:
'Tis a month before the month of May,
And the Spring comes slowly up this way.

The lovely lady, Christabel,
Whom her father loves so well,
What makes her in the wood so late,
A furlong from the castle gate?
She had dreams all yesternight
Of her own betrothéd knight;
And she in the midnight wood will pray
For the weal of her lover that 's far away.

She stole along, she nothing spoke,
The sighs she heaved were soft and low,
And naught was green upon the oak
But moss and rarest misletoe:
She kneels beneath the huge oak tree,
And in silence prayeth she.

The lady sprang up suddenly,
The lovely lady, Christabel!
It moaned as near, as near can be,
But what it is she cannot tell.—

On the other side it seems to be,
Of the huge, broad-breasted, old oak tree.

The night is chill; the forest bare;
Is it the wind that moaneth bleak?
There is not wind enough in the air
To move away the ringlet curl
From the lovely lady's cheek—
There is not wind enough to twirl
The one red leaf, the last of its clan,
That dances as often as dance it can,
Hanging so light, and hanging so high,
On the topmost twig that looks up at the sky.

Hush, beating heart of Christabel!
Jesu, Maria, shield her well!
She folded her arms beneath her cloak,
And stole to the other side of the oak.
     What sees she there?

There she sees a damsel bright,
Drest in a silken robe of white,
That shadowy in the moonlight shone:
The neck that made that white robe wan,
Her stately neck, and arms were bare;
Her blue-veined feet unsandal'd were,
And wildly glittered here and there
The gems entangled in her hair.
I guess, 'twas frightful there to see
A lady so richly clad as she—
Beautiful exceedingly!

Mary mother, save me now!
(Said Christabel,) And who art thou?

CHRISTABEL

The lady strange made answer meet,
And her voice was faint and sweet:—
Have pity on my sore distress,
I scarce can speak for weariness:
Stretch forth thy hand, and have no fear!
Said Christabel, How camest thou here?
And the lady, whose voice was faint and sweet,
Did thus pursue her answer meet:—

My sire is of a noble line,
And my name is Geraldine:
Five warriors seized me yestermorn,
Me, even me, a maid forlorn:
They choked my cries with force and fright,
And tied me on a palfrey white.
The palfrey was as fleet as wind,
And they rode furiously behind.

They spurred amain, their steeds were white:
And once we crossed the shade of night.
As sure as Heaven shall rescue me,
I have no thought what men they be;
Nor do I know how long it is
(For I have lain entranced I wis)
Since one, the tallest of the five,
Took me from the palfrey's back,
A weary woman, scarce alive.
Some muttered words his comrades spoke:
He placed me underneath this oak;
He swore they would return with haste;
Whither they went I cannot tell—
I thought I heard, some minutes past,
Sounds as of a castle bell.

263

Stretch forth thy hand (thus ended she),
And help a wretched maid to flee.

Then Christabel stretched forth her hand,
And comforted fair Geraldine:
O well, bright dame! may you command
The service of Sir Leoline;
And gladly our stout chivalry
Will he send forth and friends withal
To guide and guard you safe and free
Home to your noble father's hall.

She rose: and forth with steps they passed
That strove to be, and were not, fast.
Her gracious stars the lady blest,
And thus spake on sweet Christabel:
All our household are at rest,
The hall as silent as the cell;
Sir Leoline is weak in health,
And may not well awakened be,
But we will move as if in stealth,
And I beseech your courtesy,
This night, to share your couch with me.

They crossed the moat, and Christabel
Took the key that fitted well;
A little door she opened straight,
All in the middle of the gate;
The gate that was ironed within and without,
Where an army in battle array had marched out.
The lady sank, belike through pain,
And Christabel with might and main

CHRISTABEL

Lifted her up, a weary weight,
Over the threshold of the gate:
Then the lady rose again,
And moved, as she were not in pain.

So free from danger, free from fear,
They crossed the court: right glad they were.
And Christabel devoutly cried
To the lady by her side,
Praise we the Virgin all divine
Who hath rescued thee from thy distress!
Alas, alas! said Geraldine,
I cannot speak for weariness.
So free from danger, free from fear,
They crossed the court: right glad they were.

Outside her kennel, the mastiff old
Lay fast asleep, in moonshine cold.
The mastiff old did not awake,
Yet she an angry moan did make!
And what can ail the mastiff bitch?
Never till now she uttered yell
Beneath the eye of Christabel.
Perhaps it is the owlet's scritch:
For what can ail the mastiff bitch?

They passed the hall, that echoes still,
Pass as lightly as you will!
The brands were flat, the brands were dying,
Amid their own white ashes lying;
But when the lady passed, there came
A tongue of light, a fit of flame;

And Christabel saw the lady's eye,
And nothing else saw she thereby,
Save the boss of the shield of Sir Leoline tall,
Which hung in a murky old niche in the wall.
O softly tread, said Christabel,
My father seldom sleepeth well.

Sweet Christabel her feet doth bare,
And jealous of the listening air
They steal their way from stair to stair,
Now in glimmer, and now in gloom,
And now they pass the Baron's room,
As still as death, with stifled breath!
And now have reached her chamber door;
And now doth Geraldine press down
The rushes of the chamber floor.

The moon shines dim in the open air,
And not a moonbeam enters here.
But they without its light can see
The chamber carved so curiously,
Carved with figures strange and sweet,
All made out of the carver's brain,
For a lady's chamber meet:
The lamp with twofold silver chain
Is fastened to an angel's feet.

The silver lamp burns dead and dim;
But Christabel the lamp will trim.
She trimmed the lamp, and made it bright,
And left it swinging to and fro,
While Geraldine, in wretched plight,
Sank down upon the floor below.

CHRISTABEL

O weary lady, Geraldine,
I pray you, drink this cordial wine!
It is a wine of virtuous powers;
My mother made it of wild flowers.

And will your mother pity me,
Who am a maiden most forlorn?
Christabel answered—Woe is me!
She died the hour that I was born.
I have heard the grey-haired friar tell
How on her death-bed she did say,
That she should hear the castle-bell
Strike twelve upon my wedding-day.
O mother dear! that thou wert here!
I would, said Geraldine, she were!

But soon with altered voice, said she—
' Off, wandering mother! Peak and pine!
I have power to bid thee flee.'
Alas! what ails poor Geraldine?
Why stares she with unsettled eye?
Can she the bodiless dead espy?
And why with hollow voice cries she,
' Off, woman, off! this hour is mine—
Though thou her guardian spirit be,
Off, woman, off! 'tis given to me.'

Then Christabel knelt by the lady's side,
And raised to heaven her eyes so blue—
Alas! said she, this ghastly ride—
Dear lady! it hath wildered you!
The lady wiped her moist cold brow,
And faintly said, ' 'tis over now!'

Again the wild-flower wine she drank:
Her fair large eyes 'gan glitter bright,
And from the floor whereon she sank,
The lofty lady stood upright:
She was most beautiful to see,
Like a lady of a far countrée.

And thus the lofty lady spake—
' All they who live in the upper sky,
Do love you, holy Christabel!
And you love them, and for their sake
And for the good which me befel,
Even I in my degree will try,
Fair maiden, to requite you well.
But now unrobe yourself; for I
Must pray, ere yet in bed I lie.'

Quoth Christabel, So let it be!
And as the lady bade, did she.
Her gentle limbs did she undress,
And lay down in her loveliness.

But through her brain of weal and woe
So many thoughts moved to and fro,
That vain it were her lids to close;
So half-way from the bed she rose,
And on her elbow did recline
To look at the lady Geraldine.

Beneath the lamp the lady bowed,
And slowly rolled her eyes around;
Then drawing in her breath aloud,
Like one that shuddered, she unbound

CHRISTABEL

The cincture from beneath her breast:
Her silken robe, and inner vest,
Dropt to her feet, and full in view,
Behold! her bosom and half her side——
A sight to dream of, not to tell!
O shield her! shield sweet Christabel!

Yet Geraldine nor speaks nor stirs;
Ah! what a stricken look was hers!
Deep from within she seems half-way
To lift some weight with sick assay,
And eyes the maid and seeks delay;
Then suddenly, as one defied,
Collects herself in scorn and pride,
And lay down by the Maiden's side!—
And in her arms the maid she took,
     Ah wel-a-day!
And with low voice and doleful look
These words did say:
' In the touch of this bosom there worketh a spell,
Which is lord of thy utterance, Christabel!
Thou knowest to-night, and wilt know to-morrow,
This mark of my shame, this seal of my sorrow;
    But vainly thou warrest,
      For this is alone in
    Thy power to declare,
      That in the dim forest
    Thou heard'st a low moaning,
And found'st a bright lady, surpassingly fair;
And didst bring her home with thee in love and in charity,
To shield her and shelter her from the damp air.'

The Conclusion to Part I

It was a lovely sight to see
The lady Christabel, when she
Was praying at the old oak tree.
    Amid the jaggéd shadows
    Of mossy leafless boughs,
    Kneeling in the moonlight,
    To make her gentle vows;
Her slender palms together prest,
Heaving sometimes on her breast;
Her face resigned to bliss or bale—
Her face, oh call it fair not pale,
And both blue eyes more bright than clear,
Each about to have a tear.

With open eyes (ah woe is me!)
Asleep, and dreaming fearfully,
Fearfully dreaming, yet, I wis,
Dreaming that alone, which is—
O sorrow and shame! Can this be she,
The lady who knelt at the old oak tree?
And lo! the worker of these harms,
That holds the maiden in her arms,
Seems to slumber still and mild,
As a mother with her child.

A star hath set, a star hath risen,
O Geraldine! since arms of thine
Have been the lovely lady's prison.
O Geraldine! one hour was thine—
Thou'st had thy will! By tairn and rill,
The night-birds all that hour were still.

But now they are jubilant anew,
From cliff and tower, tu—whoo! tu—whoo!
Tu—whoo! tu—whoo! from wood and fell!

And see! the lady Christabel
Gathers herself from out her trance;
Her limbs relax, her countenance
Grows sad and soft; the smooth thin lids
Close o'er her eyes; and tears she sheds—
Large tears that leave the lashes bright!
And oft the while she seems to smile
As infants at a sudden light!

Yea, she doth smile, and she doth weep,
Like a youthful hermitess,
Beauteous in a wilderness,
Who, praying always, prays in sleep.
And, if she move unquietly,
Perchance, 'tis but the blood so free
Comes back and tingles in her feet.
No doubt, she hath a vision sweet.
What if her guardian spirit 'twere,
What if she knew her mother near?
But this she knows, in joys and woes,
That saints will aid if men will call:
For the blue sky bends over all!

Christabel, &c., 1816

111   '*Alas! they had been friends in youth*'

ALAS! they had been friends in youth;
   But whispering tongues can poison truth;
And constancy lives in realms above;
And life is thorny; and youth is vain;

And to be wroth with one we love
Doth work like madness in the brain.
And thus it chanced, as I divine,
With Roland and Sir Leoline.
Each spake words of high disdain
And insult to his heart's best brother:
They parted—ne'er to meet again!
But never either found another
To free the hollow heart from paining—
They stood aloof, the scars remaining,
Like cliffs which had been rent asunder;
A dreary sea now flows between;—
But neither heat, nor frost, nor thunder,
Shall wholly do away, I ween,
The marks of that which once hath been.

Christabel, &c., 1816

112   *Kubla Khan*

IN Xanadu did Kubla Khan
A stately pleasure-dome decree:
Where Alph, the sacred river, ran
Through caverns measureless to man
   Down to a sunless sea.
So twice five miles of fertile ground
With walls and towers were girdled round:
And there were gardens bright with sinuous rills,
Where blossomed many an incense-bearing tree;
And here were forests ancient as the hills,
Enfolding sunny spots of greenery.

KUBLA KHAN

But oh! that deep romantic chasm which slanted
Down the green hill athwart a cedarn cover!
A savage place! as holy and enchanted
As e'er beneath a waning moon was haunted
By woman wailing for her demon-lover!
And from this chasm, with ceaseless turmoil seething,
As if this earth in fast thick pants were breathing,
A mighty fountain momently was forced:
Amid whose swift half-intermitted burst
Huge fragments vaulted like rebounding hail,
Or chaffy grain beneath the thresher's flail:
And 'mid these dancing rocks at once and ever
It flung up momently the sacred river.
Five miles meandering with a mazy motion
Through wood and dale the sacred river ran,
Then reached the caverns measureless to man,
And sank in tumult to a lifeless ocean:
And 'mid this tumult Kubla heard from far
Ancestral voices prophesying war!
   The shadow of the dome of pleasure
   Floated midway on the waves;
   Where was heard the mingled measure
   From the fountain and the caves.
It was a miracle of rare device,
A sunny pleasure-dome with caves of ice!

   A damsel with a dulcimer
   In a vision once I saw:
   It was an Abyssinian maid,
   And on her dulcimer she played,
   Singing of Mount Abora.
   Could I revive within me

Her symphony and song,
    To such a deep delight 'twould win me,
That with music loud and long,
I would build that dome in air,
That sunny dome! those caves of ice!
And all who heard should see them there,
And all should cry, Beware! Beware!
His flashing eyes, his floating hair!
Weave a circle round him thrice,
And close your eyes with holy dread,
For he on honey-dew hath fed,
And drunk the milk of Paradise.

Christabel, &c., 1816

113   *The Pains of Sleep*

ERE on my bed my limbs I lay,
    It hath not been my use to pray
With moving lips or bended knees;
But silently, by slow degrees,
My spirit I to Love compose,
In humble trust mine eye-lids close,
With reverential resignation,
No wish conceived, no thought exprest,
Only a sense of supplication;
A sense o'er all my soul imprest
That I am weak, yet not unblest,
Since in me, round me, every where
Eternal Strength and Wisdom are.

But yester-night I prayed aloud
In anguish and in agony,

THE PAINS OF SLEEP

Up-starting from the fiendish crowd
Of shapes and thoughts that tortured me:
A lurid light, a trampling throng,
Sense of intolerable wrong,
And whom I scorned, those only strong!
Thirst of revenge, the powerless will
Still baffled, and yet burning still!
Desire with loathing strangely mixed
On wild or hateful objects fixed.
Fantastic passions! maddening brawl!
And shame and terror over all!
Deeds to be hid which were not hid,
Which all confused I could not know
Whether I suffered, or I did:
For all seemed guilt, remorse or woe,
My own or others still the same
Life-stifling fear, soul-stifling shame.

So two nights passed: the night's dismay
Saddened and stunned the coming day.
Sleep, the wide blessing, seemed to me
Distemper's worst calamity.
The third night, when my own loud scream
Had waked me from the fiendish dream,
O'ercome with sufferings strange and wild,
I wept as I had been a child;
And having thus by tears subdued
My anguish to a milder mood,
Such punishments, I said, were due
To natures deepliest stained with sin,—
For aye entempesting anew
The unfathomable hell within,

The horror of their deeds to view,
To know and loathe, yet wish and do!
Such griefs with such men well agree,
But wherefore, wherefore fall on me?
To be beloved is all I need,
And whom I love, I love indeed.

Christabel, &c., 1816

114 *Work without Hope*

ALL Nature seems at work. Slugs leave their lair—
The bees are stirring—birds are on the wing—
And Winter slumbering in the open air,
Wears on his smiling face a dream of Spring!
And I the while, the sole unbusy thing,
Nor honey make, nor pair, nor build, nor sing.

Yet well I ken the banks where amaranths blow,
Have traced the fount whence streams of nectar flow.
Bloom, O ye amaranths! bloom for whom ye may,
For me ye bloom not! Glide, rich streams, away!
With lips unbrightened, wreathless brow, I stroll:
And would you learn the spells that drowse my soul?
Work without Hope draws nectar in a sieve,
And Hope without an object cannot live.

Poetical Works, 1828

115 *Time, Real and Imaginary*

ON the wide level of a mountain's head,
(I knew not where, but 'twas some faery place)
Their pinions, ostrich-like, for sails out-spread,
Two lovely children run an endless race,

A sister and a brother!
This far outstripp'd the other;
Yet ever runs she with reverted face,
And looks and listens for the boy behind:
For he, alas! is blind!
O'er rough and smooth with even step he passed,
And knows not whether he be first or last.

Poetical Works, 1828

116   *Youth and Age*

VERSE, a breeze mid blossoms straying,
  Where Hope clung feeding, like a bee—
Both were mine! Life went a-maying
    With Nature, Hope, and Poesy,
      When I was young!

When I was young?—Ah, woful When!
Ah! for the change 'twixt Now and Then!
This breathing house not built with hands,
This body that does me grievous wrong,
O'er aery cliffs and glittering sands,
How lightly then it flashed along:—
Like those trim skiffs, unknown of yore,
On winding lakes and rivers wide,
That ask no aid of sail or oar,
That fear no spite of wind or tide!
Nought cared this body for wind or weather
When Youth and I lived in't together.

Flowers are lovely; Love is flower-like;
Friendship is a sheltering tree;

277

O! the joys, that came down shower-like,
Of Friendship, Love, and Liberty,
                    Ere I was old!

Ere I was old? Ah woful Ere,
Which tells me, Youth 's no longer here!
O Youth! for years so many and sweet,
'Tis known, that Thou and I were one,
I'll think it but a fond conceit—
It cannot be that Thou art gone!
Thy vesper-bell hath not yet toll'd:—
And thou wert aye a masker bold!
What strange disguise hast now put on,
To make believe, that thou art gone?
I see these locks in silvery slips,
This drooping gait, this altered size:
But Spring-tide blossoms on thy lips,
And tears take sunshine from thine eyes!
Life is but thought: so think I will
That Youth and I are house-mates still.

Dew-drops are the gems of morning,
But the tears of mournful eve!
Where no hope is, life 's a warning
That only serves to make us grieve,
                    When we are old:

That only serves to make us grieve
With oft and tedious taking-leave,
Like some poor nigh-related guest,
That may not rudely be dismist;
Yet hath outstay'd his welcome while,
And tells the jest without the smile.

Poetical Works, 1834

Epitaph

STOP, Christian passer-by!—Stop, child of God,
    And read with gentle breast. Beneath this sod
A poet lies, or that which once seem'd he.
O, lift one thought in prayer for S. T. C.;
That he who many a year with toil of breath
Found death in life, may here find life in death!
Mercy for praise—to be forgiven for fame
He ask'd, and hoped, through Christ. Do thou the same!

Poetical Works, 1834

ROBERT TANNAHILL

1774–1810

118　　　*The Braes o' Gleniffer*

KEEN blaws the wind o'er the Braes o' Gleniffer,
    The auld castle's turrets are cover'd wi' snaw;
How chang'd frae the time when I met wi' my lover
    Amang the broom bushes by Stanley green shaw:
The wild flow'rs o' simmer were spread a' sae bonnie,
    The mavis sang sweet frae the green birken tree:
But far to the camp they hae march'd my dear Johnnie,
    And now it is winter wi' nature and me.

Then ilk thing around us was blithesome and cheery,
    Then ilk thing around us was bonny and braw;
Now naething is heard but the wind whistling dreary,
    And naething is seen but the wide-spreading snaw.
The trees are a' bare, and the birds mute and dowie,
    They shake the cauld drift frae their wings as they flee,
        dowie] dull.

And chirp out their plaints, seeming wae for my Johnnie,—
    'Tis winter wi' them, and 'tis winter wi' me.

Yon cauld sleety cloud skiffs alang the bleak mountain,
    And shakes the dark firs on the stey rocky brae,
While down the deep glen bawls the snaw-flooded fountain,
    That murmur'd sae sweet to my laddie and me.
'Tis no its loud roar on the wintry wind swellin',
    'Tis no the cauld blast brings the tears i' my e'e,
For, O gin I saw but my bonny Scotch callan,
    The dark days o' winter were simmer to me!

Poems, 1807

119   ' *O are ye sleeping, Maggie?* '

                    Chorus

            ' **O** ARE ye sleeping, Maggie?
              O are ye sleeping, Maggie?
              Let me in, for loud the linn
                Is roaring o'er the warlock-craigie.

        Mirk and rainy is the night,
            No a starn in a' the corry,
        Lightnings gleam athwart the lift,
            And winds drive wi' winter's fury.
                    O are ye sleeping, Maggie?

        Fearful soughs the bour-tree bank,
            The rifted wood roars wild and dreary,
        Loud the iron yett does clank,
            And cry of howlets makes me eerie.
                    O are ye sleeping, Maggie?

skiffs] moves quickly.   stey] steep.   warlock-craigie] wizard's
crag.   bour-tree] elder-tree.   yett] gate.

' O ARE YE SLEEPING, MAGGIE ? '

Aboon my breath I darna' speak,
  For fear I rouse your waukrife daddie,
Cauld 's the blast upon my cheek,—
  O rise, rise, my bonny lady!
        O are ye sleeping, Maggie? '

She opt the door, she let him in,
  He cuist aside his dreeping plaidie;
' Blaw your warst, ye rain and win',
  Since, Maggie, now I'm in beside ye.'

Chorus

> ' Now since ye're waking, Maggie,
> Now since ye're waking, Maggie,
> What care I for howlet's cry,
> For bour-tree bank, or warlock-craigie! '

Poems, 1807

ROBERT SOUTHEY

1774–1843

120   *The Battle of Blenheim*

I

IT was a summer evening,
  Old Kaspar's work was done,
And he before his cottage door
  Was sitting in the sun,
And by him sported on the green
His little grandchild Wilhelmine.

waukrife] wakeful.

2

She saw her brother Peterkin
   Roll something large and round,
Which he beside the rivulet
   In playing there had found;
He came to ask what he had found,
That was so large, and smooth, and round.

3

Old Kaspar took it from the boy,
   Who stood expectant by;
And then the old man shook his head,
   And, with a natural sigh,
' 'Tis some poor fellow's skull,' said he,
' Who fell in the great victory.

4

' I find them in the garden,
   For there 's many here about;
And often when I go to plough,
   The ploughshare turns them out!
For many thousand men,' said he,
' Were slain in that great victory.'

5

' Now tell us what 'twas all about,'
   Young Peterkin, he cries;
And little Wilhelmine looks up
   With wonder-waiting eyes;
' Now tell us all about the war,
And what they fought each other for.'

THE BATTLE OF BLENHEIM

6

' It was the English,' Kaspar cried,
　' Who put the French to rout;
But what they fought each other for,
　I could not well make out;
But every body said,' quoth he,
' That 'twas a famous victory.

7

' My father lived at Blenheim then,
　Yon little stream hard by;
They burnt his dwelling to the ground,
　And he was forced to fly;
So with his wife and child he fled,
Nor had he where to rest his head.

8

' With fire and sword the country round
　Was wasted far and wide,
And many a childing mother then,
　And new-born baby died;
But things like that, you know, must be
At every famous victory.

9

' They say it was a shocking sight
　After the field was won;
For many thousand bodies here
　Lay rotting in the sun;
But things like that, you know, must be
After a famous victory.

10

' Great praise the Duke of Marlbro' won,
    And our good Prince Eugene.'
' Why 'twas a very wicked thing!'
    Said little Wilhelmine.
' Nay . . . nay . . . my little girl,' quoth he,
' It was a famous victory.

11

' And every body praised the Duke
    Who this great fight did win.'
' But what good came of it at last?'
    Quoth little Peterkin.
' Why that I cannot tell,' said he,
' But 'twas a famous victory.'

The Morning Post, Aug. 9, 1798;
The Annual Anthology, 1800

121 *The Old Woman of Berkeley*

THE Raven croak'd as she sate at her meal,
    And the Old Woman knew what he said,
And she grew pale at the Raven's tale,
    And sicken'd and went to her bed.

' Now fetch me my children, and fetch them with speed,'
    The Old Woman of Berkeley said,
' The Monk my son, and my daughter the Nun,
    Bid them hasten or I shall be dead.'

The Monk her son, and her daughter the Nun,
    Their way to Berkeley went,
And they have brought with pious thought
    The holy sacrament.

284

THE OLD WOMAN OF BERKELEY

The Old Woman shriek'd as they enter'd her door,
  And she cried with a voice of despair,
' Now take away the sacrament,
  For its presence I cannot bear! '

Her lip it trembled with agony,
  The sweat ran down her brow,
' I have tortures in store for evermore,
  But spare me, my children, now! '

Away they sent the sacrament,
  The fit it left her weak,
She look'd at her children with ghastly eyes,
  And faintly struggled to speak.

' All kind of sin I have rioted in,
  And the judgement now must be,
But I secured my children's souls,
  Oh! pray, my children, for me!

' I have 'nointed myself with infant's fat,
  The fiends have been my slaves,
From sleeping babes I have suck'd the breath,
And breaking by charms the sleep of death,
  I have call'd the dead from their graves.

' And the Devil will fetch me now in fire,
  My witchcrafts to atone;
And I who have troubled the dead man's grave
  Shall never have rest in my own.

' Bless, I entreat, my winding sheet,
  My children, I beg of you;
And with holy water sprinkle my shroud,
  And sprinkle my coffin too.

' And let me be chain'd in my coffin of stone,
   And fasten it strong, I implore,
With iron bars, and with three chains,
   Chain it to the church floor.

' And bless the chains and sprinkle them,
   And let fifty Priests stand round,
Who night and day the mass may say
   Where I lie on the ground.

' And see that fifty Choristers
   Beside the bier attend me,
And day and night by the tapers' light,
   With holy hymns defend me.

' Let the church bells all, both great and small,
   Be toll'd by night and day,
To drive from thence the fiends who come
   To bear my body away.

' And ever have the church door barr'd
   After the even-song;
And I beseech you, children dear,
   Let the bars and bolts be strong.

' And let this be three days and nights
   My wretched corpse to save;
Till the fourth morning keep me safe,
   And then I may rest in my grave.'

The Old Woman of Berkeley laid her down,
   And her eyes grew deadly dim,
Short came her breath, and the struggle of death
   Did loosen every limb.

THE OLD WOMAN OF BERKELEY

They blest the old woman's winding sheet
   With rites and prayers due,
With holy water they sprinkled her shroud,
   And they sprinkled her coffin too.

And they chain'd her in her coffin of stone,
   And with iron barr'd it down,
And in the church with three strong chains
   They chain'd it to the ground.

And they blest the chains and sprinkled them,
   And fifty Priests stood round,
By night and day the mass to say
   Where she lay on the ground.

And fifty sacred Choristers
   Beside the bier attend her,
Who day and night by the tapers' light
   Should with holy hymns defend her.

To see the Priests and Choristers
   It was a goodly sight,
Each holding, as it were a staff,
   A taper burning bright.

And the church bells all, both great and small,
   Did toll so loud and long;
And they have barr'd the church door hard,
   After the even-song.

And the first night the tapers' light
   Burnt steadily and clear,
But they without a hideous rout
   Of angry fiends could hear;

A hideous roar at the church door
    Like a long thunder peal;
And the Priests they pray'd, and the Choristers sung
    Louder in fearful zeal.

Loud toll'd the bell, the Priests pray'd well,
    The tapers they burnt bright,
The Monk her son, and her daughter the Nun,
    They told their beads all night.

The cock he crew, the Fiends they flew
    From the voice of the morning away;
Then undisturb'd the Choristers sing,
    And the fifty Priests they pray;
As they had sung and pray'd all night,
    They pray'd and sung all day.

The second night the tapers' light
    Burnt dismally and blue,
And every one saw his neighbour's face
    Like a dead man's face to view.

And yells and cries without arise
    That the stoutest heart might shock,
And a deafening roaring like a cataract pouring
    Over a mountain rock.

The Monk and Nun they told their beads
    As fast as they could tell,
And aye as louder grew the noise
    The faster went the bell.

Louder and louder the Choristers sung
    As they trembled more and more,
And the Priests as they pray'd to heaven for aid,
    They smote their breasts full sore.

THE OLD WOMAN OF BERKELEY

The cock he crew, the Fiends they flew
　　From the voice of the morning away;
Then undisturb'd the Choristers sing,
　　And the fifty Priests they pray;
As they had sung and pray'd all night,
　　They pray'd and sung all day.

The third night came, and the tapers' flame
　　A frightful stench did make;
And they burnt as though they had been dipt
　　In the burning brimstone lake.

And the loud commotion, like the rushing of ocean,
　　Grew momently more and more;
And strokes as of a battering ram
　　Did shake the strong church door.

The bellmen, they for very fear
　　Could toll the bell no longer;
And still as louder grew the strokes
　　Their fear it grew the stronger.

The Monk and Nun forgot their beads,
　　They fell on the ground in dismay;
There was not a single Saint in heaven
　　To whom they did not pray.

And the Choristers' song, which late was so strong,
　　Falter'd with consternation,
For the church did rock as an earthquake shock
　　Uplifted its foundation.

And a sound was heard like the trumpet's blast,
　　That shall one day wake the dead;
The strong church door could bear no more,
　　And bolts and the bars they fled;

And the taper's light was extinguish'd quite,
   And the Choristers faintly sung,
And the Priests dismay'd, panted and pray'd,
And on all Saints in heaven for aid
   They call'd with trembling tongue.

And in He came with eyes of flame,
   The Devil to fetch the dead,
And all the church with his presence glow'd
   Like a fiery furnace red.

He laid his hand on the iron chains,
   And like flax they moulder'd asunder,
And the coffin lid, which was barr'd so firm,
   He burst with his voice of thunder.

And he bade the Old Woman of Berkeley rise,
   And come with her Master away;
A cold sweat started on that cold corpse,
   At the voice she was forced to obey.

She rose on her feet in her winding sheet,
   Her dead flesh quiver'd with fear,
And a groan like that which the Old Woman gave
   Never did mortal hear.

She follow'd her Master to the church door,
   There stood a black horse there;
His breath was red like furnace smoke,
   His eyes like a meteor's glare.

The Devil he flung her on the horse,
   And he leapt up before,
And away like the lightning's speed they went,
   And she was seen no more.

They saw her no more, but her cries
    For four miles round they could hear,
And children at rest at their mothers' breast
    Started, and scream'd with fear.

Poems, vol. ii, 1799

122 *God's Judgement on a Wicked Bishop*

THE summer and autumn had been so wet,
    That in winter the corn was growing yet,
'Twas a piteous sight to see all around
The grain lie rotting on the ground.

Every day the starving poor
Crowded around Bishop Hatto's door,
For he had a plentiful last-year's store,
And all the neighbourhood could tell
His granaries were furnish'd well.

At last Bishop Hatto appointed a day
To quiet the poor without delay;
He bade them to his great Barn repair,
And they should have food for the winter there.

Rejoiced such tidings good to hear,
The poor folk flock'd from far and near;
The great Barn was full as it could hold
Of women and children, and young and old.

Then when he saw it could hold no more,
Bishop Hatto he made fast the door;
And while for mercy on Christ they call,
He set fire to the Barn and burnt them all.

' I'faith 'tis an excellent bonfire! ' quoth he,
' And the country is greatly obliged to me,
For ridding it in these times forlorn
Of Rats that only consume the corn.'

So then to his palace returned he,
And he sat down to supper merrily,
And he slept that night like an innocent man;
But Bishop Hatto never slept again.

In the morning as he enter'd the hall
Where his picture hung against the wall,
A sweat like death all over him came,
For the Rats had eaten it out of the frame.

As he look'd there came a man from his farm—
He had a countenance white with alarm;
' My Lord, I open'd your granaries this morn,
And the Rats had eaten all your corn.'

Another came running presently,
And he was pale as pale could be,
' Fly! my Lord Bishop, fly,' quoth he,
' Ten thousand Rats are coming this way, . . .
The Lord forgive you for yesterday! '

' I'll go to my tower on the Rhine,' replied he,
' 'Tis the safest place in Germany;
The walls are high and the shores are steep,
And the stream is strong and the water deep.'

Bishop Hatto fearfully hasten'd away,
And he crost the Rhine without delay,
And reach'd his tower, and barr'd with care
All the windows, doors, and loop-holes there.

GOD'S JUDGEMENT ON A WICKED BISHOP

He laid him down and closed his eyes; . . .
But soon a scream made him arise,
He started and saw two eyes of flame
On his pillow from whence the screaming came.

He listen'd and look'd; . . . it was only the Cat;
But the Bishop he grew more fearful for that,
For she sat screaming, mad with fear
At the Army of Rats that were drawing near.

For they have swum over the river so deep,
And they have climb'd the shores so steep,
And up the Tower their way is bent,
To do the work for which they were sent.

They are not to be told by the dozen or score,
By thousands they come, and by myriads and more,
Such numbers had never been heard of before,
Such a judgement had never been witness'd of yore.

Down on his knees the Bishop fell,
And faster and faster his beads did he tell,
As louder and louder drawing near
The gnawing of their teeth he could hear.

And in at the windows and in at the door,
And through the walls helter-skelter they pour,
And down from the ceiling and up through the floor,
From the right and the left, from behind and before,
From within and without, from above and below,
And all at once to the Bishop they go.

They have whetted their teeth against the stones,
And now they pick the Bishop's bones:
They gnaw'd the flesh from every limb,
For they were sent to do judgement on him!

The Morning Post, Nov. 27, 1799;
Metrical Tales, 1805

123   *The Inchcape Rock*

NO stir in the air, no stir in the sea,
    The ship was still as she could be,
Her sails from heaven received no motion,
Her keel was steady in the ocean.

Without either sign or sound of their shock
The waves flow'd over the Inchcape Rock;
So little they rose, so little they fell,
They did not move the Inchcape Bell.

The Abbot of Aberbrothok
Had placed that bell on the Inchcape Rock;
On a buoy in the storm it floated and swung,
And over the waves its warning rung.

When the Rock was hid by the surge's swell,
The mariners heard the warning bell;
And then they knew the perilous Rock,
And blest the Abbot of Aberbrothok.

The Sun in heaven was shining gay,
All things were joyful on that day;
The sea-birds scream'd as they wheel'd round,
And there was joyaunce in their sound.

THE INCHCAPE ROCK

The buoy of the Inchcape Bell was seen
A darker speck on the ocean green;
Sir Ralph the Rover walk'd his deck,
And he fixed his eye on the darker speck.

He felt the cheering power of spring,
It made him whistle, it made him sing;
His heart was mirthful to excess,
But the Rover's mirth was wickedness.

His eye was on the Inchcape float;
Quoth he, ' My men, put out the boat,
And row me to the Inchcape Rock,
And I'll plague the Abbot of Aberbrothok.'

The boat is lower'd, the boatmen row,
And to the Inchcape Rock they go;
Sir Ralph bent over from the boat,
And he cut the Bell from the Inchcape float.

Down sunk the Bell with a gurgling sound,
The bubbles rose and burst around;
Quoth Sir Ralph, ' The next who comes to the Rock
Won't bless the Abbot of Aberbrothok.'

Sir Ralph the Rover sail'd away,
He scour'd the seas for many a day;
And now grown rich with plunder'd store,
He steers his course for Scotland's shore.

So thick a haze o'erspreads the sky
They cannot see the Sun on high;
The wind hath blown a gale all day,
At evening it hath died away.

On the deck the Rover takes his stand,
So dark it is they see no land.
Quoth Sir Ralph, ' It will be lighter soon,
For there is the dawn of the rising Moon.'

' Canst hear,' said one, ' the breakers roar?
For methinks we should be near the shore.'
' Now where we are I cannot tell,
But I wish I could hear the Inchcape Bell.'

They hear no sound, the swell is strong;
Though the wind hath fallen they drift along,
Till the vessel strikes with a shivering shock,—
' Oh Christ! it is the Inchcape Rock!'

Sir Ralph the Rover tore his hair;
He curst himself in his despair;
The waves rush in on every side,
The ship is sinking beneath the tide.

But even in his dying fear
One dreadful sound could the Rover hear,
A sound as if with the Inchcape Bell,
The Devil below was ringing his knell.

The Morning Post, Oct. 19, 1803

124   *From ' The Curse of Kehama '*

(i)

I CHARM thy life
From the weapons of strife,
From stone and from wood,
From fire and from flood,

THE CURSE OF KEHAMA

From the serpent's tooth,
And the beasts of blood:
From Sickness I charm thee,
And Time shall not harm thee;
But Earth which is mine,
Its fruits shall deny thee;
And Water shall hear me,
And know thee and fly thee;
And the Winds shall not touch thee
When they pass by thee,
And the Dews shall not wet thee,
When they fall nigh thee:
And thou shalt seek Death
To release thee, in vain;
Thou shalt live in thy pain
While Kehama shall reign,
With a fire in thy heart,
And a fire in thy brain;
And Sleep shall obey me,
And visit thee never,
And the Curse shall be on thee
For ever and ever.

(ii)

A STREAM descends on Meru mountain;
None hath seen its secret fountain;
It had its birth, so Sages say,
Upon the memorable day
When Parvati presumed to lay,
In wanton play,
Her hands, too venturous Goddess, in her mirth,
On Seeva's eyes, the light and life of Earth.

Thereat the heart of the Universe stood still:
The Elements ceased their influences; the Hours
Stopt on the eternal round; Motion and Breath,
Time, Change, and Life and Death,
In sudden trance opprest, forgot their powers.
A moment, and the dread eclipse was ended;
But at the thought of Nature thus suspended,
The sweat on Seeva's forehead stood,
And Ganges thence upon the world descended,
The Holy River, the Redeeming Flood.

None hath seen its secret fountain;
But on the top of Meru Mountain
Which rises o'er the hills of earth,
In light and clouds, it hath its mortal birth.
Earth seems that pinnacle to rear
Sublime above this worldly sphere,
Its cradle, and its altar, and its throne;
And there the new-born River lies
Outspread beneath its native skies,
As if it there would love to dwell
Alone and unapproachable.
Soon flowing forward, and resign'd
To the will of the Creating Mind,
It springs at once, with sudden leap,
Down from the immeasurable steep.
From rock to rock, with shivering force rebounding,
The mighty cataract rushes; Heaven around,
Like thunder, with the incessant roar resounding,
And Meru's summit shaking with the sound.
Wide spreads the snowy foam, the sparkling spray
Dances aloft; and ever there at morning

THE CURSE OF KEHAMA

The earliest sunbeams haste to wing their way,
With rainbow wreaths the holy stream adorning;
And duly the adoring Moon at night
Sheds her white glory there,
And in the watery air
Suspends her halo-crowns of silver light.

A mountain-valley in its blessed breast
Receives the stream, which there delights to lie,
Untroubled and at rest
Beneath the untainted sky.
There in a lovely lake it seems to sleep,
And thence through many a channel dark and deep,
Their secret way the holy Waters wind,
Till, rising underneath the root
Of the Tree of Life on Hemakoot,
Majestic forth they flow to purify mankind.

(iii)

THEY sin who tell us Love can die.
With life all other passions fly,
All others are but vanity.
In Heaven Ambition cannot dwell,
Nor Avarice in the vaults of Hell ;
Earthly these passions of the Earth,
They perish where they have their birth;
But Love is indestructible.
Its holy flame for ever burneth,
From Heaven it came, to Heaven returneth;
Too oft on Earth a troubled guest,
At times deceived, at times opprest,

It here is tried and purified,
Then hath in Heaven its perfect rest:
It soweth here with toil and care,
But the harvest time of Love is there.

(*iv*)

TWO forms inseparable in unity
Hath Yamen; even as with hope or fear
The Soul regardeth him doth he appear;
For hope and fear
At that dread hour, from ominous conscience spring,
And err not in their bodings. Therefore some,
They who polluted with offences come,
Behold him as the King
Of Terrors, black of aspect, red of eye,
Reflecting back upon the sinful mind,
Heighten'd with vengeance, and with wrath divine
Its own inborn deformity.
But to the righteous Spirit how benign
His aweful countenance,
Where, tempering justice with parental love,
Goodness and heavenly grace
And sweetest mercy shine! Yet is he still
Himself the same, one form, one face, one will;
And these his twofold aspects are but one;
And change is none
In him, for change in Yamen could not be,
The Immutable is he.

He sat upon a marble sepulchre
Massive and huge, where at the Monarch's feet,

THE CURSE OF KEHAMA

The righteous Baly had his Judgement-seat.
A Golden Throne before them vacant stood;
Three human forms sustain'd its ponderous weight,
   With lifted hands outspread, and shoulders bow'd
      Bending beneath the load.
A fourth was wanting. They were of the hue
Of coals of fire; yet were they flesh and blood,
      And living breath they drew;
And their red eye-balls roll'd with ghastly stare,
As thus, for their misdeeds, they stood tormented there.

   On steps of gold those living Statues stood,
Who bore the Golden Throne. A cloud behind
   Immovable was spread; not all the light
    Of all the flames and fires of Padalon
      Could pierce its depth of night.
There Azyoruca veil'd her aweful form
In those eternal shadows: there she sate,
And as the trembling Souls, who crowd around
The Judgement-seat, received the doom of fate,
   Her giant arms, extending from the cloud,
Drew them within the darkness. Moving out
To grasp and bear away the innumerous rout,
    For ever and for ever thus were seen
The thousand mighty arms of that dread Queen.

   Here, issuing from the car, the Glendoveer
Did homage to the God, then raised his head.
     Suppliants we come, he said,
I need not tell thee by what wrongs opprest,
For nought can pass on earth to thee unknown;
  Sufferers from tyranny we seek for rest,
And Seeva bade us go to Yamen's throne;

Here, he hath said, all wrongs shall be redrest.
Yamen replied, Even now the hour draws near,
When Fate its hidden ways will manifest.
Not for light purpose would the Wisest send
His suppliants here, when we, in doubt and fear,
The aweful issue of the hour attend.
Wait ye in patience and in faith the end!

The Curse of Kehama, 1810

125   *' My days among the Dead are past '*

1

MY days among the Dead are past;
  Around me I behold,
Where'er these casual eyes are cast,
  The mighty minds of old;
My never-failing friends are they,
With whom I converse day by day.

2

With them I take delight in weal,
  And seek relief in woe;
And while I understand and feel
  How much to them I owe,
My cheeks have often been bedew'd
With tears of thoughtful gratitude.

3

My thoughts are with the Dead, with them
  I live in long-past years,
Their virtues love, their faults condemn,
  Partake their hopes and fears,

And from their lessons seek and find
Instruction with an humble mind.

4

My hopes are with the Dead, anon
   My place with them will be,
And I with them shall travel on
   Through all Futurity;
Yet leaving here a name, I trust,
That will not perish in the dust.

Poetical Works, 1837

JOHN LEYDEN

1775–1811

126   *Lords of the Wilderness*

SO the red Indian, by Ontario's side,
  Nursed hardy on the brindled panther's hide,
Who, like the bear, delights his woods to roam,
And on the maple finds at eve a home,
As fades his swarthy race, with anguish sees
The white man's cottage rise beneath his trees,
While o'er his vast and undivided lawn
The hedge-row and the bounding trench are drawn,
From their dark beds his aged forests torn,
While round him close long fields of reed-like corn:—
He leaves the shelter of his native wood,
He leaves the murmur of Ohio's flood,
And forward rushing, in indignant grief,
Where never foot has trod the falling leaf,

JOHN LEYDEN

He bends his course, where twilight reigns, sublime,
O'er forests, silent since the birth of time;
Where roll on spiral folds, immense and dun,
The ancient snakes, the favourites of the sun,
Or in the lonely vales, serene, repose;
While the clear carbuncle its lustre throws,
From each broad brow, star of a baleful sky,
Which luckless mortals only view to die!
Lords of the wilderness, since time began,
They scorn to yield their ancient sway to man.

Scenes of Infancy, 1803

CHARLES LAMB

1775–1834

127   *The Old Familiar Faces*

I HAVE had playmates, I have had companions,
In my days of childhood, in my joyful school-days,
All, all are gone, the old familiar faces,

I have been laughing, I have been carousing,
Drinking late, sitting late, with my bosom cronies,
All, all are gone, the old familiar faces.

I loved a love once, fairest among women;
Closed are her doors on me, I must not see her—
All, all are gone, the old familiar faces.

I have a friend, a kinder friend has no man;
Like an ingrate, I left my friend abruptly;
Left him, to muse on the old familiar faces.

THE OLD FAMILIAR FACES

Ghost-like, I paced round the haunts of my childhood.
Earth seemed a desart I was bound to traverse,
Seeking to find the old familiar faces.

Friend of my bosom, thou more than a brother,
Why wert not thou born in my father's dwelling?
So might we talk of the old familiar faces—

How some they have died, and some they have left me,
And some are taken from me; all are departed;
All, all are gone, the old familiar faces.

Blank Verse, 1798

128   *Parental Recollections*

A CHILD'S a plaything for an hour;
   Its pretty tricks we try
For that or for a longer space;
   Then tire, and lay it by.

But I knew one, that to itself
   All seasons could controul;
That would have mock'd the sense of pain
   Out of a grieved soul.

Thou straggler into loving arms,
   Young climber up of knees,
When I forget thy thousand ways,
   Then life and all shall cease.

Poetry for Children, 1809

129   *A Farewell to Tobacco*

MAY the Babylonish curse
      Strait confound my stammering verse,
If I can a passage see
In this word-perplexity,
Or a fit expression find,
Or a language to my mind,
(Still the phrase is wide or scant)
To take leave of thee, GREAT PLANT!
Or in any terms relate
Half my love, or half my hate:
For I hate, yet love, thee so,
That, whichever thing I shew,
The plain truth will seem to be
A constrained hyperbole,
And the passion to proceed
More from a mistress than a weed.

Sooty retainer to the vine,
Bacchus' black servant, negro fine;
Sorcerer, that mak'st us dote upon
Thy begrimed complexion,
And, for thy pernicious sake,
More and greater oaths to break
Than reclaimed lovers take
'Gainst women: thou thy siege dost lay
Much too in the female way,
While thou suck'st the lab'ring breath
Faster than kisses or than death.

A FAREWELL TO TOBACCO

Thou in such a cloud dost bind us,
That our worst foes cannot find us,
And ill fortune, that would thwart us,
Shoots at rovers, shooting at us;
While each man, thro' thy height'ning steam,
Does like a smoking Etna seem,
And all about us does express
(Fancy and wit in richest dress)
A Sicilian fruitfulness.

Thou through such a mist dost shew us,
That our best friends do not know us,
And, for those allowed features,
Due to reasonable creatures,
Liken'st us to fell Chimeras,
Monsters that, who see us, fear us;
Worse than Cerberus or Geryon,
Or, who first lov'd a cloud, Ixion.

Bacchus we know, and we allow
His tipsy rites. But what art thou,
That but by reflex can'st shew
What his deity can do,
As the false Egyptian spell
Aped the true Hebrew miracle?
Some few vapours thou may'st raise,
The weak brain may serve to amaze,
But to the reins and nobler heart
Can'st nor life nor heat impart.

Brother of Bacchus, later born,
The old world was sure forlorn,

Wanting thee, that aidest more
The god's victories than before
All his panthers, and the brawls
Of his piping Bacchanals.
These, as stale, we disallow
Or judge of *thee* meant: only thou
His true Indian conquest art;
And, for ivy round his dart,
The reformed god now weaves
A finer thyrsus of thy leaves.

Scent to match thy rich perfume
Chemic art did ne'er presume
Through her quaint alembic strain,
None so sov'reign to the brain.
Nature, that did in thee excel,
Fram'd again no second smell.
Roses, violets, but toys
For the smaller sort of boys,
Or for greener damsels meant;
Thou art the only manly scent.

Stinking'st of the stinking kind,
Filth of the mouth and fog of the mind.
Africa, that brags her foyson,
Breeds no such prodigious poison,
Henbane, nightshade, both together,
Hemlock, aconite——

                              Nay, rather,
Plant divine, of rarest virtue;
Blisters on the tongue would hurt you.

A FAREWELL TO TOBACCO

'Twas but in a sort I blam'd thee;
None e'er prosper'd who defam'd thee;
Irony all, and feigned abuse,
Such as perplext lovers use,
At a need, when, in despair
To paint forth their fairest fair,
Or in part but to express
That exceeding comeliness
Which their fancies doth so strike,
They borrow language of dislike;
And, instead of Dearest Miss,
Jewel, Honey, Sweetheart, Bliss,
And those forms of old admiring,
Call her Cockatrice and Siren,
Basilisk, and all that's evil,
Witch, Hyena, Mermaid, Devil,
Ethiop, Wench, and Blackamoor,
Monkey, Ape, and twenty more;
Friendly Trait'ress, loving Foe,—
Not that she is truly so,
But no other way they know
A contentment to express,
Borders so upon excess,
That they do not rightly wot
Whether it be pain or not.

Or as men, constrain'd to part
With what's nearest to their heart,
While their sorrow's at the height,
Lose discrimination quite,
And their hasty wrath let fall,
To appease their frantic gall,

On the darling thing whatever
Whence they feel it death to sever,
Though it be, as they, perforce,
Guiltless of the sad divorce.

    For I must (nor let it grieve thee,
Friendliest of plants, that I must) leave thee.
For thy sake, TOBACCO, I
Would do any thing but die,
And but seek to extend my days
Long enough to sing thy praise.
But as she, who once hath been
A king's consort, is a queen
Ever after, nor will bate
Any tittle of her state,
Though a widow, or divorced,
So I, from thy converse forced,
The old name and style retain,
A right Katherine of Spain;
And a seat, too, 'mongst the joys
Of the blest Tobacco boys;
Where, though I, by sour physician,
Am debarr'd the full fruition
Of thy favours, I may catch
Some collateral sweets, and snatch
Sidelong odours, that give life
Like glances from a neighbour's wife;
And still live in the by-places
And the suburbs of thy graces;
And in thy borders take delight,
An unconquer'd Canaanite.

The Reflector, No. iv, 1811;
Works, 1818

WHEN maidens such as Hester die,
    Their place ye may not well supply,
Though ye among a thousand try,
      With vain endeavour.

A month or more hath she been dead,
Yet cannot I by force be led
To think upon the wormy bed,
      And her together.

A springy motion in her gait,
A rising step, did indicate
Of pride and joy no common rate,
      That flush'd her spirit.

I know not by what name beside
I shall it call:—if 'twas not pride,
It was a joy to that allied,
      She did inherit.

Her parents held the Quaker rule,
Which doth the human feeling cool,
But she was train'd in Nature's school,
      Nature had blest her.

A waking eye, a prying mind,
A heart that stirs, is hard to bind,
A hawk's keen sight ye cannot blind,
      Ye could not Hester.

My sprightly neighbour, gone before
To that unknown and silent shore,
Shall we not meet, as heretofore,
    Some summer morning,

When from thy cheerful eyes a ray
Hath struck a bliss upon the day,
A bliss that would not go away,
    A sweet fore-warning?

Works, 1818

131   *Written at Cambridge*

I WAS not train'd in Academic bowers,
  And to those learned streams I nothing owe
Which copious from those twin fair founts do flow;
Mine have been any thing but studious hours.
Yet can I fancy, wandering 'mid thy towers,
Myself a nursling, Granta, of thy lap;
My brow seems tightening with the Doctor's cap,
And I walk *gowned;* feel unusual powers.
Strange forms of logic clothe my admiring speech,
Old Ramus' ghost is busy at my brain;
And my scull teems with notions infinite.
Be still, ye reeds of Camus, while I teach
Truths, which transcend the searching Schoolmen's vein,
And half had stagger'd that stout Stagirite!

The Examiner, August 29, 30, 1819;
Album Verses, 1830

IO! Pæan! Io! sing
   To the finny people's King.
Not a mightier Whale than this
In the vast Atlantic is;
Not a fatter fish than he
Flounders round the polar sea.
See his blubber—at his gills
What a world of drink he swills,
From his trunk, as from a spout,
Which next moment he pours out.
   Such his person—next declare,
Muse, who his companions are.—
Every fish of generous kind
Scuds aside, or slinks behind;
But about his presence keep
All the Monsters of the Deep;
Mermaids, with their tails and singing
His delighted fancy stinging;
Crooked Dolphins, they surround him,
Dog-like Seals, they fawn around him.
Following hard the progress mark,
Of the intolerant salt sea Shark.
For his solace and relief,
Flat-fish are his courtiers chief.
Last and lowest in his train,
Ink-fish (libellers of the main)
Their black liquor shed in spite:
(Such on earth *the things that write*.)
In his stomach, some do say,
No good thing can ever stay.

Had it been the fortune of it
To have swallowed that old Prophet,
Three days there he'd not have dwell'd.
But in one have been expell'd.
Hapless mariners are they,
Who beguil'd (as seamen say),
Deeming him some rock or island,
Footing sure, safe spot, and dry land,
Anchor in his scaly rind;
Soon the difference they find,
Sudden plumb he sinks beneath them;
Does to ruthless seas bequeathe them.

    Name or title, what has he?
Is he Regent of the Sea?
From this difficulty free us,
Buffon, Banks, or sage Linnæus.
With his wondrous attributes
Say, what appellation suits?
By his bulk, and by his size,
By his oily qualities,
This (or else my eyesight fails),
This should be the PRINCE OF WHALES.

The Examiner, March 22, 1812;
The Poetical Recreations of 'The Champion', 1822

133   *In my own Album*

FRESH clad from heaven in robes of white,
  A young probationer of light,
Thou wert, my soul, an Album bright,

IN MY OWN ALBUM

A spotless leaf; but thought, and care,
And friend and foe, in foul or fair,
Have ' written strange defeatures ' there;

And Time, with heaviest hand of all,
Like that fierce writing on the wall,
Hath stamp'd sad dates—he can't recal;

And error, gilding worst designs—
Like speckled snake that strays and shines—
Betrays his path by crooked lines;

And vice hath left his ugly blot;
And good resolves, a moment hot,
Fairly began—but finish'd not;

And fruitless, late remorse doth trace—
Like Hebrew lore, a backward pace—
Her irrecoverable race.

Disjointed numbers; sense unknit;
Huge reams of folly; shreds of wit;
Compose the mingled mass of it.

My scalded eyes no longer brook
Upon this ink-blurr'd thing to look—
Go, shut the leaves, and clasp the book.

The Bijou, 1828;
Album Verses, 1830

134   *On an Infant dying as soon as born*

I SAW where in the shroud did lurk
A curious frame of Nature's work.
A flow'ret crushed in the bud,
A nameless piece of Babyhood,

Was in her cradle-coffin lying;
Extinct, with scarce the sense of dying;
So soon to exchange the imprisoning womb
For darker closets of the tomb!
She did but ope an eye, and put
A clear beam forth, then strait up shut
For the long dark: ne'er more to see
Through glasses of mortality.
Riddle of destiny, who can show
What thy short visit meant, or know
What thy errand here below?
Shall we say, that Nature blind
Check'd her hand, and changed her mind,
Just when she had exactly wrought
A finish'd pattern without fault?
Could she flag, or could she tire,
Or lack'd she the Promethean fire
(With her nine moons' long workings sicken'd)
That should thy little limbs have quicken'd?
Limbs so firm, they seem'd to assure
Life of health, and days mature:
Woman's self in miniature!
Limbs so fair, they might supply
(Themselves now but cold imagery)
The sculptor to make Beauty by.
Or did the stern-eyed Fate descry,
That babe, or mother, one must die;
So in mercy left the stock,
And cut the branch; to save the shock
Of young years widow'd; and the pain,
When Single State comes back again
To the lone man who, 'reft of wife,

ON AN INFANT DYING

Thenceforward drags a maimed life?
The economy of Heaven is dark;
And wisest clerks have miss'd the mark,
Why Human Buds, like this, should fall,
More brief than fly ephemeral,
That has his day; while shrivel'd crones
Stiffen with age to stocks and stones;
And crabbed use the conscience sears
In sinners of an hundred years.
Mother's prattle, mother's kiss,
Baby fond, thou ne'er wilt miss.
Rites, which custom does impose,
Silver bells and baby clothes;
Coral redder than those lips,
Which pale death did late eclipse;
Music framed for infant's glee,
Whistle never tuned for thee;
Though thou want'st not, thou shalt have them,
Loving hearts were they which gave them.
Let not one be missing; nurse,
See them laid upon the hearse
Of infant slain by doom perverse.
Why should kings and nobles have
Pictured trophies to their grave;
And we, churls, to thee deny
Thy pretty toys with thee to lie,
A more harmless vanity?

The Gem, 1829; *Album Verses*, 1830

135   *Free Thoughts on several Eminent Composers*

SOME cry up Haydn, some Mozart,
Just as the whim bites; for my part,
I do not care a farthing candle
For either of them, or for Handel.—
Cannot a man live free and easy,
Without admiring Pergolesi?
Or thro' the world with comfort go,
That never heard of Doctor Blow?
So help me God, I hardly have;
And yet I eat, and drink, and shave,
Like other people, if you watch it,
And know no more of Stave or Crotchet,
Than did the primitive Peruvians;
Or those old ante-queer-Diluvians
That lived in the unwash'd world with Tubal,
Before that dirty blacksmith Jubal
By stroke on anvil, or by summ'at,
Found out, to his great surprise, the gamut.
I care no more for Cimarosa,
Than he did for Salvator Rosa,
Being no painter; and bad luck
Be mine, if I can bear that Gluck!
Old Tycho Brahe, and modern Herschel,
Had something in 'em; but who's Purcel?
The devil, with his foot so cloven,
For aught I care, may take Beethoven;
And, if the bargain does not suit,
I'll throw him Weber in to boot.

318

FREE THOUGHTS

There 's not the splitting of a splinter
To chuse 'twixt him last named, and Winter.
Of Doctor Pepusch old queen Dido
Knew just as much, God knows, as I do.
I would not go four miles to visit
Sebastian Bach (or Batch, which is it?);
No more I would for Bononcini.
As for Novello, or Rossini,
I shall not say a word to grieve 'em,
Because they're living; so I leave 'em.

The Monthly Repository, 1835;
Poetical Works, 1836

CHARLES LLOYD

1775–1839

136 *From 'An Essay on The Genius of Pope'*

'TIS not so much, these men more forms survey
   Than others, but they see them cloth'd with ray
From an indwelling faculty, which sheds
New grace upon them; which the spirit weds
To a communion with their very being;
So that the simple agency of seeing
Is fraught with fresh perceptions of delight;
Various in combination; infinite
In its associating quality;
And cloth'd with all the soul of sympathy.

He who has this, the touchstone sure possesses,
To find, as 'twere, with superhuman guesses,
That which, in every circumstance of life,
Accrues to man in passion's fearful strife:—
His soul is like a microcosm: he,
Largely possessing this high quality,

At once pronounces with a tact precise,
Profound, as it is accurate and nice,
What, in a given post, a given mood;
What, in society, in solitude;
Or what in sorrow, what in joy; in death;
In life; a being breathing human breath
Can feel! He can at once identify
Self with all aspects of humanity.
Talents can not give this. By process deep
This can give talents; for what man can keep,
In his own breast, a little world reflecting
' All objects of all thoughts; ' a sense detecting
All qualities, and properties of man;
All feelings which can visit life's brief span,
And not be rich in many a mental prize?
In intellectual process not be wise?
A man, by talents, abstract truth may find;
But to the abstract still will be confin'd
All his acquirements; intuitions none
In him will e'er be found; nor depths which shun
Coyly, *his* dry and scrutinizing gaze,
Who, when he ought to feel, would theories raise.
The gifted, thus, with intuition's spirit,
At once can tell whether a man inherit
This awful dower, who theoretic test
Of truth exhibits for the human breast.
It is a dower which none can simulate;
A dower, devoid of which, devoid of weight
Will be a poet's lucubrations still,
Howe'er strong talents exercise their skill.

Poetical Essays, 1821

HORATIO (HORACE) SMITH

1779–1849

AND

JAMES SMITH

1775–1839

137   *Loyal Effusion*

BY W. T. FITZGERALD

Quicquid dicunt, laudo: id rursum si negant,
Laudo id quoque.

TERENCE.

HAIL, glorious edifice, stupendous work!
God bless the Regent and the Duke of York!
Ye Muses! by whose aid I cried down Fox,
Grant me in Drury Lane a private box,
Where I may loll, cry bravo! and profess
The boundless powers of England's glorious press;
While Afric's sons exclaim, from shore to shore,
' Quashee ma boo! '—the slave-trade is no more!
In fair Arabia (happy once, now stony,
Since ruined by that arch-apostate Boney),
A phœnix late was caught: the Arab host
Long ponder'd—part would boil it, part would roast;
But while they ponder, up the pot-lid flies,
Fledged, beak'd, and claw'd, alive they see him rise
To heaven, and caw defiance in the skies.
So Drury, first in roasting flames consumed,
Then by old renters to hot water doom'd,
By Wyatt's trowel patted, plump and sleek,
Soars without wings, and caws without a beak.
Gallia's stern despot shall in vain advance
From Paris, the metropolis of France;

By this day month the monster shall not gain
A foot of land in Portugal or Spain.
See Wellington in Salamanca's field
Forces his favourite general to yield,
Breaks through his lines, and leaves his boasted Marmont
Expiring on the plain without his arm on:
Madrid he enters at the cannon's mouth,
And then the villages still further south.
Base Buonapartè, fill'd with deadly ire,
Sets, one by one, our playhouses on fire.
Some years ago he pounced with deadly glee on
The Opera House, then burnt down the Pantheon;
Nay, still unsated, in a coat of flames,
Next at Millbank he cross'd the river Thames;
Thy hatch, O Halfpenny! pass'd in a trice,
Boil'd some black pitch, and burnt down Astley's twice;
Then buzzing on through ether with a vile hum,
Turn'd to the left hand, fronting the Asylum,
And burnt the Royal Circus in a hurry—
('Twas call'd the Circus then, but now the Surrey).

Who burnt (confound his soul!) the houses twain
Of Covent Garden and of Drury Lane?
Who, while the British squadron lay off Cork
(God bless the Regent and the Duke of York!)
With a foul earthquake ravaged the Caraccas,
And raised the price of dry goods and tobaccos?
Who makes the quartern loaf and Luddites rise?
Who fills the butchers' shops with large blue flies?
Who thought in flames St. James's court to pinch?
Who burnt the wardrobe of poor Lady Finch?—
Why he, who, forging for this isle a yoke,
Reminds me of a line I lately spoke,

LOYAL EFFUSION

' The tree of freedom is the British oak.'

   Bless every man possess'd of aught to give;
Long may Long Tilney Wellesley Long Pole live;
God bless the Army, bless their coats of scarlet,
God bless the Navy, bless the Princess Charlotte;
God bless the Guards, though worsted Gallia scoff,
God bless their pig-tails, though they're now cut off;
And, oh! in Downing Street should Old Nick revel,
England's prime minister, then bless the devil!

Rejected Addresses, 1812

138   *The Baby's Debut*

BY W. W.

> Thy lisping prattle and thy mincing gait,
> All thy false mimic fooleries I hate;
> For thou art Folly's counterfeit, and she
> Who is right foolish hath the better plea:
> Nature's true idiot I prefer to thee.
>
> CUMBERLAND.

[Spoken in the character of Nancy Lake, a girl eight years of age, who is drawn upon the stage in a child's chaise by Samuel Hughes, her uncle's porter.]

MY brother Jack was nine in May,
   And I was eight on New-year's-day;
     So in Kate Wilson's shop
Papa (he 's my papa and Jack's)
Bought me, last week, a doll of wax,
     And brother Jack a top.

Jack 's in the pouts, and this it is,—
He thinks mine came to more than his;
     So to my drawer he goes,

323

Takes out the doll, and, O, my stars!
He pokes her head between the bars,
 And melts off half her nose!

Quite cross, a bit of string I beg,
And tie it to his peg-top's peg,
 And bang, with might and main,
Its head against the parlour-door:
Off flies the head, and hits the floor,
 And breaks a window-pane.

This made him cry with rage and spite:
Well, let him cry, it serves him right.
 A pretty thing, forsooth!
If he 's to melt, all scalding hot,
Half my doll's nose, and I am not
 To draw his peg-top's tooth!

Aunt Hannah heard the window break,
And cried, ' O naughty Nancy Lake,
 Thus to distress your aunt:
No Drury Lane for you to-day!'
And while Papa said, ' Pooh, she may!'
 Mamma said, ' No, she sha'n't!'

Well, after many a sad reproach,
They got into a hackney coach,
 And trotted down the street.
I saw them go: one horse was blind,
The tails of both hung down behind,
 Their shoes were on their feet.

The chaise in which poor brother Bill
Used to be drawn to Pentonville
 Stood in the lumber-room:

THE BABY'S DEBUT

I wiped the dust from off the top,
While Molly mopp'd it with a mop.
    And brush'd it with a broom.

My uncle's porter, Samuel Hughes,
Came in at six to black the shoes,
    (I always talk to Sam:)
So what does he, but takes, and drags
Me in the chaise along the flags,
    And leaves me where I am.

My father's walls are made of brick,
But not so tall and not so thick
    As these; and, goodness me!
My father's beams are made of wood,
But never, never half so good
    As those that now I see.

What a large floor! 'tis like a town!
The carpet, when they lay it down,
    Won't hide it, I'll be bound;
And there's a row of lamps!—my eye!
How they do blaze! I wonder why
    They keep them on the ground.

At first I caught hold of the wing,
And kept away; but Mr. Thing-
    umbob, the prompter man,
Gave with his hand my chaise a shove,
And said, ' Go on, my pretty love;
    Speak to 'em, little Nan.

' You've only got to curtsy, whisper, hold your chin up, laugh, and lisp,
    And then you're sure to take:

I've known the day when brats, not quite
Thirteen, got fifty pounds a-night;
   Then why not Nancy Lake?'

But while I'm speaking, where's papa?
And where's my aunt? and where's mamma?
   Where's Jack? O, there they sit!
They smile, they nod; I'll go my ways,
And order round poor Billy's chaise,
   To join them in the pit.

And now, good gentlefolks, I go
To join mamma, and see the show;
   So, bidding you adieu,
I curtsy, like a pretty miss,
And if you'll blow to me a kiss,
   I'll blow a kiss to you.

                  [*Blows a kiss, and exit.*]
                  Rejected Addresses, 1812

139   *From 'The Theatre'*

JOHN Richard William Alexander Dwyer
Was footman to Justinian Stubbs, Esquire;
But when John Dwyer listed in the Blues,
Emanuel Jennings polish'd Stubbs's shoes.
Emanuel Jennings brought his youngest boy
Up as a corn-cutter—a safe employ;
In Holywell Street, St. Pancras, he was bred
(At number twenty-seven, it is said),
Facing the pump, and near the Granby's Head:
He would have bound him to some shop in town,
But with a premium he could not come down.

THE THEATRE

Pat was the urchin's name—a red-hair'd youth,
Fonder of purl and skittle-grounds than truth.

Silence, ye gods! to keep your tongues in awe,
The Muse shall tell an accident she saw.

Pat Jennings in the upper gallery sat,
But, leaning forward, Jennings lost his hat:
Down from the gallery the beaver flew,
And spurn'd the one to settle in the two.
How shall he act? Pay at the gallery-door
Two shillings for what cost, when new, but four?
Or till half-price, to save his shilling wait,
And gain his hat again at half-past eight?
Now, while his fears anticipate a thief,
John Mullins whispers, ' Take my handkerchief.'
' Thank you,' cries Pat; ' but one won't make a line.'
' Take mine,' cried Wilson; and cried Stokes, ' Take mine.'
A motley cable soon Pat Jennings ties,
Where Spitalfields with real India vies.
Like Iris' bow, down darts the painted clue,
Starr'd, striped, and spotted, yellow, red, and blue,
Old calico, torn silk, and muslin new.
George Green below, with palpitating hand,
Loops the last 'kerchief to the beaver's band—
Upsoars the prize! The youth, with joy unfeign'd,
Regain'd the felt, and felt what he regain'd;
While to the applauding galleries grateful Pat
Made a low bow, and touch'd the ransom'd hat.

Rejected Addresses, 1812

JOSEPH BLANCO WHITE

1775-1841

140   *To Night*

MYSTERIOUS Night! when our first parent knew
    Thee from report divine, and heard thy name,
Did he not tremble for this lovely frame,
This glorious canopy of light and blue?
Yet 'neath a curtain of translucent dew,
Bathed in the rays of the great setting flame,
Hesperus with the host of heaven came,
And lo! Creation widened in man's view.
Who could have thought such darkness lay concealed
Within thy beams, O sun! or who could find,
Whilst fly and leaf and insect stood revealed,
That to such countless orbs thou mad'st us blind!
Why do we then shun death with anxious strife?
If Light can thus deceive, wherefore not Life?

The Bijou, 1828

WALTER SAVAGE LANDOR

1775-1864

141   *From ' Gebir '*

(*i*)

BUT Gebir when he heard of her approach,
    Laid by his orbéd shield, his vizor-helm,
His buckler and his corset he laid by,
And bade that none attend him: at his side
Two faithful dogs that urge the silent course,
Shaggy, deep-chested, crouched: the crocodile,
Crying, oft made them raise their flaccid ears,

328

And push their heads within their master's hand.
There was a bright'ning paleness in his face,
Such as Diana rising o'er the rocks
Shower'd on the lonely Latmian; on his brow
Sorrow there was, yet nought was there severe.
But when the royal damsel first he saw,
Faint, hanging on her handmaids, and her knees
Tottering, as from the motion of the car,
His eyes looked earnest on her; and those eyes
Shew'd, if they had not, that they might have lov'd,
For there was pity in them at that hour.
With gentle speech, and more, with gentle looks,
He sooth'd her; but, lest Pity go beyond,
And crossed Ambition lose her lofty aim,
Bending, he kisst her garment, and retir'd.
He went; nor slumber'd in the sultry noon,
When viands, couches, generous wines persuade,
And slumber most refreshes; nor at night,
When heavy dews are laden with disease;
And blindness waits not there for lingering age.
Ere morning dawn'd behind him, he arrived
At those rich meadows where young Tamar fed
The royal flocks, entrusted to his care.
Now, said he to himself, will I repose
At least this burthen on a brother's breast:
His brother stood before him: he, amaz'd,
Rear'd suddenly his head, and thus began.
' Is it thou, brother! Tamar, is it thou!
Why, standing on the valley's utmost verge,
Lookest thou on that dull and dreary shore
Where many a league Nile blackens all the sand.
And why that sadness? when I passed our sheep

The dew-drops were not shaken off the bar;
Therefore if one be wanting 'tis untold.'
   ' Yes! one is wanting, nor is that untold,'
Said Tamar, ' and this dull and dreary shore
Is neither dull nor dreary at all hours.'
Whereon, the tear stole silent down his cheek.
Silent, but not by Gebir unobserv'd:
Wondering he gazed awhile, and pitying spake:—
' Let me approach thee: does the morning light
Scatter this wan suffusion o'er thy brow,
This faint blue lustre under both thine eyes? '
   ' O brother, is this pity or reproach,'
Cried Tamar, ' cruel if it be reproach,
If pity—O how vain! '
                              ' Whate'er it be
That grieves thee, I will pity; thou but speak
And I can tell thee, Tamar, pang for pang.'
   ' Gebir! then more than brothers are we now!
Every thing—take my hand—will I confess.
I neither feed the flock, nor watch the fold;
How can I, lost in love? But, Gebir, why
That anger which has risen to your cheek?
Can other men? Could you? What, no reply!
And still more anger, and still worse conceal'd!
Are these your promises, your pity this?'
   ' Tamar, I well may pity what I feel—
Mark me aright—I feel for thee—proceed—
Relate me all.' ' Then will I all relate,'
Said the young shepherd, gladden'd from his heart.
' 'Twas evening, though not sunset, and springtide
Level with these green meadows, seem'd still higher;
'Twas pleasant: and I loosen'd from my neck

The pipe you gave me, and began to play.
O that I ne'er had learnt the tuneful art!
It always brings us enemies or love!
Well, I was playing—when above the waves
Some swimmer's head methought I saw ascend;
I, sitting still, survey'd it, with my pipe
Awkwardly held before my lips half-clos'd.
Gebir! it was a nymph! a nymph divine!
I cannot wait describing how she came,
How I was sitting, how she first assum'd
The sailor: of what happened, there remains
Enough to say, and too much to forget.
The sweet deceiver stept upon this bank
Before I was aware; for, with surprize
Moments fly rapid as with love itself.
Stooping to tune afresh the hoarsen'd reed,
I heard a rustling; and where that arose
My glance first lighted on her nimble feet.
Her feet resembled those long shells explored
By him who to befriend his steeds' dim sight
Would blow the pungent powder in their eye.
Her eyes too! O immortal Gods! her eyes
Resembled—what could they resemble—what
Ever resemble those! E'en her attire
Was not of wonted woof nor vulgar art:
Her mantle shew'd the yellow samphire-pod,
Her girdle, the dove-colour'd wave serene.
" Shepherd," said she, " and will you wrestle now
And with the sailor's hardier race engage?"
I was rejoiced to hear it, and contrived
How to keep up contention;—could I fail
By pressing not too strongly, yet to press?

331

" Whether a shepherd, as indeed you seem,
Or whether of the hardier race you boast,
I am not daunted, no: I will engage."
" But first," said she, " what wager will you lay? "
" A sheep," I answered; " add whate'er you will."
" I cannot," she replied, " make that return:
Our hided vessels, in their pitchy round
Seldom, unless from rapine, hold a sheep.
But I have sinuous shells, of pearly hue
Within, and they that lustre have imbibed
In the sun's palace porch; where when unyoked
His chariot wheel stands midway in the wave.
Shake one, and it awakens, then apply
Its polished lips to your attentive ear,
And it remembers its august abodes,
And murmurs as the ocean murmurs there.
And I have others given me by the nymphs,
Of sweeter sound than any pipe you have.—
But we, by Neptune, for no pipe contend;
This time a sheep I win, a pipe the next."
Now came she forward, eager to engage;
But first her dress, her bosom then, survey'd,
And heav'd it, doubting if she could deceive.
Her bosom seem'd, inclos'd in haze like heav'n,
To baffle touch; and rose forth undefined.
Above her knees she drew the robe succinct,
Above her breast, and just below her arms:
" This will preserve my breath, when tightly bound,
If struggle and equal strength should so constrain."
Thus, pulling hard to fasten it, she spoke,
And, rushing at me, closed. I thrill'd throughout
And seem'd to lessen and shrink up with cold.

GEBIR

Again, with violent impulse gushed my blood;
And hearing nought external, thus absorb'd,
I heard it, rushing through each turbid vein,
Shake my unsteady swimming sight in air.
Yet with unyielding though uncertain arms,
I clung around her neck; the vest beneath
Rustled against our slippery limbs entwined:
Often mine, springing with eluded force,
Started aside, and trembled, till replaced:
And when I most succeeded, as I thought,
My bosom and my throat felt so comprest
That life was almost quivering on my lips,
Yet nothing was there painful! these are signs
Of secret arts, and not of human might,
What arts I cannot tell: I only know
My eyes grew dizzy, and my strength decay'd,
I was indeed o'ercome!—with what regret,
And more, with what confusion, when I reached
The fold, and yielding up the sheep, she cried,
" This pays a shepherd to a conquering maid."
She smil'd, and more of pleasure than disdain
Was in her dimpled chin, and liberal lip,
And eyes that languished, lengthening,—just like love.
She went away; I on the wicker gate
Leant, and could follow with my eyes alone.
The sheep she carried easy as a cloak.
But when I heard its bleating, as I did,
And saw, she hastening on, its hinder feet
Struggle, and from her snowy shoulder slip,
(One shoulder its poor efforts had unveil'd,)
Then, all my passions mingling fell in tears!
Restless then ran I to the highest ground

To watch her; she was gone; gone down the tide;
And the long moonbeam on the hard wet sand
Lay like a jasper column half-uprear'd.'

Book I, ll. 49–217

(ii)

ONCE a fair city, courted then by kings,
    Mistress of nations, throng'd by palaces,
Raising her head o'er destiny, her face
Glowing with pleasure, and with palms refreshed,
Now, pointed at by Wisdom or by Wealth,
Bereft of beauty, bare of ornaments,
Stood, in the wilderness of woe, Masar.
Ere far advancing, all appear'd a plain,
Treacherous and fearful mountains, far advanced.
Her glory so gone down, at human step
The fierce hyæna, frighted from the walls,
Bristled his rising back, his teeth unsheathed,
Drew the long growl and with slow foot retired.
Yet were remaining some of ancient race,
And ancient arts were now their sole delight.
With Time's first sickle they had marked the hour
When at their incantation would the Moon
Start back, and shuddering shed blue blasted light.
The rifted rays they gather'd, and immersed
In potent portion of that wondrous wave
Which, hearing rescued Israel, stood erect,
And led her armies through his crystal gates.
    Hither—none shared her way, her counsel none—
Hied the Masarian Dalica: 'twas night,
And the still breeze fell languid on the waste.
    She, tired with journey long, and ardent thoughts,

Stopt; and before the city she descried
A female form emerge above the sands:
Intent she fix'd her eyes, and on herself
Relying, with fresh vigour bent her way;
Nor disappear'd the woman, but exclaim'd—
One hand retaining tight her folded vest—
' Stranger! who loathest life, there lies Masar.
Begone, nor tarry longer, or, ere morn,
The cormorant, in his solitary haunt
Of insulated rock or sounding cove,
Stands on thy bleached bones, and screams for prey.
My lips can scatter them a hundred leagues,
So shrivell'd in one breath, as all the sands
We tread on, could not in as many years.
Wretched who die nor raise their sepulchre!
Therefore begone.'

                But, Dalica, unawed,—
Though in her wither'd but still firm right-hand
Held up with imprecations, hoarse and deep,
Glimmer'd her brazen sickle, and inclosed
Within its figur'd curve the fading moon—
Spake thus aloud. ' By yon bright orb of Heaven,
In that most sacred moment when her beam
Guided first thither by the forked shaft,
Strikes thro the crevice of Arishtah's tower——'

  ' Sayst thou ? ' astonished cried the sorceress,
' Woman of outer darkness, fiend of death,
From what inhuman cave, what dire abyss,
Hast thou invisible that spell o'erheard?
What potent hand hath touched thy quicken'd corse,
What song dissolved thy cerements; who unclosed
Those faded eyes, and fill'd them from the stars?

But if with inextinguished light of life
Thou breathest, soul and body unamerst,
Then, whence that invocation; who hath dared
Those hallow'd words, divulging, to profane?'

    Dalica cried, ' To heaven, not earth, addrest,
Prayers for protection cannot be profane.'

    Here the pale sorceress turn'd her face aside,
Wildly, and mutter'd to herself, amazed,
' I dread her who, alone, at such an hour,
Can speak so strangely; who can thus combine
The words of reason with our gifted rites;
Yet will I speak once more.—If thou hast seen
The city of Charoba, hast thou marked
The steps of Dalica?'

                ' What then?'

                        ' The tongue
Of Dalica has then our rites divulged.'
  ' Whose rites?'

              ' Her sister's, mother's, and her own.'
' Never.'

        ' How sayst thou never? one would think,
Presumptuous, thou wert Dalica.'

                ' I am,
Woman, and who art thou?' With close embrace,
Clung the Masarian round her neck, and cried
' Art thou, then, not my sister? ah I fear
The golden lamps and jewels of a court
Deprive thine eyes of strength and purity:
O Dalica, mine watch the waning moon,
For ever patient in our mother's art,
And rest on Heaven suspended, where the founts
Of Wisdom rise, where sound the wings of Power:
336

Studies intense of strong and stern delight!
And thou too, Dalica, so many years
Wean'd from the bosom of thy native land,
Returnest back, and seekest true repose.
O what more pleasant than the short-breath'd sigh
When laying down your burden at the gate,
And dizzy with long wandering, you embrace
The cool and quiet of a homespun bed.'
　' Alas,' said Dalica, ' tho all commend
This choice, and many meet with no control,
Yet, none pursue it! Age, by Care opprest,
Feels for the couch, and drops into the grave.'

Book V, ll. 1–103

(iii)

THE long awaited day at last arrived,
　　When, linkt together by the seven-arm'd Nile,
Egypt with proud Iberia should unite.
Here the Tartesian, there the Gadite tents
Rang with impatient pleasure: here engaged
Woody Nebrissa's quiver-bearing crew,
Contending warm with amicable skill:
While they of Durius raced along the beach,
And scatter'd mud and jeers on all behind.
The strength of Bætis, too, removed the helm,
And stript the corslet off, and staunched the foot
Against the mossy maple, while they tore
Their quivering lances from the hissing wound.
Others push forth the prows of their compeers,
And the wave, parted by the pouncing beak,
Swells up the sides, and closes far astern:

The silent oars now dip their level wings,
And weary with strong stroke the whitening wave.
Others, afraid of tardiness, return.
Now, entering the still harbour, every surge
Runs with a louder murmur up their keel,
And the slack cordage rattles round the mast.
Sleepless, with pleasure and expiring fears,
Had Gebir risen ere the break of dawn,
And o'er the plains appointed for the feast
Hurried with ardent step: the swains admired
What so transversely could have swept the dew,
For never long one path had Gebir trod,
Nor long, unheeding man, one pace preserved.
Not thus Charoba. She despaired the day:
The day was present; true; yet she despair'd.
In the too tender and once tortured heart
Doubts gather strength from habit, like disease;
Fears, like the needle verging to the pole,
Tremble and tremble into certainty.
How often, when her maids with merry voice
Call'd her, and told the sleepless queen 'twas morn,
How often would she feign some fresh delay,
And tell them (tho' they saw) that she arose.
Next to her chamber, closed by cedar doors,
A bath, of purest marble, purest wave,
On its fair surface bore its pavement high.
Arabian gold enchased the crystal roof,
With fluttering boys adorn'd and girls unrobed,
These, when you touch the quiet water, start
From their aërial sunny arch, and pant
Entangled mid each other's flowery wreaths,
And each pursuing is in turn pursued.

GEBIR

Here came at last, as ever wont at morn,
Charoba: long she linger'd at the brink,
Often she sighed, and, naked as she was,
Sat down, and leaning on the couch's edge,
On the soft inward pillow of her arm
Rested her burning cheek: she moved her eyes;
She blush'd; and blushing plung'd into the wave.
    Now brazen chariots thunder thro' each street,
And neighing steeds paw proudly from delay.
While o'er the palace breathes the dulcimer,
Lute, and aspiring harp, and lisping reed;
Loud rush the trumpets, bursting through the throng,
And urge the high-shoulder'd vulgar; now are heard
Curses and quarrels and constricted blows,
Threats and defiance and suburban war.
Hark! the reiterated clangour sounds!
Now murmurs, like the sea, or like the storm,
Or like the flames on forests, move and mount
From rank to rank, and loud and louder roll,
Till all the people is one vast applause.
Yes, 'tis herself—Charoba—now the strife
To see again a form so often seen.
Feel they some partial pang, some secret void,
Some doubt of feasting those fond eyes again?
Panting imbibe they that refreshing sight
To reproduce in hour of bitterness?
She goes; the king awaits her from the camp.
Him she descried; and trembled ere he reached
Her car; but shudder'd paler at his voice.
So the pale silver at the festive board
Grows paler fill'd afresh and dew'd with wine;
So seems the tenderest herbage of the spring

To whiten, bending from a balmy gale.
The beauteous queen alighting he received,
And sighed to loose her from his arms; she hung
A little longer on them thro' her fears,
Her maidens followed her: and one that watch'd,
One that had call'd her in the morn, observ'd
How virgin passion with unfuel'd flame
Burns into whiteness; while the blushing cheek
Imagination heats and Shame imbues.

Between both nations, drawn in ranks, they pass.
The priests, with linen ephods, linen robes,
Attend their steps, some follow, some precede,
Where clothed with purple intertwined with gold
Two lofty thrones commanded land and main.
Behind and near them, numerous were the tents
As freckled clouds o'erfloat our vernal skies,
Numerous as wander in warm moonlight nights,
Along Meander's or Cayster's marsh,
Swans pliant-neckt and village storks, revered.
Throughout each nation moved the hum confused,
Like that from myriad wings, o'er Scythian cups
Of frothy milk, concreted soon with blood.
Throughout the fields the savoury smoke ascends,
And bough and branches shade the hides unbroached.
Some roll the flowery turf into a seat,
And others press the helmet—now resounds
The signal!—queen and monarch mount the thrones.
The brazen clarion hoarsens: many leagues
Above them, many to the south, the heron
Rising with hurried croak and throat outstretched,
Ploughs up the silvering surface of her plain.

Book VII, ll. 40–151; *Gebir*, 1798

On Man

IN his own image the Creator made,
His own pure sunbeam quicken'd thee, O man!
Thou breathing dial! Since thy day began
The present hour was ever markt with shade!

Poetry by the Author of Gebir, 1802

Rose Aylmer

AH what avails the sceptred race!
Ah what the form divine!
What every virtue, every grace!
Rose Aylmer, all were thine.

Rose Aylmer, whom these wakeful eyes
May weep, but never see,
A night of memories and sighs
I consecrate to thee.

Simonidea, 1806

Mother, I cannot mind my Wheel

MOTHER, I cannot mind my wheel;
My fingers ache, my lips are dry:
Oh! if you felt the pain I feel!
But oh, who ever felt as I!

No longer could I doubt him true.
All other men may use deceit;
He always said my eyes were blue,
And often swore my lips were sweet.

Simonidea, 1806

145   *Fæsulan Idyl*

HERE, where precipitate Spring with one light bound
    Into hot Summer's lusty arms expires;
And where go forth at morn, at eve, at night,
Soft airs, that want the lute to play with them,
And softer sighs, that know not what they want;
Under a wall, beneath an orange-tree
Whose tallest flowers could tell the lowlier ones
Of sights in Fiesole right up above,
While I was gazing a few paces off
At what they seemed to show me with their nods,
Their frequent whispers and their pointing shoots,
A gentle maid came down the garden-steps
And gathered the pure treasure in her lap.
I heard the branches rustle, and stept forth
To drive the ox away, or mule, or goat,
(Such I believed it must be); for sweet scents
Are the swift vehicles of stil sweeter thoughts,
And nurse and pillow the dull memory
That would let drop without them her best stores.
They bring me tales of youth and tones of love,
And 'tis and ever was my wish and way
To let all flowers live freely, and all die,
Whene'er their Genius bids their souls depart,
Among their kindred in their native place.
I never pluck the rose; the violet's head
Hath shaken with my breath upon its bank
And not reproacht me; the ever-sacred cup
Of the pure lily hath between my hands

FÆSULAN IDYL

Felt safe, unsoil'd, nor lost one grain of gold.
I saw the light that made the glossy leaves
More glossy; the fair arm, the fairer cheek
Warmed by the eye intent on its pursuit;
I saw the foot, that, altho half-erect
From its grey slipper, could not lift her up
To what she wanted: I held down a branch
And gather'd her some blossoms, since their hour
Was come, and bees had wounded them, and flies
Of harder wing were working their way thro
And scattering them in fragments under foot.
So crisp were some, they rattled unevolved,
Others, ere broken off, fell into shells,
For such appear the petals when detacht,
Unbending, brittle, lucid, white like snow,
And like snow not seen thro, by eye or sun:
Yet every one her gown received from me
Was fairer than the first. . I thought not so,
But so she praised them to reward my care.
I said: *you find the largest.*

> *This indeed,*

Cried she, *is large and sweet.*

> She held one forth,

Whether for me to look at or to take
She knew not, nor did I; but taking it
Would best have solved (and this she felt) her doubts.
I dared not touch it; for it seemed a part
Of her own self; fresh, full, the most mature
Of blossoms, yet a blossom; with a touch
To fall, and yet unfallen.

> She drew back

The boon she tendered, and then, finding not 343

The ribbon at her waist to fix it in,
Dropt it, as loth to drop it, on the rest.

Gebir, Count Julian, and other Poems, 1831

146   *' In Clementina's artless mien '*

IN Clementina's artless mien
Lucilla asks me what I see,
And are the roses of sixteen
        Enough for me?

Lucilla asks, if that be all,
    Have I not cull'd as sweet before. . .
Ah yes, Lucilla! and their fall
        I still deplore.

I now behold another scene,
    Where Pleasure beams with heaven's own light
More pure, more constant, more serene,
        And not less bright. . .

Faith, on whose breast the Loves repose,
    Whose chain of flowers no force can sever,
And Modesty who, when she goes,
        Is gone for ever.

Gebir, Count Julian, and other Poems, 1831

147   *Dirce*

STAND close around, ye Stygian set,
    With Dirce in one boat conveyed!
Or Charon, seeing, may forget
    That he is old and she a shade.

Gebir, Count Julian, and other Poems, 1831

344

IANTHE! you resolve to cross the sea!
　　A path forbidden *me*!
Remember, while the sun his blessing sheds
　　Upon the mountain-heads,
How often we have watch'd him laying down
　　His brow, and dropp'd our own
Against each other's, and how faint and short
　　And sliding the support!
What will succeed it now? Mine is unblest,
　　Ianthe! nor will rest
But on the very thought that swells with pain.
　　O bid me hope again!
O give me back what Earth, what (without you)
　　Not Heaven itself can do,
One of the golden days that we have past;
　　And let it be my last!
Or else the gift would be, however sweet,
　　Fragile and incomplete.

Gebir, Count Julian, and other Poems, 1831

149　　'*Mild is the parting year*'

MILD is the parting year, and sweet
　　The odour of the falling spray;
Life passes on more rudely fleet,
　　And balmless is its closing day.

I wait its close, I court its gloom,
　　But mourn that never must there fall
Or on my breast or on my tomb
　　The tear that would have sooth'd it all.

Gebir, Count Julian, and other Poems, 1831

150   '*So late removed from him she swore*'

SO late removed from him she swore,
    With clasping arms and vows and tears,
In life and death she would adore,
    While memory, fondness, bliss, endears . . .

Can she forswear? can she forget?
    Strike, mighty Love! strike, Vengeance! . . . soft!
Conscience must come, and bring Regret . . .
    These let her feel! . . . nor these too oft!

Gebir, Count Julian, and other Poems, 1831

151   '*Past ruin'd Ilion Helen lives*'

PAST ruin'd Ilion Helen lives,
    Alcestis rises from the shades;
Verse calls them forth; 'tis verse that gives
    Immortal youth to mortal maids.

Soon shall Oblivion's deepening veil
    Hide all the peopled hills you see,
The gay, the proud, while lovers hail
    In distant ages you and me.

The tear for fading beauty check,
    For passing glory cease to sigh;
One form shall rise above the wreck,
    One name, Ianthe, shall not die.

Gebir, Count Julian, and other Poems, 1831

346

For an Epitaph at Fiesole

L O! where the four mimosas blend their shade,
  In calm repose at last is Landor laid;
For ere he slept he saw them planted here
By her his soul had ever held most dear,
And he had lived enough when he had dried her tear.

Gebir, Count Julian, and other Poems, 1831

The Maid's Lament

I LOVED him not; and yet, now he is gone,
    I feel I am alone.
I check'd him while he spoke; yet, could he speak,
    Alas! I would not check.
For reasons not to love him once I sought,
    And wearied all my thought
To vex myself and him: I now would give
    My love could he but live
Who lately lived for me, and, when he found
    'Twas vain, in holy ground
He hid his face amid the shades of death!
    I waste for him my breath
Who wasted his for me! but mine returns,
    And this lorn bosom burns
With stifling heat, heaving it up in sleep,
    And waking me to weep
Tears that had melted his soft heart: for years
    Wept he as bitter tears!
Merciful God! such was his latest prayer,
    These may she never share!

347

Quieter is his breath, his breast more cold,
    Than daisies in the mould,
Where children spell, athwart the churchyard gate,
    His name and life's brief date.
Pray for him, gentle souls, whoe'er you be,
    And, oh! pray too for me!

Citation and Examination of William Shakespeare, 1834

154 *From Myrtis*

FRIENDS, whom she lookt at blandly from her couch
    And her white wrist above it, gem-bedewed,
Were arguing with Pentheusa: she had heard
Report of Creon's death, whom years before
She listened to, well-pleas'd; and sighs arose;
For sighs full often fondle with reproofs
And will be fondled by them.

                  When I came,
After the rest, to visit her, she said,

Myrtis! how kind! Who better knows than thou
The pangs of love? and my first love was he!

Tell me, if ever, Eros! are reveal'd
Thy secrets to the earth, have they been true
To any love who speak about the first?
What! shall these holier lights, like twinkling stars
In the few hours assign'd them, change their place,
And, when comes ampler splendour, disappear?
Idler I am, and pardon, not reply,
Implore from thee, thus questioned; well I know
Thou strikest, like Olympian Jove, but once.

Pericles and Aspasia, 1836

From Athens

1

TANAGRA! think not I forget
     Thy beautifully-storied streets;
Be sure my memory bathes yet
     In clear Thermodon, and yet greets
The blythe and liberal shepherd-boy,
Whose sunny bosom swells with joy
When we accept his matted rushes
Upheav'd with sylvan fruit; away he bounds, and blushes.

2

I promise to bring back with me
     What thou with transport wilt receive.
The only proper gift for thee,
     Of which no mortal shall bereave
In later times thy mouldering walls,
Until the last old turret falls;
A crown, a crown from Athens won,
A crown no God can wear, beside Latona's son.

3

There may be cities who refuse
     To their own child the honours due,
And look ungently on the Muse;
     But ever shall those cities rue
The dry, unyielding, niggard breast,
Offering no nourishment, no rest,
To that young head which soon shall rise
Disdainfully, in might and glory, to the skies.

4

Sweetly where cavern'd Dirce flows
　　Do white-arm'd maidens chaunt my lay,
Flapping the while with laurel-rose
　　The honey-gathering tribes away;
And sweetly, sweetly, Attick tongues
Lisp your Corinna's early songs;
　　To her with feet more graceful come
The verses that have dwelt in kindred breasts at home.

5

O let thy children lean aslant
　　Against the tender mother's knee,
And gaze into her face, and want
　　To know what magic there can be
In words that urge some eyes to dance,
While others as in holy trance
　　Look up to heaven; be such my praise!
Why linger? I must haste, or lose the Delphick bays.

Pericles and Aspasia, 1836

156　*On his own Agamemnon and Iphigeneia*

FROM eve to morn, from morn to parting night,
Father and daughter stood before my sight.
I felt the looks they gave, the words they said,
And reconducted each serener shade.
Ever shall these to me be well-spent days,
Sweet fell the tears upon them, sweet the praise.
Far from the footstool of the tragic throne,
I am tragedian in this scene alone.

Satire on Satirists, 1837

Lines to a Dragon Fly

LIFE (priest and poet say) is but a dream;
   I wish no happier one than to be laid
  Beneath a cool syringa's scented shade,
Or wavy willow, by the running stream,
  Brimful of Moral, where the Dragon Fly
  Wanders as careless and content as I.

  Thanks for this fancy, insect king,
  Of purple crest and filmy wing,
  Who with indifference givest up
  The water-lily's golden cup,
  To come again and overlook
  What I am writing in my book.
  Believe me, most who read the line
  Will read with hornier eyes than thine;
  And yet their souls shall live for ever,
  And thine drop dead into the river!
  God pardon them, O insect king,
  Who fancy so unjust a thing!

              Joseph Ablett's *Literary Hours,* 1837

158

To my child Carlino

CARLINO! what art thou about, my boy?
   Often I ask that question, though in vain;
For we are far apart: ah! therefore 'tis
I often ask it; not in such a tone
As wiser fathers do, who know too well.
Were we not children, you and I together?

Stole we not glances from each other's eyes?
Swore we not secrecy in such misdeeds?
Well could we trust each other. Tell me, then,
What thou art doing. Carving out thy name,
Or haply mine, upon my favourite seat,
With the new knife I sent thee over-sea?
Or hast thou broken it, and hid the hilt
Among the myrtles, starr'd with flowers, behind?
Or under that high throne whence fifty lilies
(With sworded tuberoses dense around)
Lift up their heads at once . . . not without fear
That they were looking at thee all the while.

    Does Cincirillo follow thee about?
Inverting one swart foot suspensively,
And wagging his dread jaw, at every chirp
Of bird above him on the olive-branch?
Frighten him then away! 'twas he who slew
Our pigeons, our white pigeons, peacock-tailed,
That fear'd not you and me . . . alas, nor him!
I flattened his striped sides along my knee,
And reasoned with him on his bloody mind,
Till he looked blandly, and half-closed his eyes
To ponder on my lecture in the shade.
I doubt his memory much, his heart a little,
And in some minor matters (may I say it?)
Could wish him rather sager. But from thee
God hold back wisdom yet for many years!
Whether in early season or in late
It always comes high priced. For thy pure breast
I have no lesson; it for me has many.
Come, throw it open then! What sports, what cares
(Since there are none too young for these) engage

352

TO MY CHILD CARLINO

Thy busy thoughts? Are you again at work,
Walter and you, with those sly labourers,
Geppo, Giovanni, Cecco, and Poeta,
To build more solidly your broken dam
Among the poplars, whence the nightingale
Inquisitively watched you all day long?
I was not of your council in the scheme,
Or might have saved you silver without end,
And sighs too without number. Art thou gone
Below the mulberry, where that cold pool
Urged to devise a warmer, and more fit
For mighty swimmers, swimming three abreast?
Or art thou panting in this summer noon
Upon the lowest step before the hall,
Drawing a slice of watermelon, long
As Cupid's bow athwart thy wetted lips
(Like one who plays Pan's pipe) and letting drop
The sable seeds from all their separate cells,
And leaving bays profound and rocks abrupt,
Redder than coral round Calypso's cave?

Pentameron and Pentalogia, 1837

THOMAS CAMPBELL

1777–1844

159   *The Pilgrim of a Day*

O H! lives there, Heaven! beneath thy dread expanse,
   One hopeless, dark idolater of Chance,
Content to feed, with pleasures unrefined,
The lukewarm passions of a lowly mind;
Who, mouldering earthward, 'reft of every trust,
In joyless union wedded to the dust,

353

Could all his parting energy dismiss,
And call this barren world sufficient bliss?
There live, alas! of heaven-directed mien,
Of cultured soul, and sapient eye serene,
Who hail thee, Man! the pilgrim of a day,
Spouse of the worm, and brother of the clay,
Frail as a leaf in Autumn's yellow bower,
Dust in the wind, or dew upon the flower;
A friendless slave, a child without a sire,
Whose mortal life and momentary fire
Lights to the grave his chance-created form,
As ocean-wrecks illuminate the storm,
And, when the gun's tremendous flash is o'er,
To night and silence sink for evermore!

The Pleasures of Hope, 1799

160   *Ye Mariners of England*

A NAVAL ODE

I

YE Mariners of England
   That guard our native seas,
Whose flag has braved, a thousand years,
The battle and the breeze—
Your glorious standard launch again
To match another foe!
And sweep through the deep,
While the stormy winds do blow,—
While the battle rages loud and long,
And the stormy winds do blow.

YE MARINERS OF ENGLAND

II

The spirits of your fathers
Shall start from every wave!
For the deck it was their field of fame,
And Ocean was their grave.
Where Blake and mighty Nelson fell
Your manly hearts shall glow,
As ye sweep through the deep,
While the stormy winds do blow,—
While the battle rages loud and long,
And the stormy winds do blow.

III

Britannia needs no bulwarks,
No towers along the steep;
Her march is o'er the mountain waves,
Her home is on the deep.
With thunders from her native oak
She quells the floods below,
As they roar on the shore
When the stormy winds do blow,—
When the battle rages loud and long
And the stormy winds do blow.

IV

The meteor flag of England
Shall yet terrific burn,
Till danger's troubled night depart
And the star of peace return.
Then, then, ye ocean warriors!
Our song and feast shall flow

To the fame of your name,
When the storm has ceased to blow,—
When the fiery fight is heard no more,
And the storm has ceased to blow.

Morning Chronicle, 1801;
Gertrude of Wyoming, 1809

161   *Hohenlinden*

ON Linden, when the sun was low,
  All bloodless lay the untrodden snow,
And dark as winter was the flow
    Of Iser, rolling rapidly.

But Linden saw another sight
When the drum beat at dead of night,
Commanding fires of death to light
    The darkness of her scenery.

By torch and trumpet fast arrayed,
Each horseman drew his battle blade,
And furious every charger neighed
    To join the dreadful revelry.

Then shook the hills with thunder riven,
Then rushed the steed to battle driven,
And louder than the bolts of heaven
    Far flashed the red artillery.

But redder yet that light shall glow
On Linden's hills of stainèd snow,
And bloodier yet the torrent flow
    Of Iser, rolling rapidly.

HOHENLINDEN

'Tis morn, but scarce yon level sun
Can pierce the war-clouds, rolling dun,
Where furious Frank and fiery Hun
    Shout in their sulphurous canopy.

The combat deepens. On, ye brave,
Who rush to glory, or the grave!
Wave, Munich! all thy banners wave,
    And charge with all thy chivalry!

Few, few shall part where many meet!
The snow shall be their winding-sheet,
And every turf beneath their feet
    Shall be a soldier's sepulchre.

Poems, 4to, 1803

162   *Lord Ullin's Daughter*

A CHIEFTAIN to the Highlands bound
    Cries ' Boatman, do not tarry!
And I'll give thee a silver pound
    To row us o'er the ferry.'

' Now who be ye would cross Lochgyle,
    This dark and stormy water? '

' O, I'm the chief of Ulva's isle,
    And this Lord Ullin's daughter.

' And fast before her father's men
    Three days we've fled together,
For, should he find us in the glen,
    My blood would stain the heather.

' His horsemen hard behind us ride;
    Should they our steps discover,
Then who will cheer my bonny bride
    When they have slain her lover? '

357

Outspoke the hardy Highland wight,
  ' I'll go, my chief! I'm ready;
It is not for your silver bright,
  But for your winsome lady.

' And, by my word! the bonny bird
  In danger shall not tarry;
So, though the waves are raging white
  I'll row you o'er the ferry.'

By this the storm grew loud apace,
  The water-wraith was shrieking;
And in the scowl of heaven each face
  Grew dark as they were speaking.

But still, as wilder blew the wind,
  And as the night grew drearer,
Adown the glen rode armèd men—
  Their trampling sounded nearer.

' O haste thee, haste ! ' the lady cries,
  ' Though tempests round us gather;
I'll meet the raging of the skies,
  But not an angry father.'

The boat has left a stormy land,
  A stormy sea before her,—
When, oh! too strong for human hand,
  The tempest gathered o'er her.

And still they rowed amidst the roar
  Of waters fast prevailing:
Lord Ullin reached that fatal shore,—
  His wrath was changed to wailing.

For sore dismayed, through storm and shade,
   His child he did discover:
One lovely hand she stretched for aid,
   And one was round her lover.

' Come back! come back! ' he cried in grief
   Across the stormy water:
' And I'll forgive your Highland chief,
   My daughter! oh my daughter! '

'Twas vain: the loud waves lashed the shore,
   Return or aid preventing;
The waters wild went o'er his child,
   And he was left lamenting.

Gertrude of Wyoming, 1809

163   *The Last Man*

ALL worldly shapes shall melt in gloom,
   The Sun himself must die,
Before this mortal shall assume
   Its Immortality!
I saw a vision in my sleep
That gave my spirit strength to sweep
   Adown the gulf of Time!
I saw the last of human mould
That shall Creation's death behold,
   As Adam saw her prime!

The Sun's eye had a sickly glare,
   The Earth with age was wan,
The skeletons of nations were
   Around that lonely man!

Some had expired in fight,—the brands
Still rusted in their bony hands;
   In plague and famine some!
Earth's cities had no sound nor tread;
And ships were drifting with the dead
   To shores where all was dumb!

Yet, prophet-like, that lone one stood
   With dauntless words and high,
That shook the sere leaves from the wood
   As if a storm passed by,
Saying, ' We are twins in death, proud Sun!
Thy face is cold, thy race is run,
   'Tis Mercy bids thee go;
For thou ten thousand thousand years
Hast seen the tide of human tears,
   That shall no longer flow.

' What though beneath thee man put forth
   His pomp, his pride, his skill,
And arts that made fire, flood, and earth
   The vassals of his will?
Yet mourn I not thy parted sway,
Thou dim discrownèd king of day:
   For all those trophied arts
And triumphs that beneath thee sprang
Healed not a passion or a pang
   Entailed on human hearts.

' Go, let oblivion's curtain fall
   Upon the stage of men,
Nor with thy rising beams recall
   Life's tragedy again.

Its piteous pageants bring not back,
Nor waken flesh upon the rack
  Of pain anew to writhe—
Stretched in disease's shapes abhorred,
Or mown in battle by the sword
  Like grass beneath the scythe.

' Even I am weary in yon skies
  To watch thy fading fire;
Test of all sumless agonies,
  Behold not me expire!
My lips that speak thy dirge of death—
Their rounded gasp and gargling breath
  To see thou shalt not boast;
The eclipse of Nature spreads my pall,—
The majesty of Darkness shall
  Receive my parting ghost!

' This spirit shall return to Him
  That gave its heavenly spark;
Yet think not, Sun, it shall be dim
  When thou thyself art dark!
No! it shall live again, and shine
In bliss unknown to beams of thine,
  By Him recalled to breath
Who captive led captivity,
Who robbed the grave of Victory,
  And took the sting from Death!

' Go, Sun, while Mercy holds me up
  On Nature's awful waste
To drink this last and bitter cup
  Of grief that man shall taste—

THOMAS CAMPBELL

Go, tell the night that hides thy face
Thou saw'st the last of Adam's race
  On Earth's sepulchral clod
The darkening universe defy
To quench his immortality
  Or shake his trust in God!'

New Monthly Magazine, August, 1823;
Poetical Works, vol. ii, 1828

? JOHN GALT

1779–1839

164   *The Canadian Boat Song*

LISTEN to me, as when ye heard our father
  Sing long ago the song of other shores—
Listen to me, and then in chorus gather
    All your deep voices as ye pull your oars:
      Fair these broad meads—these hoary woods are grand;
      But we are exiles from our fathers' land.

From the lone shieling of the misty island
  Mountains divide us, and the waste of seas—
Yet still the blood is strong, the heart is Highland,
    And we in dreams behold the Hebrides:
      Fair these broad meads, &c.

We ne'er shall tread the fancy-haunted valley,
  Where 'tween the dark hills creeps the small clear stream,
In arms around the patriarch banner rally,
    Nor see the moon on royal tombstones gleam:
      Fair these broad meads, &c.

THE CANADIAN BOAT SONG

When the bold kindred, in the time long-vanished,
  Conquered the soil and fortified the keep,
No seer foretold the children would be banished,
   That a degenerate Lord might boast his sheep:
    Fair these broad meads, &c.

Come foreign rage—let Discord burst in slaughter!
  O then for clansmen true, and stern claymore—
The hearts that would have given their blood like water,
  Beat heavily beyond the Atlantic roar:
    Fair these broad meads—these hoary woods are grand;
    But we are exiles from our fathers' land.

Blackwood's Magazine, Sept. 1829

THOMAS MOORE

1779–1852

165   ' *I pray you* '

— Tale iter omne cave.
      PROPERTIUS, lib. iv, eleg. 8.

I PRAY you, let us roam no more
  Along that wild and lonely shore,
   Where late we thoughtless stray'd;
'Twas not for us, whom heaven intends
To be no more than simple friends,
   Such lonely walks were made.

That little Bay, where turning in
From ocean's rude and angry din,
   As lovers steal to bliss,
The billows kiss the shore, and then
Flow back into the deep again,
   As though they did not kiss.

Remember, o'er its circling flood
In what a dangerous dream we stood—
    The silent sea before us,
Around us, all the gloom of grove,
That ever lent its shade to love,
    No eye but heaven's o'er us!

I saw you blush, you felt me tremble,
In vain would formal art dissemble
    All we then look'd and thought;
'Twas more than tongue could dare reveal,
'Twas ev'ry thing that young hearts feel,
    By Love and Nature taught.

I stoop'd to cull, with faltering hand,
A shell that, on the golden sand,
    Before us faintly gleam'd;
I trembling rais'd it, and when you
Had kist the shell, I kist it too—
    How sweet, how wrong it seem'd!

Oh, trust me, 'twas a place, an hour,
The worst that e'er the tempter's power
    Could tangle me or you in;
Sweet Nea, let us roam no more
Along that wild and lonely shore,
    Such walks may be our ruin.

                              Odes and Epistles, 1806

FAINTLY as tolls the evening chime
　Our voices keep tune and our oars keep time.
Soon as the woods on shore look dim,
We'll sing at St. Ann's our parting hymn.
Row, brothers, row, the stream runs fast,
The Rapids are near and the daylight 's past.

　Why should we yet our sail unfurl?
There is not a breath the blue wave to curl;
But, when the wind blows off the shore,
Oh! sweetly we'll rest our weary oar.
Blow, breezes, blow, the stream runs fast,
The Rapids are near and the daylight 's past.

　Utawas' tide! this trembling moon
Shall see us float over thy surges soon.
Saint of this green isle! hear our prayers,
Oh, grant us cool heavens and favouring airs.
Blow, breezes, blow, the stream runs fast,
The Rapids are near and the daylight 's past.

Odes and Epistles, 1806

Bendemeer

THERE 'S a bower of roses by BENDEMEER's stream,
　And the nightingale sings round it all the day long;
In the time of my childhood 'twas like a sweet dream,
　To sit in the roses and hear the bird's song.

That bower and its music I never forget,
　But oft when alone, in the bloom of the year,
I think—is the nightingale singing there yet?
　Are the roses still bright by the calm BENDEMEER?

No, the roses soon wither'd that hung o'er the wave,
　　But some blossoms were gather'd, while freshly they shone,
And a dew was distill'd from their flowers, that gave
　　All the fragrance of summer, when summer was gone.

Thus memory draws from delight, ere it dies,
　　An essence that breathes of it many a year;
Thus bright to my soul, as 'twas then to my eyes,
　　Is that bower on the banks of the calm BENDEMEER!

Lalla Rookh, 1817

168　　'*When he, who adores thee*'

WHEN he, who adores thee, has left but the name
　　Of his fault and his sorrows behind,
Oh! say wilt thou weep, when they darken the fame
　　Of a life that for thee was resign'd?
Yes, weep, and however my foes may condemn,
　　Thy tears shall efface their decree;
For Heaven can witness, though guilty to them,
　　I have been but too faithful to thee.

With thee were the dreams of my earliest love:
　　Every thought of my reason was thine;
In my last humble prayer to the Spirit above,
　　Thy name shall be mingled with mine.
Oh! blest are the lovers and friends who shall live
　　The days of thy glory to see;
But the next dearest blessing that Heaven can give
　　Is the pride of thus dying for thee.

Irish Melodies, 1807

169   ' *Believe me, if all those endearing young charms* '

BELIEVE me, if all those endearing young charms,
    Which I gaze on so fondly to-day,
Were to change by to-morrow, and fleet in my arms,
    Like fairy-gifts fading away,
Thou wouldst still be ador'd, as this moment thou art,
    Let thy loveliness fade as it will,
And around the dear ruin each wish of my heart
    Would entwine itself verdantly still.

It is not while beauty and youth are thine own,
    And thy cheeks unprofan'd by a tear
That the fervour and faith of a soul can be known,
    To which time will but make thee more dear;
No, the heart that has truly lov'd never forgets,
    But as truly loves on to the close,
As the sun-flower turns on her god, when he sets,
    The same look which she turn'd when he rose.

                        Irish Melodies, 1807

170   ' *At the mid hour of night* '

AT the mid hour of night, when stars are weeping, I fly
    To the lone vale we lov'd, when life shone warm in
        thine eye;
    And I think oft, if spirits can steal from the regions of air,
    To revisit past scenes of delight, thou wilt come to me there,
And tell me our love is remember'd, even in the sky.

Then I sing the wild song 'twas once such pleasure to hear!
When our voices commingling breath'd, like one, on the ear;
  And, as Echo far off through the vale my sad orison rolls,
  I think, oh my love! 'tis thy voice from the Kingdom of
    Souls,
Faintly answering still the notes that once were so dear.

Irish Melodies, 1813

171   '*Oft, in the stilly night*'

O FT, in the stilly night,
    Ere Slumber's chain has bound me,
Fond Memory brings the light
    Of other days around me;
      The smiles, the tears,
      Of boyhood's years,
    The words of love then spoken;
      The eyes that shone,
      Now dimm'd and gone,
    The cheerful hearts now broken!
Thus, in the stilly night,
    Ere Slumber's chain hath bound me,
Sad Memory brings the light
    Of other days around me.

When I remember all
    The friends, so link'd together,
I've seen around me fall,
    Like leaves in wintry weather;
      I feel like one,
      Who treads alone

OFT, IN THE STILLY NIGHT

Some banquet-hall deserted,
　Whose lights are fled,
　Whose garlands dead,
And all but he departed!
Thus, in the stilly night,
　Ere Slumber's chain has bound me,
Sad Memory brings the light
　Of other days around me.

Popular National Airs, 1815

172　　　*French Cookery*

AS to Marshals, and Statesmen, and all their whole lineage,
　For aught that *I* care, you may knock them to spinage;
But think, Dick, their Cooks—what a loss to mankind!
What a void in the world would their art leave behind!
Their chronometer spits—their intense salamanders—
Their ovens—their pots, that can soften old ganders,
All vanish'd for ever—their miracles o'er,
And the *Marmite Perpétuelle* bubbling no more!
Forbid it, forbid it, ye Holy Allies!

　Take whatever ye fancy—take statues, take money—
But leave them, oh leave them, their Perigueux pies,
　Their glorious goose-livers, and high pickled tunny!
Though many, I own, are the evils they've brought us,
　Though Royalty's here on her very last legs,
Yet, who can help loving the land that has taught us
　Six hundred and eighty-five ways to dress eggs?

The Fudge Family in Paris, 1818

173   *What's my thought like?*

Quest.   WHY is a Pump like V—sc—nt C—stl—r—gh?
Answ.   Because it is a slender thing of wood,
    That up and down its awkward arm doth sway,
    And coolly spout and spout and spout away,
In one weak, washy, everlasting flood!

Tom Cribb's Memorial to Congress, 1819

174   '*The Living Dog*' and
            '*The Dead Lion*'

NEXT week will be publish'd (as 'Lives' are the rage)
    The whole Reminiscences, wond'rous and strange,
Of a small puppy-dog, that liv'd once in the cage
    Of the late noble Lion at Exeter 'Change.

Though the dog is a dog of the kind they call 'sad',
    'Tis a puppy that much to good breeding pretends;
And few dogs have such opportunities had
    Of knowing how Lions behave—among friends;

How that animal eats, how he snores, how he drinks,
    Is all noted down by this Boswell so small;
And 'tis plain, from each sentence, the puppy-dog thinks
    That the Lion was no such great things after all.

Though he roar'd pretty well—this the puppy allows—
    It was all, he says, borrow'd—all second-hand roar;
And he vastly prefers his own little bow-wows
    To the loftiest war-note the Lion could pour.

370

THE LIVING DOG AND THE DEAD LION

'Tis, indeed, as good fun as a *Cynic* could ask,
 To see how this cockney-bred setter of rabbits
Takes gravely the Lord of the Forest to task,
 And judges of lions by puppy-dog habits.

Nay, fed as he was (and this makes it a dark case)
 With sops every day from the Lion's own pan,
He lifts up his leg at the noble beast's carcass,
 And—does all a dog, so diminutive, can.

However, the book's a good book, being rich in
 Examples and warnings to lions high-bred,
How they suffer small mongrelly curs in their kitchen
 Who'll feed on them living, and foul them when dead.

Cash, Corn, and Catholics, 1828

GEORGE CROLY

1780–1860

175   *A Fauxbourg*

B UT, venture on the darkness; and within
   See the stern haunt of wretchedness and sin.
The door unhinged, for winter's bitterest air,
The paper pane, the gapp'd and shaking stair,
Winding in murkiness, as to the sty
Of guilt forlorn, or base debauchery;
The chamber, tatter'd, melancholy, old,
Yet large—where plunder might its midnights hold;
And in its foulest corners, from the day
Sullen and shrunk, its lord, the Federé.
Meagre the form, the visage swart and spare,
Furrow'd with early vice and desperate care;
Hollow the cheek, the eye ferocious guile,
Yet gentle to his hard, habitual smile.

371

His end on earth, to live the doubtful day,
And glean the livre for the Sunday's play.
Heavy that chamber's air; the sunbeams fall
Scatter'd and sickly on the naked wall;
Through the time-crusted casement scarcely shown
The rafter'd roof, the floor of chilling stone,
The crazy bed, the mirror that betrays
Frameless, where vanity yet loves to gaze;
And still, the symbols of his darker trade,
The musquet, robber-pistol, sabre blade,
Hung rusting, where around the scanty fire
His squalid offspring watch its brands expire.
His glance is there;—another, statelier spot
Has full possession of his fever'd thought;
In the fierce past the fierce to-come he sees,
The day return'd of plunder'd palaces,
When faction revell'd, mobs kept throne in awe,
And the red pike at once was king and law.

Paris in 1815, 1817

EDWARD THURLOW, LORD THURLOW

1781–1829

176   *May*

MAY! queen of blossoms,
  And fulfilling flowers,
With what pretty music
  Shall we charm the hours?
Wilt thou have pipe and reed,
Blown in the open mead?
Or to the lute give heed
  In the green bowers?

MAY

Thou hast no need of us,
    Or pipe or wire,
That hast the golden bee
    Ripen'd with fire;
And many thousand more
Songsters, that thee adore,
Filling earth's grassy floor
    With new desire.

Thou hast thy mighty herds,
    Tame, and free-livers;
Doubt not, thy music too
    In the deep rivers;
And the whole plumy flight,
Warbling the day and night:
Up at the gates of light,
    See, the lark quivers!

When with the jacinth
    Coy fountains are tressed;
And for the mournful bird
    Green woods are dressed,
That did for Tereus pine;
Then shall our songs be thine,
To whom our hearts incline:
    MAY, be thou blessed!

Select Poems, 1821

373

1781–1849

177   *Battle Song*

DAY, like our souls, is fiercely dark;
        What then?   'Tis day!
We sleep no more; the cock crows—hark!
        To arms! away!
They come! they come! The knell is rung
        Of us or them.
Wide o'er their march the pomp is flung
        Of gold and gem.
What collar'd hound of lawless sway,
        To famine dear—
What pension'd slave of Attila,
        Leads in the rear?
Come they from Scythian wilds afar,
        Our blood to spill?
Wear they the livery of the Czar?
        They do his will.
Nor tassell'd silk, nor epaulet,
        Nor plume, nor torse—
No splendour gilds, all sternly met,
        Our foot and horse.
But, dark and still, we inly glow,
        Condens'd in ire!
Strike, tawdry slaves! and ye shall know
        Our gloom is fire.
In vain your pomp, ye evil powers,
        Insults the land;
Wrongs, vengeance, and *the cause* are ours,
        And God's right hand!

BATTLE SONG

Madmen! they trample into snakes
    The wormy clod!
Like fire, beneath their feet awakes
    The sword of God!
Behind, before, above, below,
        They rouse the brave;
Where'er they go, they make a foe,
        Or find a grave.

The Splendid Village, &c., 1833

178   *From ' Spirits and Men '*

I SING of men and angels, and the days
    When God repented him that he had made
Man on the earth; when crimes alone won praise;
When the few righteous were with curses paid,
And none seem'd vile as they whom truth betray'd;
Till hope despair'd her myriad sons to save,
And giant sin fill'd up their universal grave.

But these—are these the flowers of Paradise,
That bloom'd when man before his Maker stood
Off'ring his sinless thoughts in sacrifice?—
Flowers, ye remind me of rock, vale, and wood,
Haunts of my early days, and still lov'd well:
Bloom not your sisters fair in Locksley's dell?
And where the sun, o'er purple moorlands wide,
Gilds Wharncliffe's oaks, while Don is dark below?
And when the blackbird sings on Rother's side?
And where Time spares the age of Conisbro'?—
Sweet flowers, remember'd well! your hues, your breath,
Call up the dead, to combat still with death:
The spirits of my buried years arise!

Again a child, where childhood rov'd I run;
While groups of speedwell, with their bright blue eyes,
Like happy children, cluster in the sun.
Still the wan primrose hath a golden core;
The millfoil, thousand-leaf'd, as heretofore,
Displays a little world of flow'rets grey;
And tiny maids might hither come to cull
The woe-mark'd cowslip of the dewy May;
And still the fragrant thorn is beautiful.
I do not dream! Is it, indeed, a rose
That, yonder in the deep'ning sunset, glows?
Methinks the orchis of the fountain'd wold
Hath, in its well-known beauty, something new.
Do I not know thy lofty disk of gold,
Thou, that still woo'st the sun, with passion true?
No, splendid stranger! haply, I have seen
One not unlike thee, but with humbler mien,
Watching her lord. Oh, lily, fair as aught
Beneath the sky, thy pallid petals glow
In evening's blush; but evening borrows nought
Of thee, thou rival of the stainless snow—
For thou art scentless. Lo! this finger'd flower,
That round the cottage window weaves a bower,
Is not the woodbine; but that lowlier one,
With thick green leaves, and spike of dusky fire,
Enamour'd of the thatch it grows upon,
Might be the houseleek of rude Hallamshire,
And would awake, beyond divorcing seas,
Thoughts of green England's peaceful cottages.
Yes, and this blue-ey'd child of earth, that bends
Its head, on leaves with liquid diamonds set,
A heavenly fragrance in its sighing sends;

SPIRITS AND MEN

And though 'tis not one downcast violet,
Yet might it, haply, to the zephyr tell
That 'tis belov'd by village maids as well.
Thou little, dusky crimson-bosom'd bird,
Starting, but not in fear, from tree to tree!
I never erst thy plaintive love-notes heard,
Nor hast thou been a suppliant erst to me
For table crumbs, when winds bow'd branch and stem,
And leafless twigs form'd winter's diadem:—

No, thou art not the bird that haunts the grange
Storm-pinch'd, with bright black eyes and breast of flame.
I look on things familiar, and yet strange,
Known, and yet new, most like, yet not the same.
I hear a voice, ne'er heard before, repeat
Songs of the past. But nature's voice is sweet,
Wherever heard; her works, wherever seen,
Are might and beauty to the mind and eye;
To the lone heart, though oceans roll between,
She speaks of things that but with life can die;
And while, above the thundering Gihon's foam
That cottage smokes, my heart seems still at home,
In England still—though there no mighty flood
Sweeps, like a foaming earthquake, from the clouds;
But still in England, where rock-shading wood
Shelters the peasant's home, remote from crowds,
And shelter'd once as noble hearts as e'er
Dwelt in th' Almighty's form, and knew nor guilt, nor fear.

The Splendid Village, &c., 1833

179   *From ' The Impious Feast '*

(i)

Babylon

STILL in her native glory, unsubdued,
   And indestructible by force or time,
That first of mightiest cities, mistress, queen,
Even as of old, earth's boast and marvel stood;
Imperious, inaccessible, sublime:
If changed, she might be all that she had been;
No conscious doubts abased her regal eye,
Rest had not made it weak but more serene—
Those who repell'd her power, revered her majesty.
Full, at her feet, wealth's largest fountain streamed,
Dominion crowned her head; on either side
Were sceptred terror and armed strength—she seemed
Above mischance imperishably high:
Though half the nations of mankind defied,
They raged but could not harm her—fierce disdain
Beheld the rebel kingdoms storm in vain—
What were their threats to her, Bel's daughter and his pride!

Book I

(ii)

The Jew's Home

WISDOM with better thoughts prevailed; aloof
   From streets where madness walked 'twixt mirth and
    dread,
Though but a little space, his dwelling stood,
Lonely, obscure, and silent. O'er its roof,

378

And round its walls, the giant cedar spread,
Ilex and cypress mixed with palms—a wood
Of myrtle undergrowth: for shadowy grove,
Cool glade, and thicket wild had room enough,
With many a sylvan maze, and verdant solitude,
Enclosed within that mighty city's bound;
Where undisturbed the consecrated dove
Labours his hoarse endearments all day long.
And all the night yet louder strains resound—
More sweetly thrills the hereditary wrong:
That lonely bird, whose notes are grief and love,
With iterated plaints deplores her young,
Listening the cadence as it died around,
Strives to surpass herself, and still resumes the song.

Book I

(iii)

The Festival

THERE was a naked greatness in those times
Hidden with the mist of ages, or descried
Dimly at best by us from far divided climes
Whence runs apace the never-refluent tide,
Bearing their mighty wrecks beyond our ken,
Parts—and fair parts—of this fair universe.
Nearer to nature were the works of men,
Themselves more like her children. Not averse,
Estranged, perverted, reprobate—as now
The populous city wakes to pant and toil
Midst loathsome trades, confused with noise and smoke:
Across the imperial brightness of her brow
There passed no cloudy stain, no sordid soil,

No shade impure when Babylon awoke,
No scowl, O queen! of care, no look like want hadst thou!
  Before their thresholds, in the ruddy light,
Thy children swarm with fragrant boughs and flowers,
Suspending bridal coronets above:
The year begins, and spring is in her pride!
Spears are entwined with garlands—helmets bright
Gleam from the lintel—war in those soft hours
Reclines a willing guest at pleasure's side,
And lends his arms as ornaments to love.
The everlasting Serpent weds the Dove—
Thus idly dreams that old idolatry—
Bel celebrates a three-day's festival,
While pale Astarte casts the Cestus by,
Yielding the god her beauty. Earth and sky
With both rejoice, whose blessings reach to all—
Two potent sexes all their realms supply,
Whence nature hath its just fertility.

Book III

(iv)

Nineveh

SHORT seemed the space 'twixt sunset and the night:
The moon behind us in its fulness shone:
Of purest sand reposed that herbless plain
Under the purple firmament. Our sight
Reached far, yet saw no bounds—but rock or stone
Half-buried in the drifting soil, and spread
With dreary intervals, appeared alone
On earth—heaven's ever-wandering isles above.
Nor sounds were there—the dromedary's tread

THE IMPIOUS FEAST

Passed noiseless marked in dust. But she who drove,
Watched not the yellow waste, or ether blue,
Nor paused, nor hesitated; she went on
Silent and swift, till more and mightier grew
The shivered cliffs around us, one by one,
High 'bove the horizon, in a thousand forms
On either hand distinct—such shapes as fear
Might worship for relenting Gods, whose storms
Forbore awhile to vex the wilderness:
At first remote, but every hour more near,
With denser ranks, to right and left, they press;
Narrowing the dismal vale through which we ride:
Thence cries the uneasy stork and wandering owl,
The leopard crosses to their shadier side;
Or wolf turns back with half-suspended growl;
Above our heads deep croaks the ill-resting raven;
Behind, as if too late, the hyena raves.
And signs we see that men had once lived there,
Though shown in works of death—continuous graves—
Subverted urns—huge stones and deeply graven:
The sculptured dragon guards its sepulchre:
A sphynx, broad-faced, looks calmly toward the moon.
Like regal monuments they seem, and some
Imperishable still in night's clear noon
With trophied arms and granite warriors frown,
Bordering the road we travel; till we come
Straight to some mighty city, whose high towers
Are broken, and the embattled wall cast down:
Her gates stand wide—no living shapes appear—
None waits to watch or question: brightly showers
That glorious radiance o'er deserted streets,
To all but us unprofitably clear.

Through grassy court and ponderous portico
We ride—unchecked the dromedary beats
His hoof with quick and regulated sound.
At length I spake in tones subdued and low,
As fearful who should hear me: 'Tell me this—
' Since ignorance such as mine such grace has found,
' Thou yet wilt spare me if I ask amiss—
' What endless city spreads where'er we go?'
She stopped, descended, helped me to the ground,
And answered, not indeed as one who feared,
Like me, to rouse the slumberers from repose;
But so that Echo, loud at first and nigh,
Then far-remote, repeating what I heard
Each time distinct, though lessening toward their close—
Taught in that mournful name its history—
Thrice sounded ' *Nineveh* '.

Book V

(v)

Sleep

SHE paced the silent hall,
Restless both when she rose, and when she sat;
Replaced her harp now first unmusical,
Wishing for those again she wished away so late.
At length she yields to that which conquers all—
Tumultuous thoughts and painful lassitude
Subside in sleep—while hope, remembrance, dread,
Remitted for a time but not subdued,
Their transient flushes o'er her paleness shed.
One hand with rosy palm sustains her head,
Beneath its braids and glossy ringlets prest;
Earthward the other lapses. More than death

382

By far—since terror cannot reach the dead—
Is sleep like this? Death heedless to molest,
Smites hard, then passes on—he stuns and leaves
But mocks us not—he bears no festal wreath
To hide the worms that round his temples creep:
His claims are just—he neither wrongs nor grieves,
Nor can he come but once. The couch beneath
Shakes with our panting heart and hard-drawn breath;
In dreams we die and live, rejoice and weep,
Are wronged, despised, abandoned—sometimes blest,
This never long! But death perchance is sleep—
And life death's dream—if so, tired maid lie still!
The shortest error then were least and best:
Thy slumbers may be gone too soon! They came
Where nothing yet hath staid an hour if ill:
This is thy native roof—remorse or blame
Abides not here, but o'er that stainless breast—
Like clouds which leave no trace and never rest—
Dark thoughts pass swiftly unapproved by will,
Absolved from guilt, and far remote from shame.

Book VII

(vi)

Historic Time

WHO journeying when the days grow shorter, stops
At sunset to review his path, with face
Turned back from some steep eminence, may see
The autumnal landscape chilled by mists, its plains
All lost and hamlets hidden; but yet the tops
Of hills or city spires distinct—their base
Alone confounded in that hazy sea

Isle-strewn and white beneath him: Memory strains
Her vision thus o'er human things, to trace
Their past proportions through the veil which drops
Round realms and empires. Some have ceased to be
Substance and shade—not even the name remains
Of that which seemed so great when near—the rest
Are, most part, ill-discerned—both age and place
Unsettled on the chart of Time: a few
Distinct, rise higher. Her bright and glorious crest
Greece lifts above the twilight round her—free,
With many a laureate wreath of art or war,
And plumed by all the muses. Egypt's hue
Is dark, her wrinkled visage sad, the scar
Of patient servitude on neck and knee—
A feeble giantess whose mystic vest
Is lettered thick with beast, bird, fish, or star—
The signs which none may read. Our dubious view
Flits vaguely o'er a hundred near her—two
Stand broad and large before us: Rome alone
Fills the mid space pre-eminent—behind,
Far off, with head as high, old Babylon.

Book VIII
The Impious Feast, 1828

JANE TAYLOR

1783–1824

180　　　　　　*Recreation*

WE took our work, and went, you see,
　　To take an early cup of tea.
We did so now and then, to pay
The friendly debt, and so did they.

384

RECREATION

Not that our friendship burnt so bright
That all the world could see the light;
'Twas of the ordinary *genus*,
And little love was lost between us:
We lov'd, I think, about as true
As such near neighbours mostly do.

   At first, we all were somewhat dry;
Mamma felt cold, and so did I:
Indeed, that room, sit where you will,
Has draught enough to turn a mill.
' I hope you're warm,' says Mrs. G.
' O, quite so,' says mamma, *says she;*
' I'll take my shawl off by and by.'—
' This room is always warm,' *says I*.

   At last the tea came up, and so,
With that, our tongues began to go.
Now, in that house you're sure of knowing
The smallest scrap of news that 's going;
We find it *there* the wisest way
To take some care of what we say.

—Says she, ' there 's dreadful doings still
In that affair about the *will*;
For now the folks in Brewer's Street
Don't speak to *James's*, when they meet.
Poor Mrs. *Sam* sits all alone,
And frets herself to skin and bone.
For months she manag'd, she declares,
All the old gentleman's affairs;
And always let him have his way,
And never left him night nor day;

Waited and watch'd his every look,
And gave him every drop he took.
Dear Mrs. *Sam*, it was too bad!
He might have left her all he had.'

' Pray ma'am,' says I, ' has poor Miss A.
Been left as *handsome* as they say ? '
' My dear,' says she, ' 'tis no such thing,
She'd nothing but a mourning ring.
But is it not *uncommon* mean
To wear that rusty bombazeen ! '
' She had,' says I, ' the very same
Three years ago, for—what 's his name ? '—
' The Duke of *Brunswick*,—very true,
And has not bought a thread of new,
I'm positive,' said Mrs. G.—
So then we laugh'd, and drank our tea.

' So,' says mamma, ' I find it 's true
What Captain P. intends to do;
To hire that house, or else to buy—'
' Close to the tan-yard, ma'am,' says I;
' Upon my word it 's very strange,
I wish they may'nt repent the change ! '
' My dear,' says she, ' 'tis very well
You know, if *they* can bear the smell.'

' Miss F.' says I, ' is said to be
A sweet young woman, is not she ? '
' O, excellent ! I hear,' she cried;
' O, truly so ! ' mamma replied.
' How old should you suppose her, pray ?
She 's older than she looks, they say.'

RECREATION

' Really,' says I, ' she seems to me
Not more than twenty-two or three.'
' O, then you're wrong,' says Mrs. G.
' Their upper servant told our *Jane*,
She'll not see twenty-nine again.'
' Indeed, so old! I wonder why
She does not marry, then,' says I;
' So many thousands to bestow,
And such a beauty, too, you know.'
' A beauty! O, my dear Miss B.
You must be joking now,' says she;
' Her *figure* 's rather pretty,'—' Ah!
That 's what *I* say,' replied mamma.

' Miss F.' says I, ' I've understood,
Spends all her time in doing good:
The people say her coming down
Is quite a blessing to the town.'
At that our hostess fetch'd a sigh,
And shook her head; and so, says I,
' It 's very kind of her, I'm sure,
To be so generous to the poor.'
' No doubt,' says she, ' 'tis very true;
Perhaps there may be *reasons* too:—
You know some people like to pass
For *patrons* with the lower class.'

And here I break my story's thread,
Just to remark, that what she said,
Although I took the other part,
Went like a cordial to my heart.

`. Some inuendos more had pass'd,
Till out the scandal came at last.
' Come then, I'll tell you something more,'
Says she,—' Eliza, shut the door.—
I would not trust a creature here,
For all the world, but you, my dear.
Perhaps it 's false—I wish it may,
—But let it go no further, pray!'
' O,' says mamma, ' You need not fear,
We never mention what we hear.'
And so, we draw our chairs the nearer,
And whispering, lest the child should hear her,
She told a tale, at least too *long*
To be repeated in a song;
We, panting every breath between,
With curiosity and spleen.
And how we did enjoy the sport!
And echo every faint report,
And answer every candid doubt,
And turn her motives inside out,
And holes in all her virtues pick,
Till we were sated, almost sick.

—Thus having brought it to a close,
In great good-humour, we arose.
Indeed, 'twas more than time to go,
Our boy had been an hour below,
So, warmly pressing Mrs. G.
To fix a day to come to tea,
We muffled up in cloke and plaid,
And trotted home behind the lad.

Essays in Rhyme, on Morals and Manners, 1816

1784–1842

181   *'The sun rises bright in France'*

THE sun rises bright in France,
    And fair sets he;
But he has tint the blythe blink he had
    In my ain countrie.

It 's nae my ain ruin
    That weets ay my ee,
But the dear Marie I left a-hin',
    Wi' sweet bairnies three.

Fu' bonnilie lowed my ain hearth,
    An' smiled my ain Marie;
O, I've left a' my heart behind,
    In my ain countrie.

O I am leal to high heaven,
    An' it'll be leal to me,
An' there I'll meet ye a' soon
    Frae my ain countrie!

Remains of Nithsdale and Galloway Song, 1810

182   *' Hame, hame, hame '*

HAME, hame, hame, Hame fain wad I be,
    O hame, hame, hame, to my ain countrie!

When the flower is i' the bud and the leaf is on the tree,
The larks shall sing me hame in my ain countrie;
Hame, hame, hame, Hame fain wad I be,
O hame, hame, hame, to my ain countrie!

    tint] lost.   lowed] blazed.

389

The green leaf o' loyaltie 's begun for to fa',
The bonnie white rose it is withering an' a';
But I'll water 't wi' the blude of usurping tyrannie,
An' green it will grow in my ain countrie.

O there 's naught frae ruin my country can save,
But the keys o' kind heaven to open the grave,
That a' the noble martyrs wha died for loyaltie,
May rise again and fight for their ain countrie.

The great now are gane, a' wha ventured to save;
The new grass is springing on the tap o' their graves;
But the sun thro' the mirk, blinks blythe in my ee:
' I'll shine on ye yet in yere ain countrie.'

Remains of Nithsdale and Galloway Song, 1810

183   *A Wet Sheet*

A WET sheet and a flowing sea,
    A wind that follows fast
And fills the white and rustling sail
    And bends the gallant mast;
And bends the gallant mast, my boys,
    While like the eagle free
Away the good ship flies, and leaves
    Old England on the lee.

O for a soft and gentle wind!
    I heard a fair one cry;
But give to me the snoring breeze
    And white waves heaving high;
And white waves heaving high, my lads,
    The good ship tight and free—

390

A WET SHEET

The world of waters is our home,
    And merry men are we.

There 's tempest in yon hornéd moon,
    And lightning in yon cloud;
But hark the music, mariners!
    The wind is piping loud;
The wind is piping loud, my boys,
    The lightning flashes free—
While the hollow oak our palace is,
    Our heritage the sea.

WILLIAM TENNANT

1784–1848

184   *On the Road to Anster Fair*

SAY, Muse, who first, who last, on foot or steed,
  Came forth to see the sports at Anster town?
St. Andrew's sprightly students first proceed,
    Clad in their foppery of sleeveless gown;
Forth whistling from Salvador's gate they speed,
    Full many a mettlesome and fiery lown,
Forgetting Horace for a while, and Tully,
And mad to embag their limbs, and leap it beautifully. . .

Nor come they only down; in chaise or gig
    Th' endoctrin'd sage professors lolling ride,
Their heads with curl'd vastidity of wig
    Thatch'd round and round, and queerly beautified;
In silken hose is sheath'd each learned leg;
    White are their cravats, long and trimly tied.
Some say they came to jump for Maggie too,
But college records say they came the sport to view.

Next from Denino's every house and hut
  Her simply guileless people hie away;
That day the doors of parish-school were shut,
  And every scholar got his leave to play:
Down rush they, light of heart and light of foot,
  Big ploughmen, in their coats of hodden gray,
Weavers, despising now both web and treadle,
Collier, and collier's wife, and minister, and beadle.

Next, from the well-air'd ancient town of Crail,
  Go out her craftsmen with tumultuous din,
Her wind-bleach'd fishers, sturdy-limb'd and hale,
  Her in-knee'd tailors, garrulous and thin;
And some are flush'd with horns of pithy ale,
  And some are fierce with drams of smuggled gin,
While, to augment his drouth, each to his jaws
A good Crail capon holds, at which he rugs and gnaws.

And barefoot lasses, on whose ruddy face
  Unfurl'd is health's rejoicing banner seen,
Trick'd in their Sunday mutches, edged with lace,
  Tippets of white, and frocks of red and green,
Come tripping o'er the roads with jocund pace,
  Gay as May-morning, tidy, gim, and clean,
Whilst, joggling at each wench's side, her jo
Cracks many a rustic joke, his power of wit to show.

Then, jostling forward on the western road,
  Approach the folk of wind-swept Pittenweem,
So numerous that the highways, long and broad,
  One waving field of gowns and coat-tails seem;
The fat man puffing goes, oppress'd with load
  Of cumbrous flesh and corpulence extreme;

ON THE ROAD TO ANSTER FAIR

The lean man bounds along, and with his toes
Smites on the fat man's heels that slow before him goes.

St. Monance, Elie, and adjacent farms
    Turn their mechanics, fishers, farmers out;
Sunburnt and shoeless schoolboys rush in swarms,
    With childish trick, and revelry and shout;
Mothers bear little children in their arms,
    Attended by their giggling daughters stout;
Clowns, cobblers, cotters, tanners, weavers, beaux,
Hurry and hop along, in clusters and in rows.

And every husbandman round Largo Law
    Hath scrap'd his huge-wheel'd dung-cart fair and clean,
Wherein, on sacks stuff'd full of oaten straw,
    Sits the Goodwife, Tam, Katie, Jock, and Jean;
In flowers and ribbands dress'd, the horses draw
    Stoutly their creaking cumbersome machine,
As, on his cart-head, sits the Goodman proud,
And cheerily cracks his whip, and whistles clear and loud.

Then from her coal-pits Dysart vomits forth
    Her subterranean men, of colour dun,
Poor human mouldwarps! doom'd to scrape in earth,
    Cimmerian people, strangers to the sun;
Gloomy as soot, with faces grim and swarth,
    They march, most sourly leering every one,
Yet very keen at Anster Loan to share
The merriments and sports to be accomplish'd there.

Nor did Path-head detain her wrangling race
    Of weavers, toiling at their looms for bread;
For now their slippery shuttles rest a space
    From flying through their labyrinths of thread;

Their treadle-shaking feet now scour apace
   Through Gallowtown with levity of tread:
So on they pass, with sack in hand, full bent
To try their sinews' strength in dire experiment.

And long Kirkaldy from each dirty street
   Her numerous population eastward throws;
Her roguish boys with bare unstocking'd feet,
   Her rich ship-owners, generous and jocose,
Her prosperous merchants, sober and discreet,
   Her coxcombs pantaloon'd and powder'd beaux;
Her pretty lasses, tripping on their great toes,
With foreheads white as milk or any boil'd potatoes.

And from Kinghorn jump hastily along
   Her ferrymen and poor inhabitants;
And the upland hamlet where, as told in song,
   Tam Lutar play'd of yore his lively rants,
Is left dispeopled of her brose-fed throng,
   For eastward scud they now as thick as ants;
Dunfermline, too, so famed for checks and ticks,
Sends out her loom-bred men with bags and walking sticks.

And market-maids, and apron'd wives, that bring
   Their gingerbread in baskets to the Fair;
And cadgers with their creels, that hang by string
   From their lean horse' ribs, rubbing off the hair;
And crook-legg'd cripples, that on crutches swing
   Their shabby persons with a noble air;
And fiddlers, with their fiddles in their cases,
And packmen, with their packs of ribbons, gauze, and laces.

And from Kinross, whose dusty streets unpaved
   Are whirl'd through heaven on summer's windy day,

394

Whose plots of cabbage-bearing ground are laved
    By Leven's waves, that clear as crystal play,
Jog her brisk burghers, spruce and cleanly shaved,
    Her sullen cutters and her weavers gay,
Her ploughboys, in their botch'd and clumsy jackets,
Her clowns, with cobbled shoon stuck full of iron tackets.

Anster Fair, 1812

JOHN KENYON

1784–1856

185   *Champagne Rosé*

LILY on liquid roses floating—
  So floats yon foam o'er pink champagne—
Fain would I join such pleasant boating,
And prove that ruby main,
    And float away on wine!

Those seas are dangerous, greybeards swear—
Whose sea-beach is the goblet's brim;
And true it is—they drown old Care,
But what care we for him,
    So we but float on wine!

And true it is—they cross in pain,
Who sober cross the Stygian ferry;
But only make our Styx—champagne,
And we shall cross right merry,
    Floating away on wine!

Old Charon's self shall make him mellow,
Then gaily row his boat from shore;
While we, and every jovial fellow,
Hear—unconcerned—the oar,
    That dips itself in wine!

Written 1837; Poems, 1838

JAMES HENRY LEIGH HUNT

1784–1859

186 *To Hampstead*

WINTER has reached thee once again at last;
    And now the rambler, whom thy groves yet please,
Feels on his house-warm lips the thin air freeze;
While in his shrugging neck the resolute blast
Comes edging; and the leaves, in heaps down cast,
    He shuffles with his hastening foot, and sees
    The cold sky whitening through the wiry trees,
And sighs to think his loitering noons have passed.

And do I love thee less to paint thee so?
    No: this the season is of beauty still
        Doubled at heart,—of smoke with whirling glee
Uptumbling ever from the blaze below,
    And home remembered most,—and oh, loved hill,
        The second, and the last, away from thee!

Examiner, December 18, 1814;
Feast of the Poets, &c. (ed. 2), 1815

187 ' *Places of nestling green* '

A NOBLE range it was, of many a rood,
    Walled round with trees, and ending in a wood:
Indeed the whole was leafy; and it had
A winding stream about it, clear and glad,
That danced from shade to shade, and on its way
Seemed smiling with delight to feel the day.
There was the pouting rose, both red and white,
The flamy heart's-ease, flushed with purple light,
Blush-hiding strawberry, sunny-coloured box,
Hyacinth, handsome with his clustering locks,

396

PLACES OF NESTLING GREEN

The lady lily, looking gently down,
Pure lavender, to lay in bridal gown,
The daisy, lovely on both sides,—in short,
All the sweet cups to which the bees resort,
With plots of grass, and perfumed walks between
Of citron, honeysuckle and jessamine,
With orange, whose warm leaves so finely suit,
And look as if they'd shade a golden fruit;
And midst the flowers, turfed round beneath a shade
Of circling pines, a babbling fountain played,
And 'twixt their shafts you saw the water bright,
Which through the darksome tops glimmered with showering
    light.
So now you walked beside an odorous bed
Of gorgeous hues, white, azure, golden, red;
And now turned off into a leafy walk,
Close and continuous, fit for lovers' talk;
And now pursued the stream, and as you trod
Onward and onward o'er the velvet sod,
Felt on your face an air, watery and sweet,
And a new sense in your soft-lighting feet;
And then perhaps you entered upon shades,
Pillowed with dells and uplands 'twixt the glades,
Through which the distant palace, now and then,
Looked lordly forth with many-windowed ken;
A land of trees, which reaching round about,
In shady blessing stretched their old arms out,
With spots of sunny opening, and with nooks,
To lie and read in, sloping into brooks,
Where at her drink you started the slim deer,
Retreating lightly with a lovely fear.
And all about, the birds kept leafy house,

And sung and sparkled in and out the boughs;
And all about, a lovely sky of blue
Clearly was felt, or down the leaves laughed through.
And here and there, in every part, were seats,
Some in the open walks, some in retreats;
With bowering leaves o'erhead, to which the eye
Looked up half sweetly and half awfully,—
Places of nestling green, for poets made,
Where when the sunshine struck a yellow shade,
The slender trunks, to inward peeping sight
Thronged in dark pillars up the gold green light.

The Story of Rimini, 1816

188   *From ' The Nymphs '*

THERE are the fair-limbed Nymphs o' the Woods
         (Look ye
Whom kindred Fancies have brought after me!)
There are the fair-limbed Dryads, who love nooks
In the dry depth of oaks;
Or feel the air in groves, or pull green dresses
For their glad heads in rooty wildernesses;
Or on the golden turf, o'er the dark lines,
Which the sun makes when he declines,
Bend their white dances in and out the pines.
They tend all forests old, and meeting trees,
Wood, copse, or queach, or slippery dell o'erhung
With firs, and with their dusty apples strewn;
And let the visiting beams the boughs among,
And bless the trunks from clingings of disease
And wasted hearts that to the night-wind groan.
They screen the cuckoo when he sings; and teach

THE NYMPHS

The mother blackbird how to lead astray
The unformed spirit of the foolish boy
From thick to thick, from hedge to layery beech,
When he would steal the huddled nest away
Of yellow bills, up-gaping for their food,
And spoil the song of the free solitude.
And they, at sound of the brute, insolent horn,
Hurry the deer out of the dewy morn;
And take into their sudden laps with joy
The startled hare that did but peep abroad;
And from the trodden road
Help the bruised hedgehog. But when tired, they love
The back-turned pheasant, hanging from the tree
His sunny drapery;
And handy squirrel, nibbling hastily;
And fragrant-living bee,
So happy, that he will not move, not he,
Without a song; and hidden, amorous dove,
With his deep breath; and bird of wakeful glow,
Whose louder song is like the voice of life,
Triumphant o'er death's image; but whose deep,
Low, lovelier note is like a gentle wife,
A poor, a pensive, yet a happy one,
Stealing, when day-light's common tasks are done,
An hour for mother's work; and singing low,
While her tired husband and her children sleep.

Foliage, 1818

189　　　　　　*The Nile*

IT flows through old hushed Egypt and its sands,
　Like some grave mighty thought threading a dream,
　And times and things, as in that vision, seem
Keeping along it their eternal stands,—
Caves, pillars, pyramids, the shepherd bands
　That roamed through the young world, the glory extreme
　Of high Sesostris, and that southern beam,
The laughing queen that caught the world's great hands.

Then comes a mightier silence, stern and strong,
As of a world left empty of its throng,
　And the void weighs on us; and then we wake,
And hear the fruitful stream lapsing along
　Twixt villages, and think how we shall take
　Our own calm journey on for human sake.

Foliage, 1818

190　　　　　　*Epitaph on Erotion*

UNDERNEATH this greedy stone
　Lies little sweet Erotion;
Whom the Fates, with hearts as cold,
Nipped away at six years old.
Thou, whoever thou may'st be,
That hast this small field after me,
Let the yearly rites be paid
To her little slender shade;
So shall no disease or jar
Hurt thy house, or chill thy Lar;
But this tomb here be alone,
The only melancholy stone.

The Indicator, November 10, 1819;
Poetical Works, 1832

The Nun

Suggested by part of the Italian song, beginning
' Se monaca ti fai '

I

IF you become a nun, dear,
  A friar I will be;
In any cell you run, dear,
  Pray look behind for me.
The roses all turn pale, too;
The doves all take the veil, too;
  The blind will see the show:
What! you become a nun, my dear!
  I'll not believe it, no.

II

If you become a nun, dear,
  The bishop Love will be;
The Cupids every one, dear,
  Will chant ' We trust in thee: '
The incense will go sighing,
The candles fall a-dying,
  The water turn to wine:
What! you go take the vows, my dear!
  You may—but they'll be mine.

The Indicator, January 3, 1821;
Poetical Works, 1832

JAMES HENRY LEIGH HUNT

192 From ' Song of Fairies Robbing an Orchard '

WE, the Fairies, blithe and antic,
    Of dimensions not gigantic,
Though the moonshine mostly keep us,
Oft in orchards frisk and peep us.

Stolen sweets are always sweeter,
Stolen kisses much completer,
Stolen looks are nice in chapels,
Stolen, stolen, be your apples.

When to bed the world are bobbing,
Then 's the time for orchard-robbing;
Yet the fruit were scarce worth peeling,
Were it not for stealing, stealing.

Tatler, September 8, 1830;
Poetical Works, 1832

193 *A House and Grounds*

WERE this impossible, I know full well
    What sort of house should grace my garden-bell,—
A good, old country lodge, half hid with blooms
Of honied green, and quaint with straggling rooms,
A few of which, white-bedded and well swept,
For friends, whose names endear'd them, should be kept.
Of brick I'd have it, far more broad than high,
With green up to the door, and elm trees nigh;
And the warm sun should have it in his eye.

402

A HOUSE AND GROUNDS

The tiptoe traveller, peeping through the boughs
O'er my low wall, should bless the pleasant house,
And that my luck might not seem ill-bestow'd,
A bench and spring should greet him on the road.
My grounds should not be large; I like to go
To Nature for a range, and prospect too,
And cannot fancy she'll comprise for me,
Even in a park, her all-sufficiency.
Besides, my thoughts fly far; and when at rest,
Love, not a watch tower, but a lulling nest.
But all the ground I had should keep a look
Of Nature still, have birds'-nests and a brook;
One spot for flowers, the rest all turf and trees;
For I'd not grow my own bad lettuces.
I'd build a walk, however, against rain,
Long, peradventure, as my whole domain,
And so be sure of generous exercise,
The youth of age, and med'cine of the wise.
And this reminds me, that behind some screen
About my grounds, I'd have a bowling-green;
Such as in wits' and merry women's days
Suckling preferred before his walk of bays.
You may still see them, dead as haunts of fairies,
By the old seats of Killigrews and Careys,
Where all, alas, is vanished from the ring,
Wits and black eyes, the skittles and the king!

Poetical Works, 1832

194 *To an Early Primrose*

MILD offspring of a dark and sullen sire!
Whose modest form, so delicately fine,
    Was nurs'd in whirling storms,
    And cradled in the winds.

Thee, when young spring first questioned winter's sway,
And dar'd the sturdy Blust'rer to the fight,
    Thee on this bank he threw
    To mark his Victory.

In this low vale, the promise of the year,
Serene, thou openest to the nipping gale,
    Unnotic'd and alone,
    Thy tender elegance.

So Virtue blooms, brought forth amid the storms
Of chill adversity, in some lone walk
    Of life, she rears her head
    Obscure and unobserv'd;

While every bleaching breeze that on her blows,
Chastens her spotless purity of breast,
    And hardens her to bear
    Serene the ills of life.

Clifton Grove, &c., 1803

195 *Description of a Summer's Eve*

DOWN the sultry arc of day
    The burning wheels have urged their way,
And Eve along the western skies
Spreads her intermingling dyes.

DESCRIPTION OF A SUMMER'S EVE

Down the deep, the miry lane,
Creeking comes the empty wain,
And Driver on the shaft-horse sits,
Whistling now and then by fits;
And oft, with his accustom'd call,
Urging on the sluggish Ball.
The barn is still, the master's gone,
And Thresher puts his jacket on,
While Dick, upon the ladder tall,
Nails the dead kite to the wall.
Here comes shepherd Jack at last,
He has penned the sheep-cote fast,
For 'twas but two nights before,
A lamb was eaten on the moor:
His empty wallet *Rover* carries,
Nor for Jack, when near home, tarries.
With lolling tongue he runs to try,
If the horse-trough be not dry.
The milk is settled in the pans,
And supper messes in the cans;
In the hovel carts are wheeled,
And both the colts are drove a-field;
The horses are all bedded up,
And the ewe is with the tup.
The snare for Mister Fox is set,
The leaven laid, the thatching wet,
And Bess has slink'd away to talk
With Roger in the holly-walk.

Now on the settle all, but Bess,
Are set to eat their supper mess;
And little Tom, and roguish Kate,

Are swinging on the meadow-gate.
Now they chat of various things,
Of taxes, ministers, and kings,
Or else tell all the village news,
How madam did the 'squire refuse;
How parson on his tythes was bent,
And landlord oft distrained for rent.
Thus do they talk, till in the sky
The pale-ey'd moon is mounted high,
And from the alehouse drunken Ned
Had reeled—then hasten all to bed.
The mistress sees that lazy Kate
The happing coal on kitchen grate
Has laid—while master goes throughout,
Sees shutters fast, the mastiff out,
The candles safe, the hearths all clear,
And nought from thieves or fire to fear;
Then both to bed together creep,
And join the general troop of sleep.

Remains, vol. ii, 1808

196 *Song from Fragment of an Eccentric Drama*

I

DING-DONG! ding-dong!
 Merry, merry, go the bells,
Ding-dong! ding-dong!
Over the heath, over the moor, and over the dale,
 ' Swinging slow with sullen roar,'
Dance, dance away the jocund roundelay!
Ding-dong, ding-dong, calls us away.

FRAGMENT OF AN ECCENTRIC DRAMA

II

Round the oak, and round the elm,
   Merrily foot it o'er the ground!
The sentry ghost it stands aloof,
   So merrily, merrily, foot it round.
     Ding-dong! ding-dong!
     Merry, merry, go the bells
   Swelling in the nightly gale.
       The sentry ghost,
       It keeps its post,
   And soon, and soon, our sports must fail!
But let us trip the nightly ground,
While the merry, merry, bells ring round.

III

Hark! hark! the death-watch ticks!
   See, see, the winding-sheet!
     Our dance is done,
     Our race is run,
And we must lie at the alder's feet!
     Ding-dong, ding-dong,
     Merry, merry, go the bells,
Swinging o'er the weltering wave!
     And we must seek
     Our death-beds bleak,
Where the green sod grows upon the grave.

Remains, vol. i, 1808

JOHN WILSON

1785–1854

197 *Written on the banks of Wastwater during a calm*

IS this the Lake, the cradle of the storms,
  Where silence never tames the mountain-roar,
Where poets fear their self-created forms,
Or sunk in trance severe, their God adore?
Is this the Lake, for ever dark and loud
With wave and tempest, cataract and cloud?
Wondrous, O Nature! is thy sovereign power,
That gives to horror hours of peaceful mirth;
For here might beauty build her summer-bower!
Lo! where yon rainbow spans the smiling earth,
And, clothed in glory, through a silent shower
The mighty Sun comes forth, a godlike birth;
While, 'neath his loving eye, the gentle Lake
Lies like a sleeping child too blest to wake!

The Isle of Palms, &c., 1812

198 *' Come forth, come forth!'*

COME forth, come forth! it were a sin
  To stay at home to-day!
Stay no more loitering within,
  Come to the woods away!

The long green grass is filled with flowers,
  The clover's deep dim red
Is brighten'd with the morning showers,
  That on the winds have fled.

COME FORTH, COME FORTH!

Scatter'd about the deep blue sky,
 In white and flying clouds,
Some bright brief rains are all that lie
 Within those snowy shrouds.

Now, look!—our weather-glass is spread—
 The pimpernel, whose flower
Closes its leaves of spotted red
 Against a rainy hour.

That first pale green is on the trees;
 That verdure more like bloom;
Yon elm-bough hath a horde of bees,
 Lured by the faint perfume.

The cherry orchard flings on high
 Its branches, whence are strown
Blossoms like snow, but with an eye
 Dark, maiden, as thine own!

As yet our flowers are chiefly those
 Which fill the sun-touch'd bough,
Within the sleeping soil repose
 Those of the radiant brow.

But we have daisies, which, like love
 Or hope, spring everywhere;
And primroses, which droop above
 Some self-consuming care.

So sad, so spiritual, so pale,
 Born all too near the snow,
They pine for that sweet southern gale
 Which they will never know.

It is too soon for deeper shade;
    But let us skirt the wood,
The blackbird there, whose nest is made,
    Sits singing to her brood.

These pleasant hours will soon be flown;
    Love! make no more delay—
I am too glad to be alone,
    Come forth with me to-day!

Blackwood's Magazine ('Noctes Ambrosianae'), May 1834

THOMAS LOVE PEACOCK

1785–1866

199   *Beneath the Cypress Shade*

I DUG, beneath the cypress shade,
    What well might seem an elfin's grave;
And every pledge in earth I laid,
    That erst thy false affection gave.

I pressed them down the sod beneath;
    I placed one mossy stone above;
And twined the rose's fading wreath
    Around the sepulchre of love.

Frail as thy love, the flowers were dead,
    Ere yet the evening sun was set:
But years shall see the cypress spread,
    Immutable as my regret.

Written after 1806
First published in 1875

IN his last binn Sir Peter lies,
  Who knew not what it was to frown:
Death took him mellow, by surprise,
  And in his cellar stopped him down.
Through all our land we could not boast
  A knight more gay, more prompt than he,
To rise and fill a bumper toast,
  And pass it round with THREE TIMES THREE.

None better knew the feast to sway,
  Or keep Mirth's boat in better trim:
For Nature had but little clay
  Like that of which she moulded him.
The meanest guest that graced his board
  Was there the freest of the free,
His bumper toast when Peter poured,
  And passed it round with THREE TIMES THREE.

He kept at true good humour's mark,
  The social flow of pleasure's tide:
He never made a brow look dark,
  Nor caused a tear, but when he died.
No sorrow round his tomb should dwell:
  More pleased his gay old ghost would be,
For funeral song, and passing bell,
  To hear no sound but THREE TIMES THREE.

Headlong Hall, 1816

201   *Chorus*

HAIL to the Headlong! the Headlong Ap-Headlong!
All hail to the Headlong, the Headlong Ap-Headlong!
   The Headlong Ap-Headlong
   Ap-Breakneck Ap-Headlong
Ap-Cataract Ap-Pistyll Ap-Rhaiader Ap-Headlong!

The bright bowl we steep in the name of the Headlong:
Let the youths pledge it deep to the Headlong Ap-Headlong,
   And the rosy-lipped lasses
   Touch the brim as it passes,
And kiss the red tide for the Headlong Ap-Headlong!

The loud harp resounds in the hall of the Headlong:
The light step rebounds in the hall of the Headlong:
   Where shall music invite us,
   Or beauty delight us,
If not in the hall of the Headlong Ap-Headlong?

Huzza! to the health of the Headlong Ap-Headlong!
Fill the bowl, fill in floods, to the health of the Headlong!
   Till the stream ruby-glowing,
   On all sides o'erflowing,
Shall fall in cascades to the health of the Headlong!
   The Headlong Ap-Headlong
   Ap-Breakneck Ap-Headlong
Ap-Cataract Ap-Pistyll Ap-Rhaiader Ap-Headlong!

Headlong Hall, 1816

THE ivy o'er the mouldering wall
   Spreads like a tree, the growth of years:
The wild wind through the doorless hall
A melancholy music rears,
A solitary voice, that sighs,
O'er man's forgotten pageantries.

   Above the central gate, the clock,
Through clustering ivy dimly seen,
Seems, like the ghost of Time, to mock
The wrecks of power that once has been.
The hands are rusted on its face;
Even where they ceased, in years gone by,
To keep the flying moments' pace;
Fixing, in Fancy's thoughtful eye,
A point of ages passed away,
A speck of time, that owns no tie
With aught that lives and breathes to-day.

   But 'mid the rank and towering grass,
Where breezes wave, in mournful sport,
The weeds that choke the ruined court,
The careless hours, that circling pass,
Still trace upon the dialled brass
The shade of their unvarying way:
And evermore, with every ray
That breaks the clouds and gilds the air,
Time's stealthy steps are imaged there:
Even as the long-revolving years
In self-reflecting circles flow,
From the first bud the hedgerow bears,

To wintry Nature's robe of snow.
The changeful forms of mortal things
Decay and pass; and art and power
Oppose in vain the doom that flings
Oblivion on their closing hour:
While still, to every woodland vale,
New blooms, new fruits, the seasons bring,
For other eyes and lips to hail
With looks and sounds of welcoming:
As where some stream light-eddying roves
By sunny meads and shadowy groves,
Wave following wave departs for ever,
But still flows on the eternal river.

Melincourt, 1817

203 *From ' Rhododaphne '*

(i)

Larissa

OH youth, beware! that laurel-rose
   Around Larissa's evil walls
In tufts of rank luxuriance grows,
'Mid dreary valleys, by the falls
Of haunted streams; and magic knows
No herb or plant of deadlier might,
When impious footsteps wake by night
The echoes of those dismal dells,
What time the murky midnight dew
Trembles on many a leaf and blossom,
That draws from earth's polluted bosom
Mysterious virtue, to imbue

RHODODAPHNE

The chalice of unnatural spells.
Oft, those dreary rocks among,
The murmurs of unholy song,
Breathed by lips as fair as hers
By whose false hands that flower was given,
The solid earth's firm breast have riven,
And burst the silent sepulchres,
And called strange shapes of ghastly fear,
To hold, beneath the sickening moon,
Portentous parle, at night's deep noon,
With beauty skilled in mysteries drear.
Oh, youth! Larissa's maids are fair;
But the dæmons of the earth and air
Their spells obey, their councils share,
And wide o'er earth and ocean bear
Their mandates to the storms that tear
The rock-enrooted oak, and sweep
With whirlwind wings the labouring deep.
Their words of power can make the streams
Roll refluent on their mountain-springs,
Can torture sleep with direful dreams,
And on the shapes of earthly things,
Man, beast, bird, fish, with influence strange,
Breathe foul and fearful interchange,
And fix in marble bonds the form
Erewhile with natural being warm,
And give to senseless stones and stocks
Motion, and breath, and shape that mocks,
As far as nicest eye can scan,
The action and the life of man.
Beware! yet once again beware!
Ere round thy inexperienced mind,

With voice and semblance falsely fair,
A chain Thessalian magic bind,
Which never more, oh youth! believe,
Shall either earth or heaven unweave.

(ii)

Bacchus

BACCHUS by the lonely ocean
Stood in youthful semblance fair:
Summer winds, with gentle motion,
Waved his black and curling hair.
Streaming from his manly shoulders
Robes of gold and purple dye
Told of spoil to fierce beholders
In their black ship sailing by.
On the vessel's deck they placed him
Strongly bound in triple bands;
But the iron rings that braced him
Melted, wax-like, from his hands.
Then the pilot spake in terror:
' 'Tis a god in mortal form!
Seek the land; repair your error
Ere his wrath invoke the storm.'—
' Silence! '—cried the frowning master,—
' Mind the helm: the breeze is fair:
Coward! cease to bode disaster:
Leave to men the captive's care.'
While he speaks, and fiercely tightens
In the full free breeze the sail,
From the deck wine bubbling lightens,
Winy fragrance fills the gale.

Gurgling in ambrosial lustre
Flows the purple-eddying wine:
O'er the yard-arms trail and cluster
Tendrils of the mantling vine:
Grapes, beneath the broad leaves springing,
Blushing as in vintage-hours,
Droop, while round the tall mast clinging
Ivy twines its bud and flowers,
Fast with graceful berries blackening:—
Garlands hang on every oar:
Then in fear the cordage slackening,
One and all, they cry, ' To shore! '—
Bacchus changed his shape, and glaring
With a lion's eyeballs wide,
Roared: the pirate-crew, despairing,
Plunged amid the foaming tide.
Through the azure depths they flitted
Dolphins by transforming fate:
But the god the pilot pitied,
Saved, and made him rich and great.

Rhododaphne, 1818

204   *Song, by Mr. Cypress*

THERE is a fever of the spirit,
    The brand of Cain's unresting doom,
Which in the lone dark souls that bear it
    Glows like the lamp in Tullia's tomb:
Unlike the lamp, its subtle fire
    Burns, blasts, consumes its cell, the heart,
Till, one by one, hope, joy, desire,
    Like dreams of shadowy smoke depart.

417

When hope, love, life itself, are only
    Dust—spectral memories—dead and cold—
The unfed fire burns bright and lonely,
    Like that undying lamp of old:
And by that drear illumination,
    Till time its clay-built home has rent,
Thought broods on feeling's desolation—
    The soul is its own monument.

Nightmare Abbey, 1818

205   *Seamen Three*

SEAMEN three! What men be ye?
  Gotham's three wise men we be.
Whither in your bowl so free?
To rake the moon from out the sea.
The bowl goes trim. The moon doth shine.
And our ballast is old wine;
And your ballast is old wine.

Who art thou, so fast adrift?
I am he they call Old Care.
Here on board we will thee lift.
No: I may not enter there.
Wherefore so? 'Tis Jove's decree,
In a bowl Care may not be;
In a bowl Care may not be.

Fear ye not the waves that roll?
No: in charmed bowl we swim.
What the charm that floats the bowl?
Water may not pass the brim.

SEAMEN THREE

The bowl goes trim. The moon doth shine.
And our ballast is old wine;
And your ballast is old wine.

Nightmare Abbey, 1818

206 *Margaret Love Peacock*

(for her tombstone, 1826)

LONG night succeeds thy little day;
  Oh blighted blossom! can it be,
That this grey stone and grassy clay
  Have closed our anxious care of thee?

The half-form'd speech of artless thought,
  That spoke a mind beyond thy years;
The song, the dance, by nature taught;
  The sunny smiles, the transient tears;

The symmetry of face and form,
  The eye with light and life replete;
The little heart so fondly warm;
  The voice so musically sweet.

These lost to hope, in memory yet
  Around the hearts that lov'd thee cling,
Shadowing, with long and vain regret,
  The too fair promise of thy spring.

Works, i. 1875

207 *The Song of the Four Winds*

WIND from the north: the young spring day
Is pleasant on the sunny mead;
The merry harps at evening play;
The dance gay youths and maidens lead:
The thrush makes chorus from the thorn:
The mighty drinker fills his horn.

Wind from the east: the shore is still;
The mountain-clouds fly tow'rds the sea;
The ice is on the winter-rill;
The great hall fire is blazing free:
The prince's circling feast is spread:
Drink fills with fumes the brainless head.

Wind from the south: in summer shade
'Tis sweet to hear the loud harp ring;
Sweet is the step of comely maid,
Who to the bard a cup doth bring:
The black crow flies where carrion lies:
Where pignuts lurk, the swine will work.

Wind from the west: the autumnal deep
Rolls on the shore its billowy pride:
He, who the rampart's watch must keep,
Will mark with awe the rising tide:
The high springtide, that bursts its mound,
May roll o'er miles of level ground.

Wind from the west: the mighty wave
Of ocean bounds o'er rock and sand;
The foaming surges roar and rave
Against the bulwarks of the land:

THE SONG OF THE FOUR WINDS

When waves are rough, and winds are high,
Good is the land that 's high and dry.

Wind from the west: the storm-clouds rise;
The breakers rave; the whirlblasts roar,
The mingled rage of seas and skies
Bursts on the low and lonely shore:
When safety's far, and danger nigh,
Swift feet the readiest aid supply.

Misfortunes of Elphin, 1829

Song of Gwythno

STAND forth, Seithenyn: winds are high:
Look down beneath the lowering sky;
Look from the rock: what meets thy sight?
Nought but the breakers rolling white.

Stand forth, Seithenyn: winds are still:
Look from the rock and heathy hill
For Gwythno's realm: what meets thy view?
Nought but the ocean's desert blue.

Curst be the treacherous mound, that gave
A passage to the mining wave:
Curst be the cup, with mead-froth crowned,
That charmed from thought the trusted mound.

A tumult, and a cry to heaven!
The white surf breaks; the mound is riven:
Through the wide rift the ocean-spring
Bursts with tumultuous ravaging.

THOMAS LOVE PEACOCK

The western ocean's stormy might
Is curling o'er the rampart's height:
Destruction strikes with want and scorn
Presumption, from abundance born.

The tumult of the western deep
Is on the winds, affrighting sleep:
It thunders at my chamber-door;
It bids me wake, to sleep no more.

The tumult of the midnight sea
Swells inland, wildly, fearfully:
The mountain-caves respond its shocks
Among the unaccustomed rocks.

The tumult of the vext sea-coast
Rolls inland like an armed host:
It leaves, for flocks and fertile land,
But foaming waves and treacherous sand.

The wild sea rolls where long have been
Glad homes of men, and pastures green:
To arrogance and wealth succeed
Wide ruin and avenging need.

Seithenyn, come: I call in vain:
The high of birth and weak of brain
Sleeps under ocean's lonely roar
Between the rampart and the shore.

The eternal waste of waters, spread
Above his unrespected head,
The blue expanse, with foam besprent,
Is his too glorious monument.

Misfortunes of Elphin, 1829

THE mountain sheep are sweeter,
   But the valley sheep are fatter;
We therefore deemed it meeter
To carry off the latter.
We made an expedition;
We met a host, and quelled it;
We forced a strong position,
And killed the men who held it.

On Dyfed's richest valley,
Where herds of kine were browsing,
We made a mighty sally,
To furnish our carousing.
Fierce warriors rushed to meet us;
We met them, and o'erthrew them:
They struggled hard to beat us;
But we conquered them, and slew them.

As we drove our prize at leisure,
The king marched forth to catch us:
His rage surpassed all measure,
But his people could not match us.
He fled to his hall-pillars;
And, ere our force we led off,
Some sacked his house and cellars,
While others cut his head off.

We there, in strife bewildr'ing,
Spilt blood enough to swim in:
We orphaned many children,
And widowed many women.

The eagles and the ravens
We glutted with our foemen;
The heroes and the cravens,
The spearmen and the bowmen.

We brought away from battle,
And much their land bemoaned them,
Two thousand head of cattle,
And the head of him who owned them:
Ednyfed, king of Dyfed,
His head was borne before us;
His wine and beasts supplied our feasts,
And his overthrow, our chorus.

Misfortunes of Elphin, 1829

210　　　　　*Merlin's Apple-trees*

FAIR the gift to Merlin given,
　　Apple-trees seven score and seven
Equal all in age and size;
On a green hill-slope, that lies
Basking in the southern sun,
Where bright waters murmuring run.

Just beneath the pure stream flows;
High above the forest grows;
Not again on earth is found
Such a slope of orchard ground:
Song of birds, and hum of bees,
Ever haunt the apple-trees.

Lovely green their leaves in spring;
Lovely bright their blossoming:

MERLIN'S APPLE-TREES

Sweet the shelter and the shade
By their summer foliage made:
Sweet the fruit their ripe boughs hold,
Fruit delicious, tinged with gold.

Gloyad, nymph with tresses bright,
Teeth of pearl, and eyes of light,
Guards these gifts of Ceidio's son,
Gwendol, the lamented one,
Him, whose keen-edged sword no more
Flashes 'mid the battle's roar.

War has raged on vale and hill:
That fair grove was peaceful still.
There have chiefs and princes sought
Solitude and tranquil thought:
There have kings, from courts and throngs,
Turned to Merlin's wild-wood songs.

Now from echoing woods I hear
Hostile axes sounding near:
On the sunny slope reclined,
Feverish grief disturbs my mind,
Lest the wasting edge consume
My fair spot of fruit and bloom.

Lovely trees, that long alone
In the sylvan vale have grown,
Bare, your sacred plot around,
Grows the once wood-waving ground:
Fervent valour guards ye still;
Yet my soul presages ill.

THOMAS LOVE PEACOCK

Well I know, when years have flown,
Briars shall grow where ye have grown:
Them in turn shall power uproot;
Then again shall flowers and fruit
Flourish in the sunny breeze,
On my new-born apple-trees.

Misfortunes of Elphin, 1829

LUKE AYLMER CONOLLY

c. 1786–1833

211   *The Enchanted Island*

TO Rathlin's Isle I chanced to sail
     When summer breezes softly blew,
And there I heard so sweet a tale
     That oft I wished it could be true.

They said, at eve, when rude winds sleep,
     And hushed is ev'ry turbid swell,
A mermaid rises from the deep
     And sweetly tunes her magic shell.

And while she plays, rock, dell, and cave,
     In dying falls the sound retain,
As if some choral spirits gave
     Their aid to swell her witching strain.

Then summoned by that dulcet note,
     Uprising to th' admiring view,
A fairy island seems to float
     With tints of many a gorgeous hue.

THE ENCHANTED ISLAND

And glittering fanes, and lofty towers,
    All on this fairy isle are seen:
And waving trees, and shady bowers,
    With more than mortal verdure green.

And as it moves, the western sky
    Glows with a thousand varying rays;
And the calm sea, tinged with each dye,
    Seems like a golden flood of haze.

They also say, if earth or stone
    From verdant Erin's hallowed land
Were on this magic island thrown,
    For ever fixed it then would stand.

But when for this some little boat
    In silence ventures from the shore,
The mermaid sinks—hushed is the note—
    The fairy isle is seen no more.

Legendary Tales in Verse, 1813

MARY RUSSELL MITFORD

1787–1855

212   *Written in July, 1824*

HOW oft amid the heaped and bedded hay,
    Under the oak's broad shadow deep and strong,
  Have we sate listening to the noonday song
(If song it were, monotonously gay)
Which crept along the field, the summer lay
  Of the grasshopper. Summer is come in pride
  Of fruit and flower, garlanded as a bride,
And crowned with corn, and graced with length of day.
  But cold is come with her. We sit not now

MARY RUSSELL MITFORD

Listening that merry music of the earth
   Like Ariel ' beneath the blossomed bough; '
But all for chillness round the social hearth
We cluster.—Hark!—a note of kindred mirth
   Echoes!—Oh, wintery cricket, welcome thou!

Dramatic Scenes, 1827

BRYAN WALLER PROCTER

1787–1874

213   *Inscription for a Fountain*

REST! This little Fountain runs
   Thus for aye:—It never stays
For the look of summer suns,
   Nor the cold of winter days.
Whosoe'er shall wander near,
   When the Syrian heat is worst,
Let him hither come, nor fear
   Lest he may not slake his thirst:
He will find this little river
Running still as bright as ever.
Let him drink, and onwards hie,
Bearing but in thought that I,
Erotas, bade the Naiad fall,
And thank the great god Pan for all!

Songs, 1832

214   *From ' A Vision '*

This is little more than the recollection of an actual dream.

FIRST, I saw a landscape fair
   Towering in the clear blue air,
Like Ida's woody summits and sweet fields,
Where all that Nature yields

A VISION

Flourishes. Three proud shapes were seen,
Standing upon the green
Like Olympian queens descended.
One was unadorned, and one
Wore her golden tresses bound
With simple flowers; the third was crowned,
And from amidst her raven hair,
Like stars, imperial jewels shone.
—Not one of those figures divine
But might have sate in Juno's chair,
And smiled in great equality
On Jove, though the blue skies were shaken;
Or, with superior aspect, taken
From Hebe's hand nectarean wine.
And that Dardanian boy was there
Whom pale Œnone loved: his hair
Was black, and curl'd his temples round;
His limbs were free and his forehead fair,
And as he stood on a rising ground,
And back his dark locks proudly tossed,
A shepherd youth he looked, but trod
On the green sward like a god;
Most like Apollo when he played
('Fore Midas,) in the Phrygian shade,
With Pan, and to the Sylvan host.

Dramatic Scenes, ed. 2, 1820

215 *From ' English Bards and Scotch Reviewers '*

(i)

NEXT comes the dull disciple of thy school,
   That mild apostate from poetic rule,
The simple Wordsworth, framer of a lay
As soft as evening in his favourite May,
Who warns his friend ' to shake off toil and trouble,
And quit his books, for fear of growing double; '
Who, both by precept and example, shows
That prose is verse, and verse is merely prose;
Convincing all, by demonstration plain,
Poetic souls delight in prose insane;
And Christmas stories tortured into rhyme
Contain the essence of the true sublime.
Thus, when he tells the tale of Betty Foy,
The idiot mother of ' an idiot boy; '
A moon-struck, silly lad, who lost his way,
And, like his bard, confounded night with day;
So close on each pathetic part he dwells,
And each adventure so sublimely tells,
That all who view the ' idiot in his glory '
Conceive the bard the hero of the story.

Shall gentle Coleridge pass unnoticed here,
To turgid ode and tumid stanza dear?
Though themes of innocence amuse him best,
Yet still obscurity 's a welcome guest.
If Inspiration should her aid refuse
To him who takes a pixy for a muse,

Yet none in lofty numbers can surpass
The bard who soars to elegise an ass.
So well the subject suits his noble mind,
He brays the laureat of the long-ear'd kind.

(ii)

ILLUSTRIOUS Holland! hard would be his lot,
His hirelings mention'd, and himself forgot!
Holland, with Henry Petty at his back,
The whipper-in and huntsman of the pack.
Blest be the banquets spread at Holland House,
Where Scotchmen feed, and critics may carouse!
Long, long beneath that hospitable roof
Shall Grub-street dine, while duns are kept aloof.
See honest Hallam lay aside his fork,
Resume his pen, review his Lordship's work,
And, grateful for the dainties on his plate,
Declare his landlord can at least translate!
Dunedin! view thy children with delight,
They write for food—and feed because they write:
And lest, when heated with the unusual grape,
Some glowing thoughts should to the press escape,
And tinge with red the female reader's cheek,
My lady skims the cream of each critique;
Breathes o'er the page her purity of soul,
Reforms each error, and refines the whole.

English Bards and Scotch Reviewers, 1809

GEORGE GORDON, LORD BYRON

216   *Written after swimming from Sestos
               to Abydos*

IF, in the month of dark December,
    Leander, who was nightly wont
(What maid will not the tale remember?)
    To cross thy stream, broad Hellespont!

If, when the wintry tempest roar'd,
    He sped to Hero, nothing loth,
And thus of old thy current pour'd,
    Fair Venus! how I pity both!

For *me*, degenerate modern wretch,
    Though in the genial month of May,
My dripping limbs I faintly stretch,
    And think I've done a feat to-day.

But since he cross'd the rapid tide,
    According to the doubtful story,
To woo,—and—Lord knows what beside,
    And swam for Love, as I for Glory;

'Twere hard to say who fared the best:
    Sad mortals! thus the gods still plague you!
He lost his labour, I my jest;
    For he was drown'd, and I've the ague.

                              Childe Harold, 1812

(*i*)

Greece

AND yet how lovely in thine age of woe,
   Land of lost gods and godlike men, art thou!
Thy vales of evergreen, thy hills of snow,
Proclaim thee Nature's varied favourite now:
Thy fanes, thy temples to thy surface bow,
Commingling slowly with heroic earth,
Broke by the share of every rustic plough:
So perish monuments of mortal birth,
So perish all in turn, save well-recorded Worth;

Save where some solitary column mourns
Above its prostrate brethren of the cave;
Save where Tritonia's airy shrine adorns
Colonna's cliff, and gleams along the wave;
Save o'er some warrior's half-forgotten grave,
Where the gray stones and unmolested grass
Ages, but not oblivion, feebly brave;
While strangers only not regardless pass,
Lingering like me, perchance, to gaze, and sigh ' Alas! '

Yet are thy skies as blue, thy crags as wild;
Sweet are thy groves, and verdant are thy fields,
Thine olive ripe as when Minerva smiled,
And still his honey'd wealth Hymettus yields;
There the blithe bee his fragrant fortress builds,
The freeborn wanderer of thy mountain-air;
Apollo still thy long, long summer gilds,
Still in his beam Mendeli's marbles glare;
Art, Glory, Freedom fail, but Nature still is fair.

GEORGE GORDON, LORD BYRON

Where'er we tread 't is haunted, holy ground;
No earth of thine is lost in vulgar mould,
But one vast realm of wonder spreads around,
And all the Muse's tales seem truly told,
Till the sense aches with gazing to behold
The scenes our earliest dreams have dwelt upon;
Each hill and dale, each deepening glen and wold
Defies the power which crush'd thy temples gone:
Age shakes Athena's tower, but spares gray Marathon.

The sun, the soil, but not the slave, the same;
Unchanged in all except its foreign lord;
Preserves alike its bounds and boundless fame
The Battle-field, where Persia's victim horde
First bow'd beneath the brunt of Hellas' sword,
As on the morn to distant Glory dear,
When Marathon became a magic word;
Which utter'd, to the hearer's eye appear
The camp, the host, the fight, the conqueror's career,

The flying Mede, his shaftless broken bow;
The fiery Greek, his red pursuing spear;
Mountains above, Earth's, Ocean's plain below;
Death in the front, Destruction in the rear!
Such was the scene—what now remaineth here?
What sacred trophy marks the hallow'd ground,
Recording Freedom's smile and Asia's tear?
The rifled urn, the violated mound,
The dust thy courser's hoof, rude stranger! spurns around.

Canto II, stanzas lxxxv–xc
Childe Harold, I and II, 1812

434

(*ii*)

Childe Harold

WHERE rose the mountains, there to him were
    friends;
Where roll'd the ocean, thereon was his home;
Where a blue sky, and glowing clime, extends,
He had the passion and the power to roam;
The desert, forest, cavern, breaker's foam,
Were unto him companionship; they spake
A mutual language, clearer than the tome
Of his land's tongue, which he would oft forsake
For Nature's pages glass'd by sunbeams on the lake.

Like the Chaldean, he could watch the stars,
Till he had peopled them with beings bright
As their own beams; and earth, and earth-born jars,
And human frailties, were forgotten quite:
Could he have kept his spirit to that flight
He had been happy; but this clay will sink
Its spark immortal, envying it the light
To which it mounts, as if to break the link
That keeps us from yon heaven which woos us to its brink.

But in Man's dwellings he became a thing
Restless and worn, and stern and wearisome,
Droop'd as a wild-born falcon with clipt wing,
To whom the boundless air alone were home:
Then came his fit again, which to o'ercome,

435

As eagerly the barr'd-up bird will beat
His breast and beak against his wiry dome
Till the blood tinge his plumage, so the heat
Of his impeded soul would through his bosom eat.

Canto III, stanzas xiii–xv

(iii)

Waterloo

THERE was a sound of revelry by night,
  And Belgium's capital had gather'd then
Her Beauty and her Chivalry, and bright
The lamps shone o'er fair women and brave men;
A thousand hearts beat happily; and when
Music arose with its voluptuous swell,
Soft eyes look'd love to eyes which spake again,
And all went merry as a marriage bell;
But hush! hark! a deep sound strikes like a rising knell!

Did ye not hear it?—No; 't was but the wind,
Or the car rattling o'er the stony street;
On with the dance! let joy be unconfined;
No sleep till morn, when Youth and Pleasure meet
To chase the glowing Hours with flying feet—
But hark!—that heavy sound breaks in once more,
As if the clouds its echo would repeat;
And nearer, clearer, deadlier than before!
Arm! Arm! it is—it is—the cannon's opening roar!

Within a window'd niche of that high hall
Sate Brunswick's fated chieftain; he did hear
That sound the first amidst the festival,
And caught its tone with Death's prophetic ear;

And when they smiled because he deem'd it near,
His heart more truly knew that peal too well
Which stretch'd his father on a bloody bier,
And roused the vengeance blood alone could quell;
He rush'd into the field, and, foremost fighting, fell.

Ah! then and there was hurrying to and fro,
And gathering tears, and tremblings of distress,
And cheeks all pale, which but an hour ago
Blush'd at the praise of their own loveliness;
And there were sudden partings, such as press
The life from out young hearts, and choking sighs
Which ne'er might be repeated; who could guess
If ever more should meet those mutual eyes,
Since upon night so sweet such awful morn could rise!

And there was mounting in hot haste: the steed,
The mustering squadron, and the clattering car,
Went pouring forward with impetuous speed,
And swiftly forming in the ranks of war;
And the deep thunder peal on peal afar;
And near, the beat of the alarming drum
Roused up the soldier ere the morning star;
While throng'd the citizens with terror dumb,
Or whispering, with white lips—' The foe! they come! they
    come!'

And wild and high the ' Cameron's gathering ' rose!
The war-note of Lochiel, which Albyn's hills
Have heard, and heard, too, have her Saxon foes:—
How in the noon of night that pibroch thrills,
Savage and shrill! But with the breath which fills

Their mountain-pipe, so fill the mountaineers
With the fierce native daring which instils
The stirring memory of a thousand years,
And Evan's, Donald's fame rings in each clansman's ears!

And Ardennes waves above them her green leaves,
Dewy with nature's tear-drops as they pass,
Grieving, if aught inanimate e'er grieves,
Over the unreturning brave,—alas!
Ere evening to be trodden like the grass
Which now beneath them, but above shall grow
In its next verdure, when this fiery mass
Of living valour, rolling on the foe
And burning with high hope, shall moulder cold and low.

Last noon beheld them full of lusty life,
Last eve in Beauty's circle proudly gay,
The midnight brought the signal-sound of strife,
The morn the marshalling in arms,—the day
Battle's magnificently stern array!
The thunder-clouds close o'er it, which when rent
The earth is cover'd thick with other clay,
Which her own clay shall cover, heap'd and pent,
Rider and horse,—friend, foe,—in one red burial blent!

Their praise is hymn'd by loftier harps than mine:
Yet one I would select from that proud throng,
Partly because they blend me with his line,
And partly that I did his sire some wrong,
And partly that bright names will hallow song;
And his was of the bravest, and when shower'd
The death-bolts deadliest the thinn'd files along,

Even where the thickest of war's tempest lower'd,
They reach'd no nobler breast than thine, young gallant
      Howard!

There have been tears and breaking hearts for thee,
And mine were nothing had I such to give;
But when I stood beneath the fresh green tree,
Which living waves where thou didst cease to live,
And saw around me the wide field revive
With fruits and fertile promise, and the Spring
Came forth her work of gladness to contrive,
With all her reckless birds upon the wing,
I turn'd from all she brought to those she could not bring.

               Canto III, stanzas xxi–xxx

(*iv*)

Napoleon

THERE sunk the greatest, nor the worst of men,
  Whose spirit, antithetically mixt,
One moment of the mightiest, and again
On little objects with like firmness fixt;
Extreme in all things! hadst thou been betwixt,
Thy throne had still been thine, or never been;
For daring made thy rise as fall: thou seek'st
Even now to re-assume the imperial mien,
And shake again the world, the Thunderer of the scene!

Conqueror and captive of the earth art thou!
She trembles at thee still and thy wild name
Was ne'er more bruited in men's minds than now
That thou art nothing, save the jest of Fame,

Who woo'd thee once, thy vassal, and became
The flatterer of thy fierceness, till thou wert
A god unto thyself; nor less the same
To the astounded kingdoms all inert,
Who deem'd thee for a time whate'er thou didst assert.

Oh, more or less than man—in high or low,
Battling with nations, flying from the field;
Now making monarch's necks thy footstool, now
More than thy meanest soldier taught to yield;
An empire thou couldst crush, command, rebuild,
But govern not thy pettiest passion, nor,
However deeply in men's spirits skill'd,
Look through thine own, nor curb the lust of war,
Nor learn that tempted Fate will leave the loftiest star.

Yet well thy soul hath brook'd the turning tide
With that untaught innate philosophy,
Which, be it wisdom, coldness, or deep pride,
Is gall and wormwood to an enemy.
When the whole host of hatred stood hard by,
To watch and mock thee shrinking, thou hast smiled
With a sedate and all-enduring eye;—
When Fortune fled her spoil'd and favourite child,
He stood unbow'd beneath the ills upon him piled.

Sager than in thy fortunes; for in them
Ambition steel'd thee on too far to show
That just habitual scorn, which could contemn
Men and their thoughts; 't was wise to feel, not so
To wear it ever on thy lip and brow,
And spurn the instruments thou wert to use
Till they were turn'd unto thine overthrow:

'Tis but a worthless world to win or lose;
So hath it proved to thee, and all such lot who choose.

If, like a tower upon a headland rock,
Thou hadst been made to stand or fall alone,
Such scorn of man had help'd to brave the shock;
But men's thoughts were the steps which paved thy throne,
Their admiration thy best weapon shone;
The part of Philip's son was thine, not then
(Unless aside thy purple had been thrown)
Like stern Diogenes to mock at men;
For sceptred cynics earth were far too wide a den.

But quiet to quick bosoms is a hell,
And *there* hath been thy bane; there is a fire
And motion of the soul which will not dwell
In its own narrow being, but aspire
Beyond the fitting medium of desire;
And, but once kindled, quenchless evermore,
Preys upon high adventure, nor can tire
Of aught but rest; a fever at the core,
Fatal to him who bears, to all who ever bore.

This makes the madmen who have made men mad
By their contagion; Conquerors and Kings,
Founders of sects and systems, to whom add
Sophists, Bards, Statesmen, all unquiet things
Which stir too strongly the soul's secret springs,
And are themselves the fools to those they fool;
Envied, yet how unenviable! what stings
Are theirs! One breast laid open were a school
Which would unteach mankind the lust to shine or rule:

Their breath is agitation, and their life
A storm whereon they ride, to sink at last,
And yet so nursed and bigoted to strife,
That should their days, surviving perils past,
Melt to calm twilight, they feel overcast
With sorrow and supineness, and so die;
Even as a flame unfed, which runs to waste
With its own flickering, or a sword laid by,
Which eats into itself, and rusts ingloriously.

Canto III, stanzas xxxvi–xliv

(v)

Voltaire and Gibbon

THE one was fire and fickleness, a child
Most mutable in wishes, but in mind
A wit as various,—gay, grave, sage, or wild,—
Historian, bard, philosopher, combined;
He multiplied himself among mankind,
The Proteus of their talents: But his own
Breathed most in ridicule,—which, as the wind,
Blew where it listed, laying all things prone,—
Now to o'erthrow a fool, and now to shake a throne.

The other, deep and slow, exhausting thought,
And hiving wisdom with each studious year,
In meditation dwelt, with learning wrought,
And shaped his weapon with an edge severe,
Sapping a solemn creed with solemn sneer;
The lord of irony,—that master-spell,
Which stung his foes to wrath, which grew from fear,
And doom'd him to the zealot's ready Hell,
Which answers to all doubts so eloquently well.

Canto III, stanzas cvi–cvii

CHILDE HAROLD'S PILGRIMAGE

(*vi*)

I HAVE not loved the world, nor the world me;
I have not flatter'd its rank breath, nor bow'd
To its idolatries a patient knee,
Nor coin'd my cheek to smiles, nor cried aloud
In worship of an echo; in the crowd
They could not deem me one of such; I stood
Among them, but not of them; in a shroud
Of thoughts which were not their thoughts, and still could,
Had I not filed my mind, which thus itself subdued.

I have not loved the world, nor the world me,—
But let us part fair foes; I do believe,
Though I have found them not, that there may be
Words which are things, hopes which will not deceive,
And virtues which are merciful, nor weave
Snares for the failing; I would also deem
O'er others' griefs that some sincerely grieve;
That two, or one, are almost what they seem,
That goodness is no name, and happiness no dream.

Canto III, stanzas cxiii–cxiv;
Childe Harold, III, 1816

(*vii*)

I STOOD in Venice, on the Bridge of Sighs;
A palace and a prison on each hand:
I saw from out the wave her structures rise
As from the stroke of the enchanter's wand:
A thousand years their cloudy wings expand
Around me, and a dying Glory smiles
O'er the far times, when many a subject land
Look'd to the winged Lion's marble piles,
Where Venice sate in state, throned on her hundred isles!

She looks a sea Cybele, fresh from ocean,
    Rising with her tiara of proud towers
At airy distance, with majestic motion,
    A ruler of the waters and their powers:
And such she was;—her daughters had their dowers
From spoils of nations, and the exhaustless East
Pour'd in her lap all gems in sparkling showers.
    In purple was she robed, and of her feast
Monarchs partook, and deem'd their dignity increased.

In Venice Tasso's echoes are no more,
    And silent rows the songless gondolier;
Her palaces are crumbling to the shore,
    And music meets not always now the ear:
Those days are gone—but Beauty still is here.
States fall, arts fade—but Nature doth not die,
    Nor yet forget how Venice once was dear,
The pleasant place of all festivity,
The revel of the earth, the masque of Italy!

But unto us she hath a spell beyond
    Her name in story, and her long array
Of mighty shadows, whose dim forms despond
    Above the dogeless city's vanish'd sway;
Ours is a trophy which will not decay
With the Rialto; Shylock and the Moor,
    And Pierre, cannot be swept or worn away—
The keystones of the arch! though all were o'er,
For us repeopled were the solitary shore.

.   .   .   .

The Suabian sued, and now the Austrian reigns—
An Emperor tramples where an Emperor knelt;
Kingdoms are shrunk to provinces, and chains
Clank over sceptred cities; nations melt
From power's high pinnacle, when they have felt
The sunshine for a while, and downward go
Like lauwine loosen'd from the mountain's belt;
Oh for one hour of blind old Dandolo!
Th' octogenarian chief, Byzantium's conquering foe.

Before St. Mark still glow his steeds of brass,
Their gilded collars glittering in the sun;
But is not Doria's menace come to pass?
Are they not *bridled?*—Venice, lost and won,
Her thirteen hundred years of freedom done,
Sinks, like a seaweed, into whence she rose!
Better be whelm'd beneath the waves, and shun,
Even in destruction's depth, her foreign foes,
From whom submission wrings an infamous repose.

In youth she was all glory,—a new Tyre;
Her very by-word sprung from victory,
The ' Planter of the Lion,' which through fire
And blood she bore o'er subject earth and sea;
Though making many slaves, herself still free,
And Europe's bulwark 'gainst the Ottomite;
Witness Troy's rival, Candia! Vouch it, ye
Immortal waves that saw Lepanto's fight!
For ye are names no time nor tyranny can blight.

Statues of glass—all shiver'd—the long file
Of her dead Doges are declined to dust;

445

But where they dwelt, the vast and sumptuous pile
Bespeaks the pageant of their splendid trust;
Their sceptre broken, and their sword in rust,
Have yielded to the stranger: empty halls,
Thin streets, and foreign aspects, such as must
Too oft remind her who and what inthrals,
Have flung a desolate cloud o'er Venice' lovely walls.

Canto IV, stanzas i–iv, xii–xv

(*viii*)

THERE is a pleasure in the pathless woods,
    There is a rapture on the lonely shore,
There is society, where none intrudes,
By the deep Sea, and music in its roar:
I love not Man the less, but Nature more,
From these our interviews, in which I steal
From all I may be, or have been before,
To mingle with the Universe, and feel
What I can ne'er express, yet cannot all conceal.

Roll on, thou deep and dark blue Ocean—roll!
Ten thousand fleets sweep over thee in vain;
Man marks the earth with ruin—his control
Stops with the shore; upon the watery plain
The wrecks are all thy deed, nor doth remain
A shadow of man's ravage, save his own,
When, for a moment, like a drop of rain,
He sinks into thy depths with bubbling groan,
Without a grave, unknell'd, uncoffin'd, and unknown.

His steps are not upon thy paths,—thy fields
Are not a spoil for him,—thou dost arise

And shake him from thee; the vile strength he wields
For earth's destruction thou dost all despise,
Spurning him from thy bosom to the skies,
And send'st him, shivering in thy playful spray
And howling, to his Gods, where haply lies
His petty hope in some near port or bay,
And dashest him again to earth:—there let him lay.

The armaments which thunderstrike the walls
Of rock-built cities, bidding nations quake,
And monarchs tremble in their capitals,
The oak leviathans, whose huge ribs make
Their clay creator the vain title take
Of lord of thee, and arbiter of war—
These are thy toys, and, as the snowy flake,
They melt into thy yeast of waves, which mar
Alike the Armada's pride or spoils of Trafalgar.

Thy shores are empires, changed in all save thee—
Assyria, Greece, Rome, Carthage, what are they?
Thy waters wash'd them power while they were free,
And many a tyrant since; their shores obey
The stranger, slave, or savage; their decay
Has dried up realms to deserts:—not so thou;—
Unchangeable, save to thy wild waves' play,
Time writes no wrinkle on thine azure brow:
Such as creation's dawn beheld, thou rollest now.

Thou glorious mirror, where the Almighty's form
Glasses itself in tempests; in all time,—
Calm or convulsed, in breeze, or gale, or storm,
Icing the pole, or in the torrid clime
Dark-heaving—boundless, endless, and sublime,

447

The image of eternity, the throne
Of the Invisible; even from out thy slime
The monsters of the deep are made; each zone
Obeys thee; thou goest forth, dread, fathomless, alone.

And I have loved thee, Ocean! and my joy
Of youthful sports was on thy breast to be
Borne, like thy bubbles, onward: from a boy
I wanton'd with thy breakers—they to me
Were a delight; and if the freshening sea
Made them a terror—'t was a pleasing fear,
For I was as it were a child of thee,
And trusted to thy billows far and near,
And laid my hand upon thy mane—as I do here.

Canto IV, stanzas clxxviii–clxxxiv;
Childe Harold, IV, 1818

218   *From ' The Bride of Abydos '*

THE winds are high on Helle's wave,
    As on that night of stormy water
When Love, who sent, forgot to save
The young, the beautiful, the brave,
    The lonely hope of Sestos' daughter.
Oh! when alone along the sky
Her turret-torch was blazing high,
Though rising gale, and breaking foam,
And shrieking sea-birds warn'd him home;
And clouds aloft and tides below,
With signs and sounds, forbade to go,
He could not see, he would not hear,
Or sound or sign foreboding fear;
His eye but saw that light of love,
The only star it hail'd above;

THE BRIDE OF ABYDOS

His ear but rang with Hero's song,
' Ye waves, divide not lovers long!'—
That tale is old, but love anew
May nerve young hearts 'to prove as true.

The winds are high, and Helle's tide
   Rolls darkly heaving to the main;·
And Night's descending shadows hide
   That field with blood bedew'd in vain,
The desert of old Priam's pride;
   The tombs, sole relics of his reign,
All—save immortal dreams that could beguile
The blind old man of Scio's rocky isle!

    .   .   .   .   .

The night hath closed on Helle's stream,
   Nor yet hath risen on Ida's hill
That moon, which shone on his high theme:
No warrior chides her peaceful beam,
   But conscious shepherds bless it still.
Their flocks are grazing on the mound
   Of him who felt the Dardan's arrow:
That mighty heap of gather'd ground
Which Ammon's son ran proudly round,
By nations raised, by monarchs crown'd,
   Is now a lone and nameless barrow!
   Within—thy dwelling-place how narrow!
Without—can only strangers breathe
The name of him that *was* beneath:
Dust long outlasts the storied stone;
But Thou—thy very dust is gone!

                 The Bride of Abydos, Canto II, 1813

219   *Lara*

THERE was in him a vital scorn of all:
　　As if the worst had fall'n which could befall,
He stood a stranger in this breathing world,
An erring spirit from another hurl'd;
A thing of dark imaginings, that shaped
By choice the perils he by chance escaped;
But 'scaped in vain, for in their memory yet
His mind would half exult and half regret:
With more capacity for love than earth
Bestows on most of mortal mould and birth,
His early dreams of good outstripp'd the truth,
And troubled manhood follow'd baffled youth;
With thought of years in phantom chase misspent,
And wasted powers for better purpose lent;
And fiery passions that had pour'd their wrath
In hurried desolation o'er his path,
And left the better feelings all at strife
In wild reflection o'er his stormy life;
But haughty still, and loth himself to blame,
He call'd on Nature's self to share the shame,
And charged all faults upon the fleshly form
She gave to clog the soul, and feast the worm;
Till he at last confounded good and ill,
And half mistook for fate the acts of will:
Too high for common selfishness, he could
At times resign his own for others' good,
But not in pity, not because he ought,
But in some strange perversity of thought,
That sway'd him onward with a secret pride
To do what few or none would do beside;

And this same impulse would, in tempting time,
Mislead his spirit equally to crime;
So much he soar'd beyond, or sunk beneath,
The men with whom he felt condemn'd to breathe,
And long'd by good or ill to separate
Himself from all who shared his mortal state;
His mind abhorring this, had fix'd her throne
Far from the world, in regions of her own:
Thus coldly passing all that pass'd below,
His blood in temperate seeming now would flow:
Ah! happier if it ne'er with guilt had glow'd,
But ever in that icy smoothness flow'd!
'Tis true, with other men their path he walk'd,
And like the rest in seeming did and talk'd,
Nor outraged Reason's rules by flaw nor start,
His madness was not of the head, but heart;
And rarely wander'd in his speech, or drew
His thoughts so forth as to offend the view.

Lara, Canto I, 1814

220   *Summer*

SLOW sinks, more lovely ere his race be run,
  Along Morea's hills the setting sun;
Not, as in northern climes, obscurely bright,
But one unclouded blaze of living light;
O'er the hush'd deep the yellow beam he throws,
Gilds the green wave that trembles as it glows;
On old Aegina's rock and Hydra's isle
The god of gladness sheds his parting smile;
O'er his own regions lingering loves to shine,
Though there his altars are no more divine.

451

Descending fast, the mountain-shadows kiss
Thy glorious gulf, unconquer'd Salamis!
Their azure arches through the long expanse,
More deeply purpled, meet his mellowing glance,
And tenderest tints, along their summits driven,
Mark his gay course, and own the hues of heaven;
Till, darkly shaded from the land and deep,
Behind his Delphian rock he sinks to sleep.

The Corsair, Canto III, 1814

221 *' She walks in beauty '*

I

SHE walks in beauty, like the night
  Of cloudless climes and starry skies;
And all that 's best of dark and bright
  Meet in her aspect and her eyes:
Thus mellow'd to that tender light
  Which heaven to gaudy day denies.

II

One shade the more, one ray the less,
  Had half impair'd the nameless grace
Which waves in every raven tress,
  Or softly lightens o'er her face;
Where thoughts serenely sweet express
  How pure, how dear their dwelling-place.

III

And on that cheek, and o'er that brow,
  So soft, so calm, yet eloquent,
The smiles that win, the tints that glow,

But tell of days in goodness spent,
A mind at peace with all below,
  A heart whose love is innocent!

Hebrew Melodies, 1815

222 ' *Oh! snatch'd away in beauty's bloom* '

I

OH! snatch'd away in beauty's bloom,
  On thee shall press no ponderous tomb;
  But on thy turf shall roses rear
  Their leaves, the earliest of the year;
And the wild cypress wave in tender gloom:

II

And oft by yon blue gushing stream
  Shall Sorrow lean her drooping head,
And feed deep thought with many a dream,
  And lingering pause and lightly tread;
  Fond wretch! as if her step disturb'd the dead!

III

Away! we know that tears are vain,
  That death nor heeds nor hears distress:
Will this unteach us to complain?
  Or make one mourner weep the less?
And thou—who tell'st me to forget,
Thy looks are wan, thine eyes are wet.

Hebrew Melodies, 1815

453

223   *Stanzas for Music*

THERE be none of Beauty's daughters
  With a magic like thee;
And like music on the waters
  Is thy sweet voice to me:
When, as if its sound were causing
The charmed ocean's pausing,
The waves lie still and gleaming,
And the lull'd winds seem dreaming:

And the midnight moon is weaving
  Her bright chain o'er the deep;
Whose breast is gently heaving,
  As an infant's asleep:
So the spirit bows before thee,
To listen and adore thee;
With a full but soft emotion,
Like the swell of Summer's ocean.

Poems, 1816

224   ' *When we two parted* '

WHEN we two parted
  In silence and tears,
Half broken-hearted
  To sever for years,
Pale grew thy cheek and cold,
  Colder thy kiss;
Truly that hour foretold
  Sorrow to this.

WHEN WE TWO PARTED

The dew of the morning
   Sunk chill on my brow—
It felt like the warning
   Of what I feel now.
Thy vows are all broken,
   And light is thy fame:
I hear thy name spoken,
   And share in its shame.

They name thee before me,
   A knell to mine ear;
A shudder comes o'er me—
   Why wert thou so dear?
They know not I knew thee,
   Who knew thee too well:—
Long, long shall I rue thee,
   Too deeply to tell.

In secret we met—
   In silence I grieve,
That thy heart could forget,
   Thy spirit deceive.
If I should meet thee
   After long years,
How should I greet thee?—
   With silence and tears.

Poems, 1816

225 *A Sketch*

'Honest—honest Iago!
If that thou be'st a devil, I cannot kill thee.'

SHAKESPEARE.

BORN in the garret, in the kitchen bred,
Promoted thence to deck her mistress' head;
Next—for some gracious service unexpress'd,
And from its wages only to be guess'd—
Raised from the toilette to the table,—where
Her wondering betters wait behind her chair.
With eye unmoved, and forehead unabash'd,
She dines from off the plate she lately wash'd.
Quick with the tale, and ready with the lie,
The genial confidante, and general spy,
Who could, ye gods! her next employment guess—
An only infant's earliest governess!
She taught the child to read, and taught so well,
That she herself, by teaching, learn'd to spell.
An adept next in penmanship she grows,
As many a nameless slander deftly shows:
What she had made the pupil of her art,
None know—but that high Soul secured the heart,
And panted for the truth it could not hear,
With longing breast and undeluded ear.
Foil'd was perversion by that youthful mind,
Which Flattery fool'd not, Baseness could not blind,
Deceit infect not, near Contagion soil,
Indulgence weaken, nor Example spoil,
Nor master'd Science tempt her to look down
On humbler talents with a pitying frown,
Nor Genius swell, nor Beauty render vain,
Nor Envy ruffle to retaliate pain,

456

A SKETCH

Nor Fortune change, Pride raise, nor Passion bow,
Nor virtue teach austerity—till now.
Serenely purest of her sex that live,
But wanting one sweet weakness—to forgive,
Too shock'd at faults her soul can never know,
She deems that all could be like her below;
Foe to all vice, yet hardly Virtue's friend,
For Virtue pardons those she would amend.

But to the theme, now laid aside too long,
The baleful burthen of this honest song,
Though all her former functions are no more,
She rules the circle which she served before.
If mothers—none know why—before her quake;
If daughters dread her for the mothers' sake;
If early habits—those false links, which bind
At times the loftiest to the meanest mind—
Have given her power too deeply to instil
The angry essence of her deadly will;
If like a snake she steal within your walls,
Till the black slime betray her as she crawls;
If like a viper to the heart she wind,
And leave the venom there she did not find;
What marvel that this hag of hatred works
Eternal evil latent as she lurks,
To make a Pandemonium where she dwells,
And reign the Hecate of domestic hells?
Skill'd by a touch to deepen scandal's tints
With all the kind mendacity of hints,
While mingling truth with falsehood, sneers with
       smiles,
A thread of candour with a web of wiles:

A plain blunt show of briefly-spoken seeming,
To hide her bloodless heart's soul-harden'd scheming;
A lip of lies; a face form'd to conceal,
And, without feeling, mock at all who feel:
With a vile mask the Gorgon would disown,—
A cheek of parchment, and an eye of stone.
Mark, how the channels of her yellow blood
Ooze to her skin, and stagnate there to mud,
Cased like the centipede in saffron mail,
Or darker greenness of the scorpion's scale—
(For drawn from reptiles only may we trace
Congenial colours in that soul or face)—
Look on her features! and behold her mind
As in a mirror of itself defined:
Look on the picture! deem it not o'ercharged—
There is no trait which might not be enlarged:
Yet true to ' Nature's journeymen,' who made
This monster when their mistress left off trade—
This female dog-star of her little sky,
Where all beneath her influence droop or die.
Oh! wretch without a tear—without a thought,
Save joy above the ruin thou hast wrought—
The time shall come, nor long remote, when thou
Shalt feel far more than thou inflictest now;
Feel for thy vile self-loving self in vain,
And turn thee howling in unpitied pain.
May the strong curse of crush'd affections light
Back on thy bosom with reflected blight!
And make thee in thy leprosy of mind
As loathsome to thyself as to mankind!
Till all thy self-thoughts curdle into hate,
Black—as thy will for others would create:

458

Till thy hard heart be calcined into dust,
And thy soul welter in its hideous crust.
Oh, may thy grave be sleepless as the bed,
The widow'd couch of fire, that thou hast spread!
Then, when thou fain wouldst weary Heaven with prayer,
Look on thine earthly victims—and despair!
Down to the dust!—and, as thou rott'st away,
Even worms shall perish on thy poisonous clay.
But for the love I bore, and still must bear,
To her thy malice from all ties would tear—
Thy name—thy human name—to every eye
The climax of all scorn should hang on high,
Exalted o'er thy less abhorr'd compeers—
And festering in the infamy of years.

A Sketch, April 4, 1816

226 *Sonnet on Chillon*

ETERNAL Spirit of the chainless Mind!
  Brightest in dungeons, Liberty! thou art,
    For there thy habitation is the heart—
The heart which love of thee alone can bind;
And when thy sons to fetters are consign'd—
    To fetters, and the damp vault's dayless gloom,
    Their country conquers with their martyrdom,
And Freedom's fame finds wings on every wind.
Chillon! thy prison is a holy place,
    And thy sad floor an altar—for 't was trod,
Until his very steps have left a trace
    Worn, as if thy cold pavement were a sod,
By Bonnivard! May none those marks efface!
    For they appeal from tyranny to God.

Prisoner of Chillon, 1816

459

From ' The Prisoner of Chillon '

(*i*)

LAKE Leman lies by Chillon's walls:
       A thousand feet in depth below
Its massy waters meet and flow;
Thus much the fathom-line was sent
From Chillon's snow-white battlement,
    Which round about the wave inthrals:
A double dungeon wall and wave
Have made—and like a living grave
Below the surface of the lake
The dark vault lies wherein we lay,
We heard it ripple night and day;
    Sounding o'er our heads it knock'd;
And I have felt the winter's spray
Wash through the bars when winds were high
And wanton in the happy sky;
    And then the very rock hath rock'd,
    And I have felt it shake, unshock'd,
Because I could have smiled to see
The death that would have set me free.

(*ii*)

A LIGHT broke in upon my brain,—
       It was the carol of a bird;
It ceased, and then it came again,
    The sweetest song ear ever heard,

THE PRISONER OF CHILLON

And mine was thankful till my eyes
Ran over with the glad surprise,
And they that moment could not see
I was the mate of misery;
But then by dull degrees came back
My senses to their wonted track;
I saw the dungeon walls and floor
Close slowly round me as before,
I saw the glimmer of the sun
Creeping as it before had done,
But through the crevice where it came
That bird was perch'd, as fond and tame,
    And tamer than upon the tree;
A lovely bird, with azure wings,
And song that said a thousand things,
    And seem'd to say them all for me!
I never saw its like before,
I ne'er shall see its likeness more:
It seem'd like me to want a mate,
But was not half so desolate,
And it was come to love me when
None lived to love me so again,
And cheering from my dungeon's brink,
Had brought me back to feel and think.
I know not if it late were free,
    Or broke its cage to perch on mine,
But knowing well captivity,
    Sweet bird! I could not wish for thine!
Or if it were, in winged guise,
A visitant from Paradise;
For—Heaven forgive that thought! the while
Which made me both to weep and smile—

I sometimes deem'd that it might be
My brother's soul come down to me;
But then at last away it flew,
And then 'twas mortal well I knew,
For he would never thus have flown,
And left me twice so doubly lone,
Lone as the corse within its shroud,
Lone as a solitary cloud,—

   A single cloud on a sunny day,
While all the rest of heaven is clear,
A frown upon the atmosphere,
That hath no business to appear
   When skies are blue, and earth is gay.

(iii)

I MADE a footing in the wall,
It was not therefrom to escape,
For I had buried one and all
   Who loved me in a human shape;
And the whole earth would henceforth be
A wider prison unto me:
No child, no sire, no kin had I,
No partner in my misery;
I thought of this, and I was glad,
For thought of them had made me mad;
But I was curious to ascend
To my barr'd windows, and to bend
Once more, upon the mountains high,
The quiet of a loving eye.

I saw them, and they were the same,
They were not changed like me in frame;

THE PRISONER OF CHILLON

I saw their thousand years of snow
On high—their wide long lake below,
And the blue Rhone in fullest flow;
I heard the torrents leap and gush
O'er channell'd rock and broken bush;
I saw the white-wall'd distant town,
And whiter sails go skimming down;
And then there was a little isle,
Which in my very face did smile,
    The only one in view;
A small green isle, it seem'd no more,
Scarce broader than my dungeon floor,
But in it there were three tall trees,
And o'er it blew the mountain breeze,
And by it there were waters flowing,
And on it there were young flowers growing
    Of gentle breath and hue.
The fish swam by the castle wall,
And they seem'd joyous each and all;
The eagle rode the rising blast,
Methought he never flew so fast
As then to me he seem'd to fly;
And then new tears came in my eye,
And I felt troubled—and would fain
I had not left my recent chain;
And when I did descend again,
The darkness of my dim abode
Fell on me as a heavy load;
It was as is a new-dug grave,
Closing o'er one we sought to save,—
And yet my glance, too much opprest,
Had almost need of such a rest.

GEORGE GORDON, LORD BYRON

It might be months, or years, or days,
    I kept no count, I took no note,
I had no hope my eyes to raise,
    And clear them of their dreary mote;
At last men came to set me free;
    I ask'd not why, and reck'd not where;
It was at length the same to me,
Fetter'd or fetterless to be,
    I learn'd to love despair.
And thus when they appear'd at last,
And all my bonds aside were cast,
These heavy walls to me had grown
A hermitage—and all my own!
And half I felt as they were come
To tear me from a second home:
With spiders I had friendship made,
And watch'd them in their sullen trade,
Had seen the mice by moonlight play,
And why should I feel less than they?
We were all inmates of one place,
And I, the monarch of each race,
Had power to kill—yet, strange to tell!
In quiet we had learn'd to dwell;
My very chains and I grew friends,
So much a long communion tends
To make us what we are:—even I
Regain'd my freedom with a sigh.

Prisoner of Chillon, 1816

WHEN the moon is on the wave,
  And the glow-worm in the grass,
And the meteor on the grave,
  And the wisp on the morass;
When the falling stars are shooting,
And the answer'd owls are hooting,
And the silent leaves are still
In the shadow of the hill,
Shall my soul be upon thine,
With a power and with a sign.

Though thy slumber may be deep,
Yet thy spirit shall not sleep;
There are shades which will not vanish,
There are thoughts thou canst not banish;
By a power to thee unknown,
Thou canst never be alone;
Thou art wrapt as with a shroud,
Thou art gather'd in a cloud;
And for ever shalt thou dwell
In the spirit of this spell.

Though thou seest me not pass by,
Thou shalt feel me with thine eye
As a thing that, though unseen,
Must be near thee, and hath been;
And when in that secret dread
Thou hast turn'd around thy head,
Thou shalt marvel I am not
As thy shadow on the spot,
And the power which thou dost feel
Shall be what thou must conceal.

465

And a magic voice and verse
Hath baptized thee with a curse;
And a spirit of the air
Hath begirt thee with a snare;
In the wind there is a voice
Shall forbid thee to rejoice;
And to thee shall night deny
All the quiet of her sky;
And the day shall have a sun,
Which shall make thee wish it done.

Manfred, 1817

229 *Italy*

WITH all its sinful doings, I must say,
    That Italy's a pleasant place to me,
Who love to see the Sun shine every day,
    And vines (not nail'd to walls) from tree to tree
Festoon'd, much like the back scene of a play,
    Or melodrame, which people flock to see,
When the first act is ended by a dance
In vineyards copied from the south of France.

I like on Autumn evenings to ride out,
    Without being forced to bid my groom be sure
My cloak is round his middle strapp'd about,
    Because the skies are not the most secure;
I know too that, if stopp'd upon my route,
    Where the green alleys windingly allure,
Reeling with grapes red waggons choke the way,—
In England 'twould be dung, dust, or a dray.

ITALY

I also like to dine on becaficas,
    To see the Sun set, sure he'll rise to-morrow,
Not through a misty morning twinkling weak as
    A drunken man's dead eye in maudlin sorrow,
But with all Heaven t'himself; the day will break as
    Beauteous as cloudless, nor be forced to borrow
That sort of farthing candlelight which glimmers
Where reeking London's smoky caldron simmers.

I love the language, that soft bastard Latin,
    Which melts like kisses from a female mouth,
And sounds as if it should be writ on satin,
    With syllables which breathe of the sweet South,
And gentle liquids gliding all so pat in,
    That not a single accent seems uncouth,
Like our harsh northern whistling, grunting guttural,
Which we're obliged to hiss, and spit, and sputter all.

I like the women too (forgive my folly),
    From the rich peasant cheek of ruddy bronze,
And large black eyes that flash on you a volley
    Of rays that say a thousand things at once,
To the high dama's brow, more melancholy,
    But clear, and with a wild and liquid glance,
Heart on her lips, and soul within her eyes,
Soft as her clime, and sunny as her skies.

Eve of the land which still is Paradise!
    Italian beauty! didst thou not inspire
Raphael, who died in thy embrace, and vies
    With all we know of Heaven, or can desire,
In what he hath bequeath'd us?—in what guise,
    Though flashing from the fervour of the lyre,

Would *words* describe thy past and present glow,
While yet Canova can create below?

' England! with all thy faults I love thee still,'
   I said at Calais, and have not forgot it;
I like to speak and lucubrate my fill;
   I like the government (but that is not it);
I like the freedom of the press and quill;
   I like the Habeas Corpus (when we've got it);
I like a parliamentary debate,
Particularly when 'tis not too late;

I like the taxes, when they're not too many;
   I like a seacoal fire, when not too dear;
I like a beef-steak, too, as well as any;
   Have no objection to a pot of beer;
I like the weather, when it is not rainy,
   That is, I like two months of every year,
And so God save the Regent, Church, and King!
Which means that I like all and everything.

Our standing army, and disbanded seamen,
   Poor's rate, Reform, my own, the nation's debt,
Our little riots just to show we are free men,
   Our trifling bankruptcies in the Gazette,
Our cloudy climate, and our chilly women,
   All these I can forgive, and those forget,
And greatly venerate our recent glories,
And wish they were not owing to the Tories.

Beppo, 1818

U P rose the sun; the mists were curl'd
    Back from the solitary world
Which lay around, behind, before.
What booted it to traverse o'er
Plain, forest, river? Man nor brute,
Nor dint of hoof, nor print of foot,
Lay in the wild luxuriant soil;
No sign of travel, none of toil;
The very air was mute;
And not an insect's shrill small horn,
Nor matin bird's new voice was borne
From herb nor thicket. Many a werst,
Panting as if his heart would burst,
The weary brute still stagger'd on;
And still we were—or seem'd—alone.
At length, while recling on our way,
Methought I heard a courser neigh,
From out yon tuft of blackening firs.
Is it the wind those branches stirs?
No, no! from out the forest prance

    A trampling troop; I see them come!
In one vast squadron they advance!

    I strove to cry—my lips were dumb.
The steeds rush on in plunging pride;
But where are they the reins to guide?
A thousand horse, and none to ride!
With flowing tail, and flying mane,
Wide nostrils never stretch'd by pain,
Mouths bloodless to the bit or rein,

And feet that iron never shod,
And flanks unscarr'd by spur or rod,
A thousand horse, the wild, the free,
Like waves that follow o'er the sea,
    Came thickly thundering on,
As if our faint approach to meet;
The sight re-nerved my courser's feet,
A moment staggering, feebly fleet,
A moment, with a faint low neigh,
    He answer'd, and then fell;
With gasps and glazing eyes he lay,
    And reeking limbs immoveable,
        His first and last career is done!
On came the troop—they saw him stoop,
    They saw me strangely bound along
    His back with many a bloody thong:
They stop, they start, they snuff the air,
Gallop a moment here and there,
Approach, retire, wheel round and round,
Then plunging back with sudden bound,
Headed by one black mighty steed,
Who seem'd the patriarch of his breed,
    Without a single speck or hair
Of white upon his shaggy hide;
They snort, they foam, neigh, swerve aside,
And backward to the forest fly,
By instinct, from a human eye.
    They left me there to my despair,
Link'd to the dead and stiffening wretch,
Whose lifeless limbs beneath me stretch,
Relieved from that unwonted weight,
From whence I could not extricate

Nor him nor me—and there we lay,
   The dying on the dead!
I little deem'd another day
   Would see my houseless; helpless head.

Mazeppa, 1819

231   *From ' Don Juan '*

(i)

First Love

'TIS sweet to hear the watch-dog's honest bark
   Bay deep-mouth'd welcome as we draw near home;
'T is sweet to know there is an eye will mark
   Our coming, and look brighter when we come;
'T is sweet to be awaken'd by the lark,
   Or lull'd by falling waters; sweet the hum
Of bees, the voice of girls, the song of birds,
The lisp of children, and their earliest words.

Sweet is the vintage, when the showering grapes
   In Bacchanal profusion reel to earth,
Purple and gushing; sweet are our escapes
   From civic revelry to rural mirth;
Sweet to the miser are his glittering heaps,
   Sweet to the father is his first-born's birth,
Sweet is revenge—especially to women,
Pillage to soldiers, prize-money to seamen.

Sweet is a legacy, and passing sweet
   The unexpected death of some old lady
Or gentleman of seventy years complete,
   Who've made ' us youth ' wait too—too long already

471

For an estate, or cash, or country seat,
   Still breaking, but with stamina so steady
That all the Israelites are fit to mob its
Next owner for their double-damn'd postobits.

'T is sweet to win, no matter how, one's laurels,
   By blood or ink; 't is sweet to put an end
To strife; 't is sometimes sweet to have our quarrels,
   Particularly with a tiresome friend:
Sweet is old wine in bottles, ale in barrels;
   Dear is the helpless creature we defend
Against the world; and dear the schoolboy spot
We ne'er forget, though there we are forgot.

But sweeter still than this, than these, than all,
   Is first and passionate love—it stands alone,
Like Adam's recollection of his fall;
   The tree of knowledge has been pluck'd—all 's known—
And life yields nothing further to recall
   Worthy of this ambrosial sin, so shown,
No doubt in fable, as the unforgiven
Fire which Prometheus filch'd for us from heaven.

Canto I, stanzas cxxiii–cxxvii

(ii)

Poetical Commandments

IF ever I should condescend to prose,
  I'll write poetical commandments, which
Shall supersede beyond all doubt all those
   That went before; in these I shall enrich

My text with many things that no one knows,
    And carry precept to the highest pitch:
I'll call the work ' Longinus o'er a Bottle,
Or, Every Poet his *own* Aristotle.'

Thou shalt believe in Milton, Dryden, Pope;
    Thou shalt not set up Wordsworth, Coleridge, Southey;
Because the first is crazed beyond all hope,
    The second drunk, the third so quaint and mouthy:
With Crabbe it may be difficult to cope,
    And Campbell's Hippocrene is somewhat drouthy:
Thou shalt not steal from Samuel Rogers, nor
Commit—flirtation with the muse of Moore.

Thou shalt not covet Mr. Sotheby's Muse,
    His Pegasus, nor anything that 's his;
Thou shalt not bear false witness like ' the Blues '—
    (There 's one, at least, is very fond of this);
Thou shalt not write, in short, but what I choose;
    This is true criticism, and you may kiss—
Exactly as you please, or not,—the rod;
But if you don't, I'll lay it on, by G—d!

                                    Canto I, stanzas cciv–ccvi

(iii)

The Shipwreck

'TWAS twilight, and the sunless day went down
    Over the waste of waters; like a veil,
Which, if withdrawn, would but disclose the frown
    Of one whose hate is mask'd but to assail.

Thus to their hopeless eyes the night was shown,
　　And grimly darkled o'er the faces pale,
And the dim desolate deep: twelve days had Fear
Been their familiar, and now Death was here.

Some trial had been making at a raft,
　　With little hope in such a rolling sea,
A sort of thing at which one would have laugh'd,
　　If any laughter at such times could be,
Unless with people who too much have quaff'd,
　　And have a kind of wild and horrid glee,
Half epileptical, and half hysterical:—
Their preservation would have been a miracle.

At half-past eight o'clock, booms, hencoops, spars,
　　And all things, for a chance, had been cast loose
That still could keep afloat the struggling tars,
　　For yet they strove, although of no great use:
There was no light in heaven but a few stars,
　　The boats put off o'ercrowded with their crews;
She gave a heel, and then a lurch to port,
And, going down head foremost—sunk, in short.

Then rose from sea to sky the wild farewell—
　　Then shriek'd the timid, and stood still the brave—
Then some leap'd overboard with dreadful yell,
　　As eager to anticipate their grave;
And the sea yawn'd around her like a hell,
　　And down she suck'd with her the whirling wave,
Like one who grapples with his enemy,
And strives to strangle him before he die.

And first one universal shriek there rush'd,
　　Louder than the loud ocean, like a crash

Of echoing thunder; and then all was hush'd,
    Save the wild wind and the remorseless dash
Of billows; but at intervals there gush'd,
    Accompanied with a convulsive splash,
A solitary shriek, the bubbling cry
Of some strong swimmer in his agony.

Canto II, stanzas xlix–liii

(iv)

Haidée

IT was the cooling hour, just when the rounded
    Red sun sinks down behind the azure hill,
Which then seems as if the whole earth it bounded,
    Circling all nature, hush'd, and dim, and still,
With the far mountain-crescent half surrounded
    On one side, and the deep sea calm and chill,
Upon the other, and the rosy sky,
With one star sparkling through it like an eye.

And thus they wander'd forth, and hand in hand,
    Over the shining pebbles and the shells,
Glided along the smooth and harden'd sand,
    And in the worn and wild receptacles
Work'd by the storms, yet work'd as it were plann'd,
    In hollow halls, with sparry roofs and cells,
They turn'd to rest; and, each clasp'd by an arm,
Yielded to the deep twilight's purple charm.

They look'd up to the sky, whose floating glow
    Spread like a rosy ocean, vast and bright;
They gazed upon the glittering sea below,
    Whence the broad moon rose circling into sight;

They heard the waves splash, and the wind so low,
   And saw each other's dark eyes darting light
Into each other—and, beholding this,
Their lips drew near, and clung into a kiss;

A long, long kiss, a kiss of youth, and love,
   And beauty, all concentrating like rays
Into one focus, kindled from above;
   Such kisses as belong to early days,
Where heart, and soul, and sense, in concert move,
   And the blood's lava, and the pulse a blaze,
Each kiss a heart-quake,—for a kiss's strength,
I think it must be reckon'd by its length.

By length I mean duration; theirs endured
   Heaven knows how long—no doubt they never reckon'd;
And if they had, they could not have secured
   The sum of their sensations to a second:
They had not spoken; but they felt allured,
   As if their souls and lips each other beckon'd,
Which, being join'd, like swarming bees they clung—
Their hearts the flowers from whence the honey sprung.

They were alone, but not alone as they
   Who shut in chambers think it loneliness;
The silent ocean, and the starlight bay,
   The twilight glow, which momently grew less,
The voiceless sands, and dropping caves, that lay
   Around them, made them to each other press,
As if there were no life beneath the sky
Save theirs, and that their life could never die.

They fear'd no eyes nor ears on that lone beach,
   They felt no terrors from the night; they were

All in all to each other; though their speech
 Was broken words, they *thought* a language there,—
And all the burning tongues the passions teach
 Found in one sigh the best interpreter
Of nature's oracle—first love,—that all
Which Eve has left her daughters since her fall.

Canto II, stanzas clxxxiii–clxxxix
Don Juan, Cantos I and II, 1819

(v)

Lambro's Return

HE saw his white walls shining in the sun,
 His garden trees all shadowy and green;
He heard his rivulet's light bubbling run,
 The distant dog-bark; and perceived between
The umbrage of the wood so cool and dun,
 The moving figures, and the sparkling sheen
Of arms (in the East all arm)—and various dyes
Of colour'd garbs, as bright as butterflies.

  . . . . . .

And still more nearly to the place advancing,
 Descending rather quickly the declivity,
Through the waved branches, o'er the greensward glancing,
 'Midst other indications of festivity,
Seeing a troop of his domestics dancing
 Like dervises, who turn as on a pivot, he
Perceived it was the Pyrrhic dance so martial,
To which the Levantines are very partial.

And further on a group of Grecian girls,
 The first and tallest her white kerchief waving,

477

Were strung together like a row of pearls,
    Link'd hand in hand, and dancing: each too having
Down her white neck long floating auburn curls—
    (The least of which would set ten poets raving);
Their leader sang—and bounded to her song,
With choral step and voice, the virgin throng.

And here, assembled cross-legg'd round their trays,
    Small social parties just begun to dine;
Pilaus and meats of all sorts met the gaze,
    And flasks of Samian and of Chian wine,
And sherbet cooling in the porous vase;
    Above them their dessert grew on its vine,
The orange and pomegranate nodding o'er
Dropp'd in their laps, scarce pluck'd, their mellow store.

A band of children, round a snow-white ram,
    There wreathe his venerable horns with flowers;
While peaceful as if still an unwean'd lamb,
    The patriarch of the flock all gently cowers
His sober head, majestically tame,
    Or eats from out the palm, or playful lowers
His brow, as if in act to butt, and then
Yielding to their small hands, draws back again.

Their classical profiles, and glittering dresses,
    Their large black eyes, and soft seraphic cheeks,
Crimson as cleft pomegranates, their long tresses,
    The gesture which enchants, the eye that speaks,
The innocence which happy childhood blesses,
    Made quite a picture of these little Greeks;
So that the philosophical beholder
Sigh'd for their sakes—that they should e'er grow older.

478

DON JUAN

Afar, a dwarf buffoon stood telling tales
　　To a sedate grey circle of old smokers,
Of secret treasures found in hidden vales,
　　Of wonderful replies from Arab jokers,
Of charms to make good gold and cure bad ails,
　　Of rocks bewitch'd that open to the knockers,
Of magic ladies who, by one sole act,
Transform'd their lords to beasts (but that 's a fact).

Here was no lack of innocent diversion
　　For the imagination or the senses,
Song, dance, wine, music, stories from the Persian,
　　All pretty pastimes in which no offence is;
But Lambro saw all these things with aversion,
　　Perceiving in his absence such expenses,
Dreading that climax of all human ills,
The inflammation of his weekly bills.

Ah! what is man? what perils still environ
　　The happiest mortals even after dinner!
A day of gold from out an age of iron
　　Is all that life allows the luckiest sinner;
Pleasure (whene'er she sings, at least) 's a siren,
　　That lures, to flay alive, the young beginner;
Lambro's reception at his people's banquet
Was such as fire accords to a wet blanket.

He—being a man who seldom used a word
　　Too much, and wishing gladly to surprise
(In general he surprised men with the sword)
　　His daughter—had not sent before to advise
Of his arrival, so that no one stirr'd;
　　And long he paused to reässure his eyes,

In fact much more astonish'd than delighted,
To find so much good company invited.

He did not know (alas! how men will lie!)
    That a report (especially the Greeks)
Avouch'd his death (such people never die),
    And put his house in mourning several weeks,—
But now their eyes and also lips were dry;
    The bloom, too, had return'd to Haidée's cheeks.
Her tears, too, being return'd into their fount,
She now kept house upon her own account.

Hence all this rice, meat, dancing, wine, and fiddling,
    Which turn'd the isle into a place of pleasure;
The servants all were getting drunk or idling,
    A life which made them happy beyond measure.
Her father's hospitality seem'd middling,
    Compared with what Haidée did with his treasure;
'T was wonderful how things went on improving,
While she had not one hour to spare from loving.

Perhaps you think, in stumbling on this feast,
    He flew into a passion, and in fact
There was no mighty reason to be pleased;
    Perhaps you prophesy some sudden act,
The whip, the rack, or dungeon at the least,
    To teach his people to be more exact,
And that, proceeding at a very high rate,
He show'd the royal *penchants* of a pirate.

You're wrong.—He was the mildest manner'd man
    That ever scuttled ship or cut a throat,
With such true breeding of a gentleman,
    You never could divine his real thought,

No courtier could, and scarcely woman can
   Gird more deceit within a petticoat;
Pity he loved adventurous life's variety,
He was so great a loss to good society.

Canto III, stanzas xxvii, xxix–xli

(vi)

The Isles of Greece

1

THE isles of Greece, the isles of Greece!
   Where burning Sappho loved and sung,
Where grew the arts of war and peace,
   Where Delos rose, and Phœbus sprung!
Eternal summer gilds them yet,
But all, except their sun, is set.

2

The Scian and the Teian muse,
   The hero's harp, the lover's lute,
Have found the fame your shores refuse:
   Their place of birth alone is mute
To sounds which echo further west
Than your sires' ' Islands of the Blest.'

3

The mountains look on Marathon—
   And Marathon looks on the sea;
And musing there an hour alone,
   I dream'd that Greece might still be free;
For standing on the Persians' grave,
I could not deem myself a slave.

4

A king sate on the rocky brow
  Which looks o'er sea-born Salamis;
And ships, by thousands, lay below,
  And men in nations;—all were his!
He counted them at break of day—
And when the sun set where were they?

5

And where are they? and where art thou,
  My country? On thy voiceless shore
The heroic lay is tuneless now—
  The heroic bosom beats no more!
And must thy lyre, so long divine,
Degenerate into hands like mine?

6

'Tis something, in the dearth of fame,
  Though link'd among a fetter'd race,
To feel at least a patriot's shame,
  Even as I sing, suffuse my face;
For what is left the poet here?
For Greeks a blush—for Greece a tear.

7

Must *we* but weep o'er days more blest?
  Must *we* but blush?—Our fathers bled.
Earth! render back from out thy breast
  A remnant of our Spartan dead!
Of the three hundred grant but three,
To make a new Thermopylæ!

8

What, silent still? and silent all?
    Ah! no;—the voices of the dead
Sound like a distant torrent's fall,
    And answer, ' Let one living head,
But one arise,—we come, we come! '
'Tis but the living who are dumb.

9

In vain—in vain: strike other chords;
    Fill high the cup with Samian wine!
Leave battles to the Turkish hordes,
    And shed the blood of Scio's vine!
Hark! rising to the ignoble call—
How answers each bold Bacchanal!

10

You have the Pyrrhic dance as yet;
    Where is the Pyrrhic phalanx gone?
Of two such lessons, why forget
    The nobler and the manlier one?
You have the letters Cadmus gave—
Think ye he meant them for a slave?

11

Fill high the bowl with Samian wine!
    We will not think of themes like these!
It made Anacreon's song divine:
    He served—but served Polycrates—
A tyrant; but our masters then
Were still, at least, our countrymen.

12

The tyrant of the Chersonese
  Was freedom's best and bravest friend;
That tyrant was Miltiades!
  Oh! that the present hour would lend
Another despot of the kind!
Such chains as his were sure to bind.

13

Fill high the bowl with Samian wine!
  On Suli's rock, and Parga's shore,
Exists the remnant of a line
  Such as the Doric mothers bore;
And there, perhaps, some seed is sown,
The Heracleidan blood might own.

14

Trust not for freedom to the Franks—
  They have a king who buys and sells;
In native swords, and native ranks,
  The only hope of courage dwells:
But Turkish force, and Latin fraud,
Would break your shield, however broad.

15

Fill high the bowl with Samian wine!
  Our virgins dance beneath the shade—
I see their glorious black eyes shine;
  But gazing on each glowing maid,
My own the burning tear-drop laves,
To think such breasts must suckle slaves.

16

Place me on Sunium's marbled steep,
   Where nothing, save the waves and I,
May hear our mutual murmurs sweep;
   There, swan-like, let me sing and die:
A land of slaves shall ne'er be mine—
Dash down yon cup of Samian wine!

              Don Juan, Canto III, 1821

(*vii*)

Wellington

OH, Wellington! (or ' Villainton ')—for Fame
   Sounds the heroic syllables both ways;
France could not even conquer your great name,
   But punn'd it down to this facetious phrase—
Beating or beaten she will laugh the same,
   You have obtain'd great pensions and much praise:
Glory like yours should any dare gainsay,
Humanity would rise, and thunder ' Nay! '

I don't think that you used Kinnaird quite well
   In Marinèt's affair—in fact 'twas shabby,
And like some other things won't do to tell
   Upon your tomb in Westminster's old abbey.
Upon the rest 'tis not worth while to dwell,
   Such tales being for the tea-hours of some tabby;
But though your years as *man* tend fast to *zero*,
In fact your grace is still but a *young hero*.

Though Britain owes (and pays you too) so much,
   Yet Europe doubtless owes you greatly more:

You have repair'd Legitimacy's crutch,
 A prop not quite so certain as before:
The Spanish, and the French, as well as Dutch,
 Have seen, and felt, how strongly you *restore*;
And Waterloo has made the world your debtor
(I wish your bards would sing it rather better).

You are ' the best of cut-throats: '—do not start;
 The phrase is Shakspeare's, and not misapplied:—
War 's a brain-spattering, windpipe-slitting art,
 Unless her cause by right be sanctified.
If you have acted *once* a generous part,
 The world, not the world's masters, will decide,
And I shall be delighted to learn who,
Save you and yours, have gain'd by Waterloo?

I am no flatterer—you've supp'd full of flattery:
 They say you like it too—'tis no great wonder.
He whose whole life has been assault and battery,
 At last may get a little tired of thunder;
And swallowing eulogy much more than satire, he
 May like being praised for every lucky blunder,
Call'd ' Saviour of the Nations '—not yet saved,
And ' Europe's Liberator '—still enslaved.

I've done. Now go and dine from off the plate
 Presented by the Prince of the Brazils,
And send the sentinel before your gate
 A slice or two from your luxurious meals:
He fought, but has not fed so well of late.
 Some hunger, too, they say the people feels:—
There is no doubt that you deserve your ration,
But pray give back a little to the nation.

DON JUAN

I don't mean to reflect—a man so great as
   You, my lord duke! is far above reflection:
The high Roman fashion, too, of Cincinnatus,
   With modern history has but small connexion:
Though as an Irishman you love potatoes,
   You need not take them under your direction;
And half a million for your Sabine farm
Is rather dear!—I'm sure I mean no harm.

Great men have always scorn'd great recompenses:
   Epaminondas saved his Thebes, and died,
Not leaving even his funeral expenses:
   George Washington had thanks, and nought beside,
Except the all-cloudless glory (which few men's is)
   To free his country: Pitt too had his pride,
And as a high-soul'd minister of state is
Renown'd for ruining Great Britain gratis.

Never had mortal man such opportunity,
   Except Napoleon, or abused it more:
You might have freed fallen Europe from the unity
   Of tyrants, and been blest from shore to shore:
And *now*—what *is* your fame? Shall the Muse tune it ye?
   Now—that the rabble's first vain shouts are o'er?
Go! hear it in your famish'd country's cries!
Behold the world! and curse your victories!

                           Canto IX, Stanzas i–ix

(viii)

Contemporary Poets

IN twice five years the ' greatest living poet,'
　Like to the champion in the fisty ring,
Is call'd on to support his claim, or show it,
　Although 'tis an imaginary thing.
Even I—albeit I'm sure I did not know it,
　Nor sought of foolscap subjects to be king,—
Was reckon'd, a considerable time,
The grand Napoleon of the realms of rhyme.

But Juan was my Moscow, and Faliero
　My Leipsic, and my Mont Saint Jean seems Cain:
' La Belle Alliance ' of dunces down at zero,
　Now that the Lion 's fallen, may rise again:
But I will fall at least as fell my hero;
　Nor reign at all, or as a *monarch* reign;
Or to some lonely isle of gaolers go,
With turncoat Southey for my turnkey Lowe.

Sir Walter reign'd before me; Moore and Campbell
　Before and after: but now grown more holy,
The Muses upon Sion's hill must ramble
　With poets almost clergymen, or wholly:
And Pegasus has a psalmodic amble
　Beneath the very Reverend Rowley Powley,
Who shoes the glorious animal with stilts,
A modern Ancient Pistol—by the hilts!

Still he excels that artificial hard
　Labourer in the same vineyard, though the vine
Yields him but vinegar for his reward,—
　That neutralised dull Dorus of the Nine;

That swarthy Sporus, neither man nor bard;
    That ox of verse, who *ploughs* for every line:—
Cambyses' roaring Romans beat at least
The howling Hebrews of Cybele's priest.—

Then there 's my gentle Euphues; who, they say,
    Sets up for being a sort of *moral me*;
He'll find it rather difficult some day
    To turn out both, or either, it may be.
Some persons think that Coleridge hath the sway;
    And Wordsworth has supporters, two or three;
And that deep-mouth'd Bœotian ' Savage Landor '
Has taken for a swan rogue Southey's gander.

John Keats, who was kill'd off by one critique,
    Just as he really promised something great,
If not intelligible, without Greek
    Contrived to talk about the Gods of late,
Much as they might have been supposed to speak.
    Poor fellow! His was an untoward fate;
'Tis strange the mind, that fiery particle,
Should let itself be snuff'd out by an article.

Canto XI, Stanzas lv–lx

(*ix*)

Norman Abbey

IT stood embosom'd in a happy valley,
    Crown'd by high woodlands, where the Druid oak
Stood, like Caractacus, in act to rally
    His host, with broad arms 'gainst the thunderstroke,

And from beneath his boughs were seen to sally
   The dappled foresters; as day awoke,
The branching stag swept down with all his herd,
To quaff a brook which murmur'd like a bird.

Before the mansion lay a lucid lake,
   Broad as transparent, deep, and freshly fed
By a river, which its soften'd way did take
   In currents through the calmer water spread
Around: the wildfowl nestled in the brake
   And sedges, brooding in their liquid bed:
The woods sloped downwards to its brink, and stood
With their green faces fix'd upon the flood.

Its outlet dash'd into a deep cascade,
   Sparkling with foam, until again subsiding,
Its shriller echoes—like an infant made
   Quiet—sank into softer ripples, gliding
Into a rivulet: and thus allay'd,
   Pursued its course, now gleaming, and now hiding
Its windings through the woods; now clear, now blue,
According as the skies their shadows threw.

A glorious remnant of the Gothic pile
   (While yet the church was Rome's) stood half apart
In a grand arch, which once screen'd many an aisle.
   These last had disappear'd—a loss to art:
The first yet frown'd superbly o'er the soil,
   And kindled feelings in the roughest heart,
Which mourn'd the power of time's or tempest's march,
In gazing on that venerable arch.

Within a niche, nigh to its pinnacle,
   Twelve saints had once stood sanctified in stone;

But these had fallen, not when the friars fell,
    But in the war which struck Charles from his throne,
When each house was a fortalice—as tell
    The annals of full many a line undone,—
The gallant cavaliers, who fought in vain
For those who knew not to resign or reign.

But in a higher niche, alone, but crown'd,
    The Virgin-Mother of the God-born Child,
With her Son in her blessed arms, look'd round;
    Spared by some chance when all beside was spoil'd;
She made the earth below seem holy ground.
    This may be superstition, weak or wild,
But even the faintest relics of a shrine
Of any worship wake some thoughts divine.

A mighty window, hollow in the centre,
    Shorn of its glass of thousand colourings,
Through which the deepen'd glories once could enter,
    Streaming from off the sun like seraph's wings,
Now yawns all desolate: now loud, now fainter,
    The gale sweeps through its fretwork, and oft sings
The owl his anthem, where the silenced quire
Lie with their hallelujahs quench'd like fire.

But in the noontide of the moon, and when
    The wind is winged from one point of heaven,
There moans a strange unearthly sound, which then
    Is musical—a dying accent driven
Through the huge arch, which soars and sinks again.
    Some deem it but the distant echo given
Back to the night wind by the waterfall,
And harmonised by the old choral wall:

Others, that some original shape, or form
    Shaped by decay perchance, hath given the power
(Though less than that of Memnon's statue, warm
    In Egypt's rays, to harp at a fix'd hour)
To this grey ruin, with a voice to charm
    Sad, but serene, it sweeps o'er tree or tower;
The cause I know not nor can solve; but such
The fact:—I've heard it,—once perhaps too much.

Canto XIII, Stanzas lvi–lxiv

(x)

FOR me, I know nought; nothing I deny,
    Admit, reject, contemn; and what know *you*,
Except perhaps that you were born to die?
    And both may after all turn out untrue.
An age may come, Font of Eternity,
    When nothing shall be either old or new.
Death, so call'd, is a thing which makes men weep,
And yet a third of life is pass'd in sleep.

A sleep without dreams, after a rough day
    Of toil, is what we covet most; and yet
How clay shrinks back from more quiescent clay!
    The very Suicide that pays his debt
At once without instalments (an old way
    Of paying debts, which creditors regret),
Lets out impatiently his rushing breath,
Less from disgust of life than dread of death.

'Tis round him, near him, here, there, everywhere,
    And there 's a courage which grows out of fear,
Perhaps of all most desperate, which will dare
    The worst to *know* it:—when the mountains rear

Their peaks beneath your human foot, and there
    You look down o'er the precipice, and drear
The gulf of rock yawns,—you can't gaze a minute,
Without an awful wish to plunge within it.

'Tis true, you don't—but, pale and struck with terror,
    Retire: but look into your past impression!
And you will find, though shuddering at the mirror
    Of your own thoughts, in all their self-confession,
The lurking bias, be it truth or error,
    To the *unknown*; a secret prepossession,
To plunge with all your fears—but where? You know not,
And that's the reason why you do—or do not.

> Canto XIV, Stanzas iii–vi;
> *Don Juan*, Cantos IX–XIV, 1823

232   *George the Fourth in Ireland*

BUT he comes! the Messiah of royalty comes!
    Like a goodly Leviathan roll'd from the waves;
Then receive him as best such an advent becomes,
    With a legion of cooks, and an army of slaves!

He comes in the promise and bloom of threescore,
    To perform in the pageant the sovereign's part—
But long live the shamrock, which shadows him o'er!
    Could the green in his *hat* be transferr'd to his *heart*!

Could that long-wither'd spot but be verdant again,
    And a new spring of noble affections arise—
Then might freedom forgive thee this dance in thy chain,
    And this shout of thy slavery which saddens the skies.

Is it madness or meanness which clings to thee now?
　Were he God—as he is but the commonest clay,
With scarce fewer wrinkles than sins on his brow—
　Such servile devotion might shame him away.

Ay, roar in his train! let thine orators lash
　Their fanciful spirits to pamper his pride—
Not thus did thy Grattan indignantly flash
　His soul o'er the freedom implored and denied.

Ever glorious Grattan! the best of the good!
　So simple in heart, so sublime in the rest!
With all which Demosthenes wanted endued,
　And his rival or victor in all he possess'd.

Ere Tully arose in the zenith of Rome,
　Though unequall'd, preceded, the task was begun—
But Grattan sprung up like a god from the tomb
　Of ages, the first, last, the saviour, the *one* !

With the skill of an Orpheus to soften the brute;
　With the fire of Prometheus to kindle mankind;
Even Tyranny listening sate melted or mute,
　And Corruption shrunk scorch'd from the glance of his
　　mind.

The Irish Avatar, September 19, 1821

233　　　*At the Gate of Heaven*

(*i*)

Saint Peter

SAINT PETER sat by the celestial gate:
　His keys were rusty, and the lock was dull,
So little trouble had been given of late;
　Not that the place by any means was full,

AT THE GATE OF HEAVEN

But since the Gallic era ' eighty-eight '
  The devils had ta'en a longer, stronger pull,
And ' a pull altogether,' as they say
At sea—which drew most souls another way.

The angels all were singing out of tune,
  And hoarse with having little else to do,
Excepting to wind up the sun and moon,
  Or curb a runaway young star or two,
Or wild colt of a comet, which too soon
  Broke out of bounds o'er th' ethereal blue,
Splitting some planet with its playful tail,
As boats are sometimes by a wanton whale.

The guardian seraphs had retired on high,
  Finding their charges past all care below;
Terrestrial business fill'd nought in the sky
  Save the recording angel's black bureau;
Who found, indeed, the facts to multiply
  With such rapidity of vice and woe,
That he had stripp'd off both his wings in quills,
And yet was in arrear of human ills.

His business so augmented of late years,
  That he was forced, against his will no doubt,
(Just like those cherubs, earthly ministers,)
  For some resource to turn himself about,
And claim the help of his celestial peers,
  To aid him ere he should be quite worn out
By the increased demand for his remarks:
Six angels and twelve saints were named his clerks.

This was a handsome board—at least for heaven;
  And yet they had even then enough to do,

So many conquerors' cars were daily driven,
   So many kingdoms fitted up anew;
Each day too slew its thousands six or seven,
   Till at the crowning carnage, Waterloo,
They threw their pens down in divine disgust—
The page was so besmear'd with blood and dust.

This by the way; 'tis not mine to record
   What angels shrink from: even the very devil
On this occasion his own work abhorr'd,
   So surfeited with the infernal revel:
Though he himself had sharpen'd every sword,
   It almost quench'd his innate thirst of evil.
(Here Satan's sole good work deserves insertion—
'Tis, that he has both generals in reversion.)

(ii)

Michael and Satan

BUT bringing up the rear of this bright host
   A Spirit of a different aspect waved
His wings, like thunder-clouds above some coast
   Whose barren beach with frequent wrecks is paved;
His brow was like the deep when tempest-toss'd;
   Fierce and unfathomable thoughts engraved
Eternal wrath on his immortal face,
And *where* he gazed a gloom pervaded space.

As he drew near, he gazed upon the gate
   Ne'er to be enter'd more by him or Sin,
With such a glance of supernatural hate,
   As made Saint Peter wish himself within;

AT THE GATE OF HEAVEN

He patter'd with his keys at a great rate,
    And sweated through his apostolic skin:
Of course his perspiration was but ichor,
Or some such other spiritual liquor.

The very cherubs huddled all together,
    Like birds when soars the falcon; and they felt
A tingling to the tip of every feather,
    And form'd a circle like Orion's belt
Around their poor old charge; who scarce knew whither
    His guards had led him, though they gently dealt
With royal manes (for by many stories,
And true, we learn the angels all are Tories).

As things were in this posture, the gate flew
    Asunder, and the flashing of its hinges
Flung over space an universal hue
    Of many-colour'd flame, until its tinges
Reach'd even our speck of earth, and made a new
    Aurora borealis spread its fringes
O'er the North Pole; the same seen, when ice-bound,
By Captain Parry's crew, in ' Melville's Sound.'

And from the gate thrown open issued beaming
    A beautiful and mighty Thing of Light,
Radiant with glory, like a banner streaming
    Victorious from some world-o'erthrowing fight:
My poor comparisons must needs be teeming
    With earthly likenesses, for here the night
Of clay obscures our best conceptions, saving
Johanna Southcote, or Bob Southey raving.

'Twas the archangel Michael; all men know
    The make of angels and archangels, since

497

GEORGE GORDON, LORD BYRON

There 's scarce a scribbler has not one to show,
    From the fiends' leader to the angels' prince;
There also are some altar-pieces, though
    I really can't say that they much evince
One's inner notions of immortal spirits;
But let the connoisseurs explain *their* merits.

Michael flew forth in glory and in good;
    A goodly work of him from whom all glory
And good arise; the portal past—he stood;
    Before him the young cherubs and saints hoary—
(I say *young*, begging to be understood
    By looks, not years; and should be very sorry
To state, they were not older than St. Peter,
But merely that they seem'd a little sweeter).

The cherubs and the saints bow'd down before
    That arch-angelic hierarch, the first
Of essences angelical, who wore
    The aspect of a god; but this ne'er nursed
Pride in his heavenly bosom, in whose core
    No thought, save for his Master's service, durst
Intrude, however glorified and high;
He knew him but the viceroy of the sky.

He and the sombre, silent Spirit met—
    They knew each other both for good and ill;
Such was their power, that neither could forget
    His former friend and future foe; but still
There was a high, immortal, proud regret
    In either's eye, as if 'twere less their will
Than destiny to make the eternal years
Their date of war, and their ' champ clos ' the spheres.

AT THE GATE OF HEAVEN

The spirits were in neutral space, before
   The gate of heaven; like eastern thresholds is
The place where Death's grand cause is argued o'er,
   And souls despatch'd to that world or to this;
And therefore Michael and the other wore
   A civil aspect: though they did not kiss,
Yet still between his Darkness and his Brightness
There pass'd a mutual glance of great politeness.

The Archangel bow'd, not like a modern beau,
   But with a graceful Oriental bend,
Pressing one radiant arm just where below
   The heart in good men is supposed to tend;
He turn'd as to an equal, not too low,
   But kindly; Satan met his ancient friend
With more hauteur, as might an old Castilian
Poor noble meet a mushroom rich civilian.

He merely bent his diabolic brow
   An instant; and then raising it, he stood
In act to assert his right or wrong, and show
   Cause why King George by no means could or should
Make out a case to be exempt from woe
   Eternal, more than other kings, endued
With better sense and hearts, whom history mentions,
Who long have ' paved hell with their good intentions.'

(iii)

Junius

' CALL Junius!' From the crowd a shadow stalk'd,
   And at the name there was a general squeeze,
So that the very ghosts no longer walk'd
   In comfort, at their own aërial ease,

But were all ramm'd, and jamm'd (but to be balk'd,
   As we shall see), and jostled hands and knees,
Like wind compress'd and pent within a bladder,
Or like a human colic, which is sadder.

The shadow came—a tall, thin, grey-hair'd figure,
   That look'd as it had been a shade on earth;
Quick in its motions, with an air of vigour,
   But nought to mark its breeding or its birth;
Now it wax'd little, then again grew bigger,
   With now an air of gloom, or savage mirth;
But as you gazed upon its features, they
Changed every instant—to *what*, none could say.

The more intently the ghosts gazed, the less
   Could they distinguish whose the features were;
The Devil himself seem'd puzzled even to guess;
   They varied like a dream—now here, now there;
And several people swore from out the press,
   They knew him perfectly; and one could swear
He was his father: upon which another
Was sure he was his mother's cousin's brother:

Another, that he was a duke, or knight,
   An orator, a lawyer, or a priest,
A nabob, a man-midwife; but the wight
   Mysterious changed his countenance at least
As oft as they their minds; though in full sight
   He stood, the puzzle only was increased;
The man was a phantasmagoria in
Himself—he was so volatile and thin.

The moment that you had pronounced him *one*,
   Presto! his face changed, and he was another;

And when that change was hardly well put on,
  It varied, till I don't think his own mother
(If that he had a mother) would her son
  Have known, he shifted so from one to t'other;
Till guessing from a pleasure grew a task,
At this epistolary ' Iron Mask.'

For sometimes he like Cerberus would seem—
  ' Three gentlemen at once ' (as sagely says
Good Mrs. Malaprop); then you might deem
  That he was not even *one*; now many rays
Were flashing round him; and now a thick steam
  Hid him from sight—like fogs on London days:
Now Burke, now Tooke, he grew to people's fancies,
And certes often like Sir Philip Francis.

(*iv*)

Southey

AT length with jostling, elbowing, and the aid
  Of cherubim appointed to that post,
The devil Asmodeus to the circle made
  His way, and look'd as if his journey cost
Some trouble. When his burden down he laid,
  ' What 's this? ' cried Michael; ' why, 'tis not a ghost? '
' I know it,' quoth the incubus; ' but he
Shall be one, if you leave the affair to me.

' Confound the renegado! I have sprain'd
  My left wing, he 's so heavy; one would think
Some of his works about his neck were chain'd.
  But to the point; while hovering o'er the brink

501

Of Skiddaw (where as usual it still rain'd),
  I saw a taper, far below me, wink,
And stooping, caught this fellow at a libel—
No less on history than the Holy Bible.

' The former is the devil's scripture, and
  The latter yours, good Michael: so the affair
Belongs to all of us, you understand.
  I snatch'd him up just as you see him there,
And brought him off for sentence out of hand:
  I've scarcely been ten minutes in the air—
At least a quarter it can hardly be:
I dare say that his wife is still at tea.'

.   .   .   .

Now the bard, glad to get an audience, which
  By no means often was his case below,
Began to cough, and hawk, and hem, and pitch
  His voice into that awful note of woe
To all unhappy hearers within reach
  Of poets when the tide of rhyme 's in flow;
But stuck fast with his first hexameter,
Not one of all whose gouty feet would stir.

But ere the spavin'd dactyls could be spurr'd
  Into recitative, in great dismay
Both cherubim and seraphim were heard
  To murmur loudly through their long array;
And Michael rose ere he could get a word
  Of all his founder'd verses under way,
And cried, ' For God's sake stop, my friend ! 'twere best—
Non Di, non homines—you know the rest.'

AT THE GATE OF HEAVEN

A general bustle spread throughout the throng,
   Which seem'd to hold all verse in detestation;
The angels had of course enough of song
   When upon service; and the generation
Of ghosts had heard too much in life, not long
   Before, to profit by a new occasion:
The monarch, mute till then, exclaim'd, ' What! what!
Pye come again? No more—no more of that!'

The tumult grew; an universal cough
   Convulsed the skies, as during a debate,
When Castlereagh has been up long enough
   (Before he was first minister of state,
I mean—the *slaves hear now*); some cried ' Off, off!'
   As at a farce; till, grown quite desperate,
The bard Saint Peter pray'd to interpose
(Himself an author) only for his prose.

The varlet was not an ill-favour'd knave;
   A good deal like a vulture in the face,
With a hook nose and a hawk's eye, which gave
   A smart and sharper-looking sort of grace
To his whole aspect, which, though rather grave,
   Was by no means so ugly as his case;
But that, indeed, was hopeless as can be,
Quite a poetic felony ' *de se.*'

Then Michael blew his trump, and still'd the noise
   With one still greater, as is yet the mode
On earth besides; except some grumbling voice,
   Which now and then will make a slight inroad
Upon decorous silence, few will twice
   Lift up their lungs when fairly overcrow'd;

And now the bard could plead his own bad cause,
With all the attitudes of self-applause.

He said—(I only give the heads)—he said,
    He meant no harm in scribbling; 'twas his way
Upon all topics; 'twas, besides, his bread,
    Of which he butter'd both sides; 'twould delay
Too long the assembly (he was pleased to dread),
    And take up rather more time than a day,
To name his works—he would but cite a few—
' Wat Tyler '—' Rhymes on Blenheim '—' Waterloo.'

He had written praises of a regicide;
    He had written praises of all kings whatever;
He had written for republics far and wide,
    And then against them bitterer than ever;
For pantisocracy he once had cried
    Aloud, a scheme less moral than 'twas clever;
Then grew a hearty anti-jacobin—
Had turn'd his coat—and would have turn'd his skin.

He had sung against all battles, and again
    In their high praise and glory; he had call'd
Reviewing ' the ungentle craft,' and then
    Become as base a critic as e'er crawl'd—
Fed, paid, and pamper'd by the very men
    By whom his muse and morals had been maul'd:
He had written much blank verse, and blanker prose,
And more of both than anybody knows.

He had written Wesley's life:—here turning round
    To Satan, ' Sir, I'm ready to write yours,
In two octavo volumes, nicely bound,
    With notes and preface, all that most allures

AT THE GATE OF HEAVEN

The pious purchaser; and there's no ground
   For fear, for I can choose my own reviewers:
So let me have the proper documents,
That I may add you to my other saints.'

Satan bow'd, and was silent. ' Well, if you,
   With amiable modesty, decline
My offer, what says Michael? There are few
   Whose memoirs could be render'd more divine.
Mine is a pen of all work; not so new
   As it was once, but I would make you shine
Like your own trumpet. By the way, my own
Has more of brass in it, and is as well blown.

' But talking about trumpets, here's my Vision!
   Now you shall judge, all people; yes, you shall
Judge with my judgment, and by my decision
   Be guided who shall enter heaven or fall.
I settle all these things by intuition,
   Times present, past, to come, heaven, hell, and all,
Like King Alfonso. When I thus see double,
I save the Deity some worlds of trouble.'

He ceased, and drew forth an MS.; and no
   Persuasion on the part of devils, saints,
Or angels, now could stop the torrent; so
   He read the first three lines of the contents;
But at the fourth, the whole spiritual show
   Had vanish'd, with variety of scents,
Ambrosial and sulphureous, as they sprang,
Like lightning, off from his ' melodious twang.'

Those grand heroics acted as a spell:
   The angels stopp'd their ears and plied their pinions;

GEORGE GORDON, LORD BYRON

The devils ran howling, deafen'd, down to hell;
    The ghosts fled, gibbering, for their own dominions—
(For 'tis not yet decided where they dwell,
    And I leave every man to his opinions);
Michael took refuge in his trump—but, lo!
His teeth were set on edge, he could not blow!

Saint Peter, who has hitherto been known
    For an impetuous saint, upraised his keys,
And at the fifth line knock'd the poet down;
    Who fell like Phaëton, but more at ease,
Into his lake, for there he did not drown;
    A different web being by the Destinies
Woven for the Laureate's final wreath, whene'er
Reform shall happen either here or there.

He first sank to the bottom—like his works,
    But soon rose to the surface—like himself;
For all corrupted things are buoy'd like corks,
    By their own rottenness, light as an elf,
Or wisp that flits o'er a morass: he lurks,
    It may be, still, like dull books on a shelf,
In his own den, to scrawl some ' Life ' or ' Vision,'
As Welborn says—' the devil turn'd precisian.'

As for the rest, to come to the conclusion
    Of this true dream, the telescope is gone
Which kept my optics free from all delusion,
    And show'd me what I in my turn have shown;
All I saw farther, in the last confusion,
    Was, that King George slipp'd into heaven for one;
And when the tumult dwindled to a calm,
I left him practising the hundredth psalm.

The Liberal, October 15, 1822

HE who first met the Highlands' swelling blue
Will love each peak that shows a kindred hue,
Hail in each crag a friend's familiar face,
And clasp the mountain in his mind's embrace.
Long have I roamed through lands which are not mine,
Adored the Alp, and loved the Apennine,
Revered Parnassus, and beheld the steep
Jove's Ida and Olympus crown the deep:
But 'twas not all long ages' lore, nor all
Their nature held me in their thrilling thrall;
The infant rapture still survived the boy,
And Loch-na-gar with Ida look'd o'er Troy,
Mix'd Celtic memories with the Phrygian mount,
And Highland linns with Castalie's clear fount.
Forgive me, Homer's universal shade!
Forgive me, Phœbus! that my fancy stray'd;
The north and nature taught me to adore
Your scenes sublime, from those beloved before.

The Island, 1823

235   ' *So, we'll go no more a roving* '

I

SO, we'll go no more a roving
So late into the night,
Though the heart be still as loving,
And the moon be still as bright.

II

For the sword outwears its sheath,
   And the soul wears out the breast,
And the heart must pause to breathe,
   And love itself have rest.

III

Though the night was made for loving,
   And the day returns too soon,
Yet we'll go no more a roving
   By the light of the moon.

Letters and Journals, 1830

236   *Stanzas written on the road between*
Florence and Pisa

OH, talk not to me of a name great in story;
   The days of our youth are the days of our glory;
And the myrtle and ivy of sweet two-and-twenty
Are worth all your laurels, though ever so plenty.

What are garlands and crowns to the brow that is wrinkled?
'Tis but as a dead-flower with May-dew besprinkled.
Then away with all such from the head that is hoary!
What care I for the wreaths that can *only* give glory!

Oh FAME!—if I e'er took delight in thy praises,
'Twas less for the sake of thy high-sounding phrases,
Than to see the bright eyes of the dear one discover,
She thought that I was not unworthy to love her.

508

STANZAS

There chiefly I sought thee, *there* only I found thee;
Her glance was the best of the rays that surround thee;
When it sparkled o'er aught that was bright in my story,
I knew it was love, and I felt it was glory.

Written November 1821;
Letters and Journals, 1830

237   *On My Thirty-Third Birthday*

January 22, 1821

THROUGH life's dull road, so dim and dirty,
    I have dragg'd to three-and-thirty.
What have these years left to me?
Nothing—except thirty-three.

Letters and Journals, 1830

RICHARD HARRIS BARHAM

1788–1845

238   *Hon. Mr. Sucklethumbkin's Story*

The Execution

A SPORTING ANECDOTE

MY Lord Tomnoddy got up one day;
    It was half after two, He had nothing to do,
So his Lordship rang for his cabriolet.

Tiger Tim   Was clean of limb,
His boots were polish'd, his jacket was trim;
With a very smart tie in his smart cravat,
And a smart cockade on the top of his hat;

Tallest of boys, or shortest of men,
He stood in his stockings just four foot ten;
And he ask'd, as he held the door on the swing,
' Pray, did your Lordship please to ring? '

My Lord Tomnoddy he raised his head,
And thus to Tiger Tim he said,
    ' Malibran 's dead, Duvernay 's fled,
Taglioni has not yet arrived in her stead;
Tiger Tim, come, tell me true,
What may a Nobleman find to do? '—

Tim look'd up, and Tim look'd down,
He paused, and he put on a thoughtful frown,
And he held up his hat, and he peep'd in the crown;
He bit his lip, and he scratch'd his head,
He let go the handle, and thus he said,
As the door, released, behind him bang'd
' An't please you, my Lord, there 's a man to be hang'd.'

My Lord Tomnoddy jump'd up at the news,
    ' Run to M'Fuze, And Lieutenant Tregooze,
And run to Sir Carnaby Jenks, of the Blues.
    Rope-dancers a score I've seen before—
Madame Sacchi, Antonio, and Master Black-more;
    But to see a man swing At the end of a string,
With his neck in a noose, will be quite a new thing!'

My Lord Tomnoddy stept into his cab—
Dark rifle green, with a lining of drab;
    Through street and through square,
    His high-trotting mare,
Like one of Ducrow's, goes pawing the air.

HON. MR. SUCKLETHUMBKIN'S STORY

Adown Piccadilly and Waterloo Place
Went the high-trotting mare at a very quick pace;
 She produced some alarm, But did no great harm,
Save frightening a nurse with a child on her arm,
 Spattering with clay Two urchins at play,
Knocking down—very much to the sweeper's dismay—
An old woman who wouldn't get out of the way,
 And upsetting a stall Near Exeter Hall,
Which made all the pious Church-Mission folks squall,
 But eastward afar, Through Temple Bar,
My Lord Tomnoddy directs his car;
 Never heeding their squalls,
 Or their calls, or their bawls,
He passes by Waithman's Emporium for shawls,
And, merely just catching a glimpse of St. Paul's,
 Turns down the Old Bailey,
 Where in front of the gaol, he
Pulls up at the door of a gin-shop, and gaily
Cries, 'What must I fork out to-night, my trump,
For the whole first-floor of the Magpie and Stump?'

 . . . .

The clock strikes Twelve—it is dark midnight—
Yet the Magpie and Stump is one blaze of light.
 The parties are met; The tables are set;
There is 'punch,' 'cold *without*,' 'hot *with*,' 'heavy wet,'
 Ale-glasses and jugs, And rummers and mugs,
And sand on the floor, without carpets or rugs,
 Cold fowl and cigars, Pickled onions in jars,
Welsh rabbits and kidneys—rare work for the jaws!—
And very large lobsters, with very large claws;
 And there is M'Fuze, And Lieutenant Tregooze,

And there is Sir Carnaby Jenks, of the Blues,
All come to see a man ' die in his shoes! '

The clock strikes One! Supper is done,
And Sir Carnaby Jenks is full of his fun,
Singing ' Jolly companions every one! '
   My Lord Tomnoddy Is drinking gin-toddy,
And laughing at ev'ry thing, and ev'ry body.—
The clock strikes Two! and the clock strikes Three!
—' Who so merry, so merry as we? '
   Save Captain M'Fuze, Who is taking a snooze,
While Sir Carnaby Jenks is busy at work,
Blacking his nose with a piece of burnt cork.

   The clock strikes Four!— Round the debtors' door
Are gather'd a couple of thousand or more,
   As many await At the press-yard gate,
Till slowly its folding doors open, and straight
The mob divides, and between their ranks
A waggon comes loaded with posts and with planks.

   The clock strikes Five! The Sheriffs arrive,
And the crowd is so great that the street seems alive;
   But Sir Carnaby Jenks Blinks, and winks,
A candle burns down in the socket, and stinks.
   Lieutenant Tregooze Is dreaming of Jews,
And acceptances all the bill-brokers refuse;
   My Lord Tomnoddy Has drunk all his toddy,
And just as the dawn is beginning to peep,
The whole of the party are fast asleep.

Sweetly, oh! sweetly, the morning breaks,
   With roseate streaks,

HON. MR. SUCKLETHUMBKIN'S STORY

Like the first faint blush on a maiden's cheeks;
Seem'd as that mild and clear blue sky
Smiled upon all things far and nigh,
On all—save the wretch condemn'd to die!
Alack! that ever so fair a Sun
As that which its course has now begun,
Should rise on such a scene of misery!—
Should gild with rays so light and free
That dismal, dark-frowning Gallows-tree!

And hark!—a sound comes, big with fate;
The clock from St. Sepulchre's tower strikes—Eight!—
List to that low funereal bell:
It is tolling, alas! a living man's knell!—
And see!—from forth that opening door
They come—HE steps that threshold o'er
Who never shall tread upon threshold more!
—God! 'tis a fearsome thing to see
That pale wan man's mute agony,—
The glare of that wild, despairing eye,
Now bent on the crowd, now turn'd to the sky,
As though 'twere scanning, in doubt and in fear,
The path of the Spirit's unknown career:
Those pinion'd arms, those hands that ne'er
Shall be lifted again,—not even in prayer;
That heaving chest!—Enough—'tis done!
The bolt has fallen!—the spirit is gone—
For weal or for woe is known but to One!—
—Oh! 'twas a fearsome sight!—Ah me!
A deed to shudder at,—not to see.

Again that clock! 'tis time, 'tis time!
The hour is past: with its earliest chime

The cord is severed, the lifeless clay
By ' dungeon villains ' is borne away:
Nine!—'twas the last concluding stroke!
And then—my Lord Tomnoddy awoke!
And Tregooze and Sir Carnaby Jenks arose,
And Captain M'Fuze, with the black on his nose:
And they stared at each other, as much as to say,
    ' Hollo! Hollo! Here's a rum Go!
Why, Captain!—my Lord!—Here's the devil to pay!
The fellow's been cut down and taken away!

    What's to be done? We've miss'd all the fun!—
Why, they'll laugh at and quiz us all over the town,
We are all of us done so uncommonly brown!'

What *was* to be done?—'twas perfectly plain
They could not well hang the man over again:
What *was* to be done?—The man was dead!
Nought *could* be done—nought could be said;
So—my Lord Tomnoddy went home to bed!

Bentley's Miscellany, June, 1837
Ingoldsby Legends, 1840

THOMAS PRINGLE

1789–1834

239   *The Hottentot*

MILD, melancholy, and sedate, he stands,
    Tending another's flock upon the fields,
His father's once, where now the White Man builds
His home, and issues forth his proud commands.
His dark eye flashes not; his listless hands
Lean on the shepherd's staff; no more he wields
The Libyan bow—but to th'oppressor yields
Submissively his freedom and his lands.

514

THE HOTTENTOT

Has he no courage? Once he had—but, lo!
Harsh Servitude hath worn him to the bone.
No enterprise? Alas! the brand, the blow,
Have humbled him to dust—even *hope* is gone!
' He 's a base-hearted hound—not worth his food '—
His Master cries—' he has no *gratitude*! '

African Sketches, 1834

CHARLES WOLFE

1791–1823

240   *The Burial of Sir John Moore*
at Corunna

NOT a drum was heard, not a funeral note,
　　As his corse to the rampart we hurried;
Not a soldier discharged his farewell shot
　　O'er the grave where our hero we buried.

We buried him darkly at dead of night,
　　The sods with our bayonets turning;
By the struggling moonbeam's misty light
　　And the lantern dimly burning.

No useless coffin enclosed his breast,
　　Not in sheet nor in shroud we wound him;
But he lay like a warrior taking his rest
　　With his martial cloak around him.

Few and short were the prayers we said,
　　And we spoke not a word of sorrow;
But we steadfastly gazed on the face that was dead,
　　And we bitterly thought of the morrow.

515

We thought, as we hollowed his narrow bed
    And smoothed down his lonely pillow,
That the foe and the stranger would tread o'er his head.
    And we far away on the billow!

Lightly they'll talk of the spirit that's gone
    And o'er his cold ashes upbraid him,—
But little he'll reck, if they let him sleep on
    In the grave where a Briton has laid him.

But half of our heavy task was done
    When the clock struck the hour for retiring:
And we heard the distant and random gun
    That the foe was sullenly firing.

Slowly and sadly we laid him down,
    From the field of his fame fresh and gory;
We carved not a line, and we raised not a stone,
    But we left him alone with his glory.

Newry Telegraph, 19 April 1817;
Poetical Remains, 1825

241   *To Mary*

IF I had thought thou couldst have died,
    I might not weep for thee;
But I forgot, when by thy side,
    That thou couldst mortal be:
It never through my mind had past
    The time would e'er be o'er,
And I on thee should look my last,
    And thou shouldst smile no more!

TO MARY

And still upon that face I look,
    And think 'twill smile again;
And still the thought I will not brook,
    That I must look in vain.
But when I speak—thou dost not say
    What thou ne'er left'st unsaid;
And now I feel, as well I may,
    Sweet Mary, thou art dead!

If thou wouldst stay, e'en as thou art,
    All cold and all serene—
I still might press thy silent heart,
    And where thy smiles have been.
While e'en thy chill, bleak corse I have,
    Thou seemest still mine own;
But there—I lay thee in thy grave,
    And I am now alone!

I do not think, where'er thou art,
    Thou hast forgotten me;
And I, perhaps, may soothe this heart
    In thinking too of thee:
Yet there was round thee such a dawn
    Of light ne'er seen before,
As fancy never could have drawn,
    And never can restore!

Poetical Remains, 1825

EDWARD QUILLINAN

The Hour Glass

POETS loiter all their leisure,
   Culling flowers of rhyme;
Thus they twine the wreath of pleasure
   Round the glass of time:
   Twining flowers of rhyme.

Fancy's Children, ever heedless!
   Why thus bribe the hours?
Death, to prove the trouble needless,
   Withers all your flowers:
   Why then bribe the hours?

Like the Sand, so fast retreating,
   Thus your hopes shall fall;
Life and fame are just as fleeting;
   Poets, flowers, and all:
   Thus your fancies fall.

Woodcuts and Verses, 1820

HENRY HART MILMAN

The Beacons

      . . . EASTWARD far anon
Another fire rose furious up; behind
Another and another: all the hills
Each beyond each held up its crest of flame.
Along the heavens the bright and crimson hue
Widening and deepening travels on: the range

THE BEACONS

O'erleaps black Tamar, by whose ebon tide
Cornwall is bounded; and on Heytor rock,
Above the stony moorish source of Dart,
It waves a sanguine standard; Haldon burns,
And the red City glows a deeper hue.
And all the southern rocks, the moorland downs,
In those portentous characters of flame
Discourse, and bear the glaring legend on:
Even to the graves on Ambri plain, where woke
That pallid woman, and rejoic'd, and deem'd
'Twas sent to guide her to the tomb she sought.
Fast flash they up, those altars of revenge,
As though the snake-hair'd Sister torch-bearers,
Th'Eumenides, from the Tartarean depths
Were leaping on from hill to hill, on each
Leaving the tracks of their flame-dropping feet.
Or as the souls of the dead fathers, wrapt
In bright meteorous grave-clothes, had arisen,
And each sate crowning his accustom'd hill,
Radiant and mute: or the devoted isle
Had wrought down by her bold and frequent guilt
Th'Almighty's lightning shafts, now numberless
Forth raining from the lurid reeking clouds,
And smiting all the heights. On spreads the train,
Northward it breaks upon the Quantock ridge;
It reddens on the Mendip forests dark;
It looks into the cavern'd Cheddar cliffs:
The boatman on the Severn mouth awakes
And sees the waters rippling round his keel
In spots and streaks of purple light, each shore
Ablaze with all its answering hills: the streams
Run glittering down Plinlimmon's side, though thick

And moonless the wan night: and Idris stands
Like Stromboli or Ætna, where 'twas feign'd
E'er at their flashing furnace wrought the Sons
Of Vulcan, forging with eternal toil
Jove's never idle thunderbolts. And thou,
Snowdon, the king of mountains, art not dark
Amid thy vassal brethren gleaming bright.
Is it to welcome thy returning Seer,
That thus above thy clouds, above thy snows,
Thou wear'st that wreathed diadem of fire,
As to outshine the pale and winking stars?
O'er Menai's waters blue the gleaming spreads,
The Bard in Mona's secret grove beholds
A glitter on his harp-strings, and looks out
Upon the kindling cliffs of Penmanmawr.

Samor, 1818

PERCY BYSSHE SHELLEY

1792–1822

244   *Hymn to Intellectual Beauty*

I

THE awful shadow of some unseen Power
     Floats though unseen among us,—visiting
This various world with as inconstant wing
As summer winds that creep from flower to flower,—
Like moonbeams that behind some piny mountain shower,
     It visits with inconstant glance
     Each human heart and countenance;
Like hues and harmonies of evening,—
     Like clouds in starlight widely spread,—
     Like memory of music fled,—

HYMN TO INTELLECTUAL BEAUTY

Like aught that for its grace may be
Dear, and yet dearer for its mystery.

II

Spirit of BEAUTY, that dost consecrate
　　With thine own hues all thou dost shine upon
　　Of human thought or form,—where art thou gone?
Why dost thou pass away and leave our state,
This dim vast vale of tears, vacant and desolate?
　　Ask why the sunlight not for ever
　　Weaves rainbows o'er yon mountain-river,
Why aught should fail and fade that once is shown,
　　Why fear and dream and death and birth
　　Cast on the daylight of this earth
　　Such gloom,—why man has such a scope
For love and hate, despondency and hope?

III

No voice from some sublimer world hath ever
　　To sage or poet these responses given—
　　Therefore the names of Demon, Ghost, and Heaven,
Remain the records of their vain endeavour,
Frail spells—whose uttered charm might not avail to sever,
　　From all we hear and all we see,
　　Doubt, chance, and mutability.
Thy light alone—like mist o'er mountains driven,
　　Or music by the night-wind sent
　　Through strings of some still instrument,
　　Or moonlight on a midnight stream,
Gives grace and truth to life's unquiet dream.

IV

Love, Hope, and Self-esteem, like clouds depart
    And come, for some uncertain moments lent.
    Man were immortal and omnipotent,
Didst thou, unknown and awful as thou art,
Keep with thy glorious train firm state within his heart.
    Thou messenger of sympathies,
    That wax and wane in lovers' eyes—
Thou—that to human thought art nourishment,
    Like darkness to a dying flame!
    Depart not as thy shadow came,
    Depart not—lest the grave should be,
Like life and fear, a dark reality.

V

While yet a boy I sought for ghosts, and sped
    Through many a listening chamber, cave and ruin,
    And starlight wood, with fearful steps pursuing
Hopes of high talk with the departed dead.
I called on poisonous names with which our youth is fed;
    I was not heard—I saw them not—
    When musing deeply on the lot
Of life, at that sweet time when winds are wooing
    All vital things that wake to bring
    News of birds and blossoming,—
    Sudden, thy shadow fell on me;
I shrieked, and clasped my hands in ecstasy!

VI

I vowed that I would dedicate my powers
    To thee and thine—have I not kept the vow?
    With beating heart and streaming eyes, even now

522

I call the phantoms of a thousand hours
Each from his voiceless grave: they have in visioned bowers
   Of studious zeal or love's delight
   Outwatched with me the envious night—
They know that never joy illumed my brow
   Unlinked with hope that thou wouldst free
   This world from its dark slavery,
   That thou—O awful LOVELINESS,
Wouldst give whate'er these words cannot express.

VII

The day becomes more solemn and serene
   When noon is past—there is a harmony
   In autumn, and a lustre in its sky,
Which through the summer is not heard or seen,
As if it could not be, as if it had not been!
   Thus let thy power, which like the truth
   Of nature on thy passive youth
Descended, to my onward life supply
   Its calm—to one who worships thee,
   And every form containing thee,
   Whom, SPIRIT fair, thy spells did bind
To fear himself, and love all human kind.

The Examiner, 19 Jan., 1817;
Rosalind and Helen, &c., 1819

245   *Love's Philosophy*

I

THE fountains mingle with the river
   And the rivers with the Ocean,
The winds of Heaven mix for ever
   With a sweet emotion;

523

Nothing in the world is single;
   All things by a law divine
In one spirit meet and mingle.
   Why not I with thine?—

II

See the mountains kiss high Heaven
   And the waves clasp one another;
No sister-flower would be forgiven
   If it disdained its brother;
And the sunlight clasps the earth
   And the moonbeams kiss the sea:
What is all this sweet work worth
   If thou kiss not me?

The Indicator, 22 December 1819
Posthumous Poems, 1824

246   *From ' Prometheus Unbound '*

(*i*)

First Spirit

ON a battle-trumpet's blast
   I fled hither, fast, fast, fast,
'Mid the darkness upward cast.
From the dust of creeds outworn,
From the tyrant's banner torn,
Gathering 'round me, onward borne,
There was mingled many a cry—
Freedom! Hope! Death! Victory!
Till they faded through the sky;
And one sound, above, around,

PROMETHEUS UNBOUND

One sound beneath, around, above,
Was moving; 'twas the soul of Love;
'Twas the hope, the prophecy,
Which begins and ends in thee.

Second Spirit

A rainbow's arch stood on the sea,
Which rocked beneath, immovably;
And the triumphant storm did flee,
Like a conqueror, swift and proud,
Between, with many a captive cloud,
A shapeless, dark and rapid crowd,
Each by lightning riven in half:
I heard the thunder hoarsely laugh:
Mighty fleets were strewn like chaff
And spread beneath a hell of death
O'er the white waters. I alit
On a great ship lightning-split,
And speeded hither on the sigh
Of one who gave an enemy
His plank, then plunged aside to die.

Third Spirit

I sate beside a sage's bed,
And the lamp was burning red
Near the book where he had fed,
When a Dream with plumes of flame,
To his pillow hovering came,
And I knew it was the same
Which had kindled long ago
Pity, eloquence, and woe;
And the world awhile below

Wore the shade, its lustre made.
It has borne me here as fleet
As Desire's lightning feet:
I must ride it back ere morrow,
Or the sage will wake in sorrow.

Fourth Spirit

On a poet's lips I slept
Dreaming like a love-adept
In the sound his breathing kept;
Nor seeks nor finds he mortal blisses,
But feeds on the aëreal kisses
Of shapes that haunt thought's wildernesses.
He will watch from dawn to gloom
The lake-reflected sun illume
The yellow bees in the ivy-bloom,
Nor heed nor see, what things they be;
But from these create he can
Forms more real than living man,
Nurslings of immortality!
One of these awakened me,
And I sped to succour thee.

Act I

(*ii*)

Spirit

MY coursers are fed with the lightning,
They drink of the whirlwind's stream,
And when the red morning is bright'ning
    They bathe in the fresh sunbeam;
    They have strength for their swiftness I deem,
Then ascend with me, daughter of Ocean.

I desire: and their speed makes night kindle;
  I fear: they outstrip the Typhoon;
Ere the cloud piled on Atlas can dwindle
  We encircle the earth and the moon:
  We shall rest from long lābours at noon:
Then ascend with me, daughter of Ocean.

Act II, Scene IV

(*iii*)

Voice in the Air, singing.

LIFE of Life! thy lips enkindle
  With their love the breath between them;
And thy smiles before they dwindle
  Make the cold air fire; then screen them
In those looks, where whoso gazes
Faints, entangled in their mazes.

Child of Light! thy limbs are burning
  Through the vest which seems to hide them;
As the radiant lines of morning
  Through the clouds ere they divide them;
And this atmosphere divinest
Shrouds thee wheresoe'er thou shinest.

Fair are others; none beholds thee,
  But thy voice sounds low and tender
Like the fairest, for it folds thee
  From the sight, that liquid splendour,
And all feel, yet see thee never,
As I feel now, lost for ever!

Lamp of Earth! where'er thou movest
   Its dim shapes are clad with brightness,
And the souls of whom thou lovest
   Walk upon the winds with lightness,
Till they fail, as I am failing,
Dizzy, lost, yet unbewailing!

Act II, Scene V

(iv)

Demogorgon

THOU, Earth, calm empire of a happy soul,
   Sphere of divinest shapes and harmonies,
Beautiful orb! gathering as thou dost roll
   The love which paves thy path along the skies:

The Earth

I hear: I am as a drop of dew that dies.

Demogorgon

Thou, Moon, which gazest on the nightly Earth
   With wonder, as it gazes upon thee;
Whilst each to men, and beasts, and the swift birth
   Of birds, is beauty, love, calm, harmony:

The Moon

I hear: I am a leaf shaken by thee!

Demogorgon

Ye Kings of suns and stars, Dæmons and Gods,
   Aetherial Dominations, who possess
Elysian, windless, fortunate abodes
   Beyond Heaven's constellated wilderness:

A Voice from above

Our great Republic hears, we are blest, and bless.

PROMETHEUS UNBOUND

Demogorgon

Ye happy Dead, whom beams of brightest verse
  Are clouds to hide, not colours to portray,
Whether your nature is that universe
  Which once ye saw and suffered—

A Voice from beneath

Or as they
Whom we have left, we change and pass away.

Demogorgon

Ye elemental Genii, who have homes
  From man's high mind even to the central stone
Of sullen lead; from heaven's star-fretted domes
  To the dull weed some sea-worm battens on:

A confused Voice

We hear: thy words waken Oblivion.

Demogorgon

Spirits, whose homes are flesh: ye beasts and birds,
  Ye worms, and fish; ye living leaves and buds;
Lightning and wind; and ye untameable herds,
  Meteors and mists, which throng air's solitudes:—

A Voice

Thy voice to us is wind among still woods.

Demogorgon

Man, who wert once a despot and a slave;
  A dupe and a deceiver; a decay;
A traveller from the cradle to the grave
  Through the dim night of this immortal day:

All

Speak: thy strong words may never pass away.

Demogorgon

This is the day, which down the void abysm
At the Earth-born's spell yawns for Heaven's despotism,
      And Conquest is dragged captive through the deep:
Love, from its awful throne of patient power
In the wise heart, from the last giddy hour
      Of dread endurance, from the slippery, steep,
And narrow verge of crag-like agony, springs
And folds over the world its healing wings.

Gentleness, Virtue, Wisdom, and Endurance,
These are the seals of that most firm assurance
      Which bars the pit over Destruction's strength;
And if, with infirm hand, Eternity,
Mother of many acts and hours, should free
      The serpent that would clasp her with his length;
These are the spells by which to reassume
An empire o'er the disentangled doom.

To suffer woes which Hope thinks infinite;
To forgive wrongs darker than death or night;
      To defy Power, which seems omnipotent;
To love, and bear; to hope till Hope creates
From its own wreck the thing it contemplates;
      Neither to change, nor falter, nor repent;
This, like thy glory, Titan, is to be
Good, great and joyous, beautiful and free;
This is alone Life, Joy, Empire, and Victory.

Act IV
Prometheus Unbound, &c., 1820

I BRING fresh showers for the thirsting flowers,
    From the seas and the streams;
I bear light shade for the leaves when laid
    In their noonday dreams.
From my wings are shaken the dews that waken
    The sweet buds every one,
When rocked to rest on their mother's breast,
    As she dances about the sun.
I wield the flail of the lashing hail,
    And whiten the green plains under,
And then again I dissolve it in rain,
    And laugh as I pass in thunder.

I sift the snow on the mountains below,
    And their great pines groan aghast;
And all the night 'tis my pillow white,
    While I sleep in the arms of the blast.
Sublime on the towers of my skiey bowers,
    Lightning my pilot sits;
In a cavern under is fettered the thunder,
    It struggles and howls at fits;
Over earth and ocean, with gentle motion,
    This pilot is guiding me,
Lured by the love of the genii that move
    In the depths of the purple sea;
Over the rills, and the crags, and the hills,
    Over the lakes and the plains,
Wherever he dream, under mountain or stream,
    The Spirit he loves remains;
And I all the while bask in Heaven's blue smile,
    Whilst he is dissolving in rains.

The sanguine Sunrise, with his meteor eyes,
    And his burning plumes outspread,
Leaps on the back of my sailing rack,
    When the morning star shines dead;
As on the jag of a mountain crag,
    Which an earthquake rocks and swings,
An eagle alit one moment may sit
    In the light of its golden wings.
And when Sunset may breathe, from the lit sea beneath,
    Its ardours of rest and of love,
And the crimson pall of eve may fall
    From the depth of Heaven above,
With wings folded I rest, on mine aëry nest,
    As still as a brooding dove.

That orbèd maiden with white fire laden,
    Whom mortals call the Moon,
Glides glimmering o'er my fleece-like floor,
    By the midnight breezes strewn;
And wherever the beat of her unseen feet,
    Which only the angels hear,
May have broken the woof of my tent's thin roof,
    The stars peep behind her and peer;
And I laugh to see them whirl and flee,
    Like a swarm of golden bees,
When I widen the rent in my wind-built tent,
    Till the calm rivers, lakes, and seas,
Like strips of the sky fallen through me on high,
    Are each paved with the moon and these.

I bind the Sun's throne with a burning zone,
    And the Moon's with a girdle of pearl;

THE CLOUD

The volcanoes are dim, and the stars reel and swim,
  When the whirlwinds my banner unfurl.
From cape to cape, with a bridge-like shape,
  Over a torrent sea,
Sunbeam-proof, I hang like a roof,—
  The mountains its columns be.
The triumphal arch through which I march
  With hurricane, fire, and snow,
When the Powers of the air are chained to my chair,
  Is the million-coloured bow;
The sphere-fire above its soft colours wove,
  While the moist Earth was laughing below.

I am the daughter of Earth and Water,
  And the nursling of the Sky;
I pass through the pores of the ocean and shores;
  I change, but I cannot die.
For after the rain when with never a stain
  The pavilion of Heaven is bare,
And the winds and sunbeams with their convex gleams
  Build up the blue dome of air,
I silently laugh at my own cenotaph,
  And out of the caverns of rain,
Like a child from the womb, like a ghost from the tomb,
  I arise and unbuild it again.

Prometheus Unbound, &c., 1820

248   *To a Skylark*

HAIL to thee, blithe Spirit!
      Bird thou never wert,
  That from Heaven, or near it,
    Pourest thy full heart
In profuse strains of unpremeditated art.

Higher still and higher
    From the earth thou springest
Like a cloud of fire;
    The blue deep thou wingest,
And singing still dost soar, and soaring ever singest.

In the golden lightning
    Of the sunken sun,
O'er which clouds are bright'ning,
    Thou dost float and run;
Like an unbodied joy whose race is just begun.

The pale purple even
    Melts around thy flight;
Like a star of Heaven,
    In the broad daylight
Thou art unseen, but yet I hear thy shrill delight,

Keen as are the arrows
    Of that silver sphere,
Whose intense lamp narrows
    In the white dawn clear
Until we hardly see—we feel that it is there.

All the earth and air
    With thy voice is loud,
As, when night is bare,
    From one lonely cloud
The moon rains out her beams, and Heaven is overflowed.

What thou art we know not;
    What is most like thee?
From rainbow clouds there flow not
    Drops so bright to see
As from thy presence showers a rain of melody.

TO A SKYLARK

Like a Poet hidden
   In the light of thought,
Singing hymns unbidden,
   Till the world is wrought
To sympathy with hopes and fears it heeded not:

Like a high-born maiden
   In a palace-tower,
Soothing her love-laden
   Soul in secret hour
With music sweet as love, which overflows her bower:

Like a glow-worm golden
   In a dell of dew,
Scattering unbeholden
   Its aëreal hue
Among the flowers and grass, which screen it from the view!

Like a rose embowered
   In its own green leaves,
By warm winds deflowered,
   Till the scent it gives
Makes faint with too much sweet those heavy-wingèd
     thieves:

Sound of vernal showers
   On the twinkling grass,
Rain-awakened flowers,
   All that ever was
Joyous, and clear, and fresh, thy music doth surpass:

Teach us, Sprite or Bird,
   What sweet thoughts are thine:
I have never heard
   Praise of love or wine
That panted forth a flood of rapture so divine.

Chorus Hymeneal,
   Or triumphal chant,
Matched with thine would be all
   But an empty vaunt,
A thing wherein we feel there is some hidden want.

What objects are the fountains
   Of thy happy strain?
What fields, or waves, or mountains?
   What shapes of sky or plain?
What love of thine own kind? what ignorance of pain?

With thy clear keen joyance
   Languor cannot be:
Shadow of annoyance
   Never came near thee.
Thou lovest—but ne'er knew love's sad satiety.

Waking or asleep,
   Thou of death must deem
Things more true and deep
   Than we mortals dream,
Or how could thy notes flow in such a crystal stream?

We look before and after,
   And pine for what is not:
Our sincerest laughter
   With some pain is fraught;
Our sweetest songs are those that tell of saddest thought.

Yet if we could scorn
   Hate, and pride, and fear;
If we were things born
   Not to shed a tear,
I know not how thy joy we ever should come near.

Better than all measures
   Of delightful sound,
Better than all treasures
   That in books are found,
Thy skill to poet were, thou scorner of the ground!

Teach me half the gladness
   That thy brain must know,
Such harmonious madness
   From my lips would flow
The world should listen then—as I am listening now.

Prometheus Unbound, &c., 1820

249   *Ode to the West Wind*

I

O WILD West Wind, thou breath of Autumn's being,
   Thou, from whose unseen presence the leaves dead
Are driven, like ghosts from an enchanter fleeing,

Yellow, and black, and pale, and hectic red,
Pestilence-stricken multitudes: O thou,
Who chariotest to their dark wintry bed

The wingèd seeds, where they lie cold and low,
Each like a corpse within its grave, until
Thine azure sister of the Spring shall blow

Her clarion o'er the dreaming earth, and fill
(Driving sweet buds like flocks to feed in air)
With living hues and odours plain and hill:

Wild Spirit, which art moving everywhere;
Destroyer and preserver; hear, oh, hear!

3353   s   537

II

Thou on whose stream, mid the steep sky's commotion,
Loose clouds like earth's decaying leaves are shed,
Shook from the tangled boughs of Heaven and Ocean,

Angels of rain and lightning: there are spread
On the blue surface of thine aëry surge,
Like the bright hair uplifted from the head

Of some fierce Maenad, even from the dim verge
Of the horizon to the zenith's height,
The locks of the approaching storm. Thou dirge

Of the dying year, to which this closing night
Will be the dome of a vast sepulchre,
Vaulted with all thy congregated might

Of vapours, from whose solid atmosphere
Black rain, and fire, and hail will burst: oh, hear!

III

Thou who didst waken from his summer dreams
The blue Mediterranean, where he lay,
Lulled by the coil of his crystàlline streams,

Beside a pumice isle in Baiae's bay,
And saw in sleep old palaces and towers
Quivering within the wave's intenser day,

All overgrown with azure moss and flowers
So sweet, the sense faints picturing them! Thou
For whose path the Atlantic's level powers

Cleave themselves into chasms, while far below
The sea-blooms and the oozy woods which wear
The sapless foliage of the ocean, know

ODE TO THE WEST WIND

Thy voice, and suddenly grow gray with fear,
And tremble and despoil themselves: oh, hear!

IV

If I were a dead leaf thou mightest bear;
If I were a swift cloud to fly with thee;
A wave to pant beneath thy power, and share

The impulse of thy strength, only less free
Than thou, O uncontrollable! If even
I were as in my boyhood, and could be

The comrade of thy wanderings over Heaven,
As then, when to outstrip thy skiey speed
Scarce seemed a vision; I would ne'er have striven

As thus with thee in prayer in my sore need.
Oh, lift me as a wave, a leaf, a cloud!
I fall upon the thorns of life! I bleed!

A heavy weight of hours has chained and bowed
One too like thee: tameless, and swift, and proud.

V

Make me thy lyre, even as the forest is:
What if my leaves are falling like its own!
The tumult of thy mighty harmonies

Will take from both a deep, autumnal tone,
Sweet though in sadness. Be thou, Spirit fierce,
My spirit! Be thou me, impetuous one!

Drive my dead thoughts over the universe
Like withered leaves to quicken a new birth!
And, by the incantation of this verse,

539

Scatter, as from an unextinguished hearth
Ashes and sparks, my words among mankind!
Be through my lips to unawakened earth

The trumpet of a prophecy! O, Wind,
If Winter comes, can Spring be far behind?

Prometheus Unbound, &c., 1820

250   *From ' Epipsychidion '*

A SHIP is floating in the harbour now,
    A wind is hovering o'er the mountain's brow;
There is a path on the sea's azure floor,
No keel has ever ploughed that path before;
The halcyons brood around the foamless isles;
The treacherous Ocean has forsworn its wiles;
The merry mariners are bold and free:
Say, my heart's sister, wilt thou sail with me?
Our bark is as an albatross, whose nest
Is a far Eden of the purple East;
And we between her wings will sit, while Night,
And Day, and Storm, and Calm, pursue their flight,
Our ministers, along the boundless Sea,
Treading each other's heels, unheededly.
It is an isle under Ionian skies,
Beautiful as a wreck of Paradise,
And, for the harbours are not safe and good,
This land would have remained a solitude
But for some pastoral people native there,
Who from the Elysian, clear, and golden air
Draw the last spirit of the age of gold,
Simple and spirited; innocent and bold.

540

EPIPSYCHIDION

The blue Aegean girds this chosen home,
With ever-changing sound and light and foam,
Kissing the sifted sands, and caverns hoar;
And all the winds wandering along the shore
Undulate with the undulating tide:
There are thick woods where sylvan forms abide;
And many a fountain, rivulet, and pond,
As clear as elemental diamond,
Or serene morning air; and far beyond,
The mossy tracks made by the goats and deer
(Which the rough shepherd treads but once a year)
Pierce into glades, caverns, and bowers, and halls
Built round with ivy, which the waterfalls
Illumining, with sound that never fails
Accompany the noonday nightingales;
And all the place is peopled with sweet airs;
The light clear element which the isle wears
Is heavy with the scent of lemon-flowers,
Which floats like mist laden with unseen showers,
And falls upon the eyelids like faint sleep;
And from the moss violets and jonquils peep,
And dart their arrowy odour through the brain
Till you might faint with that delicious pain.
And every motion, odour, beam, and tone,
With that deep music is in unison:
Which is a soul within the soul—they seem
Like echoes of an antenatal dream.—
It is an isle 'twixt Heaven, Air, Earth, and Sea,
Cradled, and hung in clear tranquillity;
Bright as that wandering Eden Lucifer,
Washed by the soft blue Oceans of young air.
It is a favoured place. Famine or Blight,

Pestilence, War and Earthquake, never light
Upon its mountain-peaks; blind vultures, they
Sail onward far upon their fatal way:
The wingèd storms, chanting their thunder-psalm
To other lands, leave azure chasms of calm
Over this isle, or weep themselves in dew,
From which its fields and woods ever renew
Their green and golden immortality.
And from the sea there rise, and from the sky
There fall, clear exhalations, soft and bright,
Veil after veil, each hiding some delight,
Which Sun or Moon or zephyr draw aside,
Till the isle's beauty, like a naked bride
Glowing at once with love and loveliness,
Blushes and trembles at its own excess:
Yet, like a buried lamp, a Soul no less
Burns in the heart of this delicious isle,
An atom of th' Eternal, whose own smile
Unfolds itself, and may be felt, not seen
O'er the gray rocks, blue waves, and forests green,
Filling their bare and void interstices.—
But the chief marvel of the wilderness
Is a lone dwelling, built by whom or how
None of the rustic island-people know:
'Tis not a tower of strength, though with its height
It overtops the woods; but, for delight,
Some wise and tender Ocean-King, ere crime
Had been invented, in the world's young prime,
Reared it, a wonder of that simple time,
An envy of the isles, a pleasure-house
Made sacred to his sister and his spouse.
It scarce seems now a wreck of human art,

EPIPSYCHIDION

But, as it were Titanic; in the heart
Of Earth having assumed its form, then grown
Out of the mountains, from the living stone,
Lifting itself in caverns light and high:
For all the antique and learnèd imagery
Has been erased, and in the place of it
The ivy and the wild-vine interknit
The volumes of their many-twining stems;
Parasite flowers illume with dewy gems
The lampless halls, and when they fade, the sky
Peeps through their winter-woof of tracery
With moonlight patches, or star atoms keen,
Or fragments of the day's intense serene;—
Working mosaic on their Parian floors.
And, day and night, aloof, from the high towers
And terraces, the Earth and Ocean seem
To sleep in one another's arms, and dream
Of waves, flowers, clouds, woods, rocks, and all that we
Read in their smiles, and call reality.

This isle and house are mine, and I have vowed
Thee to be lady of the solitude.—
And I have fitted up some chambers there
Looking towards the golden Eastern air,
And level with the living winds, which flow
Like waves above the living waves below.—
I have sent books and music there, and all
Those instruments with which high Spirits call
The future from its cradle, and the past
Out of its grave, and make the present last
In thoughts and joys which sleep, but cannot die,
Folded within their own eternity.

Our simple life wants little, and true taste
Hires not the pale drudge Luxury, to waste
The scene it would adorn, and therefore still,
Nature with all her children haunts the hill.
The ring-dove, in the embowering ivy, yet
Keeps up her love-lament, and the owls flit
Round the evening tower, and the young stars glance
Between the quick bats in their twilight dance;
The spotted deer bask in the fresh moonlight
Before our gate, and the slow, silent night
Is measured by the pants of their calm sleep.
Be this our home in life, and when years heap
Their withered hours, like leaves, on our decay,
Let us become the overhanging day,
The living soul of this Elysian isle,
Conscious, inseparable, one. Meanwhile
We two will rise, and sit, and walk together,
Under the roof of Ionian blue weather,
And wander in the meadows, or ascend
The mossy mountains, where the blue heavens bend
With lightest winds, to touch their paramour;
Or linger, where the pebble-paven shore,
Under the quick, faint kisses of the sea
Trembles and sparkles as with ecstasy,—
Possessing and possessed by all that is
Within that calm circumference of bliss,
And by each other, till to love and live
Be one:—or, at the noontide hour, arrive
Where some old cavern hoar seems yet to keep
The moonlight of the expired night asleep,
Through which the awakened day can never peep;
A veil for our seclusion, close as night's,

Where secure sleep may kill thine innocent lights;
Sleep, the fresh dew of languid love, the rain
Whose drops quench kisses till they burn again.
And we will talk, until thought's melody
Become too sweet for utterance, and it die
In words, to live again in looks, which dart
With thrilling tone into the voiceless heart,
Harmonizing silence without a sound.
Our breath shall intermix, our bosoms bound,
And our veins beat together; and our lips
With other eloquence than words, eclipse
The soul that burns between them, and the wells
Which boil under our being's inmost cells,
The fountains of our deepest life, shall be
Confused in Passion's golden purity,
As mountain-springs under the morning sun.
We shall become the same, we shall be one
Spirit within two frames, oh! wherefore two?
One passion in twin-hearts, which grows and grew,
Till like two meteors of expanding flame,
Those spheres instinct with it become the same,
Touch, mingle, are transfigured; ever still
Burning, yet ever inconsumable:
In one another's substance finding food,
Like flames too pure and light and unimbued
To nourish their bright lives with baser prey,
Which point to Heaven and cannot pass away:
One hope within two wills, one will beneath
Two overshadowing minds, one life, one death,
One Heaven, one Hell, one immortality,
And one annihilation. Woe is me!
The wingèd words on which my soul would pierce

Into the height of Love's rare Universe,
Are chains of lead around its flight of fire—
I pant, I sink, I tremble, I expire!

Epipsychidion, 1821

251   *Adonais*

I

I WEEP for Adonais—he is dead!
O, weep for Adonais! though our tears
Thaw not the frost which binds so dear a head!
And thou, sad Hour, selected from all years
To mourn our loss, rouse thy obscure compeers,
And teach them thine own sorrow, say: ' With me
Died Adonais; till the Future dares
Forget the Past, his fate and fame shall be
An echo and a light unto eternity!'

II

Where wert thou, mighty Mother, when he lay,
When thy Son lay, pierced by the shaft which flies
In darkness? where was lorn Urania
When Adonais died? With veilèd eyes,
'Mid listening Echoes, in her Paradise
She sate, while one, with soft enamoured breath,
Rekindled all the fading melodies,
With which, like flowers that mock the corse beneath,
He had adorned and hid the coming bulk of Death.

III

Oh, weep for Adonais—he is dead!
Wake, melancholy Mother, wake and weep!
Yet wherefore? Quench within their burning bed
Thy fiery tears, and let thy loud heart keep

ADONAIS

Like his, a mute and uncomplaining sleep;
For he is gone, where all things wise and fair
Descend;—oh, dream not that the amorous Deep
Will yet restore him to the vital air;
Death feeds on his mute voice, and laughs at our despair.

IV

Most musical of mourners, weep again!
Lament anew, Urania!—He died,
Who was the Sire of an immortal strain,
Blind, old, and lonely, when his country's pride,
The priest, the slave, and the liberticide,
Trampled and mocked with many a loathèd rite
Of lust and blood; he went, unterrified,
Into the gulf of death; but his clear Sprite
Yet reigns o'er earth; the third among the sons of light.

V

Most musical of mourners, weep anew!
Not all to that bright station dared to climb;
And happier they their happiness who knew,
Whose tapers yet burn through that night of time
In which suns perished; others more sublime,
Struck by the envious wrath of man or god,
Have sunk, extinct in their refulgent prime;
And some yet live, treading the thorny road,
Which leads, through toil and hate, to Fame's serene abode.

VI

But now, thy youngest, dearest one, has perished—
The nursling of thy widowhood, who grew,
Like a pale flower by some sad maiden cherished,
And fed with true-love tears, instead of dew;

Most musical of mourners, weep anew!
Thy extreme hope, the loveliest and the last,
The bloom, whose petals nipped before they blew
Died on the promise of the fruit, is waste;
The broken lily lies—the storm is overpast.

VII

To that high Capital, where kingly Death
Keeps his pale court in beauty and decay,
He came; and bought, with price of purest breath,
A grave among the eternal.—Come away!
Haste, while the vault of blue Italian day
Is yet his fitting charnel-roof! while still
He lies, as if in dewy sleep he lay;
Awake him not! surely he takes his fill
Of deep and liquid rest, forgetful of all ill.

VIII

He will awake no more, oh, never more!—
Within the twilight chamber spreads apace
The shadow of white Death, and at the door
Invisible Corruption waits to trace
His extreme way to her dim dwelling-place;
The eternal Hunger sits, but pity and awe
Soothe her pale rage, nor dares she to deface
So fair a prey, till darkness, and the law
Of change, shall o'er his sleep the mortal curtain draw.

IX

Oh, weep for Adonais!—The quick Dreams,
The passion-wingèd Ministers of thought,
Who were his flocks, whom near the living streams
Of his young spirit he fed, and whom he taught

548

ADONAIS

The love which was its music, wander not,—
Wander no more, from kindling brain to brain,
But droop there, whence they sprung; and mourn their lot
Round the cold heart, where, after their sweet pain,
They ne'er will gather strength, or find a home again.

X

And one with trembling hands clasps his cold head,
And fans him with her moonlight wings, and cries;
' Our love, our hope, our sorrow, is not dead;
See, on the silken fringe of his faint eyes,
Like dew upon a sleeping flower, there lies
A tear some Dream has loosened from his brain.'
Lost Angel of a ruined Paradise!
She knew not 'twas her own; as with no stain
She faded, like a cloud which had outwept its rain.

XI

One from a lucid urn of starry dew
Washed his light limbs as if embalming them;
Another clipped her profuse locks, and threw
The wreath upon him, like an anadem,
Which frozen tears instead of pearls begem;
Another in her wilful grief would break
Her bow and wingèd reeds, as if to stem
A greater loss with one which was more weak;
And dull the barbèd fire against his frozen cheek.

XII

Another Splendour on his mouth alit,
That mouth, whence it was wont to draw the breath
Which gave it strength to pierce the guarded wit,
And pass into the panting heart beneath

With lightning and with music: the damp death
Quenched its caress upon his icy lips;
And, as a dying meteor stains a wreath
Of moonlight vapour, which the cold night clips,
It flushed through his pale limbs, and passed to its eclipse.

XIII

And others came . . . Desires and Adorations,
Wingèd Persuasions and veiled Destinies,
Splendours, and Glooms, and glimmering Incarnations
Of hopes and fears, and twilight Phantasies;
And Sorrow, with her family of Sighs,
And Pleasure, blind with tears, led by the gleam
Of her own dying smile instead of eyes,
Came in slow pomp;—the moving pomp might seem
Like pageantry of mist on an autumnal stream.

XIV

All he had loved, and moulded into thought,
From shape, and hue, and odour, and sweet sound,
Lamented Adonais. Morning sought
Her eastern watch-tower, and her hair unbound,
Wet with the tears which should adorn the ground,
Dimmed the aëreal eyes that kindle day;
Afar the melancholy thunder moaned,
Pale Ocean in unquiet slumber lay,
And the wild Winds flew round, sobbing in their dismay.

XV

Lost Echo sits amid the voiceless mountains,
And feeds her grief with his remembered lay,
And will no more reply to winds or fountains,
Or amorous birds perched on the young green spray,

550

ADONAIS

Or herdsman's horn, or bell at closing day;
Since she can mimic not his lips, more dear
Than those for whose disdain she pined away
Into a shadow of all sounds:—a drear
Murmur, between their songs, is all the woodmen hear.

XVI

Grief made the young Spring wild, and she threw down
Her kindling buds, as if she Autumn were,
Or they dead leaves; since her delight is flown,
For whom should she have waked the sullen year?
To Phoebus was not Hyacinth so dear
Nor to himself Narcissus, as to both
Thou, Adonais: wan they stand and sere
Amid the faint companions of their youth,
With dew all turned to tears; odour, to sighing ruth.

XVII

The spirit's sister, the lorn nightingale
Mourns not her mate with such melodious pain;
Not so the eagle, who like thee could scale
Heaven, and could nourish in the sun's domain
Her mighty youth with morning, doth complain,
Soaring and screaming round her empty nest,
As Albion wails for thee: the curse of Cain
Light on his head who pierced thy innocent breast,
And scared the angel soul that was its earthly guest!

XVIII

Ah, woe is me! Winter is come and gone,
But grief returns with the revolving year;
The airs and streams renew their joyous tone;
The ants, the bees, the swallows reappear;

Fresh leaves and flowers deck the dead Seasons' bier;
The amorous birds now pair in every brake,
And build their mossy homes in field and brere;
And the green lizard, and the golden snake,
Like unimprisoned flames, out of their trance awake.

XIX

Through wood and stream and field and hill and Ocean
A quickening life from the Earth's heart has burst
As it has ever done, with change and motion,
From the great morning of the world when first
God dawned on Chaos; in its stream immersed,
The lamps of Heaven flash with a softer light;
All baser things pant with life's sacred thirst;
Diffuse themselves; and spend in love's delight,
The beauty and the joy of their renewèd might.

XX

The leprous corpse, touched by this spirit tender,
Exhales itself in flowers of gentle breath;
Like incarnations of the stars, when splendour
Is changed to fragrance, they illumine death
And mock the merry worm that wakes beneath;
Nought we know, dies. Shall that alone which knows
Be as a sword consumed before the sheath
By sightless lightning?—the intense atom glows
A moment, then is quenched in a most cold repose.

XXI

Alas! that all we loved of him should be,
But for our grief, as if it had not been,
And grief itself be mortal! Woe is me!
Whence are we, and why are we? of what scene

552

The actors or spectators? Great and mean
Meet massed in death, who lends what life must borrow.
As long as skies are blue, and fields are green,
Evening must usher night, night urge the morrow,
Month follow month with woe, and year wake year to sorrow.

XXII

He will awake no more, oh, never more!
' Wake thou,' cried Misery, ' childless Mother, rise
Out of thy sleep, and slake, in thy heart's core,
A wound more fierce than his, with tears and sighs.'
And all the Dreams that watched Urania's eyes,
And all the Echoes whom their sister's song
Had held in holy silence, cried: ' Arise! '
Swift as a Thought by the snake Memory stung,
From her ambrosial rest the fading Splendour sprung.

XXIII

She rose like an autumnal Night, that springs
Out of the East, and follows wild and drear
The golden Day, which, on eternal wings,
Even as a ghost abandoning a bier,
Had left the Earth a corpse. Sorrow and fear
So struck, so roused, so rapt Urania;
So saddened round her like an atmosphere
Of stormy mist; so swept her on her way
Even to the mournful place where Adonais lay.

XXIV

Out of her secret Paradise she sped,
Through camps and cities rough with stone, and steel,
And human hearts, which to her aery tread
Yielding not, wounded the invisible

Palms of her tender feet where'er they fell:
And barbèd tongues, and thoughts more sharp than they,
Rent the soft Form they never could repel,
Whose sacred blood, like the young tears of May,
Paved with eternal flowers that undeserving way.

XXV

In the death-chamber for a moment Death,
Shamed by the presence of that living Might,
Blushed to annihilation, and the breath
Revisited those lips, and Life's pale light
Flashed through those limbs, so late her dear delight.
' Leave me not wild and drear and comfortless,
As silent lightning leaves the starless night!
Leave me not! ' cried Urania: her distress
Roused Death: Death rose and smiled, and met her vain
      caress.

XXVI

' Stay yet awhile! speak to me once again;
Kiss me, so long but as a kiss may live;
And in my heartless breast and burning brain
That word, that kiss, shall all thoughts else survive,
With food of saddest memory kept alive,
Now thou art dead, as if it were a part
Of thee, my Adonais! I would give
All that I am to be as thou now art!
But I am chained to Time, and cannot thence depart!

XXVII

' O gentle child, beautiful as thou wert,
Why didst thou leave the trodden paths of men
Too soon, and with weak hands though mighty heart
Dare the unpastured dragon in his den?

554

ADONAIS

Defenceless as thou wert, oh, where was then
Wisdom the mirrored shield, or scorn the spear?
Or hadst thou waited the full cycle, when
Thy spirit should have filled its crescent sphere,
The monsters of life's waste had fled from thee like deer.

XXVIII

' The herded wolves, bold only to pursue;
The obscene ravens, clamorous o'er the dead;
The vultures to the conqueror's banner true
Who feed where Desolation first has fed,
And whose wings rain contagion;—how they fled,
When, like Apollo, from his golden bow
The Pythian of the age one arrow sped
And smiled!—The spoilers tempt no second blow,
They fawn on the proud feet that spurn them lying low.

XXIX

' The sun comes forth, and many reptiles spawn;
He sets, and each ephemeral insect then
Is gathered into death without a dawn,
And the immortal stars awake again;
So is it in the world of living men:
A godlike mind soars forth, in its delight
Making earth bare and veiling heaven, and when
It sinks, the swarms that dimmed or shared its light
Leave to its kindred lamps the spirit's awful night.'

XXX

Thus ceased she: and the mountain shepherds came,
Their garlands sere, their magic mantles rent;
The Pilgrim of Eternity, whose fame
Over his living head like Heaven is bent,

An early but enduring monument,
Came, veiling all the lightnings of his song
In sorrow; from her wilds Ierne sent
The sweetest lyrist of her saddest wrong,
And Love taught Grief to fall like music from his tongue.

XXXI

Midst others of less note, came one frail Form,
A phantom among men; companionless
As the last cloud of an expiring storm
Whose thunder is its knell; he, as I guess,
Had gazed on Nature's naked loveliness,
Actaeon-like, and now he fled astray
With feeble steps o'er the world's wilderness,
And his own thoughts, along that rugged way,
Pursued, like raging hounds, their father and their prey.

XXXII

A pardlike Spirit beautiful and swift—
A Love in desolation masked;—a Power
Girt round with weakness;—it can scarce uplift
The weight of the superincumbent hour;
It is a dying lamp, a falling shower,
A breaking billow;—even whilst we speak
Is it not broken? On the withering flower
The killing sun smiles brightly: on a cheek
The life can burn in blood, even while the heart may break.

XXXIII

His head was bound with pansies overblown,
And faded violets, white, and pied, and blue;
And a light spear topped with a cypress cone,
Round whose rude shaft dark ivy-tresses grew

ADONAIS

Yet dripping with the forest's noonday dew,
Vibrated, as the ever-beating heart
Shook the weak hand that grasped it; of that crew
He came the last, neglected and apart;
A herd-abandoned deer struck by the hunter's dart.

XXXIV

All stood aloof, and at his partial moan
Smiled through their tears; well knew that gentle band
Who in another's fate now wept his own,
As in the accents of an unknown land
He sung new sorrow; sad Urania scanned
The Stranger's mien, and murmured: ' Who art thou? '
He answered not, but with a sudden hand
Made bare his branded and ensanguined brow,
Which was like Cain's or Christ's—oh! that it should be so!

XXXV

What softer voice is hushed over the dead?
Athwart what brow is that dark mantle thrown?
What form leans sadly o'er the white death-bed,
In mockery of monumental stone,
The heavy heart heaving without a moan?
If it be He, who, gentlest of the wise,
Taught, soothed, loved, honoured the departed one,
Let me not vex, with inharmonious sighs,
The silence of that heart's accepted sacrifice.

XXXVI

Our Adonais has drunk poison—oh!
What deaf and viperous murderer could crown
Life's early cup with such a draught of woe?
The nameless worm would now itself disown:

It felt, yet could escape, the magic tone
Whose prelude held all envy, hate, and wrong,
But what was howling in one breast alone,
Silent with expectation of the song,
Whose master's hand is cold, whose silver lyre unstrung.

XXXVII

Live thou, whose infamy is not thy fame!
Live! fear no heavier chastisement from me,
Thou noteless blot on a remembered name!
But be thyself, and know thyself to be!
And ever at thy season be thou free
To spill the venom when thy fangs o'erflow:
Remorse and Self-contempt shall cling to thee;
Hot Shame shall burn upon thy secret brow,
And like a beaten hound tremble thou shalt—as now.

XXXVIII

Nor let us weep that our delight is fled
Far from these carrion kites that scream below;
He wakes or sleeps with the enduring dead;
Thou canst not soar where he is sitting now.—
Dust to the dust! but the pure spirit shall flow
Back to the burning fountain whence it came,
A portion of the Eternal, which must glow
Through time and change, unquenchably the same,
Whilst thy cold embers choke the sordid hearth of shame.

XXXIX

Peace, peace! he is not dead, he doth not sleep——
He hath awakened from the dream of life—
'Tis we, who lost in stormy visions, keep
With phantoms an unprofitable strife,

And in mad trance, strike with our spirit's knife
Invulnerable nothings.—*We* decay
Like corpses in a charnel; fear and grief
Convulse us and consume us day by day,
And cold hopes swarm like worms within our living clay.

XL

He has outsoared the shadow of our night;
Envy and calumny and hate and pain,
And that unrest which men miscall delight,
Can touch him not and torture not again;
From the contagion of the world's slow stain
He is secure, and now can never mourn
A heart grown cold, a head grown gray in vain;
Nor, when the spirit's self has ceased to burn,
With sparkless ashes load an unlamented urn.

XLI

He lives, he wakes—'tis Death is dead, not he;
Mourn not for Adonais.—Thou young Dawn,
Turn all thy dew to splendour, for from thee
The spirit thou lamentest is not gone;
Ye caverns and ye forests, cease to moan!
Cease, ye faint flowers and fountains, and thou Air,
Which like a mourning veil thy scarf hadst thrown
O'er the abandoned Earth, now leave it bare
Even to the joyous stars which smile on its despair!

XLII

He is made one with Nature: there is heard
His voice in all her music, from the moan
Of thunder, to the song of night's sweet bird;
He is a presence to be felt and known

In darkness and in light, from herb and stone,
Spreading itself where'er that Power may move
Which has withdrawn his being to its own;
Which wields the world with never-wearied love,
Sustains it from beneath, and kindles it above.

XLIII

He is a portion of the loveliness
Which once he made more lovely: he doth bear
His part, while the one Spirit's plastic stress
Sweeps through the dull dense world, compelling there
All new successions to the forms they wear;
Torturing th' unwilling dross that checks its flight
To its own likeness, as each mass may bear;
And bursting in its beauty and its might
From trees and beasts and men into the Heaven's light.

XLIV

The splendours of the firmament of time
May be eclipsed, but are extinguished not;
Like stars to their appointed height they climb,
And death is a low mist which cannot blot
The brightness it may veil. When lofty thought
Lifts a young heart above its mortal lair,
And love and life contend in it, for what
Shall be its earthly doom, the dead live there
And move like winds of light on dark and stormy air.

XLV

The inheritors of unfulfilled renown
Rose from their thrones, built beyond mortal thought,
Far in the Unapparent. Chatterton
Rose pale,—his solemn agony had not

ADONAIS

Yet faded from him; Sidney, as he fought
And as he fell and as he lived and loved
Sublimely mild, a Spirit without spot,
Arose; and Lucan, by his death approved:
Oblivion as they rose shrank like a thing reproved.

XLVI

And many more, whose names on Earth are dark,
But whose transmitted effluence cannot die
So long as fire outlives the parent spark,
Rose, robed in dazzling immortality.
' Thou art become as one of us,' they cry,
' It was for thee yon kingless sphere has long
Swung blind in unascended majesty,
Silent alone amid an Heaven of Song.
Assume thy wingèd throne, thou Vesper of our throng!'

XLVII

Who mourns for Adonais? Oh, come forth,
Fond wretch! and know thyself and him aright.
Clasp with thy panting soul the pendulous Earth;
As from a centre, dart thy spirit's light
Beyond all worlds, until its spacious might
Satiate the void circumference: then shrink
Even to a point within our day and night;
And keep thy heart light lest it make thee sink
When hope has kindled hope and lured thee to the brink.

XLVIII

Or go to Rome, which is the sepulchre,
Oh, not of him, but of our joy: 'tis nought
That ages, empires, and religions there
Lie buried in the ravage they have wrought;

For such as he can lend,—they borrow not
Glory from those who made the world their prey;
And he is gathered to the kings of thought
Who waged contention with their time's decay,
And of the past are all that cannot pass away.

XLIX

Go thou to Rome,—at once the Paradise,
The grave, the city, and the wilderness;
And where its wrecks like shattered mountains rise,
And flowering weeds, and fragrant copses dress
The bones of Desolation's nakedness
Pass, till the spirit of the spot shall lead
Thy footsteps to a slope of green access
Where, like an infant's smile, over the dead
A light of laughing flowers along the grass is spread;

L

And gray walls moulder round, on which dull Time
Feeds, like slow fire upon a hoary brand;
And one keen pyramid with wedge sublime,
Pavilioning the dust of him who planned
This refuge for his memory, doth stand
Like flame transformed to marble; and beneath,
A field is spread, on which a newer band
Have pitched in Heaven's smile their camp of death,
Welcoming him we lose with scarce extinguished breath.

LI

Here pause: these graves are all too young as yet
To have outgrown the sorrow which consigned
Its charge to each; and if the seal is set,
Here, on one fountain of a mourning mind,

562

Break it not thou! too surely shalt thou find
Thine own well full, if thou returnest home,
Of tears and gall. From the world's bitter wind
Seek shelter in the shadow of the tomb.
What Adonais is, why fear we to become?

LII

The One remains, the many change and pass;
Heaven's light forever shines, Earth's shadows fly;
Life, like a dome of many-coloured glass,
Stains the white radiance of Eternity,
Until Death tramples it to fragments.—Die,
If thou wouldst be with that which thou dost seek!
Follow where all is fled!—Rome's azure sky,
Flowers, ruins, statues, music, words, are weak
The glory they transfuse with fitting truth to speak.

LIII

Why linger, why turn back, why shrink, my Heart?
Thy hopes are gone before: from all things here
They have departed; thou shouldst now depart!
A light is passed from the revolving year,
And man, and woman; and what still is dear
Attracts to crush, repels to make thee wither.
The soft sky smiles,—the low wind whispers near:
'Tis Adonais calls! oh, hasten thither,
No more let Life divide what Death can join together.

LIV

That Light whose smile kindles the Universe,
That Beauty in which all things work and move,
That Benediction which the eclipsing Curse
Of birth can quench not, that sustaining Love

563

Which through the web of being blindly wove
By man and beast and earth and air and sea,
Burns bright or dim, as each are mirrors of
The fire for which all thirst; now beams on me,
Consuming the last clouds of cold mortality.

LV

The breath whose might I have invoked in song
Descends on me; my spirit's bark is driven,
Far from the shore, far from the trembling throng
Whose sails were never to the tempest given;
The massy earth and spherèd skies are riven!
I am borne darkly, fearfully, afar;
Whilst, burning through the inmost veil of Heaven,
The soul of Adonais, like a star,
Beacons from the abode where the Eternal are.

Adonais, 1821

252   *Final Chorus*

THE world's great age begins anew,
   The golden years return,
The earth doth like a snake renew
   Her winter weeds outworn:
Heaven smiles, and faiths and empires gleam,
Like wrecks of a dissolving dream.

A brighter Hellas rears its mountains
   From waves serener far;
A new Peneus rolls his fountains
   Against the morning star.
Where fairer Tempes bloom, there sleep
Young Cyclads on a sunnier deep.

FINAL CHORUS

A loftier Argo cleaves the main,
   Fraught with a later prize;
Another Orpheus sings again,
   And loves, and weeps, and dies.
A new Ulysses leaves once more
Calypso for his native shore.

Oh, write no more the tale of Troy,
   If earth Death's scroll must be!
Nor mix with Laian rage the joy
   Which dawns upon the free:
Although a subtler Sphinx renew
Riddles of death Thebes never knew.

Another Athens shall arise,
   And to remoter time
Bequeath, like sunset to the skies,
   The splendour of its prime;
And leave, if nought so bright may live,
All earth can take or Heaven can give.

Saturn and Love their long repose
   Shall burst, more bright and good
Than all who fell, than One who rose,
   Than many unsubdued:
Not gold, not blood, their altar dowers,
But votive tears and symbol flowers.

Oh, cease! must hate and death return?
   Cease! must men kill and die?
Cease! drain not to its dregs the urn
   Of bitter prophecy.
The world is weary of the past,
Oh, might it die or rest at last!

Hellas, 1822

253   *The Indian Serenade*

I

I ARISE from dreams of thee
In the first sweet sleep of night,
When the winds are breathing low,
And the stars are shining bright:
I arise from dreams of thee,
And a spirit in my feet
Hath led me—who knows how?
To thy chamber window, Sweet!

II

The wandering airs they faint
On the dark, the silent stream—
The Champak odours fail
Like sweet thoughts in a dream;
The nightingale's complaint,
It dies upon her heart;—
As I must on thine,
Oh, belovèd as thou art!

III

Oh lift me from the grass!
I die! I faint! I fail!
Let thy love in kisses rain
On my lips and eyelids pale.
My cheek is cold and white, alas!
My heart beats loud and fast;—
Oh! press it to thine own again,
Where it will break at last.

The Liberal, ii, 1822;
Posthumous Poems, 1824

The Question

I

I DREAMED that, as I wandered by the way,
  Bare Winter suddenly was changed to Spring,
And gentle odours led my steps astray,
    Mixed with a sound of waters murmuring
Along a shelving bank of turf, which lay
    Under a copse, and hardly dared to fling
Its green arms round the bosom of the stream,
But kissed it and then fled, as thou mightest in dream.

II

There grew pied wind-flowers and violets,
  Daisies, those pearled Arcturi of the earth,
The constellated flower that never sets;
    Faint oxslips; tender bluebells, at whose birth
The sod scarce heaved; and that tall flower that wets—
    Like a child, half in tenderness and mirth—
Its mother's face with Heaven's collected tears,
When the low wind, its playmate's voice, it hears.

III

And in the warm hedge grew lush eglantine,
  Green cowbind and the moonlight-coloured may,
And cherry-blossoms, and white cups, whose wine
    Was the bright dew, yet drained not by the day;
And wild roses, and ivy serpentine,
    With its dark buds and leaves, wandering astray;
And flowers azure, black, and streaked with gold,
Fairer than any wakened eyes behold.

567

IV

And nearer to the river's trembling edge
　　There grew broad flag-flowers, purple pranked with white,
And starry river buds among the sedge,
　　And floating water-lilies, broad and bright,
Which lit the oak that overhung the hedge
　　With moonlight beams of their own watery light;
And bulrushes, and reeds of such deep green
As soothed the dazzled eye with sober sheen.

V

Methought that of these visionary flowers
　　I made a nosegay, bound in such a way
That the same hues, which in their natural bowers
　　Were mingled or opposed, the like array
Kept these imprisoned children of the Hours
　　Within my hand,—and then, elate and gay,—
I hastened to the spot whence I had come,
That I might there present it!—Oh! to whom?

The Literary Pocket Book, 1822;
Posthumous Poems, 1824

255　　*From ' Letter to Maria Gisborne '*

　　　　　　　　　　　YOU are now
In London, that great sea, whose ebb and flow
At once is deaf and loud, and on the shore
Vomits its wrecks, and still howls on for more.
Yet in its depth what treasures! You will see
That which was Godwin,—greater none than he
Though fallen—and fallen on evil times—to stand
Among the spirits of our age and land,

LETTER TO MARIA GISBORNE

Before the dread tribunal of *to come*
The foremost,—while Rebuke cowers pale and dumb
You will see Coleridge—he who sits obscure
In the exceeding lustre and the pure
Intense irradiation of a mind,
Which, with its own internal lightning blind,
Flags wearily through darkness and despair—
A cloud-encircled meteor of the air,
A hooded eagle among blinking owls.—
You will see Hunt—one of those happy souls
Which are the salt of the earth, and without whom
This world would smell like what it is—a tomb;
Who is, what others seem; his room no doubt
Is still adorned with many a cast from Shout,
With graceful flowers tastefully placed about;
And coronals of bay from ribbons hung,
And brighter wreaths in neat disorder flung;
The gifts of the most learned among some dozens
Of female friends, sisters-in-law, and cousins.
And there is he with his eternal puns,
Which beat the dullest brain for smiles, like duns
Thundering for money at a poet's door;
Alas! it is no use to say, ' I'm poor!'
Or oft in graver mood, when he will look
Things wiser than were ever read in book,
Except in Shakespeare's wisest tenderness.—
You will see Hogg,—and I cannot express
His virtues,—though I know that they are great,
Because he locks, then barricades the gate
Within which they inhabit;—of his wit
And wisdom, you'll cry out when you are bit.
He is a pearl within an oyster shell,

One of the richest of the deep;—and there
Is English Peacock, with his mountain Fair,
Turned into a Flamingo;—that shy bird
That gleams i' the Indian air—have you not heard
When a man marries, dies, or turns Hindoo,
His best friends hear no more of him?—but you
Will see him, and will like him too, I hope,
With the milk-white Snowdonian Antelope
Matched with this cameleopard—his fine wit
Makes such a wound, the knife is lost in it;
A strain too learnèd for a shallow age,
Too wise for selfish bigots; let his page,
Which charms the chosen spirits of the time,
Fold itself up for the serener clime
Of years to come, and find its recompense
In that just expectation.—Wit and sense,
Virtue and human knowledge; all that might
Make this dull world a business of delight,
Are all combined in Horace Smith.—And these,
With some exceptions, which I need not tease
Your patience by descanting on,—are all
You and I know in London.

Posthumous Poems, 1824

256   ' *A widow bird sate mourning* '

A WIDOW bird sate mourning for her love
    Upon a wintry bough;
The frozen wind crept on above,
   The freezing stream below.

There was no leaf upon the forest bare,
  No flower upon the ground,
And little motion in the air
  Except the mill-wheel's sound.

Posthumous Poems, 1824

257   *Stanzas*

WRITTEN IN DEJECTION, NEAR NAPLES

I

THE sun is warm, the sky is clear,
  The waves are dancing fast and bright,
Blue isles and snowy mountains wear
  The purple noon's transparent might,
  The breath of the moist earth is light,
Around its unexpanded buds;
  Like many a voice of one delight,
The winds, the birds, the ocean floods,
The City's voice itself, is soft like Solitude's.

II

I see the Deep's untrampled floor
  With green and purple seaweeds strown;
I see the waves upon the shore,
  Like light dissolved in star-showers, thrown:
  I sit upon the sands alone,—
The lightning of the noontide ocean
  Is flashing round me, and a tone
Arises from its measured motion,
How sweet! did any heart now share in my emotion.

571

III

Alas! I have nor hope nor health,
　　Nor peace within nor calm around,
Nor that content surpassing wealth
　　The sage in meditation found,
　　And walked with inward glory crowned—
Nor fame, nor power, nor love, nor leisure.
　　Others I see whom these surround—
Smiling they live, and call life pleasure;—
To me that cup has been dealt in another measure.

IV

Yet now despair itself is mild,
　　Even as the winds and waters are;
I could lie down like a tired child,
　　And weep away the life of care
　　Which I have borne and yet must bear,
Till death like sleep might steal on me,
　　And I might feel in the warm air
My cheek grow cold, and hear the sea
Breathe o'er my dying brain its last monotony.

V

Some might lament that I were cold,
　　As I, when this sweet day is gone,
Which my lost heart, too soon grown old,
　　Insults with this untimely moan;
　　They might lament—for I am one
Whom men love not,—and yet regret,
　　Unlike this day, which, when the sun
Shall on its stainless glory set,
Will linger, though enjoyed, like joy in memory yet.

Posthumous Poems, 1824

WHEN the lamp is shatter'd,
    The light in the dust lies dead;
  When the cloud is scatter'd,
The rainbow's glory is shed:
  When the lute is broken,
Sweet tones are remember'd not
  When the lips have spoken,
Loved accents are soon forgot.

  As music and splendour
Survive not the lamp and the lute,
  The heart's echoes render
No song when the spirit is mute—
  No song but sad dirges,
Like the wind through a ruin'd cell,
  Or the mournful surges
That ring the dead seaman's knell.

  When hearts have once mingled,
Love first leaves the well-built nest;
  The weak one is singled
To endure what it once possest.
  O Love, who bewailest
The frailty of all things here,
  Why choose you the frailest
For your cradle, your home, and your bier?

  Its passions will rock thee,
As the storms rock the ravens on high:
  Bright reason will mock thee,
Like the sun from a wintry sky.

From thy nest every rafter
Will rot, and thine eagle home
  Leave thee naked to laughter,
When leaves fall and cold winds come.

Posthumous Poems, 1824

259   *To Night*

I

SWIFTLY walk o'er the western wave,
      Spirit of Night!
Out of the misty eastern cave,
Where, all the long and lone daylight,
Thou wovest dreams of joy and fear,
Which make thee terrible and dear,—
      Swift be thy flight!

II

Wrap thy form in a mantle gray,
      Star-inwrought!
Blind with thine hair the eyes of Day;
Kiss her until she be wearied out,
Then wander o'er city, and sea, and land,
Touching all with thine opiate wand—
      Come, long-sought!

III

When I arose and saw the dawn,
      I sighed for thee;
When light rode high, and the dew was gone,
And noon lay heavy on flower and tree,
And the weary Day turned to his rest,
Lingering like an unloved guest,
      I sighed for thee.

IV

Thy brother Death came, and cried,
  Wouldst thou me?
Thy sweet child Sleep, the filmy-eyed,
Murmured like a noontide bee,
Shall I nestle near thy side?
Wouldst thou me?—And I replied,
  No, not thee!

V

Death will come when thou art dead,
  Soon, too soon—
Sleep will come when thou art fled;
Of neither would I ask the boon
I ask of thee, belovèd Night—
Swift be thine approaching flight,
  Come soon, soon!

Posthumous Poems, 1824

260   *' Music, when soft voices die '*

MUSIC, when soft voices die,
 Vibrates in the memory—
Odours, when sweet violets sicken,
Live within the sense they quicken.

Rose leaves, when the rose is dead,
Are heaped for the belovèd's bed;
And so thy thoughts, when thou art gone,
Love itself shall slumber on.

Posthumous Poems, 1824

261 *Song*

I

RARELY, rarely, comest thou,
    Spirit of Delight!
Wherefore hast thou left me now
    Many a day and night?
Many a weary night and day
'Tis since thou art fled away.

II

How shall ever one like me
    Win thee back again?
With the joyous and the free
    Thou wilt scoff at pain.
Spirit false! thou hast forgot
All but those who need thee not.

III

As a lizard with the shade
    Of a trembling leaf,
Thou with sorrow art dismayed;
    Even the sighs of grief
Reproach thee, that thou art not near,
And reproach thou wilt not hear.

IV

Let me set my mournful ditty
    To a merry measure;
Thou wilt never come for pity,
    Thou wilt come for pleasure;
Pity then will cut away
Those cruel wings, and thou wilt stay.

SONG

v

I love all that thou lovest,
   Spirit of Delight!
The fresh Earth in new leaves dressed,
   And the starry night;
Autumn evening, and the morn
When the golden mists are born.

vi

I love snow, and all the forms
   Of the radiant frost;
I love waves, and winds, and storms,
   Everything almost
Which is Nature's, and may be
Untainted by man's misery.

vii

I love tranquil solitude,
   And such society
As is quiet, wise, and good;
   Between thee and me
What difference? but thou dost possess
The things I seek, not love them less.

viii

I love Love—though he has wings,
   And like light can flee,
But above all other things,
   Spirit, I love thee—
Thou art love and life! Oh, come,
Make once more my heart thy home.

Posthumous Poems, 1824

262 *A Lament*

I

O WORLD! O life! O time!
　On whose last steps I climb,
　　Trembling at that where I had stood before;
When will return the glory of your prime?
　　No more—Oh, never more!

II

Out of the day and night
A joy has taken flight;
　　Fresh spring, and summer, and winter hoar,
Move my faint heart with grief, but with delight
　　No more—Oh, never more!

Posthumous Poems, 1824

263 ' *One word is too often profaned* '

I

O NE word is too often profaned
　For me to profane it,
One feeling too falsely disdained
　For thee to disdain it;
One hope is too like despair
　For prudence to smother,
And pity from thee more dear
　Than that from another.

II

I can give not what men call love,
　But wilt thou accept not
The worship the heart lifts above
　And the Heavens reject not,—

ONE WORD IS TOO OFTEN PROFANED

> The desire of the moth for the star,
>> Of the night for the morrow,
> The devotion to something afar
>> From the sphere of our sorrow?

Posthumous Poems, 1824

A Bridal Song

I

THE golden gates of Sleep unbar
  Where Strength and Beauty, met together.
Kindle their image like a star
  In a sea of glassy weather!
Night, with all thy stars look down,—
  Darkness, weep thy holiest dew,—
Never smiled the inconstant moon
    On a pair so true.
Let eyes not see their own delight;—
Haste, swift Hour, and thy flight
    Oft renew.

II

Fairies, sprites, and angels, keep her!
  Holy stars, permit no wrong!
And return to wake the sleeper,
    Dawn,—ere it be long!
O joy! O fear! what will be done
In the absence of the sun!
    Come along!

Posthumous Poems, 1824

265 *Arethusa*

I

ARETHUSA arose
   From her couch of snows
In the Acroceraunian mountains,—
   From cloud and from crag,
   With many a jag,
Shepherding her bright fountains.
   She leapt down the rocks,
   With her rainbow locks
Streaming among the streams;—
   Her steps paved with green
   The downward ravine
Which slopes to the western gleams;
   And gliding and springing
   She went, ever singing,
In murmurs as soft as sleep;
   The Earth seemed to love her,
   And Heaven smiled above her,
As she lingered towards the deep.

II

   Then Alpheus bold,
   On his glacier cold,
With his trident the mountains strook;
   And opened a chasm
   In the rocks—with the spasm
All Erymanthus shook.
   And the black south wind
   It unsealed behind
The urns of the silent snow,

And earthquake and thunder
  Did rend in sunder
The bars of the springs below.
  And the beard and the hair
  Of the River-god were
Seen through the torrent's sweep,
  As he followed the light
  Of the fleet nymph's flight
To the brink of the Dorian deep.

III

' Oh, save me! Oh, guide me!
  And bid the deep hide me,
For he grasps me now by the hair! '
  The loud Ocean heard,
  To its blue depth stirred,
And divided at her prayer;
  And under the water
  The Earth's white daughter
Fled like a sunny beam;
  Behind her descended
  Her billows, unblended
With the brackish Dorian stream :—
  Like a gloomy stain
  On the emerald main
Alpheus rushed behind,—
  As an eagle pursuing
  A dove to its ruin
Down the streams of the cloudy wind.

IV

Under the bowers
Where the Ocean Powers

Sit on their pearlèd thrones;
　　Through the coral woods
　　Of the weltering floods,
Over heaps of unvalued stones;
　　Through the dim beams
　　Which amid the streams
Weave a network of coloured light;
　　And under the caves,
　　Where the shadowy waves
Are as green as the forest's night:—
　　Outspeeding the shark,
　　And the sword-fish dark,
Under the Ocean's foam,
　　And up through the rifts
　　Of the mountain clifts
They passed to their Dorian home.

v

　　And now from their fountains
　　In Enna's mountains,
Down one vale where the morning basks,
　　Like friends once parted
　　Grown single-hearted,
They ply their watery tasks.
　　At sunrise they leap
　　From their cradles steep
In the cave of the shelving hill;
　　At noontide they flow
　　Through the woods below
And the meadows of asphodel;
　　And at night they sleep
　　In the rocking deep

ARETHUSA

Beneath the Ortygian shore;—
  Like spirits that lie
  In the azure sky
When they love but live no more.

Posthumous Poems, 1824

266　　　　*Hymn of Apollo*

I

THE sleepless Hours who watch me as I lie,
  Curtained with star-inwoven tapestries
From the broad moonlight of the sky,
  Fanning the busy dreams from my dim eyes,—
Waken me when their Mother, the gray Dawn,
Tells them that dreams and that the moon is gone.

II

Then I arise, and climbing Heaven's blue dome,
  I walk over the mountains and the waves,
Leaving my robe upon the ocean foam;
  My footsteps pave the clouds with fire; the caves
Are filled with my bright presence, and the air
Leaves the green Earth to my embraces bare.

III

The sunbeams are my shafts, with which I kill
  Deceit, that loves the night and fears the day;
All men who do or even imagine ill
  Fly me, and from the glory of my ray
Good minds and open actions take new might,
Until diminished by the reign of Night.

IV

I feed the clouds, the rainbows and the flowers
   With their aethereal colours; the moon's globe
And the pure stars in their eternal bowers
   Are cinctured with my power as with a robe;
Whatever lamps on Earth or Heaven may shine
Are portions of one power, which is mine.

V

I stand at noon upon the peak of Heaven,
   Then with unwilling steps I wander down
Into the clouds of the Atlantic even;
   For grief that I depart they weep and frown:
What look is more delightful than the smile
With which I soothe them from the western isle?

VI

I am the eye with which the Universe
   Beholds itself and knows itself divine;
All harmony of instrument or verse,
   All prophecy, all medicine is mine,
All light of art or nature;—to my song
Victory and praise in its own right belong.

Posthumous Poems, 1824

267   *Hymn of Pan*

I

FROM the forests and highlands
   We come, we come;
From the river-girt islands,
   Where loud waves are dumb
     Listening to my sweet pipings.

HYMN OF PAN

The wind in the reeds and the rushes,
  The bees on the bells of thyme,
The birds on the myrtle bushes,
  The cicale above in the lime,
And the lizards below in the grass,
Were as silent as ever old Tmolus was,
    Listening to my sweet pipings.

II

Liquid Peneus was flowing,
  And all dark Tempe lay
In Pelion's shadow, outgrowing
  The light of the dying day,
    Speeded by my sweet pipings.
The Sileni, and Sylvans, and Fauns,
  And the Nymphs of the woods and the waves,
To the edge of the moist river-lawns,
  And the brink of the dewy caves,
And all that did then attend and follow,
Were silent with love, as you now, Apollo,
    With envy of my sweet pipings.

III

I sang of the dancing stars.
  I sang of the daedal Earth,
And of Heaven—and the giant wars,
  And Love, and Death, and Birth,—
    And then I changed my pipings,—
Singing how down the vale of Maenalus
  I pursued a maiden and clasped a reed.
Gods and men, we are all deluded thus!
  It breaks in our bosom and then we bleed:

585

All wept, as I think both ye now would,
If envy or age had not frozen your blood,
    At the sorrow of my sweet pipings.

Posthumous Poems, 1824

268   *England in 1819*

AN old, mad, blind, despised, and dying king,—
    Princes, the dregs of their dull race, who flow
Through public scorn,—mud from a muddy spring,—
Rulers who neither see, nor feel, nor know,
But leech-like to their fainting country cling,
Till they drop, blind in blood, without a blow,—
A people starved and stabbed in the untilled field,—
An army, which liberticide and prey
Makes as a two-edged sword to all who wield,—
Golden and sanguine laws which tempt and slay;
Religion Christless, Godless—a book sealed;
A Senate,—Time's worst statute unrepealed,—
Are graves, from which a glorious Phantom may
Burst, to illumine our tempestuous day.

Poetical Works, 1839

269   *To Jane: The Invitation*

BEST and brightest, come away!
    Fairer far than this fair Day,
Which, like thee to those in sorrow,
Comes to bid a sweet good-morrow
To the rough Year just awake
In its cradle on the brake.
The brightest hour of unborn Spring,
Through the winter wandering,

TO JANE : THE INVITATION

Found, it seems, the halcyon Morn
To hoar February born.
Bending from Heaven, in azure mirth,
It kissed the forehead of the Earth,
And smiled upon the silent sea,
And bade the frozen streams be free,
And waked to music all their fountains,
And breathed upon the frozen mountains,
And like a prophetess of May
Strewed flowers upon the barren way,
Making the wintry world appear
Like one on whom thou smilest, dear.

Away, away, from men and towns,
To the wild wood and the downs—
To the silent wilderness
Where the soul need not repress
Its music lest it should not find
An echo in another's mind,
While the touch of Nature's art
Harmonizes heart to heart.
I leave this notice on my door
For each accustomed visitor:—
' I am gone into the fields
To take what this sweet hour yields;—
Reflection, you may come to-morrow,
Sit by the fireside with Sorrow.—
You with the unpaid bill, Despair,—
You, tiresome verse-reciter, Care,—
I will pay you in the grave,—
Death will listen to your stave.
Expectation too, be off!

To-day is for itself enough;
Hope, in pity mock not Woe
With smiles, nor follow where I go;
Long having lived on thy sweet food,
At length I find one moment's good
After long pain—with all your love,
This you never told me of.'

Radiant Sister of the Day,
Awake! arise! and come away!
To the wild woods and the plains,
And the pools where winter rains
Image all their roof of leaves,
Where the pine its garland weaves
Of sapless green and ivy dun
Round stems that never kiss the sun;
Where the lawns and pastures be,
And the sandhills of the sea;—
Where the melting hoar-frost wets
The daisy-star that never sets,
And wind-flowers, and violets,
Which yet join not scent to hue,
Crown the pale year weak and new;
When the night is left behind
In the deep east, dun and blind,
And the blue noon is over us,
And the multitudinous
Billows murmur at our feet,
Where the earth and ocean meet,
And all things seem only one
In the universal sun.

Poetical Works, 1839 (Second ed.)

I

NOW the last day of many days,
  All beautiful and bright as thou,
    The loveliest and the last, is dead,
Rise, Memory, and write its praise!
    Up,—to thy wonted work! come, trace
      The epitaph of glory fled,—
For now the Earth has changed its face,
  A frown is on the Heaven's brow.

II

We wandered to the Pine Forest
  That skirts the Ocean's foam,
The lightest wind was in its nest,
  The tempest in its home.
The whispering waves were half asleep,
  The clouds were gone to play,
And on the bosom of the deep
  The smile of Heaven lay;
It seemed as if the hour were one
  Sent from beyond the skies,
Which scattered from above the sun
  A light of Paradise.

III

We paused amid the pines that stood
  The giants of the waste,
Tortured by storms to shapes as rude
  As serpents interlaced,

589

And soothed by every azure breath,
    That under Heaven is blown,
To harmonies and hues beneath,
    As tender as its own;
Now all the tree-tops lay asleep,
    Like green waves on the sea,
As still as in the silent deep
    The ocean woods may be.

IV

How calm it was!—the silence there
    By such a chain was bound
That even the busy woodpecker
    Made stiller by her sound
The inviolable quietness;
    The breath of peace we drew
With its soft motion made not less
    The calm that round us grew.
There seemed from the remotest seat
    Of the white mountain waste,
To the soft flower beneath our feet,
    A magic circle traced,—
A spirit interfused around,
    A thrilling, silent life,—
To momentary peace it bound
    Our mortal nature's strife;
And still I felt the centre of
    The magic circle there
Was one fair form that filled with love
    The lifeless atmosphere.

TO JANE : THE RECOLLECTION

We paused beside the pools that lie
　　Under the forest bough,—
Each seemed as 'twere a little sky
　　Gulfed in a world below;
A firmament of purple light
　　Which in the dark earth lay,
More boundless than the depth of night,
　　And purer than the day—
In which the lovely forests grew,
　　As in the upper air,
More perfect both in shape and hue
　　Than any spreading there.
There lay the glade and neighbouring lawn,
　　And through the dark green wood
The white sun twinkling like the dawn
　　Out of a speckled cloud.
Sweet views which in our world above
　　Can never well be seen,
Were imaged by the water's love
　　Of that fair forest green.
And all was interfused beneath
　　With an Elysian glow,
An atmosphere without a breath,
　　A softer day below.
Like one beloved the scene had lent
　　To the dark water's breast,
Its every leaf and lineament
　　With more than truth expressed;
Until an envious wind crept by,
　　Like an unwelcome thought,

Which from the mind's too faithful eye
    Blots one dear image out.
Though thou art ever fair and kind,
    The forests ever green,
Less oft is peace in Shelley's mind,
    Than calm in waters, seen.

Poetical Works, 1839 (Second ed.)

271   *To the Nile*

MONTH after month the gathered rains descend
    Drenching yon secret Aethiopian dells,
And from the desert's ice-girt pinnacles
Where Frost and Heat in strange embraces blend
On Atlas, fields of moist snow half depend.
Girt there with blasts and meteors Tempest dwells
By Nile's aëreal urn, with rapid spells
Urging those waters to their mighty end.
O'er Egypt's land of Memory floods are level
And they are thine, O Nile—and well thou knowest
That soul-sustaining airs and blasts of evil
And fruits and poisons spring where'er thou flowest.
Beware, O Man—for knowledge must to thee,
Like the great flood to Egypt, ever be.

Written 4 February 1818
St. James's Magazine, March 1876;
Poetical Works, 1876

JOHN KEBLE

Morning

HUES of the rich unfolding morn,
  That, ere the glorious sun be born,
By some soft touch invisible
Around his path are taught to swell;—

Thou rustling breeze so fresh and gay,
That dancest forth at opening day,
And brushing by with joyous wing,
Wakenest each little leaf to sing;—

Ye fragrant clouds of dewy steam,
By which deep grove and tangled stream
Pay, for soft rains in season given,
Their tribute to the genial heaven;—

Why waste your treasures of delight
Upon our thankless, joyless sight;
Who day by day to sin awake,
Seldom of Heaven and you partake?

Oh! timely happy, timely wise,
Hearts that with rising morn arise!
Eyes that the beam celestial view,
Which evermore makes all things new.

New every morning is the love
Our wakening and uprising prove;
Through sleep and darkness safely brought,
Restor'd to life, and power, and thought.

JOHN KEBLE

New mercies, each returning day,
Hover around us while we pray;
New perils past, new sins forgiven,
New thoughts of God, new hopes of Heaven.

If on our daily course our mind
Be set to hallow all we find,
New treasures still, of countless price,
God will provide for sacrifice.

Old friends, old scenes, will lovelier be,
As more of Heaven in each we see:
Some softening gleam of love and prayer
Shall dawn on every cross and care.

As for some dear familiar strain
Untir'd we ask, and ask again,
Ever, in its melodious store,
Finding a spell unheard before;

Such is the bliss of souls serene,
When they have sworn, and steadfast mean,
Counting the cost, in all t' espy
Their God, in all themselves deny.

O could we learn that sacrifice,
What lights would all around us rise!
How would our hearts with wisdom talk
Along Life's dullest dreariest walk!

We need not bid, for cloister'd cell,
Our neighbour and our work farewell,
Nor strive to wind ourselves too high
For sinful man beneath the sky:

MORNING

The trivial round, the common task,
Would furnish all we ought to ask;
Room to deny ourselves; a road
To bring us, daily, nearer God.

Seek we no more; content with these,
Let present Rapture, Comfort, Ease,
As Heaven shall bid them, come and go:—
The secret this of Rest below.

Only, O Lord, in Thy dear love
Fit us for perfect Rest above;
And help us, this and every day,
To live more nearly as we pray.

The Christian Year, 1827

273 *Whitsunday*

WHEN God of old came down from Heaven,
    In power and wrath He came;
Before His feet the clouds were riven,
    Half darkness and half flame:

Around the trembling mountain's base
    The prostrate people lay;
A day of wrath, and not of grace;
    A dim and dreadful day.

But when He came the second time,
    He came in power and love,
Softer than gale at morning prime
    Hover'd His holy Dove.

JOHN KEBLE

The fires that rush'd on Sinai down
    In sudden torrents dread,
Now gently light, a glorious crown,
    On every sainted head.

Like arrows went those lightnings forth
    Wing'd with the sinner's doom,
But these, like tongues, o'er all the earth
    Proclaiming life to come:

And as on Israel's awe-struck ear
    The voice exceeding loud,
The trump, that angels quake to hear,
    Thrill'd from the deep, dark cloud;

So, when the Spirit of our God
    Came down His flock to find,
A voice from Heavèn was heard abroad,
    A rushing, mighty wind.

Nor doth the outward ear alone
    At that high warning start;
Conscience gives back th' appalling tone;
    'Tis echoed in the heart.

It fills the Church of God; it fills
    The sinful world around;
Only in stubborn hearts and wills
    No place for it is found.

To other strains our souls are set:
    A giddy whirl of sin
Fills ear and brain, and will not let
    Heaven's harmonies come in.

WHITSUNDAY

Come Lord, come Wisdom, Love, and Power,
    Open our ears to hear;
Let us not miss th' accepted hour;
    Save, Lord, by Love or Fear.

The Christian Year, 1827

FELICIA DOROTHEA HEMANS

1793-1835

274   *A Death-Hymn*

CALM on the bosom of thy God,
    Fair spirit! rest thee now!
E'en while with ours thy footsteps trod
    His seal was on thy brow.

Dust, to its narrow house beneath!
    Soul, to its place on high!
They that have seen thy look in death
    No more may fear to die.

The Siege of Valencia, 1823

275   *Foliage*

COME forth, and let us through our hearts receive
    The joy of verdure!—see, the honied lime
Showers cool green light o'er banks where wild-flowers weave
Thick tapestry; and woodbine tendrils climb
Up the brown oak from buds of moss and thyme.
The rich deep masses of the sycamore
Hang heavy with the fulness of their prime,
And the white poplar, from its foliage hoar,
Scatters forth gleams like moonlight, with each gale
That sweeps the boughs:—the chestnut flowers are past,

The crowning glories of the hawthorn fail,
But arches of sweet eglantine are cast
From every hedge:—Oh! never may we lose,
Dear friend! our fresh delight in simplest nature's hues!

Poetical Remains, 1836

276   *The Cid's Rising*

'TWAS the deep mid-watch of the silent night,
      And Leon in slumber lay,
When a sound went forth in rushing might,
      Like an army on its way!
   In the stillness of the hour,
   When the dreams of sleep have power,
      And men forget the day.

Through the dark and lonely streets it went,
      Till the slumberers woke in dread;—
The sound of a passing armament,
      With the charger's stony tread.
   There was heard no trumpet's peal,
   But the heavy tramp of steel,
      As a host's to combat led.

Through the dark and lonely streets it pass'd,
      And the hollow pavement rang,
And the towers, as with a sweeping blast,
      Rock'd to the stormy clang!
   But the march of the viewless train
   Went on to a royal fane,
      Where a priest his night-hymn sang.

598

THE CID'S RISING

There was knocking that shook the marble floor,
    And a voice at the gate, which said—
' That the Cid Ruy Diez, the Campeador,
    Was there in his arms array'd;
  And that with him, from the tomb,
  Had the Count Gonzalez come
    With a host, uprisen to aid!

' And they came for the buried king that lay
    At rest in that ancient fane;
For he must be arm'd on the battle-day,
    With them, to deliver Spain!'
  —Then the march went sounding on,
  And the Moors, by noontide sun,
    Were dust on Tolosa's plain.

Songs of the Cid, in *Works*, v. 1839

JOHN CLARE

1793–1864

277   *From ' Address to Plenty '*

'TIS not great, what I solicit;
    Was it more, thou couldst not miss it:
Now the cutting Winter 's come,
'Tis but just to find a home,
In some shelter, dry and warm,
That will shield me from the storm.
Toiling in the naked fields,
Where no bush a shelter yields,
Needy Labour dithering stands,
Beats and blows his numbing hands;

599

And upon the crumping snows
Stamps, in vain, to warm his toes.
Leaves are fled, that once had power
To resist a summer shower;
And the wind so piercing blows,
Winnowing small the drifting snows,
The summer shade of loaded bough
Would vainly boast a shelter now:
Piercing snows so searching fall,
They sift a passage through them all.
Though all 's vain to keep him warm,
Poverty must brave the storm.
Friendship none, its aid to lend:
Health alone his only friend;
Granting leave to live in pain,
Giving strength to toil in vain;
To be, while winter's horrors last,
The sport of every pelting blast.

Poems descriptive of Rural Life and Scenery, 1820

278 *Noon*

ALL how silent and how still;
Nothing heard but yonder mill:
While the dazzled eye surveys
All around a liquid blaze;
And amid the scorching gleams,
If we earnest look, it seems
As if crooked bits of glass
Seem'd repeatedly to pass.

crumping] crunching.

NOON

Oh, for a puffing breeze to blow!
But breezes are all strangers now;
Not a twig is seen to shake,
Nor the smallest bent to quake;
From the river's muddy side
Not a curve is seen to glide;
And no longer on the stream
Watching lies the silver bream,
Forcing, from repeated springs,
' Verges in successive rings.'
Bees are faint, and cease to hum;
Birds are overpower'd and dumb.
Rural voices all are mute,
Tuneless lie the pipe and flute:
Shepherds, with their panting sheep,
In the swaliest corner creep;
And from the tormenting heat
All are wishing to retreat.
Huddled up in grass and flowers,
Mowers wait for cooler hours;
And the cow-boy seeks the sedge,
Ramping in the woodland hedge,
While his cattle o'er the vales
Scamper, with uplifted tails;
Others not so wild and mad,
That can better bear the gad,
Underneath the hedge-row lunge,
Or, if nigh, in waters plunge.
Oh! to see how flowers are took,
How it grieves me when I look:
Ragged-robins, once so pink,

bent] grass-like reed, or rush.   swaliest] coolest.

Now are turn'd as black as ink,
And the leaves, being scorch'd so much,
Even crumble at the touch;
Drowking lies the meadow-sweet,
Flopping down beneath one's feet:
While to all the flowers that blow,
If in open air they grow,
Th' injurious deed alike is done
By the hot relentless sun.
E'en the dew is parched up
From the teasel's jointed cup:
O poor birds! where must ye fly,
Now your water-pots are dry?
If ye stay upon the heath,
Ye'll be choak'd and clamm'd to death.
Therefore leave the shadeless goss,
Seek the spring-head lin'd with moss;
There your little feet may stand,
Safely printing on the sand;
While, in full possession, where
Purling eddies ripple clear,
You with ease and plenty blest,
Sip the coolest and the best.
Then away! and wet your throats;
Cheer me with your warbling notes;
'Twill hot noon the more revive;
While I wander to contrive
For myself a place as good,
In the middle of a wood:
There aside some mossy bank,
Where the grass in bunches rank
       Drowking] drooping.

Lifts its down on spindles high,
Shall be where I'll choose to lie;
Fearless of the things that creep,
There I'll think, and there I'll sleep;
Caring not to stir at all,
Till the dew begins to fall.

Poems descriptive of Rural Life and Scenery, 1820

279　*The Wood-Cutter's Night Song*

WELCOME, red and roundy sun,
　　Dropping lowly in the west;
Now my hard day's work is done,
　　I'm as happy as the best.

Joyful are the thoughts of home,
　　Now I'm ready for my chair,
So, till morrow-morning 's come,
　　Bill and mittens, lie ye there!

Though to leave your pretty song,
　　Little birds, it gives me pain,
Yet to-morrow is not long,
　　Then I'm with you all again.

If I stop, and stand about,
　　Well I know how things will be.
Judy will be looking out
　　Every now-and-then for me.

So fare ye well! and hold your tongues,
　　Sing no more until I come;
They're not worthy of your songs
　　That never care to drop a crumb.

All day long I love the oaks,
    But, at nights, yon little cot,
Where I see the chimney smokes,
    Is by far the prettiest spot.

Wife and children all are there,
    To revive with pleasant looks,
Table ready set, and chair,
    Supper hanging on the hooks.

Soon as ever I get in,
    When my faggot down I fling,
Little prattlers they begin
    Teasing me to talk and sing.

Welcome, red and roundy sun,
    Dropping lowly in the west;
Now my hard day's work is done,
    I'm as happy as the best.

Joyful are the thoughts of home,
    Now I'm ready for my chair,
So, till morrow-morning 's come,
    Bill and mittens, lie ye there!

The Village Minstrel, 1821

After reading in a Letter

280   *Proposals for Building a Cottage*

BESIDE a runnel build my shed,
    With stubbles cover'd o'er;
Let broad oaks o'er its chimney spread,
    And grass-plats grace the door.

BUILDING A COTTAGE

The door may open with a string,
　　So that it closes tight;
And locks would be a wanted thing,
　　To keep out thieves at night.

A little garden, not too fine,
　　Inclose with painted pales;
And woodbines, round the cot to twine,
　　Pin to the wall with nails.

Let hazels grow, and spindling sedge,
　　Bend bowering over-head;
Dig old man's beard from woodland hedge,
　　To twine a summer shade.

Beside the threshold sods provide,
　　And build a summer seat;
Plant sweet-briar bushes by its side,
　　And flowers that blossom sweet.

I love the sparrow's ways to watch
　　Upon the cotter's sheds,
So here and there pull out the thatch,
　　That they may hide their heads.

And as the sweeping swallows stop
　　Their flights along the green,
Leave holes within the chimney-top
　　To paste their nest between.

Stick shelves and cupboards round the hut,
　　In all the holes and nooks;
Nor in the corner fail to put
　　A cupboard for the books.

　　　　spindling] tall and slender.

Along the floor some sand I'll sift,
    To make it fit to live in;
And then I'll thank ye for the gift,
    As something worth the giving.

The Village Minstrel, 1821

281   *From ' February '*

THE milkmaid singing leaves her bed,
    As glad as happy thoughts can be,
While magpies chatter o'er her head
    As jocund in the change as she:
Her cows around the closes stray,
    Nor ling'ring wait the foddering-boy;
Tossing the mole-hills in their play,
    And staring round with frolic joy.

The shepherd now is often seen
    Near warm banks o'er his hook to bend;
Or o'er a gate or stile to lean,
    Chattering to a passing friend:
Ploughmen go whistling to their toils,
    And yoke again the rested plough;
And, mingling o'er the mellow soils,
    Boys shout, and whips are noising now.

The barking dogs, by lane and wood,
    Drive sheep a-field from foddering ground;
And Echo, in her summer mood,
    Briskly mocks the cheering sound.
The flocks, as from a prison broke,
    Shake their wet fleeces in the sun,
While, following fast, a misty smoke
    Reeks from the moist grass as they run.

FEBRUARY

No more behind his master's heels
   The dog creeps on his winter-pace;
But cocks his tail, and o'er the fields
   Runs many a wild and random chase,
Following, in spite of chiding calls,
   The startled cat with harmless glee,
Scaring her up the weed-green walls,
   Or mossy mottled apple tree.

As crows from morning perches fly,
   He barks and follows them in vain;
E'en larks will catch his nimble eye,
   And off he starts and barks again,
With breathless haste and blinded guess,
   Oft following where the hare hath gone;
Forgetting, in his joy's excess,
   His frolic puppy-days are done!

The hedgehog, from his hollow root,
   Sees the wood-moss clear of snow,
And hunts the hedge for fallen fruit—
   Crab, hip, and winter-bitten sloe;
But often check'd by sudden fears,
   As shepherd-dog his haunt espies,
He rolls up in a ball of spears,
   And all his barking rage defies.

The gladden'd swine bolt from the sty,
   And round the yard in freedom run,
Or stretching in their slumbers lie
   Beside the cottage in the sun.

The young horse whinneys to his mate,
  And, sickening from the thresher's door,
Rubs at the straw-yard's banded gate,
  Longing for freedom on the moor.

The Shepherd's Calendar, 1827

282   *From ' July '*

LOUD is the Summer's busy song,
  The smallest breeze can find a tongue,
While insects of each tiny size
Grow teazing with their melodies,
Till noon burns with its blistering breath
Around, and day dies still as death.
The busy noise of man and brute
Is on a sudden lost and mute;
Even the brook that leaps along
Seems weary of its bubbling song,
And, so soft its waters creep,
Tired silence sinks in sounder sleep.
The cricket on its banks is dumb,
The very flies forget to hum;
And, save the waggon rocking round,
The landscape sleeps without a sound.
The breeze is stopt, the lazy bough
Hath not a leaf that dances now;
The tottergrass upon the hill,
And spiders' threads, are standing still;
The feathers dropt from moorhen's wing,
Which to the water's surface cling,
Are steadfast, and as heavy seem
As stones beneath them in the stream;

Hawkweed and groundsel's fanning downs
Unruffled keep their seedy crowns;
And in the oven-heated air,
Not one light thing is floating there,
Save that to the earnest eye,
The restless heat seems twittering by.
Noon swoons beneath the heat it made,
And flowers e'en wither in the shade,
Until the sun slopes in the west,
Like weary traveller, glad to rest,
On pillowed clouds of many hues;
Then nature's voice its joy renews,
And chequer'd field and grassy plain
Hum, with their summer songs again,
A requiem to the day's decline,
Whose setting sunbeams coolly shine,
As welcome to day's feeble powers
As falling dews to thirsty flowers.

The Shepherd's Calendar, 1827

283   *From ' Summer Images '*

THE green lane now I traverse, where it goes
    Nought guessing, till some sudden turn espies
Rude batter'd finger post, that stooping shows
    Where the snug mystery lies;
And then a mossy spire, with ivy crown,
    Cheers up the short surprise,
        And shows a peeping town.

I see the wild flowers, in their summer morn
    Of beauty, feeding on joy's luscious hours;
The gay convolvulus, wreathing round the thorn,
    Agape for honey showers;

609

And slender kingcup, burnished with the dew
   Of morning's early hours,
      Like gold yminted new.

And mark by rustic bridge, o'er shallow stream,
   Cow-tending boy, to toil unreconciled,
Absorbed as in some vagrant summer dream;
   Who now, in gestures wild,
Starts dancing to his shadow on the wall,
   Feeling self-gratified,
      Nor fearing human thrall.

Or thread the sunny valley laced with streams,
   Or forests rude, and the o'ershadow'd brims
Of simple ponds, where idle shepherd dreams,
   Stretching his listless limbs;
Or trace hay-scented meadows, smooth and long,
   Where joy's wild impulse swims
      In one continued song.

I love at early morn, from new mown swath,
   To see the startled frog his route pursue;
To mark while, leaping o'er the dripping path,
   His bright sides scatter dew,
The early lark that from its bustle flies,
   To hail his matin new;
      And watch him to the skies.

To note on hedgerow baulks, in moisture sprent,
   The jetty snail creep from the mossy thorn,
With earnest heed, and tremulous intent,
   Frail brother of the morn,

SUMMER IMAGES

That from the tiny bent's dew-misted leaves
    Withdraws his timid horn,
        And fearful vision weaves.

Or swallow heed on smoke-tanned chimney top,
    Wont to be first unsealing Morning's eye,
Ere yet the bee hath gleaned one wayward drop
    Of honey on his thigh;
To see him seek morn's airy couch to sing,
    Until the golden sky
        Bepaint his russet wing.

Or sauntering boy by tanning corn to spy,
    With clapping noise to startle birds away,
And hear him bawl to every passer-by
    To know the hour of day;
While the uncradled breezes, fresh and strong,
    With waking blossoms play,
        And breathe Æolian song.

I love the south-west wind, or low or loud,
    And not the less when sudden drops of rain
Moisten my glowing cheek from ebon cloud,
    Threatening soft showers again,
That over lands new ploughed and meadow grounds,
    Summer's sweet breath unchain,
        And wake harmonious sounds.

Rich music breathes in Summer's every sound;
    And in her harmony of varied greens,
Woods, meadows, hedge-rows, corn-fields, all around
    Much beauty intervenes,
Filling with harmony the ear and eye;
    While o'er the mingling scenes
        Far spreads the laughing sky.

JOHN CLARE

See, how the wind-enamoured aspen leaves
   Turn up their silver lining to the sun!
And hark! the rustling noise, that oft deceives,
   And makes the sheep-boy run:
The sound so mimics fast-approaching showers,
   He thinks the rain 's begun,
      And hastes to sheltering bowers.

But now the evening curdles dank and grey,
   Changing her watchet hue for sombre weed;
And moping owls, to close the lids of day,
   On drowsy wing proceed;
While chickering crickets, tremulous and long,
   Light's farewell inly heed,
      And give it parting song.

The pranking bat its flighty circlet makes;
   The glow-worm burnishes its lamp anew;
O'er meadows dew-besprent, the beetle wakes
   Inquiries ever new,
Teazing each passing ear with murmurs vain,
   As wanting to pursue
      His homeward path again.

Hark! 'tis the melody of distant bells
   That on the wind with pleasing hum rebounds
By fitful starts, then musically swells
   O'er the dim stilly grounds;
While on the meadow-bridge the pausing boy
   Listens the mellow sounds,
      And hums in vacant joy.

        chickering] chirping.

Now homeward-bound, the hedger bundles round
 His evening faggot, and with every stride
His leathern doublet leaves a rustling sound,
 Till silly sheep beside
His path start tremulous, and once again
 Look back dissatisfied,
   And scour the dewy plain.

The Rural Muse, 1835

284   *Sudden Shower*

BLACK grows the southern sky, betokening rain,
 And humming hive-bees homeward hurry by:
They feel the change; so let us shun the grain,
 And take the broad road while our feet are dry.
Aye there, some drops fell moistening on my face,
 And pattering on my hat—'tis coming nigh!—
Let's look about, and find a sheltering place.
 The little things around us fear the sky,
And hasten through the grass to shun the shower.
 Here stoops an ash-tree—hark! the wind gets high,
But never mind; this ivy, for an hour,
 Rain as it may, will keep us drily here:
That little wren knows well his sheltering bower,
 Nor leaves his covert, though we come so near.

The Rural Muse, 1835

285   *From ' The Flitting '*

I'VE left my own old home of homes,
 Green fields and every pleasant place;
The summer like a stranger comes,
I pause and hardly know her face.

613

I miss the hazel's happy green,
The blue bell's quiet hanging blooms,
Where envy's sneer was never seen,
Where staring malice never comes.

I miss the heath, its yellow furze,
Molehills and rabbit tracks that lead
Through beesom, ling, and teazel burrs
That spread a wilderness indeed;
The woodland oaks and all below
That their white powdered branches shield,
The mossy paths: the very crow
Croaked music in my native fields.

I sit me in my corner chair
That seems to feel itself at home,
And hear bird music here and there
From hawthorn hedge and orchard come.
I hear, but all is strange and new:
I sat on my old bench in June,
The sailing puddock's shrill ' peelew '
On Royce Wood seemed a sweeter tune.

I walk adown the narrow lane,
The nightingale is singing now,
But like to me she seems at loss
For Royce Wood and its shielding bough.
I lean upon the window sill,
The bees and summer happy seem;
Green, sunny green they shine, but still
My heart goes far away to dream

Of happiness, and thoughts arise
With home-bred pictures many a one,

puddock] kite or buzzard.

THE FLITTING

Green lanes that shut out burning skies
And old crook'd stiles to rest upon;
Above them hangs the maple tree,
Below grass swells a velvet hill,
And little footpaths sweet to see
Go seeking sweeter places still.

Written 1824–36
Poems by John Clare, 1908

286   *From ' The Cottager '*

TRUE as the church clock hand the hour pursues
   He plods about his toils and reads the news,
And at the blacksmith's shop his hour will stand
To talk of ' Lunun ' as a foreign land.
For from his cottage door in peace or strife
He ne'er went fifty miles in all his life.
His knowledge with old notions still combined
Is twenty years behind the march of mind.
He views new knowledge with suspicious eyes
And thinks it blasphemy to be so wise.
On steam's almighty tales he wondering looks
As witchcraft gleaned from old black letter books.
Life gave him comfort but denied him wealth,
He toils in quiet and enjoys his health.
He smokes a pipe at night and drinks his beer
And runs no scores on tavern screens to clear.
He goes to market all the year about
And keeps one hour and never stays it out.
E'en at St. Thomas tide old Rover's bark
Hails Dapple's trot an hour before it 's dark.

.   .   .   .

JOHN CLARE

In an old corner cupboard by the wall
His books are laid, though good, in number small,
His Bible first in place, from worth and age;
Whose grandsire's name adorns the title page,
And blank leaves once, now filled with kindred claims,
Displayed a world's epitome of names.
Parents and children and grandchildren all
Memory's affections in the lists recall.
And prayer book next, much worn,though strongly bound,
Proves him a churchman orthodox and sound.
The 'Pilgrim's Progress' and the 'Death of Abel
Are seldom missing from his Sunday table,
And prime old Tusser in his homely trim,
The first of bards in all the world with him,
And only Poet which his leisure knows:
Verse deals in fiction, so he sticks to prose.
These are the books he reads and reads again
And weekly hunts the almanacks for rain.
Here and no further learning's channels ran;
Still, neighbours prize him as the learned man.
His cottage is a humble place of rest
With one spare room to welcome every guest,
And that tall poplar pointing to the sky
His own hand planted while an idle boy,
It shades his chimney while the singing wind
Hums songs of shelter to his happy mind.
Within his cot the largest ears of corn
He ever found his picture frames adorn:
Brave Granby's head, De Grosse's grand defeat;
He rubs his hands and shows how Rodney beat.
And from the rafters upon strings depend
Bean stalks beset with pods from end to end,

THE COTTAGER

Whose numbers without counting may be seen
Wrote on the almanack behind the screen.
Around the corner upon worsted strung
Pooties in wreaths above the cupboard hung.
Memory at trifling incidents awakes
And there he keeps them for his children's sakes,
Who when as boys searched every sedgy lane,
Traced every wood and shattered clothes again,
Roaming about on rapture's easy wing
To hunt those very pooty shells in Spring.
And thus he lives too happy to be poor
While strife ne'er pauses at so mean a door.
Low in the sheltered valley stands his cot,
He hears the mountain storm and feels it not;
Winter and spring, toil ceasing ere 'tis dark,
Rests with the lamb and rises with the lark.
Content is helpmate to the day's employ
And care ne'er comes to steal a single joy.
Time, scarcely noticed, turns his hair to grey,
Yet leaves him happy as a child at play.

Written 1824–36
Poems by John Clare, 1908

287 *The Fear of Flowers*

THE nodding oxeye bends before the wind,
  The woodbine quakes lest boys their flowers should find,
And prickly dogrose spite of its array
Can't dare the blossom-seeking hand away,
While thistles wear their heavy knobs of bloom
Proud as a warhorse wears its haughty plume,

Pooties] snail shells.

And by the roadside danger's self defies;
On commons where pined sheep and oxen lie
In ruddy pomp and ever thronging mood
It stands and spreads like danger in a wood,
And in the village street where meanest weeds
Can't stand untouched to fill their husks with seed,
The haughty thistle o'er all danger towers,
In every place the very wasp of flowers.

Written 1824–36
Poems by John Clare, 1908

288 *The Old Cottagers*

THE little cottage stood alone, the pride
    Of solitude surrounded every side.
Bean fields in blossom almost reached the wall;
A garden with its hawthorn hedge was all
The space between.—Green light did pass
Through one small window, where a looking-glass
Placed in the parlour, richly there revealed
A spacious landscape and a blooming field.
The pasture cows that herded on the moor
Printed their footsteps to the very door,
Where little summer flowers with seasons blow
And scarcely gave the eldern leave to grow.
The cuckoo that one listens far away
Sung in the orchard trees for half the day;
And where the robin lives, the village guest,
In the old weedy hedge the leafy nest
Of the coy nightingale was yearly found,
Safe from all eyes as in the loneliest ground;
And little chats that in bean stalks will lie
A nest with cobwebs there will build, and fly

THE OLD COTTAGERS

Upon the kidney bean that twines and towers
Up little poles in wreaths of scarlet flowers.

There a lone couple lived, secluded there
From all the world considers joy or care,
Lived to themselves, a long lone journey trod,
And through their Bible talked aloud to God;
While one small close and cow their wants maintained,
But little needing, and but little gained.
Their neighbour's name was Peace, with her they went,
With tottering age, and dignified content,
Through a rich length of years and quiet days,
And filled the neighbouring village with their praise.

Written 1824–36
Poems by John Clare, 1920

289 *Song*

GO with your tauntings, go;
Neer think to hurt me so;
   I'll scoff at your disdain.
Cold though the winter blow,
When hills are free from snow
   It will be spring again.

So go, and fare thee well,
Nor think ye'll have to tell
   Of wounded hearts from me,
Locked up in your hearts cell.
Mine still at home doth dwell
   In its first liberty.

JOHN CLARE

Bees sip not at one flower,
Spring comes not with one shower,
  Nor shines the sun alone
Upon one favoured hour,
But with unstinted power
  Makes every day his own.

And for my freedom's sake
With such I'll pattern take,
  And rove and revel on.
Your gall shall never make
Me honied paths forsake;
  So prythee get thee gone.

And when my toil is blest
And I find a maid possest
  Of truth that's not in thee,
Like bird that finds its nest
I'll stop and take my rest;
  And love as she loves me.

Written 1824–36
Poems by John Clare, 1920

JOHN GIBSON LOCKHART

1794–1854

290   *Lament for Captain Paton*

TOUCH once more a sober measure,
  And let punch and tears be shed
For a prince of good old fellows
  That, alack-a-day! is dead,—
For a prince of worthy fellows,
  And a pretty man also,
That has left the Saltmarket

LAMENT FOR CAPTAIN PATON

In sorrow, grief, and woe.
Oh! we ne'er shall see the like of Captain Paton no mo!

His waistcoat, coat, and breeches
    Were all cut off the same web,
Of a beautiful snuff-colour,
    Or a modest genty drab;
The blue stripe in his stocking
    Round his neat slim leg did go,
And his ruffles of the cambric fine
    They were whiter than the snow.
Oh! we ne'er shall see the like of Captain Paton no mo!

His hair was curled in order,
    At the rising of the sun,
In comely rows and buckles smart
    That about his ears did run;
And before there was a toupee
    That some inches up did grow,
And behind there was a long queue
    That did o'er his shoulders flow,
Oh! we ne'er shall see the like of Captain Paton no mo!

And whenever we foregathered
    He took off his wee three-cockit,
And he proffer'd you his snuff-box,
    Which he drew from his side-pocket,
And on Burdett or Bonaparte
    He would make a remark or so,
And then along the plainstones
    Like a provost he would go.
Oh! we ne'er shall see the like of Captain Paton no mo!

JOHN GIBSON LOCKHART

In dirty days he picked well
        His footsteps with his rattan,
Oh! you ne'er could see the least speck
        On the shoes of Captain Paton;
And on entering the coffee-room,
        About *two*, all men did know
They would see him with his *Courier*
        In the middle of the row.
Oh! we ne'er shall see the like of Captain Paton no mo!

Now and then upon a Sunday
        He invited me to dine,
On a herring and a mutton-chop,
        Which his maid dressed very fine;
There was also a little Malmsey
        And a bottle of Bordeaux,
Which between me and the Captain
        Passed nimbly to and fro.
Oh! I ne'er shall take pot luck with Captain Paton no mo!

Or if a bowl was mentioned,
        The Captain he would ring
And bid Nelly run to the West Port
        And a stoup of water bring:
Then would he mix the genuine stuff
        As they made it long ago,
With limes that on his property
    —   In Trinidad did grow.
Oh! we ne'er shall taste the like of Captain Paton's punch no
        mo!

And then all the time he would discourse
        So sensible and courteous,—

LAMENT FOR CAPTAIN PATON

Perhaps talking of last sermon
    He had heard from Dr. Porteous,—
Or some little bit of scandal
    About Mrs. So-and-so,
Which he scarce could credit, having heard
    The *con* but not the *pro*.
Oh! we ne'er shall hear the like of Captain Paton no mo!

Or when the candles were brought forth
    And the night was fairly setting in,
He would tell some fine old stories
    About Minden-field or Dettingen,
How he fought with a French major
    And dispatch'd him at a blow,
While his blood ran out like water
    On the soft grass below.
Oh! we ne'er shall hear the like of Captain Paton no mo!

But at last the Captain sickened,
    And grew worse from day to day;
And all missed him in the coffee-room,
    From which now he stay'd away:
On Sabbaths, too, the Wee Kirk
    Made a melancholy show,
All for wanting of the presence
    Of our venerable beau.
Oh! we ne'er shall see the like of Captain Paton no mo!

And, in spite of all that Cleghorn
    And Corkindale could do,
It was plain from twenty symptoms,
    That death was in his view;
So the Captain made his test'ment,
    And submitted to his foe,

And we laid him by the Ram's-horn-Kirk;
   'Tis the way we all must go!
Oh! we ne'er shall see the like of Captain Paton no mo!

Join all in chorus, jolly boys!
   And let punch and tears be shed
For this prince of good old fellows,
   That, alack-a-day! is dead,—
For this prince of worthy fellows,
   And a pretty man also,
That has left the Saltmarket
   In sorrow, grief, and woe!
For it ne'er shall see the like of Captain Paton no mo!

Blackwood's Magazine, September 1819

291   *Serenade*

WHILE my lady sleepeth,
   The dark blue heaven is bright,
Soft the moonbeam creepeth
   Round her bower all night.
Thou gentle, gentle breeze,
   While my lady slumbers,
Waft lightly through the trees
   Echoes of my numbers,
Her dreaming ear to please.

Should ye, breathing numbers
   That for her I weave,
Should ye break her slumbers,
   All my soul would grieve.
Rise on the gentle breeze,
   And gain her lattice height

SERENADE

O'er yon poplar trees,
  But be your echoes light
As hum of distant bees.

All the stars are glowing
  In the gorgeous sky,
In the stream scarce flowing
  Mimic lustres lie:—
Blow, gentle, gentle breeze,
  But bring no cloud to hide
Their dear resplendencies;
  Nor chase from Zara's side
Dreams bright and pure as these.

Spanish Ballads, 1823

WILLIAM CULLEN BRYANT

1794–1878

292 *Thanatopsis*

TO him who in the love of Nature holds
    Communion with her visible forms, she speaks
A various language; for his gayer hours
She has a voice of gladness, and a smile
And eloquence of beauty, and she glides
Into his darker musings, with a mild
And healing sympathy, that steals away
Their sharpness ere he is aware. When thoughts
Of the last bitter hour come like a blight
Over thy spirit, and sad images
Of the stern agony, and shroud, and pall,
And breathless darkness, and the narrow house,
Make thee to shudder, and grow sick at heart;—
Go forth, under the open sky, and list

To Nature's teachings, while from all around—
Earth and her waters, and the depths of air,—
Comes a still voice—Yet a few days, and thee
The all-beholding sun shall see no more
In all his course; nor yet in the cold ground,
Where thy pale form was laid, with many tears,
Nor in the embrace of ocean, shall exist
Thy image. Earth, that nourished thee, shall claim
Thy growth, to be resolved to earth again,
And, lost each human trace, surrendering up
Thine individual being, shalt thou go
To mix for ever with the elements,
To be a brother to the insensible rock
And to the sluggish clod, which the rude swain
Turns with his share, and treads upon. The oak
Shall send his roots abroad, and pierce thy mould.

　　Yet not to thine eternal resting-place
Shalt thou retire alone,—nor couldst thou wish
Couch more magnificent. Thou shalt lie down
With patriarchs of the infant world—with kings,
The powerful of the earth—the wise, the good,
Fair forms, and hoary seers of ages past,
All in one mighty sepulchre. The hills
Rock-ribbed and ancient as the sun; the vales
Stretching in pensive quietness between;
The venerable woods; rivers that move
In majesty, and the complaining brooks
That make the meadows green; and, poured round all,
Old ocean's grey and melancholy waste—
Are but the solemn decorations all
Of the great tomb of man. The golden sun,

626

THANATOPSIS

The planets, all the infinite host of heaven,
Are shining on the sad abodes of death,
Through the still lapse of ages. All that tread
The globe are but a handful to the tribes
That slumber in its bosom.—Take the wings
Of· morning, traverse Barca's desert sands,
Or lose thyself in the continuous woods
Where rolls the Oregon, and hears no sound,
Save his own dashings—yet—the dead are there:
And millions in those solitudes, since first
The flight of years began, have laid them down
In their last sleep—the dead reign there alone.
So shalt thou rest, and what if thou withdraw
In silence from the living, and no friend
Take note of thy departure? All that breathe
Will share thy destiny. The gay will laugh
When thou art gone, the solemn brood of care
Plod on, and each one as before will chase
His favourite phantom; yet all these shall leave
Their mirth and their employments, and shall come,
And make their bed with thee. As the long train
Of ages glide away, the sons of men,
The youth in life's green spring, and he who goes
In the full strength of years, matron, and maid,
And the sweet babe, and the grey-headed man—
Shall one by one be gathered to thy side,
By those, who in their turn shall follow them.

So live, that when thy summons comes to join
The innumerable caravan, which moves
To that mysterious realm, where each shall take
His chamber in the silent halls of death,

Thou go not, like the quarry-slave at night,
Scourged to his dungeon, but, sustained and soothed
By an unfaltering trust, approach thy grave
Like one who wraps the drapery of his couch
About him, and lies down to pleasant dreams.

North American Review, September 1817;
Poems, 1821

293 *To a Waterfowl*

WHITHER, 'midst falling dew,
While glow the heavens with the last steps of day,
Far, through their rosy depths, dost thou pursue
    Thy solitary way?

Vainly the fowler's eye
Might mark thy distant flight to do thee wrong,
As, darkly seen against the crimson sky,
    Thy figure floats along.

Seek'st thou the plashy brink
Of weedy lake, or marge of river wide,
Or where the rocking billows rise and sink
    On the chafed ocean side?

There is a Power whose care
Teaches thy way along that pathless coast,—
The desert and illimitable air,—
    Lone wandering, but not lost.

All day thy wings have fanned,
At that far height, the cold thin atmosphere,
Yet stoop not, weary, to the welcome land,
    Though the dark night is near.

And soon that toil shall end;
Soon shalt thou find a summer home and rest,
And scream among thy fellows; reeds shall bend,
 Soon, o'er thy sheltered nest.

Thou 'rt gone, the abyss of heaven
Hath swallowed up thy form; yet, on my heart
Deeply hath sunk the lesson thou hast given,
 And shall not soon depart:

He who, from zone to zone,
Guides through the boundless sky thy certain flight,
In the long way that I must tread alone,
 Will lead my steps aright.

Poems, 1821

294   *To the Fringed Gentian*

THOU blossom bright with autumn dew,
 And coloured with the heaven's own blue,
That openest when the quiet light
Succeeds the keen and frosty night.

Thou comest not when violets lean
O'er wandering brooks and springs unseen,
Or columbines, in purple dressed,
Nod o'er the ground-bird's hidden nest;

Thou waitest late and com'st alone,
When woods are bare and birds are flown,
And frosts and shortening days portend
The aged year is near his end.

Then doth thy sweet and quiet eye
Look through its fringes to the sky,
Blue—blue—as if that sky let fall
A flower from its cerulean wall.

I would that thus, when I shall see
The hour of death draw near to me,
Hope, blossoming within my heart,
May look to heaven as I depart.

Poems, 1832

JOHN KEATS

1795–1821

295   *On first looking into Chapman's Homer*

MUCH have I travell'd in the realms of gold,
    And many goodly states and kingdoms seen;
    Round many western islands have I been
Which bards in fealty to Apollo hold.
Oft of one wide expanse had I been told
    That deep-brow'd Homer ruled as his demesne;
    Yet did I never breathe its pure serene
Till I heard Chapman speak out loud and bold:
Then felt I like some watcher of the skies
    When a new planet swims into his ken;
Or like stout Cortez when with eagle eyes
    He star'd at the Pacific—and all his men
Look'd at each other with a wild surmise—
    Silent, upon a peak in Darien.

Poems, 1817

296

From ' Sleep and Poetry '

STOP and consider! life is but a day;
A fragile dew-drop on its perilous way
From a tree's summit; a poor Indian's sleep
While his boat hastens to the monstrous steep
Of Montmorenci. Why so sad a moan?
Life is the rose's hope while yet unblown;
The reading of an ever-changing tale;
The light uplifting of a maiden's veil;
A pigeon tumbling in clear summer air;
A laughing school-boy, without grief or care,
Riding the springy branches of an elm.

Poems, 1817

297

From ' Endymion '

(i)

'A thing of beauty '

A THING of beauty is a joy for ever:
Its loveliness increases; it will never
Pass into nothingness; but still will keep
A bower quiet for us, and a sleep
Full of sweet dreams, and health, and quiet breathing.
Therefore, on every morrow, are we wreathing
A flowery band to bind us to the earth,
Spite of despondence, of the inhuman dearth
Of noble natures, of the gloomy days,
Of all the unhealthy and o'er-darkened ways
Made for our searching: yes, in spite of all,
Some shape of beauty moves away the pall

From our dark spirits. Such the sun, the moon,
Trees old and young, sprouting a shady boon
For simple sheep; and such are daffodils
With the green world they live in; and clear rills
That for themselves a cooling covert make
'Gainst the hot season; the mid forest brake,
Rich with a sprinkling of fair musk-rose blooms:
And such too is the grandeur of the dooms
We have imagined for the mighty dead;
All lovely tales that we have heard or read:
An endless fountain of immortal drink,
Pouring unto us from the heaven's brink.

Book I, ll. 1–24

(ii)

Hymn to Pan

O THOU, whose mighty palace roof doth hang
  From jagged trunks, and overshadoweth
Eternal whispers, glooms, the birth, life, death
Of unseen flowers in heavy peacefulness;
Who lov'st to see the hamadryads dress
Their ruffled locks where meeting hazels darken;
And through whole solemn hours dost sit, and hearken
The dreary melody of bedded reeds—
In desolate places, where dank moisture breeds
The pipy hemlock to strange overgrowth;
Bethinking thee, how melancholy loth
Thou wast to lose fair Syrinx—do thou now,
By thy love's milky brow!
By all the trembling mazes that she ran,
Hear us, great Pan!

632

ENDYMION

O thou, for whose soul-soothing quiet, turtles
Passion their voices cooingly 'mong myrtles,
What time thou wanderest at eventide
Through sunny meadows, that outskirt the side
Of thine enmossed realms: O thou, to whom
Broad leaved fig trees even now foredoom
Their ripen'd fruitage; yellow girted bees
Their golden honeycombs; our village leas
Their fairest blossom'd beans and poppied corn;
The chuckling linnet its five young unborn,
To sing for thee; low creeping strawberries
Their summer coolness; pent up butterflies
Their freckled wings; yea, the fresh budding year
All its completions—be quickly near,
By every wind that nods the mountain pine,
O forester divine!

Thou, to whom every fawn and satyr flies
For willing service; whether to surprise
The squatted hare while in half sleeping fit;
Or upward ragged precipices flit
To save poor lambkins from the eagle's maw;
Or by mysterious enticement draw
Bewildered shepherds to their path again;
Or to tread breathless round the frothy main,
And gather up all fancifullest shells
For thee to tumble into Naiads' cells,
And, being hidden, laugh at their out-peeping;
Or to delight thee with fantastic leaping,
The while they pelt each other on the crown
With silvery oak apples, and fir cones brown—
By all the echoes that about thee ring,
Hear us, O satyr king!

x

JOHN KEATS

O Hearkener to the loud clapping shears,
While ever and anon to his shorn peers
A ram goes bleating: Winder of the horn,
When snouted wild-boars routing tender corn
Anger our huntsmen: Breather round our farms,
To keep off mildews, and all weather harms:
Strange ministrant of undescribed sounds,
That come a swooning over hollow grounds,
And wither drearily on barren moors:
Dread opener of the mysterious doors
Leading to universal knowledge—see,
Great son of Dryope,
The many that are come to pay their vows
With leaves about their brows!

Be still the unimaginable lodge
For solitary thinkings; such as dodge
Conception to the very bourne of heaven,
Then leave the naked brain: be still the leaven,
That spreading in this dull and clodded earth,
Gives it a touch ethereal—a new birth:
Be still a symbol of immensity;
A firmament reflected in a sea;
An element filling the space between;
An unknown—but no more: we humbly screen
With uplift hands our foreheads, lowly bending,
And giving out a shout most heaven rending,
Conjure thee to receive our humble Pæan,
Upon thy Mount Lycean!

Book I, ll. 232–306

634

(*iii*)

Love and Friendship

BUT there are
Richer entanglements, enthralments far
More self-destroying, leading, by degrees,
To the chief intensity: the crown of these
Is made of love and friendship, and sits high
Upon the forehead of humanity.
All its more ponderous and bulky worth
Is friendship, whence there ever issues forth
A steady splendour; but at the tip-top,
There hangs by unseen film, an orbed drop
Of light, and that is love: its influence,
Thrown in our eyes, genders a novel sense,
At which we start and fret; till in the end,
Melting into its radiance, we blend,
Mingle, and so become a part of it,—
Nor with aught else can our souls interknit
So wingedly: when we combine therewith,
Life's self is nourish'd by its proper pith,
And we are nurtured like a pelican brood.
Aye, so delicious is the unsating food,
That men, who might have tower'd in the van
Of all the congregated world, to fan
And winnow from the coming step of time
All chaff of custom, wipe away all slime
Left by men-slugs and human serpentry,
Have been content to let occasion die,
Whilst they did sleep in love's elysium.
And, truly, I would rather be struck dumb,

Than speak against this ardent listlessness:
For I have ever thought that it might bless
The world with benefits unknowingly;
As does the nightingale, upperched high,
And cloister'd among cool and bunched leaves—
She sings but to her love, nor e'er conceives
How tiptoe Night holds back her dark-grey hood.
Just so may love, although 'tis understood
The mere commingling of passionate breath,
Produce more than our searching witnesseth:
What I know not: but who, of men, can tell
That flowers would bloom, or that green fruit would swell
To melting pulp, that fish would have bright mail,
The earth its dower of river, wood, and vale,
The meadows runnels, runnels pebble-stones,
The seed its harvest, or the lute its tones,
Tones ravishment, or ravishment its sweet
If human souls did never kiss and greet?

Book I, ll. 798–842

(*iv*)

' *Here is wine* '

HERE is wine,
Alive with sparkles—never, I aver,
Since Ariadne was a vintager,
So cool a purple: taste these juicy pears,
Sent me by sad Vertumnus, when his fears
Were high about Pomona: here is cream,
Deepening to richness from a snowy gleam;
Sweeter than that nurse Amalthea skimm'd
For the boy Jupiter: and here, undimm'd

ENDYMION

By any touch, a bunch of blooming plums
Ready to melt between an infant's gums:
And here is manna pick'd from Syrian trees,
In starlight, by the three Hesperides.

Book II, ll. 441–53

(v)[1]

TO Sorrow,
I bade good-morrow,
And thought to leave her far away behind;
But cheerly, cheerly,
She loves me dearly;
She is so constant to me, and so kind:
I would deceive her
And so leave her,
But ah! she is so constant and so kind.

Beneath my palm trees, by the river side,
I sat a weeping: in the whole world wide
There was no one to ask me why I wept,—
And so I kept
Brimming the water-lily cups with tears
Cold as my fears.

Beneath my palm trees, by the river side,
I sat aweeping: what enamour'd bride,
Cheated by shadowy wooer from the clouds,
But hides and shrouds
Beneath dark palm trees by a river side?

[1] This arrangement follows the suggestion of Mr. Robert Bridges in his introduction to Keats's Poems (Muses' Library, 1896).

And as I sat, over the light blue hills
There came a noise of revellers: the rills
Into the wide stream came of purple hue—
     'Twas Bacchus and his crew!
The earnest trumpet spake, and silver thrills
From kissing cymbals made a merry din—
     'Twas Bacchus and his kin!
Like to a moving vintage down they came,
Crown'd with green leaves, and faces all on flame;
All madly dancing through the pleasant valley,
     To scare thee, Melancholy!
O then, O then, thou wast a simple name!
And I forgot thee, as the berried holly
By shepherds is forgotten, when, in June,
Tall chesnuts keep away the sun and moon:—
     I rush'd into the folly!

Within his car, aloft, young Bacchus stood,
Trifling his ivy-dart, in dancing mood,
     With sidelong laughing;
And little rills of crimson wine imbrued
His plump white arms, and shoulders, enough white
     For Venus' pearly bite:
And near him rode Silenus on his ass,
Pelted with flowers as he on did pass
     Tipsily quaffing.

Whence came ye, merry Damsels! whence came ye!
So many, and so many, and such glee?
Why have ye left your bowers desolate,
     Your lutes, and gentler fate?—
' We follow Bacchus! Bacchus on the wing,
     A conquering!

ENDYMION

Bacchus, young Bacchus! good or ill betide,
We dance before him thorough kingdoms wide:—
Come hither, lady fair, and joined be
    To our wild minstrelsy!'

Whence came ye, jolly Satyrs! whence came ye!
So many, and so many, and such glee?
Why have ye left your forest haunts, why left
    Your nuts in oak-tree cleft?—
' For wine, for wine we left our kernel tree;
For wine we left our heath, and yellow brooms,
    And cold mushrooms;
For wine we follow Bacchus through the earth;
Great God of breathless cups and chirping mirth!—
Come hither, lady fair, and joined be
    To our mad minstrelsy!'

Over wide streams and mountains great we went,
And, save when Bacchus kept his ivy tent,
Onward the tiger and the leopard pants,
    With Asian elephants:
Onward these myriads—with song and dance,
With zebras striped, and sleek Arabians' prance,
Web-footed alligators, crocodiles,
Bearing upon their scaly backs, in files,
Plump infant laughers mimicking the coil
Of seamen, and stout galley-rowers' toil:
With toying oars and silken sails they glide,
    Nor care for wind and tide.

Mounted on panthers' furs and lions' manes,
From rear to van they scour about the plains;
A three days' journey in a moment done:
And always, at the rising of the sun,

About the wilds they hunt with spear and horn,
  On spleenful unicorn.
I saw Osirian Egypt kneel adown
  Before the vine-wreath crown!
I saw parch'd Abyssinia rouse and sing
  To the silver cymbals' ring!
I saw the whelming vintage hotly pierce
  Old Tartary the fierce!
The kings of Inde their jewel-sceptres vail,
And from their treasures scatter pearled hail;
Great Brahma from his mystic heaven groans,
  And all his priesthood moans;
Before young Bacchus' eye-wink turning pale.—
Into these regions came I following him,
Sick hearted, weary—so I took a whim
To stray away into these forests drear
  Alone, without a peer:
And I have told thee all thou mayest hear.

    Come then, Sorrow!
    Sweetest Sorrow!
Like an own babe I nurse thee on my breast:
    I thought to leave thee
    And deceive thee,
But now of all the world I love thee best.

    There is not one,
    No, no, not one
But thee to comfort a poor lonely maid;
    Thou art her mother,
    And her brother,
Her playmate, and her wooer in the shade.

                    Book IV, ll. 173–290, omitting 273–8;
                                    Endymion, 1818

FOUR seasons fill the measure of the year;
   There are four seasons in the mind of man.
He has his lusty Spring, when fancy clear
   Takes in all beauty with an easy span:
He has his Summer, when luxuriously
   Spring's honied cud of youthful thought he loves
To ruminate, and by such dreaming nigh
   His nearest unto heaven: quiet coves
His soul has in its Autumn, when his wings
   He furleth close; contented so to look
On mists in idleness—to let fair things
   Pass by unheeded as a threshold brook.
He has his Winter too of pale misfeature,
Or else he would forego his mortal nature.

Literary Pocket-Book, 1819

299 *Ode*

BARDS of Passion and of Mirth,
  Ye have left your souls on earth!
Have ye souls in heaven too,
Double lived in regions new?
Yes, and those of heaven commune
With the spheres of sun and moon;
With the noise of fountains wond'rous,
And the parle of voices thund'rous;
With the whisper of heaven's trees
And one another, in soft ease
Seated on Elysian lawns
Brows'd by none but Dian's fawns;

Underneath large blue-bells tented,
Where the daisies are rose-scented,
And the rose herself has got
Perfume which on earth is not;
Where the nightingale doth sing
Not a senseless, tranced thing,
But divine melodious truth;
Philosophic numbers smooth;
Tales and golden histories
Of heaven and its mysteries.

Thus ye live on high, and then
On the earth ye live again;
And the souls ye left behind you
Teach us, here, the way to find you,
Where your other souls are joying,
Never slumber'd, never cloying.
Here, your earth-born souls still speak
To mortals, of their little week;
Of their sorrows and delights;
Of their passions and their spites;
Of their glory and their shame;
What doth strengthen and what maim.
Thus ye teach us, every day,
Wisdom, though fled far away.

Bards of Passion and of Mirth,
Ye have left your souls on earth!
Ye have souls in heaven too,
Double-lived in regions new!

Lamia, &c., 1820

SOULS of Poets dead and gone,
What Elysium have ye known,
Happy field or mossy cavern,
Choicer than the Mermaid Tavern?
Have ye tippled drink more fine
Than mine host's Canary wine?
Or are fruits of Paradise
Sweeter than those dainty pies
Of venison? O generous food!
Drest as though bold Robin Hood
Would, with his maid Marian,
Sup and bowse from horn and can.

I have heard that on a day
Mine host's sign-board flew away,
Nobody knew whither, till
An astrologer's old quill
To a sheepskin gave the story,
Said he saw you in your glory,
Underneath a new-old sign
Sipping beverage divine,
And pledging with contented smack
The Mermaid in the Zodiac.

Souls of Poets dead and gone,
What Elysium have ye known,
Happy field or mossy cavern,
Choicer than the Mermaid Tavern?

Lamia, &c., 1820

JOHN KEATS

Stanzas

I

IN a drear-nighted December,
    Too happy, happy tree,
Thy branches ne'er remember
    Their green felicity:
    The north cannot undo them,
    With a sleety whistle through them;
    Nor frozen thawings glue them
        From budding at the prime.

II

In a drear-nighted December,
    Too happy, happy brook,
Thy bubblings ne'er remember
    Apollo's summer look;
    But with a sweet forgetting,
    They stay their crystal fretting,
    Never, never petting
        About the frozen time.

III

Ah! would 'twere so with many
    A gentle girl and boy!
But were there ever any
    Writh'd not at passed joy?
    To know the change and feel it,
    When there is none to heal it,
    Nor numbed sense to steel it,
        Was never said in rhyme.

Galignani's edition, 1829

I

ST. AGNES' Eve—Ah, bitter chill it was!
　　The owl, for all his feathers, was a-cold;
The hare limp'd trembling through the frozen grass,
And silent was the flock in woolly fold:
Numb were the Beadsman's fingers, while he told
His rosary, and while his frosted breath,
Like pious incense from a censer old,
Seem'd taking flight for heaven, without a death,
Past the sweet Virgin's picture, while his prayer he saith.

II

His prayer he saith, this patient, holy man;
Then takes his lamp, and riseth from his knees,
And back returneth, meagre, barefoot, wan,
Along the chapel aisle by slow degrees:
The sculptur'd dead, on each side, seem to freeze,
Emprison'd in black, purgatorial rails:
Knights, ladies, praying in dumb orat'ries,
He passeth by; and his weak spirit fails
To think how they may ache in icy hoods and mails.

III

Northward he turneth through a little door,
And scarce three steps, ere Music's golden tongue
Flatter'd to tears this aged man and poor;
But no—already had his deathbell rung;

645

The joys of all his life were said and sung:
His was harsh penance on St. Agnes' Eve:
Another way he went, and soon among
Rough ashes sat he for his soul's reprieve,
And all night kept awake, for sinners' sake to grieve

IV

That ancient Beadsman heard the prelude soft;
And so it chanc'd, for many a door was wide,
From hurry to and fro. Soon, up aloft,
The silver, snarling trumpets 'gan to chide:
The level chambers, ready with their pride,
Were glowing to receive a thousand guests:
The carved angels, ever eager-eyed,
Star'd, where upon their heads the cornice rests,
With hair blown back, and wings put cross-wise on their breasts.

V

At length burst in the argent revelry,
With plume, tiara, and all rich array,
Numerous as shadows haunting fairily
The brain, new stuff'd, in youth, with triumphs gay
Of old romance. These let us wish away,
And turn, sole-thoughted, to one Lady there,
Whose heart had brooded, all that wintry day,
On love, and wing'd St. Agnes' saintly care,
As she had heard old dames full many times declare.

VI

They told her how, upon St. Agnes' Eve,
Young virgins might have visions of delight,
And soft adorings from their loves receive
Upon the honey'd middle of the night,

THE EVE OF ST. AGNES

If ceremonies due they did aright;
As, supperless to bed they must retire,
And couch supine their beauties, lily white;
Nor look behind, nor sideways, but require
Of Heaven with upward eyes for all that they desire

VII

Full of this whim was thoughtful Madeline:
The music, yearning like a God in pain,
She scarcely heard: her maiden eyes divine,
Fix'd on the floor, saw many a sweeping train
Pass by—she heeded not at all: in vain
Came many a tiptoe, amorous cavalier,
And back retir'd; not cool'd by high disdain,
But she saw not: her heart was otherwhere:
She sigh'd for Agnes' dreams, the sweetest of the year.

VIII

She danc'd along with vague, regardless eyes,
Anxious her lips, her breathing quick and short:
The hallow'd hour was near at hand: she sighs
Amid the timbrels, and the throng'd resort
Of whisperers in anger, or in sport;
'Mid looks of love, defiance, hate, and scorn,
Hoodwink'd with faery fancy; all amort,
Save to St. Agnes and her lambs unshorn,
And all the bliss to be before to-morrow morn.

IX

So, purposing each moment to retire,
She linger'd still. Meantime, across the moors,
Had come young Porphyro, with heart on fire
For Madeline. Beside the portal doors,

Buttress'd from moonlight, stands he, and implores
All saints to give him sight of Madeline,
But for one moment in the tedious hours,
That he might gaze and worship all unseen;
Perchance speak, kneel, touch, kiss—in sooth such things
      have been.

X

He ventures in: let no buzz'd whisper tell:
All eyes be muffled, or a hundred swords
Will storm his heart, Love's fev'rous citadel:
For him, those chambers held barbarian hordes,
Hyena foemen, and hot-blooded lords,
Whose very dogs would execrations howl
Against his lineage: not one breast affords
Him any mercy, in that mansion foul,
Save one old beldame, weak in body and in soul.

XI

Ah, happy chance! the aged creature came,
Shuffling along with ivory-headed wand,
To where he stood, hid from the torch's flame,
Behind a broad hall-pillar, far beyond
The sound of merriment and chorus bland:
He startled her; but soon she knew his face,
And grasp'd his fingers in her palsied hand,
Saying, ' Mercy, Porphyro! hie thee from this place;
' They are all here to-night, the whole blood-thirsty race!

XII

' Get hence! get hence! there 's dwarfish Hildebrand;
' He had a fever late, and in the fit
' He cursed thee and thine, both house and land:
' Then there 's that old Lord Maurice, not a whit

648

' More tame for his gray hairs—Alas me! flit!
' Flit like a ghost away.'—' Ah, Gossip dear,
' We're safe enough; here in this arm-chair sit,
' And tell me how '—' Good Saints! not here, not here;
' Follow me, child, or else these stones will be thy bier.'

XIII

He follow'd through a lowly arched way,
Brushing the cobwebs with his lofty plume,
And as she mutter'd ' Well-a—well-a-day! '
He found him in a little moonlight room,
Pale, lattic'd, chill, and silent as a tomb.
' Now tell me where is Madeline,' said he,
' O tell me, Angela, by the holy loom
' Which none but secret sisterhood may see,
' When they St. Agnes' wool are weaving piously.

XIV

' St. Agnes! Ah! it is St. Agnes' Eve—
' Yet men will murder upon holy days:
' Thou must hold water in a witch's sieve,
' And be liege-lord of all the Elves and Fays,
' To venture so: it fills me with amaze
' To see thee, Porphyro!—St. Agnes' Eve!
' God's help! my lady fair the conjuror plays
' This very night: good angels her deceive!
' But let me laugh awhile, I've mickle time to grieve.'

XV

Feebly she laugheth in the languid moon,
While Porphyro upon her face doth look,
Like puzzled urchin on an aged crone
Who keepeth clos'd a wond'rous riddle-book,

As spectacled she sits in chimney nook.
But soon his eyes grew brilliant, when she told
His lady's purpose; and he scarce could brook
Tears, at the thought of those enchantments cold,
And Madeline asleep in lap of legends old.

XVI

Sudden a thought came like a full-blown rose,
Flushing his brow, and in his pained heart
Made purple riot: then doth he propose
A stratagem, that makes the beldame start:
' A cruel man and impious thou art:
' Sweet lady, let her pray, and sleep, and dream
' Alone with her good angels, far apart
' From wicked men like thee. Go, go!—I deem
' Thou canst not surely be the same that thou didst seem.'

XVII

' I will not harm her, by all saints I swear,'
Quoth Porphyro: ' O may I ne'er find grace
' When my weak voice shall whisper its last prayer,
' If one of her soft ringlets I displace,
' Or look with ruffian passion in her face:
' Good Angela, believe me by these tears;
' Or I will, even in a moment's space,
' Awake, with horrid shout, my foemen's ears,
' And beard them, though they be more fang'd than wolves
    and bears.'

XVIII

' Ah! why wilt thou affright a feeble soul?
' A poor, weak, palsy-stricken, churchyard thing,

650

' Whose passing-bell may ere the midnight toll;
' Whose prayers for thee, each morn and evening,
' Were never miss'd.'—Thus plaining, doth she bring
A gentler speech from burning Porphyro;
So woful, and of such deep sorrowing,
That Angela gives promise she will do
Whatever he shall wish, betide her weal or woe.

XIX

Which was, to lead him, in close secrecy,
Even to Madeline's chamber, and there hide
Him in a closet, of such privacy
That he might see her beauty unespied,
And win perhaps that night a peerless bride,
While legion'd fairies pac'd the coverlet,
And pale enchantment held her sleepy-eyed.
Never on such a night have lovers met,
Since Merlin paid his Demon all the monstrous debt.

XX

' It shall be as thou wishest,' said the Dame:
' All cates and dainties shall be stored there
' Quickly on this feast-night: by the tambour frame
' Her own lute thou wilt see: no time to spare,
' For I am slow and feeble, and scarce dare
' On such a catering trust my dizzy head.
' Wait here, my child, with patience; kneel in prayer
' The while: Ah! thou must needs the lady wed,
' Or may I never leave my grave among the dead.'

XXI

So saying, she hobbled off with busy fear.
The lover's endless minutes slowly pass'd;

The dame return'd, and whisper'd in his ear
To follow her; with aged eyes aghast
From fright of dim espial. Safe at last,
Through many a dusky gallery, they gain
The maiden's chamber, silken, hush'd, and chaste;
Where Porphyro took covert, pleas'd amain.
His poor guide hurried back with agues in her brain.

XXII

Her falt'ring hand upon the balustrade,
Old Angela was feeling for the stair,
When Madeline, St. Agnes' charmed maid,
Rose, like a mission'd spirit, unaware:
With silver taper's light, and pious care,
She turn'd, and down the aged gossip led
To a safe level matting. Now prepare,
Young Porphyro, for gazing on that bed;
She comes, she comes again, like ring-dove fray'd and fled.

XXIII

Out went the taper as she hurried in;
Its little smoke, in pallid moonshine, died:
She clos'd the door, she panted, all akin
To spirits of the air, and visions wide:
No uttered syllable, or, woe betide!
But to her heart, her heart was voluble,
Paining with eloquence her balmy side;
As though a tongueless nightingale should swell
Her throat in vain, and die, heart-stifled, in her dell.

XXIV

A casement high and triple-arch'd there was,
All garlanded with carven imag'ries

THE EVE OF ST. AGNES

Of fruits, and flowers, and bunches of knot-grass,
And diamonded with panes of quaint device,
Innumerable of stains and splendid dyes,
As are the tiger-moth's deep-damask'd wings;
And in the midst, 'mong thousand heraldries,
And twilight saints, and dim emblazonings,
A shielded scutcheon blush'd with blood of queens and kings.

XXV

Full on this casement shone the wintry moon,
And threw warm gules on Madeline's fair breast,
As down she knelt for heaven's grace and boon;
Rose-bloom fell on her hands, together prest,
And on her silver cross soft amethyst,
And on her hair a glory, like a saint:
She seem'd a splendid angel, newly drest,
Save wings, for heaven:—Porphyro grew faint:
She knelt, so pure a thing, so free from mortal taint.

XXVI

Anon his heart revives: her vespers done,
Of all its wreathed pearls her hair she frees;
Unclasps her warmed jewels one by one;
Loosens her fragrant boddice; by degrees
Her rich attire creeps rustling to her knees:
Half-hidden, like a mermaid in sea-weed,
Pensive awhile she dreams awake, and sees,
In fancy, fair St. Agnes in her bed,
But dares not look behind, or all the charm is fled.

XXVII

Soon, trembling in her soft and chilly nest,
In sort of wakeful swoon, perplex'd she lay,

Until the poppied warmth of sleep oppress'd
Her soothed limbs, and soul fatigued away;
Flown, like a thought, until the morrow-day;
Blissfully haven'd both from joy and pain;
Clasp'd like a missal where swart Paynims pray;
Blinded alike from sunshine and from rain,
As though a rose should shut, and be a bud again.

XXVIII

Stol'n to this paradise, and so entranced,
Porphyro gazed upon her empty dress,
And listen'd to her breathing, if it chanced
To wake into a slumberous tenderness;
Which when he heard, that minute did he bless,
And breath'd himself: then from the closet crept,
Noiseless as fear in a wide wilderness,
And over the hush'd carpet, silent, stept,
And 'tween the curtains peep'd, where, lo!—how fast she
slept.

XXIX

Then by the bed-side, where the faded moon
Made a dim, silver twilight, soft he set
A table, and, half anguish'd, threw thereon
A cloth of woven crimson, gold, and jet:—
O for some drowsy Morphean amulet!
The boisterous, midnight, festive clarion,
The kettle-drum, and far-heard clarionet,
Affray his ears, though but in dying tone:—
The hall door shuts again, and all the noise is gone.

THE EVE OF ST. AGNES

And still she slept an azure-lidded sleep,
In blanched linen, smooth, and lavender'd,
While he from forth the closet brought a heap
Of candied apple, quince, and plum, and gourd;
With jellies soother than the creamy curd,
And lucent syrops, tinct with cinnamon;
Manna and dates, in argosy transferr'd
From Fez; and spiced dainties, every one,
From silken Samarcand to cedar'd Lebanon.

These delicates he heap'd with glowing hand
On golden dishes and in baskets bright
Of wreathed silver: sumptuous they stand
In the retired quiet of the night,
Filling the chilly room with perfume light.—
' And now, my love, my seraph fair, awake!
' Thou art my heaven, and I thine eremite:
' Open thine eyes, for meek St. Agnes' sake,
' Or I shall drowse beside thee, so my soul doth ache.'

Thus whispering, his warm, unnerved arm
Sank in her pillow. Shaded was her dream
By the dusk curtains:—'twas a midnight charm
Impossible to melt as iced stream:
The lustrous salvers in the moonlight gleam;
Broad golden fringe upon the carpet lies:
It seem'd he never, never could redeem
From such a stedfast spell his lady's eyes;
So mus'd awhile, entoil'd in woofed phantasies.

XXXIII

Awakening up, he took her hollow lute,—
Tumultuous,—and, in chords that tenderest be,
He play'd an ancient ditty, long since mute,
In Provence call'd, ' La belle dame sans mercy: '
Close to her ear touching the melody;—
Wherewith disturb'd, she utter'd a soft moan:
He ceased—she panted quick—and suddenly
Her blue affrayed eyes wide open shone:
Upon his knees he sank, pale as smooth-sculptured stone.

XXXIV

Her eyes were open, but she still beheld,
Now wide awake, the vision of her sleep:
There was a painful change, that nigh expell'd
The blisses of her dream so pure and deep
At which fair Madeline began to weep,
And moan forth witless words with many a sigh;
While still her gaze on Porphyro would keep;
Who knelt, with joined hands and piteous eye,
Fearing to move or speak, she look'd so dreamingly.

XXXV

' Ah, Porphyro! ' said she, ' but even now
' Thy voice was at sweet tremble in mine ear,
' Made tuneable with every sweetest vow;
' And those sad eyes were spiritual and clear:
' How chang'd thou art! how pallid, chill, and drear!
' Give me that voice again, my Porphyro,
' Those looks immortal, those complainings dear!
' Oh leave me not in this eternal woe,
' For if thou diest, my Love, I know not where to go.'

THE EVE OF ST. AGNES

Beyond a mortal man impassion'd far
At these voluptuous accents, he arose,
Ethereal, flush'd, and like a throbbing star
Seen mid the sapphire heaven's deep repose;
Into her dream he melted, as the rose
Blendeth its odour with the violet,—
Solution sweet: meantime the frost-wind blows
Like Love's alarum pattering the sharp sleet
Against the window-panes; St. Agnes' moon hath set.

XXXVII

'Tis dark: quick pattereth the flaw-blown sleet:
' This is no dream, my bride, my Madeline!'
'Tis dark: the iced gusts still rave and beat:
' No dream, alas! alas! and woe is mine!
' Porphyro will leave me here to fade and pine.—
' Cruel! what traitor could thee hither bring?
' I curse not, for my heart is lost in thine
' Though thou forsakest a deceived thing;—
' A dove forlorn and lost with sick unpruned wing.'

' My Madeline! sweet dreamer! lovely bride!
' Say, may I be for aye thy vassal blest?
' Thy beauty's shield, heart-shap'd and vermeil dyed?
' Ah, silver shrine, here will I take my rest
' After so many hours of toil and quest,
' A famish'd pilgrim,—sav'd by miracle.
' Though I have found, I will not rob thy nest
' Saving of thy sweet self; if thou think'st well
' To trust, fair Madeline, to no rude infidel.

XXXIX

' Hark! 'tis an elfin-storm from faery land,
' Of haggard seeming, but a boon indeed:
' Arise—arise! the morning is at hand;—
' The bloated wassaillers will never heed:—
' Let us away, my love, with happy speed;
' There are no ears to hear, or eyes to see,—
' Drown'd all in Rhenish and the sleepy mead:
' Awake! arise! my love, and fearless be,
' For o'er the southern moors I have a home for thee.'

XL

She hurried at his words, beset with fears,
For there were sleeping dragons all around,
At glaring watch, perhaps, with ready spears—
Down the wide stairs a darkling way they found.—
In all the house was heard no human sound.
A chain-droop'd lamp was flickering by each door;
The arras, rich with horseman, hawk, and hound,
Flutter'd in the besieging wind's uproar;
And the long carpets rose along the gusty floor.

XLI

They glide, like phantoms, into the wide hall;
Like phantoms, to the iron porch, they glide;
Where lay the Porter, in uneasy sprawl,
With a huge empty flaggon by his side:
The wakeful bloodhound rose, and shook his hide,
But his sagacious eye an inmate owns:
By one, and one, the bolts full easy slide:—
The chains lie silent on the footworn stones;—
The key turns, and the door upon its hinges groans.

658

XLII

And they are gone: ay, ages long ago
These lovers fled away into the storm.
That night the Baron dreamt of many a woe,
And all his warrior-guests, with shade and form
Of witch, and demon, and large coffin-worm,
Were long be-nightmar'd. Angela the old
Died palsy-twitch'd, with meagre face deform;
The Beadsman, after thousand aves told,
For aye unsought for slept among his ashes cold.

Lamia, &c., 1820

303   *To Autumn*

I

SEASON of mists and mellow fruitfulness,
Close bosom-friend of the maturing sun;
Conspiring with him how to load and bless
    With fruit the vines that round the thatch-eves run;
To bend with apples the moss'd cottage-trees,
    And fill all fruit with ripeness to the core;
        To swell the gourd, and plump the hazel shells
    With a sweet kernel; to set budding more,
And still more, later flowers for the bees,
Until they think warm days will never cease,
        For Summer has o'er-brimm'd their clammy cells.

II

Who hath not seen thee oft amid thy store?
    Sometimes whoever seeks abroad may find
Thee sitting careless on a granary floor,
    Thy hair soft-lifted by the winnowing wind;

Or on a half-reap'd furrow sound asleep,
  Drows'd with the fume of poppies, while thy hook
    Spares the next swath and all its twined flowers:
And sometimes like a gleaner thou dost keep
  Steady thy laden head across a brook;
  Or by a cyder-press, with patient look,
    Thou watchest the last oozings hours by hours.

III

Where are the songs of Spring? Ay, where are they?
  Think not of them, thou hast thy music too,—
While barred clouds bloom the soft-dying day,
  And touch the stubble-plains with rosy hue;
Then in a wailful choir the small gnats mourn
  Among the river sallows, borne aloft
    Or sinking as the light wind lives or dies;
And full-grown lambs loud bleat from hilly bourn;
  Hedge-crickets sing; and now with treble soft
  The red-breast whistles from a garden-croft;
    And gathering swallows twitter in the skies.

Lamia, &c., 1820

304   *Ode on a Grecian Urn*

I

THOU still unravish'd bride of quietness,
    Thou foster-child of silence and slow time,
Sylvan historian, who canst thus express
  A flowery tale more sweetly than our rhyme:
What leaf-fring'd legend haunts about thy shape
  Of deities or mortals, or of both,

ODE ON A GRECIAN URN

In Tempe or the dales of Arcady?
What men or gods are these? What maidens loth?
What mad pursuit? What struggle to escape?
What pipes and timbrels? What wild ecstasy?

II

Heard melodies are sweet, but those unheard
Are sweeter; therefore, ye soft pipes, play on;
Not to the sensual ear, but, more endear'd,
Pipe to the spirit ditties of no tone:
Fair youth, beneath the trees, thou canst not leave
Thy song, nor ever can those trees be bare;
Bold Lover, never, never canst thou kiss,
Though winning near the goal—yet, do not grieve;
She cannot fade, though thou hast not thy bliss,
For ever wilt thou love, and she be fair!

III

Ah, happy, happy boughs! that cannot shed
Your leaves, nor ever bid the Spring adieu;
And, happy melodist, unwearied,
For ever piping songs for ever new;
More happy love! more happy, happy love!
For ever warm and still to be enjoy'd,
For ever panting, and for ever young;
All breathing human passion far above,
That leaves a heart high-sorrowful and cloy'd,
A burning forehead, and a parching tongue.

IV

Who are these coming to the sacrifice?
To what green altar, O mysterious priest,

661

Lead'st thou that heifer lowing at the skies,
    And all her silken flanks with garlands drest?
What little town by river or sea shore,
    Or mountain-built with peaceful citadel,
      Is emptied of this folk, this pious morn?
And, little town, thy streets for evermore
    Will silent be; and not a soul to tell
      Why thou art desolate, can e'er return.

v

O Attic shape! Fair attitude! with brede
    Of marble men and maidens overwrought,
With forest branches and the trodden weed;
    Thou, silent form, dost tease us out of thought
As doth eternity: Cold Pastoral!
    When old age shall this generation waste,
      Thou shalt remain, in midst of other woe
Than ours, a friend to man, to whom thou say'st,
    ' Beauty is truth, truth beauty,'—that is all
      Ye know on earth, and all ye need to know.

Annals of the Fine Arts, 1820;
Lamia, &c., 1820

305   *Ode to a Nightingale*

MY heart aches, and a drowsy numbness pains
    My sense, as though of hemlock I had drunk,
Or emptied some dull opiate to the drains
    One minute past, and Lethe-wards had sunk:
'Tis not through envy of thy happy lot,
    But being too happy in thine happiness,—

ODE TO A NIGHTINGALE

That thou, light-winged Dryad of the trees,
    In some melodious plot
Of beechen green, and shadows numberless,
    Singest of summer in full-throated ease.

O, for a draught of vintage! that hath been
    Cool'd a long age in the deep-delved earth,
Tasting of Flora and the country green,
    Dance, and Provençal song, and sunburnt mirth!
O for a beaker full of the warm South,
    Full of the true, the blushful Hippocrene,
      With beaded bubbles winking at the brim,
        And purple-stained mouth;
    That I might drink, and leave the world unseen,
    And with thee fade away into the forest dim:

Fade far away, dissolve, and quite forget
    What thou among the leaves hast never known,
The weariness, the fever, and the fret
    Here, where men sit and hear each other groan;
Where palsy shakes a few, sad, last gray hairs,
    Where youth grows pale, and spectre-thin, and dies;
      Where but to think is to be full of sorrow
        And leaden-eyed despairs,
    Where Beauty cannot keep her lustrous eyes,
    Or new Love pine at them beyond to-morrow.

Away! away! for I will fly to thee,
    Not charioted by Bacchus and his pards,
But on the viewless wings of Poesy,
    Though the dull brain perplexes and retards:
Already with thee! tender is the night,
    And haply the Queen-Moon is on her throne,

Cluster'd around by all her starry Fays;
But here there is no light,
Save what from heaven is with the breezes blown
Through verdurous glooms and winding mossy ways.

I cannot see what flowers are at my feet,
Nor what soft incense hangs upon the boughs,
But, in embalmed darkness, guess each sweet
Wherewith the seasonable month endows
The grass, the thicket, and the fruit-tree wild;
White hawthorn, and the pastoral eglantine;
Fast fading violets cover'd up in leaves;
And mid-May's eldest child,
The coming musk-rose, full of dewy wine,
The murmurous haunt of flies on summer eves.

Darkling I listen; and, for many a time
I have been half in love with easeful Death,
Call'd him soft names in many a mused rhyme,
To take into the air my quiet breath;
Now more than ever seems it rich to die,
To cease upon the midnight with no pain,
While thou art pouring forth thy soul abroad
In such an ecstasy!
Still wouldst thou sing, and I have ears in vain—
To thy high requiem become a sod.

Thou wast not born for death, immortal Bird!
No hungry generations tread thee down;
The voice I hear this passing night was heard
In ancient days by emperor and clown:
Perhaps the self-same song that found a path
Through the sad heart of Ruth, when, sick for home,

She stood in tears amid the alien corn;
　　The same that oft-times hath
Charm'd magic casements, opening on the foam
　　Of perilous seas, in faery lands forlorn.

Forlorn! the very word is like a bell
　　To toll me back from thee to my sole self!
Adieu! the fancy cannot cheat so well
　　As she is fam'd to do, deceiving elf.
Adieu! adieu! thy plaintive anthem fades
　　Past the near meadows, over the still stream,
　　　　Up the hill-side; and now 'tis buried deep
　　　　In the next valley-glades:
　　Was it a vision, or a waking dream?
　　Fled is that music:—Do I wake or sleep?

Annals of the Fine Arts, 1820;
Lamia, &c., 1820

306　　　　　*Ode to Psyche*

O GODDESS! hear these tuneless numbers, wrung
　　By sweet enforcement and remembrance dear,
And pardon that thy secrets should be sung
　　Even into thine own soft-conched ear:
Surely I dreamt to-day, or did I see
　　The winged Psyche with awaken'd eyes?
I wander'd in a forest thoughtlessly,
　　And, on the sudden, fainting with surprise,
Saw two fair creatures, couched side by side
　　In deepest grass, beneath the whisp'ring roof
　　Of leaves and trembled blossoms, where there ran
　　　　A brooklet, scarce espied:

'Mid hush'd, cool-rooted flowers, fragrant-eyed,
 Blue, silver-white, and budded Tyrian,
They lay calm-breathing on the bedded grass;
 Their arms embraced, and their pinions too;
 Their lips touch'd not, but had not bade adieu,
As if disjoined by soft-handed slumber,
And ready still past kisses to outnumber
 At tender eye-dawn of aurorean love:
  The winged boy I knew;
 But who wast thou, O happy, happy dove?
  His Psyche true!

O latest born and loveliest vision far
 Of all Olympus' faded hierarchy!
Fairer than Phœbe's sapphire-region'd star,
 Or Vesper, amorous glow-worm of the sky;
Fairer than these, though temple thou hast none,
  Nor altar heap'd with flowers;
Nor virgin-choir to make delicious moan
  Upon the midnight hours;
No voice, no lute, no pipe, no incense sweet
 From chain-swung censer teeming;
No shrine, no grove, no oracle, no heat
 Of pale-mouth'd prophet dreaming.

O brightest! though too late for antique vows,
 Too, too late for the fond believing lyre,
When holy were the haunted forest boughs,
 Holy the air, the water, and the fire;
Yet even in these days so far retir'd
 From happy pieties, thy lucent fans,
 Fluttering among the faint Olympians,
I see, and sing, by my own eyes inspired.

ODE TO PSYCHE

So let me be thy choir, and make a moan
    Upon the midnight hours;
Thy voice, thy lute, thy pipe, thy incense sweet
    From swinged censer teeming;
Thy shrine, thy grove, thy oracle, thy heat
    Of pale-mouth'd prophet dreaming.

Yes, I will be thy priest, and build a fane
    In some untrodden region of my mind,
Where branched thoughts, new grown with pleasant pain,
    Instead of pines shall murmur in the wind:
Far, far around shall those dark-cluster'd trees
    Fledge the wild-ridged mountains steep by steep;
And there by zephyrs, streams, and birds, and bees,
    The moss-lain Dryads shall be lull'd to sleep;
And in the midst of this wide quietness
A rosy sanctuary will I dress
With the wreath'd trellis of a working brain,
    With buds, and bells, and stars without a name,
With all the gardener Fancy e'er could feign,
    Who breeding flowers, will never breed the same:
And there shall be for thee all soft delight
    That shadowy thought can win,
A bright torch, and a casement ope at night,
    To let the warm Love in!

Lamia, &c., 1820

307 *From ' Hyperion '*

A Fragment

(i)

DEEP in the shady sadness of a vale
    Far sunken from the healthy breath of morn,
Far from the fiery noon, and eve's one star,
Sat gray-hair'd Saturn, quiet as a stone,
Still as the silence round about his lair;
Forest on forest hung about his head
Like cloud on cloud. No stir of air was there,
Not so much life as on a summer's day
Robs not one light seed from the feather'd grass,
But where the dead leaf fell, there did it rest.
A stream went voiceless by, still deadened more
By reason of his fallen divinity
Spreading a shade: the Naiad 'mid her reeds
Press'd her cold finger closer to her lips.

Along the margin-sand large foot-marks went,
No further than to where his feet had stray'd,
And slept there since. Upon the sodden ground
His old right hand lay nerveless, listless, dead,
Unsceptred; and his realmless eyes were closed;
While his bow'd head seem'd list'ning to the Earth,
His ancient mother, for some comfort yet.

It seem'd no force could wake him from his place:
But there came one, who with a kindred hand
Touch'd his wide shoulders, after bending low
With reverence, though to one who knew it not.
She was a Goddess of the infant world;

By her in stature the tall Amazon
Had stood a pigmy's height: she would have ta'en
Achilles by the hair and bent his neck;
Or with a finger stay'd Ixion's wheel.
Her face was large as that of Memphian sphinx,
Pedestal'd haply in a palace court,
When sages look'd to Egypt for their lore.
But oh! how unlike marble was that face:
How beautiful, if sorrow had not made
Sorrow more beautiful than Beauty's self.
There was a listening fear in her regard,
As if calamity had but begun;
As if the vanward clouds of evil days
Had spent their malice, and the sullen rear
Was with its stored thunder labouring up.
One hand she press'd upon that aching spot
Where beats the human heart, as if just there,
Though an immortal, she felt cruel pain:
The other upon Saturn's bended neck
She laid, and to the level of his ear
Leaning with parted lips, some words she spake
In solemn tenour and deep organ tone:
Some mourning words, which in our feeble tongue
Would come in these like accents; O how frail
To that large utterance of the early Gods!
' Saturn, look up!—though wherefore, poor old King?
' I have no comfort for thee, no not one:
' I cannot say, " O wherefore sleepest thou? "
' For heaven is parted from thee, and the earth
' Knows thee not, thus afflicted, for a God;
' And ocean too, with all its solemn noise,
' Has from thy sceptre pass'd; and all the air

' Is emptied of thine hoary majesty.
' Thy thunder, conscious of the new command,
' Rumbles reluctant o'er our fallen house;
' And thy sharp lightning in unpractis'd hands
' Scorches and burns our once serene domain.
' O aching time! O moments big as years!
' All as ye pass swell out the monstrous truth,
' And press it so upon our weary griefs
' That unbelief has not a space to breathe.
' Saturn, sleep on:—O thoughtless, why did I
' Thus violate thy slumbrous solitude?
' Why should I ope thy melancholy eyes?
' Saturn, sleep on! while at thy feet I weep.'

   As when, upon a tranced summer-night,
Those green-rob'd senators of mighty woods,
Tall oaks, branch-charmed by the earnest stars,
Dream, and so dream all night without a stir,
Save from one gradual solitary gust
Which comes upon the silence, and dies off,
As if the ebbing air had but one wave;
So came these words and went; the while in tears
She touch'd her fair large forehead to the ground,
Just where her falling hair might be outspread
A soft and silken mat for Saturn's feet.
One moon, with alteration slow, had shed
Her silver seasons four upon the night,
And still these two were postured motionless,
Like natural sculpture in cathedral cavern;
The frozen God still couchant on the earth,
And the sad Goddess weeping at his feet:
Until at length old Saturn lifted up

His faded eyes, and saw his kingdom gone,
And all the gloom and sorrow of the place,
And that fair kneeling Goddess.

Book I, ll. 1–92

(ii)

BUT one of the whole mammoth-brood still kept
His sov'reignty, and rule, and majesty;—
Blazing Hyperion on his orbed fire
Still sat, still snuff'd the incense, teeming up
From man to the sun's God; yet unsecure:
For as among us mortals omens drear
Fright and perplex, so also shuddered he—
Not at dog's howl, or gloom-bird's hated screech,
Or the familiar visiting of one
Upon the first toll of his passing-bell,
Or prophesyings of the midnight lamp;
But horrors, portion'd to a giant nerve,
Oft made Hyperion ache. His palace bright
Bastion'd with pyramids of glowing gold,
And touch'd with shade of bronzed obelisks,
Glar'd a blood-red through all its thousand courts,
Arches, and domes, and fiery galleries;
And all its curtains of Aurorian clouds
Flush'd angerly: while sometimes eagle's wings,
Unseen before by Gods or wondering men,
Darken'd the place; and neighing steeds were heard,
Not heard before by Gods or wondering men.
Also, when he would taste the spicy wreaths
Of incense, breath'd aloft from sacred hills,
Instead of sweets, his ample palate took
Savour of poisonous brass and metal sick:

671

And so, when harbour'd in the sleepy west,
After the full completion of fair day,—
For rest divine upon exalted couch
And slumber in the arms of melody,
He pac'd away the pleasant hours of ease
With stride colossal, on from hall to hall;
While far within each aisle and deep recess,
His winged minions in close clusters stood,
Amaz'd and full of fear; like anxious men
Who on wide plains gather in panting troops,
When earthquakes jar their battlements and towers.
Even now, while Saturn, rous'd from icy trance,
Went step for step with Thea through the woods,
Hyperion, leaving twilight in the rear,
Came slope upon the threshold of the west;
Then, as was wont, his palace-door flew ope
In smoothest silence, save what solemn tubes,
Blown by the serious Zephyrs, gave of sweet
And wandering sounds, slow-breathed melodies;
And like a rose in vermeil tint and shape,
In fragrance soft, and coolness to the eye,
That inlet to severe magnificence
Stood full blown, for the God to enter in.

Book I, ll. 164–212

(iii)

JUST at the self-same beat of Time's wide wings
Hyperion slid into the rustled air,
And Saturn gain'd with Thea that sad place
Where Cybele and the bruised Titans mourn'd.
It was a den where no insulting light
Could glimmer on their tears; where their own groans

They felt, but heard not, for the solid roar
Of thunderous waterfalls and torrents hoarse,
Pouring a constant bulk, uncertain where.
Crag jutting forth to crag, and rocks that seem'd
Ever as if just rising from a sleep,
Forehead to forehead held their monstrous horns;
And thus in thousand hugest phantasies
Made a fit roofing to this nest of woe.
Instead of thrones, hard flint they sat upon,
Couches of rugged stone, and slaty ridge
Stubborn'd with iron. All were not assembled:
Some chain'd in torture, and some wandering.
Cœus, and Gyges, and Briareüs,
Typhon, and Dolor, and Porphyrion,
With many more, the brawniest in assault,
Were pent in regions of laborious breath;
Dungeon'd in opaque element, to keep
Their clenched teeth still clench'd, and all their limbs
Lock'd up like veins of metal, crampt and screw'd;
Without a motion, save of their big hearts
Heaving in pain, and horribly convuls'd
With sanguine feverous boiling gurge of pulse.
Mnemosyne was straying in the world;
Far from her moon had Phœbe wandered;
And many else were free to roam abroad,
But for the main, here found they covert drear.
Scarce images of life, one here, one there,
Lay vast and edgeways; like a dismal cirque
Of Druid stones, upon a forlorn moor,
When the chill rain begins at shut of eve,
In dull November, and their chancel vault,
The Heaven itself, is blinded throughout night.

Each one kept shroud, nor to his neighbour gave
Or word, or look, or action of despair.
Creüs was one; his ponderous iron mace
Lay by him, and a shatter'd rib of rock
Told of his rage, ere he thus sank and pined.
Iäpetus another; in his grasp,
A serpent's plashy neck; its barbed tongue
Squeez'd from the gorge, and all its uncurl'd length
Dead; and because the creature could not spit
Its poison in the eyes of conquering Jove.
Next Cottus: prone he lay, chin uppermost,
As though in pain; for still upon the flint
He ground severe his skull, with open mouth
And eyes at horrid working. Nearest him
Asia, born of most enormous Caf,
Who cost her mother Tellus kèener pangs,
Though feminine, than any of her sons:
More thought than woe was in her dusky face,
For she was prophesying of her glory;
And in her wide imagination stood
Palm-shaded temples, and high rival fanes,
By Oxus or in Ganges' sacred isles.
Even as Hope upon her anchor leans,
So leant she, not so fair, upon a tusk
Shed from the broadest of her elephants.
Above her, on a crag's uneasy shelve,
Upon his elbow rais'd, all prostrate else,
Shadow'd Enceladus; once tame and mild
As grazing ox unworried in the meads;
Now tiger-passion'd, lion-thoughted, wroth,
He meditated, plotted, and even now
Was hurling mountains in that second war,

Not long delay'd, that scar'd the younger Gods
To hide themselves in forms of beast and bird.
Not far hence Atlas; and beside him prone
Phorcus, the sire of Gorgons. Neighbour'd close
Oceanus, and Tethys, in whose lap
Sobb'd Clymene among her tangled hair.
In midst of all lay Themis, at the feet
Of Ops the queen all clouded round from sight;
No shape distinguishable, more than when
Thick night confounds the pine-tops with the clouds:
And many else whose names may not be told.

Book II, 1–81

(iv)

—APOLLO then,
With sudden scrutiny and gloomless eyes,
Thus answer'd, while his white melodious throat
Throbb'd with the syllables.—' Mnemosyne!
' Thy name is on my tongue, I know not how;
' Why should I tell thee what thou so well seest?
' Why should I strive to show what from thy lips
' Would come no mystery? For me, dark, dark,
' And painful vile oblivion seals my eyes:
' I strive to search wherefore I am so sad,
' Until a melancholy numbs my limbs;
' And then upon the grass I sit, and moan,
' Like one who once had wings.—O why should I
' Feel curs'd and thwarted, when the liegeless air
' Yields to my step aspirant? why should I
' Spurn the green turf as hateful to my feet?
' Goddess benign, point forth some unknown thing:
' Are there not other regions than this isle?

675

' What are the stars? There is the sun, the sun!
' And the most patient brilliance of the moon!
' And stars by thousands! Point me out the way
' To any one particular beauteous star,
' And I will flit into it with my lyre,
' And make its silvery splendour pant with bliss.
' I have heard the cloudy thunder: Where is power?
' Whose hand, whose essence, what divinity
' Makes this alarum in the elements,
' While I here idle listen on the shores
' In fearless yet in aching ignorance?
' O tell me, lonely Goddess, by thy harp,
' That waileth every morn and eventide,
' Tell me why thus I rave, about these groves!
' Mute thou remainest—mute! yet I can read
' A wondrous lesson in thy silent face:
' Knowledge enormous makes a God of me.
' Names, deeds, grey legends, dire events, rebellions,
' Majesties, sovran voices, agonies,
' Creations and destroyings, all at once
' Pour into the wide hollows of my brain,
' And deify me, as if some blithe wine
' Or bright elixir peerless I had drunk,
' And so become immortal.'—Thus the God,
While his enkindled eyes, with level glance
Beneath his white soft temples, stedfast kept
Trembling with light upon Mnemosyne.
Soon wild commotions shook him, and made flush
All the immortal fairness of his limbs;
Most like the struggle at the gate of death;
Or liker still to one who should take leave
Of pale immortal death, and with a pang

As hot as death's is chill, with fierce convulse
Die into life: so young Apollo anguish'd:
His very hair, his golden tresses famed
Kept undulation round his eager neck.
During the pain Mnemosyne upheld
Her arms as one who prophesied.—At length
Apollo shriek'd;—and lo! from all his limbs
Celestial   .   .   .   .   .   .

  .   .   .   .   .   .

Book III, ll. 79–136
Lamia, &c., 1820

308   *La Belle Dame sans Merci*

I

O WHAT can ail thee Knight at arms
    Alone and palely loitering?
The sedge is withered from the Lake
    And no birds sing!

II

O what can ail thee Knight at arms
    So haggard, and so woe begone?
The squirrel's granary is full
    And the harvest 's done.

III

I see a lily on thy brow
    With anguish moist and fever dew,
And on thy cheeks a fading rose
    Fast withereth too—

IV

I met a Lady in the Meads
   Full beautiful, a faery's child;
Her hair was long, her foot was light
   And her eyes were wild—

V

I made a Garland for her head,
   And bracelets too, and fragrant Zone:
She look'd at me as she did love
   And made sweet moan—

VI

I set her on my pacing steed
   And nothing else saw all day long
For sidelong would she bend and sing
   A faery's song—

VII

She found me roots of relish sweet
   And honey wild and manna dew
And sure in language strange she said
   I love thee true—

VIII

She took me to her elfin grot
   And there she wept and sigh'd full sore,
And there I shut her wild wild eyes
   With kisses four.

IX

And there she lulled me asleep,
   And there I dream'd Ah Woe betide!
The latest dream I ever dreamt
   On the cold hill side.

LA BELLE DAME SANS MERCI

X

I saw pale Kings, and Princes too
 Pale warriors death pale were they all
Who cried, La belle dame sans merci
 Thee hath in thrall.

XI

I saw their starv'd lips in the gloam
 With horrid warning gaped wide,
And I awoke, and found me here
 On the cold hill's side.

XII

And this is why I sojourn here
 Alone and palely loitering;
Though the sedge is withered from the Lake
 And no birds sing— . . .

Indicator, 10 May 1820 ;
Milnes's *Life, Letters, &c., of John Keats*, 1848, vol. ii

309 *The Eve of Saint Mark*

UPON a Sabbath-day it fell;
 Twice holy was the Sabbath-bell,
That call'd the folk to evening prayer;
The city streets were clean and fair
From wholesome drench of April rains;
And, on the western window panes,
The chilly sunset faintly told
Of unmatur'd green vallies cold,
Of the green thorny bloomless hedge,
Of rivers new with spring-tide sedge,
Of primroses by shelter'd rills,
And daisies on the aguish hills.

Twice holy was the Sabbath-bell:
The silent streets were crowded well
With staid and pious companies,
Warm from their fire-side orat'ries;
And moving, with demurest air,
To even-song, and vesper prayer.
Each arched porch, and entry low,
Was fill'd with patient folk and slow,
With whispers hush, and shuffling feet,
While play'd the organ loud and sweet.

The bells had ceas'd, the prayers begun,
And Bertha had not yet half done
A curious volume, patch'd and torn,
That all day long, from earliest morn,
Had taken captive her two eyes,
Among its golden broideries;
Perplex'd her with a thousand things,—
The stars of Heaven, and angels' wings,
Martyrs in a fiery blaze,
Azure saints in silver rays,
Moses' breastplate, and the seven
Candlesticks John saw in Heaven,
The winged Lion of Saint Mark,
And the Covenantal Ark,
With its many mysteries,
Cherubim and golden mice.
Bertha was a maiden fair,
Dwelling in th' old Minster-square;
From her fire-side she could see,
Sidelong, its rich antiquity,
Far as the Bishop's garden-wall;

THE EVE OF SAINT MARK

Where sycamores and elm-trees tall,
Full-leav'd, the forest had outstript,
By no sharp north-wind ever nipt,
So shelter'd by the mighty pile.
Bertha arose, and read awhile,
With forehead 'gainst the window-pane.
Again she try'd, and then again,
Until the dusk eve left her dark
Upon the legend of St. Mark.
From plaited lawn-frill, fine and thin,
She lifted up her soft warm chin,
With aching neck and swimming eyes,
And daz'd with saintly imageries.

All was gloom, and silent all,
Save now and then the still foot-fall
Of one returning homewards late,
Past the echoing minster-gate.

The clamorous daws, that all the day
Above tree-tops and towers play,
Pair by pair had gone to rest,
Each in its ancient belfry-nest,
Where asleep they fall betimes,
To music of the drowsy chimes.

All was silent, all was gloom,
Abroad and in the homely room:
Down she sat, poor cheated soul!
And struck a lamp from the dismal coal;
Lean'd forward, with bright drooping hair
And slant book, full against the glare.
Her shadow, in uneasy guise,
Hover'd about, a giant size,

On ceiling-beam and old oak chair,
The parrot's cage, and panel square;
And the warm angled winter screen,
On which were many monsters seen,
Call'd doves of Siam, Lima mice,
And legless birds of Paradise,
Macaw, and tender Avadavat,
And silken-furr'd Angora cat.
Untir'd she read, her shadow still
Glower'd about, as it would fill
The room with wildest forms and shades,
As though some ghostly queen of spades
Had come to mock behind her back,
And dance, and ruffle her garments black.
Untir'd she read the legend page,
Of holy Mark, from youth to age,
On land, on sea, in pagan chains,
Rejoicing for his many pains.
Sometimes the learned eremite,
With golden star, or dagger bright,
Referr'd to pious poesies
Written in smallest crow-quill size
Beneath the text; and thus the rhyme
Was parcell'd out from time to time:
' Gif ye wol stonden hardie wight—
Amiddes of the blacke night—
Righte in the churche porch, pardie
Ye wol behold a companie
Appouchen thee full dolourouse
For sooth to sain from everich house
Be it in City or village
Wol come the Phantom and image

THE EVE OF SAINT MARK

Of ilka gent and ilka carle
Whom coldè Deathè hath in parle
And wol some day that very year
Touchen with foulè venime spear
And sadly do them all to die—
Hem all shalt thou see verilie—
And everichon shall by thee pass
All who must die that year Alas.
Als writith he of swevenis,
Man han beforne they wake in bliss,
Whanne that hir friendes thinke hem bound
In crimped shroude farre under grounde;
And how a litling child mote be
A saint er its nativitie,
Gif that the modre (God her blesse!)
Kepen in solitarinesse,
And kissen devoute the holy croce.
Of Goddes love, and Sathan's force,—
He writith; and thinges many mo:
Of swiche thinges I may not show.
Bot I must tellen verilie
Somdel of Saintè Cicilie,
And chieflie what he auctorethe
Of Saintè Markis life and dethe: '

At length her constant eyelids come
Upon the fervent martyrdom;
Then lastly to his holy shrine,
Exalt amid the tapers' shine
At Venice,—

Milnes's *Life, Letters, &c., of John Keats*, 1848, vol. ii
with 16 lines since discovered

310 *Written on a Blank Page in Shakespeare's Poems, facing ' A Lover's Complaint '*

BRIGHT Star, would I were stedfast as thou art—
   Not in lone splendour hung aloft the night,
And watching, with eternal lids apart,
   Like nature's patient, sleepless Eremite,
The moving waters at their priestlike task
   Of pure ablution round earth's human shores,
Or gazing on the new soft-fallen mask
   Of snow upon the mountains and the moors—
No—yet still stedfast, still unchangeable,
   Pillow'd upon my fair love's ripening breast,
To feel for ever its soft fall and swell,
   Awake for ever in a sweet unrest,
Still, still to hear her tender-taken breath,
And so live ever—or else swoon to death.

      Milnes's *Life, Letters, &c., of John Keats,* 1848, vol. ii

311 *To the Nile*

SON of the old moon-mountains African!
   Chief of the Pyramid and Crocodile!
   We call thee fruitful, and, that very while,
A desert fills our seeing's inward span;
   Nurse of swart nations since the world began,
     Art thou so fruitful? or dost thou beguile
     Such men to honour thee, who, worn with toil,
   Rest for a space 'twixt Cairo and Decan?

O may dark fancies err! they surely do;
 'Tis ignorance that makes a barren waste
Of all beyond itself, thou dost bedew
 Green rushes like our rivers, and dost taste
The pleasant sun-rise, green isles hast thou too,
 And to the sea as happily dost haste.

   Milnes's *Life, Letters, &c., of John Keats*, 1848, vol. i

312   *To Homer*

STANDING aloof in giant ignorance,
 Of thee I hear and of the Cyclades,
As one who sits ashore and longs perchance
 To visit dolphin-coral in deep seas.
So thou wast blind;—but then the veil was rent,
 For Jove uncurtain'd Heaven to let thee live,
And Neptune made for thee a spumy tent,
 And Pan made sing for thee his forest-hive;
Aye on the shores of darkness there is light,
 And precipices show untrodden green,
There is a budding morrow in midnight,
 There is a triple sight in blindness keen;
Such seeing hadst thou, as it once befel
To Dian, Queen of Earth, and Heaven, and Hell.

   Milnes's *Life, Letters, &c., of John Keats*, 1848, vol. ii

313   *To Sleep*

O SOFT embalmer of the still midnight,
 Shutting, with careful fingers and benign,
Our gloom-pleas'd eyes, embower'd from the light,
 Enshaded in forgetfulness divine:

JOHN KEATS

O soothest Sleep! if so it please thee, close
  In midst of this thine hymn my willing eyes,
Or wait the ' Amen,' ere thy poppy throws
  Around my bed its lulling charities.
Then save me, or the passed day will shine
Upon my pillow, breeding many woes,—
  Save me from curious Conscience, that still lords
Its strength for darkness, burrowing like a mole;
  Turn the key deftly in the oiled wards,
And seal the hushed Casket of my Soul.

          Milnes' *Life, Letters, &c., of John Keats*, 1848, vol. ii

314   ' *When I have fears* '

WHEN I have fears that I may cease to be
    Before my pen has glean'd my teeming brain,
Before high-piled books, in charactery,
  Hold like rich garners the full ripen'd grain;
When I behold, upon the night's starr'd face,
  Huge cloudy symbols of a high romance,
And think that I may never live to trace
  Their shadows, with the magic hand of chance;
And when I feel, fair creature of an hour,
  That I shall never look upon thee more,
Never have relish in the faery power
  Of unreflecting love;—then on the shore
Of the wide world I stand alone, and think
Till love and fame to nothingness do sink.

          Milnes' *Life, Letters, &c., of John Keats*, 1848, vol. ii

315 *Fragment of an Ode to Maia, written on May Day, 1818*

MOTHER of Hermes! and still youthful Maia!
      May I sing to thee
As thou wast hymned on the shores of Baiæ?
      Or may I woo thee
In earlier Sicilian? or thy smiles
Seek as they once were sought, in Grecian isles,
By bards who died content on pleasant sward,
   Leaving great verse unto a little clan?
O, give me their old vigour, and unheard
   Save of the quiet Primrose, and the span
       Of heaven and few ears,
Rounded by thee, my song should die away
       Content as theirs,
Rich in the simple worship of a day.

     Milnes' Life, Letters, &c., of John Keats, 1848, vol. i

316 *From ' The Fall of Hyperion '*

A Dream

(*i*)

METHOUGHT I stood where trees of every clime,
   Palm, myrtle, oak, and sycamore, and beech,
With plantain, and spice-blossoms, made a screen;
In neighbourhood of fountains (by the noise
Soft-showering in mine ears), and, (by the touch
Of scent,) not far from roses. Turning round,
I saw an arbour with a drooping roof
Of trellis vines, and bells, and larger blooms,

Like floral censers, swinging light in air;
Before its wreathed doorway, on a mound
Of moss, was spread a feast of summer fruits,
Which, nearer seen, seem'd refuse of a meal
By angel tasted or our Mother Eve;
For empty shells were scatter'd on the grass,
And grape-stalks but half bare, and remnants more,
Sweet-smelling, whose pure kinds I could not know.
Still was more plenty than the fabled horn
Thrice emptied could pour forth, at banqueting
For Proserpine return'd to her own fields,
Where the white heifers low. And appetite
More yearning than on Earth I ever felt
Growing within, I ate deliciously;
And, after not long, thirsted, for thereby
Stood a cool vessel of transparent juice,
Sipp'd by the wander'd bee, the which I took,
And, pledging all the mortals of the world,
And all the dead whose names are in our lips,
Drank. That full draught is parent of my theme.
No Asian poppy nor elixir fine
Of the soon-fading jealous Caliphat;
No poison gender'd in close monkish cell,
To thin the scarlet conclave of old men,
Could so have rapt unwilling life away.
Among the fragrant husks and berries crush'd,
Upon the grass I struggled hard against
The domineering potion; but in vain:
The cloudy swoon came on, and down I sank,
Like a Silenus on an antique vase.
How long I slumber'd 'tis a chance to guess.
When sense of life return'd, I started up

THE FALL OF HYPERION

As if with wings; but the fair trees were gone,
The mossy mound and arbour were no more:
I look'd around upon the carved sides
Of an old sanctuary with roof august,
Builded so high, it seem'd that filmed clouds
Might spread beneath, as o'er the stars of heaven;
So old the place was, I remember'd none
The like upon the Earth: what I had seen
Of grey cathedrals, buttress'd walls, rent towers,
The superannuations of sunk realms,
Or Nature's rocks toil'd hard in waves and winds,
Seem'd but the faulture of decrepit things
To that eternal domed Monument.—
Upon the marble at my feet there lay
Store of strange vessels, and large draperies,
Which needs had been of dyed asbestos wove,
Or in that place the moth could not corrupt,
So white the linen, so, in some, distinct
Ran imageries from a sombre loom.
All in a mingled heap confus'd there lay
Robes, golden tongs, censer and chafing-dish,
Girdles, and chains, and holy jewelries.

Turning from these with awe, once more I rais'd
My eyes to fathom the space every way;
The embossed roof, the silent massy range
Of columns north and south, ending in mist
Of nothing, then to eastward, where black gates
Were shut against the sunrise evermore.—
Then to the west I look'd, and saw far off
An image, huge of feature as a cloud,
At level of whose feet an altar slept,

To be approach'd on either side by steps,
And marble balustrade, and patient travail
To count with toil the innumerable degrees.
Towards the altar sober-paced I went,
Repressing haste, as too unholy there;
And, coming nearer, saw beside the shrine
One minist'ring; and there arose a flame.—
When in mid-way the sickening East wind
Shifts sudden to the south, the small warm rain
Melts out the frozen incense from all flowers,
And fills the air with so much pleasant health
That even the dying man forgets his shroud;—
Even so that lofty sacrificial fire,
Sending forth Maian incense, spread around
Forgetfulness of everything but bliss,
And clouded all the altar with soft smoke.

Book I, ll. 19–105

(ii)

'NONE can usurp this height,' return'd that shade,
    ' But those to whom the miseries of the world
' Are misery, and will not let them rest.
' All else who find a haven in the world,
' Where they may thoughtless sleep away their days,
' If by a chance into this fane they come,
' Rot on the pavement where thou rotted'st half.'—
' Are there not thousands in the world,' said I,
Encourag'd by the sooth voice of the shade,
' Who love their fellows even to the death,
' Who feel the giant agony of the world,
' And more, like slaves to poor humanity,
' Labour for mortal good? I sure should see

' Other men here; but I am here alone.'
' Those whom thou spak'st of are no vision'ries,'
Rejoin'd that voice—' They are no dreamers weak,
' They seek no wonder but the human face;
' No music but a happy-noted voice—
' They come not here, they have no thought to come—
' And thou art here, for thou art less than they—
' What benefit canst thou, or all thy tribe,
' To the great world? Thou art a dreaming thing,
' A fever of thyself—think of the Earth;
' What bliss even in hope is there for thee?
' What haven? every creature hath its home;
' Every sole man hath days of joy and pain,
' Whether his labours be sublime or low—
' The pain alone; the joy alone; distinct:
' Only the dreamer venoms all his days,
' Bearing more woe than all his sins deserve.
' Therefore, that happiness be somewhat shar'd,
' Such things as thou art are admitted oft
' Into like gardens thou didst pass erewhile,
' And suffer'd in these temples: for that cause
' Thou standest safe beneath this statue's knees.'
' That I am favour'd for unworthiness,
' By such propitious parley medicin'd
' In sickness not ignoble, I rejoice,
' Aye, and could weep for love of such award.'
So answer'd I, continuing, ' If it please,
' Majestic shadow, tell me: sure not all
' Those melodies sung into the World's ear
' Are useless: sure a poet is a sage;
' A humanist, physician to all men.
' That I am none I feel, as vultures feel

' They are no birds when eagles are abroad.
' What am I then: Thou spakest of my tribe:
' What tribe?' The tall shade veil'd in drooping white
Then spake, so much more earnest, that the breath
Moved the thin linen folds that drooping hung
About a golden censer from the hand
Pendent—' Art thou not of the dreamer tribe?
' The poet and the dreamer are distinct,
' Diverse, sheer opposite, antipodes.
' The one pours out a balm upon the World,
' The other vexes it.'

Book I, ll. 147–202;
Milnes' *Life, Letters, &c., of John Keats*, 1867

JEREMIAH JOHN CALLANAN

1795–1829

317   *The Outlaw of Loch Lene*

From the Irish

O MANY a day have I made good ale in the glen,
 That came not of stream, or malt;—like the brewing of
   men.
My bed was the ground; my roof, the greenwood above,
And the wealth that I sought one far kind glance from my love.

Alas! on that night when the horses I drove from the field,
That I was not near from terror my angel to shield.
She stretched forth her arms,—her mantle she flung to the
   wind,
And swam o'er Loch Lene, her outlawed lover to find.

O would that a freezing sleet-wing'd tempest did sweep,
And I and my love were alone, far off on the deep;

692

I'd ask not a ship, or a bark, or pinnace, to save,—
With her hand round my waist, I'd fear not the wind or the
    wave.

'Tis down by the lake where the wild tree fringes its sides,
The maid of my heart, my fair one of Heaven resides;—
I think as at eve she wanders its mazes along,
The birds go to sleep by the sweet wild twist of her song.

The Recluse of Inchidmy, 1830

GEORGE DARLEY

1795–1846

318   *Wherefore, unlaurelled Boy*

WHEREFORE, unlaurelled Boy,
    Whom the contemptuous Muse will not inspire,
With a sad kind of joy,
    Still sing'st thou to thy solitary lyre?

The melancholy winds
    Pour through unnumbered reeds their idle woes,
And every Naiad finds
    A stream to weep her sorrow as it flows.

Her sighs unto the air
    The wood-maid's native oak doth broadly tell,
And Echo's fond despair
    Intelligible rocks re-syllable.

Wherefore then should not I,
    Albeit no haughty Muse my breast inspire,
Fated of grief to die,
    Impart it to a solitary lyre?

Labours of Idleness, 1826

319 *Dirge*

WAIL! wail ye o'er the dead!
    Wail! wail ye o'er her!
Youth's ta'en, and Beauty's fled,
    O then deplore her!

Strew! strew ye, Maidens! strew
    Sweet flowers and fairest!
Pale rose, and pansy blue,
    Lily the rarest!
           Wail! wail ye, &c.

Lay, lay her gently down
    On her moss pillow,
While we our foreheads crown
    With the sad willow!
           Wail! wail ye, &c.

Raise, raise the song of wo,
    Youths, to her honour!
Fresh leaves, and blossoms throw,
    Virgins, upon her!
           Wail! wail ye, &c.

Round, round the cypress bier
    Where she lies sleeping,
On every turf a tear,
    Let us go weeping!
           Wail! wail ye, &c.

Sylvia, or, The May Queen, 1827

I'VE taught thee Love's sweet lesson o'er,
A task that is not learn'd with tears:
Was Sylvia e'er so blest before
In her wild, solitary years?
　　Then what does he deserve, the Youth,
　　Who made her con so dear a truth!

Till now in silent vales to roam,
Singing vain songs to heedless flowers,
Or watch the dashing billows foam,
Amid thy lonely myrtle bowers,
　　To weave light crowns of various hue,—
　　Were all the joys thy bosom knew.

The wild bird, though most musical,
Could not to thy sweet plaint reply;
The streamlet, and the waterfall,
Could only weep when thou did'st sigh!
　　Thou could'st not change one dulcet word
　　Either with billow, or with bird.

For leaves, and flowers, but these alone,
Winds have a soft discoursing way;
Heav'n's starry talk is all its own,—
It dies in thunder far away.
　　E'en when thou would'st the Moon beguile
　　To speak,—she only deigns to smile!

Now, birds and winds, be churlish still,
Ye waters keep your sullen roar,

Stars be as distant as ye will,—
Sylvia need court ye now no more:
    In Love there is society
    She never yet could find with ye!

            Sylvia, or, The May Queen, 1827

321   *It is not Beauty I demand*

IT is not Beauty I demand,
    A crystal brow, the moon's despair,
Nor the snow's daughter, a white hand,
    Nor mermaid's yellow pride of hair.

Tell me not of your starry eyes,
    Your lips that seem on roses fed,
Your breasts where Cupid tumbling lies,
    Nor sleeps for kissing of his bed.

A bloomy pair of vermeil cheeks,
    Like Hebe's in her ruddiest hours,
A breath that softer music speaks
    Than summer winds a-wooing flowers.

These are but gauds; nay, what are lips?
    Coral beneath the ocean-stream,
Whose brink when your adventurer sips
    Full oft he perisheth on them.

And what are cheeks but ensigns oft
    That wave hot youth to fields of blood?
Did Helen's breast though ne'er so soft,
    Do Greece or Ilium any good?

IT IS NOT BEAUTY I DEMAND

Eyes can with baleful ardour burn,
 Poison can breath that erst perfumed,
There 's many a white hand holds an urn
 With lovers' hearts to dust consumed.

For crystal brows—there 's naught within,
 They are but empty cells for pride;
He who the Syren's hair would win
 Is mostly strangled in the tide.

Give me, instead of beauty's bust,
 A tender heart, a loyal mind,
Which with temptation I could trust,
 Yet never linked with error find.

One in whose gentle bosom I
 Could pour my secret heart of woes,
Like the care-burthened honey-fly
 That hides his murmurs in the rose.

My earthly comforter! whose love
 So indefeasible might be,
That when my spirit won above
 Hers could not stay for sympathy.

The Literary Gazette, 12 April 1828

322   *From ' Nepenthe '*

(i)

OVER a bloomy land, untrod
 By heavier foot than bird or bee
Lays on the grassy-bosomed sod,
 I passed one day in reverie:
High on his unpavilioned throne
The heaven's hot tyrant sat alone,

And like the fabled king of old
Was turning all he touched to gold.
The glittering fountains seemed to pour
Steep downward rills of molten ore,
Glassily tinkling smooth between
Broom-shaded banks of golden green,
And o'er the yellow pasture straying
Dallying still yet undelaying,
In hasty trips from side to side
Footing adown their steepy slide
Headlong, impetuously playing
With the flowery border pied,
That edged the rocky mountain stair,
They pattered down incessant there,
To lowlands sweet and calm and wide.
With golden lip and glistening bell
Burned every bee-cup on the fell,
Whate'er its native un-sunned hue,
Snow-white or crimson or cold blue;
Even the black lustres of the sloe
Glanced as they sided to the glow;
And furze in russet frock arrayed
With saffron knots, like shepherd maid,
Broadly tricked out her rough brocade.
The singed mosses curling here,
A golden fleece too short to shear!
Crumbled to sparkling dust beneath
My light step on that sunny heath.

Light! for the ardour of the clime
Made rare my spirit, that sublime
Bore me as buoyant as young Time

NEPENTHE

Over the green Earth's grassy prime,
Ere his slouch'd wing caught up her slime;
And sprang I not from clay and crime,
Had from those humming beds of thyme
Lifted me near the starry chime
To learn an empyrean rhyme.

No melody beneath the moon
Sweeter than this deep runnel tune!
Here on the greensward grown hot gray,
Crisp as the unshorn desert hay,
Where his moist pipe the dulcet rill
For humorous grasshopper doth fill,
That spits himself from blade to blade
By long o'er-rest uneasy made;
Here, ere the stream by fountain pushes
Lose himself brightly in the rushes
With butterfly path among the bushes,
I'll lay me, on these mosses brown,
Murmuring beside his murmurs down,
And from the liquid tale he tells
Glean out some broken syllables,
Or close mine eyes in dreamy swoon,
As by hoarse-winding deep Gihoon
Soothes with the hum his idle pain
The melancholy Tartar swain,
Sole mark on that huge-meadowed plain!

(ii)

O BLEST unfabled Incense Tree,
That burns in glorious Araby,
With red scent chalicing the air,
Till earth-life grow Elysian there!

GEORGE DARLEY

Half buried to her flaming breast
In this bright tree, she makes her nest,
Hundred-sunned Phœnix! when she must
Crumble at length to hoary dust!

Her gorgeous death-bed! her rich pyre
Burnt up with aromatic fire!
Her urn, sight high from spoiler men!
Her birthplace when self-born again!

The mountainless green wilds among,
Here ends she her unechoing song!
With amber tears and odorous sighs
Mourned by the desert where she dies!

Laid like the young fawn mossily
In sun-green vales of Araby,
I woke hard by the Phœnix tree
That with shadeless boughs flamed over me;
And upward called by a dumb cry
With moonbroad orbs of wonder, I
Beheld the immortal Bird on high
Glassing the great sun in her eye.
Stedfast she gazed upon his fire,
Still her destroyer and her sire!
As if to his her soul of flame
Had flown already, whence it came;
Like those that sit and glare so still,
Intense with their death struggle, till
We touch, and curdle at their chill!—
But breathing yet while she doth burn,
The deathless Daughter of the sun!

NEPENTHE

Slowly to crimson embers turn
    The beauties of the brightsome one;
O'er the broad nest her silver wings
Shook down their wasteful glitterings;
Her brinded neck high-arched in air
Like a small rainbow faded there;
But brighter glowed her plumy crown
Mouldering to golden ashes down;
With fume of sweet woods, to the skies,
Pure as a Saint's adoring sighs,
Warm as a prayer in Paradise,
Her life-breath rose in sacrifice!
The while with shrill triumphant tone
Sounding aloud, aloft, alone,
Ceaseless her joyful deathwail she
Sang to departing Araby!

(iii)

O, FAST her amber blood doth flow
    From the heart-wounded Incense Tree,
Fast as earth's deep-embosomed woe
    In silent rivulets to the sea!

Beauty may weep her fair first-born,
    Perchance in as resplendent tears,
Such golden dewdrops bow the corn
    When the stern sickleman appears.

But oh! such perfume to a bower
    Never allured sweet-seeking bee,
As to sip fast that nectarous shower
    A thirstier minstrel drew in me!

GEORGE DARLEY

(iv)

THOU whose thrilling hand in mine
Makes it tremble as unbid,
Whose dove-drooping eyes divine
Curtain Love beneath their lid!
Fairest Anthea! thou whose grace
Leads me enchantedly along
Till the sweet windings that we trace
Seem like the image of a song!
Blithest Anthea! thou I ween
Of this jocund choir the queen,
From thy beauty still more rare,
And a more earth-spurning air,
If forsooth my reeling vision
Hold thee steadily, and this
Be not my mind's insane misprision,
Drunk with the essence-drop of bliss!
Small matter!—while the dream be bright!
Surely thou with form so light
Must be some creature born for winging
Where the chimes of Heaven are ringing,
And sweet cherub faces singing
Requiems to ascending souls
Where each orb of glory rolls!
Bind me, oh bind me next thy heart,
So shall we to the skies depart,
And like a twin-star fixt in ether,
Burn with immortal flame together!

That be our emprised rest,
Eyry where birds of Eden nest,

NEPENTHE

Warbling hymns in Wonder's ear!
We still walk this lowly sphere,
Lost in the heaven's crystalline mere
More than in ocean one small tear.
Wherefore, without vain delay,
Haste, Anthea! haste away
To those highest peaks the sun
Steps with glittering sandal on,
That this bosom-fire as fast.
As his, breathe forth in the clear vast!

Bright-haired Spirit! Golden Brow!
Onward to far Ida now!
Leaving these garden lands below
In sea-born dews to steep their glow:
Caria and Lycia, dulcet climes!
Beds of flowers whose odour limes
The o'erflying fast far bird, their thrall
Hovering entranced till he fall;
Broad Mæonia's streamy vales
Winding beneath us, white with swans
Borne by their downy-swelling sails;
Each her lucid beauty scans,
Bending her slow beak round, and sees
Her grandeur as she floats along
Gracefully ruffled by the breeze,
And troats for joy, too proud for song.
Leave we the downlands, tho' be there
Joy a lifelong sojourner;
There for ever wildwood numbers
Poured in Doric strains dilute
Thro' the unlaborious flute

Soothe Disquiet to his slumbers;
In his rosebed sleeps the bee,
Lulled by Lydian melody,
Half the honied morn in vain!
Idler still than Doric swain,
Steeped in double sweetness he
Hums, as he dreams, his wildwood strain.
The Mysian vineplucker sings i' the tree,
And Ionia's echoing train
Of reapers, bending down the lea,
Make rich the winds with minstrelsy.

(v)

LIST no more the ominous din,
  Let us plunge deep Helle in!
Thracia hollos!—what to us
Sky-dejected Icarus?
Shall we less than those wild kine
That swam this shallow salt confine,
Venture to show how mere a span
Keeps continental man from man?
Welcome, gray Europe, native clime
Of clouds, and cliffs yet more sublime!
Gray Europe, on whose Alpine head
The Northwind makes his snowy bed,
And fostered in that savage form
Lies down a blast and wakes a storm!
Up! up! to shrouded Rhodope
That seems in the white waste to be
An ice-rock in a foaming sea!
This inward rage, this eating flame,

NEPENTHE

Turns into fiery dust my frame;
Thro' my red nostril and my teeth
In sulphury fumes I seem to breathe
My dragon soul, and fain would quench
This drouth in some o'erwhelming drench!
Up! to the frostbound waterfalls,
That hang in waves the mountain walls!
Down tumbling ever and anon
With long-pent thunders loosed in one,
Thro' the deep valleys where of yore
The Deluge his wide channels wore.
Hark! thro' each green and gateless door,
Valley to echoing valley calls
Me, steep up, higher to the sun!
Hark! while we stand in mute astound,
Cloud-battled high Pangæus hoar
With earthquake voice and ocean roar
Keeps the pale region trembling round!
Upward! each loftier height we gain,
I spurn it like the basest plain
Trod by the fallen in hell's profound!
Illoo, great Hemus! Hemus old,
Half earth into his girdle rolled,
Swells against heaven!—Up! up! the stars
Wheel near his goal their glittering cars;
Ambition's mounting-step sublime
To vault beyond the sphere of Time
Into Eternity's bright clime!
Where this fierce joy
I feel shall aye subside,
Like a swoln bubble on the ocean tide,
Into the River of Bliss, Elysium-wide;

And all annoy
Lie drowned with it for ever there,
And never ebbing Life's soft stream with confluent wave
My floating Spirit bear
Among those calm Beatitudes and fair,
That lave
Their angel forms, with pure luxuriance free,
In thy rich ooze and amber-molten sea,
Slow-flooding to the one deep choral stave—
Eterne Tranquillity!
All-blessing, blest, eterne Tranquillity!

Strymon! heaven-descended stream!
Valley along, thy silver sand
Broader and broader yet doth gleam,
Spreading into ocean's strand,
Over whose white verge the storm
With his wide-swaying loomy arm
Weaves his mournful tapestry,
Slowly let down from sky to sea.
Strymon! up thy craggy banks
'Mid the pinewood's wavering ranks,
What terrible howl ascends? What blaze
Of torches blackening the coil'd haze
With grim contrast of smoky rays?
What hideous features 'mid the flare,
Lit with yellow laughter? Where,
Ah! where my boon Circean band
Quiring round me hand in hand?—
Furies, avaunt! that dismal joy
Breeds me horrible annoy!
Avaunt, she-wolves! with rabid yell

Riving the very seams of hell
To swallow me and your rout as well!
Flee, flee, my wretched soul, from these
Erinnys and Eumenides,
Bacchants no more, but raging brood
Of fiends to feast them on hot blood!—
Down! down! and shelter me in the flood!

' Hollo after!—to living shreds tear him!—hollo after!
To the ravenous wild winds share him!—hollo after!
    Our rite he spurns,
    From our love he turns,
Hurl him the glassy crags down! hollo after!
    With your torches blast him,
    To the broken waves cast him,
    Head and trunk far asunder!—
    With a bellow like thunder
Hollo after! hollo after! hollo after!'

Dull in the Drowner's ear
Bubbled amid far ocean these sad echoes drear.

In the caves of the deep—Hollo! hollo!—
Lost Youth!—o'er and o'er fleeting billows!—
Hollo! hollo!—without all ruth!—
In the foam's cold shroud!—Hollo! hollo!
To his everlasting sleep!—Lost Youth!

(*vi*)

SOLITARY wayfarer!
Minstrel winged of the green wild!
What dost thou delaying here,
Like a wood-bewildered child

Weeping to his far-flown troop,
Whoop! and plaintive whoop! and whoop!
Now from rock and now from tree,
Bird! methinks thou whoop'st to me,
Flitting before me upward still
With clear warble, as I've heard
Oft on my native Northern hill
No less wild and lone a bird,
Luring me with his sweet chee-chee
Up the mountain crags which he
Tript as lightly as a bee,
O'er steep pastures, far among
Thickets and briary lanes along,
Following still a fleeting song!—
If such my errant nature, I
Vainly to curb or coop it try
Now that the sundrop thro' my frame
Kindles another soul of flame!
Whoop on, whoop on, thou canst not wing
Too fast or far, thou well-named thing,
Hoopoe, if of that tribe which sing
Articulate in the desert ring!

(*vii*)

LO! in the mute, mid wilderness,
    What wondrous Creature?—of no kind:—
His burning lair doth largely press—
Gaze fixt—and feeding on the wind?
His fell is of the desert dye,
And tissue adust, dun-yellow and dry,
Compact of living sands; his eye

708

Black luminary, soft and mild,
With its dark lustre cools the wild.
From his stately forehead springs,
Piercing to heaven, a radiant horn!
Lo, the compeer of lion-kings,
The steed self-armed, the Unicorn!
Ever heard of, never seen,
With a main of sands between
Him and approach; his lonely pride
To course his arid arena wide,
Free as the hurricane, or lie here,
Lord of his couch as his career!—
Wherefore should this foot profane
His sanctuary, still domain?
Let me turn, ere eye so bland
Perchance be fire-shot, like heaven's brand,
To wither my boldness! Northward now,
Behind the white star on his brow
Glittering straight against the sun,
Far athwart his lair I run.

Nepenthe, 1835

323   *Serenade of a Loyal Martyr*

SWEET in her green cell the flower of beauty slumbers,
  Lull'd by the faint breezes sighing through her hair;
Sleeps she and hears not the melancholy numbers
  Breathed to my sad lute amid the lonely air.

Down from the high cliffs the rivulet is teeming
  To wind round the willow banks that lure him from above:
O that in tears from my rocky prison streaming,
  I too could glide to the bower of my love!

Ah! where the woodbines with sleepy arms have wound her,
   Opes she her eyelids at the dream of my lay,
Listening, like the dove, while the fountains echo round her,
   To her lost mate's call in the forests far away?

Come then, my bird! For the peace thou ever bearest,
   Still heaven's messenger of comfort to me,
Come!—this fond bosom, my faithfullest! my fairest!
   Bleeds with its death-wound, but deeper yet for thee.

                              Athenaeum, 23 January 1836

324   *The Sea-Ritual*

PRAYER unsaid, and mass unsung,
   Deadman's dirge must still be rung:
      Dingle-dong, the dead-bells sound!
      Mermen chant his dirge around!

Wash him bloodless, smoothe him fair,
Stretch his limbs and sleek his hair:
      Dingle-dong, the dead-bells go!
      Mermen swing them to and fro!

In the wormless sands shall he
Feast for no foul gluttons be:
      Dingle-dong, the dead-bells toll;
      Mermen ring his requiem-knoll!

We must with a tombstone brave
Shut the shark out of his grave:
      Dingle-dong, the dead-bells chime;
      Mermen keep the tune and time!

Such a slab will we lay o'er him,
All the dead shall rise before him!
    Dingle-dong, the dead-bells boom;
    Mermen lay him in his tomb!

The Tribute, 1837

325   *The Mermaidens' Vesper-Hymn*

TROOP home to silent grots and caves!
   Troop home! and mimic as you go
The mournful winding of the waves
   Which to their dark abysses flow.

At this sweet hour, all things beside
   In amorous pairs to covert creep;
The swans that brush the evening tide
   Homeward in snowy couples keep.

In his green den the murmuring seal
   Close by his sleek companion lies;
While singly we to bedward steal,
   And close in fruitless sleep our eyes.

In bowers of love men take their rest,
   In loveless bowers we sigh alone,—
With bosom-friends are others blest,
   But we have none! but we have none!

The Tribute, 1837

326 *Cui Bono?*

WHAT is hope? A smiling rainbow
  Children follow through the wet;
'Tis not here, still yonder, yonder:
  Never urchin found it yet.

What is life? A thawing iceboard
  On a sea with sunny shore;—
Gay we sail; it melts beneath us;
  We are sunk, and seen no more.

What is Man? A foolish baby,
  Vainly strives, and fights, and frets;
Demanding all, deserving nothing;—
  One small grave is what he gets.

Fraser's Magazine, September 1830

327 *Adieu*

LET time and chance combine, combine,
  Let time and chance combine;
The fairest love from heaven above,
That love of yours was mine,
                    My dear,
That love of yours was mine.

The past is fled and gone, and gone,
The past is fled and gone;
If nought but pain to me remain,
I'll fare in memory on,
                    My dear,
I'll fare in memory on.

ADIEU

The saddest tears must fall, must fall,
The saddest tears must fall;
In weal or woe, in this world below,
I love you ever and all,

        My dear,

I love you ever and all.

A long road full of pain, of pain,
A long road full of pain;
One soul, one heart, sworn ne'er to part,—
We ne'er can meet again,

        My dear,

We ne'er can meet again.

Hard fate will not allow, allow,
Hard fate will not allow;
We blessed were as the angels are,—
Adieu for ever, now,

        My dear,

Adieu for ever now.

Written 1823–33;
Critical and Miscellaneous Essays, 1839

HARTLEY COLERIDGE

1796–1849

328   *Sonnets*

To a Friend

WHEN we were idlers with the loitering rills,
   The need of human love we little noted:
Our love was nature; and the peace that floated
On the white mist, and dwelt upon the hills,

713

To sweet accord subdued our wayward wills:
One soul was ours, one mind, one heart devoted,
That, wisely doating, ask'd not why it doated,
And ours the unknown joy, which knowing kills.
But now I find, how dear thou wert to me;
That man is more than half of nature's treasure,
Of that fair Beauty which no eye can see,
Of that sweet music which no ear can measure;
And now the streams may sing for others' pleasure,
The hills sleep on in their eternity.

329 *' Whither is gone '*

WHITHER is gone the wisdom and the power
    That ancient sages scatter'd with the notes
Of thought-suggesting lyres? The music floats
In the void air; e'en at this breathing hour,
In every cell and every blooming bower
The sweetness of old lays is hovering still:
But the strong soul, the self-constraining will,
The rugged root that bare the winsome flower
Is weak and wither'd. Were we like the Fays
That sweetly nestle in the fox-glove bells,
Or lurk and murmur in the rose-lipp'd shells
Which Neptune to the earth for quit-rent pays,
Then might our pretty modern Philomels
Sustain our spirits with their roundelays.

330 *' Long time a child '*

LONG time a child, and still a child, when years
    Had painted manhood on my cheek, was I;
For yet I lived like one not born to die;
A thriftless prodigal of smiles and tears,

No hope I needed, and I knew no fears.
But sleep, though sweet, is only sleep, and waking,
I waked to sleep no more, at once o'ertaking
The vanguard of my age, with all arrears
Of duty on my back. Nor child, nor man,
Nor youth, nor sage, I find my head is grey,
For I have lost the race I never ran:
A rathe December blights my lagging May;
And still I am a child, tho' I be old,
Time is my debtor for my years untold.

331 *November*

THE mellow year is hasting to its close;
   The little birds have almost sung their last,
Their small notes twitter in the dreary blast—
That shrill-piped harbinger of early snows;
The patient beauty of the scentless rose,
Oft with the Morn's hoar crystal quaintly glass'd,
Hangs, a pale mourner for the summer past,
And makes a little summer where it grows:
In the chill sunbeam of the faint brief day
The dusky waters shudder as they shine,
The russet leaves obstruct the straggling way
Of oozy brooks, which no deep banks define,
And the gaunt woods, in ragged, scant array,
Wrap their old limbs with sombre ivy twine.

332 *From Country to Town*

'TIS strange to me, who long have seen no face
   That was not like a book whose every page
I knew by heart, a kindly common-place—
And faithful record of progressive age—

To wander forth, and view an unknown race;
Of all that I have been, to find no trace,
Not footstep of my by-gone pilgrimage.
Thousands I pass, and no one stays his pace
To tell me that the day is fair, or rainy—
Each one his object seeks with anxious chase,
And I have not a common hope with any—
Thus like one drop of oil upon a flood,
In uncommunicating solitude—
Single am I amid the countless many.

Poems, 1833.

333   *Song*

SHE is not fair to outward view
    As many maidens be,
Her loveliness I never knew
    Until she smil'd on me;
Oh! then I saw her eye was bright,
A well of love, a spring of light.

But now her looks are coy and cold,
    To mine they ne'er reply,
And yet I cease not to behold
    The love-light in her eye:
Her very frowns are fairer far,
Than smiles of other maidens are.

Poems, 1833

334   *Reply*

AH—well it is—since she is gone,
    She can return no more,
To see the face so dim and wan,
    That was so warm before.

REPLY

Familiar things would all seem strange,
  And pleasure past be woe;
A record sad of ceaseless change,
  Is all the world below.

The very hills, they are not now
  The hills which once they were;
They change as we are changed, or how
  Could we the burden bear?

Ye deem the dead are ashy pale,
  Cold denizens of gloom—
But what are ye, who live to wail,
  And weep upon their tomb?

She pass'd away, like morning dew,
  Before the sun was high;
So brief her time, she scarcely knew
  The meaning of a sigh.

As round the rose its soft perfume,
  Sweet love around her floated;
Admired she grew—while mortal doom
  Crept on, unfear'd, unnoted.

Love was her guardian Angel here,
  But love to death resign'd her;
Tho' love was kind, why should we fear,
  But holy death is kinder?

Poems, 1833

335 *Sonnet to ——*

THE trees in Sherwood forest are old and good,—
    The grass beneath them now is dimly green;
  Are they deserted all? Is no young mien
With loose-slung bugle met within the wood:
No arrow found,—foil'd of its antler'd food,—
    Struck in the oak's rude side? Is there nought seen,
    To mark the revelries which there have been,—
In the sweet days of merry Robin Hood?
Go there, with Summer, and with evening,—go
    In the soft shadows like some wandering man,—
And thou shalt far amid the forest know
The archer men in green, with belt and bow,
    Feasting on pheasant, river-fowl, and swan,
    With Robin at their head, and Marian.

John Hunt's *Yellow Dwarf*, 21 February 1813;
The Garden of Florence, 1821

336 *Farewell to the Muses*

I HAVE no chill despondence that I am
    Self banished from those rolls of honoring men
That keep a temperate eye on airy Fame
And write songs to her with a golden pen.
I do not wail because the Muses keep
    Their secrets on the top of Helicon
Nor do I in my wayward moments weep
    That from my Youth, Romance is past and gone.
My boat is trimm'd—my sail is set—And I
Shall coast the shallows of the tide of Time

And rest me happily—where others lie,
Who pass oblivious days. No feelings climb
Ambitiously within me. Sweet Farewell
Be to the Nymphs that on the old Hill dwell.

Written 14 February 1818;
The Letters of John Keats (ed. Buxton Forman), 1901

337   *Peter Bell: A Lyrical Ballad*

I do affirm that I am the REAL SIMON PURE.—*Bold Stroke for
a Wife.*

I

IT is the thirty-first of March,
    A gusty evening—half-past seven;
The moon is shining o'er the larch,
A simple shape—a cock'd-up arch,
Rising bigger than a star,
Though the stars are thick in Heaven.

II

Gentle moon! how canst thou shine
Over graves and over trees,
With as innocent a look
As my own grey eyeball sees,
When I gaze upon a brook?

III

Od's me! how the moon doth shine:
It doth make a pretty glitter,
Playing in the waterfall;
As when Lucy Gray doth litter
Her baby-house with bugles small.

719

IV

Beneath the ever blessed moon
An old man o'er an old grave stares,
You never look'd upon his fellow;
His brow is covered with grey hairs,
As though they were an umbrella.

V

He hath a noticeable look,
This old man hath—this grey old man;
He gazes at the graves, and seems,
With over waiting, over wan,
Like Susan Harvey's pan of creams.

VI

'T is Peter Bell—'t is Peter Bell,
Who never stirreth in the day;
His hand is wither'd—he is old!
On Sundays he is us'd to pray,
In winter he is very cold.

VII

I've seen him in the month of August,
At the wheatfield, hour by hour,
Picking ear,—by ear,—by ear,—
Through wind,—and rain,—and sun,—and shower,
From year,—to year,—to year,—to year.

VIII

You never saw a wiser man,
He knows his Numeration Table;
He counts the sheep of Harry Gill,
Every night that he is able,
When the sheep are on the hill.

PETER BELL: A LYRICAL BALLAD

IX

Betty Foy—*My* Betty Foy,—
Is the aunt of Peter Bell;
And credit me, as I would have you,
Simon Lee was once his nephew,
And his niece is Alice Fell.

X

He is rurally related;
Peter Bell hath country cousins,
(He had once a worthy mother)
Bells and Peters by the dozens,
But Peter Bell he hath no brother.

XI

Not a brother owneth he,
Peter Bell he hath no brother,
His mother had no other son,
No other son e'er call'd her mother;
Peter Bell hath brother none.

XII

Hark! the churchyard brook is singing
Its evening song amid the leaves;
And the peering moon doth look
Sweetly on that singing brook,
Round and sad as though it grieves.

XIII

Peter Bell doth lift his hand,
That thin hand, which in the light
Looketh like to oiled paper;
Paper oiled,—oily bright,—
And held up to a waxen taper.

   .   .   .   .   .

JOHN HAMILTON REYNOLDS

XVIII

I the poet of the mountain,
Of the waterfall and fell,
I the mighty mental medlar,
I the lonely lyric pedlar,
I the Jove of Alice Fell,

XIX

I the Recluse—a gentle man,
A gentle man—a simple creature,
Who would not hurt—God shield the thing,—
The merest, meanest May-bug's wing,
Am tender in my tender nature.

XX

I do doat on my dear wife,
On the linnet, on the worm,
I can see sweet written salads
Growing in the Lyric Ballads,
And always find them green and firm.

XXI

Peter Bell is laughing now,
Like a dead man making faces;
Never saw I smile so old,
On face so wrinkled and so cold,
Since the Idiot Boy's grimaces.

XXII

He is thinking of the moors,
Where I saw him in his breeches
Ragged though they were, a pair
Fit for a grey old man to wear;
Saw him poking,—gathering leeches.

722

XXIII

And gather'd leeches are to him,
To Peter Bell, like gather'd flowers;
They do yield him such delight,
As roses poach'd from porch at night,
Or pluck'd from oratoric bowers.

XXIV

How that busy smile doth hurry
O'er the cheek of Peter Bell;
He is surely in a flurry,
Hurry skurry—hurry skurry,
Such delight I may not tell.

XXV

His stick is made of wilding wood,
His hat was formerly of felt,
His duffel cloak of wool is made,
His stockings are from stock in trade,
His belly 's belted with a belt.

XXVI

His father was a bellman once,
His mother was a beldame old;
They kept a shop at Keswick Town,
Close by the Bell, (beyond the Crown,)
And pins and peppermint they sold.

XXVII

He is stooping now about
O'er the gravestones one and two;
The clock is now a striking eight,
Four more hours and 't will be late,
And Peter Bell hath much to do.

XXVIII

O'er the gravestones three and four.
Peter stoopeth old and wise;
He counteth with a wizard glee
The graves of all his family,
While the hooting owlet cries.

XXIX

Peter Bell, he readeth ably,
All his letters he can tell;
Roman W,—Roman S,
In a minute he can guess,
Without the aid of Dr. Bell.

XXX

Peter keeps a gentle pony,
But the pony is not here;
Susan who is very tall,
And very sick and sad withal,
Rides it slowly far and near.

XXXI

Hark! the voice of Peter Bell,
And the belfry bell is knelling;
It soundeth drowsily and dead,
As though a corse th' ' Excursion ' read;
Or Martha Ray her tale was telling.

XXXII

Do listen unto Peter Bell,
While your eyes with tears do glisten:
Silence! his old eyes do read
All, on which the boys do tread
When holidays do come—Do listen!

PETER BELL: A LYRICAL BALLAD

XXXIII

The ancient Marinere lieth here,
Never to rise, although he pray'd,—
But all men, all, must have their fallings;
And, like the Fear of Mr. Collins,
He died ' of sounds himself had made '.

XXXIV

Dead mad mother,—Martha Ray,
Old Matthew too, and Betty Foy,
Lack-a-daisy! here's a rout full;
Simon Lee whose age was doubtful,
Simon even the Fates destroy.

XXXV

Harry Gill is gone to rest,
Goody Blake is food for maggot;
They lie sweetly side by side,
Beautiful as when they died;
Never more shall she pick faggot.

XXXVI

Still he reads, and still the moon
On the churchyard's mounds doth shine;
The brook is still demurely singing,
Again the belfry bell is ringing,
'T is nine o'clock, six, seven, eight, nine!

XXXVII

Patient Peter pores and proses
On, from simple grave to grave;
Here marks the children snatch'd to heaven,
None left to blunder ' we are seven ';—
Even Andrew Jones no power could save.

JOHN HAMILTON REYNOLDS

XXXVIII

What a Sexton's work is here,
Lord! the Idiot Boy is gone;
And Barbara Lewthwaite's fate the same,
And cold as mutton is her lamb;
And Alice Fell is bone by bone.

XXXIX

And tears are thick with Peter Bell,
Yet still he sees one blessed tomb;
Tow'rds it he creeps with spectacles,
And bending on his leather knees,
He reads the *Lake*iest Poet's doom.

XL

The letters printed are by fate,
The death they say was suicide;
He reads—' Here lieth W. W.
Who never more will trouble you, trouble you ':
The old man smokes who 't is that died.

XLI

Go home, go home—old Man, go home;
Peter, lay thee down at night,
Thou art happy, Peter Bell,
Say thy prayers for Alice Fell,
Thou hast seen a blessed sight.

XLII

He quits that moonlight yard of skulls,
And still he feels right glad, and smiles
With moral joy at that old tomb;
Peter's cheek recalls its bloom,

And as he creepeth by the tiles,
He mutters ever—' W. W.
Never more will trouble you, trouble you.'

Here endeth the ballad of Peter Bell.

Peter Bell, 1819

338 ### Sonnet

SWEET poets of the gentle antique line,
  That made the hue of beauty all eterne,
  And gave earth's melodies a silver turn,—
Where did you steal your art so right divine?—
Sweetly ye memoried every golden twine
  Of your ladies' tresses:—teach me how to spurn
  Death's lone decaying and oblivion stern
From the sweet forehead of a lady mine.
The golden clusters of enamouring hair
  Glow'd in poetic pictures sweetly well;—
Why should not tresses dusk, that are so fair
  On the live brow, have an eternal spell
In poesy?—dark eyes are dearer far
  Than orbs that mock the hyacinthine-bell.

The Garden of Florence, 1821

THOMAS HOOD

1799–1845

339 ### The Last Man

'TWAS in the year two thousand and one,
  A pleasant morning of May,
I sat on the gallows-tree all alone,
  A chaunting a merry lay,—
To think how the pest had spared my life,
  To sing with the larks that day!

When up the heath came a jolly knave,
Like a scarecrow, all in rags:
It made me crow to see his old duds
All abroad in the wind, like flags:—
So up he came to the timbers' foot
And pitch'd down his greasy bags.—

Good Lord! how blythe the old beggar was!
At pulling out his scraps,—
The very sight of his broken orts
Made a work in his wrinkled chaps:
' Come down,' says he, ' you Newgate bird,
And have a taste of my snaps! '——

Then down the rope, like a tar from the mast,
I slided, and by him stood;
But I wished myself on the gallows again
When I smelt that beggar's food,
A foul beef-bone and a mouldy crust;
' Oh! ' quoth he, ' the heavens are good! '

Then after this grace he cast him down:
Says I, ' You'll get sweeter air
A pace or two off, on the windward side,'
For the felons' bones lay there.
But he only laugh'd at the empty skulls,
And offered them part of his fare.

' I never harm'd *them*, and they won't harm me:
Let the proud and the rich be cravens! '
I did not like that strange beggar man,
He look'd so up at the heavens.
Anon he shook out his empty old poke;
' There 's the crumbs,' saith he, ' for the ravens! '

THE LAST MAN

It made me angry to see his face,
It had such a jesting look;
But while I made up my mind to speak,
A small case-bottle he took:
Quoth he, ' though I gather the green water-cress,
My drink is not of the brook! '

Full manners-like he tender'd the dram;
Oh, it came of a dainty cask!
But, whenever it came to his turn to pull,
' Your leave, good sir, I must ask;
But I always wipe the brim with my sleeve,
When a hangman sups at my flask! '

And then he laugh'd so loudly and long,
The churl was quite out of breath;
I thought the very Old One was come
To mock me before my death,
And wish'd I had buried the dead men's bones
That were lying about the heath!

But the beggar gave me a jolly clap—
' Come, let us pledge each other,
For all the wide world is dead beside,
And we are brother and brother—
I've a yearning for thee in my heart,
As if we had come of one mother.

' I've a yearning for thee in my heart
That almost makes me weep,
For as I pass'd from town to town
The folks were all stone-asleep,—
But when I saw thee sitting aloft,
It made me both laugh and leap! '

Now a curse (I thought) be on his love,
And a curse upon his mirth,—
An' if it were not for that beggar man
I'd be the King of the earth,—
But I promis'd myself an hour should come
To make him rue his birth—

So down we sat and bous'd again
Till the sun was in mid-sky,
When, just when the gentle west-wind came,
We hearken'd a dismal cry;
' Up, up, on the tree,' quoth the beggar man,
' Till these horrible dogs go by! '

And, lo! from the forest's far-off skirts,
They came all yelling for gore,
A hundred hounds pursuing at once,
And a panting hart before,
Till he sunk down at the gallows' foot,
And there his haunches they tore!

His haunches they tore, without a horn
To tell when the chase was done;
And there was not a single scarlet coat
To flaunt it in the sun!—
I turn'd, and look'd at the beggar man,
And his tears dropt one by one!

And with curses sore he chid at the hounds,
Till the last dropt out of sight,
Anon, saith he, ' Let's down again,
And ramble for our delight,
For the world 's all free, and we may choose
A right cozie barn for to-night! '

THE LAST MAN

With that, he set up his staff on end,
And it fell with the point due West;
So we far'd that way to a city great,
Where the folks had died of the pest—
It was fine to enter in house and hall
Wherever it liked me best;

For the porters all were stiff and cold,
And could not lift their heads;
And when we came where their masters lay,
The rats leapt out of the beds;
The grandest palaces in the land
Were as free as workhouse sheds.

But the beggar man made a mumping face,
And knocked at every gate:
It made me curse to hear how he whined,
So our fellowship turned to hate,
And I bade him walk the world by himself,
For I scorn'd so humble a mate!

So *he* turn'd right, and *I* turn'd left,
As if we had never met;
And I chose a fair stone house for myself,
For the city was all to let;
And for three brave holidays drank my fill
Of the choicest that I could get.

And because my jerkin was coarse and worn,
I got me a properer vest;
It was purple velvet, stitch'd o'er with gold,
And a shining star at the breast!—
'Twas enough to fetch old Joan from her grave
To see me so purely drest!

But Joan was dead and under the mould,
And every buxom lass;
In vain I watch'd, at the window pane
For a Christian soul to pass!
But sheep and kine wander'd up the street,
And browz'd on the new-come grass.—

When lo! I spied the old beggar man,
And lustily he did sing!—
His rags were lapp'd in a scarlet cloak,
And a crown he had like a King;
So he stept right up before my gate
And danc'd me a saucy fling!

Heaven mend us all!—but, within my mind,
I had killed him then and there;
To see him lording so braggart-like
That was born to his beggar's fare,
And how he had stolen the royal crown
His betters were meant to wear.

But God forbid that a thief should die
Without his share of the laws!
So I nimbly whipt my tackle out,
And soon tied up his claws,—
I was judge myself, and jury, and all,
And solemnly tried the cause.

But the beggar man would not plead, but cried
Like a babe without its corals,
For he knew how hard it is apt to go
When the law and a thief have quarrels,—
There was not a Christian soul alive
To speak a word for his morals.

THE LAST MAN

Oh, how gaily I doff'd my costly gear,
And put on my work-day clothes;
I was tired of such a long Sunday life,—
And never was one of the sloths;
But the beggar man grumbled a weary deal,
And made many crooked mouths.

So I haul'd him off to the gallows' foot,
And blinded him in his bags;
'Twas a weary job to have him up,
For a doom'd man always lags;
But by ten of the clock he was off his legs
In the wind, and airing his rags!

So there he hung, and there I stood,
The LAST MAN left alive,
To have my own will of all the earth:
Quoth I, now I shall thrive!
But when was ever honey made
With one bee in a hive?

My conscience began to gnaw my heart,
Before the day was done,
For other men's lives had all gone out,
Like candles in the sun!—
But it seem'd as if I had broke, at last,
A thousand necks in one!

So I went and cut his body down
To bury it decentlie;—
God send there were any good soul alive
To do the like by me!
But the wild dogs came with terrible speed,
And bade me up the tree!

My sight was like a drunkard's sight,
And my head began to swim,
To see their jaws all white with foam,
Like the ravenous ocean brim;—
But when the wild dogs trotted away
Their jaws were bloody and grim!

Their jaws were bloody and grim, good Lord!
But the beggar man, where was he ?—
There was naught of him but some ribbons of rags
Below the gallows' tree!—
I know the Devil, when I am dead,
Will send his hounds for me!—

I've buried my babies one by one,
And dug the deep hole for Joan,
And covered the faces of kith and kin,
And felt the old churchyard stone
Go cold to my heart, full many a time,
But I never felt so lone!

For the lion and Adam were company,
And the tiger him beguiled:
But the simple kine are foes to my life,
And the household brutes are wild.
If the veriest cur would lick my hand,
I could love it like a child!

And the beggar man's ghost besets my dream,
At night to make me madder,—
And my wretched conscience within my breast,
Is like a stinging adder;—
I sigh when I pass the gallows' foot,
And look at the rope and ladder!—

For hanging looks sweet,—but, alas! in vain
My desperate fancy begs,—
I must turn my cup of sorrows quite up,
And drink it to the dregs,—
For there is not another man alive,
In the world, to pull my legs!

Whims and Oddities, 1826

340   *Fair Ines*

I

O SAW ye not fair Ines?
    She's gone into the West,
To dazzle when the sun is down,
And rob the world of rest:
She took our daylight with her,
The smiles that we love best,
With morning blushes on her cheek,
And pearls upon her breast.

II

O turn again, fair Ines,
Before the fall of night,
For fear the Moon should shine alone,
And stars unrivall'd bright;
And blessed will the lover be
That walks beneath their light,
And breathes the love against thy cheek
I dare not even write!

III

Would I had been, fair Ines,
That gallant cavalier,

Who rode so gaily by thy side,
And whisper'd thee so near!—
Were there no bonny dames at home
Or no true lovers here,
That he should cross the seas to win
The dearest of the dear ?

IV

I saw thee, lovely Ines,
Descend along the shore,
With bands of noble gentlemen,
And banners wav'd before;
And gentle youth and maidens gay,
And snowy plumes they wore;—
It would have been a beauteous dream,
—If it had been no more!

V

Alas, alas, fair Ines,
She went away with song,
With Music waiting on her steps,
And shoutings of the throng;
But some were sad, and felt no mirth,
But only Music's wrong,
In sounds that sang Farewell, Farewell,
To her you've loved so long.

VI

Farewell, farewell, fair Ines,
That vessel never bore
So fair a lady on its deck,
Nor danc'd so light before,—

Alas for pleasure on the sea,
And sorrow on the shore!
The smile that blest one lover's heart
Has broken many more!

The Plea of the Midsummer Fairies, 1827

Ode

Autumn

I

I SAW old Autumn in the misty morn
Stand shadowless like Silence, listening
To silence, for no lonely bird would sing
Into his hollow ear from woods forlorn,
Nor lowly hedge nor solitary thorn;—
Shaking his languid locks all dewy bright
With tangled gossamer that fell by night,
      Pearling his coronet of golden corn.

II

Where are the songs of Summer ?—With the sun,
Oping the dusky eyelids of the south,
Till shade and silence waken up as one,
And Morning sings with a warm odorous mouth.
Where are the merry birds ?—Away, away,
On panting wings through the inclement skies,
      Lest owls should prey
      Undazzled at noon-day,
And tear with horny beak their lustrous eyes.

III

Where are the blooms of Summer?—In the west,
Blushing their last to the last sunny hours,

When the mild Eve by sudden Night is prest
Like tearful Proserpine, snatch'd from her flow'rs
    To a most gloomy breast.
Where is the pride of Summer,—the green prime,—
The many, many leaves all twinkling?—Three
    On the moss'd elm; three on the naked lime
Trembling,—and one upon the old oak tree!
    Where is the Dryads' immortality?—
Gone into mournful cypress and dark yew,
Or wearing the long gloomy Winter through
    In the smooth holly's green eternity.

IV

The squirrel gloats on his accomplish'd hoard,
The ants have brimm'd their garners with ripe grain,
    And honey bees have stor'd
The sweets of Summer in their luscious cells;
The swallows all have wing'd across the main;
But here the Autumn melancholy dwells,
    And sighs her tearful spells
Amongst the sunless shadows of the plain.
      Alone, alone,
      Upon a mossy stone,
She sits and reckons up the dead and gone
With the last leaves for a love-rosary,
Whilst all the wither'd world looks drearily,
Like a dim picture of the drowned past
In the hush'd mind's mysterious far away,
Doubtful what ghostly thing will steal the last
Into that distance, grey upon the grey.

ODE

v

O go and sit with her, and be o'ershaded
Under the languid downfall of her hair:
She wears a coronal of flowers faded
Upon her forehead, and a face of care;—
There is enough of wither'd every where
To make her bower,—and enough of gloom;
There is enough of sadness to invite,
If only for the rose that died,—whose doom
Is Beauty's,—she that with the living bloom
Of conscious cheeks most beautifies the light;—
There is enough of sorrowing, and quite
Enough of bitter fruits the earth doth bear,—
Enough of chilly droppings for her bowl;
Enough of fear and shadowy despair,
To frame her cloudy prison for the soul!

The Plea of the Midsummer Fairies, 1827

342   *Ruth*

SHE stood breast high amid the corn,
  Clasp'd by the golden light of morn,
Like the sweetheart of the sun,
Who many a glowing kiss had won.

On her cheek an autumn flush,
Deeply ripened;—such a blush
In the midst of brown was born,
Like red poppies grown with corn.

Round her eyes her tresses fell,
Which were blackest none could tell,
But long lashes veil'd a light,
That had else been all too bright.

And her hat, with shady brim,
Made her tressy forehead dim;—
Thus she stood amid the stooks,
Praising God with sweetest looks:—

Sure, I said, heav'n did not mean,
Where I reap thou shouldst but glean,
Lay thy sheaf adown and come,
Share my harvest and my home.

The Plea of the Midsummer Fairies, 1827

343   *I remember, I remember*

I

I REMEMBER, I remember,
  The house where I was born,
The little window where the sun
Came peeping in at morn;
He never came a wink too soon,
Nor brought too long a day,
But now, I often wish the night
Had borne my breath away!

II

I remember, I remember,
The roses, red and white,
The vi'lets, and the lily-cups,
Those flowers made of light!
The lilacs where the robin built,
And where my brother set
The laburnum on his birthday,—
The tree is living yet!

III

I remember, I remember,
Where I was used to swing,
And thought the air must rush as fresh
To swallows on the wing;
My spirit flew in feathers then,
That is so heavy now,
And summer pools could hardly cool
The fever on my brow!

IV

I remember, I remember,
The fir trees dark and high;
I used to think their slender tops
Were close against the sky:
It was a childish ignorance,
But now 'tis little joy
To know I'm farther off from heav'n
Than when I was a boy.

The Plea of the Midsummer Fairies, 1827

344   *On Mistress Nicely, a Pattern for Housekeepers*

SHE was a woman peerless in her station,
  With household virtues wedded to her name;
  Spotless in linen, grass-bleach'd in her fame,
And pure and clear-starch'd in her conversation;
Thence in my Castle of Imagination
  She dwells for evermore, the dainty dame,
  To keep all airy draperies from shame,
And all dream furnitures in preservation:

741

There walketh she with keys quite silver bright,
In perfect hose, and shoes of seemly black,
    Apron and stomacher of lily-white,
And decent order follows in her track:
    The burnish'd plate grows lustrous in her sight,
And polish'd floors and tables shine her back.

The Plea of the Midsummer Fairies, 1827

345   '*It is not Death*'

IT is not death, that sometime in a sigh
    This eloquent breath shall take its speechless flight;
That sometime these bright stars, that now reply
In sunlight to the sun, shall set in night;
That this warm conscious flesh shall perish quite,
And all life's ruddy springs forget to flow;
That thoughts shall cease, and the immortal spright
Be lapp'd in alien clay and laid below;
It is not death to know this,—but to know
That pious thoughts, which visit at new graves
In tender pilgrimage, will cease to go
So duly and so oft,—and when grass waves
Over the past-away, there may be then
No resurrection in the minds of men.

The Plea of the Midsummer Fairies, 1827

346   *Silence*

THERE is a silence where hath been no sound,
    There is a silence where no sound may be,
    In the cold grave—under the deep deep sea,
Or in wide desert where no life is found,

Which hath been mute, and still must sleep profound;
   No voice is hush'd—no life treads silently,
   But clouds and cloudy shadows wander free,
That never spoke, over the idle ground:
But in green ruins, in the desolate walls
   Of antique palaces, where Man hath been,
Though the dun fox, or wild hyena, calls,
   And owls, that flit continually between,
Shriek to the echo, and the low winds moan,
There the true Silence is, self-conscious and alone.

The Plea of the Midsummer Fairies, 1827

347   *From ' The Plea of the Midsummer*
Fairies '

(i)

Titania

MEANWHILE the Queen with many piteous drops,
   Falling like tiny sparks full fast and free,
Bedews a pathway from her throne;—and stops
Before the foot of her arch enemy,
And with her little arms enfolds his knee,
That shows more gristly from that fair embrace;
But she will ne'er depart. ' Alas! ' quoth she,
' My painful fingers I will here enlace
Till I have gain'd your pity for our race.

' What have we ever done to earn this grudge,
And hate—(if not too humble for thy hating ?)—
Look o'er our labours and our lives, and judge
If there be any ills of our creating;

For we are very kindly creatures, dating
With nature's charities still sweet and bland:—
O think this murder worthy of debating!'—
Herewith she makes a signal with her hand,
To beckon some one from the Fairy band.

Anon I saw one of those elfin things,
Clad all in white like any chorister,
Come fluttering forth on his melodious wings,
That made soft music at each little stir,
But something louder than a bee's demur
Before he lights upon a bunch of broom,
And thus 'gan he with Saturn to confer,—
And O his voice was sweet, touch'd with the gloom
Of that sad theme that argued of his doom!

Quoth he, ' We make all melodies our care,
That no false discords may offend the Sun,
Music's great master—tuning every where
All pastoral sounds and melodies, each one
Duly to place and season, so that none
May harshly interfere. We rouse at morn
The shrill sweet lark; and when the day is done,
Hush silent pauses for the bird forlorn,
That singeth with her breast against a thorn.

' We gather in loud choirs the twittering race,
That make a chorus with their single note;
And tend on new-fledged birds in every place,
That duly they may get their tunes by rote;
And oft, like echoes, answering remote,

744

We hide in thickets from the feather'd throng,
And strain in rivalship each throbbing throat,
Singing in shrill responses all day long,
Whilst the glad truant listens to our song.

' Wherefore, great King of Years, as thou dost love
The raining music from a morning cloud,
When vanish'd larks are carolling above,
To wake Apollo with their pipings loud;—
If ever thou hast heard in leafy shroud
The sweet and plaintive Sappho of the dell,
Show thy sweet mercy on this little crowd,
And we will muffle up the sheepfold bell
Whene'er thou listenest to Philomel.'

(ii)

Tender Babes

THEN saith another, ' We are kindly things,
And like her offspring nestle with the dove,—
Witness these hearts embroider'd on our wings,
To show our constant patronage of love:—
We sit at even, in sweet bow'rs above
Lovers, and shake rich odours on the air,
To mingle with their sighs; and still remove
The startling owl, and bid the bat forbear
Their privacy, and haunt some other where.

' And we are near the mother when she sits
Beside her infant in its wicker bed;
And we are in the fairy scene that flits
Across its tender brain: sweet dreams we shed,

745

And whilst the tender little soul is fled
Away, to sport with our young elves, the while
We touch the dimpled cheek with roses red,
And tickle the soft lips until they smile,
So that their careful parents they beguile.

' O then, if ever thou hast breathed a vow
At Love's dear portal, or at pale moon-rise
Crush'd the dear curl on a regardful brow
That did not frown thee from thy honey prize—
If ever thy sweet son sat on thy thighs,
And wooed thee from thy careful thoughts within
To watch the harmless beauty of his eyes,
Or glad thy fingers on his smooth soft skin,
For Love's dear sake, let us thy pity win! '

Then Saturn fiercely thus:—' What joy have I
In tender babes, that have devour'd mine own,
Whenever to the light I heard them cry,
Till foolish Rhea cheated me with stone?
Whereon, till now, is my great hunger shown,
In monstrous dints of my enormous tooth;
And,—but the peopled world is too full grown
For hunger's edge,—I would consume all youth
At one great meal, without delay or ruth!

' For I am well nigh craz'd and wild to hear
How boastful fathers taunt me with their breed,
Saying, We shall not die nor disappear,
But in these other selves, ourselves succeed,
Ev'n as ripe flowers pass into their seed
Only to be renew'd from prime to prime,
All of which boastings I am forced to read,

Besides a thousand challenges to Time
Which bragging lovers have compil'd in rhyme.

' Wherefore, when they are sweetly met o' nights,
There will I steal, and with my hurried hand
Startle them suddenly from their delights
Before the next encounter hath been plann'd,
Ravishing hours in little minutes spann'd;
But when they say farewell, and grieve apart,
Then like a leaden statue I will stand,
Meanwhile their many tears encrust my dart,
And with a ragged edge cut heart from heart.'

(iii)

Shakespeare

HERE he lets go the struggling imp, to clutch
His mortal engine with each grisly hand,
Which frights the elfin progeny so much,
They huddle in a heap, and trembling stand
All round Titania, like the queen bee's band,
With sighs and tears and very shrieks of woe!—
Meanwhile, some moving argument I plann'd,
To make the stern Shade merciful,—when lo!
He drops his fatal scythe without a blow!

For, just at need, a timely Apparition
Steps in between, to bear the awful brunt;
Making him change his horrible position,
To marvel at this comer, brave and blunt,
That dares Time's irresistible affront,
Whose strokes have scarr'd even the gods of old;—
Whereas this seem'd a mortal, at mere hunt

For coneys, lighted by the moonshine cold,
Or stalker of stray deer, stealthy and bold.

Who, turning to the small assembled fays,
Doffs to the lily queen his courteous cap,
And holds her beauty for a while in gaze,
With bright eyes kindling at this pleasant hap;
And thence upon the fair moon's silver map,
As if in question of this magic chance,
Laid like a dream upon the green earth's lap;
And then upon old Saturn turns askance,
Exclaiming, with a glad and kindly glance:—

' Oh, these be Fancy's revellers by night!
Stealthy companions of the downy moth—
Diana's motes, that flit in her pale light,
Shunners of sunbeams in diurnal sloth;—
These be the feasters on night's silver cloth,—
The gnat with shrilly trump is their convener,
Forth from their flowery chambers, nothing loth,
With lulling tunes to charm the air serener,
Or dance upon the grass to make it greener.

' These be the pretty genii of the flow'rs,
Daintily fed with honey and pure dew—
Midsummer's phantoms in her dreaming hours,
King Oberon, and all his merry crew,
The darling puppets of romance's view;
Fairies, and sprites, and goblin elves we call them,
Famous for patronage of lovers true;—
Nor harm they act, neither shall harm befall them,
So do not thus with crabbed frowns appal them.'

748

THE PLEA OF THE MIDSUMMER FAIRIES

O what a cry was Saturn's then!—it made
The fairies quake. ' What care I for their pranks,
However they may lovers choose to aid,
Or dance their roundelays on flow'ry banks?—
Long must they dance before they earn my thanks,—
So step aside, to some far safer spot,
Whilst with my hungry scythe I mow their ranks,
And leave them in the sun, like weeds, to rot,
And with the next day's sun to be forgot.'

Anon, he raised afresh his weapon keen;
But still the gracious Shade disarm'd his aim,
Stepping with brave alacrity between,
And made his sere arm powerless and tame.
His be perpetual glory, for the shame
Of hoary Saturn in that grand defeat!—
But I must tell, how here Titania came
With all her kneeling lieges, to entreat
His kindly succour, in sad tones, but sweet.

Saying, ' Thou seest a wretched queen before thee,
The fading power of a failing land,
Who for her kingdom kneeleth to implore thee,
Now menac'd by this tyrant's spoiling hand;
No one but thee can hopefully withstand
That crooked blade, he longeth so to lift.
I pray thee blind him with his own vile sand,
Which only times all ruins by its drift,
Or prune his eagle wings that are so swift.

' Or take him by that sole and grizzled tuft,
That hangs upon his bald and barren crown;
And we will sing to see him so rebuff'd,
And lend our little mights to pull him down,

And make brave sport of his malicious frown,
For all his boastful mockery o'er men;
For thou wast born I know for this renown,
By my most magical and inward ken,
That readeth ev'n at Fate's forestalling pen.

' Nay, by the golden lustre of thine eye,
And by thy brow's most fair and ample span,
Thought's glorious palace, fram'd for fancies high,
And by thy cheek thus passionately wan,
I know the signs of an immortal man,—
Nature's chief darling, and illustrious mate,
Destin'd to foil old Death's oblivious plan,
And shine untarnish'd by the fogs of Fate,
Time's famous rival till the final date!

' O shield us then from this usurping Time,
And we will visit thee in moonlight dreams;
And teach thee tunes, to wed unto thy rhyme,
And dance about thee in all midnight gleams,
Giving thee glimpses of our magic schemes,
Such as no mortal's eye hath ever seen;
And, for thy love to us in our extremes,
Will ever keep thy chaplet fresh and green,
Such as no poet's wreath hath ever been!

' And we'll distil thee aromatic dews,
To charm thy sense, when there shall be no flow'rs;
And flavour'd syrops in thy drinks infuse,
And teach the nightingale to haunt thy bow'rs.
And with our games divert thy weariest hours,
With all that elfin wits can e'er devise.
And, this churl dead, there'll be no hasting hours

To rob thee of thy joys, as now joy flies: '—
Here she was stopp'd by Saturn's furious cries.

Whom therefore, the kind Shade rebukes anew,
Saying, ' Thou haggard Sin, go forth, and scoop
Thy hollow coffin in some churchyard yew,
Or make th' autumnal flow'rs turn pale, and droop;
Or fell the bearded corn, till gleaners stoop
Under fat sheaves,—or blast the piny grove;—
But here thou shalt not harm this pretty groupe,
Whose lives are not so frail and feebly wove,
But leas'd on Nature's loveliness and love.

' 'Tis these that free the small entangled fly,
Caught in the venom'd spider's crafty snare;—
These be the petty surgeons that apply
The healing balsams to the wounded hare,
Bedded in bloody fern, no creature's care!—
These be providers for the orphan brood,
Whose tender mother hath been slain in air,
Quitting with gaping bill her darling's food,
Hard by the verge of her domestic wood.

' 'Tis these befriend the timid trembling stag,
When, with a bursting heart beset with fears,
He feels his saving speed begin to flag;
For then they quench the fatal taint with tears,
And prompt fresh shifts in his alarum'd ears,
So piteously they view all bloody morts;
Or if the gunner, with his arm, appears,
Like noisy pyes and jays, with harsh reports,
They warn the wild fowl of his deadly sports.

mort] dead body.

' For these are kindly ministers of nature,
To soothe all covert hurts and dumb distress;
Pretty they be, and very small of stature,—
For mercy still consorts with littleness;—
Wherefore the sum of good is still the less,
And mischief grossest in this world of wrong;—
So do these charitable dwarfs redress
The tenfold ravages of giants strong,
To whom great malice and great might belong.

' Likewise to them are Poets much beholden
For secret favours in the midnight glooms;
Brave Spenser quaff'd out of their goblets golden,
And saw their tables spread of prompt mushrooms,
And heard their horns of honeysuckle blooms
Sounding upon the air most soothing soft,
Like humming bees busy about the brooms,—
And glanc'd this fair queen's witchery full oft,
And in her magic wain soared far aloft.

' Nay I myself, though mortal, once was nurs'd
By fairy gossips, friendly at my birth,
And in my childish ear glib Mab rehears'd
Her breezy travels round our planet's girth,
Telling me wonders of the moon and earth;
My gramarye at her grave lap I conn'd,
Where Puck hath been conven'd to make me mirth;
I have had from Queen Titania tokens fond,
And toy'd with Oberon's permitted wand.

' With figs and plums and Persian dates they fed me,
And delicate cates after my sunset meal,
And took me by my childish hand, and led me
By craggy rocks crested with keeps of steel,

Whose awful bases deep dark woods conceal,
Staining some dead lake with their verdant dyes:
And when the West sparkled at Phœbus' wheel,
With fairy euphrasy they purg'd mine eyes,
To let me see their cities in the skies.

' 'Twas they first school'd my young imagination
To take its flights like any new-fledg'd bird,
And show'd the span of winged meditation
Stretch'd wider than things grossly seen or heard.
With sweet swift Ariel how I soar'd and stirr'd
The fragrant blooms of spiritual bow'rs!
'Twas they endear'd what I have still preferr'd,
Nature's blest attributes and balmy pow'rs,
Her hills and vales and brooks, sweet birds and flow'rs!

' Wherefore with all true loyalty and duty
Will I regard them in my honouring rhyme,
With love for love, and homages to beauty,
And magic thoughts gather'd in night's cool clime,
With studious verse trancing the dragon Time,
Strong as old Merlin's necromantic spells;
So these dear monarchs of the summer's prime
Shall live unstartled by his dreadful yells,
Till shrill larks warn them to their flowery cells.'

The Plea of the Midsummer Fairies, 1827

348   *The Death-Bed*

WE watch'd her breathing thro' the night,
    Her breathing soft and low,
As in her breast the wave of life
Kept heaving to and fro!

So silently we seemed to speak—
So slowly moved about!
As we had lent her half our powers
To eke her living out!

Our very hopes belied our fears,
Our fears our hopes belied—
We thought her dying when she slept,
And sleeping when she died!

For when the morn came dim and sad—
And chill with early showers,
Her quiet eyelids closed—she had
Another morn than ours!

Englishman's Magazine, August 1831

349 *Domestic Didactics by an Old Servant*

The Broken Dish

WHAT 'S life but full of care and doubt,
    With all its fine humanities,
With parasols we walk about,
    Long pigtails and such vanities.

We plant pomegranate trees and things,
    And go in gardens sporting,
With toys and fans of peacock's wings
    To painted ladies courting.

We gather flowers of every hue,
    And fish in boats for fishes,
Build summer-houses painted blue,—
    But life 's as frail as dishes.

Walking about their groves of trees,
  Blue bridges and blue rivers,
How little thought them two Chinese,
  They'd both be smash'd to shivers!

Published in *Hood's Own*, 1839

JOHN MOULTRIE

1799–1874

350   *The Fairy Maimounè*

SHE came on Earth soon after the creation,
  And was akin to Oberon, 'tis said:
In Faeryland received her education,
  But never yet had been induced to wed,
Though she was woo'd by half the Elfin nation—
  But still a free and roving life she led;
And sought diversion for her gentle mind
Chiefly among the haunts of humankind.

There was a deep and solitary well in
  The palace where the Prince was now confined,
Which served this lovely Fairy for a dwelling,
  A spot just suited to a Fairy's mind;
Much like the fountain where Narcissus fell in
  Love with her own fair face, and pined, and pined
To death (the passion 's not at all uncommon
In Man, and very prevalent in woman).

Beneath this fountain's fresh and bubbling water,
  Unfathomably deep, the livelong day,
This wondrous Fairy, Time's most radiant daughter,
  In unimaginable visions lay;

Where never earthly care or sorrow sought her,
　　But o'er her head did the wild waters play,
And flitting spirits of the Earth and Air
Scattered sweet dreams and lulling music there.

For she was well beloved by all th' immortal
　　Beings that roam through Ocean, Earth, or Sky;
And oft would blessed spirits pass the portal
　　Of the vast Eden of Eternity
To be her slaves, and to her did resort all
　　Angelic thoughts, each heavenly phantasy,
That mortals may not know—all came to bless
This gentle Being's dreams of happiness.

And all around that fountain, the pure air
　　Breathed of her presence; every leaf was hung
With music, and each flower that blossom'd there
　　A fine and supernatural fragrance flung
On the glad sense; and thither did repair
　　Garlanded maids, and lovers fond and young;
And by the side of the low-murmuring stream
Would youthful poets lay them down to dream.

And ever on that spot the rays of Morning
　　Fell thickest, and the Sun's meridian light
Sparkled and danced amid the waves, adorning
　　The crystal chamber of the sleeping Sprite.
But when proud Dian walk'd, with maiden scorn, in
　　The Eastern skies, and the sweet dews of Night
Lay heavy on the Earth, that Sprite arose
Fresh from the visions of the day's repose.

And then, she gaily wander'd through the world,
　　Where'er her fancy led her, and would stray

(The sails of her bright meteor-wings unfurl'd)
    Through many a populous city, and survey
The chambers of the sleeping; oft she curl'd
    The locks of young chaste maidens, as they lay,
And lit new lustre in their sleeping eyes,
And breathed upon their cheeks the bloom of Paradise.

And she would scatter o'er the Poet's brain
    (As he lay smiling through swift-springing tears)
A strange and unintelligible train
    Of fancies, and ring loud into his ears
A long, mysterious, and perplexing strain
    Of music, or combine the joy of years
In half an hour of slumber; till he started
From such sweet visions, weeping and wild-hearted.

And, in her mirthful moments, would she seek
    The bachelor's room, and spoil his lonely rest;
Or with old maids play many a wicked freak;
    Or rattle loudly at the miser's chest,
Till he woke trembling; she would often wreak
    Her vengeance on stern fathers who repress'd
Their children's young and innocent loves, and sold
(Like our two Kings) their happiness for gold.

           The Etonian, August 1821; *Poems*, 1837

351   *From 'Sir Launfal'*

BUT here, at starting, I must just premise
    (Lest any reader should look grave and cold)
That 'tis not my intention to disguise
    A tale immoral in decorous mould.

JOHN MOULTRIE

Approach not me, ye cockneys, good and wise,
   And other great philosophers, who hold
That Epicurus is Man's best physician,
And chastity a ' monkish superstition.'

Think not to gain, in me, a new recruit—
   You'll find yourselves mistaken I assure you;
I hate your doctrines, and your rhymes to boot,
   And tell you, in plain terms, I can't endure you;
I'd thresh you soundly, if I'd time to do't,
   And thought a canto's horse-whipping would cure you,—
Though, I confess, 'twould grieve me to affront
That cleverest coxcomb in the world, Leigh Hunt.

I'll spare thy weaker brethren for thy sake—
   I love thee, when I laugh at thee, sweet Leigh;
But do, my gentle Indicator, take
   A friend's advice, and soon recross the sea.
How canst thou tarry with the jaded rake,
   The heartless bard, the hoary debauchee,
The impotent reviler, who 's unfurl'd
His Atheist banner to reform the world?

With all thy follies, *thou* wast still sincere,
   And gentle (save in politics) though blind
And very often silly, and, I fear,
   Hast done some harm among the cockney kind;
But what in that same misanthropic peer,
   What, in the name of wonder, couldst thou find,
What could induce thee to suppose that he
Would make a good *enthusiast*, simple Leigh?

Thou wast a faithful and a fit Achates,
   Once, to a great Æneas, Percy Shelley—
758

SIR LAUNFAL

A vast, though erring spirit, whose sad fate is
   A thing which I deplore—but let me tell ye,
You made yourself a monstrous ninny gratis
   With that same funeral pile—he might as well lie,
Methinks, beneath the turf o'ergrown with flowers,
As dance among the winds and thunder-showers.

However, he and you of course knew best;
   His life, at least, was suited to his end,—
His obsequies to both—so let them rest;
   But how Achates could at once descend
From His to Byron's friendship, I protest,
   Is what it puzzles me to comprehend;
Take care, sweet Leigh, or you'll afford the Tories
A handle to invent ill-natured stories.

They'll say—I shan't believe 'em—but they'll say
   That Leigh 's become what once he most abhorr'd,
Has thrown his independence all away,
   And dubb'd himself toad-eater to a Lord;
And though, of course, you'll hit as hard as they,
   I fear you'll find it difficult to ward
Their poison'd arrows off—you'd best come back,
Before the Cockney kingdom goes to wrack.

The Examiner's grown dull as well as dirty,
   The Indicator's sick, the Liberal dead;—
I hear its readers were some six-and-thirty,
   But really 'twas too stupid to be read.
'Tis plain your present partnership has hurt ye:
   Poor brother John ' looks up and is not fed;'
For scarce a soul will purchase or get through one
E'en of his shilling budgets of Don Juan.

JOHN MOULTRIE

Poor brother John!—poor Cockneys!—but I've spent
  More time upon you now than you deserve,
Because your King for better things was meant,
  And shows, on most occasions, pluck and nerve;
I hope, sincerely, he may yet repent;
  For you, sweet Cockneys, these few hints must serve—
Perhaps, I may expand them, by and by,
But have, at present, other fish to fry.

Poems, 1837

THOMAS BABINGTON MACAULAY

1800–1859

352   *Ivry*

NOW glory to the Lord of Hosts, from whom all glories
      are!
And glory to our sovereign liege, King Henry of Navarre!
Now let there be the merry sound of music and of dance,
  Through thy corn-fields green, and sunny vines, oh pleasant
      land of France!
And thou, Rochelle, our own Rochelle, proud city of the
      waters,
Again let rapture light the eyes of all thy mourning daughters.
As thou wert constant in our ills, be joyous in our joy,
For cold, and stiff, and still are they who wrought thy walls
      annoy.
Hurrah! hurrah! a single field hath turned the chance of war,
Hurrah! hurrah! for Ivry, and Henry of Navarre.

Oh! how our hearts were beating, when, at the dawn of day,
We saw the army of the League drawn out in long array;
With all its priest-led citizens, and all its rebel peers,
And Appenzel's stout infantry, and Egmont's Flemish spears.

IVRY

There rode the brood of false Lorraine, the curses of our land;
And dark Mayenne was in the midst, a truncheon in his hand:
And, as we looked on them, we thought of Seine's empurpled
    flood,
And good Coligni's hoary hair all dabbled with his blood;
And we cried unto the living God, who rules the fate of war,
To fight for His own holy name, and Henry of Navarre.

The king is come to marshal us, in all his armour drest,
And he has bound a snow-white plume upon his gallant crest.
He looked upon his people, and a tear was in his eye;
He looked upon the traitors, and his glance was stern and high.
Right graciously he smiled on us, as rolled from wing to wing,
Down all our line, a deafening shout, ' God save our lord the
    King.'
' An if my standard-bearer fall, as fall full well he may,
For never saw I promise yet of such a bloody fray,
Press where ye see my white plume shine, amidst the ranks
    of war,
And be your oriflamme to-day the helmet of Navarre.'

Hurrah! the foes are moving! Hark to the mingled din
Of fife, and steed, and trump, and drum, and roaring culverin.
The fiery Duke is pricking fast across St. André's plain,
With all the hireling chivalry of Guelders and Almayne.
Now by the lips of those ye love, fair gentlemen of France,
Charge for the golden lilies,—upon them with the lance.
A thousand spurs are striking deep, a thousand spears in rest,
A thousand knights are pressing close behind the snow-white
    crest;
And in they burst, and on they rushed, while, like a guiding
    star,
Amidst the thickest carnage blazed the helmet of Navarre.

Now, God be praised, the day is ours. Mayenne hath turned
his rein.
D'Aumale hath cried for quarter. The Flemish count is slain.
Their ranks are breaking like thin clouds before a Biscay gale;
The field is heaped with bleeding steeds, and flags, and cloven
mail.
And then we thought on vengeance, and, all along our van,
' Remember Saint Bartholomew,' was passed from man to
man.
But out spake gentle Henry, ' No Frenchman is my foe:
Down, down with every foreigner, but let your brethren go.'
Oh! was there ever such a knight, in friendship or in war,
As our sovereign lord, King Henry, the soldier of Navarre!

Ho! maidens of Vienna; ho! matrons of Lucerne!
Weep, weep, and rend your hair for those who never shall
return.
Ho! Philip, send, for charity, thy Mexican pistoles,
That Antwerp monks may sing a mass for thy poor spear-
men's souls.
Ho! gallant nobles of the League, look that your arms be
bright;
Ho! burghers of Saint Genevieve, keep watch and ward
to-night.
For our God hath crushed the tyrant, our God hath raised
the slave,
And mocked the counsel of the wise, and the valour of the
brave.
Then glory to his holy name, from whom all glories are;
And glory to our sovereign lord, King Henry of Navarre.

Knight's Quarterly Magazine, January 1824;
Lays of Ancient Rome, 1848

ATTEND, all ye who list to hear our noble England's praise,
I tell of the thrice famous deeds she wrought in ancient days,
When that great fleet invincible against her bore in vain
The richest spoils of Mexico, the stoutest hearts of Spain.

It was about the lovely close of a warm summer day,
There came a gallant merchant ship full sail to Plymouth bay.
Her crew had seen Castile's black fleet, beyond Aurigny's isle,
At earliest twilight, on the waves lie heaving many a mile.
At sunrise she escaped their van, by God's especial grace;
And the tall Pinta, till the noon, had held her close in chase.

Forthwith a guard at every gun was placed along the wall;
The beacon blazed upon the roof of Edgecumbe's lofty hall;
Many a light fishing bark put out to pry along the coast;
And with loose rein and bloody spur rode inland many a post.
With his white hair unbonneted the stout old sheriff comes;
Behind him march the halberdiers, before him sound the drums;
His yeomen, round the market-cross, make clear an ample space,
For there behoves him to set up the standard of her Grace.
And haughtily the trumpets peal, and gaily dance the bells,
As slow upon the labouring wind the royal blazon swells.
Look how the lion of the sea lifts up his ancient crown,
And underneath his deadly paw treads the gay lilies down.
So stalked he when he turned to flight, on that famed Picard field,
Bohemia's plume, and Genoa's bow, and Cæsar's eagle shield:

So glared he when at Agincourt in wrath he turned to bay,
And crushed and torn beneath his claws the princely hunters
    lay.
Ho! strike the flag-staff deep, sir knight: ho! scatter flowers,
    fair maids:
Ho! gunners, fire a loud salute: ho! gallants, draw your
    blades:
Thou, sun, shine on her joyously! ye breezes waft her wide:
Our glorious SEMPER EADEM,—the banner of our pride.

The freshening breeze of eve unfurled that banner's massy
    fold,
The parting gleam of sunshine kissed that haughty scroll of
    gold:
Night sank upon the dusky beach, and on the purple sea;—
Such night in England ne'er had been, nor e'er again shall
    be.
From Eddystone to Berwick bounds, from Lynn to Milford
    bay,
That time of slumber was as bright and busy as the day:
For swift to east and swift to west the warning radiance
    spread;
High on St. Michael's Mount it shone—it shone on Beachy
    Head.
Far on the deep the Spaniard saw, along each southern shire,
Cape beyond cape, in endless range, those twinkling points
    of fire:
The fisher left his skiff to rock on Tamar's glittering waves;
The rugged miners poured to war from Mendip's sunless
    caves.
O'er Longleat's towers, o'er Cranbourne's oaks, the fiery
    herald flew;

And roused the shepherds of Stonehenge, the rangers of
 Beaulieu.
Right sharp and quick the bells all night rang out from Bristol
 town;
And ere the day three hundred horse had met on Clifton
 down.

The sentinel on Whitehall gate looked forth into the night,
And saw o'erhanging Richmond-hill the streak of blood-red
 light.
Then bugle's note and cannon's roar the death-like silence
 broke,
And with one start, and with one cry, the royal city woke.
At once on all her stately gates arose the answering fires:
At once the wild alarum clashed from all her reeling spires:
From all the batteries of the Tower pealed loud the voice of
 fear;
And all the thousand masts of Thames sent back a louder
 cheer:
And from the furthest wards was heard the rush of hurrying
 feet,
And the broad streams of flags and pikes dashed down each
 roaring street:
And broader still became the blaze, and louder still the din,
As fast from every village round the horse came spurring in:
And eastward straight, from wild Blackheath, the warlike
 errand went,
And roused in many an ancient hall the gallant squires of
 Kent.

Southward from Surrey's pleasant hills flew those bright
 couriers forth;

High on bleak Hampstead's swarthy moor they started for
    the north.
And on, and on, without a pause, untired they bounded still,
All night from tower to tower they sprang;—they sprang
    from hill to hill,
Till the proud peak unfurled the flag o'er Darwin's rocky
    dales,
Till, like volcanoes, flared to heaven the stormy hills of Wales;
Till twelve fair counties saw the blaze on Malvern's lonely
    height;
Till streamed in crimson on the wind the Wrekin's crest of
    light;
Till, broad and fierce, the star came forth on Ely's stately fane,
And tower and hamlet rose in arms o'er all the boundless
    plain;
Till Belvoir's lordly terraces the sign to Lincoln sent,
And Lincoln sped the message on o'er the wide vale of Trent;
Till Skiddaw saw the fire that burned on Gaunt's embattled
    pile,
And the red glare on Skiddaw roused the burghers of Carlisle.

                Friendship's Offering, 1833;
                Lays of Ancient Rome, 1848

354   *Sermon in a Churchyard*

LET pious Damon take his seat,
    With mincing step and languid smile,
And scatter from his 'kerchief sweet,
    Sabæan odours o'er the aisle;
And spread his little jewelled hand,
    And smile round all the parish beauties,
And pat his curls, and smooth his band,
    Meet prelude to his saintly duties.

SERMON IN A CHURCHYARD

Let the thronged audience press and stare,
  Let stifled maidens ply the fan,
Admire his doctrines, and his hair,
  And whisper, ' What a good young man! '
While he explains what seems most clear,
  So clearly that it seems perplexed;
I'll stay and read my sermon here;
  And skulls, and bones, shall be the text.

Art thou the jilted dupe of fame?
  Dost thou with jealous anger pine
When'er she sounds some other name,
  With fonder emphasis than thine?
To thee I preach; draw near; attend!
  Look on these bones, thou fool, and see
Where all her scorns and favours end,
  What Byron is, and thou must be.

Dost thou revere, or praise, or trust
  Some clod like those that here we spurn;
Some thing that sprang like thee from dust,
  And shall like thee to dust return?
Dost thou rate statesmen, heroes, wits,
  At one sear leaf, or wandering feather?
Behold the black, damp, narrow pits,
  Where they and thou must lie together.

Dost thou beneath the smile or frown
  Of some vain woman bend thy knee?
Here take thy stand, and trample down
  Things that were once as fair as she.
Here rave of her ten thousand graces,
  Bosom, and lip, and eye, and chin,

While, as in scorn, the fleshless faces
    Of Hamiltons and Waldegraves grin.

Whate'er thy losses or thy gains,
    Whate'er thy projects or thy fears,
Whate'er the joys, whate'er the pains
    That prompt thy baby smiles and tears;
Come to my school and thou shalt learn,
    In one short hour of placid thought,
A stoicism, more deep, more stern,
    Than ever Zeno's porch hath taught.

The plots and feats of those that press
    To seize on titles, wealth, or power,
Shall seem to thee a game of chess,
    Devised to pass a tedious hour.
What matters it to him who fights
    For shows of unsubstantial good,
Whether his Kings and Queens and Knights
    Be things of flesh, or things of wood?

We check, and take; exult, and fret;
    Our plans extend, our passions rise,
Till in our ardour we forget
    How worthless is the victor's prize.
Soon fades the spell, soon comes the night:
    Say will it not be then the same,
Whether we played the white or black,
    Whether we lost or won the game?

Dost thou among these hillocks stray,
    O'er some dear idol's tomb to moan?
Know that thy foot is on the clay
    Of hearts once wretched as thy own.

SERMON IN A CHURCHYARD

How many a father's anxious scheme,
  How many rapturous thoughts of lovers,
How many a mother's cherished dreams,
  The swelling turf before thee covers!

Here for the living, and the dead,
  The weepers and the friends they weep,
Hath been ordained the same cold bed,
  The same dark night, the same long sleep;
Why shouldest thou writhe, and sob, and rave
  O'er those with whom thou soon must be?
Death his own sting shall cure—the grave
  Shall vanquish its own victory.

Here learn that all the griefs and joys,
  Which now torment, which now beguile,
Are children's hurts, and children's toys,
  Scarce worthy of one bitter smile.
Here learn that pulpit, throne and press,
  Sword, sceptre, lyre, alike are frail;
That science is a blind man's guess,
  And History a nurse's tale.

Here learn that glory and disgrace,
  Wisdom and folly, pass away,
That mirth hath its appointed space,
  That sorrow is but for a day;
That all we love, and all we hate,
  That all we hope, and all we fear,
Each mood of mind, each turn of fate
  Must end in dust and silence here.

Written 1825;
Miscellaneous Writings, vol. ii, 1860

355 *The Battle of Naseby,*

by Obadiah Bind-their-kings-in-chains-and-their-
nobles-with-links-of-iron, Serjeant in Ireton's Regiment.

OH! wherefore come ye forth, in triumph from the North,
With your hands, and your feet, and your raiment all
red?
And wherefore doth your rout send forth a joyous shout?
And whence be the grapes of the wine-press which ye
tread?

Oh evil was the root, and bitter was the fruit,
And crimson was the juice of the vintage that we trod;
For we trampled on the throng of the haughty and the strong,
Who sate in the high places and slew the saints of God.

It was about the noon of a glorious day of June
That we saw their banners dance and their cuirasses shine,
And the Man of Blood was there, with his long essenced hair,
And Astley, and Sir Marmaduke, and Rupert of the Rhine.

Like a servant of the Lord, with his Bible and his sword,
The General rode along us to form us for the fight,
When a murmuring sound broke out, and swell'd into a shout,
Among the godless horsemen upon the tyrant's right.

And hark! like the roar of the billows on the shore,
The cry of battle rises along their charging line!
For God! for the Cause! for the Church! for the Laws!
For Charles King of England, and Rupert of the Rhine!

The furious German comes, with his clarions and his drums,
His bravoes of Alsatia and pages of Whitehall;
They are bursting on our flanks. Grasp your pikes:—close
your ranks:—
For Rupert never comes but to conquer or to fall.

770

THE BATTLE OF NASEBY

They are here:—they rush on.—We are broken:—we are
    gone:—
  Our left is borne before them like stubble on the blast.
O Lord, put forth thy might! O Lord, defend the right!
  Stand back to back, in God's name, and fight it to the last.

Stout Skippon hath a wound:—the centre hath given
    ground:—
  Hark! hark!—What means the trampling of horsemen
    on our rear?
Whose banner do I see, boys? 'Tis he, thank God, 'tis he,
    boys.
  Bear up another minute. Brave Oliver is here.

Their heads all stooping low, their points all in a row,
  Like a whirlwind on the trees, like a deluge on the dykes,
Our cuirassiers have burst on the ranks of the Accurst,
  And at a shock have scattered the forest of his pikes.

Fast, fast, the gallants ride, in some safe nook to hide
  Their coward heads, predestined to rot on Temple-Bar,
And he—he turns, he flies,—shame on those cruel eyes
  That bore to look on torture, and dare not look on war.

Ho! comrades, scour the plain: and, ere ye strip the slain,
  First give another stab to make your quest secure,
Then shake from sleeves and pockets their broad-pieces and
    lockets,
  The tokens of the wanton, the plunder of the poor.

Fools, your doublets shone with gold, and your hearts were
    gay and bold,
  When you kissed your lily hands to your lemans to-day;
And to-morrow shall the fox, from her chambers in the rocks,
  Lead forth her tawny cubs to howl above the prey.

Where be your tongues that late mocked at heaven and hell
    and fate,
    And the fingers that once were so busy with your blades,
Your perfum'd satin clothes, your catches and your oaths,
    Your stage-plays and your sonnets, your diamonds and
    your spades?

Down, down, for ever down with the mitre and the crown,
    With the Belial of the court, and the Mammon of the Pope;
There is woe in Oxford Halls: there is wail in Durham's
    Stalls:
    The Jesuit smites his bosom: the Bishop rends his cope.

And She of the seven hills shall mourn her children's ills,
    And tremble when she thinks on the edge of England's
    sword;
And the Kings of earth in fear, shall shudder when they hear
    What the hand of God hath wrought for the Houses and
    the Word.

Knight's Quarterly Magazine, April 1824

SIR HENRY TAYLOR
1800–1886

356   *Elena's Song*

QUOTH tongue of neither maid nor wife
    To heart of neither wife nor maid,
Lead we not here a jolly life
    Betwixt the shine and shade?

Quoth heart of neither maid nor wife
    To tongue of neither wife nor maid,
Thou wag'st but I am worn with strife,
    And feel like flowers that fade.

Philip van Artevelde, Part II, 1834

JANE BAILLIE WELSH CARLYLE

1801–1866

357 *To a Swallow building under our Eaves*

THOU too hast travelled, little fluttering thing—
Hast seen the world, and now thy weary wing
    Thou too must rest.
But much, my little bird, couldst thou but tell,
I'd give to know why here thou lik'st so well
    To build thy nest.

For thou hast passed fair places in thy flight;
A world lay all beneath thee where to light;
    And, strange thy taste,
Of all the varied scenes that met thine eye—
Of all the spots for building 'neath the sky—
    To choose this waste.

Did fortune try thee? was thy little purse
Perchance run low, and thou, afraid of worse,
    Felt here secure?
Ah, no! thou need'st not gold, thou happy one!
Thou know'st it not. Of all God's creatures, man
    Alone is poor!

What was it, then? some mystic turn of thought,
Caught under German eaves, and hither brought,
    Marring thine eye
For the world's loveliness, till thou art grown
A sober thing that dost but mope and moan
    Not knowing why?

Nay, if thy mind be sound, I need not ask,
Since here I see thee working at thy task
    With wing and beak.

JANE BAILLIE WELSH CARLYLE

A well-laid scheme doth that small head contain,
At which thou work'st, brave bird, with might and main,
      Nor more need'st seek.

In truth, I rather take it thou hast got
By instinct wise much sense about thy lot,
      And hast small care
Whether an Eden or a desert be
Thy home so thou remain'st alive and free
      To skim the air.

God speed thee, pretty bird; may thy small nest
With little ones all in good time be blest.
      I love thee much;
For well thou managest that life of thine,
While I! Oh, ask not what I do with mine!
      Would I were such!

Written *c*. 1832. From Froude's *Thomas Carlyle:
First Forty Years*, 1882

WILLIAM BARNES

1801–1886

358   *Liady-Day an' Ridden House*

E ES, twer at Liady-Day, ya know,
  I come vrom Gullybrook to Stowe.
At Liady-Day I took my pack
O' rottletraps, an' turn'd my back
Upon the wold thick woaken door
That had inzide ō'n long avore
The muost that, thieze zide o' the griave,
I'd live to have, or die to siave;
My children an' my vier-pliace,
An' Molly wi' her cheerful fiace.

      Ridden] moving.

LIADY-DAY AN' RIDDEN HOUSE

An' ridden house is sich a caddle,
That I shont want to have noo muore ō't
Not eet a bit, ya mid be sure ō't,—
I'd rather kip upon oone staddle.

Well zoo, ya know, in marnen we
Got up so riathe as we could zee,
An' borried uncle's wold hoss *Dragon*,
To bring the wold ramshackle-waggon
An' luoad: an' vust begun a-packèn
The bedsteads, an the ruopes an' zackèn;
An' then put up the girt yarm-chair,
An' cuoffer vull ov ethen-ware,
An vier-dogs, an' copper kettle;
Wi pots an sasspans big an little;
An' other *th*ings bezide; an' then
Al' up o' top o' tha' agen,
The long woak table buoard to eat
Our tiaties an' our bit o' meat.—
Var he ther wou'den be noo doèn
'ithout at al—an' then we tied
Upon the riaves along the zide
The long woak stools belongen too en;
An' put betwix his lags turn'd up'ard
The zalt box an' the carner cup-b'ard.
An' then we laid the wold clock kiase
Al' dumb a*th*irt upon his fiace,
Var al' the works, I needen tell ye,
Wer took out ov his head an' belly.
An' then we put upon the pack
The settle, flat upon his back;

staddle] a wooden framework on which a rick is built.
riathe] early.   riaves] sloping side-ledges.

775

An' a'ter he, a-tied in pairs,
Oon in another, al' the chairs;
An' beds an' other *th*ings bezide;
An' at the very top, a-tied,
The children's little stools did lie,
Wi' lags a-turn'd tȯwards the sky.
An' zoo we luoded up our scroff,
An' tied it vast, an' started off.
An',—as the waggon diden car al'
We had to car—the buttel-barrel
An' cheese-press, wi' a pâil an' viat
Or two, an' cistern var to get
The milk in, an' a view *th*ings muore,
Wer al' a-carr'd the day avore.

And when we *th*ought the *th*ings wer out,
An' went in var to look about
In holes an' carners, var to vind
What odd oones wer aleft behind,
The holler wind did whissle round
About the empty rooms, an' sound
So dismal, that I zaid to Molly
Did miake I veel quite melancholy.
Var when a man da liave the heth
Wher vust his children drā'd ther breath,
Ar where thā grow'd, an' had ther fun,
An' *th*ings wer oonce a-zaid an' done
That he da mind, da touch his heart
A little bit, I'll ānswer var't;
Zoo ridden house is sich a caddle,
That I wou'd rather kip my staddle.

Dorset County Chronicle, 1833

scroff] broken faggots, firewood.   viat] cheese vat.

776

JOHN HENRY NEWMAN

1801–1890

359   *Light in the Darkness*

LEAD, kindly Light, amid the encircling gloom,
      Lead Thou me on!
The night is dark, and I am far from home—
      Lead Thou me on!
Keep Thou my feet; I do not ask to see
The distant scene,—one step enough for me.

I was not ever thus, nor prayed that Thou
      Shouldst lead me on.
I loved to choose and see my path; but now,
      Lead Thou me on!
I loved the garish day, and, spite of fears,
Pride ruled my will; remember not past years.

So long Thy power hath blest me, sure it still
      Will lead me on,
O'er moor and fen, o'er crag and torrent, till
      The night is gone;
And with the morn those Angel faces smile
Which I have loved long since, and lost awhile.

Lyra Apostolica, 1836

360   *Rest*

THEY are at rest:
    We may not stir the heaven of their repose
By rude invoking voice, or prayer addrest
      In waywardness to those,
Who in the mountain grots of Eden lie,
And hear the fourfold river as it murmurs by.

77

They hear it sweep
In distance down the dark and savage vale;
But they at rocky bed, or current deep,
        Shall never more grow pale;
They hear, and meekly muse, as fain to know
How long untired, unspent, that giant stream shall flow.

        And soothing sounds
Blend with the neighbouring waters as they glide,
Posted along the haunted garden's bounds,
        Angelic forms abide,—
Echoing, as words of watch, o'er lawn and grove
The verses of that hymn which Seraphs chant above.

Lyra Apostolica, 1836

361   *The Discovery*

I SAW thee once, and nought discerned
    For stranger to admire;
A serious aspect, but it burned
    With no unearthly fire.

Again I saw, and I confessed
    Thy speech was rare and high;
And yet it vexed my burdened breast,
    And scared, I knew not why.

I saw once more, and awe-struck gazed
    On face, and form, and air;
God's living glory round thee blazed—
    A Saint—a Saint was there!

Lyra Apostolica, 1836

362

The Zeal of Jehu

*T*HOU to wax fierce
   In the cause of the LORD,
To threat and to pierce
   With the heavenly sword;
Anger and Zeal,
   And the Joy of the brave,
Who bade *thee* to feel,
   Sin's slave.

The Altar's pure flame
   Consumes as it soars;
Faith meetly may blame,
   For it serves and adores.
Thou warnest and smitest!
   Yet CHRIST must atone
For a soul that thou slightest—
   Thine own.

Lyra Apostolica, 1836

363

The Elements

*M*AN is permitted much
   To scan and learn
In Nature's frame;
Till he well-nigh can tame
Brute mischiefs, and can touch
Invisible things, and turn
All warring ills to purposes of good.
Thus as a God below,
   He can control

And harmonise what seems amiss to flow,
   As severed from the whole
   And dimly understood.

But o'er the elements
   One Hand alone,
   One Hand has sway.
What influence day by day
In straiter belt prevents
The impious Ocean, thrown
Alternate o'er the ever-sounding shore?
   Or who has eye to trace
   How the Plague came?
Forerun the doublings of the Tempest's race?
   Or the Air's weight and flame
   On a set scale explore?

Thus GOD has willed
That man, when fully skilled,
   Still gropes in twilight dim;
   Encompassed all his hours
     By fearfullest powers
     Inflexible to him;
   That so he may discern
     His feebleness,
   And e'en for earth's success
   To HIM in wisdom turn,
Who holds for us the Keys of either home,
   Earth and the world to come.

               Lyra Apostolica, 1836

364 *A Letter of Advice*

From Miss Medora Trevilian, at Padua, to Miss Araminta
Vavasour, in London.

> Enfin, monsieur, un homme aimable;
> Voilà pourquoi je ne saurais l'aimer.—SCRIBE.

YOU tell me you're promised a lover,
  My own Araminta, next week;
Why cannot my fancy discover
  The hue of his coat and his cheek?
Alas! if he look like another,
  A vicar, a banker, a beau,
Be deaf to your father and mother,
  My own Araminta, say 'No!'

Miss Lane, at her Temple of Fashion,
  Taught us both how to sing and to speak,
And we loved one another with passion,
  Before we had been there a week:
You gave me a ring for a token;
  I wear it wherever I go;
I gave you a chain,—is it broken?
  My own Araminta, say 'No!'

O think of our favourite cottage,
  And think of our dear Lalla Rookh!
How we shared with the milkmaids their pottage,
  And drank of the stream from the brook;
How fondly our loving lips faltered
  'What further can grandeur bestow?'
My heart is the same;—is yours altered?
  My own Araminta, say 'No!'

Remember the thrilling romances
   We read on the bank in the glen;
Remember the suitors our fancies
   Would picture for both of us then.
They wore the red cross on their shoulder,
   They had vanquished and pardoned their foe—
Sweet friend, are you wiser or colder?
   My own Araminta, say ' No! '

You know, when Lord Rigmarole's carriage
   Drove off with your cousin Justine,
You wept, dearest girl, at the marriage,
   And whispered ' How base she has been ! '
You said you were sure it would kill you,
   If ever your husband looked so;
And you will not apostatize,—will you?
   My own Araminta, say ' No! '

When I heard I was going abroad, love,
   I thought I was going to die;
We walked arm in arm to the road, love,
   We looked arm in arm to the sky;
And I said ' When a foreign postilion
   Has hurried me off to the Po,
Forget not Medora Trevilian:
   My own Araminta, say " No! " '

We parted! but sympathy's fetters
   Reach far over valley and hill;
I muse o'er your exquisite letters,
   And feel that your heart is mine still;
And he who would share it with me, love,—
   The richest of treasures below,—

A LETTER OF ADVICE

If he 's not what Orlando should be, love,
  My own Araminta, say ' No! '

If he wears a top-boot in his wooing,
  If he comes to you riding a cob,
If he talks of his baking or brewing,
  If he puts up his feet on the hob,
If he ever drinks port after dinner,
  If his brow or his breeding is low,
If he calls himself ' Thompson ' or ' Skinner ',
  My own Araminta, say ' No! '

If he studies the news in the papers
  While you are preparing the tea,
If he talks of the damps or the vapours
  While moonlight lies soft on the sea,
If he 's sleepy while you are capricious,
  If he has not a musical ' Oh! '
If he does not call Werther delicious,—
  My own Araminta, say ' No! '

If he ever sets foot in the City
  Among the stockbrokers and Jews,
If he has not a heart full of pity,
  If he don't stand six feet in his shoes,
If his lips are not redder than roses,
  If his hands are not whiter than snow,
If he has not the model of noses,—
  My own Araminta, say ' No! '

If he speaks of a tax or a duty,
  If he does not look grand on his knees,
If he 's blind to a landscape of beauty,
  Hills, valleys, rocks, waters, and trees,

If he dotes not on desolate towers,
    If he likes not to hear the blast blow,
If he knows not the language of flowers,—
    My own Araminta, say ' No! '

He must walk—like a god of old story
    Come down from the home of his rest;
He must smile—like the sun in his glory
    On the buds he loves ever the best;
And oh! from its ivory portal
    Like music his soft speech must flow!—
If he speak, smile, or walk like a mortal,
    My own Araminta, say ' No! '

Don't listen to tales of his bounty,
    Don't hear what they say of his birth,
Don't look at his seat in the county,
    Don't calculate what he is worth;
But give him a theme to write verse on,
    And see if he turns out his toe;
If he 's only an excellent person,—
    My own Araminta, say ' No! '

                    New Monthly Magazine, December 1828

365   *The Vicar*

SOME years ago, ere time and taste
    Had turned our parish topsy-turvy,
When Darnel Park was Darnel Waste,
    And roads as little known as scurvy,
The man who lost his way, between
    St. Mary's Hill and Sandy Thicket,
Was always shown across the green,
    And guided to the Parson's wicket.

THE VICAR

Back flew the bolt of lissom lath;
 Fair Margaret, in her tidy kirtle,
Led the lorn traveller up the path,
 Through clean-clipt rows of box and myrtle;
And Don and Sancho, Tramp and Tray,
 Upon the parlour steps collected,
Wagged all their tails, and seemed to say—
 ' Our master knows you—you're expected.'

Uprose the Reverend Dr. Brown,
 Uprose the Doctor's winsome marrow;
The lady laid her knitting down,
 Her husband clasped his ponderous Barrow;
Whate'er the stranger's caste or creed,
 Pundit or Papist, saint or sinner,
He found a stable for his steed,
 And welcome for himself, and dinner.

If, when he reached his journey's end,
 And warmed himself in Court or College,
He had not gained an honest friend
 And twenty curious scraps of knowledge,—
If he departed as he came,
 With no new light on love or liquor,—
Good sooth, the traveller was to blame,
 And not the Vicarage, nor the Vicar.

His talk was like a stream, which runs
 With rapid change from rocks to roses:
It slipped from politics to puns,
 It passed from Mahomet to Moses;
Beginning with the laws which keep
 The planets in their radiant courses,

And ending with some precept deep
    For dressing eels, or shoeing horses.

He was a shrewd and sound Divine,
    Of loud Dissent the mortal terror;
And when, by dint of page and line,
    He 'stablished Truth, or startled Error,
The Baptist found him far too deep;
    The Deist sighed with saving sorrow;
And the lean Levite went to sleep,
    And dreamed of tasting pork to-morrow.

His sermon never said or showed
    That Earth is foul, that Heaven is gracious,
Without refreshment on the road
    From Jerome, or from Athanasius:
And sure a righteous zeal inspired
    The hand and head that penned and planned them,
For all who understood admired,
    And some who did not understand them.

He wrote, too, in a quiet way,
    Small treatises, and smaller verses,
And sage remarks on chalk and clay,
    And hints to noble Lords—and nurses;
True histories of last year's ghost,
    Lines to a ringlet, or a turban,
And trifles for the Morning Post,
    And nothings for Sylvanus Urban.

He did not think all mischief fair,
    Although he had a knack of joking;
He did not make himself a bear,
    Although he had a taste for smoking;

THE VICAR

And when religious sects ran mad,
   He held, in spite of all his learning,
That if a man's belief is bad,
   It will not be improved by burning.

And he was kind, and loved to sit
   In the low hut or garnished cottage,
And praise the farmer's homely wit,
   And share the widow's homelier pottage:
At his approach complaint grew mild;
   And when his hand unbarred the shutter,
The clammy lips of fever smiled
   The welcome which they could not utter.

He always had a tale for me
   Of Julius Caesar, or of Venus;
From him I learnt the rule of three,
   Cat's cradle, leap-frog, and *Quae genus*:
I used to singe his powdered wig,
   To steal the staff he put such trust in,
And make the puppy dance a jig,
   When he began to quote Augustine.

Alack the change! in vain I look
   For haunts in which my boyhood trifled,—
The level lawn, the trickling brook,
   The trees I climbed, the beds I rifled:
The church is larger than before;
   You reach it by a carriage entry;
It holds three hundred people more,
   And pews are fitted up for gentry.

Sit in the Vicar's seat: you'll hear
   The doctrine of a gentle Johnian,

Whose hand is white, whose tone is clear,
    Whose phrase is very Ciceronian.
Where is the old man laid?—look down,
    And construe on the slab before you,
' *Hic jacet GVLIELMVS BROWN,*
    Vir nulla non donandus lauru.'

                    New Monthly Magazine, March 1829

366   *School and Schoolfellows*

                    Floreat Etona.

TWELVE years ago I made a mock
    Of filthy trades and traffics:
I wondered what they meant by stock;
    I wrote delightful sapphics;
I knew the streets of Rome and Troy,
    I supped with Fates and Furies,—
Twelve years ago I was a boy,
    A happy boy, at Drury's.

Twelve years ago!—how many a thought
    Of faded pains and pleasures
Those whispered syllables have brought
    From Memory's hoarded treasures!
The fields, the farms, the bats, the books,
    The glories and disgraces,
The voices of dear friends, the looks
    Of old familiar faces!

Kind Mater smiles again to me,
    As bright as when we parted;
I seem again the frank, the free,
    Stout-limbed, and simple-hearted!

SCHOOL AND SCHOOLFELLOWS

Pursuing every idle dream,
    And shunning every warning;
With no hard work but Bovney stream,
    No chill except Long Morning:

Now stopping Harry Vernon's ball
    That rattled like a rocket;
Now hearing Wentworth's ' Fourteen all! '
    And striking for the pocket;
Now feasting on a cheese and flitch,—
    Now drinking from the pewter;
Now leaping over Chalvey ditch,
    Now laughing at my tutor.

Where are my friends? I am alone;
    No playmate shares my beaker:
Some lie beneath the churchyard stone,
    And some—before the Speaker;
And some compose a tragedy,
    And some compose a rondo;
And some draw sword for Liberty,
    And some draw pleas for John Doe.

Tom Mill was used to blacken eyes
    Without the fear of sessions;
Charles Medlar loathed false quantities,
    As much as false professions;
Now Mill keeps order in the land,
    A magistrate pedantic;
And Medlar's feet repose unscanned
    Beneath the wide Atlantic.

Wild Nick, whose oaths made such a din,
    Does Dr. Martext's duty;

And Mullion, with that monstrous chin,
 Is married to a Beauty;
And Darrell studies, week by week,
 His Mant, and not his Manton;
And Ball, who was but poor at Greek,
 Is very rich at Canton.

And I am eight-and-twenty now;—
 The world's cold chains have bound me;
And darker shades are on my brow,
 And sadder scenes around me:
In Parliament I fill my seat,
 With many other noodles;
And lay my head in Jermyn Street,
 And sip my hock at Boodle's.

But often, when the cares of life
 Have set my temples aching,
When visions haunt me of a wife,
 When duns await my waking,
When Lady Jane is in a pet,
 Or Hoby in a hurry,
When Captain Hazard wins a bet,
 Or Beaulieu spoils a curry,—

For hours and hours I think and talk
 Of each remembered hobby;
I long to lounge in Poets' Walk,
 To shiver in the lobby;
I wish that I could run away
 From House, and Court, and Levee,
Where bearded men appear to-day
 Just Eton boys grown heavy,—

That I could bask in childhood's sun
    And dance o'er childhood's roses,
And find huge wealth in one pound one,
    Vast wit in broken noses,
And play Sir Giles at Datchet Lane,
    And call the milk-maids Houris,—
That I could be a boy again,—
    A happy boy,—at Drury's.

Written 1829;
Poetical Works, New York, 1844

367 *The Covenanter's Lament for Bothwell Brigg*

THE men of sin prevail!
Once more the prince of this world lifts his horn;
Judah is scattered, as the chaff is borne
    Before the stormy gale.

Where are our brethren? where
The good and true, the terrible and fleet?
They whom we loved, with whom we sat at meat,
    With whom we kneeled in prayer?

Mangled and marred they lie
Upon the bloody pillow of their rest;
Stern Dalzell smiles, and Clavers with a jest
    Spurs his fierce charger by.

So let our foes rejoice;
We to the Lord, who hears their impious boasts,
Will call for comfort; to the God of hosts
    We will lift up our voice.

WINTHROP MACKWORTH PRAED

Give ear unto our song;
For we are wandering o'er our native land
As sheep that have no shepherd; and the hand
Of wicked men is strong.

Only to thee we bow:
Our lips have drained the fury of thy cup;
And the deep murmurs of our hearts go up
To Heaven for vengeance now.

Avenge,—oh! not our years
Of pain and wrong, the blood of martyrs shed,
The ashes heaped upon the hoary head,
The maiden's silent tears,

The babe's bread torn away,
The harvest blasted by the war steed's hoof,
The red flame wreathing o'er the cottage roof,
Judge not for these to-day!—

Is not thine own dread rod
Mocked by the proud, thy holy book disdained,
Thy name blasphemed, thy temple courts profaned?—
Avenge thyself, O God!

Break Pharaoh's iron crown;
Bind with new chains their nobles and their kings;
Wash from thine house the blood of unclean things,
And hurl their Dagon down!

Come in thine own good time!
We will abide; we have not turned from thee,
Though in a world of grief our portion be,
Of bitter grief, and crime.

Be thou our guard and guide!
Forth from the spoiler's synagogue we go,
That we may worship where the torrents flow
    And where the whirlwinds ride.

From lonely rocks and caves
We will pour forth our sacrifice of prayer.—
On, brethren, to the mountains! Seek we there
    Safe temples, quiet graves!

Written 1830; *Poetical Works,* 1864

368   *One More Quadrille*

NOT yet, not yet; it 's hardly four;
    Not yet; we'll send the chair away;
Mirth still has many smiles in store,
    And love has fifty things to say.
Long leagues the weary Sun must drive,
    Ere pant his hot steeds o'er the hill;
The merry stars will dance till five;
    One more quadrille,—one more quadrille!

'Tis only thus, 'tis only here
    That maids and minstrels may forget
The myriad ills they feel or fear,
    Ennui, taxation, cholera, debt;
With daylight busy cares and schemes
    Will come again to chafe or chill;
This is the fairy land of dreams;
    One more quadrille,—one more quadrille!

What tricks the French in Paris play,
    And what the Austrians are about,
And whether that tall knave, Lord Grey,
    Is staying in, or going out;

WINTHROP MACKWORTH PRAED

And what the House of Lords will do,
   At last, with that eternal Bill,
I do not care a rush,—do you?
   One more quadrille,—one more quadrille!

My book don't sell, my play don't draw,
   My garden gives me only weeds;
And Mr. Quirk has found a flaw—
   Deuce take him—in my title-deeds;
My Aunt has scratched her nephew's name
   From that sweet corner in her will;
My dog is dead, my horse is lame;
   One more quadrille,—one more quadrille!

Not yet, not yet; it is not late;
   Don't whisper it to sister Jane;
Your brother, I am sure, will wait;
   Papa will go to cards again.
Not yet, not yet. Your eyes are bright,
   Your step is like a wood-nymph's, still.
Oh no, you can't be tired, to-night!
   One more quadrille,—one more quadrille!

            Written, 1832; *Select Poems*, 1909

SARA COLERIDGE

                     1802–1852

369   ' *O sleep, my babe* '

O SLEEP, my babe, hear not the rippling wave,
   Nor feel the breeze that round thee lingering strays,
To drink thy balmy breath,
And sigh one long farewell.

794

'O SLEEP, MY BABE'

Soon shall it mourn above thy wat'ry bed,
And whisper to me on the wave-beat shore,
    Deep murm'ring in reproach,
    Thy sad untimely fate.

Ere those dear eyes had open'd on the light,
In vain to plead, thy coming life was sold,
    O! wakened but to sleep,
    Whence it can wake no more!

A thousand and a thousand silken leaves
The tufted beech unfolds in early spring,
    All clad in tenderest green,
    All of the self-same shape:

A thousand infant faces, soft and sweet,
Each year sends forth, yet every mother views
    Her last not least beloved
    Like its dear self alone.

No musing mind hath ever yet foreshaped
The face to-morrow's sun shall first reveal,
    No heart hath e'er conceived
    What love that face will bring.

O sleep, my babe, nor heed how mourns the gale
To part with thy soft locks and fragrant breath,
    As when it deeply sighs
    O'er autumn's latest bloom.

Phantasmion, 1837

370 *'He came unlook'd for'*

HE came unlook'd for, undesir'd,
   A sun-rise in the northern sky:
More than the brightest dawn admir'd,
Tc shine and then for ever fly.

His love, conferr'd without a claim,
Perchance was like the fitful blaze,
Which lives to light a steadier flame,
And, while that strengthens, fast decays.

Glad fawn along the forest springing,
Gay birds that breeze-like stir the leaves,
Why hither haste, no message bringing,
To solace one that deeply grieves?

Thou star that dost the skies adorn
So brightly heralding the day,
Bring one more welcome than the morn,
Or still in night's dark prison stay.

Phantasmion, 1837

371 *'I was a brook'*

I WAS a brook in straitest channel sent,
   Forcing 'mid rocks and stones my toilsome way,
A scanty brook in wandering well-nigh spent;
But now with thee, rich stream, conjoin'd I stray,
Through golden meads the river sweeps along,
Murmuring its deep full joy in gentlest undersong.

'I WAS A BROOK'

I crept through desert moor and gloomy glade,
My waters ever vex'd, yet sad and slow,
My waters ever steep'd in baleful shade:
But, whilst with thee, rich stream, conjoined I flow,
E'en in swift course the river seems to rest,
Blue sky, bright bloom, and verdure imag'd on its breast.

And, whilst with thee I roam through regions bright
Beneath kind love's serene and gladsome sky,
A thousand happy things that seek the light,
Till now in darkest shadow forc'd to lie,
Up through the illumin'd waters nimbly run,
To show their forms and hues in the all revealing sun.

Phantasmion, 1837

RICHARD HURRELL FROUDE

1803–1836

372   *Weakness of Nature*

LORD, I have fasted, I have prayed,
    And sackcloth has my girdle been,
To purge my soul I have essayed
    With hunger blank and vigil keen;
O GOD of Mercy! why am I
Still haunted by the self I fly?'

Sackcloth is a girdle good,
    O bind it round thee still:
Fasting, it is Angel's food,
    And JESUS loved the night-air chill;
Yet think not prayer and fast were given
To make one step 'twixt earth and Heaven.

Lyra Apostolica, 1836

THOMAS LOVELL BEDDOES

1803–1849

373 *From 'Death's Jest-Book; or The Fool's Tragedy'*

(i)

Song from the ship

TO sea, to sea! The calm is o'er;
  The wanton water leaps in sport,
And rattles down the pebbly shore;
  The dolphin wheels, the sea-cows snort,
And unseen Mermaids' pearly song
Comes bubbling up, the weeds among.
  Fling broad the sail, dip deep the oar:
  To sea, to sea! the calm is o'er.

To sea, to sea! our wide-winged bark
  Shall billowy cleave its sunny way,
And with its shadow, fleet and dark,
  Break the caved Tritons' azure day,
Like mighty eagle soaring light
O'er antelopes on Alpine height.
  The anchor heaves, the ship swings free,
  The sails swell full. To sea, to sea!

Act I

(ii)

A voice from the waters

THE swallow leaves her nest,
  The soul my weary breast;
But therefore let the rain
  On my grave

Fall pure; for why complain?
Since both will come again
   O'er the wave.

The wind dead leaves and snow
Doth hurry to and fro;
And, once, a day shall break
   O'er the wave,
When a storm of ghosts shall shake
The dead, until they wake
   In the grave.

Act I

(iii)

Dirge

IF thou wilt ease thine heart
  Of love and all its smart,
    Then sleep, dear, sleep;
And not a sorrow
   Hang any tear on your eyelashes;
    Lie still and deep,
   Sad soul, until the sea-wave washes
The rim o' the sun to-morrow,
    In eastern sky.

But wilt thou cure thine heart
Of love and all its smart,
    Then die, dear, die;
'Tis deeper, sweeter,
   Than on a rose bank to lie dreaming

799

With folded eye;
And then alone, amid the beaming
Of love's stars, thou'lt meet her
In eastern sky.

Act II

(iv)

Song

OLD Adam, the carrion crow,
  The old crow of Cairo;
He sat in the shower, and let it flow
  Under his tail and over his crest;
    And through every feather
    Leaked the wet weather;
  And the bough swung under his nest;
  For his beak it was heavy with marrow.
    Is that the wind dying? O no;
    It's only two devils, that blow
    Through a murderer's bones, to and fro,
      In the ghosts' moonshine.

Ho! Eve, my grey carrion wife,
  When we have supped on kings' marrow,
Where shall we drink and make merry our life?
  Our nest it is queen Cleopatra's skull,
    'Tis cloven and cracked,
    And battered and hacked,
  But with tears of blue eyes it is full:
  Let us drink then, my raven of Cairo.

Is that the wind dying? O no;
It 's only two devils, that blow
Through a murderer's bones, to and fro,
  In the ghosts' moonshine..

Act V, Scene IV.
Death's Jest-Book, or The Fool's Tragedy,
written 1825–6; published 1850

374   *Song*

H OW many times do I love thee, dear?
    Tell me how many thoughts there be
      In the atmosphere
      Of a new-fall'n year,
Whose white and sable hours appear
    The latest flake of Eternity:
So many times do I love thee, dear.

How many times do I love again?
    Tell me how many beads there are
      In a silver chain
      Of evening rain,
Unravelled from the tumbling main,
    And threading the eye of a yellow star:
So many times do I love again.

Torrismond, written before 1825
Poems, posthumous and collected, 1851

375   *The Phantom-Wooer*

                    I

A GHOST, that loved a lady fair,
    Ever in the starry air
  Of midnight at her pillow stood;
And, with a sweetness skies above

801

The luring words of human love,
  Her soul the phantom wooed.
Sweet and sweet is their poisoned note,
The little snakes of silver throat,
In mossy skulls that nest and lie,
Ever singing ' die, oh! die '.

II

Young soul, put off your flesh, and come
With me into the quiet tomb,
  Our bed is lovely, dark, and sweet;
The earth will swing us, as she goes,
Beneath our coverlid of snows,
  And the warm leaden sheet.
Dear and dear is their poisoned note,
The little snakes of silver throat,
In mossy skulls that nest and lie,
Ever singing ' die, oh! die '.

Written before 1837
Poems, posthumous and collected, 1851

376   *The Reason Why*

I

I LOVE thee and I love thee not,
  I love thee, yet I'd rather not,
All of thee, yet I know not what.
    A flowery eye as tender,
    A swan-like neck as slender,
    And on it a brown little spot
      For tears to fall afraid on,
      And kisses to be paid on,

THE REASON WHY

Have other maidens too.
Then why love I, love, none but you?
If I could find the reason why,
Methinks my love would quickly die.

II

Aye, knew I how to hate thee, maid,
I'd hate thee for I knew not what,
Excepting that I'd rather not
    Be thy friend or foeman;
    For thou'rt the only woman,
      On whom to think my heart's afraid;
        For, if I would abhor thee,
        The more must I long for thee.
    What others force me to,
      I turn me from; why not from you?
If I could find the reason why,
Methinks my love would quickly die.

III

Yet should'st thou cease my heart to move
To longings, that I'd rather not,
And tried I hate, I know not what
    My heart would do for mourning;
    Love I—it bursts, love scorning.
    O loveliest hate, most hateful love,
      This combat and endeavour
      Is what enslaves me ever.
    I'll neither of the two,
      Or hate or love the love of you.
And now I've found the reason why,
I know my love can never die.

Written 1825–6
Poems, posthumous and collected, 1851

Dream-Pedlary

I

IF there were dreams to sell,
  What would you buy?
Some cost a passing bell;
  Some a light sigh,
That shakes from Life's fresh crown
Only a rose-leaf down.
If there were dreams to sell,
Merry and sad to tell,
And the crier rung the bell,
  What would you buy?

II

A cottage lone and still,
  With bowers nigh,
Shadowy, my woes to still,
  Until I die.
Such pearl from Life's fresh crown
Fain would I shake me down.
Were dreams to have at will,
This would best heal my ill,
  This would I buy.

III

But there were dreams to sell,
  Ill didst thou buy;
Life is a dream, they tell,
  Waking, to die.
Dreaming a dream to prize,
Is wishing ghosts to rise;

DREAM-PEDLARY

And, if I had the spell
    To call the buried well,
Which one would I?

IV

If there are ghosts to raise,
    What shall I call,
Out of hell's murky haze,
    Heaven's blue pall?
Raise my loved long-lost boy
To lead me to his joy.
    There are no ghosts to raise;
    Out of death lead no ways;
        Vain is the call.

V

Know'st thou not ghosts to sue?
    No love thou hast.
Else lie, as I will do,
    And breathe thy last.
So out of Life's fresh crown
Fall like a rose-leaf down.
    Thus are the ghosts to woo;
    Thus are all dreams made true,
        Ever to last!

Written before 1837
Poems, posthumous and collected, 1851

EDWARD MOXON

1801–1858

378 *The Nightingale*

LONE midnight-soothing melancholy bird,
    That send'st such music to my sleepless soul,
Chaining her faculties in fast controul,

Few listen to thy song; yet I have heard,
When Man and Nature slept, nor aspen stirred,
   Thy mournful voice, sweet vigil of the sleeping—
And liken'd thee to some angelic mind,
   That sits and mourns for erring mortals weeping.
The genius, not of groves, but of mankind,
   Watch at this solemn hour o'er millions keeping.
   In Eden's bowers, as mighty poets tell,
Did'st thou repeat, as now, that wailing call—
   Those sorrowing notes might seem, sad Philomel,
Prophetic to have mourned of *man* the *fall*.

Sonnets, 1830

379   *Moonlight*

HOW sweet the moon is climbing heaven's hill!
   The night seems just as if for gallants made;
   Her silver light gives courage, while the shade
In dim disguise the Lover hides. How still,
And yet how musical! Methinks I hear
   A voice in every tree, as tho' they lov'd;
   And at this hour towards each other mov'd:
So loving seems the night, so soft, and clear.
Groves, streams, dells, flowers, in solemn silence sleep;
   While from yon terrace, or high castled tower,
   A pale light glimmers, which bespeaks the bower
Where Love expectant breathless watch doth keep;
   Herself the star, eclipsing those above her,
   That shines, and to her chamber lights her Lover.

Sonnets, 1830

THE cygnet crested on the purple water;
   The fawn at play beside its graceful dam;
On cowslip bank, in spring, the artless lamb;
The hawthorn robed in white, May's fragrant daughter;
   The willow weeping o'er the silent stream;
The rich laburnum with its golden show;
   The fairy vision of a poet's dream;
On summer eve earth's many-coloured bow;
   Diana at her bath; Aurora bright;
The dove that sits and singeth o'er her woes;
   The star of eve; the lily, child of light;
Fair Venus' self, as from the sea she rose!
   Imagine these, and I in truth will prove
   They are not half so fair as she I love.

Sonnets, 1835

ROBERT STEPHEN HAWKER

1803–1875

381   *The Song of the Western Men*

A GOOD sword and a trusty hand!
   A merry heart and true!
King James's men shall understand
   What Cornish lads can do!

And have they fix'd the where and when?
   And shall Trelawny die?
Here's twenty thousand Cornish men
   Will see the reason why!

Out spake their captain brave and bold,
    A merry wight was he:
' If London Tower were Michael's hold,
    We'll set Trelawny free!

' We'll cross the Tamar, land to land,
    The Severn is no stay,—
All side by side, and hand to hand,
    And who shall bid us nay!

' And when we come to·London Wall,
    A pleasant sight to view,
Come forth! Come forth! ye Cowards all,
    To better men than you!

' Trelawny he 's in keep and hold,
    Trelawny he may die,
But here 's twenty thousand Cornish bold
    Will see the reason why! '

Royal Devonport Telegraph, 2 September 1826;
Records of the Western Shore, 1832

382   *Death Song*

THERE lies a cold corpse upon the sands
    Down by the rolling sea;
Close up the eyes and straighten the hands
    As a Christian man's should be.

Bury it deep, for the good of my soul,
    Six feet below the ground;
Let the sexton come and the death-bell toll
    And good men stand around.

Lay it among the church-yard stones,
   Where the priest hath blest the clay:
I cannot leave the unburied bones,
   And I fain would go my way.

Written 1835; first published 1869

383   *The Silent Tower of Bottreaux*

TINTADGEL bells ring o'er the tide!
   The boy leans on his vessel's side;
He hears that sound, and dreams of home
Soothe the wild orphan of the foam.
    ' Come to thy God in time!'
    Thus saith their pealing chime:
    ' Youth, manhood, old-age, past,
    Come to thy God at last.'

But why are Bottreaux' echoes still?
Her Tower stands proudly on the hill:—
Yet the strange chough that home hath found,
The lamb lies sleeping on the ground!
    ' Come to thy God in time!'
    Should be her answering chime—
    ' Come to thy God at last!'
    Should echo on the blast.

The ship rode down with courses free,
The daughter of a distant sea:
Her sheet was loose, her anchor stor'd—
The merry Bottreaux' bells on board.
    ' Come to thy God in time!'
    Rung out Tintadgel chime—
    ' Youth, manhood, old-age, past,
    Come to thy God at last!'

The Pilot heard his native bells
Hung on the breeze in fitful swells;
' Thank God! ' with reverent brow, he cried,
' We'll make the shore with Evening's tide! '
    ' Come to thy God in time! '
    It was his marriage chime;—
    ' Youth, manhood, old-age, past '—
    His bell must ring at last!

' Thank God, thou whining knave, on land!
' But thank, at sea, the steersman's hand;
' The captain's voice above the gale—
' Thank the good ship and ready sail! '
    ' Come to thy God in time! '
    Sad grew the boding chime;
    ' Come to thy God at last! '
    Boom'd heavy on the blast!

Up rose that sea! as if it heard
The mighty Master's signal word!
What thrills the Captain's whitening lip?
The Deathgroans of his sinking ship.
    ' Come to thy God in time! '
    Swung deep the funeral-chime—
    ' Grace, Mercy, Kindness, past,
    ' Come to thy God at last! '

Long did the rescued Pilot tell
When grey hairs o'er his forehead fell,
While those around would hear and weep,
That fearful judgment of the deep!
    ' Come to thy God in time! '
    He read his native chime;—

THE SILENT TOWER OF BOTTREAUX

    ' Youth, manhood, old-age, past,'
    His bell rung out at last!

Still, when the storm of Bottreaux' waves
Is waking in his weedy caves,
Those bells, that sullen surges hide,
Peal their deep tones beneath the tide!
    ' Come to thy God in time!'
    Thus saith the ocean-chime;—
    ' Storm, billow, whirlwind past,
    ' Come to thy God at last!'

              Records of the Western Shore, 1832

CHARLES WHITEHEAD
                             1804–1862

384   *A Summer Storm*

As when, of amorous night uncertain birth,
    The giant of still noontide, weary grown,
Crawls sultrily along the steaming earth,
    And basks him in the meadows sunbeam-strown,
    Anon, his brow collapses to a frown,
Unto his feet he springs, and bellows loud,
    With uncouth rage pulls the rude tempest down,
Shatters the woods, beneath his fury bow'd,
And hunts the frighted winds, and huddles cloud on cloud.

Nor rests, but by the heat to madness stung,
    With headlong speed tramples the golden grain,
And, at a bound, over the mountains flung,
    Grasps the reluctant thunder by the mane,
    And drags it back, girt with a sudden chain
Of thrice-brac'd lightning; now, more fiercely dire,
    Slipt from its holds, flies down the hissing rain;

CHARLES WHITEHEAD

The labouring welkin teems with leaping fire
That strikes the straining oak, and smites the glimmering spire.

And yet at length appeas'd he sinks, and spent,
   Gibbers far off over the misty hills,
And the stain'd sun, through a cloud's jagged rent,
   Goes down, and all the west with glory fills;
   A fresher bloom the odorous earth distils,
A richer green reviving nature spreads,
   The water-braided rainbow melting, spills
Her liquid light into the air, and sheds
Her lovely hues upon the flowers' dejected heads.

The Solitary, 1831

FRANCIS SYLVESTER MAHONY
1804–1866

385   *The Bells of Shandon*

WITH deep affection and recollection
   I often think of the Shandon bells,
Whose sounds so wild would, in the days of childhood,
   Fling round my cradle their magic spells—
On this I ponder, where'er I wander,
   And thus grow fonder, sweet Cork, of thee;
     With thy bells of Shandon,
     That sound so grand on
The pleasant waters of the river Lee.

I have heard bells chiming full many a clime in,
   Tolling sublime in cathedral shrine;
While at a glib rate brass tongues would vibrate,
   But all their music spoke nought like thine;

THE BELLS OF SHANDON

For memory dwelling on each proud swelling
  Of thy belfry knelling its bold notes free,
     Made the bells of Shandon
     Sound far more grand on
  The pleasant waters of the river Lee.

I have heard bells tolling ' old Adrian's mole ' in,
  Their thunder rolling from the Vatican,
And cymbals glorious, swinging uproarious
  In the gorgeous turrets of Notre Dame;
But thy sounds were sweeter than the dome of Peter
  Flings o'er the Tiber, pealing solemnly.
     Oh! the bells of Shandon
     Sound far more grand on
  The pleasant waters of the river Lee.

There 's a bell in Moscow, while on tower and kiosk o!
  In St. Sophia the Turkman gets,
And loud in air, calls men to prayer,
  From the tapering summit of tall minarets.
Such empty phantom I freely grant them,
  But there is an anthem more dear to me,—
     'Tis the bells of Shandon,
     That sound so grand on
  The pleasant waters of the river Lee.

Fraser's Magazine, August 1834;
The Reliques of Father Prout, 1836

1807–1867

386 *The Charming Woman*

SO Miss Myrtle is going to marry?
   What a number of hearts she will break!
There's Lord George, and Tom Brown, and Sir Harry,
   Who are dying of love for her sake!
'Tis a match that we all must approve,—
   Let gossips say all that they can!
For indeed she's a charming woman,
   And he's a most fortunate man!

Yes, indeed, she's a charming woman,
   And she reads both Latin and Greek,—
And I'm told that she solved a problem
   In Euclid before she could speak!
Had she been but a daughter of mine,
   I'd have taught her to hem and to sew,—
But her mother (a charming woman)
   Couldn't think of such trifles, you know!

Oh, she's really a charming woman!
   But, perhaps, a little too thin;
And no wonder such very late hours
   Should ruin her beautiful skin!
And her shoulders are rather too bare,
   And her gown's nearly up to her knees,
But I'm told that these charming women
   May dress themselves just as they please!

Yet, she's really a charming woman!
   But, I thought I observed, by the bye,
A something—that's rather uncommon,—
   In the flash of that very bright eye?

THE CHARMING WOMAN

It may be a mere fancy of mine,
 Tho' her voice has a very sharp tone,—
But I'm told that these charming women
 Are inclined to have wills of their own!

She sings like a bullfinch or linnet,
 And she talks like an Archbishop too;
Can play you a rubber and win it,—
 If she's got nothing better to do!
She can chatter of Poor-Laws and Tithes,
 And the value of labour and land,—
'Tis a pity when charming women
 Talk of things which they don't understand!

I'm told that she hasn't a penny,
 Yet her gowns would make Maradan stare;
And I feel her bills must be many,—
 But that's only her husband's affair!
Such husbands are very uncommon,
 So regardless of prudence and pelf,—
But they say such a charming woman
 Is a fortune, you know, in herself.

She's brothers and sisters by dozens,
 And all charming people, they say!
And several tall Irish cousins,
 Whom she loves in a sisterly way.
O young men, if you'd take my advice,
 You would find it an excellent plan,—
Don't marry a charming woman,
 If you are a sensible man.

     Written 1835; *Songs, Poems, and Verses,* 1894

Recollections of Burgos

MOST like some agèd king it seemed to me,
 Who had survived his old regality,
Poor and deposed, but keeping still his state,
In all he had before of truly great;
With no vain wishes and no vain regret,
But his enforcèd leisure soothing yet
With meditation calm and books and prayer,
For all was sober and majestic there—
The old Castilian, with close finger tips
Pressing his folded mantle to his lips;
The dim cathedral's cross-surmounted pile,
With carved recess, and cool and shadowy aisle,
The walks of poplar by the river's side,
That wound by many a straggling channel wide;
And seats of stone, where one might sit and weave
Visions, till well-nigh tempted to believe
That life had few things better to be done,
And many worse, than sitting in the sun
To lose the hours, and wilfully to dim
Our half-shut eyes, and veil them till might swim
The pageant by us, smoothly as the stream
And unremembered pageant of a dream.

A castle crowned a neighbouring hillock's nest,
But now the moat was level with the rest,
And all was fallen of this place of power,
All heaped with formless stone, save one round tower,
And here and there a gateway low and old,
Figured with antique shape of warrior bold.

And then behind this eminence the sun
Would drop serenely, long ere day was done;
And one who climbed that height might see again
A second setting o'er the fertile plain
Beyond the town, and glittering in his beam,
Wind far away that poplar-skirted stream.

The Story of Justin Martyr, &c., 1835

388 *Gibraltar*

ENGLAND, we love thee better than we know—
And this I learned, when after wandering long
'Mid people of another stock and tongue,
I heard again thy martial music blow,
And saw thy gallant children to and fro
Pace, keeping ward at one of those huge gates,
Which like twin giants watch the Herculean straits:
When first I came in sight of that brave show,
It made my very heart within me dance,
To think that thou thy proud foot shouldst advance
Forward so far into the mighty sea;
Joy was it and exultation to behold
Thine ancient standard's rich emblazonry,
A glorious picture by the wind unrolled.

The Story of Justin Martyr, &c., 1835

389   *Sonnet*

In a pass of Bavaria between the Walchen and the
Waldensee

'His voice was as the sound of many waters.'

A SOUND of many waters!—now I know
      To what was likened the large utterance sent
By Him who 'mid the golden lampads went:
Innumerable streams, above, below;
Some seen, some heard alone, with headlong flow
Come rushing; some with smooth and sheer descent,
Some dashed to foam and whiteness, but all blent
Into one mighty music. As I go,
The tumult of a boundless gladness fills
My bosom, and my spirit leaps and sings:
Sounds and sights are there of the ancient hills,
The eagle's cry, or when the mountain flings
Mists from its brow, but none of all these things
Like the one voice of multitudinous rills.

The Story of Justin Martyr, &c., 1835

390   '*Lord, many times*'

L ORD, many times I am aweary quite
      Of mine own self, my sin, my vanity—
Yet be not thou, or I am lost outright,
            Weary of me.

And hate against myself I often bear,
      And enter with myself in fierce debate:
Take thou my part against myself, nor share
            In that just hate.

'LORD, MANY TIMES'

Best friends might loathe us, if what things perverse
    We knew of our own selves, they also knew:
Lord, Holy One! if thou who knowest worse
    Should loathe us too!

Sabbation, &c., 1838

391   *From ' A Century of Couplets '*

WHO praises God the most, what says he more than he
    Who silent is, yet who would therefore silent be?

.   .   .   .   .   .

Merely thyself, oh man, thou canst not long abide,
But presently for less or greater must decide.

.   .   .   .   .   .

Owe no man aught save love, but that esteem a debt
Which thou must ever pay, well pleased to owe it yet.

Rear highly as thou wilt thy branches in the air,
But that thy roots descend as deep in earth have care.

Sin, not till it is left, will duly sinful seem;
A man must waken first, ere he can tell his dream.

.   .   .   .   .   .

Would'st thou do harm, and still unharmed thyself abide?
None struck another yet, except through his own side.

.   .   .   .   .   .

Before the eyes of men let duly shine thy light
But ever let thy life's best part be out of sight.

.   .   .   .   .   .

We children are from earth weaned hardly, so Heaven strews
Some wormwood on earth's breasts, as tenderest mothers use.

.   .   .   .   .   .

RICHARD CHENEVIX TRENCH

Things earthly we must know ere love them: 'tis alone
Things heavenly that must be first loved and after known.

. . . . .

All noblest things are still the commonest, every place
Has water, light, and air, and God's abounding grace.

. . . . .

He is not wholly lost, who yet keeps love for aught,
Large fire from smallest spark has many times been brought.

Sabbation, &c., 1838

CHARLES TENNYSON TURNER
1808–1879

392   *A Summer Twilight*

IT is a Summer gloaming, balmy-sweet,
  A gloaming brighten'd by an infant moon,
Fraught with the fairest light of middle June;
The lonely garden echoes to my feet,
And hark! O hear I not the gentle dews,
Fretting the silent forest in his sleep?
Or does the stir of housing insects creep
Thus faintly on mine ear? Day's many hues
Waned with the paling light and are no more,
And none but drowsy pinions beat the air:
The bat is hunting softly by my door,
And, noiseless as the snow-flake, leaves his lair;
O'er the still copses flitting here and there,
Wheeling the self-same circuit o'er and o'er.

Sonnets, 1830

EDGAR ALLAN POE

1809–1849

393

The Lake

IN youth's spring it was my lot
　　To haunt of the wide earth a spot
The which I could not love the less;
So lovely was the loneliness
Of a wild lake, with black rock bound,
And the tall pines that tower'd around.

But when the night had thrown her pall
Upon that spot—as upon all,
And the wind would pass me by
In its stilly melody,
My infant spirit would awake
To the terror of the lone lake.

Yet that terror was not fright—
But a tremulous delight,
And a feeling undefined,
Springing from a darken'd mind.
Death was in that poison'd wave
And in its gulf a fitting grave
For him who thence could solace bring
To his dark imagining;
Whose wildering thought could even make
An Eden of that dim lake.

Tamerlane and other Poems, 1827

394

To Helen

HELEN, thy beauty is to me
　　Like those Nicean barks of yore,
That gently, o'er a perfumed sea,
　　The weary, wayworn wanderer bore
　　To his own native shore.

On desperate seas long wont to roam,
　Thy hyacinth hair, thy classic face,
Thy Naiad airs have brought me home
　To the glory that was Greece
And the grandeur that was Rome.

Lo! in yon brilliant window-niche
　How statue-like I see thee stand,
　The agate lamp within thy hand!
Ah, Psyche, from the regions which
　Are Holy Land!

Poems, 1831

395　　　*The Doomed City*

LO! Death hath rear'd himself a throne
　In a strange city, all alone,
Far down within the dim West—
And the good, and the bad, and the worst, and the best,
Have gone to their eternal rest.

There shrines, and palaces, and towers
Are—not like anything of ours—
O! no—O! no—*ours* never loom
To heaven with that ungodly gloom!
Time-eaten towers that tremble not!
Around, by lifting winds forgot,
Resignedly beneath the sky
The melancholy waters lie.

A heaven that God doth not contemn
With stars is like a diadem
We liken our ladies' eyes to them—

THE DOOMED CITY

But there! that everlasting pall!
It would be mockery to call
Such dreariness a heaven at all.

Yet tho' no holy rays come down
On the long night-time of that town,
Light from the lurid, deep sea
Streams up the turrets silently—

Up thrones—up long-forgotten bowers
Of sculptured ivy and stone flowers—
Up domes—up spires—up kingly halls—
Up fanes—up Babylon-like walls—
Up many a melancholy shrine,
Whose entablatures intertwine
The mask—the viol—and the vine.

There open temples—open graves
Are on a level with the waves—
But not the riches there that lie
In each idol's diamond eye,
Not the gaily-jewell'd dead
Tempt the waters from their bed:
For no ripples curl, alas!
Along that wilderness of glass—
No swellings hint that winds may be
Upon a far-off happier sea:
So blend the turrets and shadows there
That all seem pendulous in air,
While from the high towers of the town
Death looks gigantically down.

But lo! a stir is in the air!
The wave! there is a ripple there!

As if the towers had thrown aside,
In slightly sinking, the dull tide—
As if the turret-tops had given
A vacuum in the filmy Heaven:
The waves have now a redder glow—
The very hours are breathing low—
And when, amid no earthly moans,
Down, down that town shall settle hence,
Hell, rising from a thousand thrones,
Shall do it reverence,
And Death to some more happy clime
Shall give his undivided time.

Poems, 1831

396   *To One in Paradise*

THOU wast all that to me, love,
    For which my soul did pine—
A green isle in the sea, love,
    A fountain and a shrine,
All wreathed with fairy fruits and flowers,
    And all the flowers were mine.

Ah, dream too bright to last!
    Ah, starry Hope! that didst arise
But to be overcast!
    A voice from out the Future cries,
' On! on!'—but o'er the Past
    (Dim gulf!) my spirit hovering lies
Mute, motionless, aghast!

For, alas! alas! with me
    The light of Life is o'er!

TO ONE IN PARADISE

' No more—no more—no more— '
(Such language holds the solemn sea
    To the sands upon the shore)
Shall bloom the thunder-blasted tree
    Or the stricken eagle soar!

And all my days are trances,
    And all my nightly dreams
Are where thy grey eye glances,
    And where thy footstep gleams—
In what ethereal dances,
    By what eternal streams.

The Southern Literary Messenger, July 1835

RICHARD MONCKTON MILNES, BARON HOUGHTON

1809–1885

397   *Two Angels*

(*Playing on Instruments*)

WE and the little cheerful goldfinch,
    Percht above that blessèd seat,—
He above and we below,—
We with voices and sweet viols,
He with chirping voice alone,—
Glorify the happy Mother,
Glorify the holy Child.
Now that our great heavenly Master
Has put on this wondrous semblance
Of a humble mortal infant,
We, the Angels of his presence,
Are become as simple children,

And beside him watch, admiring
All his innocence and beauty,
Lulling him to downy slumbers
With remembrances of Heaven.

Memorials of a Residence on the Continent, 1838

398   *The Venetian Serenade*

WHEN along the light ripple the far serenade
    Has accosted the ear of each passionate maid,
She may open the window that looks on the stream,—
She may smile on her pillow and blend it in dream;
Half in words, half in music, it pierces the gloom,
' I am coming—Stalì—but you know not for whom!
        Stalì—not for whom!'

Now the tones become clearer, you hear more and more
How the water divided returns on the oar,—
Does the prow of the gondola strike on the stair?
Do the voices and instruments pause and prepare?
Oh! they faint on the ear as the lamp on the view,
' I am passing—Premì—but I stay not for you!
        Premì—not for you!'

Then return to your couch, you who stifle a tear,
Then awake not, fair sleeper—believe he is here;
For the young and the loving no sorrow endures,
If to-day be another's, to-morrow is yours;—
May, the next time you listen, your fancy be true,
' I am coming—Sciàr—and for you and to you!
        Sciàr—and to you!'

Memorials of a Residence on the Continent, 1838

ALFRED TENNYSON

1809–1892

399   *The Kraken*

BELOW the thunders of the upper deep;
     Far far beneath in the abysmal sea,
His antient, dreamless, uninvaded sleep
The Kraken sleepeth: faintest sunlights flee
About his shadowy sides: above him swell
Huge sponges of millennial growth and height;
And far away into the sickly light,
From many a wondrous grot and secret cell
Unnumbered and enormous polypi
Winnow with giant fins the slumbering green.
There hath he lain for ages and will lie
Battening upon huge seaworms in his sleep,
Until the latter fire shall heat the deep;
Then once by men and angels to be seen,
In roaring he shall rise and on the surface die.

                 Poems, chiefly Lyrical, 1830

400   *Song.—The Owl*

I

WHEN cats run home and light is come,
     And dew is cold upon the ground,
And the far-off stream is dumb,
     And the whirring sail goes round,
     And the whirring sail goes round;
       Alone and warming his five wits,
       The white owl in the belfry sits.

II

When merry milkmaids click the latch,
    And rarely smells the newmown hay,
And the cock hath sung beneath the thatch
    Twice or thrice his roundelay,
    Twice or thrice his roundelay:
        Alone and warming his five wits,
        The white owl in the belfry sits.

Poems chiefly Lyrical, 1830

401   *To* — —

I

ALL good things have not kept aloof,
    Nor wander'd into other ways:
I have not lacked thy mild reproof,
    Nor golden largess of thy praise,
    But life is full of weary days.

II

Shake hands, my friend, across the brink
    Of that deep grave to which I go.
Shake hands once more: I cannot sink
    So far—far down, but I shall know
    Thy voice, and answer from below.

III

When, in the darkness over me
    The fourhanded mole shall scrape,
Plant thou no dusky cypresstree,
    Nor wreathe thy cap with doleful crape,
    But pledge me in the flowing grape.

TO ——

IV

And when the sappy field and wood
   Grow green beneath the showery gray,
And rugged barks begin to bud,
    And through damp holts, newflushed with May,
    Ring sudden laughters of the Jay;

V

Then let wise Nature work her will
   And on my clay her darnels grow.
Come only, when the days are still,
    And at my headstone whisper low,
    And tell me if the woodbines blow,

VI

If thou art blest, my mother's smile
   Undimmed, if bees are on the wing:
Then cease, my friend, a little while,
    That I may hear the throstle sing
    His bridal song, the boast of spring.

VII

Sweet as the noise in parchèd plains
   Of bubbling wells that fret the stones,
(If any sense in me remains),
    Thy words will be; thy cheerful tones
    As welcome to my crumbling bones.

Poems, 1833

The Lady of Shalott

PART THE FIRST

ON either side the river lie
   Long fields of barley and of rye,
That clothe the wold, and meet the sky.
And thro' the field the road runs by
          To manytowered Camelot.
The yellowleavèd waterlily,
The greensheathèd daffodilly,
Tremble in the water chilly,
          Round about Shalott.

Willows whiten, aspens shiver,
The sunbeam-showers break and quiver
In the stream that runneth ever
By the island in the river,
          Flowing down to Camelot.
Four gray walls and four gray towers
Overlook a space of flowers,
And the silent isle imbowers
          The Lady of Shalott.

Underneath the bearded barley,
The reaper, reaping late and early,
Hears her ever chanting cheerly,
Like an angel, singing clearly,
          O'er the stream of Camelot.
Piling the sheaves in furrows airy,
Beneath the moon, the reaper weary
Listening whispers, ' 'tis the fairy
          Lady of Shalott.'

THE LADY OF SHALOTT

The little isle is all inrailed
With a rose-fence, and overtrailed
With roses: by the marge unhailed
The shallop flitteth silkensailed,
>> Skimming down to Camelot.
A pearlgarland winds her head:
She leaneth on a velvet bed,
Full royally apparellèd,
>> The Lady of Shalott.

Part the Second

No time hath she to sport and play:
A charmèd web she weaves alway.
A curse is on her, if she stay
Her weaving, either night or day,
>> To look down to Camelot.
She knows not what the curse may be;
Therefore she weaveth steadily,
Therefore no other care hath she,
>> The Lady of Shalott.

She lives with little joy or fear.
Over the water, running near,
The sheepbell tinkles in her ear.
Before her hangs a mirror clear,
>> Reflecting towered Camelot.
And, as the mazy web she whirls,
She sees the surly village-churls.
And the red cloaks of market-girls,
>> Pass onward from Shalott.

Sometimes a troop of damsels glad,
An abbot on an ambling pad,

Sometimes a curly shepherd lad,
Or longhaired page, in crimson clad,
   Goes by to towered Camelot.
And sometimes thro' the mirror blue,
The knights come riding, two and two.
She hath no loyal knight and true,
   The Lady of Shalott.

But in her web she still delights
To weave the mirror's magic sights:
For often thro' the silent nights
A funeral, with plumes and lights
   And music, came from Camelot.
Or, when the moon was overhead,
Came two young lovers, lately wed:
' I am half-sick of shadows,' said
   The Lady of Shalott.

Part the Third

A bowshot from her bower-eaves,
He rode between the barleysheaves,
The sun came dazzling thro' the leaves,
And flamed upon the brazen greaves
   Of bold Sir Launcelot.
A redcross knight for ever kneeled
To a lady in his shield,
That sparkled on the yellow field,
   Beside remote Shalott.

The gemmy bridle glittered free,
Like to some branch of stars we see

THE LADY OF SHALOTT

Hung in the golden galaxy.
The bridle-bells rang merrily,
    As he rode down from Camelot.
And, from his blazoned baldric slung,
A mighty silver bugle hung,
And, as he rode, his armour rung,
    Beside remote Shalott.

All in the blue unclouded weather,
Thickjewelled shone the saddle-leather.
The helmet, and the helmet-feather
Burned like one burning flame together,
    As he rode down from Camelot.
As often thro' the purple night,
Below the starry clusters bright,
Some bearded meteor, trailing light,
    Moves over green Shalott.

His broad clear brow in sunlight glowed.
On burnished hooves his warhorse trode.
From underneath his helmet flowed
His coalblack curls, as on he rode,
    As he rode down from Camelot.
From the bank, and from the river,
He flashed into the crystal mirror,
' Tirra lirra, tirra lirra,'
    Sang Sir Launcelot.

She left the web: she left the loom:
She made three paces thro' the room:
She saw the waterflower bloom:
She saw the helmet and the plume:
    She looked down to Camelot.

Out flew the web, and floated wide,
The mirror cracked from side to side,
' The curse is come upon me,' cried
      The Lady of Shalott.

PART THE FOURTH

In the stormy eastwind straining
The pale-yellow woods were waning,
The broad stream in his banks complaining,
Heavily the low sky raining
      Over towered Camelot;
Outside the isle a shallow boat
Beneath a willow lay afloat,
Below the carven stern she wrote,
      The Lady of Shalott.

A cloudwhite crown of pearl she dight,
All raimented in snowy white
That loosely flew, (her zone in sight,
Clasped with one blinding diamond bright,)
      Her wide eyes fixed on Camelot,
Though the squally eastwind keenly
Blew, with folded arms serenely
By the water stood the queenly
      Lady of Shalott.

With a steady, stony glance—
Like some bold seer in a trance,
Beholding all his own mischance,
Mute, with a glassy countenance—
      She looked down to Camelot.

THE LADY OF SHALOTT

It was the closing of the day,
She loosed the chain, and down she lay,
The broad stream bore her far away,
      The Lady of Shalott.

As when to sailors while they roam,
By creeks and outfalls far from home,
Rising and dropping with the foam,
From dying swans wild warblings come,
      Blown shoreward; so to Camelot
Still as the boathead wound along
The willowy hills and fields among,
They heard her chanting her deathsong,
      The Lady of Shalott.

A longdrawn carol, mournful, holy,
She chanted loudly, chanted lowly,
Till her eyes were darkened wholly,
And her smooth face sharpened slowly
      Turned to towered Camelot:
For ere she reached upon the tide
The first house by the waterside,
Singing in her song she died,
      The Lady of Shalott.

Under tower and balcony,
By gardenwall and gallery,
A pale, pale corpse she floated by,
Deadcold, between the houses high,
      Dead into towered Camelot.
Knight and burgher, lord and dame,
To the plankèd wharfage came:
Below the stern they read her name,
      ' The Lady of Shalott.'

They crossed themselves, their stars they blest,
Knight, minstrel, abbot, squire and guest.
There lay a parchment on her breast,
That puzzled more than all the rest,
   The wellfed wits at Camelot.
' *The web was woven curiously,*
The charm is broken utterly,
Draw near and fear not—this is I,
   The Lady of Shalott.'

        Poems, 1833

403 —— *A Dream of Fair Women*

AS when a man, that sails in a balloon,
  Downlooking sees the solid shining ground
Stream from beneath him in the broad blue noon,—
  Tilth, hamlet, mead and mound:

And takes his flags and waves them to the mob,
  That shout below, all faces turned to where
Glows rubylike the far-up crimson globe,
  Filled with a finer air:

So, lifted high, the Poet at his will
  Lets the great world flit from him, seeing all,
Higher thro' secret splendours mounting still,
  Selfpoised, nor fears to fall,

Hearing apart the echoes of his fame.
  While I spoke thus, the seedsman, memory,
Sowed my deepfurrowed thought with many a name,
  Whose glory will not die.

A DREAM OF FAIR WOMEN

I read, before my eyelids dropt their shade,
  ' *The legend of good women*,' long ago
Sung by the morningstar of song, who made
  His music heard below,

Dan Chaucer, the first warbler, whose sweet breath
  Preluded those melodious bursts, that fill
The spacious times of great Elizabeth
  With sounds that echo still.

And, for awhile, the knowledge of his art
  Held me above the subject, as strong gales
Hold swollen clouds from raining, tho' my heart,
  Brimful of those wild tales,

Charged both mine eyes with tears. In every land
  I saw, wherever light illumineth,
Beauty and anguish walking hand in hand
  The downward slope to death.

In every land I thought that, more or less,
  The stronger sterner nature overbore
The softer, uncontrolled by gentleness
  And selfish evermore:

And whether there were any means whereby,
  In some far aftertime, the gentler mind
Might reassume its just and full degree
  Of rule among mankind.

Those far-renownèd brides of ancient song
  Peopled the hollow dark, like burning stars,
And I heard sounds of insult, shame, and wrong,
  And trumpets blown for wars;

And clattering flints battered with clanging hoofs:
    And I saw crowds in columned sanctuaries;
And forms that screamed at windows and on roofs
    Of marble palaces;

Corpses across the threshold; heroes tall
    Dislodging pinnacle and parapet
Upon the tortoise creeping to the wall;
    Lances in ambush set;

And high shrinedoors burst thro' with heated blasts
    That run before the fluttering tongues of fire,
White surf windscattered over sails and masts,
    And ever climbing higher,

Squadrons and squares of men in brazen plates,
    Scaffolds, still sheets of water, divers woes,
Ranges of glimmering vaults with iron grates,
    And hushed seraglios.

So shape chased shape as swift as, when to land
    Bluster the winds and tides the selfsame way,
Crisp foamflakes scud along the level sand,
    Torn from the fringe of spray.

I started once, or seemed to start in pain,
    Resolved on noble things, and strove to speak,
As when a great thought strikes along the brain,
    And flushes all the cheek.

And once my arm was lifted to hew down
    A cavalier from off his saddlebow,
That bore a lady from a leaguered town;
    And then, I know not how,

A DREAM OF FAIR WOMEN

All those sharp fancies, by downlapsing thought
　　Streamed onward, lost their edges, and did creep
Rolled on each other, rounded, smoothed, and brought
　　Into the gulfs of sleep.

At last methought that I had wandered far
　　In an old wood: freshwashed in coolest dew,
The maiden splendours of the morningstar
　　Shook in the stedfast blue.

Enormous elmtree-boles did stoop and lean
　　Upon the dusky brushwood underneath
Their broad curved branches, fledged with clearest green,
　　New from its silken sheath.

The dim red morn had died, her journey done,
　　And with dead lips smiled at the twilight plain,
Half-fall'n across the threshold of the sun,
　　Never to rise again.

There was no motion in the dumb dead air,
　　Not any song of bird or sound of rill.
Gross darkness of the inner sepulchre
　　Is not so deadly still

As that wide forest. Clasping jasmine turned
　　Its twinèd arms festooning tree to tree,
And at the root thro' lush green grasses burned
　　The red anemone.

I knew the flowers, I knew the leaves, I knew
　　The tearful glimmer of the languid dawn
On those long, rank, dark woodwalks drenched in dew,
　　Leading from lawn to lawn.

839

ALFRED TENNYSON

The smell of violets, hidden in the green,
    Poured back into my empty soul and frame
The times when I remember to have been
    Joyful and free from blame.

And from within me a clear undertone
    Thrilled thro' mine ears in that unblissful clime:
' Pass freely thro'! the wood is all thine own,
    Until the end of time.'

At length I saw a lady within call,
    Stiller than chiselled marble, standing there,
A daughter of the gods, divinely tall,
    And most divinely fair.

Her loveliness with shame and with surprise
    Froze my swift speech: she turning on my face
The starlike sorrows of immortal eyes,
    Spoke slowly in her place.

' I had great beauty: ask thou not my name:
    No one can be more wise than destiny.
Many drew swords and died. Where'er I came
    I brought calamity.'

' No marvel, sovran lady! in fair field,
    Myself for such a face had boldly died,'
I answered free; and turning I appealed
    To one that stood beside.

But she, with sick and scornful looks averse,
    To her full height her stately stature draws;
' My youth,' she said, ' was blasted with a curse:
    This woman was the cause.

A DREAM OF FAIR WOMEN

‘ I was cut off from hope in that sad place,
    Which yet to name my spirit loathes and fears:
My father held his hand upon his face;
    I, blinded with my tears,

‘ Still strove to speak—my voice was thick with sighs
    As in a dream. Dimly I could descry
The stern blackbearded kings with wolfish eyes,
    Waiting to see me die.

‘ The tall masts quivered as they lay afloat,
    The temples and the people and the shore.
One drew a sharp knife thro’ my tender throat
    Slowly,—and nothing more.’

Whereto the other with a downward brow:
    ‘ I would the white cold heavyplunging foam,
Whirled by the wind, had rolled me deep below,
    Then when I left my home.’

Her slow full words sank thro’ the silence drear,
    As thunderdrops fall on a sleeping sea:
Sudden I heard a voice that cried, ‘ Come here,
    That I may look on thee.’

I turning saw, throned on a flowery rise,
    One sitting on a crimson scarf unrolled;
A queen, with swarthy cheeks and bold black eyes,
    Browbound with burning gold.

She, flashing forth a haughty smile, began:
    ‘ I governed men by change, and so I sway’d
All moods. ’Tis long since I have seen a man.
    Once, like the moon, I made

' The evershifting currents of the blood
 According to my humour ebb and flow.
I have no men to govern in this wood:
 That makes my only woe.

' Nay—yet it chafes me that I could not bend
 One will; nor tame and tutor with mine eye
That dull coldblooded Caesar. Prythee, friend,
 Where is Mark Antony?

' By him great Pompey dwarfs and suffers pain,
 A mortal man before immortal Mars;
The glories of great Julius lapse and wane,
 And shrink from suns to stars.

' That man, of all the men I ever knew,
 Most touched my fancy. O! what days and nights
We had in Egypt, ever reaping new
 Harvest of ripe delights,

' Realmdraining revels! Life was one long feast.
 What wit! what words! what sweet words, only made
Less sweet by the kiss that broke 'em, liking best
 To be so richly stayed!

' What dainty strifes, when fresh from war's alarms,
 My Hercules, my gallant Antony,
My mailèd captain leapt into my arms,
 Contented there to die!

' And in those arms he died: I heard my name
 Sighed forth with life: then I shook off all fear:
Oh what a little snake stole Caesar's fame!
 What else was left? look here! '

842

A DREAM OF FAIR WOMEN

(With that she tore her robe apart, and half
    The polished argent of her breast to sight
Laid bare. Thereto she pointed with a laugh,
    Showing the aspick's bite.)

' I died a Queen. The Roman soldier found
    Me lying dead, my crown about my brows,
A name for ever!—lying robed and crowned,
    Worthy a Roman spouse.'

Her warbling voice, a lyre of widest range
    Touched by all passion, did fall down and glance
From tone to tone, and glided thro' all change
    Of liveliest utterance.

When she made pause I knew not for delight;
    Because with sudden motion from the ground
She raised her piercing orbs, and filled with light
    The interval of sound.

Still with their fires Love tipt his keenest darts;
    As once they drew into two burning rings
All beams of Love, melting the mighty hearts
    Of captains and of kings.

Slowly my sense undazzled. Then I heard
    A noise of some one coming thro' the lawn,
And singing clearer than the crested bird,
    That claps his wings at dawn.

' The torrent brooks of hallowed Israel
    From craggy hollows pouring, late and soon,
Sound all night long, in falling thro' the dell,
    Far-heard beneath the moon.

' The balmy moon of blessèd Israel
    Floods all the deepblue gloom with beams divine:
All night the splintered crags that wall the dell
    With spires of silver shine.'

As one, that museth where broad sunshine laves
    The lawn by some cathedral, thro' the door
Hearing the holy organ rolling waves
    Of sound on roof and floor

Within, and anthem sung, is charmed and tied
    To where he stands,—so stood I, when that flow
Of music left the lips of her that died
    To save her father's vow;

The daughter of the warrior Gileadite,
    A maiden pure; as when she went along
From Mizpeh's towered gate with welcome light,
    With timbrel and with song.

My words leapt forth: ' Heaven heads the count of crimes
    With that wild oath.' She rendered answer high:
' Not so, nor once alone; a thousand times
    I would be born and die.

' Single I grew, like some green plant, whose root
    Creeps to the garden waterpipes beneath,
Feeding the flower; but ere my flower to fruit
    Changed, I was ripe for death.

' My God, my land, my father—these did move
    Me from my bliss of life, that Nature gave,
Lowered softly with a threefold cord of love
    Down to a silent grave.

A DREAM OF FAIR WOMEN

' And I went mourning, " no fair Hebrew boy
    Shall smile away my maiden blame among
The Hebrew mothers "—emptied of all joy,
    Leaving the dance and song,

' Leaving the olivegardens far below,
    Leaving the promise of my bridal bower,
The valleys of grapeloaded vines that glow
    Beneath the battled tower.

' The light white cloud swam over us. Anon
    We heard the lion roaring in his den:
We saw the large white stars rise one by one,
    Or, from the darkened glen,

' Saw God divide the night with flying flame,
    And thunder on the everlasting hills.
I heard Him, for He spake, and grief became
    A solemn scorn of ills.

' When the next moon was rolled into the sky,
    Strength came to me that equalled my desire.
How beautiful a thing it was to die
    For God and for my sire!

' It comforts me in this one thought to dwell—
    That I subdued me to my father's will;
Because the kiss he gave me, ere I fell,
    Sweetens the spirit still.

' Moreover it is written that my race
    Hewed Ammon, hip and thigh, from Aroer
On Arnon unto Minneth.' Here her face
    Glowed, as I looked at her.

She locked her lips: she left me where I stood:
    ' Glory to God,' she sang, and past afar,
Thridding the sombre boskage of the wood,
    Toward the morningstar.

Losing her carol I stood pensively,
    As one that from a casement leans his head,
When midnight bells cease ringing suddenly,
    And the old year is dead.

' Alas! alas!' a low voice, full of care,
    Murmured beside me: ' Turn and look on me:
I am that Rosamond, whom men call fair,
    If what I was I be.

' Would I had been some maiden coarse and poor!
    O me! that I should ever see the light!
Those dragon eyes of angered Eleanor
    Do hunt me, day and night.'

She ceased in tears, fallen from hope and trust:
    To whom the Egyptian: ' O, you tamely died!
You should have clung to Fulvia's waist, and thrust
    The dagger thro' her side.'

With that sharp sound the white dawn's creeping beams,
    Stol'n to my brain, dissolved the mystery
Of folded sleep. The captain of my dreams
    Ruled in the eastern sky.

Morn broadened on the borders of the dark,
    Ere I saw her, that in her latest trance
Clasped her dead father's heart, or Joan of Arc,
    A light of ancient France;

Or her, who knew that Love can vanquish Death,
    Who kneeling, with one arm about her king,
Drew forth the poison with her balmy breath,
    Sweet as new buds in Spring.

No memory labours longer from the deep
    Goldmines of thought to lift the hidden ore
That glimpses, moving up, than I from sleep
    To gather and tell o'er

Each little sound and sight. With what dull pain
    Compassed, how eagerly I sought to strike
Into that wondrous track of dreams again!
    But no two dreams are like.

As when a soul laments, which hath been blest,
    Desiring what is mingled with past years,
In yearnings that can never be exprest
    By signs or groans or tears;

Because all words, tho' culled with choicest art,
    Failing to give the bitter of the sweet,
Wither beneath the palate, and the heart
    Faints, faded by its heat.

Poems, 1833

404   *The Lotos-Eaters*

'COURAGE!' he said, and pointed toward the land,
    'This mounting wave will roll us shoreward soon.'
In the afternoon they came unto a land,
In which it seemèd always afternoon.
All round the coast the languid air did swoon,
Breathing like one that hath a weary dream.

ALFRED TENNYSON

Above the valley burned the golden moon;
And like a downward smoke, the slender stream
Along the cliff to fall and pause and fall did seem.

A land of streams! some, like a downward smoke,
Slowdropping veils of thinnest lawn, did go;
And some thro' wavering lights and shadows broke,
Rolling a slumbrous sheet of foam below.
They saw the gleaming river's seaward flow
From the inner land: far off, three mountaintops,
Three thundercloven thrones of oldest snow,
Stood sunsetflushed: and, dewed with showery drops,
Upclomb the shadowy pine above the woven copse.

The charmèd sunset lingered low adown
In the red West: thro' mountain clefts the dale
Was seen far inland, and the yellow down
Bordered with palm, and many a winding vale
And meadow, set with slender galingale;
A land where all things always seemed the same!
And round about the keel with faces pale,
Dark faces pale against that rosy flame,
The mildeyed melancholy Lotos-eaters came.

Branches they bore of that enchanted stem,
Laden with flower and fruit, whereof they gave
To each, but whoso did receive of them,
And taste, to him the gushing of the wave
Far far away did seem to mourn and rave
On alien shores; and if his fellow spake,
His voice was thin, as voices from the grave;
And deep-asleep he seemed, yet all awake,
And music in his ears his beating heart did make.

THE LOTOS-EATERS

They sat them down upon the yellow sand,
Between the sun and moon upon the shore;
And sweet it was to dream of Fatherland,
Of child, and wife, and slave; but evermore
Most weary seemed the sea, weary the oar,
Weary the wandering fields of barren foam.
Then some one said, ' We will return no more; '
And all at once they sang, ' Our island home
Is far beyond the wave; we will no longer roam.'

Choric Song

I

There is sweet music here that softer falls
Than petals from blown roses on the grass,
Or nightdews on still waters between walls
Of shadowy granite, in a gleaming pass.
Music that gentlier on the spirit lies,
Than tir'd eyelids upon tir'd eyes;
Music that brings sweet sleep down from the blissful skies.
Here are cool mosses deep,
And thro' the moss the ivies creep,
And in the stream the longleaved flowers weep,
And from the craggy ledge the poppy hangs in sleep.

II

Why are we weighed upon with heaviness,
And utterly consumed with sharp distress,
While all things else have rest from weariness?
All things have rest: why should *we* toil alone,
We only toil, who are the first of things,

And make perpetual moan,
Still from one sorrow to another thrown:
Nor ever fold our wings,
And cease from wanderings;
Not steep our brows in slumber's holy balm;
Nor hearken what the inner spirit sings,
' There is no joy but calm! '
Why should we only toil, the roof and crown of things?

III

Lo! in the middle of the wood,
The folded leaf is wooed from out the bud
With winds upon the branch, and there
Grows green and broad, and takes no care,
Sunsteeped at noon, and in the moon
Nightly dewfed; and turning yellow
Falls, and floats adown the air.
Lo! sweetened with the summer light,
The fulljuiced apple, waxing overmellow,
Drops in a silent autumn night.
All its allotted length of days,
The flower ripens in its place,
Ripens and fades, and falls, and hath no toil,
Fastrooted in the fruitful soil.

IV

Hateful is the darkblue sky,
Vaulted o'er the darkblue sea.
Death is the end of life; ah! why
Should life all labour be?
Let us alone. Time driveth onward fast,
And in a little while our lips are dumb.

THE LOTOS-EATERS

Let us alone. What is it that will last?
All things are taken from us, and become
Portions and parcels of the dreadful Past.
Let us alone. What pleasure can we have
To war with evil? Is there any peace
In ever climbing up the climbing wave?
All things have rest, and ripen toward the grave
In silence, ripen, fall and cease.
Give us long rest or death, dark death, or dreamful ease!

v

How sweet it were, hearing the downward stream,
With halfshut eyes ever to seem
Falling asleep in a halfdream!
To dream and dream, like yonder amber light,
Which will not leave the myrrhbush on the height;
To hear each other's whispered speech;
Eating the Lotos, day by day,
To watch the crisping ripples on the beach,
And tender curving lines of creamy spray:
To lend our hearts and spirits wholly
To the influence of mildminded melancholy;
To muse and brood, and live again in memory,
With the old faces of our infancy
Heaped over with a mound of grass,
Two handfuls of white dust, shut in an urn of brass:

vi

Or, propt on lavish beds of amaranth and moly,
How sweet (while warm airs lull us, blowing lowly,)
With halfdropt eyelids still,
Beneath a heaven dark and holy,

To watch the long bright river drawing slowly
His waters from the purple hill—
To hear the dewy echoes calling
From cave to cave thro' the thicktwined vine—
To watch the emeraldcoloured water falling
Thro' many a wov'n acanthus-wreath divine!
Only to hear and see the far-off sparkling brine,
Only to hear were sweet, stretched out beneath the pine.

VII

The Lotos blooms below the flowery peak:
The Lotos blows by every winding creek:
All day the wind breathes low with mellower tone:
Thro' every hollow cave and alley lone
Round and round the spicy downs the yellow Lotos-dust is
    blown.
We have had enough of motion,
Weariness and wild alarm,
Tossing on the tossing ocean,
Where the tuskèd seahorse walloweth
In a stripe of grassgreen calm,
At noon tide beneath the lee;
And the monstrous narwhale swalloweth
His foamfountains in the sea.
Long enough the winedark wave our weary bark did carry
This is lovelier and sweeter,
Men of Ithaca, this is meeter,
In the hollow rosy vale to tarry,
Like a dreamy Lotos-eater, a delirious Lotos-eater!
We will eat the Lotos, sweet
As the yellow honeycomb,
In the valley some, and some

THE LOTOS-EATERS

On the ancient heights divine;
And no more roam,
On the loud hoar foam,
To the melancholy home
At the limit of the brine,
The little isle of Ithaca, beneath the day's decline.
We'll lift no more the shattered oar,
No more unfurl the straining sail;
With the blissful Lotos-eaters pale
We will abide in the golden vale
Of the Lotos-land, till the Lotos fail;
We will not wander more.
Hark! how sweet the horned ewes bleat
On the solitary steeps,
And the merry lizard leaps,
And the foamwhite waters pour;
And the dark pine weeps,
And the lithe vine creeps,
And the heavy melon sleeps
On the level of the shore:
Oh! islanders of Ithaca, we will not wander more.
Surely, surely slumber is more sweet than toil, the shore
Than labour in the ocean, and rowing with the oar,
Oh! islanders of Ithaca, we will return no more.

Poems, 1833

405

Mariana

' Mariana in the moated grange.'—*Measure for Measure.*

WITH blackest moss the flowerplots
  Were thickly crusted, one and all,
The rusted nails fell from the knots
  That held the peach to the gardenwall.

ALFRED TENNYSON

The broken sheds looked sad and strange,
    Unlifted was the clinking latch,
    Weeded and worn the ancient thatch
Upon the lonely moated grange.
        She only said ' My life is dreary,
            He cometh not,' she said;
        She said ' I am aweary, aweary;
            I would that I were dead! '

Her tears fell with the dews at even,
    Her tears fell ere the dews were dried,
She could not look on the sweet heaven,
    Either at morn or eventide.
After the flitting of the bats,
    When thickest dark did trance the sky,
    She drew her casementcurtain by,
And glanced athwart the glooming flats.
        She only said ' The night is dreary,
            He cometh not,' she said:
        She said ' I am aweary, aweary,
            I would that I were dead! '

Upon the middle of the night,
    Waking she heard the nightfowl crow:
The cock sung out an hour ere light:
    From the dark fen the oxen's low
Came to her: without hope of change,
    In sleep she seemed to walk forlorn,
    Till cold winds woke the gray-eyed morn
About the lonely moated grange.
        She only said, ' The day is dreary,
            He cometh not,' she said;

MARIANA

She said, ' I am aweary, aweary,
   I would that I were dead! '

About a stonecast from the wall
   A sluice with blackened waters slept,
And o'er it many, round and small,
   The clustered marishmosses crept.
Hard by a poplar shook alway,
   All silvergreen with gnarled bark,
   For leagues no other tree did dark
The level waste, the rounding grey.
     She only said, ' My life is dreary,
      He cometh not,' she said;
     She said, ' I am aweary, aweary,
      I would that I were dead! '

And ever when the moon was low,
   And the shrill winds were up an' away,
In the white curtain, to and fro,
   She saw the gusty shadow sway.
But when the moon was very low,
   And wild winds bound within their cell,
   The shadow of the poplar fell
Upon her bed, across her brow.
     She only said, ' The night is dreary,
      He cometh not,' she said;
     She said, ' I am aweary, aweary,
      I would that I were dead! '

All day within the dreamy house,
   The doors upon their hinges creaked,
The blue fly sung i' the pane; the mouse
   Behind the mouldering wainscot shrieked,

Or from the crevice peered about.
　　Old faces glimmered through the doors,
　　Old footsteps trod the upper floors,
Old voices called her from without.
　　　　She only said, ' My life is dreary,
　　　　　　He cometh not,' she said;
　　　　She said, ' I am aweary, aweary,
　　　　　　I would that I were dead! '

The sparrow's chirrup on the roof,
　　The slow clock ticking, and the sound
Which to the wooing wind aloof
　　The poplar made, did all confound
Her sense; but most she loathed the hour
　　When the thickmoted sunbeam lay
　　Athwart the chambers, and the day
Downsloped was westering in his bower.
　　　　Then, said she, ' I am very dreary,
　　　　　　He will not come,' she said;
　　　　She wept, ' I am aweary, aweary,
　　　　　　Oh God, that I were dead! '

Poems, chiefly Lyrical, 1830

406　　　　　　　　　*Œnone*

THERE is a dale in Ida, lovelier
　　Than any in old Ionia, beautiful
With emerald slopes of sunny sward, that lean
Above the loud glenriver, which hath worn
A path thro' steepdown granite walls below
Mantled with flowering tendriltwine. In front
The cedarshadowy valleys open wide.

ŒNONE

Far-seen, high over all the Godbuilt wall
And many a snowycolumned range divine,
Mounted with awful sculptures—men and Gods,
The work of Gods—bright on the darkblue sky
The windy citadel of Ilion
Shone, like the crown of Troas. Hither came
Mournful Œnone wandering forlorn
Of Paris, once her playmate. Round her neck,
Her neck all marblewhite and marblecold,
Floated her hair or seemed to float in rest.
She, leaning on a vine-entwinèd stone,
Sang to the stillness, till the mountain-shadow
Sloped downward to her seat from the upper cliff.

    ' O mother Ida, manyfountained Ida,
Dear mother Ida, hearken ere I die.
The grasshopper is silent in the grass,
The lizard with his shadow on the stone
Sleeps like a shadow, and the scarletwinged
Cicala in the noonday leapeth not
Along the water-rounded granite-rock.
The purple flower droops: the golden bee
Is lilycradled: I alone awake.
My eyes are full of tears, my heart of love,
My heart is breaking and my eyes are dim,
And I am all aweary of my life.

    ' O mother Ida, manyfountained Ida,
Dear mother Ida, hearken ere I die.
Hear me O Earth, hear me O Hills, O Caves
That house the cold crowned snake! O mountain brooks,
I am the daughter of a River-God,

ALFRED TENNYSON

Hear me, for I will speak, and build up all
My sorrow with my song, as yonder walls
Rose slowly to a music slowly breathed,
A cloud that gathered shape: for it may be
That, while I speak of it, a little while
My heart may wander from its deeper woe.

' O mother Ida, manyfountained Ida,
Dear mother Ida, hearken ere I die.
Aloft the mountain lawn was dewydark,
And dewydark aloft the mountain pine;
Beautiful Paris, evilhearted Paris,
Leading a jetblack goat whitehorned, whitehooved,
Came up from reedy Simois all alone.

' O mother Ida, hearken ere I die.
I sate alone: the goldensandalled morn
Rosehued the scornful hills: I sate alone
With downdropt eyes: whitebreasted like a star
Fronting the dawn he came: a leopard skin
From his white shoulder drooped: his sunny hair
Clustered about his temples like a God's:
And his cheek brightened, as the foambow brightens
When the wind blows the foam; and I called out,
' Welcome Apollo, welcome home Apollo,
Apollo, my Apollo, loved Apollo.'

' Dear mother Ida, hearken ere I die.
He, mildly smiling, in his milkwhite palm
Close-held a golden apple, lightningbright
With changeful flashes, dropt with dew of Heaven
Ambrosially smelling. From his lip,
Curved crimson, the fullflowing river of speech
Came down upon my heart.

ŒNONE

       ' " My own Œnone,
Beautifulbrowed Œnone, mine own soul,
Behold this fruit, whose gleaming rind ingrav'n
' For the most fair,' in aftertime may breed
Deep evilwilledness of heaven and sore
Heartburning toward hallowed Ilion;
And all the colour of my afterlife
Will be the shadow of today. Today
Here and Pallas and the floating grace
Of laughterloving Aphrodite meet
In manyfolded Ida to receive
This meed of beauty, she to whom my hand
Award the palm. Within the green hillside,
Under yon whispering tuft of oldest pine,
Is an ingoing grotto, strown with spar
And ivymatted at the mouth, wherein
Thou unbeholden may'st behold, unheard
Hear all, and see thy Paris judge of Gods."

  ' Dear mother Ida, hearken ere I die.
It was the deep midnoon: one silvery cloud
Had lost his way between the piney hills.
They came—all three—the Olympian goddesses:
Naked they came to the smoothswarded bower,
Lustrous with lilyflower, violeteyed
Both white and blue, with lotetree-fruit thickset,
Shadowed with singing pine; and all the while,
Above, the overwandering ivy and vine
This way and that in many a wild festoon
Ran riot, garlanding the gnarlèd boughs
With bunch and berry and flower thro' and thro'.
On the treetops a golden glorious cloud

Leaned, slowly dropping down ambrosial dew.
How beautiful they were, too beautiful
To look upon! but Paris was to me
More lovelier than all the world beside.

   ' O mother Ida, hearken ere I die.
First spake the imperial Olympian
With archèd eyebrow smiling sovranly,
Fulleyèd Here. She to Paris made
Proffer of royal power, ample rule
Unquestioned, overflowing revenue
Wherewith to embellish state, " from many a vale
And riversundered champaign clothed with corn,
Or upland glebe wealthy in oil and wine—
Honour and homage, tribute, tax and toll,
From many an inland town and haven large,
Mast-thronged below her shadowing citadel
In glassy bays among her tallest towers."

   ' O mother Ida, hearken ere I die.
Still she spake on and still she spake of power
" Which in all action is the end of all.
Power fitted to the season, measured by
The height of the general feeling, wisdomborn
And throned of wisdom—from all neighbour crowns
Alliance and allegiance evermore.
Such boon from me Heaven's Queen to thee kingborn,
A shepherd all thy life and yet kingborn,
Should come most welcome, seeing men, in this
Only are likest gods, who have attained
Rest in a happy place and quiet seats
Above the thunder, with undying bliss
In knowledge of their own supremacy;

The changeless calm of undisputed right,
The highest height and topmost strength of power.'

' Dear mother Ida, hearken ere I die.
She ceased, and Paris held the costly fruit
Out at arm's-length, so much the thought of power
Flattered his heart: but Pallas where she stood
Somewhat apart, her clear and barèd limbs
O'erthwarted with the brazenheaded spear
Upon her pearly shoulder leaning cold;
The while, above, her full and earnest eye
Over her snowcold breast and angry cheek
Kept watch, waiting decision, made reply.

' " Selfreverence, selfknowledge, selfcontrol
Are the three hinges of the gates of Life,
That open into power, everyway
Without horizon, bound or shadow or cloud.
Yet not for power (power of herself
Will come uncalled-for) but to live by law
Acting the law we live by without fear,
And, because right is right, to follow right
Were wisdom, in the scorn of consequence.
(Dear mother Ida, hearken ere I die.)
Not as men value gold because it tricks
And blazons outward life with ornament,
But rather as the miser, for itself.
Good for selfgood doth half destroy selfgood.
The means and end, like two coiled snakes, infect
Each other, bound in one with hateful love.
So both into the fountain and the stream
A drop of poison falls. Come hearken to me,

861

And look upon me and consider me,
So shalt thou find me fairest, so endurance,
Like to an athlete's arm, shall still become
Sinewed with motion, till thine active will
(As the dark body of the Sun robed round
With his own ever-emanating lights)
Be flooded o'er with her own effluences,
And thereby grow to freedom."

                   ' Here she ceased
And Paris pondered. I cried out, " Oh Paris,
Give it to Pallas! " but he heard me not,
Or hearing would not hear me, woe is me!

  ' O mother Ida, manyfountained Ida,
Dear mother Ida, hearken ere I die.
Idalian Aphrodite oceanborn,
Fresh as the foam, newbathed in Paphian wells,
With rosy slender fingers upward drew
From her warm brow and bosom her dark hair
Fragrant and thick, and on her head upbound
In a purple band: below her lucid neck
Shone ivorylike, and from the ground her foot
Gleamed rosywhite, and o'er her rounded form
Between the shadows of the vinebunches
Floated the glowing sunlights, as she moved.

  ' Dear mother Ida, hearken ere I die.
She with a subtle smile in her mild eyes,
The herald of her triumph, drawing nigh
Half whispered in his ear, " I promise thee
The fairest and most loving wife in Greece."
I only saw my Paris raise his arm:
I only saw great Here's angry eyes,

ŒNONE

As she withdrew into the golden cloud,
And I was left alone within the bower;
And from that time to this I am alone.
And I shall be alone until I die.

'Yet, mother Ida, hearken ere I die.
Fairest—why fairest wife? am I not fair?
My love hath told me so a thousand times.
Methinks I must be fair, for yesterday,
When I passed by, a wild and wanton pard,
Eyed like the eveningstar, with playful tail
Crouched fawning in the weed. Most loving is she?
Ah me, my mountain-shepherd, that my arms
Were wound about thee, and my hot lips prest
Close—close to thine in that quickfalling dew
Of fruitful kisses, thick as Autumn-rains
Flash in the pools of whirling Simois.

'Dear mother Ida, hearken ere I die.
They came, they cut away my tallest pines—
My dark tall pines, that plumed the craggy ledge
High over the blue gorge, or lower down
Filling greengulphèd Ida, all between
The snowy peak and snowwhite cataract
Fostered the callow eaglet—from beneath
Whose thick mysterious boughs in the dark morn
The panther's roar came muffled, while I sat
Low in the valley. Never, nevermore
Shall lone Œnone see the morning mist
Sweep thro' them—never see them overlaid
With narrow moonlit slips of silver cloud,
Between the loud stream and the trembling stars.

' Oh! mother Ida, hearken ere I die.
Hath he not sworn his love a thousand times,
In this green valley, under this green hill,
Ev'n on this hand, and sitting on this stone?
Sealed it with kisses? watered it with tears?
Oh happy tears, and how unlike to these!
Oh happy Heaven, how can'st thou see my face?
Oh happy earth, how can'st thou bear my weight?
Oh death, death, death, thou everfloating cloud,
There are enough unhappy on this earth,
Pass by the happy souls, that love to live:
I pray thee, pass before my light of life,
And shadow all my soul, that I may die.
Thou weighest heavy on the heart within,
Weigh heavy on my eyelids—let me die.

' Yet, mother Ida, hear me ere I die.
I will not die alone, for fiery thoughts
So shape themselves within me, more and more,
Whereof I catch the issue, as I hear
Dead sounds at night come from the inmost hills,
Like footsteps upon wool. I dimly see
My far-off doubtful purpose, as a mother
Conjectures of the features of her child
Ere it is born. I will not die alone.

' Dear mother Ida, hearken ere I die.
Hear me, O earth. I will not die alone,
Lest their shrill, happy laughter come to me
Walking the cold and starless road of Death
Uncomforted, leaving my ancient love
With the Greek woman. I will rise and go
Down into Troy, and ere the stars come forth

Talk with the wild Cassandra, for she says
A fire dances before her, and a sound
Rings ever in her ears of armèd men.
What this may be I know not, but I know
That, wheresoe'er I am by night and day,
All earth and air seem only burning fire.'

Poems, 1833

ARTHUR HENRY HALLAM

1811–1833

407 *On the Picture of the Three Fates in
the Palazzo Pitti, at Florence*

usually ascribed to Michael Angiolo

NONE but a Tuscan hand could fix ye here
    In rigidness of sober colouring.
Pale are ye, mighty Triad, not with fear,
    But the most awful knowledge, that the spring
Is in you of all birth, and act, and sense.
    I sorrow to behold ye: pain is blent
With your aloof and loveless permanence,
    And your high princedom seems a punishment.
The cunning limner could not personate
    Your blind control, save in th' aspect of grief;
So does the thought repugn of sovran fate.
    Let him gaze here who trusts not in the love
    Toward which all being solemnly doth move:
More this grand sadness tells, than forms of fairest life.

Remains, 1834

865

1812–1889

From ' Pauline '

(i)

Shelley

SUN-TREADER—life and light be thine for ever;
Thou art gone from us—years go by—and spring
Gladdens, and the young earth is beautiful,
Yet thy songs come not—other bards arise,
But none like thee—they stand—thy majesties,
Like mighty works which tell some Spirit there
Hath sat regardless of neglect and scorn,
Till, its long task completed, it hath risen
And left us, never to return: and all
Rush in to peer and praise when all in vain.
The air seems bright with thy past presence yet,
But thou art still for me, as thou hast been
When I have stood with thee, as on a throne
With all thy dim creations gathered round
Like mountains,—and I felt of mould like them,
And creatures of my own were mixed with them,
Like things half-lived, catching and giving life.
But thou art still for me, who have adored,
Tho' single, panting but to hear thy name,
Which I believed a spell to me alone,
Scarce deeming thou wert as a star to men—
As one should worship long a sacred spring
Scarce worth a moth's flitting, which long grasses cross,
And one small tree embowers droopingly,
Joying to see some wandering insect won,
To live in its few rushes—or some locust

To pasture on its boughs—or some wild bird
Stoop for its freshness from the trackless air,
And then should find it but the fountain-head,
Long lost, of some great river—washing towns
And towers, and seeing old woods which will live
But by its banks, untrod of human foot,
Which, when the great sun sinks, lie quivering
In light as some thing lieth half of life
Before God's foot—waiting a wondrous change
—Then girt with rocks which seek to turn or stay
Its course in vain, for it does ever spread
Like a sea's arm as it goes rolling on,
Being the pulse of some great country—so
Wert thou to me—and art thou to the world.

(ii)

Andromeda

AND she is with me—years roll, I shall change,
But change can touch her not—so beautiful
With her dark eyes, earnest and still, and hair
Lifted and spread by the salt-sweeping breeze;
And one red-beam, all the storm leaves in heaven,
Resting upon her eyes and face and hair,
As she awaits the snake on the wet beach,
By the dark rock, and the white wave just breaking
At her feet; quite naked and alone,—a thing
You doubt not, nor fear for, secure that God
Will come in thunder from the stars to save her.

(iii)
Water and Air

NIGHT, and one single ridge of narrow path
  Between the sullen river and the woods
Waving and muttering—for the moonless night
Has shaped them into images of life,
Like the upraising of the giant-ghosts,
Looking on earth to know how their sons fare.
Thou art so close by me, the roughest swell
Of wind in the tree-tops hides not the panting
Of thy soft breasts; no—we will pass to morning—
Morning—the rocks, and vallies, and old woods.
How the sun brightens in the mist, and here,—
Half in the air, like creatures of the place,
Trusting the element—living on high boughs
That swing in the wind—look at the golden spray,
Flung from the foam-sheet of the cataract,
Amid the broken rocks—shall we stay here
With the wild hawks?—no, ere the hot noon come
Dive we down—safe;—see this our new retreat
Walled in with a sloped mound of matted shrubs,
Dark, tangled, old and green—still sloping down
To a small pool whose waters lie asleep
Amid the trailing boughs turned water-plants,
And tall trees over-arch to keep us in,
Breaking the sunbeams into emerald shafts,
And in the dreamy water one small group
Of two or three strange trees are got together,
Wondering at all around—as strange beasts herd
Together far from their own land—all wildness—
No turf nor moss, for boughs and plants pave all,
And tongues of bank go shelving in the waters,

PAULINE

Where the pale-throated snake reclines his head,
And old grey stones lie making eddies there;
The wild mice cross them dry-shod—deeper in—
Shut thy soft eyes—now look—still deeper in:
This is the very heart of the woods—all round,
Mountain-like, heaped above us; yet even here
One pond of water gleams—far off the river
Sweeps like a sea, barred out from land; but one—
One thin clear sheet has over-leaped and wound
Into this silent depth, which gained, it lies
Still, as but let by sufferance; the trees bend
O'er it as wild men watch a sleeping girl,
And thro' their roots long creeping plants stretch out
Their twined hair, steeped and sparkling; farther on,
Tall rushes and thick flag-knots have combined
To narrow it; so, at length, a silver thread
It winds, all noiselessly, thro' the deep wood,
Till thro' a cleft way, thro' the moss and stone,
It joins its parent-river with a shout.
Up for the glowing day—leave the old woods:
See, they part, like a ruined arch, the sky!
Nothing but sky appears, so close the root
And grass of the hill-top level with the air—
Blue sunny air, where a great cloud floats, laden
With light, like a dead whale that white birds pick,
Floating away in the sun in some north sea.
Air, air—fresh life-blood—thin and searching air—
The clear, dear breath of God, that loveth us:
Where small birds reel and winds take their delight.
Water is beautiful, but not like air.
See, where the solid azure waters lie,
Made as of thickened air, and down below

The fern-ranks, like a forest spread themselves,
As tho' each pore could feel the element;
Where the quick glancing serpent winds his way—
Float with me there, Pauline, but not like air.

Pauline, 1833

409 *From ' Paracelsus '*

Songs

(i)

HEAP cassia, sandal-buds, and stripes
   Of labdanum, and aloe-balls,
Smear'd with dull nard an Indian wipes
   From out her hair: such balsam falls
From tall trees where tired winds are fain,
Spent with the vast and howling main,
To treasure half their island-gain;
And strew faint sweetness from some old
   Egyptian's fine worm-eaten shroud,
Which breaks to dust when once unroll'd;
   Or shredded perfume, like a cloud
   From closet long to quiet vow'd,
With moth'd and dropping arras hung,
Mouldering her lute and books among,
As when a queen, long dead, was young.

(ii)

OVER the sea our galleys went,
   Cleaving prows in order brave,
With speeding wind and a bounding wave—
   A gallant armament:
Each bark built out of a forest-tree,
   Left leafy and rough as first it grew,
And nail'd all over the gaping sides,

PARACELSUS

Within and without, with black-bull hides,
Seeth'd in fat and suppled in flame;
So each good ship was rude to see,
Rude and bare to outward view,
    But each upbore a stately tent:
Cedar-pales in scented row
Kept out the flakes of dancing brine:
An awning droop'd the mast below,
That neither noon-tide nor star-shine
Nor moonlight cold which maketh mad,
    Might pierce the regal tenement.
When the sun dawn'd, gay and glad
We set the sail and plied the oar;
But when the night-wind blew like breath,
For joy of one day's voyage more,
We sang together on the wide sea,
Like men at peace on a peaceful shore;
Each sail was loosed to the wind so free,
Each helm made sure by the twilight star,
And in a sleep as calm as death,
We, the voyagers from afar,
    Lay stretch'd—each weary crew
In a circle round its wondrous tent,
Whence gleam'd soft light and curl'd rich scent,
    And with light and perfume, music too:
At morn we started beside the mast,
And still each ship was sailing fast!
Now one morn land appeared!—a speck
    Dim trembling betwixt sea and sky—
Not so the isles our voyage must find
    Should meet our longing eye;
But the heaving sea was black behind

Many a night and many a day,
And land, though but a rock, was nigh;
So we broke the cedar pales away,
And let the purple flap in the wind:
   And a statue bright was on every deck!
We shouted, every man of us,
And steer'd right into the harbour thus,
With pomp and pæan glorious.

A hundred shapes of lucid stone!
   All day we built its shrine for each—
A shrine of rock for every one—
Nor paused till in the westering sun
   We sate together on the beach
To sing, because our task was done;
When lo! what shouts and merry songs!
What laughter all the distance stirs!
A loaded raft, and happy throngs
Of gentle islanders!
' Our isles are just at hand,' they cried;
   ' Like cloudlets faint in even sleeping,
' Our temple-gates are open'd wide,
   ' Our olive-groves thick shade are keeping
' For these majestic forms,' they cried.
Then we awoke with sudden start
From our deep dream, and knew, too late,
How bare the rock, how desolate,
Which had received our precious freight:
   Yet we called out—' Depart!
' Our gifts, once given, must here abide.
   ' Our work is done; we have no heart
To mar our work,' we cried.

PARACELSUS

(*iii*)

Festus. Thus the Mayne glideth
Where my love abideth;
Sleep's no softer: it proceeds
On through lawns, on through meads,
On and on, whate'er befall,
Meandering and musical,
Though the niggard pasturage
Bears not on its shaven edge
Aught but weeds and waving grasses
To behold it as it passes,
Save here and there a scanty patch
Of primroses, too faint to catch
A weary bee.

. . . . .

Fest.   And scarce it pushes
Its gentle way through strangling rushes,
Where the glossy king-fisher
Flutters when noon-heats are near,
Glad the shelving banks to shun,
Red and steaming in the sun,
Where the shrew-mouse with pale throat
Burrows, and the speckled stoat,
Where the quick sand-pipers flit
In and out the soft and wet
Clay that breeds them, brown as they.
Nought disturbs its quiet way,
Save some lazy stork that springs,
Trailing it with legs and wings,
Whom the shy fox from the hill
Arouses . . .

INDEX OF AUTHORS

The references are to the numbers of the poems

874

INDEX OF AUTHORS

INDEX OF FIRST LINES

INDEX OF FIRST LINES

INDEX OF FIRST LINES

883

INDEX OF FIRST LINES

INDEX OF FIRST LINES

PRINTED IN GREAT BRITAIN AT THE UNIVERSITY PRESS, OXFORD
BY VIVIAN RIDLER, PRINTER TO THE UNIVERSITY

INDEX OF FIRST LINES

PRINTED IN GREAT BRITAIN AT THE UNIVERSITY PRESS, OXFORD
BY VIVIAN RIDLER, PRINTER TO THE UNIVERSITY